Praise for the Second Edition

"This may be the most clearly written narrative-style coverage of the topic that I have encountered and one of the most complete that is not solely a reference work.

"[The book] has forced me to think differently about some of these topics and how they build on one another. It's almost like when I studied LISP way back when and it turned all my thinking about programming on its head. Thank you! It is a privilege to review this.

"This is one of the better-crafted tech books I've reviewed across two decades. The exercises consistently help the reader focus on specific things in the text and gently struggle and learn concepts that might otherwise slip through the cracks. I failed to find any exercise that I would delete and can't think of any I would add."

— *Matthew Helmke, Linux author and consultant*

Praise for the First Edition

"This is an excellent introduction to Linux programming. The topics are well chosen and lucidly presented. I learned things myself, especially about internationalization, and I've been at this for quite a while."

— *Chet Ramey, coauthor and maintainer of the Bash shell*

"This is a good introduction to Linux programming. Arnold's technique of showing how experienced programmers use the Linux programming interfaces is a nice touch, much more useful than the canned programming examples found in most books."

— *Ulrich Drepper, project lead, GNU C library*

"A gentle yet thorough introduction to the art of UNIX system programming, *Linux Programming by Example* uses code from a wide range of familiar programs to illustrate each concept it teaches. Readers will enjoy an interesting mix of in-depth API descriptions and portability guidelines, and will come away well prepared to begin reading and writing systems applications. *Heartily recommended.*"

— *Jim Meyering, coauthor and maintainer of the GNU Core Utility Programs*

Linux Application Development by Example

The Fundamental APIs

Second Edition

Arnold Robbins

Addison-Wesley
Hoboken, New Jersey

Cover image: JIN KANSA/stock.adobe.com
Figure 17.1: Ubuntu

Visit us on the Web: informit.com

Library of Congress Control Number: 2025944250

ISBN-13: 978-0-13-532552-0
ISBN-10: 0-13-532552-8

1 2025

Contents

Foreword xv
Preface xvii

PART I Files and Users 1

Chapter 1 Introduction 3
1.1 The Linux/Unix File Model 3
1.1.1 Files and Permissions 3
1.1.2 Directories and File Names 5
1.1.3 Executable Files 6
1.1.4 Devices 7
1.2 The Linux/Unix Process Model 7
1.2.1 Pipes: Hooking Processes Together 9
1.3 Standard C versus Original C 9
1.4 Why GNU Programs Are Better 13
1.4.1 Program Design 13
1.4.2 Program Behavior 14
1.4.3 C Code Programming 14
1.4.4 Things That Make a GNU Program Better 15
1.4.5 Parting Thoughts about the *GNU Coding Standards* 17
1.5 Portability Revisited 17
1.5.1 Why Be Portable? 17
1.5.2 Portability Recommendations 17
1.6 Some Words about Coding Style 18
1.7 Artificial Intelligence Isn't Intelligent 19
1.8 Suggested Reading 19
1.9 Summary 20
Exercises 21

Chapter 2 Arguments, Options, and the Environment 23
2.1 Option and Argument Conventions 23
2.1.1 POSIX Conventions 24
2.1.2 GNU Long Options 26

2.2 Basic Command-Line Processing 26
2.2.1 The V7 `echo` Program 27
2.3 Option Parsing: `getopt()` and `getopt_long()` 28
2.3.1 Single-Letter Options 29
2.3.2 GNU `getopt()` and Option Ordering 31
2.3.3 Long Options 32
2.4 The Environment 37
2.4.1 Environment Management Functions 38
2.4.2 The Entire Environment: `environ` 39
2.4.3 GNU `env` 40
2.5 Summary 49
Exercises 49

Chapter 3 User-Level Memory Management 51
3.1 Linux/Unix Address Space 51
3.2 Memory Allocation 55
3.2.1 Library Calls: `malloc()`, `calloc()`, `realloc()`, `free()` 55
3.2.2 String Copying: `strdup()` 71
3.2.3 System Calls: `brk()` and `sbrk()` 72
3.2.4 Lazy Programmer Calls: `alloca()` 73
3.2.5 Address Space Examination 74
3.3 Summary 76
Exercises 77

Chapter 4 Files and File I/O 79
4.1 Introducing the Linux/Unix I/O Model 79
4.2 Presenting a Basic Program Structure 79
4.3 Determining What Went Wrong 81
4.3.1 Values for `errno` 82
4.3.2 Error Message Style 86
4.4 Doing Input and Output 87
4.4.1 Understanding File Descriptors 87
4.4.2 Opening and Closing Files 88
4.4.3 Reading and Writing 91
4.4.4 Example: Unix `cat` 94
4.5 Random Access: Moving Around within a File 96
4.6 Creating Files 101
4.6.1 Specifying Initial File Permissions 101
4.6.2 Controlling Default Permissions with `umask()` 102
4.6.3 Creating Files with `creat()` 103
4.6.4 Revisiting `open()` 104
4.7 Forcing Data to Disk 106
4.8 Setting File Length 107

4.9 Summary 108
Exercises 109

Chapter 5 Directories and File Metadata 111
5.1 Considering Directory Contents 111
5.1.1 Definitions 111
5.1.2 Directory Contents 113
5.1.3 Hard Links 114
5.1.4 File Renaming 117
5.1.5 File Removal 118
5.1.6 Symbolic Links 119
5.2 Creating and Removing Directories 121
5.3 Reading Directories 123
5.3.1 Basic Directory Reading 124
5.3.2 BSD Directory Positioning Functions 129
5.4 Obtaining Information about Files 130
5.4.1 Linux File Types 130
5.4.2 Retrieving File Information 131
5.4.3 Linux Only: Specifying Higher-Precision File Times 135
5.4.4 Determining File Type 135
5.4.5 Working with Symbolic Links 141
5.5 Avoiding Race Conditions: `openat()` and Friends 144
5.6 Changing Ownership, Permission, and Modification Times 145
5.6.1 Changing File Ownership: `chown()`, `fchown()`, and `lchown()` 146
5.6.2 Changing Permissions: `chmod()` and `fchmod()` 147
5.6.3 Using `fchown()` and `fchmod()` for Security 147
5.6.4 Changing Timestamps: `utime()` and Successors 148
5.7 Summary 151
Exercises 153

Chapter 6 General Library Interfaces—Part 1 155
6.1 Times and Dates 155
6.1.1 Retrieving the Current Time: `time()` and `difftime()` 156
6.1.2 Breaking Down Times: `gmtime()` and `localtime()` 157
6.1.3 Formatting Dates and Times 159
6.1.4 Converting a Broken-Down Time to a `time_t` 164
6.1.5 Parsing a Date and Time into a `struct tm` 166
6.1.6 Getting Time-Zone Information 168
6.2 Sorting and Searching Functions 171
6.2.1 Sorting: `qsort()` 171
6.2.2 Binary Searching: `bsearch()` 180
6.3 User and Group Names 190
6.3.1 User Database 190
6.3.2 Group Database 193

6.4 Terminals: `isatty()` 196
6.5 Suggested Reading 196
6.6 Summary 197
Exercises 198

Chapter 7 Putting It All Together: `ls` 201
7.1 V7 `ls` Options 201
7.2 V7 `ls` Code 202
7.3 Summary 218
Exercises 218

Chapter 8 Filesystems and Directory Walks 221
8.1 Mounting and Unmounting Filesystems 221
8.1.1 Reviewing the Background 221
8.1.2 Looking at Different Filesystem Types 224
8.1.3 Mounting Filesystems: `mount` 225
8.1.4 Unmounting Filesystems: `umount` 228
8.2 Files for Filesystem Administration 228
8.2.1 Using Mount Options 230
8.2.2 Working with Mounted Filesystems: `getmntent()` 231
8.3 Retrieving Per-Filesystem Information 234
8.3.1 POSIX Style: `statvfs()` and `fstatvfs()` 235
8.3.2 Linux Style: `statfs()` and `fstatfs()` 242
8.4 Moving Around in the File Hierarchy 247
8.4.1 Changing Directory: `chdir()` and `fchdir()` 247
8.4.2 Getting the Current Directory: `getcwd()` 248
8.4.3 Processing a File Hierarchy: `fts_open()` and Friends 250
8.5 Processing a File Hierarchy: GNU `du` 261
8.6 Changing the Root Directory: `chroot()` 269
8.7 Summary 270
Exercises 271

PART II Processes, Networking, and Internationalization **273**

Chapter 9 Process Management and Pipes 275
9.1 Process Creation and Management 275
9.1.1 Creating a Process: `fork()` 275
9.1.2 Identifying a Process: `getpid()` and `getppid()` 279
9.1.3 Setting Process Priority: `nice()` 282
9.1.4 Starting New Programs: The `exec()` Family 283
9.1.5 Terminating a Process 289
9.1.6 Recovering a Child's Exit Status 293

9.2 Process Groups 300
9.2.1 Job Control Overview 300
9.2.2 Process Group Identification: getpgrp() and getpgid() 301
9.2.3 Process Group Setting: setpgid() and setpgrp() 302
9.3 Basic Interprocess Communication: Pipes and FIFOs 302
9.3.1 Pipes 303
9.3.2 FIFOs 306
9.4 File Descriptor Management 307
9.4.1 Duplicating Open Files: dup() and dup2() 307
9.4.2 Creating Nonlinear Pipelines: /dev/fd/XX 314
9.4.3 Managing File Attributes: fcntl() 315
9.5 Example: Two-Way Pipes in gawk 323
9.6 Suggested Reading 327
9.7 Summary 328
Exercises 330

Chapter 10 Signals 333
10.1 Introduction 333
10.2 Signal Actions 333
10.3 Standard C Signals: signal() and raise() 334
10.3.1 The signal() Function 334
10.3.2 Sending Signals Programmatically: raise() 337
10.4 Signal Handlers in Action 337
10.4.1 Traditional Systems 337
10.4.2 BSD and GNU/Linux 340
10.4.3 Ignoring Signals 340
10.4.4 Restartable System Calls 341
10.4.5 Race Conditions and sig_atomic_t (ISO C) 344
10.4.6 Additional Caveats 346
10.4.7 Our Story So Far, Episode I 346
10.5 The System V Release 3 Signal APIs: sigset() et al. 349
10.6 POSIX Signals 350
10.6.1 Uncovering the Problem 351
10.6.2 Signal Sets: sigset_t and Related Functions 351
10.6.3 Managing the Signal Mask: sigprocmask() et al. 352
10.6.4 Catching Signals: sigaction() 353
10.6.5 Retrieving Pending Signals: sigpending() 357
10.6.6 Making Functions Interruptible: siginterrupt() 357
10.6.7 Sending Signals: kill() and killpg() 358
10.6.8 Our Story So Far, Episode II 360
10.7 Signals for Interprocess Communication 360
10.8 Important Special-Purpose Signals 363
10.8.1 Alarm Clocks: sleep(), alarm(), and SIGALRM 363
10.8.2 Job Control Signals 365
10.8.3 Parental Supervision: Three Different Strategies 366

10.9 Signals across `fork()` and `exec()` 378
10.10 Summary 379
Exercises 381

Chapter 11 Permissions and User and Group ID Numbers 383
11.1 Checking Permissions 383
11.1.1 Real and Effective IDs 383
11.1.2 Setuid and Setgid Bits 384
11.2 Retrieving User and Group IDs 385
11.3 Checking as the Real User: `access()` 388
11.4 Setting Extra Permission Bits for Directories 391
11.4.1 Default Group for New Files and Directories 391
11.4.2 Directories and the Sticky Bit 392
11.5 Setting Real and Effective IDs 393
11.5.1 Changing the Group Set 393
11.5.2 Changing the Real and Effective IDs 394
11.5.3 Using the Setuid and Setgid Bits 396
11.6 Working with All Three IDs: `getresuid()` and `setresuid()` (Linux) 398
11.7 Crossing a Security Minefield: Setuid `root` 399
11.8 Suggested Reading 400
11.9 Summary 401
Exercises 403

Chapter 12 Resource Limits 405
12.1 Introduction 405
12.2 System Limits: `sysconf()`, `pathconf()`, and `fpathconf()` 405
12.2.1 How It Works 405
12.2.2 System Configuration Constants: `sysconf()` 406
12.2.3 Filesystem Limitations: `pathconf()` and `fpathconf()` 409
12.3 Getting Configuration String Variables: `confstr()` 411
12.4 Basic Process Limits: `ulimit()` 413
12.5 Hard and Soft Limits: `getrlimit()` and `setrlimit()` 414
12.6 Summary 417
Exercises 418

Chapter 13 General Library Interfaces—Part 2 419
13.1 Assertion Statements: `assert()` 419
13.2 Low-Level Memory: The `memXXX()` Functions 423
13.2.1 Setting Memory: `memset()` 423
13.2.2 Copying Memory: `memcpy()`, `memmove()`, and `memccpy()` 423
13.2.3 Comparing Memory Blocks: `memcmp()` 425
13.2.4 Searching for a Byte Value: `memchr()` 426
13.3 Temporary Files 426
13.3.1 Generating Temporary File Names (Bad) 426

13.3.2 Creating and Opening Temporary Files (Good) 430
13.3.3 Using the TMPDIR Environment Variable 433
13.4 Committing Suicide: abort() 434
13.5 Nonlocal Gotos 435
13.5.1 Using Standard Functions: setjmp() and longjmp() 435
13.5.2 Handling Signal Masks: sigsetjmp() and siglongjmp() 437
13.5.3 Observing Important Caveats 438
13.6 Pseudorandom Numbers 442
13.6.1 Standard C: rand() and srand() 443
13.6.2 POSIX Functions: random() and srandom() 445
13.6.3 The /dev/random and /dev/urandom Special Files 447
13.6.4 Using getrandom() Instead of /dev/urandom 449
13.6.5 Cryptographically Secure Random Numbers 450
13.7 Metacharacter Expansions 450
13.7.1 Simple Pattern Matching: fnmatch() 451
13.7.2 File Name Expansion: glob() and globfree() 453
13.7.3 Shell Word Expansion: wordexp() and wordfree() 458
13.8 Regular Expressions 459
13.9 Suggested Reading 467
13.10 Summary 468
Exercises 469

Chapter 14 Sockets and Basic Networking **473**
14.1 Introduction, with a Little Bit of History 473
14.2 Networking Technologies 474
14.3 Internet Building Blocks 474
14.3.1 IPv4 Addresses 475
14.3.2 IPv6 Addresses 475
14.3.3 Addresses and Interfaces 476
14.3.4 Network Byte Order 476
14.4 Networking and Client/Server 477
14.5 Basic Structure of a Server Program 478
14.5.1 Creating a Socket: socket() 478
14.5.2 Associating the Socket with an Address: bind() 481
14.5.3 Waiting for a Connection: listen() 482
14.5.4 Starting a Conversation: accept() 483
14.5.5 Running the Application: read()/write() 484
14.5.6 Cleaning Up: close() and shutdown() 485
14.5.7 Identifying the Ends of a Connection 485
14.5.8 Example Server Code: ftpd 486
14.6 Basic Structure of a Client Program 488
14.6.1 Creating a Socket: socket() 489
14.6.2 Making the Call: connect() 489
14.6.3 Example Client Code: ftp 489

14.7 Specialized Send and Receive Functions 492
14.7.1 Using `send()` and `recv()` 493
14.7.2 Connectionless Communication: UDP Sockets 494
14.8 Handling Multiple Open Connections: `select()` 494
14.8.1 Example Code: 4.4 BSD `inetd` 496
14.9 `pselect()`: A Smarter Version of `select()` 501
14.10 Unix-Domain Sockets 502
14.11 Suggested Reading 502
14.12 Summary 503
Exercises 504

Chapter 15 Internationalization and Localization 507
15.1 Introduction 507
15.2 Locales and the C Library 508
15.2.1 Locale Categories and Environment Variables 508
15.2.2 Setting the Locale: `setlocale()` 510
15.2.3 String Collation: `strcoll()` and `strxfrm()` 512
15.2.4 Low-Level Numeric and Monetary Formatting: `localeconv()` 515
15.2.5 High-Level Numeric and Monetary Formatting: `strfmon()` and `printf()` 519
15.2.6 Example: Formatting Numeric Values in `gawk` 521
15.2.7 Formatting Date and Time Values: `ctime()` and `strftime()` 523
15.2.8 Other Locale Information: `nl_langinfo()` 524
15.3 Dynamic Translation of Program Messages 526
15.3.1 Setting the Text Domain: `textdomain()` 527
15.3.2 Translating Messages: `gettext()` 527
15.3.3 Working with Plurals: `ngettext()` 528
15.3.4 Making `gettext()` Easy to Use 529
15.3.5 Rearranging Word Order with `printf()` 533
15.3.6 Testing Translations in a Private Directory 534
15.3.7 Setting the Output Codeset 534
15.3.8 Preparing Internationalized Programs 535
15.3.9 Creating Translations 536
15.4 Can You Spell That for Me, Please? 540
15.4.1 Wide Characters 541
15.4.2 Multibyte Character Encodings 545
15.4.3 Converting Bytes to Wide Characters 545
15.4.4 Converting Wide Characters to Bytes 550
15.4.5 Languages 552
15.4.6 Conclusion 553
15.5 Suggested Reading 553
15.6 Summary 553
Exercises 555

Chapter 16 Extended Interfaces 557
16.1 Allocating Aligned Memory: `posix_memalign()` and `memalign()` 557
16.2 Locking Files 558
16.2.1 File Locking Concepts 558
16.2.2 POSIX Locking: `fcntl()` and `lockf()` 559
16.2.3 BSD Locking: `flock()` 565
16.2.4 Mandatory Locking 566
16.3 More Precise Times 567
16.3.1 Microsecond Times: `gettimeofday()` 567
16.3.2 Nanosecond Times: `clock_gettime()` 569
16.3.3 Interval Timers: `setitimer()` and `getitimer()` 570
16.3.4 More Exact Pauses: `nanosleep()` 573
16.4 Advanced Searching with Binary Trees 575
16.4.1 Introduction to Binary Trees 575
16.4.2 Tree Management Functions 577
16.4.3 Tree Insertion: `tsearch()` 578
16.4.4 Tree Lookup and Use of a Returned Pointer: `tfind()` and `tsearch()` 579
16.4.5 Tree Traversal: `twalk()` 581
16.4.6 Tree Node Removal and Tree Deletion: `tdelete()` and `tdestroy()` 585
16.5 Summary 586
Exercises 587

PART III Debugging and Final Project 589

Chapter 17 Debugging 591
17.1 First Things First 591
17.2 Compilation for Debugging 592
17.3 GDB Basics 593
17.3.1 Getting a `core` File 594
17.3.2 Running GDB 597
17.3.3 Setting Breakpoints, Single-Stepping, and Setting Watchpoints 599
17.3.4 Escaping the Line-at-a-Time Jail 603
17.3.5 Repeatable, Reversable Debugging with `rr` 604
17.3.6 Honorable Mention: `lldb` 605
17.4 Programming for Debugging 606
17.4.1 Compile-Time Debugging Code 606
17.4.2 Runtime Debugging Code 622
17.5 Debugging Tools I: A Modern `lint` 632
17.6 Debugging Tools II: Memory Allocation Debuggers 633
17.6.1 Valgrind: A Versatile Tool 634
17.6.2 Address Sanitizer 644
17.7 Asking for Help 650
17.8 Software Testing 651

17.9 Debugging Rules 653
17.10 Suggested Reading 655
17.11 Summary 656
Exercises 657

Chapter 18 A Project That Ties Everything Together 659
18.1 Project Description 659
18.2 Suggested Reading 661

PART IV Appendices 663

Appendix A Teach Yourself Programming in Ten Years 665

Appendix B Caldera Ancient UNIX License 671

Appendix C GNU General Public License 673

Appendix D License for the One True Awk 685

Appendix E License for 4.4 BSD Code 687

Index 689

Foreword

Everyone remembers when they started programming. You could have started in elementary school, high school or college (like me), or before. You could have been a hobbyist, finding interesting things on the Internet and wanting to tinker. Maybe you started as part of a job.

Either way, it wasn't long before you found C, attracted by its spare elegance, its economy of expression, and the power it afforded to do surprisingly complex things. Whether you started with the "Hello, World" program—something of a koan in the C universe—from *The C Programming Language*, or a different book, or no book at all, you quickly discovered that the path to good programming practices was to understand the power of the programming environment and learn from well-written programs that used it. But where to find them?

This is the book for you.

This book fills the gap between learning C and its syntax and being able to use it to write useful applications in the GNU/Linux environment. You'll find its explanations of the APIs clear and coherent, and its use of existing programs to show how everything fits together illustrative.

Arnold Robbins has distilled years of programming practice into this volume, and shared tidbits of his own experiences, mistakes, and solutions. After reading, I'm confident that you'll appreciate the GNU/Linux environment and what you can do with it.

It's something I wish I had had way back when I first started to learn and program in C. I think it will become an essential part of your programming journey.

— Chet Ramey
Novelty, Ohio
USA

Preface

One of the best ways to learn about programming is to read well-written programs. This book teaches the fundamental Linux system APIs—those that form the core of any significant program—by presenting code from production programs that you use every day.

By looking at concrete programs, you not only can see how to use the Linux APIs but also can examine the real-world issues (performance, portability, robustness) that arise in writing software.

While the book's title is *Linux Application Development by Example*, everything we cover, unless otherwise noted, applies to other Unix-derived systems as well.[1] In particular, we focus on GNU/Linux systems. In general we use "Linux" to mean the Linux kernel, and "GNU/Linux" to mean the total system (kernel, libraries, tools). Also, we often say "Linux" when we mean all of Linux, GNU/Linux, and Unix; if something is specific to one system or the other, we mention it explicitly.

Audience

This book is intended for the person who understands programming and is familiar with the basics of C, at least on the level of *The C Programming Language* by Brian Kernighan and Dennis Ritchie. (Java, Python, and Go programmers wishing to read this book should understand C pointers, since C code makes heavy use of them.) The examples use both the 1999 version of Standard C and Original C.[2]

In particular, you should be familiar with all C operators, control-flow structures, variable and pointer declarations and use, the string management functions, the use of `exit()`, and the `<stdio.h>` suite of functions for file input/output.

You should understand the basic concepts of *standard input*, *standard output*, and *standard error*, and the fact that all C programs receive an array of character strings representing invocation options and arguments. You should also be familiar with the fundamental command-line tools, such as `cd`, `cp`, `date`, `ln`, `ls`, `man` (and `info` if you have it), `rmdir`, and `rm`; the use of long and short command-line options; environment variables; and I/O redirection, including pipes.

[1]Systems derived from the original Unix source code, such as Solaris, HP-UX, and AIX, can today be classified as legacy systems. However, there are a number of BSD-derived systems in active development, such as NetBSD, FreeBSD, and OpenBSD, along with many others.

[2]Although there are newer C standards, we don't need any of the features they offer.

We assume that you want to write programs that work not just under GNU/Linux but across the range of Unix-like systems. To that end, we mark each interface as to its availability (GLIBC systems only, or defined by POSIX, and so on), and portability advice forms an integral part of the text.

The programming taught here may be at a lower level than you're used to; that's OK. The system calls are the fundamental building blocks for higher operations and are thus low level by nature. This in turn dictates our use of C: the APIs were designed for use from C, and code that interfaces them to higher-level languages, such as C++, Java, Python, or Go, will necessarily be lower level in nature, and most likely, written in C. It may help to remember that "low level" doesn't mean "bad," it just means "more challenging."

What You Will Learn

Fundamentals may get old, but they usually don't become wrong.
— Grant Taylor

This book focuses on the basic APIs that form the core of Linux programming, the *fundamental* things you need to know to write software that makes good use of the GNU/Linux and POSIX APIs:

- Arguments, options, and the environment
- Memory management
- File input/output
- File metadata
- Processes and signals
- Interprocess communication
- Users and groups
- Resource limits
- Programming support (sorting, argument parsing, and so on)
- Basic networking
- Internationalization
- Debugging

We have purposely kept the list of topics short. We believe that it is intimidating to try to learn "all there is to know" from a single book. Most readers prefer smaller, more focused books, and the best Unix books are all written that way.[3]

[3] Although this book isn't exactly small, we've seen several POSIX programming books that are easily twice as big.

We have also made an effort to avoid too much information (TMI), giving you exactly what you need to do your work: no less, but also no more.

The APIs we cover include both system calls and library functions. Indeed, at the C level, both appear as simple function calls. A *system call* is a direct request for system services, such as reading or writing a file or creating a process. A *library function*, on the other hand, runs at the user level, possibly never requesting any services from the operating system. System calls are documented in section 2 of the online reference manual and library functions are documented in section 3. (As with the online manual pages for commands, you access the manual pages for system calls and library functions with the `man` command.)

Our goal is to teach you the use of the Linux APIs by example, in particular through the use, wherever possible, of both original Unix source code and the GNU utilities. Unfortunately, there aren't as many self-contained examples as we thought there'd be. Thus, we have written numerous small demonstration programs as well. We stress programming principles, especially those aspects of GNU programming such as "no arbitrary limits," that make the GNU utilities into exceptional programs.

The choice of everyday programs to study is deliberate. If you've been using GNU/Linux for any length of time, you already understand what programs such as `ls` and `cp` do; it then becomes easy to dive straight into *how* the programs work, without having to spend a lot of time learning *what* they do.

Occasionally, we present both higher-level and lower-level ways of doing things. Usually the higher-level standard interface is implemented in terms of the lower-level interface or construct. We hope that such views of what's "under the hood" will help you understand how things work; for all the code you write, you should always use the higher-level, standard interface.

Similarly, we sometimes introduce functions that provide certain functionality and then recommend (with a stated reason) that these functions be avoided! The primary reason for this approach is so that you'll be able to recognize these functions when you see them and thus understand the code using them. A well-rounded knowledge of a topic requires understanding not just what you can do, but what you should and should not do.

Finally, each chapter concludes with suggested readings and exercises. Some of the exercises involve modifying or writing code. Others are more in the category of "thought experiments" or "Why do you think ...?" We recommend that you do all of them—they will help cement your understanding of the material.

Small Is Beautiful: Unix Programs

Hoare's law:
Inside every large program is a small program struggling to get out.
— C. A. R. Hoare

Initially, we planned to teach the Linux API by using the code from the GNU utilities. However, the modern versions of even simple command-line programs (like `mv` and `cp`) are large and many-featured. This is particularly true of the GNU variants of the standard utilities, which allow long and short options, do everything required by POSIX, and often have additional, seemingly unrelated options as well (like output highlighting).

It then becomes reasonable to ask, "Given such a large and confusing forest, how can we focus on the one or two important trees?" In other words, if we present the current full-featured program, will it be possible to see the underlying core operation of the program?

That is when *Hoare's law*[4] inspired us to look to the original Unix programs for example code. The original V7 Unix utilities are small and straightforward, making it easy to see what's going on and to understand how the system calls are used. (V7 was released around 1979; it is the common ancestor of all modern Unix systems, including GNU/Linux and the BSD systems.)

For many years, Unix source code was protected by copyrights and trade secret license agreements, making it difficult to use for study and impossible to publish. This is still true of all commercial Unix source code. However, in 2002, Caldera (currently operating as SCO) made the original Unix code (through V7 and 32V Unix) available under an Open Source–style license (see Appendix B, "Caldera Ancient UNIX License," page 671). This makes it possible for us to include the code from the early Unix system in this book.

Standards

Throughout the book we refer to several different formal standards. A *standard* is a document describing how something works. Formal standards exist for many things; for example, the shape, placement, and meaning of the holes in the electrical outlet in your wall are defined by a formal standard so that all the power cords in your country work in all the outlets.

So, too, do formal standards for computing systems define how they are supposed to work; this enables developers and users to know what to expect from their software and enables them to complain to their vendor when software doesn't work.

Of interest to us here are:

[4] This famous statement was made at *The International Workshop on Efficient Production of Large Programs* in Jabłonna, Poland, August 10–14, 1970.

1. *ISO/IEC International Standard 9899:1999 Programming Languages — C, second edition, 1999.* The second formal standard for the C programming language.
2. *ISO/IEC International Standard 14882:2024 Programming Languages — C++, 2024.* The current formal standard for the C++ programming language.
3. *The Open Group Base Specifications Issue 8, IEEE Std 1003.1™–2024 edition.*[5] The current version of the POSIX standard; it describes the behavior expected of Unix and Unix-like systems. This edition covers both the system call and library interface, as seen by the C/C++ programmer, and the shell and utilities interface, seen by the user. It consists of several volumes:

   - *Base Definitions.* The definitions of terms, facilities, and header files.
   - *System Interfaces.* The system calls and library functions. POSIX terms them all "functions."
   - *Shell and Utilities.* The shell language and utilities available for use with shell programs and interactively.
   - *Rationale.* Explanations and rationales for the choice of facilities that are or are not included in the standard.

Although language standards aren't exciting reading, you may wish to consider purchasing a copy of the C standard, as it provides the final definition of the language. Copies can be purchased from ANSI[6] and from ISO.[7] (The PDF version of the C standard is quite affordable.)

The POSIX standard is available online. The standard is intended for implementation on both Unix and Unix-like systems, as well as on non-Unix systems. Thus, the base functionality it provides is a subset of what Unix systems have. However, the POSIX standard also defines optional *extensions*—additional functionality, for example, for threads or real-time support. Of most importance to us is the *X/Open System Interface* (XSI) extension, which describes facilities from historical Unix systems.

Throughout the book, we mark each API as to its availability: ISO C, POSIX, XSI, GLIBC only, or nonstandard but commonly available.

Features and Power: GNU Programs

Restricting ourselves to just the original Unix code would have made an interesting history book, but it would not have been very useful a quarter of the way into the twenty-first century. Modern programs do not have the same constraints (memory, CPU power, disk space and speed) that the early Unix systems did. Furthermore, they need to operate in a multilingual world—ASCII and American English aren't enough.

[5] `https://pubs.opengroup.org/onlinepubs/9799919799/`

[6] `http://www.ansi.org`

[7] `http://www.iso.ch`

More importantly, one of the primary freedoms expressly promoted by the Free Software Foundation (FSF) and the GNU Project[8] is the "freedom to study." GNU programs are intended to provide a large corpus of well-written programs that journeyman programmers can use as a source from which to learn.

By using GNU programs, we want to meet both goals: show you well-written, modern code from which you will learn how to write good code and how to use the APIs well.

We believe that GNU software is better because it is free (in the sense of "freedom," not "free beer"). But it's also recognized that GNU software is often *technically* better than the corresponding Unix counterparts, and we devote space in Section 1.4, "Why GNU Programs Are Better," page 13, to explaining why.

A number of the GNU code examples come from `gawk` (GNU `awk`). The main reason is that it's a program with which we're very familiar, and therefore it was easy to pick examples from it. We don't otherwise make any special claims about it.

Summary of Chapters

Driving a car is a holistic process that involves multiple simultaneous tasks. In many ways, Linux programming is similar, requiring that you understand multiple aspects of the API, such as file I/O, file metadata, directories, storage of time information, and so on.

The first part of the book looks at enough of these individual items to enable studying the first significant program, the V7 `ls`. Then we complete the discussion of files and users by looking at file hierarchies and the way filesystems work and are used.

Chapter 1, "Introduction," page 3,
describes the Unix and Linux file and process models, looks at the differences between Original C and 1999 Standard C, and provides an overview of the principles that make GNU programs generally better than standard Unix programs. The chapter also includes advice on programming style, and some thoughts on the use of AI for software development.

Chapter 2, "Arguments, Options, and the Environment," page 23,
describes how a C program accesses and processes command-line arguments and options and explains how to work with the environment.

Chapter 3, "User-Level Memory Management," page 51,
provides an overview of the different kinds of memory in use and available in a running process. User-level memory management is central to every nontrivial application, so it's important to understand it early on.

Chapter 4, "Files and File I/O," page 79,
discusses basic file I/O, showing how to create and use files. This understanding is important for everything else that follows.

[8] `http://www.gnu.org`

Chapter 5, "Directories and File Metadata," page 111,
describes how directories, hard links, and symbolic links work. It then describes file metadata, such as owners, permissions, and so on, as well as covering how to work with directories.

Chapter 6, "General Library Interfaces—Part 1," page 155,
looks at the first set of general programming interfaces that we need so that we can make effective use of a file's metadata.

Chapter 7, "Putting It All Together: `ls`*," page 201,*
ties together everything seen so far by looking at the V7 `ls` program.

Chapter 8, "Filesystems and Directory Walks," page 221,
describes how filesystems are mounted and unmounted and how a program can tell what is mounted on the system. It also describes how a program can easily "walk" an entire file hierarchy, taking appropriate action for each object it encounters.

The second part of the book deals with process creation and management, interprocess communication with pipes and signals, user and group IDs, resource limits, additional general programming interfaces, and basic networking. Next, the book describes internationalization with GNU `gettext` and then several advanced APIs.

Chapter 9, "Process Management and Pipes," page 275,
looks at process creation, program execution, IPC with pipes, and file descriptor management, including nonblocking I/O.

Chapter 10, "Signals," page 333,
discusses signals, a simplistic form of interprocess communication. Signals also play an important role in a parent process's management of its children.

Chapter 11, "Permissions and User and Group ID Numbers," page 383,
looks at how processes and files are identified, how permission checking works, and how the setuid and setgid mechanisms work.

Chapter 12, "Resource Limits," page 405,
describes the ways in which processes may use system resources, and in particular how they may be constrained from using too many resources.

Chapter 13, "General Library Interfaces—Part 2," page 419,
looks at the rest of the general APIs; many of these are more specialized than the first general set of APIs.

Chapter 14, "Sockets and Basic Networking," page 473,
introduces the basic facilities for communication between processes on different computers.

Chapter 15, "Internationalization and Localization," page 507,
explains how to enable your programs to work in multiple languages, with almost no pain.

Chapter 16, "Extended Interfaces," page 557,
describes several extended versions of interfaces covered in previous chapters, as well as covering file locking in full detail.

The third part rounds off the book with a chapter on debugging, since (almost) no one gets things right the first time, and we suggest a final project to cement your knowledge of the APIs covered in this book.

Chapter 17, "Debugging," page 591,
describes the basics of the GDB debugger, transmits as much of our programming experience in this area as possible, and looks at several useful tools for doing different kinds of debugging.

Chapter 18, "A Project That Ties Everything Together," page 659,
presents a significant programming project that makes use of just about everything covered in the book.

Several appendices cover topics of interest, including the licenses for the source code used in this book.

Appendix A, "Teach Yourself Programming in Ten Years," page 665,
invokes the famous saying "Rome wasn't built in a day." Similarly, Linux/Unix expertise and understanding come only with time and practice. With that in mind, we have included this essay by Peter Norvig, which we highly recommend.

Appendix B, "Caldera Ancient UNIX License," page 671,
covers the Unix source code used in this book.

Appendix C, "GNU General Public License," page 673,
covers the GNU source code used in this book.

Appendix D, "License for the One True Awk," page 685,
covers the source code from the One True Awk that is used in this book.

Appendix E, "License for 4.4 BSD Code," page 687,
covers the source code from the 4.4 BSD distribution that is used in this book.

Typographical Conventions

Like all books on computer-related topics, we use certain typographical conventions to convey information. *Definitions* or first uses of terms appear in italics, like the word "Definitions" at the beginning of this sentence. Italics are also used for *emphasis*, for citations of other works, and for commentary in examples. Variable items such as arguments or file names, appear *like this*. Occasionally, we use a bold font when a point needs to be made **strongly**.

Things that exist on a computer are in a constant-width font, such as file names (`foo.c`) and command names (`ls`, `grep`). Short snippets that you type are additionally enclosed in single quotes: '`ls -l *.c`'.

`$` and `>` are the default Bourne shell primary and secondary prompts and are used to display interactive examples. *`User input`* appears in a different font from regular `computer output` in examples. Examples look like this:

```
$ ls -l *.texi          Look at files. Option is letter l, not numeral "one"
-rw-rw-r-- 1 arnold arnold  33165 Apr 24 18:03 00-preface.texi
-rw-rw-r-- 1 arnold arnold  48622 Apr 24 18:05 01-intro.texi
-rw-rw-r-- 1 arnold arnold  65930 Apr 23 22:43 02-cmdline.texi
...
```

We prefer the Bourne shell and its variants (`ksh93`, Bash) over the C shell; thus, all our examples show only the Bourne shell. Be aware that quoting and line-continuation rules are different in the C shell; if you use it, you're on your own![9]

When referring to functions in programs, we append an empty pair of parentheses to the function's name: `printf()`, `strcpy()`. When referring to a manual page (accessible with the `man` command), we follow the standard Unix convention of writing the command or function name in italics and the section in parentheses after it, in regular type: *awk*(1), *printf*(3).

Where to Get Unix and GNU Source Code

You may wish to have copies of the programs we use in this book for your own experimentation and review. All the source code is available over the Internet, and your GNU/Linux distribution contains the source code for the GNU utilities.

Unix Code

Archives of various "ancient" versions of Unix are maintained by the UNIX Heritage Society (TUHS).[10]

Of most interest is that it is possible to browse the archive of old Unix source code on the Web. Start with `http://www.tuhs.org/UnixTree/`. Almost all the example code in this book is from the Seventh Edition Research UNIX System, also known as "V7."

The TUHS site is physically located in Australia, although there are mirrors of the archive around the world—see `http://www.tuhs.org/archive_sites.html`. This page also indicates that the archive is available for mirroring with `rsync`. (See `http://rsync.samba.org/` if you don't have `rsync`; it's standard on GNU/Linux systems.)

As of the time of this writing, you will need about 6.5–7 gigabytes of disk to copy the entire archive. To copy the archive, create an empty directory, and in it, run the following commands:

[9] See the *csh*(1) and *tcsh*(1) manpages and the book *Using `csh` & `tcsh`*, by Paul DuBois (O'Reilly & Associates, 1995), ISBN-13: 978-1-56592-132-0.

[10] `http://www.tuhs.org`

```
mkdir Applications Distributions Documentation Tools

rsync -avz minnie.tuhs.org::UA_Root             .
rsync -avz minnie.tuhs.org::UA_Applications    Applications
rsync -avz minnie.tuhs.org::UA_Distributions   Distributions
rsync -avz minnie.tuhs.org::UA_Documentation   Documentation
rsync -avz minnie.tuhs.org::UA_Tools           Tools
```

(For your convenience, these commands are available in a script named `get-tuhs-files.sh` in the `ch-01-intro` directory of the book's GitHub repository.)

It's interesting to note that V7 code does not contain any copyright or permission notices in it. The authors wrote the code primarily for themselves and their research, leaving the permission issues to AT&T's corporate licensing department.

GNU Code

If you're using GNU/Linux, then your distribution will have come with source code, presumably in whatever packaging format it uses (Red Hat RPM files, Debian DEB files, Slackware `.tar.gz` files, etc.). The examples in the book are from the GNU Coreutils, version 9.4. You can search for the appropriate source package for your distribution, if you like. Or follow the instructions in the next few paragraphs to retrieve the code.

If you prefer to retrieve the files yourself from the GNU FTP site, you will find them at `https://ftp.gnu.org/gnu/coreutils/coreutils-9.4.tar.gz`.[11]

You can use either `wget` or `curl` to retrieve the file:

```
$ wget https://ftp.gnu.org/gnu/coreutils/coreutils-9.4.tar.gz
... lots of output here as file is retrieved ...
```

Alternatively, you can use good old-fashioned `ftp`[12] to retrieve the file:

```
$ ftp ftp.gnu.org                                   Connect to the GNU ftp site
Trying 209.51.188.20:21 ...
Connected to ftp.gnu.org.
220 GNU FTP server ready.
Name (ftp.gnu.org:arnold): anonymous                Use anonymous ftp
...                                                 Site notice deleted
230 Login successful.
Remote system type is UNIX.
Using binary mode to transfer files.
ftp> cd /gnu/coreutils                              Change to the Coreutils directory
250 Directory successfully changed.
ftp> bin
200 Switching to Binary mode.
ftp> get coreutils-9.4.tar.gz                       Retrieve the file
```

[11] The tar file is also available compressed with `xz`; this file is somewhat smaller than the one compressed with `gzip`.

[12] Note that the FSF prefers you use HTTPS instead of FTP; their server indicates that they will eventually disable FTP access.

```
local: coreutils-9.4.tar.gz remote: coreutils-9.4.tar.gz
229 Entering Extended Passive Mode (|||25110|)
150 Opening BINARY mode data connection for coreutils-9.4.tar.gz (14714577 bytes).
100% |***********************************| 14369 KiB  792.25 KiB/s    00:00 ETA
226 Transfer complete.
14714577 bytes received in 00:18 (785.75 KiB/s)
ftp> quit                                                    Log off
221 Goodbye.
```

Once you have the file, extract it as follows:

```
$ gzip -dc < coreutils-9.4.tar.gz | tar -xvpf -          Extract files
... lots of output here as files are extracted ...
```

Systems using GNU `tar` may use this incantation:

```
$ tar -xvpzf coreutils-9.4.tar.gz                        Extract files
... lots of output here as files are extracted ...
```

In compliance with the GNU General Public License, here is the copyright information for all GNU programs quoted in this book: all the programs are "free software; you can redistribute it and/or modify it under the terms of the GNU General Public License as published by the Free Software Foundation; either version 3 of the License, or (at your option) any later version." See Appendix C, "GNU General Public License," page 673, for the text of the GNU General Public License.

Coreutils 9.4 file	**Copyright dates**
`lib/safe-read.c`	Copyright © 1993–1994, 1998, 2002–2006, 2009–2023
`lib/safe-write.c`	Copyright © 2002, 2009–2023
`src/du.c`	Copyright © 1988–2023
`src/env.c`	Copyright © 1986–2023
`src/install.c`	Copyright © 1989–2023
`src/link.c`	Copyright © 2001–2023
`src/ls.c`	Copyright © 1985–2023
`src/sort.c`	Copyright © 1988–2023
`src/stdbuf.c`	Copyright © 2009–2023
`src/system.h`	Copyright © 1989–2023

Gawk 3.0.0 file	**Copyright dates**
`posix/gawkmisc.c`	Copyright © 1986, 1988, 1989, 1991–1995

Gawk 3.0.6 file	**Copyright dates**
`eval.c`	Copyright © 1986, 1988, 1989, 1991–2000

Gawk 3.1.8 file	**Copyright dates**
`eval.c`	Copyright © 1986, 1988, 1989, 1991–2010
`io.c`	Copyright © 1986, 1988, 1989, 1991–2010

Gawk 5.3.0 file	**Copyright dates**
`awk.h`	Copyright © 1986, 1988, 1989, 1991–2023
`builtin.c`	Copyright © 1986, 1988, 1989, 1991–2023
`io.c`	Copyright © 1986, 1988, 1989, 1991–2023
`main.c`	Copyright © 1986, 1988, 1989, 1991–2023
`node.c`	Copyright © 1986, 1988, 1989, 1991–2001, 2003–2015, 2017–2019, 2021–2023
`posix/gawkmisc.c`	Copyright © 1986, 1988, 1989, 1991–1998, 2001–2004, 2011, 2021–2023

Gawk 5.3.1 file	**Copyright dates**
`printf.c`	Copyright © 1986, 1988, 1989, 1991–2024

Gettext 0.22.5 file	**Copyright dates**
`gettext.h`	Copyright © 1995–1998, 2000–2002, 2004–2006, 2009–2020

GLIBC 2.35 file	**Copyright dates**
`/usr/include/locale.h`	Copyright © 1991–2002

Make 4.4.1 file	**Copyright dates**
`read.c`	Copyright © 1988–2023

We use a few examples from the One True AWK, published by Brian Kernighan. Appendix D, "License for the One True Awk," page 685, presents its license. Here is the copyright information for it:

One True Awk file	**Copyright dates**
`awk.h`	Copyright © 1997
`b.c`	Copyright © 1997

Example code from 4.2 BSD used in Section 14.5.8, "Example Server Code: `ftpd`," page 486, is covered by the Caldera Open Source license.

Finally, we use some example code from 4.4 BSD. The license for this code is in Appendix E, "License for 4.4 BSD Code," page 687. Here is the relevant copyright information.

4.4 BSD file	**Copyright dates**
`ftp.c`	Copyright © 1985, 1989, 1993
`inetd.c`	Copyright © 1983, 1991

Where to Get the Example Programs

The example programs are available on GitHub. You can get them from `https://github.com/arnoldrobbins/LinuxByExample-2e`. Errata for the book will be available there as well.

Acknowledgments for the Second Edition

Thanks to Debra Williams and Mark Taub for endorsing a new edition of this book.

Thanks to Chet Ramey for answering questions about macOS, POSIX, and other things. I thank him also for his kind words in the Foreword.

Thanks to Nelson H. F. Beebe for answering questions related to Solaris and other Unix systems. Thanks to Geoff Clare for help with questions related to POSIX.

Gavin Smith and Patrice Dumas currently maintain and develop the Texinfo markup language and its toolset, which I used to write the book. I thank them.

Thanks to Matthew Helmke, Professor Brian Kernighan, Chet Ramey, and Miriam Robbins for their technical reviews of this edition. Their comments materially improved the entire text. As for the previous edition, any remaining errors are mine.

I thank Arthur Johnson for his amazing copyediting, and Chuti Prasertsith for the fantastic cover design. Thanks to the production team headed by Julie Nahil and Sumitra Boopalan.

Once again, my deepest gratitude and love to my wife, Miriam, for her support and encouragement during the book's writing.

— Nof Ayalon, ISRAEL
September 2025

Acknowledgments for the First Edition

Writing a book is lots of work, and doing it well requires help from many people. Dr. Brian W. Kernighan, Dr. Doug McIlroy, Peter Memishian, and Peter van der Linden reviewed the initial book proposal. David J. Agans, Fred Fish, Don Marti, Jim Meyering, Peter Norvig, and Julian Seward provided reprint permission for various items quoted throughout the book. Thanks to Geoff Collyer, Ulrich Drepper, Yosef Gold, Dr. C. A. R. (Tony) Hoare, Dr. Manny Lehman, Jim Meyering, Dr. Dennis M. Ritchie, Julian Seward, Henry Spencer, and Dr. Wladyslaw M. Turski, who provided much useful general information. Thanks also to the other members of the GNITS gang: Karl Berry, Akim DeMaille, Ulrich Drepper, Greg McGary, Jim Meyering, François Pinard, and Tom Tromey, who all provided helpful feedback about good programming practice. Karl Berry, Alper Ersoy, and Dr. Nelson H. F. Beebe provided valuable technical help with the Texinfo and DocBook/XML toolchains.

Good technical reviewers not only make sure that an author gets his facts right, but they also ensure that he thinks carefully about his presentation. Dr. Nelson H. F. Beebe, Geoff Collyer, Russ Cox, Ulrich Drepper, Dr. Brian W. Kernighan, Randy Lechlitner, Peter Memishian, Jim Meyering, Chet Ramey, and Louis Taber acted as technical reviewers for the entire book. Dr. Michael Brennan provided helpful comments on Chapter 15.

[This is Chapter 17 in the current edition.] Both the prose and many of the example programs benefited from their reviews. I hereby thank all of them. As most authors usually say here, "Any remaining errors are mine."

I would especially like to thank Mark Taub of Pearson Education for initiating this project, for his enthusiasm for the series, and for his help and advice as the book moved through its various stages. Anthony Gemmellaro did a phenomenal job of realizing my concept for the cover, and Gail Cocker's interior design is beautiful. Fay Gemmellaro made the production process enjoyable, instead of a chore. Dmitry and Alina Kirsanov did the figures, page layout, and indexing; they were a pleasure to work with.

Finally, my deepest gratitude and love to my wife, Miriam, for her support and encouragement during the book's writing.

— Nof Ayalon, ISRAEL
April 2004

Part I

Files and Users

Chapter 1

Introduction

If there is one phrase that summarizes the primary GNU/Linux (and therefore Unix) concepts, it's "files and processes." In this chapter we review the Linux file and process models. These are important to understand because the system calls are almost all concerned with modifying some attribute or part of the state of a file or a process.

Next, because we'll be examining code in both styles, we briefly review the major difference between 1999 Standard C and Original C. Next, we discuss at some length the programming principles that make GNU programs "better"; we'll see these principles in use in the code. After that, we discuss a few general issues related to programming style, and then discourse some about the use of artificial intelligence for software development.

This chapter contains a number of intentional simplifications. The full details are covered as we progress through the book. If you're already a Linux wizard, please forgive us.

1.1 The Linux/Unix File Model

One of the driving goals in the original Unix design was *simplicity*. Simple concepts are easy to learn and use. When the concepts are translated into simple APIs, simple programs are then easy to design, write, and get correct. In addition, simple code is often smaller and more efficient than more complicated designs, and it is easier to maintain and modify.

The quest for simplicity was driven by two factors. From a technical point of view, the original PDP-11 minicomputers on which Unix was developed had a small address space: 64 kilobytes total on the smaller systems, 64 KB of code and 64 KB of data on the large ones. These restrictions applied not just to regular programs (so-called *user-level* code), but to the operating system itself (*kernel-level* code). Thus, "Small Is Beautiful" not only aesthetically, but also because there was no other choice!

The second factor was a negative reaction to contemporary commercial operating systems, which were needlessly complicated, with obtuse command languages, multiple kinds of file I/O, and little generality or symmetry. (Steve Johnson once remarked that "Using TSO is like trying to kick a dead whale down a beach." TSO was one of the obtuse mainframe time-sharing systems just described.)

1.1.1 Files and Permissions

The Unix file model is as simple as it gets: a file is a linear stream of bytes. Period. The operating system imposes no preordained structure on files: no fixed or varying record sizes, no indexed files, nothing. The interpretation of file contents is entirely up to the application. (This isn't quite true, as we'll see shortly, but it's close enough for a start.)

Once you have a file, you can do three things with the file's data: read it, write it, or execute it.

Unix was designed for time-sharing minicomputers; this implies a multiuser environment from the get-go. Once there are multiple users, it must be possible to specify a file's permissions: perhaps user `jane` is user `fred`'s boss, and `jane` doesn't want `fred` to read the latest performance evaluations.

For file permission purposes, users are classified into three distinct categories: *user*, or the owner of a file; *group*, or the group of users associated with this file (discussed shortly); and *other*, meaning anybody else. For each of these categories, *every* file has separate read, write, and execute permission bits associated with it, yielding a total of nine permission bits. This shows up in the first field of the output of '`ls -l`':

```
$ ls -l progex.texi
-rw-rw-r-- 1 arnold arnold 5100 Jan 25 14:55 progex.texi
```

Here, `arnold` and `arnold` are the owner and group of `progex.texi`, and `-rw-rw-r--` are the file type and permissions. The first character is a dash for regular files, a `d` for directories, or one of a small set of other characters for other kinds of files that aren't important at the moment. Each subsequent group of three characters represents read, write, and execute permission for the owner, group, and "other," respectively.

In this example, `progex.texi` is readable and writable by the owner and group, and readable by other. The dashes indicate absent permissions; thus the file is not executable by anyone, nor is it writable by "other."

The owner and group of a file are stored as numeric values known as the *user ID* (UID) and *group ID* (GID); standard library functions that we present later in the book make it possible to print the values as human-readable names.

A file's owner can change the permission by using the `chmod` (change mode) command. (As such, file permissions are sometimes referred to as the "file mode.") A file's group and owner can be changed with the `chgrp` (change group) and `chown` (change owner) commands, respectively.[1]

Group permissions were intended to support cooperative work: although one person in a group or department may own a particular file, it may be that everyone in that group needs to be able to modify it. (Consider a collaborative marketing paper or data from a survey.)

When the system goes to check a file access (usually upon opening a file), if the UID of the process matches that of the file, the owner permissions apply. If those permissions deny the operation (say, a write to a file with `-r--rw-rw-` permissions), the operation fails; Unix and Linux do not proceed to test the group and other permissions.[2] The same is true if the UID is different but the GID matches; if the group permissions deny the operation, it fails.

Unix and Linux support the notion of a *superuser*: a user with special privileges. This user is known as `root` and has the UID of zero. `root` is allowed to do *anything*; all bets are off,

[1] Some systems allow regular users to change the ownership on their files to someone else, thus "giving them away." The details are standardized by POSIX but are a bit messy. Typical GNU/Linux configurations do not allow it.

[2] The owner can always change the permission, of course. Most users don't disable write permission for themselves.

all doors are open, all drawers are unlocked.[3] (This can have significant security implications, which we touch on throughout the book but do not cover exhaustively.) Thus, even if a file is mode `----------`, `root` can still read and write the file. (One exception is that the file can't be executed. But as `root` can add execute permission, the restriction doesn't prevent anything.)

The user/group/other, read/write/execute permissions model is simple, yet flexible enough to cover most situations. More powerful but more complicated models exist and are implemented on different systems, but none of them are well enough standardized and broadly enough implemented to be worth discussing in a general-purpose text like this one.

1.1.2 Directories and File Names

Once you have a file, you need someplace to keep it. This is the purpose of the *directory* (known as a "folder" on Windows and Mac systems). A directory is a special kind of file that associates file names with particular collections of file metadata, known as *inodes*. Directories are special because they can only be updated by the operating system, by the system calls described in Chapter 4, "Files and File I/O," page 79. They are also special in that the operating system dictates the format of directory entries.

File names may contain any valid 8-bit byte except the `/` (forward slash) character and ASCII NUL, the character whose bits are all zero. Early Unix systems limited file names to 14 bytes; modern systems allow individual file names to be up to 255 bytes.

The inode contains all the information about a file except its name: the type, owner, group, permissions, size, and modification and access times. It also stores the locations of the disk blocks containing the file's data. All of these are data *about* the file, not the file's data itself, thus the term *metadata*.

Read, write, and execute have slightly different meanings for directories than they do for files. Read permission means the ability to search the directory—that is, to look through it to see what files it contains. Write permission is the ability to create *and remove* files in the directory. Execute permission is the ability to go through a directory when opening or otherwise accessing a contained file or subdirectory.

NOTE

If you have write permission on a directory, you can remove files in that directory, even if they don't belong to you! When used interactively, the `rm` command notices this, and asks you for confirmation in such a case.

The `/tmp` directory has write permission for everyone, but your files in `/tmp` are quite safe because `/tmp` usually has the so-called sticky bit set on it:

```
$ ls -ld /tmp
drwxrwxrwt 19 root root 36864 Nov 12 06:54 /tmp
```

Note the `t` is the last position of the first field. On most directories this position has an `x` in it. With the sticky bit set, only you, as the file's owner or `root`, may remove your files. (We discuss this in more detail in Section 11.4.2, "Directories and the Sticky Bit," page 392.)

---

[3] There are some rare exceptions to this rule, all of which are beyond the scope of this book.

1.1.3 Executable Files

Remember we said that the operating system doesn't impose a structure on files? Well, we've already seen that that was a white lie when it comes to directories, and that's also the case for binary executable files. To run a program, the kernel has to know what part of a file represents instructions (code) and what part represents data. This leads to the notion of an *object file format*, which is the definition for how these things are laid out within a file on disk.

Although the kernel will only run files laid out in the proper format, it is up to user-level utilities to create these files. The compiler for a programming language (such as C, C++, Fortran, Go, or Rust) creates object files, and then a linker or loader (usually named `ld`) binds the object files with library routines to create the final executable. Note that even if a file has all the right bits in all the right places, the kernel won't run it if the appropriate execute permission bit (or at least one execute bit for `root`) isn't turned on.

Because the compiler, assembler, and loader are user-level tools, it's (relatively) easy to change object file formats as needs develop over time; it's only necessary to "teach" the kernel about the new format, and then that format can be used. The part that loads executables is relatively small, and this isn't an impossible task. Thus Unix object file formats have evolved over time. The original format was known as `a.out` (Assembler OUTput). The next format, still used on some commercial systems, is known as COFF (Common Object File Format), and the current, most widely used format is ELF (Extensible Linking Format). Modern GNU/Linux, BSD systems, and Solaris use ELF.

The kernel recognizes that an executable file contains binary object code by looking at the first few bytes of the file for special *magic numbers*. These are sequences of two or four bytes that the kernel recognizes as being special. For backward compatibility, modern Unix systems recognize multiple formats. ELF files begin with the four characters `"\177ELF"`.

Besides binary executables, the kernel also supports executable *scripts*. Such a file also begins with a magic number—in this case, the two regular characters `#!`. A script is a program executed by an interpreter, such as the shell, `awk`, Perl, Python, or Ruby. The `#!` line provides the full path to the interpreter and, optionally, a single argument:

```
#! /usr/bin/awk -f
BEGIN { print "hello, world" }
```

Let's assume the above contents are in a file named `hello.awk` and that the file is executable. When you type '`hello.awk`', the kernel runs the program as if you had typed '`/usr/bin/awk -f hello.awk`'. Any additional command-line arguments are also passed on to the program. In this case, `awk` runs the program and prints the universally known `hello, world` message.

The `#!` mechanism is an elegant way of hiding the distinction between binary executables and script executables. If `hello.awk` is renamed to just `hello`, the user typing '`hello`' can't tell (and indeed shouldn't have to know) that `hello` isn't a binary executable program.

1.1.4 Devices

One of Unix's most notable innovations was the unification of file I/O and device I/O.[4] Devices appear as files in the filesystem, regular permissions apply to their access, and the same I/O system calls are used for opening, reading, writing, and closing them. All of the "magic" to make devices look like files is hidden in the kernel. This is just another aspect of the driving simplicity principle in action; we might phrase it as *no special cases for user code.*

Two devices appear frequently in everyday use, particularly at the shell level: `/dev/null` and `/dev/tty`.

`/dev/null` is the "bit bucket." All data sent to `/dev/null` is discarded by the operating system, and attempts to read from it always return end-of-file (EOF) immediately.

`/dev/tty` is the process's current controlling terminal—the one to which it listens when a user types the interrupt character (typically CTRL-C) or performs job control (CTRL-Z).

GNU/Linux systems, and many modern Unix systems, supply `/dev/stdin`, `/dev/stdout`, and `/dev/stderr` devices, which provide a way to name the open files each process inherits upon startup.

Other devices represent real hardware, such as disk drives, DVD drives, and serial ports. There are also software devices, such as pseudo-ttys, that are used for networking logins and windowing systems. `/dev/console` represents the system console, a particular hardware device on minicomputers. On modern computers, `/dev/console` is the screen and keyboard, but it could be a serial port. Serial port consoles are still found on embedded systems.

Unfortunately, device-naming conventions are not standardized, and each operating system has different names for tapes, disks, and so on. (Fortunately, that's not an issue for what we cover in this book.) Devices have either a `b` or a `c` in the first character of '`ls -l`' output:

```
$ ls -l /dev/tty /dev/zero /dev/nvme0n1
brw-rw---- 1 root disk 259, 0 Nov 11 18:54 /dev/nvme0n1
crw-rw-rw- 1 root tty    5, 0 Nov 11 19:15 /dev/tty
crw-rw-rw- 1 root root   1, 5 Nov 11 18:54 /dev/zero
```

The initial `b` represents block devices, and a `c` represents character devices. Device files are discussed further in Section 5.4, "Obtaining Information about Files," page 130.

1.2 The Linux/Unix Process Model

A process is a running program.[5] Processes have the following attributes:

- A unique process identifier (the PID)
- A parent process (with an associated identifier, the PPID)
- Permission identifiers (UID, GID, group set, and so on)

[4] This feature first appeared in Multics, but Multics was never widely used.

[5] Processes can be suspended, in which case they are not "running"; however, neither are they terminated. In any case, in the early stages of the climb up the learning curve, it pays not to be too pedantic.

- A process group identifier
- An address space, separate from those of all other processes
- A program running in that address space
- A current working directory (`.`)
- A current root directory (`/`; changing this is an advanced topic)
- A set of open files, directories, or both
- A permissions-to-deny mask for use in creating new files
- A set of strings representing the environment
- A scheduling priority (an advanced topic)
- Settings for signal disposition (an advanced topic)
- Usually, but not always, a controlling terminal (also an advanced topic)

When the `main()` function begins execution, all of these things have already been put in place for the running program. System calls are available to query and change each of the above items; covering them is the purpose of this book.

New processes are always created by an existing process. The existing process is termed the *parent*, and the new process is termed the *child*. Upon booting, the kernel handcrafts the first, primordial process, which runs the program `/sbin/init`; it has process ID `1` and serves several administrative functions. All other processes are descendants of `init`. (`init`'s parent is the kernel, often listed as process ID `0`.)

The child-to-parent relationship is one-to-one; each process has only one parent, and thus it's easy to find out the PID of the parent. The parent-to-child relationship is one-to-many; any given process can create a potentially unlimited number of children. Thus, there is no easy way for a process to find out the PIDs of all its children. (In practice, it's not necessary, anyway.) A parent process can arrange to be notified when a child process terminates ("dies"), and it can also explicitly wait for such an event.

Each process's address space (memory) is separate from that of every other. Unless two processes have made an explicit arrangement to share memory, one process cannot affect the address space of another. This is important; it provides a basic level of security and system reliability. (For efficiency, the system arranges to share the read-only executable code of the same program among all the processes running that program. This is transparent to the user and to the running program.)

The current working directory is the one to which relative pathnames (those that don't start with a `/`) are relative. This is the directory you are "in" after you issue a '`cd` *`someplace`*' command to the shell.

By convention, all programs start out with three files already open: standard input, standard output, and standard error. These are where input comes from, output goes to, and error messages go to, respectively. In the course of this book, we will see how these are put in place. A parent process can open additional files and have them already available for a child process; the child will have to know they're there, either by way of some convention or by a command-line argument or environment variable.

The *environment* is a set of strings, each of the form '`name=value`'. Functions exist for querying and setting environment variables, and child processes inherit the environment of their parents. Typical environment variables are things like `PATH` and `HOME` in the shell. Many programs look for the existence and value of specific environment variables in order to control their behavior.

It is important to understand that a single process may execute multiple programs during its lifetime. Unless explicitly changed, *all* of the other system-maintained attributes (current directory, open files, PID, etc.) remain the same.

The separation of "starting a new process" from "choosing which program to run in the process" is a key Unix innovation. It makes many operations simple and straightforward. Other operating systems that combine the two operations are less general and more complicated to use.

1.2.1 Pipes: Hooking Processes Together

You've undoubtedly used the pipe construct ('`|`') in the shell to connect two or more running programs. A pipe acts like a file: one process writes to it using the normal write operation, and the other process reads from it using the read operation. The processes don't (usually) know that their input/output is a pipe and not a regular file.

Just as the kernel hides the "magic" for devices, making them act like regular files, so too does the kernel do the work for pipes, arranging to pause the pipe's writer when the pipe fills up and to pause the reader when no data is waiting to be read.

The file I/O paradigm with pipes thus acts as a key mechanism for connecting running programs; no temporary files are needed. Again, this is generality and simplicity at work: no special cases for user code.

1.3 Standard C versus Original C

For many years, the de facto definition of C was found in the first edition of the book *The C Programming Language* by Brian Kernighan and Dennis Ritchie. This book described C as it existed for Unix and on the systems to which the Bell Labs developers had ported it. Throughout this book, we refer to it as "Original C," although it's also common for it to be referred to as "K&R C," after the book's two authors. (Dennis Ritchie designed and implemented C.)

The 1990 ISO Standard for C formalized the language's definition, including the functions in the C library (such as `printf()` and `fopen()`). The C standards committee did an admirable job of standardizing existing practice and avoided inventing new features, with one notable exception (and a few minor ones). The most visible change in the language was the use of *function prototypes*, borrowed from C++.

Standard C, C++, and the Java programming language use function prototypes for function declarations and definitions. A prototype describes not only the function's return value but also the number and type of its arguments. With prototypes, a compiler can do complete type checking at the point of a function call. Consider the following example, a function to return the sine of an angle given in degrees:

```
/* ch-intro-sindegrees.c --- do sin(), converting from degrees */

#include <math.h>

#define PI  3.1415927

double
sin_degrees(double degrees)
{
    degrees = fmod(degrees, 360.0); // pull into range 0-360, like degrees %= 360

    double circle_fraction = degrees / 360.0;
    double radians = circle_fraction * 2.0 * PI;    // convert to radians

    return sin(radians);
}
```

As is good practice for a library function, there is a header file to declare the function:

```
/* ch-intro-sindegrees.h --- do sin(), converting from degrees */

extern double sin_degrees(double degrees);
```

Here's a test program that uses it:

```
/* ch-intro-sindegrees-test1.c --- test sin_degrees() function */

#include <stdio.h>
#include <stdlib.h>
#include <math.h>

#include "ch-intro-sindegrees.h"

#define PI  3.1415927

/* main --- test it */

int
main(void)
{
    double radians = PI * 0.25; // 1/4 PI = 45 degrees

    printf("sin(%lf) = %lf\n", radians, sin(radians));
    printf("sin_degrees(45) = %lf\n", sin_degrees(45));

    exit(EXIT_SUCCESS);
}
```

Let's compile the pieces and run the program:

```
$ gcc -c ch-intro-sindegrees.c
$ gcc -c ch-intro-sindegrees-test1.c
$ gcc ch-intro-sindegrees-test1.o ch-intro-sindegrees.o -lm \
>     -o ch-intro-sindegrees-test1
$ ch-intro-sindegrees-test1
sin(0.785398) = 0.707107
sin_degrees(45) = 0.707107
```

So far, so good—this is what we expect to see. What's the big deal? First, take a look at the call to `sin_degrees()` on line 19: '`sin_degrees(45)`'. We've passed an `int`, but the function expects a `double`. Because of the prototype, the compiler knows to automatically convert `45` into `45.0` before making the call. And if we made an erroneous call, such as '`sin_degrees("45")`', the compiler gives us a very explicit error diagnostic:

```
$ gcc -c ch-intro-sindegrees-test-bad.c
ch-intro-sindegrees-test-bad.c: In function 'main':
ch-intro-sindegrees-test-bad.c:19:55: error: incompatible type for argument 1 of 'sin_degrees'
   19 |         printf("sin_degrees(45) = %lf\n", sin_degrees("45"));
      |                                                       ^~~~
      |                                                       |
      |                                                       char *
In file included from ch-intro-sindegrees-test-bad.c:7:
ch-intro-sindegrees.h:3:34: note: expected 'double' but argument is of type 'char *'
    3 | extern double sin_degrees(double degrees);
      |                           ~~~~~~~~~~~~~~
```

Contrast the way things work with function prototypes to how they worked without them. In Original C, you declared a function with its return type, but without the ability to provide information about the parameters:

```
extern double sin_degrees();
```

Here's the same test program, but with just such a declaration, instead of including the header:

```
/* ch-intro-sindegrees-test2.c --- test sin_degrees() function */

#include <stdio.h>
#include <stdlib.h>
#include <math.h>

extern double sin_degrees();

#define PI  3.1415927

/* main --- test it */
```

```
12
13 int
14 main(void)
15 {
16     double radians = PI * 0.25; // 1/4 PI = 45 degrees
17
18     printf("sin(%lf) = %lf\n", radians, sin(radians));
19     printf("sin_degrees(45) = %lf\n", sin_degrees(45));
20
21     exit(EXIT_SUCCESS);
22 }
```

The primary difference is line 7. Here's what happens when we compile and run the code:

```
$ gcc -c ch-intro-sindegrees-test2.c
$ gcc ch-intro-sindegrees-test2.o ch-intro-sindegrees.o -lm \
>       -o ch-intro-sindegrees-test2
$ ch-intro-sindegrees-test2
sin(0.785398) = 0.707107                Correct results
sin_degrees(45) = 0.000000              Incorrect results!
```

Here, the compiler didn't know to convert `45` to `45.0`, and thus we get a really wrong result.

Such erroneous calls generally led to hard-to-find runtime problems (such as segmentation faults, whereby the program dies), and the Unix `lint` program was created to deal with these kinds of things.

Original C also differed from Standard C in how function definitions were written. Function definitions list the parameter names in the function header, and then declare the parameters before the function body. Parameters of type `int` didn't have to be declared, and if a function returns `int`, that didn't have to be declared either:

```
myfunc(a, b, c, d)                      Return type is int
struct my_struct *a, *b;
double c;                               Note, no declaration of parameter d
{
    ...
}
```

So, although function prototypes were a radical departure from existing practice, their additional type checking was deemed too important to be without, and they were added to the language with little opposition.

In 1990 Standard C, code written in the original style, for both declarations and definitions, is valid. This makes it possible to continue to compile millions of lines of existing code with a standard-conforming compiler. New code, obviously, should be written with prototypes because of the improved possibilities for compile-time error checking.

1999 Standard C continues to allow original-style declarations and definitions. However, the "implicit `int`" rule was removed; functions must have a return type, and all parameters must be declared.

Furthermore, when a program called a function that had not been formally declared, Original C would create an implicit declaration for the function, giving it a return type of `int`. 1990 Standard C did the same, additionally noting that it had no information about the parameters. 1999 Standard C no longer provides this "auto-declare" feature.

Other notable additions in Standard C are the `const` keyword, also from C++, and the `volatile` keyword, which the committee invented. 1999 C introduced a Boolean type (`bool` and the `<stdbool.h>` header), making C code considerably cleaner. For the code you'll see in this book, understanding the different function declaration and definition syntaxes is the most important thing.

For V7 code using original-style definitions, we have added comments showing the equivalent prototype. Otherwise, we have left the code alone, preferring to show it exactly as it was originally written and as you'll see it if you download the code yourself.

There have been a number of revisions to the C standard since 1999. However, none of the programs in this book need any of the major new features added to the language in those standards, nor do they affect our discussion or use of the fundamental Linux/Unix APIs. For that reason, we stick to using 1999 C in our examples.

1.4 Why GNU Programs Are Better

What is it that makes a GNU program a GNU program?[6] What makes GNU software "better" than other (free or non-free) software? The most obvious difference is the GNU General Public License (GPL), which describes the distribution terms for GNU software. But this is usually not the reason you hear people saying, "Get the GNU version of `xyz`, it's much better." GNU software is generally more robust, and performs better, than standard Unix versions. In this section we look at some of the reasons why, and at the document that describes the principles of GNU software design.

The *GNU Coding Standards* manual describes how to write software for the GNU project. It covers a range of topics. You can read the *GNU Coding Standards* online at `https://www.gnu.org/prep/standards.html`. See the online version for pointers to the source files in other formats.

In this section, we describe only those parts of the *GNU Coding Standards* that relate to program design and implementation.

1.4.1 Program Design

Chapter 3 of the *GNU Coding Standards* provides general advice about program design. The four main issues are compatibility (with standards and Unix), the language to write in, reliance on nonstandard features of other programs (in a word, "none"), and the meaning of "portability."

[6] This section is adapted from an article by the author that appeared in Issue 16 of *Linux Journal*. (See `https://www.linuxjournal.com/article/1135`.) Reprinted and adapted by permission.

Compatibility with Standard C and POSIX—and, to a lesser extent, with Berkeley Unix—is an important goal. But it's not an overriding one. The general idea is to provide all necessary functionality, with command-line options to provide a strict ISO or POSIX mode.

C is the preferred language for writing GNU software since it is the most commonly available language. Although the coding standards prefer C over C++, C++ is now commonplace too. One widely used GNU package written in C++ is `groff` (GNU `troff`). With GCC supporting C++, it has been our experience that installing `groff` from source is not difficult. These days, though, people tend to just use the package manager provided by their GNU/Linux distribution.

The standards state that portability is a bit of a red herring. GNU utilities are ultimately intended to run on the GNU kernel with the GNU C Library.[7] But since the kernel isn't finished yet and users are using GNU tools on non-GNU systems, portability is desirable, just not paramount. The standards recommend using Autoconf for achieving portability among different Unix systems.

1.4.2 Program Behavior

Chapter 4 of the *GNU Coding Standards* provides general advice about program behavior. We will return to look at one of its sections in detail, below. The chapter focuses on program design, formatting error messages, writing libraries (by making them reentrant), and standards for the command-line interface.

Error message formatting is important since several tools, notably Emacs, use the error messages to help you go straight to the point in the source file or data file at which an error occurred.

GNU utilities should use a function named `getopt_long()` for processing the command line. This function provides command-line option parsing for both traditional Unix-style options ('`gawk -F: ...`') and GNU-style long options ('`gawk --field-separator=: ...`'). All programs should provide `--help` and `--version` options, and when a long name is used in one program, it should be used the same way in other GNU programs. To this end, there is a rather exhaustive list of long options used by current GNU programs.

As a simple yet obvious example, `--verbose` is spelled exactly the same way in *all* GNU programs. Contrast this with `-v`, `-V`, `-d`, etc., in many Unix programs. Most of Chapter 2, "Arguments, Options, and the Environment," page 23, is devoted to the mechanics of argument and option parsing.

1.4.3 C Code Programming

The most substantive part of the *GNU Coding Standards* is Chapter 5, which describes how to write C code, covering things like formatting the code, using comments correctly, using C cleanly, naming your functions and variables, and declaring, or not declaring, standard system functions that you wish to use.

Code formatting is a religious issue; many people have different styles that they prefer. We have more to say about this in Section 1.6, "Some Words about Coding Style," page 18.

---

[7] This statement refers to the HURD kernel, which, sadly, has been under development for decades. GCC and GNU C Library (GLIBC) development takes place on Linux-based systems today.

What we find important about the chapter on C coding is that the advice is good for *any* C coding, not just if you happen to be working on a GNU program. So, if you're just learning C, or even if you've been working in C (or C++) for a while, we recommend this chapter to you since it encapsulates many years of experience.

1.4.4 Things That Make a GNU Program Better

We now examine the section titled "Writing Robust Programs" in Chapter 4, "Program Behavior for All Programs," in the *GNU Coding Standards*. This section provides the principles of software design that make GNU programs better than their Unix counterparts. We quote selected parts of the chapter, with some examples of cases in which these principles have paid off.

> Avoid arbitrary limits on the length or number of *any* data structure, including file names, lines, files, and symbols, by allocating all data structures dynamically. In most Unix utilities, "long lines are silently truncated." This is not acceptable in a GNU utility.

This rule is perhaps the single most important rule in GNU software design—*no arbitrary limits*. All GNU utilities should be able to manage arbitrary amounts of data.

While this requirement perhaps makes it harder for the programmer, it makes things much better for the user. At one point, we had a `gawk` user who regularly ran an `awk` program on more than 650,000 files (no, that's not a typo) to gather statistics. `gawk` would grow to over 192 megabytes of data space, and the program ran for around seven CPU hours. He would not have been able to run his program using another `awk` implementation.[8]

Mike Haertel, the original author of GNU `grep`, recently had this to say about the "no arbitrary limits" principle:

> I used to think the GNU standard was merely a luxury or a "how to distinguish GNU from Unix for legal reasons" thing, but nowadays, in the era of buffer overrun attacks, it has proven to be quite important.

We couldn't agree more! Continuing on with the text:

> Utilities reading files should not drop NUL characters, or any other nonprinting characters. Programs should work properly with multibyte character encodings, such as UTF-8. You can use libiconv to deal with a range of encodings.[9]

It is also well known that Emacs can edit any arbitrary file, including files containing binary data!

> Check every system call for an error return, unless you know you wish to ignore errors. Include the system error text (from `strerror` or equivalent) in *every* error

[8] This situation occurred circa 1993; the truism is even more obvious today, as users process gigabytes of log files with `gawk`.

[9] Section 15.4, "Can You Spell That for Me, Please?," page 540, provides an overview of multibyte characters and encodings.

> message resulting from a failing system call, as well as the name of the file if any and the name of the utility. Just "cannot open foo.c" or "stat failed" is not sufficient.

Checking every system call provides robustness. This is another case in which life is harder for the programmer but better for the user. An error message detailing what exactly went wrong makes finding and solving any problems much easier.[10]

Finally, we quote from Chapter 1 of the *GNU Coding Standards*, which discusses how to write your program differently from the way a Unix program may have been written:

> For example, Unix utilities were generally optimized to minimize memory use; if you go for speed instead, your program will be very different. You could keep the entire input file in memory and scan it there instead of using stdio. Use a smarter algorithm discovered more recently than the Unix program. Eliminate use of temporary files. Do it in one pass instead of two (we did this in the assembler).
>
> Or, on the contrary, emphasize simplicity instead of speed. For some applications, the speed of today's computers makes simpler algorithms adequate.
>
> Or go for generality. For example, Unix programs often have static tables or fixed-size strings, which make for arbitrary limits; use dynamic allocation instead. Make sure your program handles NULs and other funny characters in the input files. Add a programming language for extensibility and write part of the program in that language.
>
> Or turn some parts of the program into independently usable libraries. Or use a simple garbage collector instead of tracking precisely when to free memory, or use a new GNU facility such as obstacks.

An excellent example of the difference an algorithm can make is GNU `diff`. One of our system's early incarnations was an AT&T 3B1: a system with a MC68010 processor, a whopping two megabytes of memory, and 80 megabytes of disk. We did (and do) lots of editing on the manual for `gawk`, a file that today is almost 48,000 lines long (although at the time, it was only in the 10,000 lines range). We used to use '`diff -c`' quite frequently to look at our changes. On this slow system, switching to GNU `diff` made a stunning difference in the amount of time it took for the context diff to appear. The difference was almost entirely due to the better algorithm that GNU `diff` uses.

The final paragraph mentions the idea of structuring a program as an independently usable library, with a command-line wrapper or other interface around it. One example of this is GDB, the GNU Debugger, which is implemented as a command-line tool on top of a debugging library. This implementation makes it possible to write a graphical debugging interface on top of the basic debugging functionality. (GDB is presented later in this book; see Chapter 17, "Debugging," page 591.)

---

[10]The mechanics of checking for and reporting errors are discussed in Section 4.3, "Determining What Went Wrong," page 81.

1.4.5 Parting Thoughts about the *GNU Coding Standards*

The *GNU Coding Standards* manual is a worthwhile document to read if you wish to develop new GNU software, enhance existing GNU software, or just learn how to be a better programmer. The principles and techniques it espouses are what make GNU software the preferred choice of the Unix community.

1.5 Portability Revisited

1.5.1 Why Be Portable?

You may be wondering, "Why so much emphasis on portable code? What's in it for me?" These are both good questions.

First, it's often just as easy to be portable as not. In today's environment with standard-conforming compilers and systems, writing portable code has never been easier. In a way, that's what this book is all about. (Admittedly, this is a "why not be portable?" sort of answer.)

Second, having portable code *increases* your user base. Most developers like having more users. If you're writing commercial software, more users means more sales. If you're writing Free or Open Source software, more users means more joy in making the world a better place.

Third, simply put, portable code is higher-quality code. And who doesn't like to write high-quality code?

Finally, it's just really cool to see your code being used across multiple systems. In today's world, besides GNU/Linux, there are macOS, the BSD systems, legacy Unix systems, and even OpenVMS and IBM's z/OS. It's possible to have your program run on all of these.

1.5.2 Portability Recommendations

Portability can be something of a holy grail—always sought after, but not always obtainable. There are several aspects to writing portable code. The *GNU Coding Standards* manual discusses many of them. But there are others as well. Keep portability in mind at both higher and lower levels as you develop. We recommend these practices:

Code to standards.

Although it can be challenging, it pays to be familiar with the formal standards for the language you're using. In particular, pay attention to the ISO standards for C and C++ since most Linux programming is done in one of those two languages.

Also, the POSIX standard for library and system call interfaces, while large, has broad industry support. Writing to POSIX greatly improves the chances of successfully moving your code to other systems besides GNU/Linux. This standard is quite readable; it distills decades of experience and good practice.

Pick the best interface for the job.

If a standard interface does what you need, use it in your code. Use Autoconf to detect an unavailable interface, and supply a replacement version of it for deficient systems.

(For example, some older systems lack the `memmove()` function, which is fairly easy to code by hand or to pull from the GLIBC library.)

Isolate portability problems behind new interfaces.
Sometimes you may need to do operating-system-specific tasks that apply on some systems but not on others. (For example, on some systems, each program has to expand command-line wildcards instead of the shell doing it.) Create a new interface that does nothing on systems that don't need it but does the correct thing on systems that do.

Use Autoconf for configuration.
In this context, *configuration* means determining if a system supports certain features or APIs. Programs often use `#ifdef` for this. However, it's better to avoid `#ifdef` if possible. If not, bury it in low-level library code. Use Autoconf to do the checking for the tests to be performed with `#ifdef`.

Do use `#ifdef` *for optional features.*
If there are actual features that are optional, use `#ifdef` for them, with command-line options to your `configure` program to enable or disable them. In general, though, having too many `#ifdef`s makes code hard to read and maintain.

1.6 Some Words about Coding Style

A *coding style* is a (formal or informal) specification for how developers should lay out their code. This refers to the placement and indentation of braces, the use of spaces around operators and keywords and in function calls, and many other aspects of "style."

In the C and C++ worlds, there are many different coding styles. These can be and have been the subject of much debate among adherents of different styles, often leading to "religious wars."

The most important points about coding styles are:

- To have one. Using a consistent coding style makes code easier to read and maintain, for you and for others in your team.
- To stay consistent with the coding style of the code you're working on, *even if you don't like it*. The worst thing that can happen when working with someone else's code is for you to reformat it to your liking and then try to get the original authors to accept your changes. They won't do it.

We personally don't like the FSF's style, and if you look at `gawk`, which we maintain, you'll see it's formatted in standard K&R style (the code layout style used in both editions of the landmark Kernighan and Ritchie book). But this is the only variation in `gawk` from this part of the coding standards.

Nevertheless, even though we don't like the FSF's style, we feel that when modifying some other program, sticking to the coding style already used is of the utmost importance. The *GNU Coding Standards* also makes this point. (Sometimes there is no detectable consistent coding style, in which case the program is probably overdue for a trip through GNU `indent`.)

In this book, we present original code exactly as it was written, be it Unix source code or programs from the GNU project.

However, for the examples that we wrote, the coding style is slightly modified from the standard "K&R" formatting style. We use tab stops of four spaces for readability in the printed text (but real TABs in the code), and we follow the convention of the *GNU Coding Standards* in placing the function names in function definitions at the beginning of a line.

1.7 Artificial Intelligence Isn't Intelligent

As we're preparing this book to go to press, the current hot topic in the software industry is generative artificial intelligence (AI). AI is clearly affecting the industry, but it's unclear if it's for better or for worse.

Many people who aren't familiar with the nitty-gritty of developing high-quality software seem to think that using AI will let them develop their products without hiring programmers and/or by firing their current development staff. (We've read a few horror stories where this didn't work out very well.)

And yes, AI may let you create something that does a particular job in a very short time, and it may even work (for now). But people who write software for a living understand that it's not so easy. Is the code generated by AI likely to be correct? Is it understandable and maintainable? Can it be modified easily down the road when new requirements arise? The answer is most likely "no."

If you are just learning to develop software, or have been doing it for only a short while, the temptation to take a shortcut via AI may be overwhelming. We strongly suggest that you don't give in to it.

There is no substitute for human knowledge, reasoning, and experience. AI isn't "intelligent" in the way that you are. It has no understanding and no judgment.

At best, you might make use of AI as a "coding assistant" in an integrated development environment (IDE), where it might suggest reasonable completions for code as you type it. But *you* should always be the one guiding the machine, and not the other way around.

Finally, we offer these questions for your consideration: If you always let AI do your work for you, how will you ever grow and develop as a professional? Will you really take pride in your work? Will you be exercising your creative abilities to the utmost? Won't you be easier to replace by AI than someone who actually understands what they are doing? We suggest that you think hard about these issues.

1.8 Suggested Reading

1. *The C Programming Language*, 2nd ed., by Brian W. Kernighan and Dennis M. Ritchie. Pearson, 1988. ISBN-13: 978-0-13-110362-7.

   This is the "bible" for C, covering the 1990 version of Standard C. It is a rather dense book, with lots of information packed into a startlingly small number of pages. You may need to read it through more than once; doing so is well worth the trouble.

2. *C: A Reference Manual*, 5th ed., by Samuel P. Harbison III and Guy L. Steele, Jr. Pearson, 2002. ISBN-13: 978-0-13-089592-9.

   This book is also a classic. It covers Original C as well as the 1990 and 1999 standards. It makes a valuable companion to *The C Programming Language*. It covers many important items, such as internationalization-related types and library functions, that aren't in the Kernighan and Ritchie book.

3. *Notes on Programming in C*, by Rob Pike, February 21, 1989. This article is available on the Web from many sites; perhaps the most widely cited location is `https://www.lysator.liu.se/c/pikestyle.html`. (Many other useful articles are available from one level up: `https://www.lysator.liu.se/c/`.)

   Rob Pike worked for many years at the Bell Labs research center, where C and Unix were invented, and where he did pioneering development. His notes distill many years of experience into a "philosophy of clarity in programming" that is well worth reading.

4. Another document of interest is the *Recommended C Style and Coding Standards*, originally written at the Bell Labs Indian Hill site. One location for it is `https://www.doc.ic.ac.uk/lab/cplus/cstyle.html`.

5. The *Google C++ Style Guide*[11] may be worth investigating, as many of its points also apply to C.

6. For one (very experienced) person's first-hand view on using AI, see `https://testprincipia.com/lft/coding-with-ai-no-skills-needed/`. The author's conclusions are interesting.

1.9 Summary

- "Files and processes" summarizes the Linux/Unix worldview. The treatment of files as byte streams and devices as files, and the use of standard input, output and error, simplify program design and unify the data access model. The permissions model is simple, yet flexible, applying to both files and directories.
- Processes are running programs, that have user and group identifiers associated with them for permission checking, as well as other attributes such as open files and a current working directory.
- The most visible difference between Standard C and Original C is the use of function prototypes for stricter type checking. A good C programmer should be able to read original-style code, since many existing programs use it. New code should be written using prototypes.
- The *GNU Coding Standards* manual describes how to write GNU programs. It provides numerous valuable techniques and guiding principles for producing robust, usable

[11] `https://google.github.io/styleguide/cppguide.html`

software. The "no arbitrary limits" principle is perhaps the single most important of these. This document is required reading for serious programmers.

- Making programs portable is a significant challenge. Guidelines and tools help, but ultimately experience is needed too.
- Having a coding style is more important than the details of what the style are. Keeping the coding style consistent makes code easier to read and maintain.
- Artificial intelligence (AI) isn't intelligent in the way you are. It appears tempting and easy to the novice. Be wary, and use it carefully, if and when you do use it.

Exercises

1. Read and comment on the article *The GNU Project*,[12] by Richard M. Stallman, originally written in August 1998.
2. Do an Internet search for different C coding–style standards. Compare some of them to the code in this book. Try taking a moderately sized program and reformatting it in different ways using the `indent` program. Which style do you like the most, and why?

[12] `https://www.gnu.org/gnu/thegnuproject.html`

Chapter 2

Arguments, Options, and the Environment

Command-line option and argument interpretation is usually the first task of any program. This chapter examines how C (and C++) programs access their command-line arguments, describes standard routines for parsing options, and takes a look at the environment.

2.1 Option and Argument Conventions

The word *arguments* has two meanings. The more technical definition is "all the 'words' on the command line." For example:

```
$ ls main.c opts.c process.c
```

Here, the user typed four "words." All four words are made available to the program as its arguments.

The second definition is more informal: arguments are all the words on the command line *except* the command name. By default, Unix shells separate arguments from each other with *whitespace* (spaces or tab characters). Quoting allows arguments to include whitespace:

```
$ echo here are lots    of spaces
here are lots of spaces                        The shell "eats" the spaces
$ echo "here are lots    of spaces"
here are lots    of spaces                     Spaces are preserved
```

Quoting is transparent to the running program; `echo` never sees the double-quote characters. (Double and single quotes are different in the shell; a discussion of the rules is beyond the scope of this book, which focuses on C programming. However, a simple rule is that text within double quotes is subject to further interpretation by the shell, whereas text within single quotes is not.)

Arguments can be further classified as *options* or *operands*. In the previous two examples all the arguments were operands: files for `ls` and raw text for `echo`.

Options are special arguments that each program interprets. Options change a program's behavior, or they provide information to the program. By ancient and (almost) universally adhered to convention, options start with a dash (a.k.a. a hyphen or minus sign) and consist of a single letter. *Option arguments* are information needed by an option, as opposed to regular

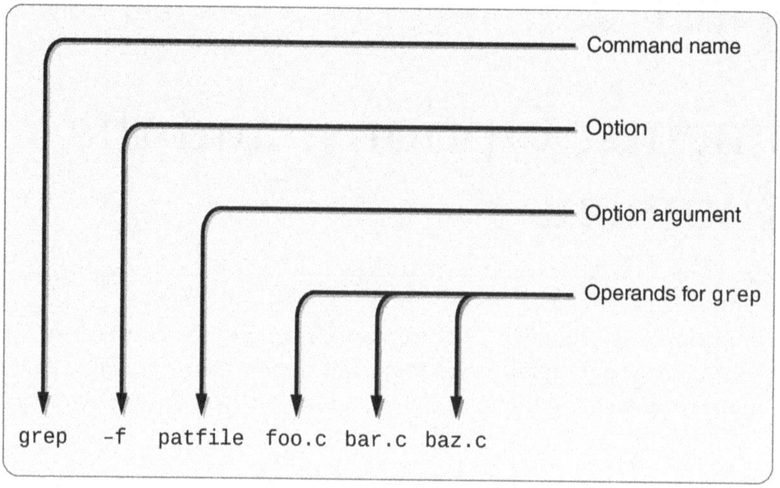

Figure 2.1: Command-line components

operand arguments. For example, the `grep` program's `-f` option means "use the contents of the following file as a list of patterns to search for." See Figure 2.1.

Thus, `patfile` is not a data file to search; rather, it's for use by `grep` in defining the list of patterns to search for.

2.1.1 POSIX Conventions

The POSIX standard describes a number of conventions that standard-conforming programs adhere to. Nothing requires that your programs adhere to these conventions, but it's a good idea for them to do so: Linux and Unix users the world over understand and use these conventions, and if your program doesn't follow them, your users will be unhappy. (Or you won't have any users!) Furthermore, the functions we discuss later in this chapter relieve you of the burden of manually adhering to these conventions for each program you write. Here they are, paraphrased from the standard:

1. Program names should have no less than two and no more than nine characters.
2. Program names should consist only of lowercase letters and digits.
3. Option names should be single alphanumeric characters. Multidigit options should not be allowed. For vendors implementing the POSIX utilities, the `-W` option is reserved for vendor-specific options.
4. All options should begin with a '`-`' character.
5. For options that don't require option arguments, it should be possible to group multiple options after a single '`-`' character. (For example, '`foo -a -b -c`' and '`foo -abc`' should be treated the same way.)
6. When an option does require an option argument, the argument should be separated from the option by a space (for example, '`grep -f patfile`').

The standard, however, does allow for historical practice, whereby sometimes the option and the operand could be in the same string: '`fgrep -fpatfile`'. In practice, the `getopt()` and `getopt_long()` functions interpret '`-fpatfile`' as '`-f patfile`', not as '`-f -p -a -t ...`'. (We present the `getopt()` and `getopt_long()` functions in Section 2.3, "Option Parsing: `getopt()` and `getopt_long()`," page 28.)

7. Option arguments should not be optional.

   This means that when a program documents an option as requiring an option argument, that option's argument must always be present or else the program fails. GNU `getopt()` does provide for optional option arguments since they're occasionally useful.

8. If an option takes an argument that may have multiple values, the program should receive that argument as a single string, with values separated by commas or whitespace.

   For example, suppose a hypothetical program `myprog` requires a list of users for its `-u` option. Then, it should be invoked in one of these two ways:

   ```
   myprog -u "arnold,joe,jane"        Separate with commas
   myprog -u "arnold joe jane"        Separate with whitespace
   ```

   In such a case, you're on your own as far as splitting out and processing each value (that is, there is no standard routine), but doing so manually is usually straightforward.

9. Options should come first on the command line, before operands. Unix versions of `getopt()` enforce this convention. GNU `getopt()` does not by default, although you can tell it to.

10. The special argument '`--`' indicates the end of all options. Any subsequent arguments on the command line are treated as operands, even if they begin with a dash.

11. The order in which options are given should not matter. However, for mutually exclusive options, when one option overrides the setting of another, then (so to speak) the last one wins. If an option that has arguments is repeated, the program should process the arguments in order. For example, '`myprog -u arnold -u jane`' is the same as '`myprog -u "arnold,jane"`'. (You have to enforce this yourself; `getopt()` doesn't help you.)

12. It is OK for the order of operands to matter to a program. Each program should document such things.

13. Programs that read or write named files should treat the single argument '`-`' as meaning standard input or standard output, as is appropriate for the program.

14. Options that don't take arguments may also be grouped together in a single argument, preceded by a single '`-`'. (It's not clear what this guideline really adds, as it seems similar to Guideline 5.)

Note that many standard programs don't follow all of the preceding conventions. The primary reason is historical compatibility; many such programs predate the codifying of these conventions.

2.1.2 GNU Long Options

As we saw in Section 1.4.2, "Program Behavior," page 14, GNU programs are encouraged to use long options of the form `--help`, `--verbose`, and so on. Such options, since they start with two hyphens, do not conflict with the POSIX conventions. They also can be easier to remember, and they provide the opportunity for consistency across all GNU utilities. (For example, `--help` is the same everywhere, as compared with `-h` for "help," `-i` for "information," and so on.) GNU long options have their own conventions, implemented by the `getopt_long()` function:

1. For programs implementing POSIX utilities, every short (single-letter) option should also have a long option.
2. Additional GNU-specific long options need not have a corresponding short option, but we recommend that they do.
3. Long options can be abbreviated to the shortest string that remains unique. For example, if there are two options `--verbose` and `--verbatim`, the shortest possible abbreviations are `--verbo` and `--verba`.
4. Option arguments are separated from long options either by whitespace or by an `=` sign—for example, `--sourcefile=/some/file` or `--sourcefile /some/file` is OK.
5. Options and arguments may be interspersed with operands on the command line; `getopt_long()` will rearrange things so that all options are processed and then all operands are available sequentially. (This behavior can be suppressed.)
6. Option arguments can be optional. For such options, the argument is deemed to be present if it's in the same string as the option. This works only for short options. For example, if `-x` is such an option, given '`foo -xYANKEES -y`', the argument to `-x` is '`YANKEES`'. For '`foo -x -y`', there is no argument to `-x`.
7. Programs can choose to allow long options to begin with a single dash. (This is common with many X Window programs.)

Much of this will become clearer when we examine `getopt_long()` later in the chapter.

The *GNU Coding Standards* manual devotes considerable space to listing all the long and short options used by GNU programs. If you're writing a program that accepts long options, see if option names already in use might make sense for you to use as well.

2.2 Basic Command-Line Processing

A C program accesses its command-line arguments through its parameters, `argc` and `argv`. The `argc` parameter is an integer, indicating the number of arguments there are, including the command name. There are two common ways to declare `main()`, varying in how `argv` is declared:

```
int main(int argc, char *argv[])
{
    ...
}
```

```
int main(int argc, char **argv)
{
    ...
}
```

Practically speaking, there's no difference between the two declarations, although the first is conceptually clearer: `argv` is an array of pointers to characters. The second is more commonly used: `argv` is a pointer to a pointer. Also, the second definition is technically more correct, and it is what we use. Figure 2.2 depicts this situation.

By convention, `argv[0]` is the program's name. (For details, see Section 9.1.4.4, "Program Names and `argv[0]`," page 286.) Subsequent entries are the command-line arguments. The final entry in the `argv` array is a `NULL` pointer.

`argc` indicates how many arguments there are; since C is zero-based, it is always true that '`argv[argc] == NULL`'. Because of this, particularly in Unix code, you will see different ways of checking for the end of arguments, such as looping until a counter is greater than or equal to `argc`, or until '`argv[i] == 0`', or while '`*argv != NULL`', and so on. These are all equivalent. (We have a mild preference for testing '`argv[i] != NULL`'.)

2.2.1 The V7 `echo` Program

Perhaps the simplest example of command-line processing is the V7 `echo` program, which prints its arguments to standard output, separated by spaces and terminated with a newline. If the first argument is `-n`, then the trailing newline is omitted. (This is used for prompting from shell scripts.) Here's the code:[1]

```
#include <stdio.h>

main(argc, argv)                    int main(int argc, char **argv)
int argc;
```

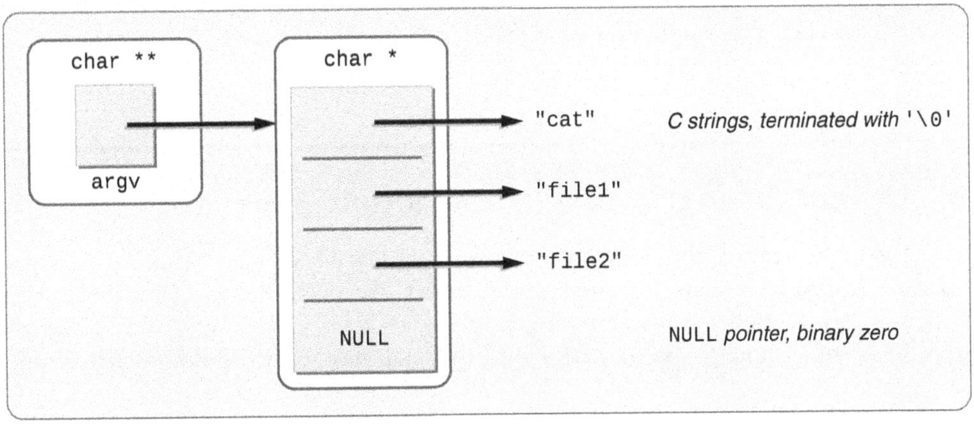

Figure 2.2: Memory for argv

[1] See `/usr/src/cmd/echo.c` in the V7 distribution. It's also in the book's GitHub repository.

```
5  char *argv[];
6  {
7      register int i, nflg;
8
9      nflg = 0;
10     if(argc > 1 && argv[1][0] == '-' && argv[1][1] == 'n') {
11         nflg++;
12         argc--;
13         argv++;
14     }
15     for(i=1; i<argc; i++) {
16         fputs(argv[i], stdout);
17         if (i < argc-1)
18             putchar(' ');
19     }
20     if(nflg == 0)
21         putchar('\n');
22     exit(0);
23 }
```

Only 23 lines! There are two points of interest. First, decrementing `argc` and simultaneously incrementing `argv` (lines 12 and 13) are common ways of skipping initial arguments. Second, the check for `-n` (line 10) is simplistic. `-no-newline-at-the-end` also works. (Compile it and try it!)

Manual option parsing is common in V7 code because the `getopt()` function hadn't been invented yet.

Finally, here and in other places throughout the book, we see use of the `register` keyword. At one time, this keyword provided a hint to the compiler that the given variables should be placed in CPU registers, if possible. Use of this keyword is obsolete; modern compilers all base register assignment on analysis of the source code, ignoring the `register` keyword. We've chosen to leave code that uses it alone, but you should be aware that `register` has no real use anymore.[2]

2.3 Option Parsing: `getopt()` and `getopt_long()`

Circa 1980, for System III, the Unix Support Group within AT&T noted that each Unix program used ad hoc techniques for parsing arguments. To make things easier for users and developers, they developed most of the conventions we listed earlier. (The statement in the System III *intro*(1) manpage is considerably less formal than what's in the POSIX standard, though.)

[2] When we asked Jim Meyering, the Coreutils maintainer, about instances of `register` in the GNU Coreutils, he gave us an interesting response, explaining that he removes them when modifying code, but otherwise leaves them alone to make it easier to integrate changes submitted against existing versions. As of this writing, some instances of `register` still remain in the code base.

The Unix Support Group also developed the `getopt()` function, along with several external variables, to make it easy to write code that follows the standard conventions. The GNU `getopt_long()` function supplies a compatible version of `getopt()`, as well as making it easy to parse long options of the form described earlier.

2.3.1 Single-Letter Options

The `getopt()` function is declared as follows:

```
#include <unistd.h>                                    POSIX

int getopt(int argc, char *const argv[], const char *optstring);

extern char *optarg;
extern int optind, opterr, optopt;
```

The arguments `argc` and `argv` are normally passed straight from those of `main()`. `optstring` is a string of option letters. If any letter in the string is followed by a colon, then that option is expected to have an argument.

To use `getopt()`, call it repeatedly from a `while` loop until it returns `-1`. Each time that it finds a valid option letter, it returns that letter. If the option takes an argument, `optarg` is set to point to it. Consider a program that accepts a `-a` option that doesn't take an argument and a `-b` option that does:

```
int oc;               /* option character */
char *b_opt_arg;

while ((oc = getopt(argc, argv, "ab:")) != -1) {
    switch (oc) {
    case 'a':
        /* handle -a, set a flag, whatever */
        break;
    case 'b':
        /* handle -b, get arg value from optarg */
        b_opt_arg = optarg;
        break;
    case ':':
        ...         /* error handling, see text */
    case '?':
    default:
        ...         /* error handling, see text */
    }
}
```

As it works, `getopt()` sets several variables that control error handling:

`char *optarg`
: The argument for an option, if the option accepts one.

`int optind`
: The current index in `argv`. When the `while` loop has finished, remaining operands are found in `argv[optind]` through `argv[argc-1]`. (Remember that '`argv[argc] == NULL`'.)

`int opterr`
: When this variable is nonzero (which it is by default), `getopt()` prints its own error messages for invalid options and for missing option arguments.

`int optopt`
: When an invalid option character is found, `getopt()` returns either a `'?'` or a `':'` (see below), and `optopt` contains the invalid character that was found.

People being human, it is inevitable that programs will be invoked incorrectly, either with an invalid option or with a missing option argument. In the normal case, `getopt()` prints its own messages for these cases and returns the `'?'` character. However, you can change its behavior in two ways.

First, by setting `opterr` to `0` before invoking `getopt()`, you can force `getopt()` to remain silent when it finds a problem.

Second, if the *first* character in the `optstring` argument is a colon, then `getopt()` is silent *and* it returns a different character depending upon the error, as follows:

Invalid argument
: `getopt()` returns a `'?'` and `optopt` contains the invalid option character. (This is the normal behavior.)

Missing option argument
: `getopt()` returns a `':'`. If the first character of `optstring` is not a colon, then `getopt()` returns a `'?'`, making this case indistinguishable from the invalid argument case.

Thus, making the first character of `optstring` a colon is a good idea since it allows you to distinguish between "invalid argument" and "missing option argument." The cost is that using the colon also silences `getopt()`, forcing you to supply your own error messages. Here is the previous example, this time with error message handling:

```
int oc;             /* option character */
char *b_opt_arg;

while ((oc = getopt(argc, argv, ":ab:")) != -1) {
    switch (oc) {
    case 'a':
        /* handle -a, set a flag, whatever */
        break;
    case 'b':
        /* handle -b, get arg value from optarg */
        b_opt_arg = optarg;
        break;
```

```
        case ':':
            /* missing option argument */
            fprintf(stderr, "%s: option `-%c' requires an argument\n",
                    argv[0], optopt);
            break;
        case '?':
        default:
            /* invalid option */
            fprintf(stderr, "%s: option `-%c' is invalid: ignored\n",
                    argv[0], optopt);
            break;
        }
}
```

A word about flag or option variable naming conventions: much Unix code uses names of the form `xflg` for any given option letter *x* (see, for example, `nflg` in the V7 `echo`; `xflag` is also common). This may be great for the program's author, who happens to know what the *x* option does without having to check the documentation, and it's OK if there aren't a lot of options. But it's unkind to someone else trying to read the code who doesn't know the meaning of all the option letters by heart. It is much better to use variable names that convey each option's meaning, such as `no_newline` for `echo`'s `-n` option.

2.3.2 GNU getopt() and Option Ordering

The standard `getopt()` function stops looking for options as soon as it encounters a command-line argument that doesn't start with a '`-`'. GNU `getopt()` is different: it scans the entire command line looking for options. As it goes along, it *permutes* (rearranges) the elements of `argv`, so that when it's done, all the options have been moved to the front and code that proceeds to examine `argv[optind]` through `argv[argc-1]` works correctly. In all cases, the special argument '`--`' terminates option scanning.

You can change the default behavior by using a special first character in `optstring`, as follows:

`optstring[0] == '+'`
: GNU `getopt()` behaves like standard `getopt()`; it returns options in the order in which they are found, stopping at the first nonoption argument. This will also be true if `POSIXLY_CORRECT` exists in the environment.

`optstring[0] == '-'`
: GNU `getopt()` returns *every* command-line argument, whether or not it represents an argument. In this case, for each such argument, the function returns the integer `1` and sets `optarg` to point to the string.

As for standard `getopt()`, if the first character of `optstring` is a `':'`, then GNU `getopt()` distinguishes between "invalid option" and "missing option argument" by returning `'?'` or `':'`, respectively. The `':'` in `optstring` can be the second character if the first character is `'+'` or `'-'`.

Finally, if an option letter in `optstring` is followed by *two* colon characters, then that option is allowed to have an optional option argument. (Say that three times fast!) Such an argument is deemed to be present if it's in the same `argv` element as the option, or it's deemed absent otherwise. In the case that it's absent, GNU `getopt()` returns the option letter and sets `optarg` to `NULL`. For example, given

```
while ((c = getopt(argc, argv, "ab::")) != 1)
    ...
```

for `-bYANKEES`, the return value is `'b'`, and `optarg` points to `"YANKEES"`, while for a plain `-b` or '`-b YANKEES`', the return value is still `'b'` but `optarg` is set to `NULL`. In the latter case, `"YANKEES"` is a separate command-line argument. (If you're confused, don't worry about it too much.)

2.3.3 Long Options

The `getopt_long()` function handles the parsing of long options of the form described earlier. An additional routine, `getopt_long_only()`, works identically, but it is used for programs where *all* options are long and options begin with a single '`-`' character. Otherwise, both work just like the simpler GNU `getopt()` function. (For brevity, whenever we say "`getopt_long()`," it's as if we'd said "`getopt_long()` and `getopt_long_only()`.") Here are the declarations, from the GNU/Linux *getopt*(3) manpage:

```
#include <getopt.h>                                          GLIBC

int getopt_long(int argc, char *const argv[],
                const char *optstring,
                const struct option *longopts, int *longindex);

int getopt_long_only(int argc, char *const argv[],
                     const char *optstring,
                     const struct option *longopts, int *longindex);
```

The first three arguments are the same as for `getopt()`. The next argument is a pointer to an array of `struct option`, which we refer to as the *long options table* and which is described shortly. The `longindex` parameter, if not set to `NULL`, points to a variable that is filled in with the index in `longopts` of the long option that was found. This is useful for error diagnostics, for example.

2.3.3.1 Long Options Table

Long options are described with an array of `struct option` structures. The `struct option` is declared in `<getopt.h>`; it looks like this:

```
struct option {
    const char *name;
    int has_arg;
    int *flag;
    int val;
};
```

The elements in the structure are as follows:

`const char *name`
: This is the name of the option, *without* any leading dashes—for example, `"help"` or `"verbose"`.

`int has_arg`
: This describes whether the long option has an argument, and if so, what kind of argument. The value must be one of those presented in Table 2.1.

  The symbolic constants are macros for the numeric values given in the table. While the numeric values work, the symbolic constants are considerably easier to read, and you should use them instead of the corresponding numbers in any code that you write.

`int *flag`
: If this pointer is `NULL`, then `getopt_long()` returns the value in the `val` field of the structure. If it's not `NULL`, the variable it points to is filled in with the value in `val` and `getopt_long()` returns `0`. If the `flag` isn't `NULL` but the long option is never seen, then the pointed-to variable is not changed.

`int val`
: This is the value to return if the long option is seen or to load into `*flag` if `flag` is not `NULL`. Typically, if `flag` is not `NULL`, then `val` is a true/false value, such as `1` or `0`. On the other hand, if `flag` is `NULL`, then `val` is usually a character constant. If the long option corresponds to a short one, the character constant should be the same one that appears in the `optstring` argument for this option. (All of this will become clearer shortly when we see some examples.)

Each long option has a single entry with the values appropriately filled in. The last element in the array should have zeros for all the values. The array need not be sorted; `getopt_long()` does a linear search. However, sorting it by long name may make it easier for a programmer to read.

The use of `flag` and `val` seems confusing at first encounter. Let's step back for a moment and examine why it works the way it does. Most of the time, option processing consists of setting different flag variables when different option letters are seen, like so:

Table 2.1: Values for `has_arg`

Symbolic constant	Numeric value	Meaning
`no_argument`	`0`	The option does not take an argument.
`required_argument`	`1`	The option requires an argument.
`optional_argument`	`2`	The option's argument is optional.

```
while ((c = getopt(argc, argv, ":af:hv")) != -1) {
    switch (c) {
    case 'a':
        do_all = true;
        break;
    case 'f':
        myfile = optarg;
        break;
    case 'h':
        do_help = true;
        break;
    case 'v':
        do_verbose = true;
        break;
    ...                    Error handling code here
    }
}
```

When `flag` is not `NULL`, `getopt_long()` *sets the variable for you.* This reduces the three cases in the previous `switch` to one case. Here is an example long options table and the code to go with it:

```
int do_all, do_help, do_verbose;    /* option variables, logically of type bool */
char *myfile;

struct option longopts[] = {
   { "all",      no_argument,       & do_all,     1   },
   { "file",     required_argument, NULL,         'f' },
   { "help",     no_argument,       & do_help,    1   },
   { "verbose",  no_argument,       & do_verbose, 1   },
   { 0, 0, 0, 0 }
};
...
do_all = do_help = do_verbose = false;

while ((c = getopt_long(argc, argv, ":f:", longopts, NULL)) != -1) {
    switch (c) {
    case 'f':
        myfile = optarg;
        break;
    case 0:
        /* getopt_long() has set a variable, just keep going */
        break;
    ...                    Error handling code here
    }
}
```

Notice that the value passed for the optstring argument no longer contains 'a', 'h', or 'v'. This means that the corresponding short options are not accepted. To allow both long and short options, you would have to restore the corresponding cases from the first example to the switch.

Practically speaking, you should write your programs such that each short option also has a corresponding long option. In this case, it's easiest to have flag be NULL and val be the corresponding single letter.

2.3.3.2 Long Options, POSIX Style

The POSIX standard reserves the -W option for vendor-specific features. Thus, by definition, -W isn't portable across different systems.

If W appears in the optstring argument followed by a semicolon (note: *not* a colon), then getopt_long() treats -Wlongopt the same as --longopt. Thus, in the previous example, change the call to be:

```
while ((c = getopt_long(argc, argv, ":f:W;", longopts, NULL)) != -1) {
```

So, -Wall is the same as --all and -Wfile=myfile is the same as --file=myfile. The use of a semicolon makes it possible for a program to use -W as a regular option, if desired. (For example, GCC uses it as a regular option, whereas gawk uses it for POSIX conformance.)

2.3.3.3 getopt_long() Return Value Summary

As should be clear by now, getopt_long() provides a flexible mechanism for option parsing. Table 2.2 summarizes the possible return values and their meaning.

Finally, we enhance the previous example code, showing the full switch statement:

```
int do_all, do_help, do_verbose;    /* option variables, logically of type bool */
char *myfile, *user;                /* input file, user name */

struct option longopts[] = {
   { "all",      no_argument,       & do_all,     1   },
   { "file",     required_argument, NULL,         'f' },
```

Table 2.2: getopt_long() return values

Return code	Meaning
0	getopt_long() has set a flag as found in the long option table.
1	optarg points at a plain command-line argument.
'?'	Invalid option.
':'	Missing option argument.
'x'	Option character 'x'.
-1	End of options.

```
    { "help",    no_argument,       & do_help,    1   },
    { "verbose", no_argument,       & do_verbose, 1   },
    { "user"   , optional_argument, NULL,         'u' },
    { 0, 0, 0, 0 }
};
...
do_all = do_help = do_verbose = false;
while ((c = getopt_long(argc, argv, ":ahvf:u::W;", longopts, NULL)) != -1) {
    switch (c) {
    case 'a':
        do_all = true;
        break;
    case 'f':
        myfile = optarg;
        break;
    case 'h':
        do_help = true;
        break;
    case 'u':
        if (optarg != NULL)
           user = optarg;
        else
           user = "root";
        break;
    case 'v':
        do_verbose = true;
        break;
    case 0:     /* getopt_long() has set a variable, just keep going */
        break;
#if 0
    case 1:
        /*
         * Use this case if getopt_long() should go through all
         * arguments.  If so, add a leading '-' character to optstring.
         * Actual code, if any, goes here.
         */
        break;
#endif
    case ':':   /* missing option argument */
        fprintf(stderr, "%s: option `-%c' requires an argument\n",
                argv[0], optopt);
        break;
    case '?':
    default:    /* invalid option */
        fprintf(stderr, "%s: option `-%c' is invalid: ignored\n",
```

```
                argv[0], optopt);
        break;
    }
}
```

The code that is `#ifdef`'ed out handles a special case that was discussed earlier; see Section 2.3.2, "GNU `getopt()` and Option Ordering," page 31.

In your programs, you may wish to have comments for each option letter explaining what each one does. However, if you've used a descriptive variable name for each option letter, comments are not as necessary. (Compare `do_verbose` to `vflg`.)

2.3.3.4 GNU `getopt()` or `getopt_long()` in User Programs

You may wish to use GNU `getopt()` or `getopt_long()` in your own programs and have them run on non-Linux systems. That's OK; just copy the source files from a GNU program or from the GNU C Library sources. You can get them via the Git source code control system.[3] The source files are `getopt.h`, `getopt.c`, and `getopt1.c` in the `glibc/posix` directory. They are licensed under the GNU Lesser General Public License, which allows library functions to be included even in proprietary programs. You should include a copy of the file `COPYING.LIB` with your program, along with the files `getopt.h`, `getopt.c`, and `getopt1.c`.

Include the source files in your distribution, and compile them along with any other source files. In your source code that calls `getopt_long()`, use '`#include <getopt.h>`', not '`#include "getopt.h"`'. Then, when compiling, add `-I.` to the C compiler's command line. That way, the local copy of the header file will be found first.

2.4 The Environment

The *environment* is a set of '*`name=value`*' pairs for each program. These pairs are termed *environment variables*. Each *name* consists of one or more alphanumeric characters or underscores ('_'), but the name may not start with a digit. (This rule is enforced by the shell; the C API can put anything it wants to into the environment, at the likely cost of confusing subsequent programs.)

A running program inherits its environment from the process that started it. Typically this is a shell. When a running program changes the value of an environment variable, the new value is seen by that program and any new processes that it creates, but the original value in the parent program is not affected.

Environment variables are often used to control program behavior. For example, if `POSIXLY_CORRECT` exists in the environment, many GNU programs disable extensions or historical behavior that isn't compatible with the POSIX standard.

You can decide (and should document) the environment variables that your program will use to control its behavior. For example, you may wish to use an environment variable for debugging options instead of a command-line argument. The advantage of using environment

[3] Use '`git clone git://sourceware.org/git/glibc.git`'.

variables is that users can set them in their startup file and not have to remember to always supply a particular set of command-line options.

Of course, the disadvantage to using environment variables is that they can *silently* change a program's behavior. Jim Meyering, the maintainer of the Coreutils, put it this way:

> It makes it easy for the user to customize how the program works without changing how the program is invoked. That can be both a blessing and a curse. If you write a script that depends on your having a certain environment variable set, but then have someone else use that same script, it may well fail (or worse, silently produce invalid results) if that other person doesn't have the same environment settings.

Chet Ramey, the Bash maintainer, adds that if you write a script that calls a program that depends on a particular environment variable, it's good practice to assume the variable will be unset when your script starts.

2.4.1 Environment Management Functions

Several functions let you retrieve, change, or remove the values of environment variables. Here are the declarations:

```
#include <stdlib.h>

char *getenv(const char *name);                   ISO C: Retrieve environment variable
int setenv(const char *name, const char *value,   POSIX: Set environment variable
           int overwrite);
int putenv(char *string);                         XSI: Set environment variable using string
void unsetenv(const char *name);                  POSIX: Remove environment variable
int clearenv(void);                               Common: Clear entire environment
```

The `getenv()` function is the one you will use 99 percent of the time. The argument is the environment variable name to look up, such as `"HOME"` or `"PATH"`. If the variable exists, `getenv()` returns a pointer to the character string value. If not, it returns `NULL`. For example:

```
char *pathval;

/* Look for PATH; if not present, supply a default value */
if ((pathval = getenv("PATH")) == NULL)
    pathval = "/bin:/usr/bin:/usr/local/bin";
```

Occasionally, environment variables exist, but with empty values. In this case, the return value will be non-`NULL`, but the first character pointed to will be the zero byte, which is the C string terminator, `'\0'`. Your code should be careful to check that the return value pointed to is not `NULL`. Even if it isn't `NULL`, also check that the string is not empty if you intend to use its value for something. In any case, don't just blindly use the returned value.

To change an environment variable or to add a new one to the environment, use `setenv()`:

```
if (setenv("PATH", "/bin:/usr/bin:/usr/local/bin", true) != 0) {
    /* handle failure */
}
```

It's possible that a variable already exists in the environment. If the third argument is true (nonzero),[4] then the supplied value overwrites the previous one. Otherwise, it doesn't. The return value is `-1` if there was no memory for the new variable, and `0` otherwise. `setenv()` makes private copies of both the variable name and the new value for storing in the environment.

A simpler alternative to `setenv()` is `putenv()`, which takes a single "*name=value*" string and places it in the environment:

```
if (putenv("PATH=/bin:/usr/bin:/usr/local/bin") != 0) {
    /* handle failure */
}
```

`putenv()` blindly replaces any previous value for the same variable. Also, and perhaps more importantly, the string passed to `putenv()` is placed *directly* into the environment. This means that if your code later modifies this string (for example, if it was an array, not a string constant), the environment is modified also. This in turn means that you should *not* use a local variable as the parameter for `putenv()`. For all these reasons, `setenv()` is preferred.

NOTE

The GNU `putenv()` has an additional (documented) quirk to its behavior: if the argument string is just a name, without an = character and value, the named variable is *removed*.

The `unsetenv()` function removes a variable from the environment:

```
unsetenv("PATH");
```

Finally, the `clearenv()` function clears the environment entirely:

```
if (clearenv() != 0) {
    /* handle failure */
}
```

This function is not standardized by POSIX, although it's available in GNU/Linux and in several commercial Unix variants. You should use it if your application must be very security conscious and you want it to build its own environment entirely from scratch. If `clearenv()` is not available, the GNU/Linux *clearenv*(3) manpage recommends using '`environ = NULL;`' to accomplish the task.

2.4.2 The Entire Environment: `environ`

The correct way to deal with the environment is through the functions described in the previous section. However, it's worth a look at how things are managed "under the hood."

The external variable `environ` provides access to the environment in the same way that `argv` provides access to the command-line arguments. You must declare the variable yourself. Although standardized by POSIX, `environ` is purposely not declared by any standardized header file. (This seems to evolve from historical practice.) Here is the declaration:

```
extern char **environ;    /* Look Ma, no header file! */          POSIX
```

[4] Original C didn't have Boolean variables, using zero for `false` and nonzero for `true`—thus the use of `int` for the type of `overwrite`. However, modern C's `true` and `false` can and should be used in cases like this.

Like `argv`, the final element in `environ` is `NULL`. There is no "environment count" variable that corresponds to `argc`, however. This simple program prints out the entire environment:

```
/* ch-cmdline-printenv.c --- Print out the environment. */

#include <stdio.h>

extern char **environ;     // no header, declare manually

int
main(int argc, char **argv)
{
    int i;

    if (environ != NULL)
        for (i = 0; environ[i] != NULL; i++)
            printf("%s\n", environ[i]);

    return 0;
}
```

Although it's unlikely to happen, this program makes sure that `environ` isn't `NULL` before attempting to use it.

Variables are kept in the environment in random order. Although some Unix shells keep the environment sorted by variable name, there is no formal requirement that this be so, and many shells don't keep them sorted.

As something of a quirk of the implementation, you can access the environment by declaring a *third* parameter to `main()`:

```
int
main(int argc, char **argv, char **envp)
{
    ...
}
```

You can then use `envp` as you would have used `environ`. Although you may see this occasionally in old code, we don't recommend its use; `environ` is the official, standard, portable way to access the entire environment, should you need to do so.

Chet Ramey mentions that modifying `environ` is one way to change the behavior of library functions that use environment variables (such as the locale; see Section 15.2.1, "Locale Categories and Environment Variables," page 508). However, we would recommend using `setenv()` or `putenv()` for that purpose, along with an appropriate comment.

2.4.3 GNU env

To round off the chapter, here are selected portions from the GNU version of the `env` command. This command adds variables to the environment for the duration of one command.

It can also be used to clear the environment for that command or to remove specific environment variables. The program serves double duty for us, since it demonstrates both `getopt_long()` and several of the functions discussed in this section. Here is how the program is invoked:

```
$ env --help
Usage: env [OPTION]... [-] [NAME=VALUE]... [COMMAND [ARG]...]
Set each NAME to VALUE in the environment and run COMMAND.

Mandatory arguments to long options are mandatory for short options too.
  -i, --ignore-environment  start with an empty environment
  -0, --null           end each output line with NUL, not newline
  -u, --unset=NAME     remove variable from the environment
  -C, --chdir=DIR      change working directory to DIR
  -S, --split-string=S  process and split S into separate arguments;
                        used to pass multiple arguments on shebang lines
      --block-signal[=SIG]    block delivery of SIG signal(s) to COMMAND
      --default-signal[=SIG]  reset handling of SIG signal(s) to the default
      --ignore-signal[=SIG]   set handling of SIG signal(s) to do nothing
      --list-signal-handling  list non default signal handling to stderr
  -v, --debug          print verbose information for each processing step
      --help     display this help and exit
      --version  output version information and exit

A mere - implies -i.  If no COMMAND, print the resulting environment.

SIG may be a signal name like 'PIPE', or a signal number like '13'.
Without SIG, all known signals are included.  Multiple signals can be
comma-separated.  An empty SIG argument is a no-op.

Exit status:
  125  if the env command itself fails
  126  if COMMAND is found but cannot be invoked
  127  if COMMAND cannot be found
  -    the exit status of COMMAND otherwise

GNU coreutils online help: <https://www.gnu.org/software/coreutils/>
Full documentation <https://www.gnu.org/software/coreutils/env>
or available locally via: info '(coreutils) env invocation'
```

As you can see, env accepts a number of options that aren't really related to modifying the environment, such as changing the directory and modifying signal settings.[5] (We cover signals

[5] These features have been added over the years. Every new feature complicates a program; this goes against the grain of the "Small Is Beautiful" approach we advocated in the preface.

in Chapter 10, “Signals,” page 333. A “shebang line” is the `#!` line for executable scripts, as discussed in Section 1.1.3, “Executable Files,” page 6.) For now, we focus on those parts of the code that manipulate the environment.

Here are some sample invocations:

`$ env - myprog arg1` *Clear environment, run program with args*

`$ env - PATH=/bin:/usr/bin myprog arg1` *Clear environment, add PATH, run program*

`$ env -u IFS PATH=/bin:/usr/bin myprog arg1` *Unset IFS, add PATH, run program*

The code begins with a standard GNU copyright statement and explanatory comment. We have omitted both for brevity. (The copyright statement is discussed in Appendix C, “GNU General Public License,” page 673. The `--help` output shown previously is enough to understand how the program works.) Following the copyright and comments are header includes and declarations:

```
#include <config.h>
#include <stdio.h>
#include <sys/types.h>
#include <getopt.h>
#include <c-ctype.h>
#include <signal.h>

#include "system.h"
#include "operand2sig.h"
#include "quote.h"
#include "sig2str.h"

/* The official name of this program (e.g., no 'g' prefix).  */
#define PROGRAM_NAME "env"
...
static char const shortopts[] = "+C:iS:u:v0" C_ISSPACE_CHARS;

/* For long options that have no equivalent short option, use a
   non-character as a pseudo short option, starting with CHAR_MAX + 1.  */
enum
{
  DEFAULT_SIGNAL_OPTION = CHAR_MAX + 1,
  IGNORE_SIGNAL_OPTION,
  BLOCK_SIGNAL_OPTION,
  LIST_SIGNAL_HANDLING_OPTION,
};

```

```
88 static struct option const longopts[] =
89 {
90   {"ignore-environment", no_argument, nullptr, 'i'},
91   {"null", no_argument, nullptr, '0'},
92   {"unset", required_argument, nullptr, 'u'},
93   {"chdir", required_argument, nullptr, 'C'},
94   {"default-signal", optional_argument, nullptr, DEFAULT_SIGNAL_OPTION},
95   {"ignore-signal",  optional_argument, nullptr, IGNORE_SIGNAL_OPTION},
96   {"block-signal",   optional_argument, nullptr, BLOCK_SIGNAL_OPTION},
97   {"list-signal-handling", no_argument, nullptr,  LIST_SIGNAL_HANDLING_OPTION},
98   {"debug", no_argument, nullptr, 'v'},
99   {"split-string", required_argument, nullptr, 'S'},
100  {GETOPT_HELP_OPTION_DECL},
101  {GETOPT_VERSION_OPTION_DECL},
102  {nullptr, 0, nullptr, 0}
103 };
```

The GNU Coreutils contain a large number of programs, many of which perform the same common tasks (for example, argument parsing). To make maintenance easier, many common idioms are defined as macros. `GETOPT_HELP_OPTION_DECL` and `GETOPT_VERSION_OPTION_DECL` (lines 100 and 101) are two such macros. We examine their definitions shortly. The first function, `usage()`, prints the usage information and exits. It is large, and merely prints the text shown earlier, so we omit its body here:

```
void
usage (int status)
{
...
}
```

For now, we skip the intervening code and move on to `main()`. The first part of `main()` declares variables and sets up the internationalization as follows:

- `initialize_main()` (line 756) handles command-line wildcarding and I/O redirection on some non-POSIX systems.
- The functions `setlocale()`, `bindtextdomain()`, and `textdomain()` (lines 758–760) are all discussed in Chapter 15, "Internationalization and Localization," page 507.
- `initialize_exit_failure()` (line 762) sets up a global variable named `exit_failure` with the desired exit status; this variable is used throughout the Coreutils for printing error messages and then exiting.
- The call to `atexit()` on line 763 (see Section 9.1.5.3, "Exiting Functions," page 290) registers a Coreutils library function to be run that flushes all pending output and closes `stdout`, reporting a message if there are problems.

- Finally, calling `initialize_signals()` (line 765) sets up the default signal handling:

```
748 int
749 main (int argc, char **argv)
750 {
751   int optc;
752   bool ignore_environment = false;
753   bool opt_nul_terminate_output = false;
754   char const *newdir = nullptr;
755
756   initialize_main (&argc, &argv);
757   set_program_name (argv[0]);
758   setlocale (LC_ALL, "");
759   bindtextdomain (PACKAGE, LOCALEDIR);
760   textdomain (PACKAGE);
761
762   initialize_exit_failure (EXIT_CANCELED);
763   atexit (close_stdout);
764
765   initialize_signals ();
```

The next bit processes the command-line arguments, using `getopt_long()`:

```
767   while ((optc = getopt_long (argc, argv, shortopts, longopts, nullptr)) != -1)
768     {
769       switch (optc)
770         {
771         case 'i':
772           ignore_environment = true;
773           break;
774         case 'u':
775           append_unset_var (optarg);
776           break;
777         case 'v':
778           dev_debug = true;
779           break;
780         case '0':
781           opt_nul_terminate_output = true;
782           break;
783         case DEFAULT_SIGNAL_OPTION:
784           parse_signal_action_params (optarg, true);
785           parse_block_signal_params (optarg, false);
786           break;
787         case IGNORE_SIGNAL_OPTION:
788           parse_signal_action_params (optarg, false);
789           break;
```

```
790         case BLOCK_SIGNAL_OPTION:
791           parse_block_signal_params (optarg, true);
792           break;
793         case LIST_SIGNAL_HANDLING_OPTION:
794           report_signal_handling = true;
795           break;
796         case 'C':
797           newdir = optarg;
798           break;
799         case 'S':
800           parse_split_string (optarg, &optind, &argc, &argv);
801           break;
802         case ' ': case '\t': case '\n': case '\v': case '\f': case '\r':
803           /* These are undocumented options.  Attempt to detect
804              incorrect shebang usage with extraneous space, e.g.:
805                 #!/usr/bin/env -i command
806              In which case argv[1] == "-i command".  */
807           error (0, 0, _("invalid option -- '%c'"), optc);
808           error (0, 0, _("use -[v]S to pass options in shebang lines"));
809           usage (EXIT_CANCELED);
810
811         case_GETOPT_HELP_CHAR;
812         case_GETOPT_VERSION_CHAR (PROGRAM_NAME, AUTHORS);
813         default:
814           usage (EXIT_CANCELED);
815         }
816     }
817
818   if (optind < argc && STREQ (argv[optind], "-"))
819     {
820       ignore_environment = true;
821       ++optind;
822     }
```

Of particular note is the action for the -u option (lines 774–775). This unsets the given environment variable by calling `append_unset_var()`, which appends the variable to a dynamically created array of variables to be unset. We show that function shortly.

Here are the macros, from `src/system.h` in the Coreutils distribution, that define the declarations we saw earlier and the '`case_GETOPT_xxx`' macros used above (lines 811–812):

```
/* Factor out some of the common --help and --version processing code.  */

/* These enum values cannot possibly conflict with the option values
   ordinarily used by commands, including CHAR_MAX + 1, etc.  Avoid
   CHAR_MIN - 1, as it may equal -1, the getopt end-of-options value.  */
enum
```

```
{
  GETOPT_HELP_CHAR = (CHAR_MIN - 2),
  GETOPT_VERSION_CHAR = (CHAR_MIN - 3)
};

#define GETOPT_HELP_OPTION_DECL \
  "help", no_argument, nullptr, GETOPT_HELP_CHAR
#define GETOPT_VERSION_OPTION_DECL \
  "version", no_argument, nullptr, GETOPT_VERSION_CHAR
#define GETOPT_SELINUX_CONTEXT_OPTION_DECL \
  "context", optional_argument, nullptr, 'Z'

#define case_GETOPT_HELP_CHAR            \
  case GETOPT_HELP_CHAR:                 \
    usage (EXIT_SUCCESS);                \
    break;
...
#define case_GETOPT_VERSION_CHAR(Program_name, Authors)          \
  case GETOPT_VERSION_CHAR:                                      \
    version_etc (stdout, Program_name, PACKAGE_NAME, Version, Authors,  \
                 (char *) nullptr);                              \
    exit (EXIT_SUCCESS);                                         \
    break;
```

The upshot of this code is that `--help` prints the usage message and `--version` prints version information. Both exit successfully. (“Success” and “failure” exit statuses are described in Section 9.1.5.1, “Defining Process Exit Status,” page 289.) Given that the Coreutils have dozens of utilities, it makes sense to factor out and standardize as much repetitive code as possible.

Returning to `env.c`:

```
  if (ignore_environment)
    {
      devmsg ("cleaning environ\n");
      static char *dummy_environ[] = { nullptr };
      environ = dummy_environ;
    }
  else
    unset_envvars ();

  char *eq;
  while (optind < argc && (eq = strchr (argv[optind], '=')))
    {
      devmsg ("setenv:   %s\n", argv[optind]);

      if (putenv (argv[optind]))
```

```
839         {
840           *eq = '\0';
841           error (EXIT_CANCELED, errno, _("cannot set %s"),
842                  quote (argv[optind]));
843         }
844       optind++;
845     }
846
847   bool program_specified = optind < argc;
...
861   if (! program_specified)
862     {
863       /* Print the environment and exit.  */
864       char *const *e = environ;
865       while (*e)
866         printf ("%s%c", *e++, opt_nul_terminate_output ? '\0' : '\n');
867       return EXIT_SUCCESS;
868     }
```

Lines 824–831 deal with either emptying the environment entirely (lines 827–828) or unsetting the variables requested via the `-u` option (line 831). We show `unset_envvars()` shortly. The `devmsg()` ("developer message") function prints debugging messages if such were requested via the `-v` option.

Lines 833–845 add any new variables to the environment by calling `putenv()`.

Upon reaching line 847, if nothing is left on the command line, we know that `env` is supposed to print the new environment, and exit. It does so (lines 861–868). The intervening lines aren't of interest at the moment, so we've omitted them.

If arguments are left, they represent a command name to run and arguments to pass to that new command. This is done with the `execvp()` system call (line 893), which *replaces* the current program with the new one. (This call is discussed in Section 9.1.4, "Starting New Programs: The `exec()` Family," page 283; don't worry about the details for now.) If this call returns to the current program, it *failed*. In such a case, `env` prints an error message and exits:

```
893   execvp (argv[optind], &argv[optind]);
894
895   int exit_status = errno == ENOENT ? EXIT_ENOENT : EXIT_CANNOT_INVOKE;
896   error (0, errno, "%s", quote (argv[optind]));
897
898   if (exit_status == EXIT_ENOENT && strpbrk (argv[optind], C_ISSPACE_CHARS))
899     error (0, 0, _("use -[v]S to pass options in shebang lines"));
900
901   main_exit (exit_status);
902 }
```

Line 895 sets the exit status. The constants `EXIT_ENOENT` and `EXIT_CANNOT_INVOKE` are defined in `src/system.h` as follows:

```
/* Exit statuses for programs like 'env' that exec other programs.  */
enum
{
  EXIT_TIMEDOUT = 124, /* Time expired before child completed.  */
  EXIT_CANCELED = 125, /* Internal error prior to exec attempt.  */
  EXIT_CANNOT_INVOKE = 126, /* Program located, but not usable.  */
  EXIT_ENOENT = 127 /* Could not find program to exec.  */
};
```

The last two exit status values, `126` and `127`, conform to POSIX. `127` means the program that `execvp()` attempted to run didn't exist. (`ENOENT` means the file doesn't have an entry in the directory.) `126` means that the file exists, but something else went wrong.

Here are the two functions that handle unsetting environment variables. `append_unset_var()` adds the variable to an array that can grow dynamically (discussed in Chapter 3, "User-Level Memory Management," page 51). `unset_envvars()` loops over the array, calling `unsetenv()` for each element:

```
static void
append_unset_var (char const *var)
{
  if (usvars_used == usvars_alloc)
    usvars = x2nrealloc (usvars, &usvars_alloc, sizeof *usvars);
  usvars[usvars_used++] = var;
}

static void
unset_envvars (void)
{
  for (idx_t i = 0; i < usvars_used; ++i)
    {
      devmsg ("unset:    %s\n", usvars[i]);

      if (unsetenv (usvars[i]))
        error (EXIT_CANCELED, errno, _("cannot unset %s"),
               quote (usvars[i]));
    }
}
```

2.5 Summary

- C programs access their command-line arguments through the parameters `argc` and `argv`. The `getopt()` function provides a standard way for consistent parsing of options and their arguments. The GNU version of `getopt()` provides some extensions, and `getopt_long()` and `getopt_long_only()` make it possible to easily parse long-style options.
- The environment is a set of '*name=value*' pairs that each program inherits from its parent. Programs can, at their author's whim, use environment variables to change their behavior, in addition to any command-line arguments. Standard routines (`getenv()`, `setenv()`, `putenv()`, and `unsetenv()`) exist for retrieving environment variable values, changing them, or removing them. If necessary, the entire environment is available through the external variable `environ` or by adding the `char **envp` third argument to `main()`. The latter technique is discouraged.

Exercises

1. If you compile the V7 `echo.c` today, you'll get a lot of warnings. Revise the code to use modern C language constructs until it compiles cleanly. Make sure that it still works the same as well.
2. Assume a program accepts options `-a`, `-b`, and `-c`, and that `-b` requires an argument. It accepts `--` to end option processing. Write the manual argument parsing code for this program, without using `getopt()` or `getopt_long()`. Make sure that `-ac` works, as do `-bYANKEES`, `-b YANKEES`, and `-abYANKEES`. Test your program.
3. Implement `getopt()`. For the first version, don't worry about the case in which '`optstring[0] == ':'`'. You may also ignore `opterr`.
4. Add code for '`optstring[0] == ':'`' and `opterr` to your version of `getopt()`.
5. Print and read the GNU `getopt.h`, `getopt.c`, and `getopt1.c` files.
6. Write a program that declares both `environ` and `envp` and compares their values.
7. Download the Coreutils 5.0 distribution (from April, 2003) from the GNU distribution site.[6] Compare its version of `env.c` to the current one. How do you feel about all the additional code in the current version?
8. Parsing command-line arguments and options is a wheel that many people can't refrain from reinventing. Besides `getopt()` and `getopt_long()`, you may wish to examine different argument-parsing packages, such as:

[6] `https://ftp.gnu.org/gnu/coreutils/coreutils-5.0.tar.gz`

- The *Plan 9 from Bell Labs arg*(2) argument-parsing library.[7]
- Argp.[8]
- AutoOpts.[9]
- Cargs.[10]
- GNU Gengetopt.[11]

9. How many other option-parsing packages can you find by searching on the Internet, or in source code sites such as GitHub and SourceForge?
10. Extra credit: Why can't a C compiler completely ignore the `register` keyword? Hint: what operation *cannot* be applied to a `register` variable?

---

[7] `https://9p.io/magic/man2html/2/arg`
[8] `https://sourceware.org/glibc/manual/latest/html_node/Argp.html`
[9] `https://autogen.sourceforge.net/autoopts.html`
[10] `https://likle.github.io/cargs`
[11] `https://ftp.gnu.org/gnu/gengetopt/`

Chapter 3

User-Level Memory Management

Without memory for storing data, it's impossible for a program to get any work done. (Or rather, it's impossible to get any *useful* work done.) Real-world programs can't afford to rely on fixed-size buffers or arrays of data structures. They have to be able to handle inputs of varying sizes, from small to large. This in turn leads to the use of *dynamically allocated memory*—memory allocated at runtime instead of at compile time. This is how the GNU "no arbitrary limits" principle is put into action.

Because dynamically allocated memory is such a basic building block for real-world programs, we cover it early, before looking at everything else there is to do. Our discussion focuses exclusively on the user-level view of the process and its memory and has nothing to do with CPU architecture.

3.1 Linux/Unix Address Space

For a working definition, we've said that a *process* is a running program. This means that the operating system has loaded the executable file for the program into memory, has arranged for it to have access to its command-line arguments and environment variables, and has started it running. A process has five conceptually different areas of memory allocated to it:

Code
: Often referred to as the *text segment*, this is the area in which the executable instructions reside. Linux and Unix arrange things so that multiple running instances of the same program share their code if possible; only one copy of the instructions for the same program resides in memory at any time. (This is transparent to the running programs.) The portion of the executable file containing the text segment is the *text section*.

Initialized data
: Global and `static` data that are initialized with nonzero values live in the *data segment*. Each process running the same program has its own data segment. The portion of the executable file containing the data segment is the *data section*.

Zero-initialized data
: Global and `static` data that are initialized to zero by default are kept in what is colloquially called the *BSS* area of the process.[1] Each process running the same program

[1] BSS is an acronym for "Block Started by Symbol," a mnemonic from the IBM 7094 assembler. The IBM 7094 was introduced in September 1962.

has its own BSS area. When running, the BSS data is placed in the data segment. In the executable file, it is stored in the *BSS section*.

The format of a Linux/Unix executable is such that only variables that are initialized to a nonzero value occupy space in the executable's disk file. Thus, a large array declared '`static char somebuf[2048];`', which is automatically zero-filled, does not take up 2 KB worth of disk space. (Some compilers have options that let you place zero-initialized data into the data segment.)

Heap

The *heap* is where dynamic memory (obtained by `malloc()` and friends) comes from. As memory is allocated on the heap, the process's address space grows, as you can see by watching a running program with the `ps` command.

Although it is possible to give memory back to the system and shrink a process's address space, this is rarely done.[2] (We distinguish between releasing no-longer-needed dynamic memory and shrinking the address space; this is discussed in more detail later in this chapter.)

It is typical for the heap to "grow upward." This means that successive items that are added to the heap are added at addresses that are numerically greater than previous items. It is also typical for the heap to start immediately after the BSS area of the data segment.

Stack

The *stack segment* is where local variables are allocated. Local variables are all variables declared inside the opening left brace of a function body (or other left brace) that aren't defined as `static`.

On most architectures, function parameters are also placed on the stack, as well as "invisible" bookkeeping information generated by the compiler, such as room for a function return value and storage for the return address representing the return from a function to its caller. (Some architectures do all this with registers.)

It is the use of a stack for function parameters and return values that makes it convenient to write *recursive* functions (functions that call themselves).

Variables stored on the stack "disappear" when the function containing them returns; the space on the stack is reused for subsequent function calls.

On most modern architectures, the stack "grows downward," meaning that items deeper in the call chain are at numerically lower addresses.

When a program is running, the initialized data, BSS, and heap areas are usually placed into a single contiguous area: the data segment. The stack segment and code segment are separate from the data segment and from each other. This is illustrated in Figure 3.1.

---

[2] Some allocators do release memory back to the system when an allocation is "large" (for whatever definition of "large"). But you shouldn't count on this.

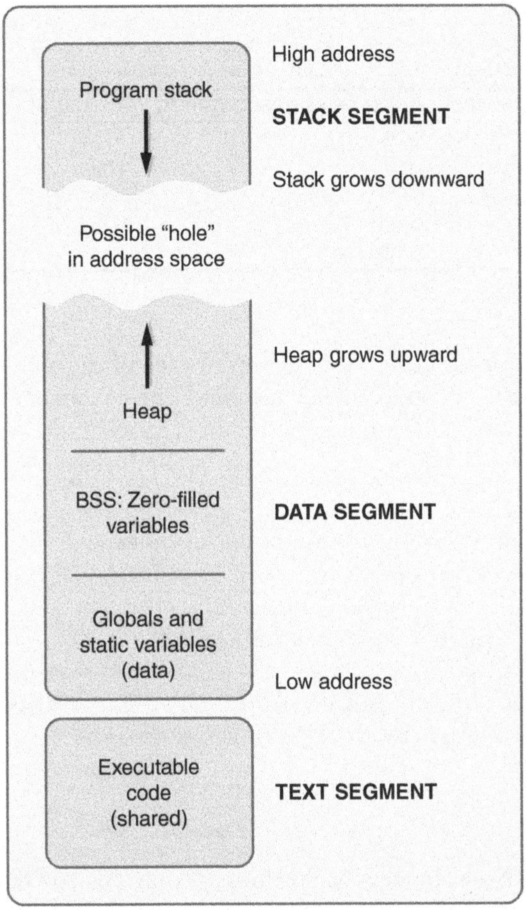

Figure 3.1: Linux/Unix process address space

Although it's theoretically possible for the stack and heap to grow into each other, the operating system prevents that event, and any program that tries to make it happen is asking for trouble. This is particularly true on modern systems, where process address spaces are large and the gap between the top of the stack and the end of the heap is a big one.

The different memory areas can have different hardware memory protection assigned to them. For example, the text segment might be marked "execute only," whereas the data and stack segments would have execute permission disabled. This practice can prevent certain kinds of security attacks. The details, of course, are hardware and operating-system specific and likely to change over time. Of note is that both Standard C and C++ allow `const` items to be placed in read-only memory. The relationship among the different segments is summarized in Table 3.1.

Table 3.1: Executable program segments and their locations

Program memory	Address space segment	Executable file section
Code	Text	Text
Initialized data	Data	Data
BSS	Data	BSS
Heap	Data	
Stack	Stack	

The `size` program prints out the size in bytes of each of the text, data, and BSS sections, along with the total size in decimal and hexadecimal (the `ch-memory-memaddr.c` program is shown later in this chapter; see Section 3.2.5, "Address Space Examination," page 74):

```
$ cc -O ch-memory-memaddr.c -o ch-memory-memaddr          Compile the program
$ ls -l ch-memory-memaddr                                 Show total size
-rwxrwxr-x 1 arnold arnold 16240 May 25 13:11 ch-memory-memaddr
$ size ch-memory-memaddr                                  Show component sizes
   text    data     bss     dec     hex filename
   2648     628      12    3288     cd8 ch-memory-memaddr
$ strip ch-memory-memaddr                                 Remove symbols
$ ls -l ch-memory-memaddr                                 Show total size again
-rwxrwxr-x 1 arnold arnold 14480 May 25 13:12 ch-memory-memaddr
$ size  ch-memory-memaddr                                 Component sizes haven't changed
   text    data     bss     dec     hex filename
   2648     628      12    3288     cd8 ch-memory-memaddr
```

The total size of what gets loaded into memory is only 3,288 bytes, in a file that is 16,240 bytes long. Most of that space is occupied by the *symbols*, a list of the program's variables and function names. (The symbols are not loaded into memory when the program runs.) The `strip` program removes some of the symbols from the object file. This can save disk space for a large program, at the cost of making it impossible to debug a core dump[3] should one occur. (On modern systems this isn't worth the trouble; don't use `strip`.) Even after removing the symbols, the file is still larger than what gets loaded into memory since the object file format maintains additional data about the program, such as what shared libraries it may use, if any.[4]

Finally, we'll mention that *threads* represent multiple threads of execution within a *single* address space. Typically, each thread has its own stack, and a way to get *thread local* data—that is, dynamically allocated data for private use by the thread. We don't otherwise cover threads in this book, since they are an advanced topic.

---

[3] A *core dump* is the memory image of a running process created when the process terminates unexpectedly. It may be used later for debugging. Unix systems named the file `core`. The name on GNU/Linux systems can vary based on settings made by the particular distribution; see Section 17.3.1, "Getting a `core` File," page 594.

[4] The description here is a deliberate simplification. Running programs occupy much more space than the `size` program indicates, since shared libraries are included in the address space. Also, the data segment will grow as a program allocates memory.

3.2 Memory Allocation

Four library functions form the basis for dynamic memory management from C. We describe them first, followed by descriptions of the two system calls upon which these library functions are built. The C library functions in turn are usually used to implement other library functions that allocate memory and the C++ `new` and `delete` operators.

Finally, we discuss a function that you may see used frequently, but that we don't recommend.

3.2.1 Library Calls: `malloc()`, `calloc()`, `realloc()`, `free()`

Dynamic memory is allocated by either the `malloc()` function or the `calloc()` function. These functions return pointers to the allocated memory. Once you have a block of memory of a certain initial size, you can change its size with the `realloc()` function. Dynamic memory is released with the `free()` function.

Debugging the use of dynamic memory is an important topic in its own right. We discuss tools for this purpose in Section 17.6, "Debugging Tools II: Memory Allocation Debuggers," page 633.

3.2.1.1 Examining C Language Details

Here are the function declarations from the GNU/Linux *malloc*(3) manpage:

```
#include <stdlib.h>                                          ISO C

void *calloc(size_t nmemb, size_t size);     Allocate and zero-fill
void *malloc(size_t size);                   Allocate raw memory
void free(void *ptr);                        Release memory
void *realloc(void *ptr, size_t size);       Change size of existing allocation
```

The allocation functions all return type `void *`. This is a *typeless* or *generic pointer*; all you can do with such a pointer is cast it to a different type and assign it to a typed pointer. Examples are coming up.

The type `size_t` is an unsigned integral type that represents amounts of memory. It is used for dynamic memory allocation, and we see many uses of it throughout the book. On most modern systems, `size_t` is `unsigned long`, but it's better to use `size_t` explicitly than to use a plain `unsigned` integral type.

The `ptrdiff_t` type is used for address calculations in pointer arithmetic, such as calculating where in an array a pointer may be pointing:

```
#define MAXBUF ...
char *p;
char buf[MAXBUF];
ptrdiff_t where;
```

```
p = buf;
while (some condition) {
    ...
    p += something;
    ...
    where = p - buf;    /* what index are we at? */
}
```

The <stdlib.h> header file declares many of the standard C library routines and types (such as `size_t`), and it also defines the preprocessor constant `NULL`, which represents the "null" or invalid pointer. (This is a zero value, such as `0` or '`((void *) 0)`'. In C, however, you should always use `NULL`. Older C++ code used `0` explicitly. Modern C++ provides a built-in null pointer, called `nullptr`, and that's what you should use if you're working in C++.)

3.2.1.2 Initially Allocating Memory: `malloc()`

Memory is allocated initially with `malloc()`. The value passed in is the total number of bytes requested. The return value is a pointer to the newly allocated memory, or `NULL` if memory could not be allocated. In the latter event, `errno` will be set to indicate the error. (`errno` is a special variable that system calls and library functions set to indicate what went wrong. It's described in Section 4.3, "Determining What Went Wrong," page 81.) For example, suppose we wish to allocate a variable number of some structure. The code looks something like this:

```
struct coord {                          /* 3D coordinates */
    int x, y, z;
} *coordinates;
unsigned int count;                      /* how many we need */
size_t amount;                           /* total amount of memory */

/* ... determine count somehow... */
amount = count * sizeof(struct coord);  /* how many bytes to allocate */

coordinates = (struct coord *) malloc(amount);  /* get the space */
if (coordinates == NULL) {
    /* report error, recover, or give up */
}
/* ... use coordinates ... */
```

The steps shown here are quite boilerplate. The order is as follows:

1. Declare a pointer of the proper type to point to the allocated memory.
2. Calculate the size *in bytes* of the memory to be allocated. This involves multiplying a count of objects needed by the size of the individual object. This size in turn is retrieved from the C `sizeof` operator, which exists for this purpose (among others). Thus, while the size of a particular `struct` may vary across compilers and architectures, `sizeof` always returns the correct value, and the source code remains correct and portable.

When allocating arrays for character strings or other data of type `char`, it is not necessary to multiply by `sizeof(char)`, since by definition this is always `1`. But it won't hurt anything either.

3. Allocate the storage by calling `malloc()`, assigning the function's return value to the pointer variable. It is good practice to cast the return value of `malloc()` to that of the variable being assigned to. In C it's not required (although the compiler may generate a warning). We strongly recommend *always* casting the return value.

   Note that in C++, assignment of a pointer value of one type to a pointer of another type does requires a cast, whatever the context. For dynamic memory management, C++ programs should use `new` and `delete`, to avoid type problems, and not `malloc()` and `free()`.

4. Check the return value. *Never* assume that memory allocation will succeed. If the allocation fails, `malloc()` returns `NULL`. If the returned value is `NULL` and you use it without checking, your program will immediately die from a *segmentation violation* (or *segfault*), which is an attempt to use memory not in your address space.

   If you check the return value, you can at least print a diagnostic message and terminate gracefully. Or you can attempt some other method of recovery.

Once we've allocated memory and set `coordinates` to point to it, we can then treat `coordinates` as if it were an array, although it's really a pointer:

```
int cur_x, cur_y, cur_z;
size_t an_index;
an_index = something;
cur_x = coordinates[an_index].x;
cur_y = coordinates[an_index].y;
cur_z = coordinates[an_index].z;
```

The compiler generates correct code for indexing through the pointer to retrieve the members of the structure at `coordinates[an_index]`.

NOTE

The memory returned by `malloc()` is *not* initialized. It can contain any random garbage. You should immediately initialize the memory with valid data or at least with zeros. To do the latter, use `memset()` (discussed in Section 13.2, "Low-Level Memory: The `memXXX()` Functions," page 423):

```
memset(coordinates, '\0', amount);
```

Another option is to use `calloc()`, described shortly.

Geoff Collyer recommends the following technique for allocating memory:

```
some_type *pointer;

pointer = malloc(count * sizeof(*pointer));
```

This approach guarantees that `malloc()` will allocate the correct amount of memory without your having to consult the declaration of `pointer`. If `pointer`'s type later changes, the `sizeof` operator automatically ensures that the count of bytes to allocate stays correct. (Geoff's technique omits the cast that we just discussed. Having the cast there also ensures a diagnostic if `pointer`'s type changes and the call to `malloc()` isn't updated.)

3.2.1.3 Releasing Memory: `free()`

When you're done using the memory, you "give it back" by using the `free()` function. The single argument is a pointer previously obtained from one of the other allocation routines:

```
free(coordinates);
coordinates = NULL;     /* not required, but a good idea */
```

Once `free(coordinates)` is called, the memory pointed to by `coordinates` is *off-limits*. It now "belongs" to the allocation subroutines, and they are free to manage it as they see fit. They can change the contents of the memory or even release it from the process's address space!

It is safe (although useless) to pass a null pointer to `free()`. There are several common errors to watch out for with `free()`:

Accessing freed memory

If unchanged, `coordinates` continues to point at memory that no longer belongs to the application. This is called a *dangling pointer*. In many systems, you can get away with continuing to access this memory, at least until the next time more memory is allocated or freed. In many others, though, such access won't work.

In sum, accessing freed memory is a bad idea: it's not portable or reliable, and the *GNU Coding Standards* disallows it. For this reason, it's a good idea to immediately set the program's pointer variable to `NULL`. If you then accidentally attempt to access freed memory, your program will immediately fail with a segmentation fault (before you've released it to the world, we hope).

Freeing the same pointer twice

This causes "undefined behavior." Once the memory has been handed back to the allocation routines, they may merge the freed block with other free storage under management. Freeing something that's already been freed is likely to lead to confusion or crashes at best, and so-called double frees have been known to lead to security problems. GLIBC systems often diagnose double frees at runtime. This helps some, in that at least you know the cause of a program's crash.

Passing a pointer not obtained from `malloc()`, `calloc()`, *or* `realloc()`

This seems obvious, but it's important nonetheless. Even passing in a pointer to somewhere in the middle of dynamically allocated memory is bad:

```
free(coordinates + 10);          /* Release all but first 10 elements. */
```

This call won't work, and it's likely to lead to disastrous consequences, such as a crash. (This is because many `malloc()` implementations keep "bookkeeping" information *in front of* the returned data. When `free()` goes to use that information, it will find invalid data there. Other implementations have the bookkeeping information at the end of the allocated chunk; the same issues apply.)

Buffer overruns and underruns
Accessing memory outside an allocated chunk also leads to undefined behavior, again because this is likely to be bookkeeping information or possibly memory that's not even in the address space. Writing into such memory is much worse, since it's likely to destroy the bookkeeping data.

Failure to free memory
Any dynamic memory that's not needed should be released. In particular, memory that is allocated inside loops or recursive or deeply nested function calls should be carefully managed and released. Failure to take care leads to *memory leaks*, whereby the process's memory can grow without bounds; eventually, the process dies from lack of memory.

This situation can be particularly pernicious if memory is allocated per input record or as some other function of the input: the memory leak won't be noticed when run on small inputs but can suddenly become obvious (and embarrassing) when run on large ones. This error is even worse for systems that must run continuously, such as telephone switching systems. A memory leak that crashes such a system can lead to significant monetary or other damage.

Even if the program never dies for lack of memory, constantly growing programs suffer in performance, because the operating system has to manage keeping in-use data in physical memory. In the worst case, this can lead to behavior known as *thrashing*, whereby the operating system is so busy moving the contents of the address space into and out of physical memory that no real work gets done.

While it's possible for `free()` to hand released memory back to the system and shrink the process address space, this is almost never done. Instead, the released memory is kept available for allocation by the next call to `malloc()`, `calloc()`, or `realloc()`.

Given that released memory continues to reside in the process's address space, it may pay to zero it out before releasing it. Security-sensitive programs may choose to do this, for example.

See Section 17.6, "Debugging Tools II: Memory Allocation Debuggers," page 633, for discussion of two very useful dynamic-memory debugging tools.

3.2.1.4 Changing Size: `realloc()`

Dynamic memory has a significant advantage over statically declared arrays, which is that it's possible to use exactly as much memory as you need, and no more. It's not necessary to declare a global, `static`, or automatic array of some fixed size and hope that it's (a) big enough and (b) not too big. Instead, you can allocate exactly as much as you need, no more and no less. (The trade-off is that this memory must be managed directly by you, the programmer. This is almost always worthwhile, especially for production programs.)

Additionally, it's possible to change the size of a dynamically allocated memory area. Although it's possible to shrink a block of memory, more typically, the block is grown. Changing the size is handled with `realloc()`. Continuing with the `coordinates` example, typical code goes like this:

```
int new_count;
size_t new_amount;
struct coord *newcoords;

/* set new_count, for example: */
new_count = count * 2;          /* double the storage */
new_amount = new_count * sizeof(struct coord);

newcoords = (struct coord *) realloc(coordinates, new_amount);
if (newcoords == NULL) {
    /* report error, recover, or give up */
}

coordinates = newcoords;
/* continue using coordinates ... */
```

As with `malloc()`, the steps are boilerplate in nature and are similar in concept:

1. Compute the new size to allocate, in bytes.
2. Call `realloc()` with the original pointer obtained from `malloc()` (or from `calloc()` or an earlier call to `realloc()`) and the new size.
3. Cast and assign the return value of `realloc()`. More discussion of this shortly.
4. As for `malloc()`, *check the return value* to make sure it's not `NULL`. Any memory allocation routine can fail.

When growing a block of memory, `realloc()` often allocates a new block of the right size, copies the data from the old block into the new one, and returns a pointer to the new one.

When shrinking a block of data, `realloc()` can often just update the internal bookkeeping information and return the same pointer. This saves having to copy the original data. However, if this happens, *don't try to use the memory beyond the new size!* It's possible that the released part of the memory is now reserved for later allocation, or even that it was removed from the address space!

In either case, you can assume that if `realloc()` doesn't return `NULL`, the old data has been copied for you into the new memory. Furthermore, the old pointer is no longer valid, as if you had called `free()` with it, and you should not use it. This is true of all pointers into that block of data, not just the particular one used to call `realloc()`.

You may have noticed that our example code used a separate variable to point to the changed storage block. It would be possible (but a bad idea) to use the same initial variable, like so:

```
coordinates = realloc(coordinates, new_amount);
```

This is a bad idea for the following reason. When `realloc()` returns `NULL`, the original pointer is still valid; it's safe to continue using that memory. However, if you reuse the same variable and `realloc()` returns `NULL`, you've now *lost* the pointer to the original memory. That memory can no longer be used. More importantly, that memory can no longer be freed! This creates a memory leak, which is to be avoided.

There are some special cases for the Standard C version of `realloc()`: When the `ptr` argument is `NULL`, `realloc()` acts like `malloc()` and allocates a fresh block of storage. When the `size` argument is `0`, `realloc()` acts like `free()` and *releases* the memory that `ptr` points to. Because (a) this can be confusing and (b) older systems don't implement this feature, we recommend using `malloc()` when you mean `malloc()` and `free()` when you mean `free()`.

NOTE

The 2024 standard for C changes the behavior of `realloc()` such that if `size` is `0`, *the behavior is undefined*. This is a terrible change, one that is likely to break vast amounts of existing code. Because of this, our advice in the previous paragraph—to use `malloc()` when you mean `malloc()` and `free()` when you mean `free()`—becomes even more important.

Here is another, fairly subtle, "gotcha."[5] Consider a routine that maintains a `static` pointer to some dynamically allocated data, which the routine occasionally has to grow. It may also maintain automatic (that is, local) pointers into this data. (For brevity, we omit error-checking code. In production code, don't do that.) For example:

```
void manage_table(void)
{
    static struct table *table;
    struct table *cur, *p;
    int i;
    size_t count;

    ...
    table = (struct table *) malloc(count * sizeof(struct table));
    /* fill table */
    cur = & table[i];         /* point at i'th item */
    ...
    cur->i = j;               /* use pointer */
    ...
    if (some condition) {     /* need to grow table */
        count += count/2;
        p = (struct table *) realloc(table, count * sizeof(struct table));
        table = p;
    }
```

---

[5]It is derived from real-life experience with `gawk`.

```
    cur->i = j;             /* PROBLEM 1: update table element */

    other_routine();        /* PROBLEM 2: see text */
    cur->j = k;             /* PROBLEM 2: see text */
    ...
}
```

This looks straightforward; `manage_table()` allocates the data, uses it, changes the size, and so on. But there are some problems that don't jump off the page (or the screen) when you are looking at this code.

In the line marked '`PROBLEM 1`', the `cur` pointer is used to update a table element. However, `cur` was assigned on the basis of the *initial* value of `table`. If *some condition* was true and `realloc()` returned a different block of memory, `cur` now points into the original, freed memory! Whenever `table` changes, any pointers into the memory need to be updated too. What's missing here is the statement '`cur = & table[i];`' after `table` is reassigned following the call to `realloc()`.

The two lines marked '`PROBLEM 2`' are even more subtle. In particular, suppose `other_routine()` makes a *recursive* call to `manage_table()`. The `table` variable could be changed again, completely invisibly! Upon return from `other_routine()`, the value of `cur` could once again be invalid.

One might think (as we did) that the only solution is to be aware of this and supply a suitably commented reassignment to `cur` after the function call. However, Brian Kernighan kindly set us straight. If we use indexing, the pointer maintenance issue doesn't even arise:

```
table = (struct table *) malloc(count * sizeof(struct table));
/* fill table */
...
table[i].i = j;          /* Update a member of the i'th element */
...
if (some condition) {   /* need to grow table */
    count += count/2;
    p = (struct table *) realloc(table, count * sizeof(struct table));
    table = p;
}

table[i].i = j;          /* PROBLEM 1 goes away */
other_routine();         /* Recursively calls us, modifies table */
table[i].j = k;          /* PROBLEM 2 goes away also */
```

Using indexing doesn't solve the problem if you have a *global* copy of the original pointer to the allocated data; in that case, you still have to worry about updating your global structures after calling `realloc()`.

NOTE

As with `malloc()`, when you grow a piece of memory, the newly allocated memory returned from `realloc()` is not zero-filled. You must clear it yourself with `memset()` if that's necessary, since `realloc()` only allocates the fresh memory; it doesn't do anything else.

Here is an example function, from the One True Awk,[6] which grows a table and initializes the newly allocated memory to zero:

```
1  static void resize_gototab(fa *f, int state)
2  {
3      size_t new_size = f->gototab[state].allocated * 2;
4      gtte *p = (gtte *) realloc(f->gototab[state].entries, new_size * sizeof(gtte));
5      if (p == NULL)
6          overflo(__func__);
7
8      // need to initialized the new memory to zero
9      size_t orig_size = f->gototab[state].allocated;     // 2nd half of new mem
                                                                   is this size
10     memset(p + orig_size, 0, orig_size * sizeof(gtte)); // clean it out
11
12     f->gototab[state].allocated = new_size;          // update gototab info
13     f->gototab[state].entries = p;
14 }
```

Line numbers are from the beginning of the function, not the file. Line 3 computes the new size and line 4 calls `realloc()`. Lines 9 and 10 handle initializing the new memory. The details of the data types in play here are unimportant; what is noteworthy is the use of pointer arithmetic ('`p + orig_size`') to find the start of the new memory, and the fact that we are zeroing it out. We return to this function and the use of dynamic memory in Section 17.6.1.1, "Valgrind Example: `gototab` in the One True Awk," page 642. The bug described there is related to what we just mentioned, that you need to initialize memory from `realloc()`. We examine related functions that use the allocated data in Section 6.2, "Sorting and Searching Functions," page 171.

3.2.1.5 Allocating and Zero-Filling: `calloc()`

The `calloc()` function is a straightforward wrapper around `malloc()`. Its primary advantage is that it zeros the dynamically allocated memory. It also performs the size calculation for you by taking as parameters the number of items and the size of each:

```
coordinates = (struct coord *) calloc(count, sizeof(struct coord));
```

Conceptually, at least, the `calloc()` code is fairly simple. Here is one possible implementation:

---

[6] https://github.com/onetrueawk/awk

```
void *calloc(size_t nmemb, size_t size)
{
    void *p;
    size_t total;

    total = nmemb * size;                    Compute size
    p = malloc(total);                       Allocate the memory

    if (p != NULL)                           If it worked ...
        memset(p, '\0', total);              Fill it with zeros

    return p;                                Return value is NULL or pointer
}
```

Many experienced programmers prefer to use `calloc()` because then there's never any question about the contents of the newly allocated memory.

Also, if you know you'll need zero-filled memory, you should use `calloc()`, because it's possible that the memory `malloc()` returns is already zero-filled. Although you, the programmer, can't know this, `calloc()` can know about it and avoid the call to `memset()`.

3.2.1.6 Summarizing from the *GNU Coding Standards*

To summarize, here is what the *GNU Coding Standards* has to say about using the memory allocation routines:

> Check every call to `malloc` or `realloc` to see if it returned `NULL`. Check `realloc` even if you are making the block smaller; in a system that rounds block sizes to a power of 2, `realloc` may get a different block if you ask for less space.
>
> You must expect `free` to alter the contents of the block that was freed. Anything you want to fetch from the block, you must fetch before calling `free`.

In two short paragraphs, Richard Stallman has distilled the important principles for doing dynamic memory management with `malloc()`. It is the use of dynamic memory and the "no arbitrary limits" principle that makes GNU programs so robust and more capable than their Unix counterparts.

We do wish to point out that the C standard requires `realloc()` to *not* destroy the original block if it returns `NULL`.

3.2.1.7 Using Private Allocators

The `malloc()` suite is a general-purpose memory allocator. It has to be able to handle requests for arbitrarily large or small amounts of memory and do all the bookkeeping when different chunks of allocated memory are released. If your program does considerable dynamic memory allocation, you may thus find that it spends a large proportion of its time in the `malloc()` functions.

One thing you can do is write a *private allocator*—a set of functions or macros that allocates large chunks of memory from `malloc()` and then parcels out small chunks one at a time. This technique is particularly useful if you allocate many individual instances of the same relatively small structure.

For example, `gawk` uses this technique. From the file `awk.h` in the `gawk` distribution:

```
#define getblock(p, id, ty)  (void) ((p = (ty) nextfree[id].freep) ? \
            (ty) (nextfree[id].freep = ((struct block_item *) p)->freep) \
            : (p = (ty) more_blocks(id)))
#define freeblock(p, id) (void) (((struct block_item *) p)->freep = nextfree[id].freep, \
                    nextfree[id].freep = (struct block_item *) p)
```

The `nextfree` variable points to a linked list of `block_item` structures. The `getblock()` macro pulls the first structure off the list if one is there. Otherwise, it calls `more_blocks()` to allocate a new list of free `block_item`ss. The `freeblock()` macro releases a `block_item` by putting it at the head of the list.

NOTE

When first writing your application, do it the simple way: use `malloc()` and `free()` directly. *Only if* profiling your program shows you that it's spending a significant amount of time in the memory allocation functions should you consider writing a private allocator.

3.2.1.8 Example: Reading Arbitrarily Long Lines

Since this is, after all, *Linux Application Development by Example*, it's time for a real-life example. The following code is the `readline()` function[7] from GNU Make 4.4.1.[8] It can be found in the file `read.c`.

Following the "no arbitrary limits" principle, lines in a `Makefile` can be of any length. Thus, this routine's primary job is to read lines of any length and make sure that they fit into the buffer being used.

A secondary job is to deal with continuation lines. As in C, lines that end with a backslash logically continue to the next line. The strategy used is to maintain a buffer. As many lines as will fit in the buffer are kept there, with pointers keeping track of the start of the buffer, the current line, and the next line. Here is the structure:

```
struct ebuffer
  {
    char *buffer;       /* Start of the current line in the buffer.  */
    char *bufnext;      /* Start of the next line in the buffer.  */
    char *bufstart;     /* Start of the entire buffer.  */
    size_t size;        /* Malloc'd size of buffer. */
    FILE *fp;           /* File, or NULL if this is an internal buffer.  */
    floc floc;          /* Info on the file in fp (if any).  */
  };
```

[7] This function should not be confused with the `readline` library used by Bash, GDB, and other programs.
[8] `https://ftp.gnu.org/gnu/make/make-4.4.1.tar.gz`

The `size` field tracks the size of the entire buffer, and `fp` is the `FILE` pointer for the input file. The `floc` structure isn't of interest for studying the routine.

The `readline()` function returns the number of lines in the buffer (the line numbers here are relative to the start of the function, not the source file):

```
1  static long
2  readline (struct ebuffer *ebuf)
3  {
4    char *p;
5    char *end;
6    char *start;
7    long nlines = 0;
8
9    /* The behaviors between string and stream buffers are different enough to
10      warrant different functions.  Do the Right Thing.  */
11
12   if (!ebuf->fp)
13     return readstring (ebuf);
14
15   /* When reading from a file, we always start over at the beginning of the
16      buffer for each new line.  */
17
18   p = start = ebuf->bufstart;
19   end = p + ebuf->size;
20   *p = '\0';
```

The initial part declares variables, and if the input is coming from a string (such as from the expansion of a macro), the code hands things off to a different function, `readstring()` (lines 12 and 13). The test '`!ebuf->fp`' (line 12) is a shorter (and less clear, in our opinion) test for a null pointer; it's the same as '`ebuf->fp == NULL`'.

Lines 18–20 initialize the pointers, and insert a NUL byte, which is the C string terminator character, at the end of the buffer. The function then starts a loop (lines 22–93), which runs as long as there is more input:

```
22   while (fgets (p, (int) (end - p), ebuf->fp) != 0)
23     {
24       char *p2;
25       size_t len;
26       int backslash;
27
28       len = strlen (p);
29       if (len == 0)
30         {
31           /* This only happens when the first thing on the line is a '\0'.
32              It is a pretty hopeless case, but (wonder of wonders) Athena
33              lossage strikes again!  (xmkmf puts NULs in its makefiles.)
```

```
34              There is nothing really to be done; we synthesize a newline so
35              the following line doesn't appear to be part of this line.  */
36           O (error, &ebuf->floc,
37              _("warning: NUL character seen; rest of line ignored"));
38           p[0] = '\n';
39           len = 1;
40         }
```

The `fgets()` function (line 22) takes a pointer to a buffer, a count of bytes to read, and a `FILE *` variable for the file to read from. It reads one less than the count so that it can terminate the buffer with `'\0'`. This function is good since it allows you to avoid buffer overflows. It stops upon encountering a newline or end-of-file, and if the newline is there, it's placed in the buffer. It returns `NULL` on failure or the (pointer) value of the first argument on success.

In this case, the arguments are a pointer to the free area of the buffer, the amount of room left in the buffer, and the `FILE` pointer to read from.

The comment on lines 31–35 is self-explanatory; if a zero byte is encountered, the program prints an error message and pretends it was an empty line. Line 36 prints the error using a macro named `O()` (capital letter "O," probably short for "output"). The string argument on line 37 is wrapped in a macro named `_()`, discussed in Section 15.3.4.1, "Portable Programs: `"gettext.h"`," page 530. After compensating for the NUL byte (lines 29–40), the code continues:

```
42       /* Jump past the text we just read.  */
43       p += len;
44
45       /* If the last char isn't a newline, the whole line didn't fit into the
46          buffer.  Get some more buffer and try again.  */
47       if (p[-1] != '\n')
48         goto more_buffer;
49
50       /* We got a newline, so add one to the count of lines.  */
51       ++nlines;
```

Lines 42–51 increment the pointer into the buffer past the data just read. The code then checks whether the last character read was a newline. The construct `p[-1]` (line 47) looks at the character *in front of* `p`, just as `p[0]` is the current character and `p[1]` is the next. This looks strange at first, but if you translate it into terms of pointer math, `*(p-1)`, it makes more sense, and the indexing form is possibly easier to read.

If the last character was not a newline, this means that we've run out of space, and the code goes off (with `goto`) to get more (line 48). Otherwise, the line count is incremented.

Lines 53–61 deal with input lines that follow the Microsoft convention of ending with a Carriage Return–Line Feed (CR-LF) combination, and not just a Line Feed (or newline), which is the Linux/Unix convention:

```
53 #if !defined(WINDOWS32) && !defined(__MSDOS__) && !defined(__EMX__)
54       /* Check to see if the line was really ended with CRLF; if so ignore
55          the CR.  */
```

```
      if ((p - start) > 1 && p[-2] == '\r')
        {
          --p;
          memmove (p-1, p, strlen (p) + 1);
        }
#endif
```

Note that the `#ifdef` *excludes* the code on Microsoft and OS/2 systems (the check for `__EMX__`); the `<stdio.h>` library on those systems handles this conversion automatically. This is also true of other non-Unix systems that support Standard C. Continuing on:

```
      backslash = 0;
      for (p2 = p - 2; p2 >= start; --p2)
        {
          if (*p2 != '\\')
            break;
          backslash = !backslash;
        }

      if (!backslash)
        {
          p[-1] = '\0';
          break;
        }

      /* It was a backslash/newline combo.  If we have more space, read
         another line.  */
      if (end - p >= 80)
        continue;

      /* We need more space at the end of our buffer, so realloc it.
         Make sure to preserve the current offset of p.  */
    more_buffer:
      {
        size_t off = p - start;
        ebuf->size *= 2;
        start = ebuf->buffer = ebuf->bufstart = xrealloc (start, ebuf->size);
        p = start + off;
        end = start + ebuf->size;
        *p = '\0';
      }
    }
```

So far we've dealt with the mechanics of getting at least one complete line into the buffer. The next chunk handles the case of a continuation line. It has to make sure, though, that the final backslash isn't part of multiple backslashes at the end of the line. It tracks whether the total number of such backslashes is odd or even by toggling the `backslash` variable from `0` to `1` and back (lines 63–69). We note that this code hasn't changed in decades(!); it still follows the original C convention of using integers for Boolean values, instead of using `bool`.

If the number is even, the test '`!backslash`' (line 71) will be true. In this case, the final newline is replaced with a NUL byte, and the code leaves the loop.

On the other hand, if the number is odd, then the line contained an even number of backslash pairs (representing escaped backslashes, \\ as in C), and a final backslash-newline combination.[9] In this case, if at least 80 free bytes are left in the buffer, the program `continue`s around the loop to read another line (lines 79–80). (The use of the magic number `80` isn't great; it would have been better to define and use a symbolic constant.)

Upon reaching line 84, the program needs more space in the buffer. Here's where the dynamic memory management comes into play. Note the comment about preserving `p` (lines 82–83); we discussed this earlier in terms of reinitializing pointers into dynamic memory. `end` is also reset. Line 88 resizes the memory.

Note that here the function being called is `xrealloc()`. Many GNU programs use "wrapper" functions around `malloc()` and `realloc()` that automatically print an error message and exit if the standard routines return `NULL`. Such a wrapper might look like this:

```
extern const char *myname;    /* set in main() */

void *
xrealloc(void *ptr, size_t amount)
{
    void *p = realloc(ptr, amount);

    if (p == NULL) {
        fprintf(stderr, "%s: out of memory! could not get %z bytes\n",
                        myname, amount);
        exit(1);
    }

    return p;
}
```

Thus, if `xrealloc()` returns, it's guaranteed to return a valid pointer. (This strategy complies with the "check every call for errors" principle while avoiding the code clutter that comes with doing so using the standard routines directly.) In addition, this allows valid use of the construct '`ptr = xrealloc(ptr, new_size)`', which we otherwise warned against earlier.

Note that it is not always appropriate to use such a wrapper. If you wish to handle errors yourself, you shouldn't use it. On the other hand, if running out of memory is always a fatal error, then such a wrapper is quite handy. And, you can even mix and match, calling the

[9] This code has the scent of practical experience about it; it wouldn't be surprising to learn that earlier versions simply checked for a final backslash before the newline, until someone complained that it didn't work when there were multiple backslashes at the end of the line.

wrapper functions when an error is fatal, but calling `malloc()` and/or `realloc()` directly, when not.

Finally, the `readline()` routine checks for I/O errors, and then returns a descriptive return value:

```
95    if (ferror (ebuf->fp))
96      pfatal_with_name (ebuf->floc.filenm);
97
98    /* If we found some lines, return how many.
99       If we didn't, but we did find _something_, that indicates we read the last
100      line of a file with no final newline; return 1.
101      If we read nothing, we're at EOF; return -1.  */
102
103   return nlines ? nlines : p == ebuf->bufstart ? -1 : 1;
104 }
```

Determining the return value via nested `?:` operators isn't the best style; if in any case you're going to do something like that, spread it across multiple lines and indent the nested test. The function `pfatal_with_name()` (line 96) doesn't return.

3.2.1.9 Reading Entire Lines: `getline()` and `getdelim()`

Now that you've seen how to read an arbitrary-length line, you can breathe a sigh of relief that you don't have to write such a function for yourself. Since 2008, POSIX has provided two functions to do this for you:[10]

```
#include <stdio.h>                                          POSIX

ssize_t getline(char **lineptr, size_t *n, FILE *stream);
ssize_t getdelim(char **lineptr, size_t *n, int delim, FILE *stream);
```

The return value of both functions is of type `ssize_t`. An `ssize_t` is a "signed `size_t`." It's meant for the same use as a `size_t`, but for places where you need to be able to hold negative values as well.

Both functions manage dynamic storage for you, ensuring that the buffer containing an input line is always big enough to hold the input line. They differ in that `getline()` reads until a newline character and `getdelim()` uses a user-provided delimiter character. The common arguments are as follows:

`char **lineptr`
: A pointer to a `char *` pointer to hold the address of a dynamically allocated buffer. It should be initialized to `NULL` if you want `getline()` to do all the work. Otherwise, it should point to storage previously obtained from `malloc()`.

---

[10] These functions were initially provided by GLIBC, but have since been standardized.

`size_t *n`
: An indication of the size of the buffer. If you allocated your own buffer, `*n` should contain the buffer's size. Both functions update `*n` to the new buffer size if they change it.

`FILE *stream`
: The open file from which to get input characters.

The functions return `-1` upon end-of-file or error. The strings hold the terminating newline or delimiter (if there was one), as well as a terminating zero byte. Using `getline()` is easy, as shown in `ch-memory-getline.c`:

```
/* ch-memory-getline.c --- demonstrate getline(). */

#include <stdio.h>

/* main --- read a line and echo it back out until EOF. */

int
main(void)
{
    char *line = NULL;
    size_t size = 0;
    ssize_t ret;

    while ((ret = getline(& line, & size, stdin)) != -1)
        printf("(%lu) %s", size, line);

    return 0;
}
```

Here it is in action, showing the size of the buffer. The third input and output lines are purposely long, to force `getline()` to grow the buffer; thus, they wrap around:

```
$ ch-memory-getline                                    Run the program
this is a line
(120) this is a line
And another line.
(120) And another line.
A lllllllllllllllllooooooooooooooooooooooooooooooooonnnnnnnnnnnnnnnnnngggg
ggggggg    llliiiiiiiiiiiiiiiiiiinnnnnnnnnnnnnnnnnnnnneeeeeeeeeee
(240) A lllllllllllllllllooooooooooooooooooooooooooooooooonnnnnnnnnnnnnnng
nnngggggggggg    llliiiiiiiiiiiiiiiiiiinnnnnnnnnnnnnnnnnnnnneeeeeeeeeee
```

3.2.2 String Copying: `strdup()`

One extremely common operation is to allocate storage for a copy of a string. It's so common that many programs provide a simple function for it instead of using inline code, and often that function is named `strdup()`:

```
#include <string.h>

/* strdup --- malloc() storage for a copy of string and copy it */

char *
strdup(const char *str)
{
    size_t len;
    char *copy;

    len = strlen(str) + 1;     /* include room for terminating '\0' */
    copy = malloc(len);

    if (copy != NULL)
        strcpy(copy, str);

    return copy;               /* returns NULL if error */
}
```

Since 2001, the POSIX standard has included `strdup()`. Originally it was an XSI extension; now it is a normative part of the standard. It is also included in the 2024 ISO standard for C:

```
#include <string.h>                                  POSIX, ISO C 2024

char *strdup(const char *str);                 Duplicate str
char *strndup(const char *s, size_t size);     Duplicate up to size bytes
```

The return value is `NULL` if there was an error or a pointer to dynamically allocated storage holding a copy of `str`. The returned value should be freed with `free()` when it's no longer needed.

`strndup()` is similar to `strdup()`, but it copies up to a maximum of `size` bytes and then appends a terminating zero.

3.2.3 System Calls: `brk()` and `sbrk()`

The four routines we've covered (`malloc()`, `calloc()`, `realloc()`, and `free()`) are the standard, portable functions to use for dynamic memory management.

On Unix systems, the standard functions are implemented on top of two additional, very primitive routines, which directly change the size of a process's address space. We present them here to help you understand how GNU/Linux and Unix work (going "under the hood" again); it is highly unlikely that you will ever need to use these functions in a regular program. They are declared as follows:

```
#include <unistd.h>                                  Common

int brk(void *end_data_segment);
void *sbrk(intptr_t increment);
```

The `brk()` system call actually changes the process's address space. The address is a pointer representing the end of the data segment (really the heap area, as shown earlier in Figure 3.1). Its argument is an absolute logical address representing the new end of the address space. It returns `0` on success or `-1` on failure.

The `sbrk()` function is easier to use; its argument is the increment in bytes by which to change the address space. By calling it with an increment of `0`, you can determine where the address space currently ends. Thus, to increase your address space by 32 bytes, use code like this:

```
char *p = (char *) sbrk(0);      /* get current end of address space */
if (brk(p + 32) < 0) {
    /* handle error */
}
/* else, change worked */
```

Practically speaking, you would not use `brk()` directly. Instead, you would use `sbrk()` exclusively to grow (or even shrink) the address space. (We show how to do this shortly, in Section 3.2.5, "Address Space Examination," page 74.)

Even more practically, you should *never* use these routines. A program using them can't then use `malloc()` also, and this is a big problem, since many parts of the standard library rely on being able to use `malloc()`. Using `brk()` or `sbrk()` is thus likely to lead to hard-to-find program crashes.

But it's worth knowing about the low-level mechanics, and indeed, the `malloc()` suite of routines is often implemented with `sbrk()` and `brk()`.

3.2.4 Lazy Programmer Calls: `alloca()`

Danger, Will Robinson! Danger!
— B-9, the Robot

There is one additional memory allocation function that you should know about. We discuss it *only* so that you'll understand it when you see it, but you should *not* use it in new programs! This function is named `alloca()`; it's declared as follows:

```
/* Header on GNU/Linux, possibly not all Unix systems */        Common
#include <alloca.h>

void *alloca(size_t size);
```

The `alloca()` function allocates `size` bytes from the *stack*. What's nice about this is that the allocated storage disappears when the function returns. There's no need to explicitly free it because it goes away automatically, just as local variables do.

At first glance, `alloca()` seems like a programming panacea; memory can be allocated that doesn't have to be managed at all. Like the Dark Side of the Force, this is indeed seductive. And it is similarly to be avoided, for the following reasons:

- The function is nonstandard; it is not included in any formal standard, either ISO C or POSIX.

- The function is not portable. Although it exists on many Unix systems and GNU/Linux, it doesn't exist on non-Unix systems. This is a problem, since it's often important for code to be multiplatform, above and beyond just Linux and Unix.
- On some systems, `alloca()` can't even be implemented. All the world is not an Intel x86 processor, nor is all the world GCC.
- An earlier version of the *alloca*(3) manpage states: "The `alloca` function is machine and compiler dependent. *On many systems its implementation is buggy.* Its use is discouraged."
- Quoting from the manpage again: "On many systems `alloca` cannot be used inside the list of arguments of a function call, because the stack space reserved by `alloca` would appear on the stack in the middle of the space for the function arguments."
- The use of `alloca()` encourages sloppy coding. Careful and correct memory management isn't hard; you just to have to think about what you're doing and plan ahead.

GCC generally uses a built-in version of the function that operates by using inline code. As a result, there are other consequences of `alloca()`. Quoting again from the manpage:

> The fact that the code is inlined means that it is impossible to take the address of this function, or to change its behavior by linking with a different library.
>
> The inlined code often consists of a single instruction adjusting the stack pointer, and does not check for stack overflow. Thus, there is no `NULL` error return.

The manual page doesn't go quite far enough in describing the problem with GCC's built-in `alloca()`. If there's a stack overflow, the return value is *garbage*. And you have no way to tell! This flaw makes GCC's `alloca()` impossible to use in robust code.

All of this should convince you to stay away from `alloca()` for any new code that you may write. If you're going to have to write portable code using `malloc()` and `free()` anyway, there's no reason to also write code using `alloca()`.

3.2.5 Address Space Examination

The following program, `ch-memory-memaddr.c`, summarizes everything we've seen about the address space. It does many things that you should not do in practice, such as call `alloca()` or use `brk()` and `sbrk()` directly:

```
/*
 * ch-memory-memaddr.c --- Show address of code, data, and stack sections,
 *                         as well as BSS and dynamic memory.
 */

#include <stdio.h>
#include <malloc.h>     /* for definition of ptrdiff_t on GLIBC */
#include <unistd.h>
#include <alloca.h>     /* for demonstration only */
```

```

extern void afunc(void);    /* a function for showing stack growth */

int bss_var;            /* auto init to 0, should be in BSS */
int data_var = 42;      /* init to nonzero, should be data */

int
main(int argc, char **argv) /* arguments aren't used */
{
    char *p, *b, *nb;

    printf("Text Locations:\n");
    printf("\tAddress of main: %p\n", main);
    printf("\tAddress of afunc: %p\n", afunc);

    printf("Stack Locations:\n");
    afunc();

    p = (char *) alloca(32);
    if (p != NULL) {
        printf("\tStart of alloca()'ed array: %p\n", p);
        printf("\tEnd of alloca()'ed array: %p\n", p + 31);
    }

    printf("Data Locations:\n");
    printf("\tAddress of data_var: %p\n", & data_var);

    printf("BSS Locations:\n");
    printf("\tAddress of bss_var: %p\n", & bss_var);

    b = sbrk((ptrdiff_t) 32);   /* grow address space */
    nb = sbrk((ptrdiff_t) 0);
    printf("Heap Locations:\n");
    printf("\tInitial end of heap: %p\n", b);
    printf("\tNew end of heap: %p\n", nb);

    b = sbrk((ptrdiff_t) -16);  /* shrink it */
    nb = sbrk((ptrdiff_t) 0);
    printf("\tFinal end of heap: %p\n", nb);
}

/* afunc --- demonstrate stack growth via recursion */

void
afunc(void)
```

```
55 {
56     static int level = 0;           /* recursion level */
57     auto int stack_var;             /* automatic variable, on stack */
58
59     if (++level == 3)               /* avoid infinite recursion */
60         return;
61
62     printf("\tStack level %d: address of stack_var: %p\n",
63             level, & stack_var);
64     afunc();                        /* recursive call */
65 }
```

This program prints the locations of the two functions `main()` and `afunc()` (lines 22–23). It then shows how the stack grows downward, letting `afunc()` (lines 53–65) print the address of successive instantiations of its local variable `stack_var`. (`stack_var` is purposely declared `auto`, to emphasize that it's on the stack.) It next shows the location of memory allocated by `alloca()` (lines 28–32). Finally, it prints the locations of data and BSS variables (lines 34–38), and then of memory allocated directly through `sbrk()` (lines 40–48). Here are the results when the program is run on a 64-bit Intel GNU/Linux system:

```
$ ch-memory-memaddr
Text Locations:
    Address of main: 0x62c25b15a20f
    Address of afunc: 0x62c25b15a1a9
Stack Locations:
    Stack level 1: address of stack_var: 0x7ffd0a9b0654
    Stack level 2: address of stack_var: 0x7ffd0a9b0634     Stack grows downward
    Start of alloca()'ed array: 0x7ffd0a9b0640
    End of alloca()'ed array: 0x7ffd0a9b065f                Addresses are on the stack
Data Locations:
    Address of data_var: 0x62c25b15d010
BSS Locations:
    Address of bss_var: 0x62c25b15d018                      BSS is above data variables
Heap Locations:
    Initial end of heap: 0x62c27042b000                     Heap is immediately above BSS
    New end of heap: 0x62c27042b020                         And grows upward
    Final end of heap: 0x62c27042b010                       Address spaces can shrink
```

3.3 Summary

- Every Linux (and Unix) program has different memory areas. They are stored in separate parts of the executable program's disk file. Some of the sections are loaded into the same part of memory when the program is run. All running copies of the same program share the executable code (the text segment). The `size` program shows the sizes of the different areas for relocatable object files and fully linked executable files.

- The address space of a running program may have holes in it, and the size of the address space can change as memory is allocated and released. On modern systems, address `0` is not part of the address space, so don't attempt to dereference `NULL` pointers.
- At the C level, memory is allocated or reallocated with one of `malloc()`, `calloc()`, or `realloc()`. Memory is freed with `free()`. It is unusual for freed memory to be removed from the address space; instead, it is reused for later allocations.
- You should not use `realloc()` to allocate new memory or to free previously allocated memory.
- Extreme care must be taken to
  - Free only memory received from the allocation routines,
  - Free such memory once and only once,
  - Free unused memory, and
  - Not "leak" any dynamically allocated memory.
- POSIX provides the `strdup()` function as a convenience, as does the 2024 ISO C standard. POSIX also provides `getline()` and `getdelim()` for reading arbitrary-length lines.
- The low-level system call interface functions `brk()` and `sbrk()` provide direct but primitive access to memory allocation and deallocation. Unless you are writing your own storage allocator, you should not use them.
- The `alloca()` function for allocating memory on the stack exists, but it is not recommended. Like being able to recognize poison ivy, you should know it only so that you'll know to avoid it.

Exercises

1. Starting with the structure

```
struct line {
    size_t buflen;
    char *buf;
    FILE *fp;
};
```

write your own `readline()` function that will read a line of any length. Don't worry about backslash continuation lines. Instead of using `fgets()` to read lines, use `getc()` to read characters one at a time.

2. Does your function preserve the terminating newline? Explain why or why not.
3. How does your function handle lines that end in CR-LF?
4. How do you initialize the structure? With a separate routine? With a documented requirement for specific values in the structure?
5. How do you indicate end-of-file? How do you indicate that an I/O error has occurred? For errors, should your function print an error message? Explain why or why not.
6. Write a program that uses your function to test it, and another program to generate input data to the first program. Test your function.
7. Rewrite your function to use `fgets()` and test it. Is the new code more complex or less complex? How does its performance compare to the `getc()` version?
8. Study the V7 *end*(3) manpage (`/usr/man/man3/end.3` in the V7 distribution; a PDF version is in the GitHub repository). Does it shed any light on how '`sbrk(0)`' might work?
9. Enhance `ch-memory-memaddr.c` to print out the location of the arguments and the environment. In which part of the address space do they reside?

Chapter 4

Files and File I/O

This chapter describes basic file operations: opening and creating files, reading and writing them, moving around in them, and closing them. Along the way it presents the standard mechanisms for detecting and reporting errors. The chapter ends by describing how to force file data and metadata to disk and set a file's length.

4.1 Introducing the Linux/Unix I/O Model

The Linux/Unix API model for I/O is straightforward. It can be summed up in four words: open, read, write, close. In fact, those are the names of the system calls: `open()`, `read()`, `write()`, and `close()`. Here are their declarations:

POSIX

```
#include <sys/types.h>
#include <sys/stat.h>          /* for mode_t */
#include <fcntl.h>             /* for flags for open() */
#include <unistd.h>            /* for ssize_t */

int open(const char *pathname, int flags, mode_t mode);
ssize_t read(int fd, void *buf, size_t count);
ssize_t write(int fd, const void *buf, size_t count);
int close(int fd);
```

In the next and subsequent sections, we illustrate the model by writing a *very* simple version of `cat`. It's so simple that it doesn't even have options; all it does is concatenate the contents of the named files to standard output. It does do minimal error reporting. Once it's written, we compare it to the V7 `cat`.

We present the program top-down, starting with the command line. In succeeding sections, we present error reporting and then get down to brass tacks, showing how to do actual file I/O.

4.2 Presenting a Basic Program Structure

Our version of `cat` follows a structure that is generally useful. The first part starts with an explanatory comment, header includes, declarations, and the `main()` function:

```
1  /*
2   * ch-fileio-cat.c --- Demonstrate open(), read(), write(), close(),
3   *                     errno and strerror().
4   */
5
6  #include <stdio.h>       /* for fprintf(), stderr, BUFSIZ */
7  #include <errno.h>       /* declare errno */
8  #include <fcntl.h>       /* for flags for open() */
9  #include <string.h>      /* declare strerror() */
10 #include <unistd.h>      /* for ssize_t */
11 #include <sys/types.h>
12 #include <sys/stat.h>    /* for mode_t */
13
14 char *myname;
15 int process(char *file);
16
17 /* main --- loop over file arguments */
18
19 int
20 main(int argc, char **argv)
21 {
22     int i;
23     int errs = 0;
24
25     myname = argv[0];
26
27     if (argc == 1)
28         errs = process("-");
29     else
30         for (i = 1; i < argc; i++)
31             errs += process(argv[i]);
32
33     return (errs != 0);
34 }
```

... continued later in the chapter ...

The `myname` variable (line 14) is used later for error messages; `main()` sets it to the program name (`argv[0]`) as its first action (line 25). Then `main()` loops over the arguments. For each argument, it calls a function named `process()` to do the work.

When given the file name - (a single dash, or minus sign), Unix `cat` reads standard input instead of trying to open a file named -. In addition, with no arguments, `cat` reads standard input. `ch-fileio-cat` implements both of these behaviors. The check for '`argc == 1`' (line 27) is true when there are no file name arguments; in this case, `main()` passes `"-"` to `process()`. Otherwise, `main()` loops over all the arguments, treating them as files to be processed. If one of them happens to be `"-"`, the program then processes standard input.

If `process()` returns a nonzero value, it means that something went wrong. Errors are added up in the `errs` variable (lines 28 and 31). When `main()` ends, it returns `0` if there weren't any errors, and `1` if there were (line 33). This is a fairly standard convention, whose meaning is discussed in more detail in Section 9.1.5.1, "Defining Process Exit Status," page 289.

The structure presented in `main()` is quite generic: `process()` could do anything we want to the file. For example (ignoring the special use of `"-"`), `process()` could just as easily remove files as concatenate them!

Before looking at the `process()` function, we have to describe how system call errors are represented and then how I/O is done. The `process()` function itself is presented in Section 4.4.3, "Reading and Writing," page 91.

4.3 Determining What Went Wrong

If anything can go wrong, it will.
— Murphy's Law

Be prepared.
— The Boy Scouts

Errors can occur anytime. Disks can fill up, users can enter invalid data, the server on a network from which a file is being read can crash, the network can die, and so on. It is important to *always* check every operation for success or failure.

The basic Linux system calls almost universally return `-1` on error, and `0` or a positive value on success. This lets you know that the operation has succeeded or failed:

```
int result;

result = some_system_call(param1, param2);
if (result < 0) {
    /* error occurred, do something */
} else
    /* all ok, proceed */
```

Knowing that an error occurred isn't enough. It's necessary to know *what* error occurred. For that, each process has a predefined variable named `errno`. Whenever a system call fails, `errno` is set to one of a set of predefined error values. `errno` and the predefined values are declared in the `<errno.h>` header file:

```
#include <errno.h>                                          ISO C

extern int errno;
```

`errno` itself may be a macro that *acts like* an `int` variable; it need not be a real integer. In particular, in threaded environments, each thread will have its own private version of `errno`. Practically speaking, though, for all the system calls and functions in this book, you can treat `errno` like a simple `int`. (At least on GLIBC systems, you can even take its address, although there isn't any reason to do so.)

4.3.1 Values for `errno`

The POSIX standard defines a large number of possible values for `errno`. Many of these are related to networking, IPC, or other specialized tasks. The manpage for each system call describes the possible `errno` values that can occur; thus, you can write code to check for particular errors and handle them specially if need be. The possible values are defined by symbolic constants. (If you have the `moreutils` package installed on your GNU/Linux system, you can use the command '`errno -l`' to list the available `errno` names, values, and descriptions.)

Table 4.1 lists the constants provided by GLIBC on the author's Intel GNU/Linux system.[1] In general, the numeric values used by GLIBC do not vary among architectures, but they may vary on other Unix-like systems. In your code, you should *always* use the symbolic names.

Many systems provide other error values as well, and older systems may not have all the errors listed in the table. You should check your local *intro*(2) and *errno*(2) manpages for the full story.

NOTE

`errno` should be examined *only* after an error has occurred and before further system calls are made. Its initial value is `0`. However, nothing changes `errno` between errors, meaning that a successful system call does *not* reset it to `0`.

Even if a system call never fails, some user-space library routines set `errno`. Thus, a common idiom is to set `errno` to `0` before calling an API of interest and then check it after the API returns.

Initially, we use `errno` only for error checking. There are two useful functions for error reporting. The first is `perror()`:

```
#include <stdio.h>                                        ISO C

void perror(const char *s);
```

The `perror()` function prints a program-supplied string, followed by a colon, and then a string describing the value of `errno`:

```
if (some_system_call(param1, param2) < 0) {
    perror("system call failed");
    return 1;
}
```

[1] The values `41` and `58` are missing. This seems to be because `EWOULDBLOCK` and `EDEADLOCK` were originally distinct values, and not aliases for `EAGAIN` and `EDEADLK`, respectively.

Table 4.1: GLIBC values for `errno`

Name	Numeric value	Meaning
`EPERM`	1	Operation not permitted.
`ENOENT`	2	No such file or directory.
`ESRCH`	3	No such process.
`EINTR`	4	Interrupted system call.
`EIO`	5	Input/output error.
`ENXIO`	6	No such device or address.
`E2BIG`	7	Argument list too long.
`ENOEXEC`	8	Exec format error.
`EBADF`	9	Bad file descriptor.
`ECHILD`	10	No child processes.
`EAGAIN`	11	Resource temporarily unavailable.
`EWOULDBLOCK`		Alias for `EAGAIN`.
`ENOMEM`	12	Cannot allocate memory.
`EACCES`	13	Permission denied.
`EFAULT`	14	Bad address.
`ENOTBLK`	15	Block device required.
`EBUSY`	16	Device or resource busy.
`EEXIST`	17	File exists.
`EXDEV`	18	Invalid cross-device link.
`ENODEV`	19	No such device.
`ENOTDIR`	20	Not a directory.
`EISDIR`	21	Is a directory.
`EINVAL`	22	Invalid argument.
`ENFILE`	23	Too many open files in system.
`EMFILE`	24	Too many open files.
`ENOTTY`	25	Inappropriate `ioctl` for device.
`ETXTBSY`	26	Text file busy.
`EFBIG`	27	File too large.
`ENOSPC`	28	No space left on device.
`ESPIPE`	29	Illegal seek.
`EROFS`	30	Read-only filesystem.
`EMLINK`	31	Too many links.
`EPIPE`	32	Broken pipe.
`EDOM`	33	Numerical argument out of domain.
`ERANGE`	34	Numerical result out of range.
`EDEADLK`	35	Resource deadlock avoided.
`EDEADLOCK`		Alias for `EDEADLK`.
`ENAMETOOLONG`	36	File name too long.
`ENOLCK`	37	No locks available.
`ENOSYS`	38	Function not implemented.
`ENOTEMPTY`	39	Directory not empty.
`ELOOP`	40	Too many levels of symbolic links.
`ENOMSG`	42	No message of desired type.
`EIDRM`	43	Identifier removed.

(*continued*)

Table 4.1: GLIBC values for `errno` (*continued*)

Name	Numeric value	Meaning
`ECHRNG`	44	Channel number out of range.
`EL2NSYNC`	45	Level 2 not synchronized.
`EL3HLT`	46	Level 3 halted.
`EL3RST`	47	Level 3 reset.
`ELNRNG`	48	Link number out of range.
`EUNATCH`	49	Protocol driver not attached.
`ENOCSI`	50	No CSI structure available.
`EL2HLT`	51	Level 2 halted.
`EBADE`	52	Invalid exchange.
`EBADR`	53	Invalid request descriptor.
`EXFULL`	54	Exchange full.
`ENOANO`	55	No anode.
`EBADRQC`	56	Invalid request code.
`EBADSLT`	57	Invalid slot.
`EBFONT`	59	Bad font file format.
`ENOSTR`	60	Device not a stream.
`ENODATA`	61	No data available.
`ETIME`	62	Timer expired.
`ENOSR`	63	Out of streams resources.
`ENONET`	64	Machine is not on the network.
`ENOPKG`	65	Package not installed.
`EREMOTE`	66	Object is remote.
`ENOLINK`	67	Link has been severed.
`EADV`	68	Advertise error.
`ESRMNT`	69	Srmount error.
`ECOMM`	70	Communication error on send.
`EPROTO`	71	Protocol error.
`EMULTIHOP`	72	Multihop attempted.
`EDOTDOT`	73	RFS specific error.
`EBADMSG`	74	Bad message.
`EOVERFLOW`	75	Value too large for defined data type.
`ENOTUNIQ`	76	Name not unique on network.
`EBADFD`	77	File descriptor in bad state.
`EREMCHG`	78	Remote address changed.
`ELIBACC`	79	Can not access a needed shared library.
`ELIBBAD`	80	Accessing a corrupted shared library.
`ELIBSCN`	81	`.lib` section in `a.out` corrupted.
`ELIBMAX`	82	Attempting to link in too many shared libraries.
`ELIBEXEC`	83	Cannot exec a shared library directly.
`EILSEQ`	84	Invalid or incomplete multibyte or wide character.
`ERESTART`	85	Interrupted system call should be restarted.
`ESTRPIPE`	86	Streams pipe error.
`EUSERS`	87	Too many users.
`ENOTSOCK`	88	Socket operation on non-socket.
`EDESTADDRREQ`	89	Destination address required.

(*continued*)

Table 4.1: GLIBC values for `errno` (*continued*)

Name	Numeric value	Meaning
`EMSGSIZE`	90	Message too long.
`EPROTOTYPE`	91	Protocol wrong type for socket.
`ENOPROTOOPT`	92	Protocol not available.
`EPROTONOSUPPORT`	93	Protocol not supported.
`ESOCKTNOSUPPORT`	94	Socket type not supported.
`ENOTSUP`	95	Operation not supported.
`EOPNOTSUPP`		Alias for `ENOTSUP`.
`EPFNOSUPPORT`	96	Protocol family not supported.
`EAFNOSUPPORT`	97	Address family not supported by protocol.
`EADDRINUSE`	98	Address already in use.
`EADDRNOTAVAIL`	99	Cannot assign requested address.
`ENETDOWN`	100	Network is down.
`ENETUNREACH`	101	Network is unreachable.
`ENETRESET`	102	Network dropped connection on reset.
`ECONNABORTED`	103	Software caused connection abort.
`ECONNRESET`	104	Connection reset by peer.
`ENOBUFS`	105	No buffer space available.
`EISCONN`	106	Transport endpoint is already connected.
`ENOTCONN`	107	Transport endpoint is not connected.
`ESHUTDOWN`	108	Cannot send after transport endpoint shutdown.
`ETOOMANYREFS`	109	Too many references: cannot splice.
`ETIMEDOUT`	110	Connection timed out.
`ECONNREFUSED`	111	Connection refused.
`EHOSTDOWN`	112	Host is down.
`EHOSTUNREACH`	113	No route to host.
`EALREADY`	114	Operation already in progress.
`EINPROGRESS`	115	Operation now in progress.
`ESTALE`	116	Stale file handle.
`EUCLEAN`	117	Structure needs cleaning.
`ENOTNAM`	118	Not a XENIX named type file.
`ENAVAIL`	119	No XENIX semaphores available.
`EISNAM`	120	Is a named type file.
`EREMOTEIO`	121	Remote I/O error.
`EDQUOT`	122	Disk quota exceeded.
`ENOMEDIUM`	123	No medium found.
`EMEDIUMTYPE`	124	Wrong medium type.
`ECANCELED`	125	Operation canceled.
`ENOKEY`	126	Required key not available.
`EKEYEXPIRED`	127	Key has expired.
`EKEYREVOKED`	128	Key has been revoked.
`EKEYREJECTED`	129	Key was rejected by service.
`EOWNERDEAD`	130	Owner died.
`ENOTRECOVERABLE`	131	State not recoverable.
`ERFKILL`	132	Operation not possible due to RF-kill.
`EHWPOISON`	133	Memory page has hardware error.

We prefer the `strerror()` function, which takes an error value parameter and returns a pointer to a string describing the error:

```
#include <string.h>                                          ISO C

char *strerror(int errnum);
```

`strerror()` provides maximum flexibility in error reporting, since `fprintf()` makes it possible to print the error in any way we like:

```
if (some_system_call(param1, param2) < 0) {
    fprintf(stderr, "%s: %d, %d: some_system_call failed: %s\n",
            argv[0], param1, param2, strerror(errno));
    return 1;
}
```

You will see many examples of both functions throughout the book.

4.3.2 Error Message Style

C provides several special macros for use in error reporting. The most widely used are `__FILE__` and `__LINE__`, which expand to the name of the source file and the current line number in that file. These have been available in C almost since its beginning. C99 defines an additional predefined identifier, `__func__`, which represents the name of the current function as a character string. The macros are used like this:

```
if (some_system_call(param1, param2) < 0) {
    fprintf(stderr, "%s: %s (%s: %d): some_system_call(%d, %d) failed: %s\n",
        argv[0], __func__, __FILE__, __LINE__,
        param1, param2, strerror(errno));
    return 1;
}
```

Here, the error message includes not only the program's name but also the function name, source file name, and line number. The full list of identifiers useful for diagnostics is provided in Table 4.2.

The use of `__FILE__` and `__LINE__` was quite popular in the early days of Unix, when most people had source code and could find the error and fix it. As Unix systems became

Table 4.2: C99 diagnostic identifiers

Identifier	C version	Meaning
`__DATE__`	C90	Date of compilation in the form `"Mmm nn yyyy"`.
`__FILE__`	Original	Source file name in the form `"program.c"`.
`__LINE__`	Original	Source file line number in the form `42`.
`__TIME__`	C90	Time of compilation in the form `"hh:mm:ss"`.
`__func__`	C99	Name of current function, as if declared `const char __func__[] = "name"`.

more commercial, use of these identifiers gradually diminished, since knowing the source code location isn't of much help to someone who has only a binary executable.

Today, although GNU/Linux systems come with source code, said source code often isn't installed by default. Thus, using these identifiers for error messages doesn't seem to provide much additional value. The *GNU Coding Standards* document doesn't even mention them.

On the other hand, Chet Ramey argues that using them is of value to the developer, as long as the user includes the information when reporting a problem. You can decide for yourself what to do.

4.4 Doing Input and Output

All I/O in Linux is accomplished through *file descriptors*. This section introduces file descriptors, describes how to obtain and release them, and explains how to do I/O with them.

4.4.1 Understanding File Descriptors

A *file descriptor* is an integer value. Valid file descriptors start at `0` and go up to some system-defined limit. These integers are in fact simple indexes into each process's table of open files. (This table is maintained inside the operating system; it is not accessible to a running program.) On most modern systems, the size of the table is large. The command '`ulimit -n`' prints the value:

```
$ ulimit -n
1024
```

From C, the maximum number of open files is returned by the `getdtablesize()` (get descriptor table size) function:

Common

```
#include <unistd.h>

int getdtablesize(void);
```

This small program prints the result of the function:

```
/* ch-fileio-maxfds.c --- Demonstrate getdtablesize(). */

#include <stdio.h>      /* for fprintf(), stderr, BUFSIZ */
#include <stdlib.h>     /* for exit() */
#include <unistd.h>     /* for getdtablesize() */

int
main(int argc, char **argv)
{
    printf("max fds: %d\n", getdtablesize());
    exit(EXIT_SUCCESS);
}
```

When compiled and run, the program unsurprisingly prints the same value as printed by `ulimit`:

```
$ ch-fileio-maxfds
max fds: 1024
```

File descriptors are held in normal `int` variables; it is typical to see declarations of the form '`int fd`' for use with I/O system calls. There is no predefined type for file descriptors.

In the usual case, every program starts running with three file descriptors already opened for it. These are standard input, standard output, and standard error, on file descriptors `0`, `1`, and `2`, respectively. (If not otherwise redirected, each one is connected to your keyboard and screen.)

> **Obvious Manifest Constants: An Oxymoron?**
>
> When working with file-descriptor-based system calls and the standard input, output, and error, it is common practice to use the integer constants `0`, `1`, and `2` directly in code. In the overwhelming majority of cases, such *manifest constants* are a bad idea. You never know what the meaning is of some random integer constant and whether the same constant used elsewhere is related to it or not. To this end, the POSIX standard requires the definition of the following *symbolic constants* in `<unistd.h>`:
>
> | | |
> |---|---|
> | `STDIN_FILENO` | The "file number" for standard input: `0`. |
> | `STDOUT_FILENO` | The file number for standard output: `1`. |
> | `STDERR_FILENO` | The file number for standard error: `2`. |
>
> However, in our humble opinion, using these macros is overkill. First, it's *painful* to type 12 or 13 characters instead of just one. Second, the use of `0`, `1`, and `2` is *so* standard and *so* well known that there's really no grounds for confusion as to the meaning of these particular manifest constants.
>
> On the other hand, use of these constants leaves no doubt as to what was intended. Consider this statement:
>
> ```
> int fd = 0;
> ```
>
> Is `fd` being initialized to refer to standard input, or is the programmer being careful to initialize their variables to a reasonable value? You can't tell.
>
> One approach (as recommended by Geoff Collyer) is to use the following `enum` definition:
>
> ```
> enum { Stdin, Stdout, Stderr };
> ```
>
> These constants can then be used in place of `0`, `1`, and `2`. They are both readable and easier to type.

4.4.2 Opening and Closing Files

New file descriptors are obtained (among other sources) from the `open()` system call. This system call opens a file for reading or writing and returns a new file descriptor for subsequent operations on the file. We saw the declaration earlier:

Table 4.3: Flag values for `open()`

Symbolic constant	Value	Meaning
`O_RDONLY`	0	Open file only for reading; writes will fail.
`O_WRONLY`	1	Open file only for writing; reads will fail.
`O_RDWR`	2	Open file for reading and writing.

POSIX

```
#include <sys/types.h>
#include <sys/stat.h>
#include <fcntl.h>
#include <unistd.h>

int open(const char *pathname, int flags, mode_t mode);
```

The three arguments are as follows:

`const char *pathname`
: A C string, representing the name of the file to open.

`int flags`
: The bitwise-OR of one or more of the constants defined in `<fcntl.h>`. We describe them shortly.

`mode_t mode`
: The permissions mode of a file being created. This is discussed later in the chapter; see Section 4.6, "Creating Files," page 101. When opening an existing file, omit this parameter.[2]

The return value from `open()` is either the new file descriptor or `-1` to indicate an error, in which case `errno` will be set. For simple I/O, the `flags` argument should be one of the values in Table 4.3.

We will see example code shortly. Additional values for `flags` are described in Section 4.6, "Creating Files," page 101. Much early Unix code didn't use the symbolic values. Instead, the numeric values were used. Today this is considered bad practice, but we present the values so that you'll recognize their meanings if you see them.

The `close()` system call closes a file: the entry for it in the system's file descriptor table is marked as unused, and no further operations may be done with that file descriptor. The declaration is

POSIX

```
#include <unistd.h>

int close(int fd);
```

[2] `open()` is one of the few *variadic* system calls—system calls that take a variable number of arguments.

The return value is `0` on success, `-1` on error. There isn't much you can do if an error does occur, other than report it. Errors closing files are unusual but not unheard of, particularly for files being accessed over a network. Thus, it's good practice to check the return value, particularly for files opened for writing.

If you choose to ignore the return value, specifically cast it to `void` to signify that you don't care about the result:

```
(void) close(fd);        /* throw away return value */
```

The flip side of this advice is that too many casts to `void` tend to the clutter the code. For example, despite the "always check the return value" principle, it's exceedingly rare to see code that checks the return value of `printf()` or bothers to cast it to `void`. As with many aspects of C programming, experience and judgment should be applied here too.

As mentioned, the number of open files, while large, is limited, and you should always close files when you're done with them. If you don't, you will eventually run out of file descriptors, a situation that makes your program less robust.

The system closes all open files when a process exits, but—except for `0`, `1`, and `2`—it's bad form to rely on this.

When `open()` returns a new file descriptor, it always returns the lowest unused integer value. *Always.* Thus, if file descriptors `0`–`6` are open and the program closes file descriptor `5`, then the next call to `open()` returns `5`, not `7`. This behavior is important; we see later in the book how it's used to cleanly implement many important Unix features, such as I/O redirection and piping.

4.4.2.1 Mapping `FILE *` Variables to File Descriptors

The Standard I/O library functions and `FILE *` variables from `<stdio.h>`, such as `stdin`, `stdout`, and `stderr`, are built on top of the file-descriptor-based system calls.

Occasionally, it's useful to directly access the file descriptor associated with a `<stdio.h>` file pointer if you need to do something not defined by the ISO C standard. The `fileno()` function returns the underlying file descriptor:

```
#include <stdio.h>                                    POSIX

int fileno(FILE *stream);
```

We will see an example later, in Section 4.4.4, "Example: Unix `cat`," page 94.

4.4.2.2 Closing All Open Files

Open files are inherited by child processes from their parent processes. They are, in effect, *shared*. In particular, the position in the file is shared. We leave the details for discussion later, in Section 9.1.1.2, "File Descriptor Sharing," page 277.

Since programs can inherit open files, you may occasionally see programs that close all their files in order to start out with a "clean slate." In particular, code like this is typical:

```
int i;

/* leave 0, 1, and 2 alone */
for (i = 3; i < getdtablesize(); i++)
    (void) close(i);
```

Assume that the result of `getdtablesize()` is 1,024. This code works, but it makes (1,024 − 3) * 2 = 2,042 system calls. 1,020 of them are needless, since the return value from `getdtablesize()` doesn't change. Here is a better way to write this code:

```
int i, fds;

for (i = 3, fds = getdtablesize(); i < fds; i++)
    (void) close(i);
```

Such an optimization does not affect the readability of the code, and it can make a difference, particularly on slow systems. In general, it's worth looking for cases in which a loop computes the same result repeatedly, to see if such a computation can't be pulled out of the loop. In all such cases, though, be sure that you (a) preserve the code's correctness and (b) preserve its readability!

We cast the return value from `close()` to `void` since in this case we don't care about it, as we mentioned earlier in Section 4.4.2, "Opening and Closing Files," page 88. In fact, in this particular instance, it's likely that most of the file descriptors aren't open, and that `close()` will therefore fail more often than it will succeed.

4.4.3 Reading and Writing

I/O is accomplished with the `read()` and `write()` system calls, respectively:

POSIX

```
#include <sys/types.h>
#include <sys/stat.h>
#include <fcntl.h>
#include <unistd.h>

ssize_t read(int fd, void *buf, size_t count);
ssize_t write(int fd, const void *buf, size_t count);
```

Each function is about as simple as can be. The arguments are the file descriptor for the open file, a pointer to a buffer to read data into or to write data from, and the number of bytes to read or write.

The return value is the number of bytes actually read or written. (This number can be smaller than the requested amount: for a read operation this happens when fewer than `count` bytes are left in the file, and for a write operation it happens if a disk fills up or some other error occurs.) The return value is `-1` if an error occurred, in which case `errno` indicates the error. When `read()` returns `0`, it means that end-of-file has been reached.

We can now show the rest of the code for `ch-fileio-cat`. The `process()` routine uses `0` if the input file name is `"-"`, for standard input (lines 50 and 51). Otherwise, it opens the given file:

```
36 /*
37  * process --- do something with the file, in this case,
38  *             send it to stdout (fd 1).
39  *             Returns 0 if all OK, 1 otherwise.
40  */
41
42 int
43 process(char *file)
44 {
45     int fd;
46     ssize_t rcount, wcount;
47     char buffer[BUFSIZ];
48     int errors = 0;
49
50     if (strcmp(file, "-") == 0)
51         fd = 0;
52     else if ((fd = open(file, O_RDONLY)) < 0) {
53         fprintf(stderr, "%s: %s: cannot open for reading: %s\n",
54                 myname, file, strerror(errno));
55         return 1;
56     }
```

The buffer `buffer` (line 47) is of size `BUFSIZ`; this constant is defined by `<stdio.h>` to be a reasonable block size for I/O. Although the value for `BUFSIZ` varies across systems, code that uses this constant is clean and portable.

The core of the routine is the following loop, which repeatedly reads data until either end-of-file or an error is encountered:

```
58     while ((rcount = read(fd, buffer, sizeof buffer)) > 0) {
59         wcount = write(1, buffer, rcount);
60         if (wcount != rcount) {
61             fprintf(stderr, "%s: %s: write error: %s\n",
62                     myname, file, strerror(errno));
63             errors++;
64             break;
65         }
66     }
```

The attempt to write data happens only if the return value from `read()` (in `rcount`) is greater than zero—that is, only if we know that there is indeed data in the buffer to be written out.

The `rcount` and `wcount` variables (line 46) are of type `ssize_t`, "signed `size_t`," which allows them to hold negative values. Note that the count value passed to `write()` is the return value from `read()` (line 59). While we want to read fixed-size `BUFSIZ` chunks, it is unlikely that the file itself is a multiple of `BUFSIZ` bytes big. When the final smaller chunk of bytes is read from the file, the return value indicates how many bytes of `buffer` received new data. Only those bytes should be copied to standard output, not the entire buffer.

The test '`wcount != rcount`' on line 60 is the correct way to check for write errors; if some, but not all, of the data were written, then `wcount` would be positive but smaller than `rcount`.

Finally, `process()` checks for read errors (lines 68–72) and then attempts to close the file. In the (unlikely) event that `close()` fails (line 75), it prints an error message. Avoiding the close of standard input isn't strictly necessary in this program, but it's a good habit to develop for writing larger programs, in case other code elsewhere wants to do something with it, or if a child program will inherit it. The last statement (line 82) returns `1` if there were errors, `0` otherwise:

```
68      if (rcount < 0) {
69          fprintf(stderr, "%s: %s: read error: %s\n",
70                  myname, file, strerror(errno));
71          errors++;
72      }
73
74      if (fd != 0) {
75          if (close(fd) < 0) {
76              fprintf(stderr, "%s: %s: close error: %s\n",
77                  myname, file, strerror(errno));
78              errors++;
79          }
80      }
81
82      return (errors != 0);
83  }
```

`ch-fileio-cat` checks every system call for errors. While this is tedious, it provides robustness (or at least clarity): when something goes wrong, `ch-fileio-cat` prints an error message that is as specific as possible. The combination of `errno` and `strerror()` makes this easy to do. That's it for `ch-fileio-cat`—only 83 lines of code!

To sum up, there are several points to understand about Unix I/O:

I/O is uninterpreted.
: The I/O system calls merely move bytes around. They do no interpretation of the data; all interpretation is up to the user-level program. This makes reading and writing binary structures just as easy as reading and writing lines of text (easier, really, although using binary data introduces portability problems).

I/O is flexible.
: You can read or write as many bytes at a time as you like. You can even read and write data one byte at a time, although doing so for large amounts of data is more expensive than doing so in large chunks.

I/O is simple.
The three-valued return (negative for error, zero for end-of-file, positive for a count) makes programming straightforward and obvious.

I/O can be partial.
Both `read()` and `write()` can transfer fewer bytes than requested. Application code (that is, *your* code) must always be aware of this.

4.4.4 Example: Unix cat

As promised, here is the V7 version of `cat`.[3] It begins by checking for options. The V7 `cat` accepts a single option, `-u`, for doing unbuffered output.

The basic design is similar to the one shown above; it loops over the files named by the command-line arguments and reads each file, one character at a time, sending the characters to standard output. Unlike our version, it uses the `<stdio.h>` facilities. In many ways code using the Standard I/O library is easier to read and write, since all buffering issues are hidden by the library:

```
/*
 * Concatenate files.
 */

#include <stdio.h>
#include <sys/types.h>
#include <sys/stat.h>

char    stdbuf[BUFSIZ];

main(argc, argv)                              int main(int argc, char **argv)
char **argv;
{
    int fflg = 0;
    register FILE *fi;
    register c;                               register int c;
    int dev, ino = -1;
    struct stat statb;

    setbuf(stdout, stdbuf);
    for( ; argc>1 && argv[1][0]=='-'; argc--,argv++) {
        switch(argv[1][1]) {                  Process options
        case 0:
            break;
        case 'u':
            setbuf(stdout, (char *)NULL);
```

[3]See `/usr/src/cmd/cat.c` in the V7 distribution. A copy is included in the book's GitHub repository. The program compiles without change under GNU/Linux.

```
27                  continue;
28              }
29              break;
30          }
31          fstat(fileno(stdout), &statb);              Lines 31–36 explained in Chapter 5
32          statb.st_mode &= S_IFMT;
33          if (statb.st_mode!=S_IFCHR && statb.st_mode!=S_IFBLK) {
34              dev = statb.st_dev;
35              ino = statb.st_ino;
36          }
37          if (argc < 2) {
38              argc = 2;
39              fflg++;
40          }
41          while (--argc > 0) {                         Loop over files
42              if (fflg || (*++argv)[0]=='-' && (*argv)[1]=='\0')
43                  fi = stdin;
44              else {
45                  if ((fi = fopen(*argv, "r")) == NULL) {
46                      fprintf(stderr, "cat: can't open %s\n", *argv);
47                      continue;
48                  }
49              }
50              fstat(fileno(fi), &statb);               Lines 50–56 explained in Chapter 5
51              if (statb.st_dev==dev && statb.st_ino==ino) {
52                  fprintf(stderr, "cat: input %s is output\n",
53                     fflg?"-": *argv);
54                  fclose(fi);
55                  continue;
56              }
57              while ((c = getc(fi)) != EOF)            Copy file contents to stdout
58                  putchar(c);
59              if (fi!=stdin)
60                  fclose(fi);
61          }
62          return(0);
63      }
```

Of note is that the program always exits successfully (line 62); it could have been written to note errors and indicate them in `main()`'s return value. (The mechanics of process exiting and the meaning of different exit status values are discussed in Section 9.1.5.1, "Defining Process Exit Status," page 289.)

The code dealing with the `struct stat` and the `fstat()` function (lines 31–36 and 50–56) is undoubtedly opaque, since we haven't yet covered these functions, and won't until the next chapter. (But do note the use of `fileno()` on line 50 to get at the underlying file descriptor associated with the `FILE *` variables.) The idea behind the code is to make sure that no input file is the same as the output file. This is intended to prevent infinite file growth, in case of a command like this:

```
$ cat myfile >> myfile          Append one copy of myfile onto itself?
```

And indeed, the check works:

```
$ echo hi > myfile              Create a file
$ v7cat myfile >> myfile        Attempt to append it onto itself
cat: input myfile is output
```

If you try this with `ch-fileio-cat`, it will keep running, and `myfile` will keep growing until you interrupt it. The GNU version of `cat` does perform the check. Note that something like the following is beyond `cat`'s control:

```
$ v7cat < myfile > myfile
cat: input - is output
$ ls -l myfile
-rw-r--r--    1 arnold   devel          0 Mar 24 14:17 myfile
```

In this case, it's too late because *the shell* truncates `myfile` (with the `>` operator) before `cat` ever gets a chance to examine the file!

Section 5.4.2, "Retrieving File Information," page 131, explains the `struct stat` and the system calls related to it. In Section 5.4.4.2, "The V7 cat Revisited," page 140, we review how lines 31–36 and 50–56 of the V7 `cat.c` make use of the `stat` structure and the related system calls.

4.5 Random Access: Moving Around within a File

So far, we have discussed *sequential* I/O, whereby data is read or written beginning at the front of the file and continuing until the end. Often, this is all a program needs to do. However, it is possible to do *random access* I/O—that is, read data from an arbitrary position in the file, without having to read everything before that position first.

The *offset* of a file descriptor is the position within an open file at which the next read or write will occur. A program sets the offset with the `lseek()` system call:

```
#include <sys/types.h>     /* for off_t */                          POSIX
#include <unistd.h>        /* declares lseek() and whence values */

off_t lseek(int fd, off_t offset, int whence);
```

The type `off_t` (offset type) is a signed integer type representing byte positions (offsets from the beginning) within a file. On 32-bit systems, the type is usually a `long`. However, many

Table 4.4: `whence` values for `lseek()`

Symbolic constant	Value	Meaning
SEEK_SET	0	`offset` is absolute, that is, relative to the beginning of the file.
SEEK_CUR	1	`offset` is relative to the current position in the file.
SEEK_END	2	`offset` is relative to the end of the file.

modern systems allow very large files, in which case `off_t` may be a more unusual type, such as a C99 `int64_t` or some other *extended* type. `lseek()` takes three arguments, as follows:

`int fd`
: The file descriptor for the open file.

`off_t offset`
: A position to move to. The interpretation of this value depends on the `whence` parameter. `offset` can be positive or negative: negative values move toward the front of the file; positive values move toward the end of the file.

`int whence`
: Describes the location in the file that `offset` is relative to. See Table 4.4.

Much old code uses the numeric values shown in Table 4.4. However, any new code you write should use the symbolic values, whose meanings are clearer.

The meaning of the values and their effects upon file position are shown in Figure 4.1. Assuming that the file has 3,000 bytes and that the current offset is `2000` before each call to `lseek()`, the new position after each call is as shown.

Negative offsets relative to the beginning of the file are meaningless; they fail with an "invalid argument" error.

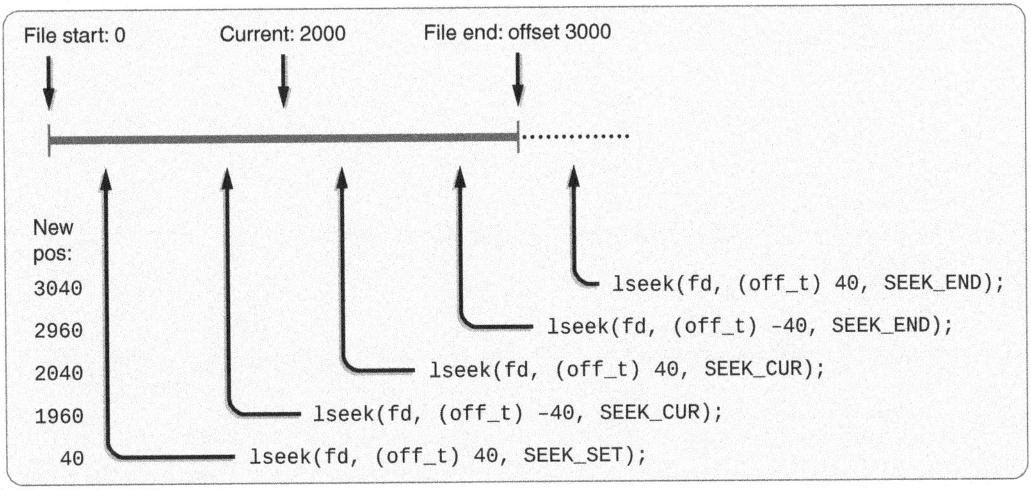

Figure 4.1: Offsets for `lseek()`

The return value is the new position in the file. Thus, to find out where in the file you are, use the following:

```
off_t curpos;
...
curpos = lseek(fd, (off_t) 0, SEEK_CUR);
```

The `l` in `lseek()` stands for `long`. `lseek()` was introduced in V7 Unix when file sizes were extended; V6 had a simple `seek()` system call. As a result, much old documentation (and code) treats the `offset` parameter as if it had type `long`, and instead of a cast to `off_t`, it's not unusual to see an `L` suffix on constant offset values:

```
curpos = lseek(fd, 0L, SEEK_CUR);
```

On systems with a Standard C compiler, where `lseek()` is declared with a prototype, such old code continues to work since the compiler automatically promotes the `0L` from `long` to `off_t` if they are different types.

One interesting and important aspect of `lseek()` is that it is possible to seek beyond the end of a file. Any data that is subsequently written at that point goes into the file, but with a "gap" or "hole" between the data at the previous end of the file and the new data. Data in the gap reads as if it is all zeros.

The following program demonstrates the creation of holes. It writes three instances of a `struct` at the beginning, middle, and far end of a file. The offsets chosen (lines 16–18, the third element of each structure) are arbitrary but big enough to demonstrate the point:

```
1  /* ch-fileio-holes.c --- Demonstrate lseek() and holes in files. */
2
3  #include <stdio.h>        /* for fprintf(), stderr, BUFSIZ */
4  #include <errno.h>        /* declare errno */
5  #include <fcntl.h>        /* for flags for open() */
6  #include <string.h>       /* declare strerror() */
7  #include <unistd.h>       /* for ssize_t */
8  #include <sys/types.h>    /* for off_t, etc. */
9  #include <sys/stat.h>     /* for mode_t */
10
11 struct person {
12     char name[10];        /* first name */
13     char id[10];          /* ID number */
14     off_t pos;            /* position in file, for demonstration */
15 } people[] = {
16     { "arnold", "123456789", 0 },
17     { "miriam", "987654321", 10240 },
18     { "joe",    "192837465", 81920 },
19 };
20
21 int
22 main(int argc, char **argv)
```

```
23 {
24     int fd;
25     int i, j;
26
27     if (argc < 2) {
28         fprintf(stderr, "usage: %s file\n", argv[0]);
29         return 1;
30     }
31
32     fd = open(argv[1], O_RDWR|O_CREAT|O_TRUNC, 0666);
33     if (fd < 0) {
34         fprintf(stderr, "%s: %s: cannot open for read/write: %s\n",
35                 argv[0], argv[1], strerror(errno));
36         return 1;
37     }
38
39     j = sizeof(people) / sizeof(people[0]);     /* count of elements */
```

Lines 27–30 make sure that the program was invoked properly. Lines 32–37 open the named file and verify that the open succeeded. The parameters and flags for `open()` are discussed in the next section.

The calculation on line 39 of `j`, the array element count, uses a lovely, portable trick: the number of elements is the size of the entire array divided by the size of the first element. The beauty of this idiom is that it's always right—no matter how many elements you add to or remove from such an array, the compiler will figure it out. It also doesn't require a terminating *sentinel* element—that is, one in which all the fields are set to zero, `NULL`, or some such.

The work is done by a loop (lines 41–55), which seeks to the byte offset given in each structure (line 42) and then writes the structure out (line 49):

```
41     for (i = 0; i < j; i++) {
42         if (lseek(fd, people[i].pos, SEEK_SET) < 0) {
43             fprintf(stderr, "%s: %s: seek error: %s\n",
44                 argv[0], argv[1], strerror(errno));
45             (void) close(fd);
46             return 1;
47         }
48
49         if (write(fd, & people[i], sizeof(people[i])) != sizeof(people[i])) {
50             fprintf(stderr, "%s: %s: write error: %s\n",
51                 argv[0], argv[1], strerror(errno));
52             (void) close(fd);
53             return 1;
54         }
55     }
56
57     /* all ok here */
```

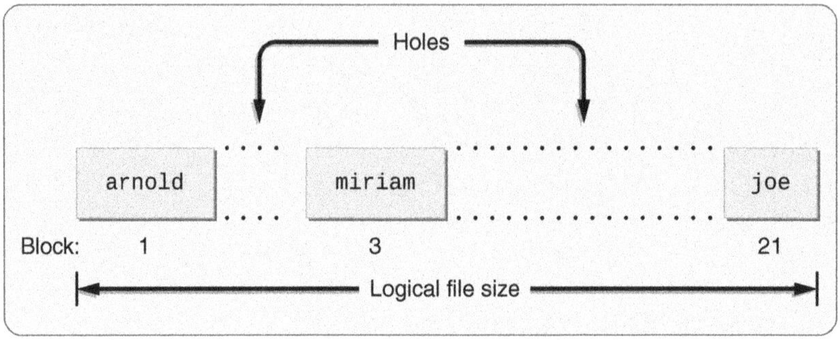

Figure 4.2: Holes in a file

```
    (void) close(fd);
    return 0;
}
```

Here are the results when the program is run:

```
$ ch-fileio-holes peoplelist                Run the program
$ ls -ls peoplelist                         Show size and blocks used
12 -rw-rw-r-- 1 arnold arnold 81952 May 25 15:29 peoplelist
$ echo 81952 / 4096 | bc -l                 Show blocks if no holes
20.00781250000000000000
```

We happen to know that each disk block in the file uses 4,096 bytes. (How we know that is discussed in Section 5.4.2, "Retrieving File Information," page 131. For now, take it as a given.) The final `bc` command indicates that a file of size 81,952 bytes needs 21 disk blocks. However, the `-s` option to `ls`, which tells us how many blocks a file really uses, shows that the file uses only 12 blocks![4] The missing blocks in the file are the holes. This is illustrated in Figure 4.2.

NOTE

`ch-fileio-holes.c` does direct binary I/O. This nicely illustrates the beauty of random access I/O: you can treat a disk file as if it were a very large array of binary data structures.

In practice, storing live data by using binary I/O is a design decision that you should consider carefully. For example, suppose you need to move the data to a system using different byte orders for integers, or using different floating-point formats? Or to a system with different alignment requirements for structure members? Ignoring such issues can become significantly costly, since later on you may need to write conversion programs, modify your original code, or make other changes in a production system.

[4] At least three of these blocks contain the data that we wrote out; the others are for use by the operating system in keeping track of where the data resides.

4.6 Creating Files

As described earlier, `open()` apparently opens existing files only. This section describes how brand-new files are created. There are two choices: `creat()` and `open()` with additional flags. Initially, `creat()` was the only way to create a file, but `open()` was later enhanced with this functionality as well. Both mechanisms require specification of the initial file permissions.

4.6.1 Specifying Initial File Permissions

As a GNU/Linux user, you are familiar with file permissions as printed by '`ls -l`': read, write, and execute for each of user (the file's owner), group, and other. The various combinations are often expressed in octal, particularly for the `chmod` and `umask` commands. For example, file permissions `-rw-r--r--` is equivalent to octal `0644` and `-rwxr-xr-x` is equivalent to octal `0755`. (The leading `0` is C's notation for octal values.)

When you create a file, you must know the protections to be given to the new file. You can do this as a raw octal number if you choose, and indeed it's not uncommon to see such numbers in older code. However, it is better to use a bitwise-OR of one or more of the symbolic constants from `<sys/stat.h>`, described in Table 4.5.

The following fragment shows how to create variables representing permissions `-rw-r--r--` and `-rwxr-xr-x` (`0644` and `0755`, respectively):

```
mode_t rw_mode, rwx_mode;

rw_mode  = S_IRUSR | S_IWUSR | S_IRGRP | S_IROTH;            /* 0644 */
rwx_mode = S_IRWXU | S_IRGRP | S_IXGRP | S_IROTH | S_IXOTH;  /* 0755 */
```

Table 4.5: POSIX symbolic constants for file modes

Symbolic constant	Value	Meaning
`S_IRWXU`	`00700`	User read, write, and execute permission.
`S_IRUSR`	`00400`	User read permission.
`S_IREAD`		Same as `S_IRUSR`.
`S_IWUSR`	`00200`	User write permission.
`S_IWRITE`		Same as `S_IWUSR`.
`S_IXUSR`	`00100`	User execute permission.
`S_IEXEC`		Same as `S_IXUSR`.
`S_IRWXG`	`00070`	Group read, write, and execute permission.
`S_IRGRP`	`00040`	Group read permission.
`S_IWGRP`	`00020`	Group write permission.
`S_IXGRP`	`00010`	Group execute permission.
`S_IRWXO`	`00007`	Other read, write, and execute permission.
`S_IROTH`	`00004`	Other read permission.
`S_IWOTH`	`00002`	Other write permission.
`S_IXOTH`	`00001`	Other execute permission.

Table 4.6: Additional POSIX symbolic constants for file modes

Symbolic constant	Value	Meaning
`S_ISUID`	`04000`	Set user ID.
`S_ISGID`	`02000`	Set group ID.
`S_ISVTX`	`01000`	Save text.

Older code used `S_IREAD`, `S_IWRITE`, and `S_IEXEC` together with bit shifting to produce the same results:

```
mode_t rw_mode, rwx_mode;

rw_mode  = (S_IREAD|S_IWRITE) | (S_IREAD >> 3) | (S_IREAD >> 6); /* 0644 */
rwx_mode = (S_IREAD|S_IWRITE|S_IEXEC) |
          ((S_IREAD|S_IEXEC) >> 3) | ((S_IREAD|S_IEXEC) >> 6);  /* 0755 */
```

Unfortunately, neither notation is incredibly clear. The modern version is preferred since each permission bit has its own name and there is less opportunity to do the bitwise operations incorrectly.

The additional permission bits shown in Table 4.6 are available for use when you are changing a file's permission, but they should not be used when you initially create a file. Whether these bits may be included varies wildly by operating system. It's best not to try; rather, you should explicitly change the permissions after the file is created. (Changing permissions is described in Section 5.6.2, "Changing Permissions: `chmod()` and `fchmod()`," page 147. The meanings of these bits is discussed in Chapter 11, "Permissions and User and Group ID Numbers," page 383.)

4.6.2 Controlling Default Permissions with `umask()`

When standard utilities create files, the default permissions they use are `-rw-rw-rw-` (or `0666`). Because most users prefer to avoid having files that are world-writable, each process carries with it a *umask*. The umask is a set of permission bits indicating those bits that should never be allowed *when new files are created*. (The umask is not used when changing permissions.) Conceptually, the operation that occurs is

```
actual_permissions = (requested_permissions & (~umask));
```

The umask is usually set by the `umask` command in `$HOME/.profile` when you log in. From a C program, it's set with the `umask()` system call:

```
#include <sys/types.h>                                    POSIX
#include <sys/stat.h>

mode_t umask(mode_t mask);
```

The return value is the old umask. Thus, to determine the current mask, you must set it to a value and then reset it (or change it, as desired):

```
mode_t mask = umask(0);        /* retrieve current mask */
(void) umask(mask);            /* restore it */
```

Here is an example of the umask in action, at the shell level:

```
$ umask                                      Show the current mask
0022
$ touch newfile                              Create a file
$ ls -l newfile                              Show permissions of new file
-rw-r--r--    1 arnold   devel           0 Mar 24 15:43 newfile
$ umask 0                                    Set mask to empty
$ touch newfile2                             Create a second file
$ ls -l newfile2                             Show permissions of new file
-rw-rw-rw-    1 arnold   devel           0 Mar 24 15:44 newfile2
```

4.6.3 Creating Files with `creat()`

The `creat()`[5] system call creates new files. It is declared as follows:

```
#include <sys/types.h>                                            POSIX
#include <sys/stat.h>
#include <fcntl.h>

int creat(const char *pathname, mode_t mode);
```

The `mode` argument represents the permissions for the new file (as discussed in the previous section). The file named by `pathname` is created, with the given permission as modified by the umask. It is opened for writing (only), and the return value is the file descriptor for the new file, or `-1` if there was a problem. In this case, `errno` indicates the error. If the file already exists, it will be truncated when opened.

In all other respects, file descriptors returned by `creat()` are the same as those returned by `open()`; they're used for writing and seeking and must be closed with `close()`:

```
int fd, count;

/* Error checking omitted for brevity */
fd = creat("/some/new/file", 0666);
count = write(fd, "some data\n", 10);
(void) close(fd);
```

---

[5] Yes, that's how it's spelled. Ken Thompson, one of the two "fathers" of Unix, was once asked what he would have done differently if he had it to do over again. He replied that he would have spelled `creat()` with an "e." Indeed, that is exactly what he did for the *Plan 9 from Bell Labs* operating system.

Table 4.7: Additional POSIX flags for `open()`

Flag	Meaning
`O_APPEND`	Force all writes to occur at the end of the file.
`O_CREAT`	Create the file if it doesn't exist.
`O_EXCL`	When used with `O_CREAT`, cause `open()` to fail if the file already exists or is a symbolic link.
`O_TRUNC`	Truncate the file (set it to zero length) if it exists.

4.6.4 Revisiting `open()`

You may recall the declaration for `open()`:

```
int open(const char *pathname, int flags, mode_t mode);
```

Earlier, we said that when opening a file for plain I/O, we could ignore the `mode` argument. Having seen `creat()`, though, you can probably guess that `open()` can also be used for creating files and that the `mode` argument is used in this case.

Besides the `O_RDONLY`, `O_WRONLY`, and `O_RDWR` flags, additional flags may be bitwise-OR'd when `open()` is called. The POSIX standard mandates a number of these additional flags. Table 4.7 presents the flags that are used for most mundane applications.

Given `O_APPEND` and `O_TRUNC`, you can imagine how the shell might open or create files corresponding to the > and >> operators. For example:

```
int fd;
extern char *filename;
mode_t mode = S_IRUSR|S_IWUSR|S_IRGRP|S_IWGRP|S_IROTH|S_IWOTH;    /* 0666 */

fd = open(filename, O_CREAT|O_WRONLY|O_TRUNC, mode);              /* for > */

fd = open(filename, O_CREAT|O_WRONLY|O_APPEND, mode);             /* for >> */
```

Note that the `O_EXCL` flag would *not* be used here, since for both > and >>, it's not an error for the file to exist. Remember also that the system applies the umask to the requested permissions.

Also, it's easy to see that, at least conceptually, `creat()` could be written this easily:

```
int creat(const char *path, mode_t mode)
{
    return open(path, O_CREAT|O_WRONLY|O_TRUNC, mode);
}
```

(In fact, the POSIX standard says that `creat()` shall behave as if implemented in exactly that way!)

NOTE

If a file is opened with `O_APPEND`, all data will be written at the end of the file, even if the current position has been reset with `lseek()`.

Table 4.8: Additional advanced POSIX flags for `open()`

Flag	Meaning
`O_CLOEXEC`	Set the close-on-exec flag for the returned file descriptor (see Section 9.4.3.1, "The Close-on-Exec and Close-on-Fork Flags," page 316).
`O_CLOFORK`	Set the close-on-fork flag for the returned file descriptor (see Section 9.4.3.1, "The Close-on-Exec and Close-on-Fork Flags," page 316).
`O_DIRECTORY`	Fail if the specified file name is not a directory.
`O_EXEC`	Open for execute only. See the discussion of `fexecve()` in Section 9.1.4, "Starting New Programs: The `exec()` Family," page 283. On GNU/Linux, use the Linux-specific `O_PATH` instead of `O_EXEC`.
`O_NOCTTY`	If the device being opened is a terminal, it does not become the process's controlling terminal. (This is a more advanced topic, discussed briefly in Section 9.2.1, "Job Control Overview," page 300.)
`O_NOFOLLOW`	Fail if the specified file name is a symbolic link.
`O_NONBLOCK`	Disable blocking of I/O operations in certain cases (see Section 9.4.3.5, "Nonblocking I/O for Pipes and FIFOs," page 320).
`O_SEARCH`	Open a directory for searching only.
`O_TTY_INIT`	If the device being opened is a terminal, initialize its settings to reasonable values. As of this writing, Linux does not seem to support this flag.
`O_DSYNC`	Ensure that data written to a file makes it all the way to physical storage before `write()` returns.
`O_RSYNC`	Ensure that any data that `read()` would read, which may have been written to the file being read, has made it all the way to physical storage before `read()` returns.
`O_SYNC`	Like `O_DSYNC`, but it also ensures that all file metadata, such as access times, has also been written to physical storage.

Modern systems provide additional flags whose uses are more specialized. Table 4.8 describes them briefly.

The `O_DSYNC`, `O_RSYNC`, and `O_SYNC` flags need some explanation. Unix systems (including Linux) maintain an internal cache of disk blocks, called the *buffer cache*. When the `write()` system call returns, the data passed to the operating system has been copied to a buffer in the buffer cache. It is not necessarily written out to the disk.

The buffer cache provides considerable performance improvement: since disk I/O is often an order of magnitude or more slower than CPU and memory operations, programs would slow down considerably if they had to wait for every write to go all the way through to the disk. In addition, if data has recently been written to a file, a subsequent read of that same data will find the information already in the buffer cache, where it can be returned immediately instead of having to wait for an I/O operation to read it from the disk.

Unix systems also do *read-ahead*; since most reads are sequential, upon reading one block, the operating system will read several more consecutive disk blocks so that their information will already be in the buffer cache when a program asks for it. If multiple programs are reading the same file, they all benefit since they will all get their data from the same copy of the file's disk blocks in the buffer cache.

All of this caching is wonderful, but of course there's no free lunch. While data is in the buffer cache, and before it has been written to disk, there's a small, but very real, window in which disaster can strike—for example, if the power goes out. Modern disk drives exacerbate this problem: many have their own internal buffers, so while data may have made it to the drive, it may not have made it onto the media when the power goes out! This can be a significant issue for small systems that aren't in a data center with controlled power or that don't have an uninterruptible power supply (UPS).[6]

For most applications, the chance that data in the buffer cache might be inadvertently lost is acceptably small. However, for some applications, *any* such chance is not acceptable. Thus, the notion of *synchronous I/O* was added to Unix systems, whereby a program can be guaranteed that if a system call has returned, the data is safely written on a physical storage device.

The `O_DSYNC` flag guarantees data integrity; the data and any other information that the operating system needs to find the data are written to disk before `write()` returns. However, metadata, such as access and modification times, may not be written to disk. The `O_SYNC` flag requires that metadata also be written to disk before `write()` returns. (Here too there is no free lunch; synchronous writes can seriously affect the performance of a program, slowing it down noticeably.)

The `O_RSYNC` flag is for data reads: if `read()` finds data in the buffer cache that was scheduled for writing to disk, then `read()` won't return that data until it has been written to disk. The other two flags can affect this: in particular, `O_SYNC` will cause `read()` to wait until the file metadata has been written out as well.

NOTE

Linux implements `O_SYNC` and `O_DSYNC`. It doesn't implement the `O_RSYNC` semantics, instead treating it the same as `O_SYNC`. Furthermore, Linux defines additional flags that are Linux specific and intended for specialized uses. We describe two of these flags in Section 5.5, "Avoiding Race Conditions: `openat()` and Friends," page 144. Check the GNU/Linux *open*(2) manpage for more information.

4.7 Forcing Data to Disk

Earlier, we described the `O_DSYNC`, `O_RSYNC`, and `O_SYNC` flags for `open()`. We noted that using these flags could slow a program down since each `write()` does not return until all data has been written to physical media.

[6]If you don't have a UPS and you use your system for critical work, we highly recommend investing in one. You should also be doing regular backups. Laptop systems have their own battery, which allows them to keep working during short power outages, but if left unattended, they eventually turn themselves off when their battery drains entirely.

For a slightly higher risk level, we can have our cake and eat it too. We do this by opening a file without one of the `O_xSYNC` flags and then using one of the following two system calls at whatever point it's necessary to have the data safely moved to physical storage:

```
#include <unistd.h>

int fsync(int fd);                                    POSIX FSC
int fdatasync(int fd);                                POSIX SIO
```

The `fdatasync()` system call is like `O_DSYNC`: it forces all file data to be written to the final physical device. The `fsync()` system call is like `O_SYNC`, forcing not just file data but also file metadata to physical storage. The `fsync()` call is more portable; it has been around in the Unix world for longer and is more likely to exist across a broad range of systems.

You can use these calls with `<stdio.h>` file pointers by first calling `fflush()` and then using `fileno()` to obtain the underlying file descriptor. Here is an `fpsync()` function that can be used to wrap both operations in one call; it returns `0` on success:

```
/* fpsync --- sync a stdio FILE * variable */

int
fpsync(FILE *fp)
{
    if (fp == NULL || fflush(fp) == EOF || fsync(fileno(fp)) < 0)
        return -1;

    return 0;
}
```

Technically, both of these calls are extensions to the base POSIX standard: `fsync()` in the "File Synchronization" extension (FSC), and `fdatasync()` in the "Synchronized Input and Output" extension. Nevertheless, you can use them on a GNU/Linux system without any problem.

4.8 Setting File Length

Two system calls make it possible to adjust the size of a file:

```
#include <unistd.h>
#include <sys/types.h>

int truncate(const char *path, off_t length);         POSIX XSI
int ftruncate(int fd, off_t length);                  POSIX
```

The functions differ in their parameters: `truncate()` takes a file name argument, whereas `ftruncate()` works on an open file descriptor. (The *xxx*`()` and `f`*xxxx*`()` naming convention for system call pairs that work on a file name or file descriptor is common. We see several examples in this and subsequent chapters.) For both, the `length` argument is the new size of the file.

This system call originated in 4.2 BSD Unix, and in early systems could only be used to shorten a file's length, hence the name. On modern systems, including Linux, the name is a misnomer, since it's possible to extend the length of a file with these calls, not just shorten a file.

For these calls, the file being truncated must have write permission (for `truncate()`), or have been opened for writing (for `ftruncate()`). If the file is being shortened, any data past the new end of the file is lost. (Thus, you can't shorten the file, lengthen it again, and expect to find the original data.) If the file is extended, as with data written after an `lseek()`, the data between the old end of the file and the new end of the file reads as zeros.

These calls are very different from '`open(file, ...|O_TRUNC, mode)`'. The latter truncates a file completely, throwing away all its data. These calls simply set the file's absolute length to the given value.

These functions are fairly specialized; they're used only nine times in all of the GNU Coreutils code.

4.9 Summary

- When a system call fails, it usually returns `-1`, and the global variable `errno` is set to a predefined value indicating the problem. The functions `perror()` and `strerror()` can be used for reporting errors.
- Files are manipulated by small integers called file descriptors. File descriptors for standard input, standard output, and standard error are inherited from a program's parent process. Others are obtained with `open()` or `creat()`. They are closed with `close()`, and `getdtablesize()` returns the maximum number of allowed open files. The value of the umask (set with `umask()`) affects the permissions given to new files created with `creat()` or the `O_CREAT` flag for `open()`.
- The `read()` and `write()` system calls read and write data, respectively. Their interface is simple. In particular, they do no interpretation of the data; files are linear streams of bytes. The `lseek()` system call provides random access I/O: the ability to move around within a file.
- Additional flags for `open()` provide for synchronous I/O, whereby data makes it all the way to the physical storage media before `write()` or `read()` return. Data can also be forced to disk on a controlled basis with `fsync()` or `fdatasync()`.
- The `truncate()` and `ftruncate()` system calls set the absolute length of a file.

Exercises

1. Using just `open()`, `read()`, `write()`, and `close()`, write a simple `copy` program that copies the file named by its first argument to the file named by its second.
2. Enhance the `copy` program to accept `"-"` to mean "standard input" if used as the first argument and "standard output" if used as the second argument. Does '`copy - -`' work correctly?
3. Look at the *proc*(5) manpage on a GNU/Linux system, and in particular the *fd* subsection. Do an '`ls -l /dev/fd`' and examine the files in the `/proc/self/fd` directly. If `/dev/stdin` and friends had been around in the early versions of Unix, how would that have simplified the code for the V7 `cat` program? (Many other modern Unix systems have a `/dev/fd` directory or filesystem. If you're not using GNU/Linux, see what you can discover about your Unix version.)
4. Even though you don't understand it yet, try to copy the code segment from the V7 `cat.c` that uses the `struct stat` and the `fstat()` function into `ch-fileio-cat.c` so that it too reports an error for '`cat file >> file`'.
5. (Easy.) Assuming the existence of `strerror()`, write your own version of `perror()`.
6. What is the result of '`ulimit -n`' on your system?
7. Write a simple version of the `umask` program, named `myumask`, that takes an octal mask on the command line. Use `strtol()` with a base of `8` to convert the character string command-line argument into an integer value. Change the umask to the new mask with the `umask()` system call.

   Compile and run `myumask`, and then examine the value of the umask with the regular `umask` command. Explain the results. (Hint: in Bash, enter '`type umask`'.)
8. Change the simple `copy` program you wrote earlier to use `open()` with the `O_SYNC` flag. Using the `time` command, compare the performance of the original version and the new version on a large file.
9. For `ftruncate()`, we said that the file must have been opened for writing. How can a file be open for writing when the file itself doesn't have write permission?
10. Write a `truncate` program whose usage is '<code>truncate *file length*</code>'.

Chapter 5

Directories and File Metadata

This chapter continues the climb up the learning curve toward the next plateau: understanding directories and information about files.

In this chapter we explore how file information is stored in a directory, how directories themselves are read, created, and removed, what information about files is available, and how to retrieve it. Finally, we explore other ways to update file metadata, such as the owner, group, permissions, and access and modification times.

5.1 Considering Directory Contents

All Unix systems, including Linux, use the same conceptual design for storing file information on disk. Although there is considerable variation in the implementation of the design, the interface at the C level remains consistent, making it possible to write portable programs that compile and run on many different systems.

5.1.1 Definitions

We start the discussion by defining some terms:

Partition

A unit of physical storage. *Physical partitions* are typically either part of a disk or an entire disk. Modern systems make it possible to create *logical partitions* from multiple physical ones.

Filesystem

A partition (physical or logical) that contains file data and *metadata*, information about files (as opposed to the file contents, which is information *in* the files). Such metadata includes file ownership, permissions, size, and so on, as well as information for use by the operating system in locating file contents.

You place filesystems "in" partitions (a one-to-one correspondence) by writing standard information in them. This is done with a user-level program, such as `mke2fs` on GNU/Linux, or `newfs` on Unix. (The Unix `mkfs` command makes filesystems but is difficult to use directly. `newfs` calls it with the correct parameters. If your system is a Unix system, see the *newfs*(8) and *mkfs*(8) manpages for the details.)

Some filesystems exist only in memory, such as those for `/run` and `/proc`. Their data is ephemeral, disappearing when the system shuts down.

For the most part, GNU/Linux and Unix hide the existence of filesystems and partitions. (Further details are given in Section 8.1, "Mounting and Unmounting Filesystems," page 221). Everything is accessed by pathnames, without reference to which disk a file lives on. (Contrast this with almost every other commercial operating system, such as OpenVMS, or the default behavior of any Microsoft system.)

Inode

Short for "index node" and initially abbreviated as "i-node," a small block of information describing everything about a file *except* the file's name(s). The number of inodes, and thus the number of unique files per filesystem, is set and made permanent when the filesystem is created. '`df -i`' can tell you how many inodes you have and how many are used.

Device

In the context of files, filesystems, and file metadata, a unique number representing an in-use ("mounted") filesystem. The (device, inode) pair *uniquely* identifies a file: two different files are guaranteed to have different (device, inode) pairs. This is discussed in more detail later in this chapter.

Directory

A special file, containing a list of (inode number, name) pairs. Directories can be opened for reading but not for writing; the operating system makes all the changes to a directory's contents.

Conceptually, each disk block contains either some number of inodes, or file data. Each inode in turn contains pointers to the blocks that contain the file's data. See Figure 5.1.

The figure shows all the inode blocks at the front of the partition and the data blocks after them. Early Unix filesystems were indeed organized this way. However, while all modern

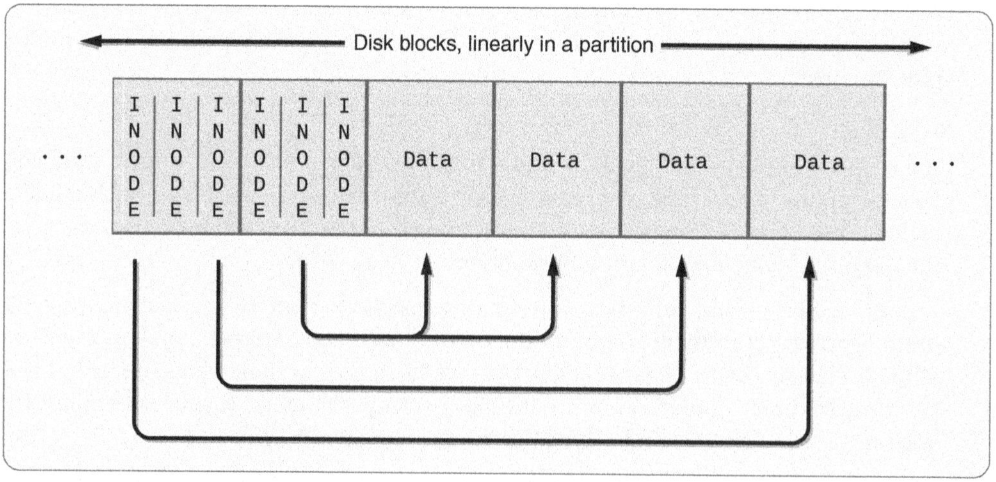

Figure 5.1: Conceptual view of inode and data blocks

systems still have inodes and data blocks, the organization has changed for improved efficiency and robustness. The details vary from system to system, and even within GNU/Linux systems there are multiple kinds of filesystems, but the concepts are the same.

5.1.2 Directory Contents

Directories make the connection between a file name and an inode. Directory entries contain an inode number and a file name. They also contain additional bookkeeping information that is not of interest to us here. See Figure 5.2.

Early Unix systems had two-byte inode numbers and up to 14-byte file names. Here are the entire contents of the V7 `/usr/include/sys/dir.h`:

```
#ifndef DIRSIZ
#define DIRSIZ  14
#endif
struct  direct
{
        ino_t   d_ino;
        char    d_name[DIRSIZ];
};
```

An `ino_t` is defined in the V7 `<sys/types.h>` as '`typedef unsigned int ino_t;`'. Since a PDP-11 `int` is 16 bits, so too is the `ino_t`. This organization made it easy to read directories directly; since the size of an entry was fixed, the code was simple. (The only thing to watch out for was that a full 14-character `d_name` was not NUL-terminated.)

Directory content management was also easy for the system. When a file was removed from a directory, the system replaced the inode number with a binary zero, signifying that the "slot" in the directory was unused. New files could then reuse the empty slot. This helped keep the size of directory files themselves reasonable. (By convention, inode number `1` is unused; inode number `2` is always the first usable inode. More details are provided in the sidebar "Root Inode Numbers," page 224, in Section 8.1.1, "Reviewing the Background," page 221.)

Modern systems provide long file names. Each directory entry is of variable length, with a common limit of 255 bytes for the file name component of the directory. Later on, we show

23	`.`
19	`..`
42	`guide`
0	`tempdata`
37	`.profile`

Figure 5.2: Conceptual directory contents

how to read a directory's contents on a modern system. On 32-bit GNU/Linux systems, an inode is 32 bits long, whereas on 64-bit systems, it's 64 bits long. (With the proper packages installed, you can use '`gcc -m32`' to build a 32-bit executable, even on a 64-bit system. Such executables have an `ino_t` that is 32 bits long, whereas regular 64-bit executables have an `ino_t` that is 64 bits long!)

As an aside, the nature of directories explains why the error for "no such file or directory" is `ENOENT`: there is no entry in the directory for the requested file.

5.1.3 Hard Links

When a file is created with `open()` or `creat()`, the system finds an unused inode and assigns it to the new file. It creates the directory entry for the file, with the file's name and inode number in it. The `-i` option to `ls` shows the inode number:

```
$ echo hello, world > message                        Create new file
$ ls -il message                                     Show inode number too
9438482 -rw-rw-r-- 1 arnold arnold 13 Dec  3 21:49 message
```

Since directory entries associate file names with inodes, it is possible for one file to have multiple names. Each directory entry referring to the same inode is called a *link*, or *hard link*, to the file. Links are created with the `ln` command. The usage is '`ln oldfile newfile`':

```
$ ln message msg                                     Create a link
$ cat msg                                            Show contents of new name
hello, world
$ ls -il msg message                                 Show inode numbers
9438482 -rw-rw-r-- 2 arnold arnold 13 Dec  3 21:49 message
9438482 -rw-rw-r-- 2 arnold arnold 13 Dec  3 21:49 msg
```

The output shows that the inode numbers of the two files are the same, and the third field in the long output is now `2`. This field is the *link count*, which reports how many links (directory entries referring to the inode) the file has.

It cannot be emphasized enough: *hard links all refer to the same file*. If you change one file, you have changed the others:

```
$ echo "Hi, how ya doin' ?" > msg                    Change file by new name
$ cat message                                        Show contents by old name
Hi, how ya doin' ?
$ ls -il message msg                                 Show info. Size changed
9438482 -rw-rw-r-- 2 arnold arnold 19 Dec  3 21:50 message
9438482 -rw-rw-r-- 2 arnold arnold 19 Dec  3 21:50 msg
```

Although we've created two links to the same file in a single directory, hard links are not restricted to being in the same directory; they can be in any other directory on the same filesystem. (This is discussed a bit more in Section 5.1.6, "Symbolic Links," page 119.)

Additionally, you can create a link to a file you don't own as long as you have write permission in the directory in which you're creating the link. (Such a file retains all the attributes of the original file: the owner, permissions, and so on. This is because it *is* the original file;

it has only acquired an additional name.) You can even create a link to a file you can't read or write, although there won't be much that you can do with that link! User-level code cannot create a hard link to a directory.

Once a link is removed, creating a new file by the same name as the original file creates a new file:

```
$ rm message                                          Remove old name
$ echo "What's happenin?" > message                   Reuse the name
$ ls -il msg message                                  Show information
9438483 -rw-rw-r-- 1 arnold arnold 17 Dec  3 21:50 message
9438482 -rw-rw-r-- 1 arnold arnold 19 Dec  3 21:50 msg
```

Notice that the link counts for both files are now equal to `1`.

At the C level, links are created with the `link()` system call:

```
#include <unistd.h>                                   POSIX

int link(const char *oldpath, const char *newpath);
```

The return value is `0` if the link was created successfully, or `-1` otherwise, in which case `errno` reflects the error. An important failure case is one in which `newpath` already exists. The system won't remove it for you, since attempting to do so can cause inconsistencies in the filesystem.

5.1.3.1 The GNU `link` Program

The `ln` program is complicated and large. However, the GNU Coreutils contain a simple `link` program that just calls `link()` on its first two arguments. The following example shows the code from `link.c`, with some irrelevant parts deleted; line numbers relate to the actual file:

```
/* Implementation overview:

   Simply call the system 'link' function */

  ... #include statements omitted for brevity ...

/* The official name of this program (e.g., no 'g' prefix).  */
#define PROGRAM_NAME "link"

#define AUTHORS proper_name ("Michael Stone")

void
usage (int status)
{
  ... omitted for brevity ...
}

int
```

```
57 main (int argc, char **argv)
58 {
59   initialize_main (&argc, &argv);
60   set_program_name (argv[0]);
61   setlocale (LC_ALL, "");
62   bindtextdomain (PACKAGE, LOCALEDIR);
63   textdomain (PACKAGE);
64
65   atexit (close_stdout);
66
67   parse_gnu_standard_options_only (argc, argv, PROGRAM_NAME, PACKAGE_NAME,
68                                    Version, true, usage, AUTHORS,
69                                    (char const *) nullptr);
70
71   if (argc < optind + 2)
72     {
73       if (argc < optind + 1)
74         error (0, 0, _("missing operand"));
75       else
76         error (0, 0, _("missing operand after %s"), quote (argv[optind]));
77       usage (EXIT_FAILURE);
78     }
79
80   if (optind + 2 < argc)
81     {
82       error (0, 0, _("extra operand %s"), quote (argv[optind + 2]));
83       usage (EXIT_FAILURE);
84     }
85
86   if (link (argv[optind], argv[optind + 1]) != 0)
87     error (EXIT_FAILURE, errno, _("cannot create link %s to %s"),
88            quoteaf_n (0, argv[optind + 1]), quoteaf_n (1, argv[optind]));
89
90   return EXIT_SUCCESS;
91 }
```

Lines 59–70 are typical Coreutils boilerplate, setting up internationalization (lines 61–63), the final action upon exit, and parsing the arguments. Lines 71–84 make sure that `link` is called with only two arguments. The `link()` system call itself occurs on line 86. (The `quote()` and `quoteaf_n()` functions provide quoting of the arguments in a style suitable for the current locale; the details aren't important here.)

5.1.3.2 Dot and Dot-Dot

Rounding off the discussion of links, let's look at how the `.` and `..` special names are managed. They are really just hard links. In the first case, `.` (dot) is a hard link to the directory containing it, and `..` (dot-dot) is a hard link to the parent directory. The operating system creates these links for you; as mentioned earlier, user-level code cannot create a hard link to a directory. This example illustrates the links:

```
$ pwd                                              Show current directory
/tmp
$ ls -ldi /tmp                                     Show its inode number
2359297 drwxrwxrwt 16 root root 40960 Dec  3 21:48 /tmp
$ mkdir x                                          Create a new directory
$ ls -ldi x                                        And show its inode number
2359352 drwxrwxr-x 2 arnold arnold 4096 Dec  3 21:56 x
$ ls -ldi x/. x/..                                 Show . and .. inode numbers
2359352 drwxrwxr-x  2 arnold arnold  4096 Dec  3 21:56 x/.
2359297 drwxrwxrwt 17 root   root   40960 Dec  3 21:56 x/..
```

The root's parent directory (`/..`) is a special case; we defer discussion of it until Chapter 8, "Filesystems and Directory Walks," page 221.

5.1.4 File Renaming

Given the way in which directory entries map names to inode numbers, renaming a file is conceptually quite easy:

1. If the new name for the file names an existing file, remove the existing link first. In the case that this was the only link to the file, the file itself is also removed, meaning that its inode can be reused, and the disk blocks it occupied are freed.
2. Create a new link to the file by the new name.
3. Remove the old name (link) for the file. (Removing names is discussed in the next section.)

Early versions of the `mv` command did work this way. However, when done this way, file renaming is not *atomic*; that is, it doesn't happen in one uninterruptible operation. And on a heavily loaded system, a malicious user could take advantage of race conditions, subverting the rename operation and substituting a different file for the original one.[1]

For this reason, 4.2 BSD introduced the `rename()` system call:

```
#include <stdio.h>                                         ISO C

int rename(const char *oldpath, const char *newpath);
```

On Linux systems, the renaming operation is atomic; the manpage states:

> If `newpath` already exists, it will be atomically replaced, so that there is no point at which another process attempting to access `newpath` will find it missing. However, there will probably be a window in which both `oldpath` and `newpath` refer to the file being renamed.

[1] A *race condition* is a situation in which details of timing can produce unintended side effects or bugs. In this case, the directory is, for a short period of time, in an inconsistent state, and it is this inconsistency that introduces the vulnerability.

> If `newpath` exists but the operation fails for some reason, `rename()` guarantees to leave an instance of `newpath` in place.

As with other system calls, a `0` return indicates success, and a return value of `-1` indicates an error.

5.1.5 File Removal

Removing a file means removing the file's entry in the directory and decrementing the file's link count (maintained in the inode). The contents of the file, and the disk blocks holding them, are not freed until the link count reaches zero.

The system call is named `unlink()`:

```
#include <unistd.h>                                          POSIX

int unlink(const char *pathname);
```

Given our discussion of file links, the name makes sense; this call removes the given link (directory entry) for the file. It returns `0` on success and `-1` on error.

The ability to remove a file requires write permission only for the directory and not for the file itself. This fact can be confusing, particularly for new Linux/Unix users. However, since the operation is one on the directory, this makes sense; it is the directory's contents that are being modified, not the file's contents.[2]

5.1.5.1 Using ISO C: `remove()`

ISO C provides the `remove()` function for removing files; this is intended to be a general function, usable on any system that supports ISO C, not just Unix and GNU/Linux:

```
#include <stdio.h>                                           ISO C

int remove(const char *pathname);
```

While not technically a system call, the return value is in the same vein: `0` on success and `-1` on error, with `errno` reflecting the value.

On GNU/Linux, `remove()` uses the `unlink()` system call to remove files, and the `rmdir()` system call (discussed later in the chapter) to remove directories.

5.1.5.2 Removing Open Files

Since the earliest days of Unix, it has been possible to remove open files. Simply call `unlink()` with the file name after a successful call to `open()` or `creat()`.

At first glance, this seems to be a strange thing to do. Since the system frees the data blocks when a file's link count goes to zero, is it even possible to use the open file?

---

[2]Indeed, the file's *metadata* is changed (the number of links), but that does not affect any other file attribute, nor does it affect the file's contents. Updating the link count is the only operation on a file that doesn't involve checking the file's permissions.

The answer is yes, you can continue to use the open file normally. The system knows that the file is open, and therefore it delays the release of the file's storage until the last file descriptor on the file is closed. Once the file is completely unused, the storage is freed.

This operation also happens to be a useful one—it is an easy way for a program to get temporary file storage that is guaranteed to be both private and automatically released when no longer needed:

```
/* Obtaining private temporary storage, error checking omitted for brevity */
int fd;
mode_t mode = O_CREAT|O_EXCL|O_TRUNC|O_RDWR;

fd = open("/tmp/myfile", mode, 0000);          Open the file
unlink("/tmp/myfile");                         Remove it

... continue to use file ...
close(fd);                                     Close file, free storage
```

One example of such a use is by a shell, for so-called *here documents* in shell scripts.

The downside to this approach is that it's also possible for a runaway application to fill up a filesystem with an open but anonymous file, in which case the system administrator has to try to find and kill the process. In olden days, a reboot and filesystem consistency check might have been required; thankfully, this is exceedingly rare on modern systems.

5.1.6 Symbolic Links

We started the chapter with a discussion of partitions, filesystems, and inodes. We also saw that directory entries associate names with inode numbers. Because directory entries contain no other information, hard links are restricted to files *within the same filesystem*. This has to be; there is no way to distinguish inode `2341` on one filesystem from inode `2341` on another filesystem. Here is what happens when we try:

```
$ mount                                  Show filesystems in use
...
/dev/nvme0n1p3 on / type ext4 (rw,relatime,errors=remount-ro)
/dev/nvme0n1p4 on /home type ext4 (rw,relatime)
...
$ ls -li /tmp/message                    Earlier example was on filesystem for /
9438483 -rw-rw-r-- 1 arnold arnold 17 Dec  3 21:50 /tmp/message
$ cat /tmp/message
Hi, how ya doin' ?
$ /bin/pwd                               Current directory is on a different filesystem
/home/arnold
$ ln /tmp/message .                      Attempt the link
ln: failed to create hard link './message' => '/tmp/message': Invalid cross-device link
```

Large systems often have many partitions, both on physically attached local disks and on remotely mounted network filesystems. The hard-link restriction to the same filesystem is inconvenient, for example, if some files or directories must be moved to a new location, but old software uses a hard-coded file name for the old location.

To get around this restriction, 4.2 BSD introduced *symbolic links*. A symbolic link (also called a *soft link*) is a special kind of file (just as a directory is a special kind of file). The contents of the file are the *pathname* of the file being "pointed to." All modern Unix systems, including Linux, provide symbolic links; indeed, they are now part of POSIX.

Symbolic links may refer to any file anywhere on the system. They may also refer to directories. They can do so using absolute or relative pathnames. This makes it easy to move directories from place to place, with a symbolic link left behind in the original location pointing to the new location.

When processing a file name, the system notices symbolic links and instead performs the action on the pointed-to file or directory. Symbolic links are created with the `-s` option to `ln`:

```
$ /bin/pwd                                           Where are we
/home/arnold                                         On a different filesystem
$ ln -s /tmp/message ./hello                         Create a symbolic link
$ cat hello                                          Use it
Hi, how ya doin' ?
$ ls -l hello                                        Show information about it
lrwxrwxrwx    1 arnold   devel      12 May  4 16:41 hello -> /tmp/message
```

The file pointed to by the link need not exist. The system detects this at runtime and acts appropriately:

```
$ rm /tmp/message                                    Remove pointed-to file
$ cat ./hello                                        Attempt to use it by the soft link
cat: ./hello: No such file or directory
$ echo hi again > hello                              Create new file contents
$ ls -l /tmp/message                                 Show pointed-to file info ...
-rw-r--r--    1 arnold   devel       9 May  4 16:45 /tmp/message
$ cat /tmp/message                                   ... and contents
hi again
```

Symbolic links are created with the `symlink()` system call:

```
#include <unistd.h>                                                    POSIX

int symlink(const char *oldpath, const char *newpath);
```

The `oldpath` argument names the pointed-to file or directory, and `newpath` is the name of the symbolic link to be created. The return value is `0` on success and `-1` on error; see your *symlink*(2) manpage for the possible `errno` values.

Symbolic links have their disadvantages:

- They take up extra disk space, requiring a separate inode and data block. Hard links take up only a directory slot.

- They add overhead. The kernel has to work harder to resolve a pathname containing symbolic links.
- They can introduce "loops." Consider the following:

```
$ rm -f a b                                  Make sure 'a' and 'b' don't exist
$ ln -s a b                                  Symlink old file 'a' to new file 'b'
$ ln -s b a                                  Symlink old file 'b' to new file 'a'
$ cat a                                      What happens?
cat: a: Too many levels of symbolic links
```

  The kernel has to be able to detect this case and produce an error message.
- They are easy to break. If you move the pointed-to file to a different location or rename it, the symbolic link is no longer valid. This can't happen with a hard link.

5.2 Creating and Removing Directories

Creating and removing directories is straightforward. The two system calls are `mkdir()` and `rmdir()`, respectively:

```
#include <sys/types.h>                                   POSIX
#include <sys/stat.h>

int mkdir(const char *pathname, mode_t mode);

#include <unistd.h>                                      POSIX

int rmdir(const char *pathname);
```

Both return `0` on success and `-1` on error, with `errno` set appropriately. For `mkdir()`, the `mode` argument represents the permissions to be applied to the directory. It is completely analogous to the `mode` arguments for `creat()` and `open()` discussed in Section 4.6, "Creating Files," page 101.

These system calls were added in 4.2 BSD for the same atomicity reasons as discussed earlier for `rename()` (see Section 5.1.4, "File Renaming," page 117).

Both functions handle the `.` and `..` in the directory being created or removed. A directory must be empty before it can be removed; `errno` is set to `ENOTEMPTY` if the directory isn't empty. (In this case, "empty" means the directory contains only `.` [dot] and `..` [dot-dot].)

New directories, like all files, are assigned a group ID number. Unfortunately, how this works is complicated. We delay discussion until Section 11.4.1, "Default Group for New Files and Directories," page 391.

Both functions work *one directory level at a time*. If `/somedir` exists and `/somedir/sub1` does not, '`mkdir("/somedir/sub1/sub2")`' fails. Each component in a long pathname has to be created individually (thus the `-p` option to the `mkdir` command—see *mkdir*(1)).

Also, if `pathname` ends with a `/` character, `mkdir()` and `rmdir()` will fail on some systems and succeed on others. The following program, `ch-fileinfo-trymkdir.c`, demonstrates both aspects:

```
/* ch-fileinfo-trymkdir.c --- Demonstrate mkdir() behavior.
                              Courtesy of Nelson H. F. Beebe. */

#include <stdio.h>              // for printf(), etc.
#include <errno.h>              // for errno
#include <stdlib.h>             // for EXIT_SUCCESS
#include <string.h>             // for strerror()
#include <sys/types.h>          // for mode_t type
#include <sys/stat.h>           // for mkdir()

/* do_test --- test the results from mkdir(2) */

void
do_test(const char *path)
{
    int retcode;

    errno = 0;
    retcode = mkdir(path, 0755);
    printf("mkdir(\"%s\") returns %d: errno = %d [%s]\n",
            path, retcode, errno, strerror(errno));
}

/* main --- run the tests */

int
main(void)
{
    do_test("/tmp/t1/t2/t3/t4");            Attempt creation in subdirs
    do_test("/tmp/t1/t2/t3");
    do_test("/tmp/t1/t2");
    do_test("/tmp/t1");

    do_test("/tmp/u1");                     Make subdirs
    do_test("/tmp/u1/u2");
    do_test("/tmp/u1/u2/u3");
    do_test("/tmp/u1/u2/u3/u4");

    do_test("/tmp/v1/");                    How is trailing '/' handled?
    do_test("/tmp/v1/v2/");
    do_test("/tmp/v1/v2/v3/");
    do_test("/tmp/v1/v2/v3/v4/");
```

```

    return (EXIT_SUCCESS);
}
```

Here are the results under GNU/Linux:

```
$ ch-fileinfo-trymkdir
mkdir("/tmp/t1/t2/t3/t4") returns -1: errno = 2 [No such file or directory]
mkdir("/tmp/t1/t2/t3") returns -1: errno = 2 [No such file or directory]
mkdir("/tmp/t1/t2") returns -1: errno = 2 [No such file or directory]
mkdir("/tmp/t1") returns 0: errno = 0 [Success]
mkdir("/tmp/u1") returns 0: errno = 0 [Success]
mkdir("/tmp/u1/u2") returns 0: errno = 0 [Success]
mkdir("/tmp/u1/u2/u3") returns 0: errno = 0 [Success]
mkdir("/tmp/u1/u2/u3/u4") returns 0: errno = 0 [Success]
mkdir("/tmp/v1/") returns 0: errno = 0 [Success]
mkdir("/tmp/v1/v2/") returns 0: errno = 0 [Success]
mkdir("/tmp/v1/v2/v3/") returns 0: errno = 0 [Success]
mkdir("/tmp/v1/v2/v3/v4/") returns 0: errno = 0 [Success]
```

Note how GNU/Linux accepts a trailing slash. Not all systems do.

5.3 Reading Directories

On the original Unix systems, reading directory contents was easy. A program opened the directory with `open()` and read binary `struct direct` structures directly, 16 bytes at a time. The following fragment of code is from the V7 `rmdir` program,[3] lines 60–74; it shows the check for the directory being empty:

```
60  if((fd = open(name,0)) < 0) {
61      fprintf(stderr, "rmdir: %s unreadable\n", name);
62      ++Errors;
63      return;
64  }
65  while(read(fd, (char *)&dir, sizeof dir) == sizeof dir) {
66      if(dir.d_ino == 0) continue;
67      if(!strcmp(dir.d_name, ".") || !strcmp(dir.d_name, ".."))
68          continue;
69      fprintf(stderr, "rmdir: %s not empty\n", name);
70      ++Errors;
71      close(fd);
72      return;
73  }
74  close(fd);
```

[3] See `/usr/src/cmd/rmdir.c` in the V7 distribution. A copy is included in the book's GitHub repository.

Line 60 opens the directory for reading (a second argument of `0`, equal to `O_RDONLY`). Line 65 reads the `struct direct`. Line 66 is the check for an empty directory slot; that is, one with an inode number of `0`. Lines 67 and 68 check for `.` (dot) and `..` (dot-dot). Upon reaching line 69, we know that some other file name has been seen and, therefore, that the directory isn't empty.

(The test '`!strcmp(s1, s2)`' is a shorter way of saying '`strcmp(s1, s2) == 0`'—that is, testing that the strings are equal. For what it's worth, we consider the '`!strcmp(s1, s2)`' form to be poor style. As Henry Spencer once said, "`strcmp()` is not a Boolean!")

When 4.2 BSD introduced a new filesystem format that allowed longer file names and provided better performance, it also introduced several new functions to provide a directory-reading abstraction. This suite of functions is usable no matter what the underlying filesystem and directory organization are. The basic parts of it are what is standardized by POSIX, and programs using it are portable across GNU/Linux and Unix systems.

5.3.1 Basic Directory Reading

Directory entries are represented by a `struct dirent` (*not* the same as the V7 `struct direct`!):

```
struct dirent {
    ...
    ino_t d_ino;              /* XSI extension --- see text */
    char  d_name[...];        /* See text on the size of this array */
    ...
};
```

For portability, POSIX specifies only the `d_name` field, which is a zero-terminated array of bytes representing the file name part of the directory entry. POSIX does provide the `d_ino` field as an XSI extension. The size of `d_name` is not specified by the standard, other than to say that there may be at most `NAME_MAX` bytes before the terminating zero. (`NAME_MAX` is defined in `<limits.h>`.)

In practice, since file names can be of variable length and `NAME_MAX` is usually fairly large (like 255), the `struct dirent` contains additional members that aid in the bookkeeping of variable-length directory entries on disk. These additional members are not relevant for everyday code.

The following functions provide the directory-reading interface:

```
#include <sys/types.h>                                    POSIX
#include <dirent.h>

DIR *opendir(const char *name);          Open a directory for reading
struct dirent *readdir(DIR *dir);        Return one struct dirent at a time
int closedir(DIR *dir);                  Close an open directory
void rewinddir(DIR *dirp);               Return to the front of a directory
```

The `DIR` type is analogous to the `FILE` type in `<stdio.h>`. It is an *opaque type*, meaning that application code is not supposed to know what's inside it; its contents are for use by the other directory routines. If opendir() returns NULL, the named directory could not be opened for reading and errno is set to indicate the error.

Once you have an open DIR * variable, it can be used to retrieve a pointer to a struct dirent representing the next directory entry. readdir() returns NULL upon end-of-file or error.

Finally, closedir() is analogous to the fclose() function in <stdio.h>; it closes the open DIR * variable. The rewinddir() function can be used to start over at the beginning of a directory.

With these routines in hand (or at least in the C library), we can write a simple catdir program that "cats" the contents of a directory. Such a program is presented in ch-fileinfo-catdir.c:

```
1  /* ch-fileinfo-catdir.c --- Demonstrate opendir(), readdir(), closedir(). */
2
3  #include <stdio.h>              /* for printf() etc. */
4  #include <errno.h>              /* for errno */
5  #include <string.h>             /* for strerror() */
6  #include <sys/types.h>          /* for system types */
7  #include <dirent.h>             /* for directory functions */
8
9  char *myname;
10 int process(char *dir);
11
12 /* main --- loop over directory arguments */
13
14 int
15 main(int argc, char **argv)
16 {
17     int i;
18     int errs = 0;
19
20     myname = argv[0];
21
22     if (argc == 1)
23         errs = process(".");    /* default to current directory */
24     else
25         for (i = 1; i < argc; i++)
26             errs += process(argv[i]);
27
28     return (errs != 0);
29 }
```

This program is quite similar to ch-fileio-cat.c (see Section 4.2, "Presenting a Basic Program Structure," page 79); the main() function is almost identical. The primary difference is that it defaults to using the current directory if there are no arguments (lines 22–23):

```
31 /*
32  * process --- do something with the directory, in this case,
33  *             print inode/name pairs on standard output.
34  *             Returns 0 if all ok, 1 otherwise.
35  */
36
37 int
38 process(char *dir)
39 {
40     DIR *dp;
41     struct dirent *ent;
42
43     if ((dp = opendir(dir)) == NULL) {
44         fprintf(stderr, "%s: %s: cannot open for reading: %s\n",
45                 myname, dir, strerror(errno));
46         return 1;
47     }
48
49     errno = 0;
50     while ((ent = readdir(dp)) != NULL)
51         printf("%8ld %s\n", ent->d_ino, ent->d_name);
52
53     if (errno != 0) {
54         fprintf(stderr, "%s: %s: reading directory entries: %s\n",
55                 myname, dir, strerror(errno));
56         return 1;
57     }
58
59     if (closedir(dp) != 0) {
60         fprintf(stderr, "%s: %s: closedir: %s\n",
61                 myname, dir, strerror(errno));
62         return 1;
63     }
64
65     return 0;
66 }
```

The `process()` function does all the work, and the majority of it is error-checking code. The heart of the function is lines 50 and 51:

```
while ((ent = readdir(dp)) != NULL)
    printf("%8ld %s\n", ent->d_ino, ent->d_name);
```

This loop reads directory entries, one at a time, until `readdir()` returns `NULL`. The loop body prints the inode number and file name of each entry. Here's what happens when the program is run:

```
$ ch-fileinfo-catdir                Default to current directory
 9205291 14-extended.texi
 9205287 10-signals.texi
 9209448 part3.texi
 9208660 15-debugging.texi
 9207317 07-ls.texi
 9209450 progex.texi
 9207328 BB-caldera.texi
 9205286 .
 9205295 AA-21-days.texi
 ...
```

The output is not sorted in any way; it represents the linear contents of the directory. (We describe how to sort the directory contents in Section 6.2, "Sorting and Searching Functions," page 171.) Note that `.` and `..` aren't necessarily the first entries in the directory!

5.3.1.1 Portability Considerations

There are several portability considerations. First, as we just saw, you should not assume that the first two entries returned by `readdir()` will always be `.` (dot) and `..` (dot-dot). Many filesystems use directory organizations that are different from that of the original Unix design, and `.` and `..` could be in the middle of the directory or may not even be present.[4]

Second, the POSIX standard is silent about possible values for `d_ino`. It does say that the returned structures represent directory entries for files; this implies that empty slots are not returned by `readdir()`, and thus the GNU/Linux `readdir()` implementation doesn't bother returning entries when '`d_ino == 0`'; it continues to the next valid directory entry.

So, on GNU/Linux and Unix systems at least, it is unlikely that `d_ino` will ever be zero. However, it is best to avoid using this field entirely if you can.

Finally, some systems use `d_fileno` instead of `d_ino` inside the `struct dirent`. Be aware of this if you have to port directory-reading code to such systems.

Indirect System Calls

Don't try this at home, kids!
— Mr. Wizard

Many system calls, such as `open()`, `read()`, and `write()`, are meant to be called directly from user-level application code—in other words, from code that you, as a GNU/Linux developer, would write.

[4] GNU/Linux and other Unix-style operating systems are capable of mounting filesystems from many non-Unix operating systems, such as Microsoft FAT-32 and NTFS filesystems. Assumptions about Unix filesystems don't apply in such cases.

However, other system calls exist only to make it possible to implement higher-level, standard library functions and should *not* be called directly. The GNU/Linux `getdents()` system call is one such; it reads multiple directory entries into a buffer provided by the caller—in this case, the code that implements `readdir()`. The `readdir()` code then returns valid directory entries one at a time from the buffer, refilling the buffer as needed.

In current GLIBC versions, these for-library-use-only system calls often do not have user-callable functions. The original `getdents()` call is like this, although a newer `getdents64()` system call may be called directly. From the *getdents*(2) manpage:

```
NAME
       getdents, getdents64 - get directory entries
SYNOPSIS
       long getdents(unsigned int fd, struct linux_dirent *dirp,
                     unsigned int count);

       #define _GNU_SOURCE        /* See feature_test_macros(7) */
       #include <dirent.h>

       ssize_t getdents64(int fd, void *dirp, size_t count);

       Note: There is no glibc wrapper for getdents(); see NOTES.
```

Any system call whose manpage indicates that "there is no glibc wrapper" should not be called directly.

In the case of `getdents()`, many other Unix systems have a similar system call, sometimes with the same name, sometimes with a different name. Thus, trying to use these calls would only lead to a massive portability mess anyway; you're much better off in all cases using `readdir()`, whose interface is well defined, standard, and portable.

The 2024 POSIX standard adds a `posix_getdents()` call, which is different from Linux's `getdents()`. Nonetheless, we stand by our recommendation to just use `readdir()`; the API is considerably cleaner and easy to use.

5.3.1.2 Mapping between `DIR *` Objects and File Descriptors

POSIX provides two functions for translating between file descriptors and `DIR *` objects:

```
#include <dirent.h>                                    POSIX

int  dirfd(DIR *dp);
DIR *fdopendir(int fd);
```

`int dirfd(DIR *dp)`

Extract the underlying file descriptor from the open `DIR *` object `dp`. This works just like the `fileno()` function (or macro) from `<stdio.h>`. The underlying file descriptor may then be used with the regular system calls that work on file descriptors. `dirfd()` is

Table 5.1: Values for `d_type`

Name	Meaning
`DT_BLK`	Block device file.
`DT_CHR`	Character device file.
`DT_DIR`	Directory.
`DT_FIFO`	FIFO or named pipe.
`DT_LNK`	Symbolic link.
`DT_REG`	Regular file.
`DT_SOCK`	Socket.
`DT_UNKNOWN`	Unknown file type.
`DT_WHT`	Whiteout entry (BSD systems only).

often implemented as a macro. It was part of the original directory reading API defined by BSD Unix.

`DIR *fdopendir(int fd)`
: This function is like `opendir()`, but you hand it a file descriptor that was opened on a directory with `open()`. (You can `open()` a directory and attempt to read the directory entries directly, but it's messy, as was pointed out earlier, in the sidebar "Indirect System Calls," page 127.)

Once you have used `fdopendir()` to obtain a `DIR *`, you should use `closedir()` to close it; doing so closes the underlying original file descriptor.

5.3.1.3 Linux and BSD Directory Entries

Although we said that you should only use the `d_ino` and `d_name` members of the `struct dirent`, it's worth knowing about the `d_type` member in the BSD and Linux `struct dirent`. This is an `unsigned char` value that stores the type of the file named by the directory entry:

```
struct dirent {
    ...
    ino_t d_ino;                /* As before */
    char  d_name[...];          /* As before */
    unsigned char d_type;       /* Linux and modern BSD */
    ...
};
```

`d_type` can have any of the values described in Table 5.1.

Knowing the file's type just by reading the directory entry is very handy; it can save a possibly expensive `stat()` system call. (The `stat()` call is described shortly, in Section 5.4.2, "Retrieving File Information," page 131.)

5.3.2 BSD Directory Positioning Functions

Occasionally, it's useful to mark the current position in a directory so you can return to it later. For example, you might be writing code that traverses a directory tree and wish to recursively enter each subdirectory as you come across it. (How to distinguish files from directories is discussed in the next section.) For this reason, the original BSD interface included two additional routines:

```
#include <dirent.h>                                    POSIX XSI

long telldir(DIR *dir);                   Return current position
void seekdir(DIR *dir, long offset);      Move to given position
```

These routines are similar to the `ftell()` and `fseek()` functions in `<stdio.h>`. They return the current position in a directory and set the current position to a previously retrieved value, respectively.

These routines are included in the XSI part of the POSIX standard, since they make sense only for directories that are implemented with linear storage of directory entries.

Besides the assumptions made about the underlying directory structure, these routines are riskier to use than the simple directory-reading routines. This is because the contents of a directory might be changing dynamically: as files are added to or removed from a directory, the operating system adjusts the contents of the directory. Since directory entries are of variable length, it may be that the absolute offset saved at an earlier time no longer represents the start of a directory entry! Thus we recommend that you don't use these functions unless you have to.

5.4 Obtaining Information about Files

Reading a directory to retrieve file names is only half the battle. Once you have a file name, you need to know how to retrieve the other information associated with the file, such as the file's type, its permissions, its owner, and so on.

5.4.1 Linux File Types

Linux (and Unix) supports the following kinds of file types:

Regular files
: As the name implies; used for data, executable programs, and anything else you might like. In an '`ls -l`' listing, they show up with a '`-`' in the first character of the permissions (mode) field.

Directories
: Special files for associating file names with inodes. In an '`ls -l`' listing, they show up with a `d` in the first character of the permissions field.

Symbolic links
: As described earlier in the chapter. In an '`ls -l`' listing, they show up with an `l` (letter "ell," not numeral "one") in the first character of the permissions field.

Devices

Files representing both physical hardware devices and software pseudo-devices. There are two kinds:

Block devices

Devices on which I/O happens in chunks of some fixed physical record size, such as disk drives and tape drives. Access to such devices goes through the kernel's buffer cache. In an '`ls -l`' listing, they show up with a `b` in the first character of the permissions field.

Character devices

Also known as *raw* devices. Originally, character devices were those on which I/O happened a few bytes at a time, such as terminals. However, the character device is also used for direct I/O to block devices such as tapes and disks, bypassing the buffer cache.[5] In an '`ls -l`' listing, they show up with a `c` in the first character of the permissions field.

Named pipes

Also known as *FIFOs* ("first-in first-out") files. These special files act like pipes—data written into them by one program can be read by another; no data go to or from the disk. FIFOs are created with the `mkfifo` command; they are discussed in Section 9.3.2, "FIFOs," page 306. In an '`ls -l`' listing, they show up with a `p` in the first character of the permissions field.

Sockets

Similar in purpose to named pipes,[6] they are managed with the socket interprocess communication (IPC) system calls, discussed in Chapter 14, "Sockets and Basic Networking," page 473. In an '`ls -l`' listing, they show up with an `s` in the first character of the permissions field.

5.4.2 Retrieving File Information

Three system calls return information about files:

```
#include <sys/types.h>                                          POSIX
#include <sys/stat.h>
#include <unistd.h>

int stat(const char *file_name, struct stat *buf);
int fstat(int filedes, struct stat *buf);
int lstat(const char *file_name, struct stat *buf);
```

The `stat()` function accepts a pathname and returns information about the given file. It *follows* symbolic links; that is, when applied to a symbolic link, `stat()` returns information

[5]Linux uses the block device for disks exclusively. Other systems use both.

[6]Named pipes and sockets were developed independently by the System V and BSD Unix groups, respectively. As Unix systems reconverged, both kinds of files became universally available.

about the pointed-to file, not about the link itself. For those times when you want to know if a file is a symbolic link, use the `lstat()` function instead; it does not follow symbolic links.

The `fstat()` function retrieves information about an already open file. It is particularly useful for file descriptors `0`, `1`, and `2` (standard input, output, and error), which are already open when a process starts up. However, it can be applied to any open file. (An open file descriptor will never relate to a symbolic link; make sure you understand why.)

The value passed in as the second parameter should be the address of a `struct stat`, declared in `<sys/stat.h>`. As with the `struct dirent`, the `struct stat` contains at least the following members:

```
struct stat {
    ...
    dev_t           st_dev;     /* device */
    ino_t           st_ino;     /* inode */
    mode_t          st_mode;    /* type and protection */
    nlink_t         st_nlink;   /* number of hard links */
    uid_t           st_uid;     /* user ID of owner */
    gid_t           st_gid;     /* group ID of owner */
    dev_t           st_rdev;    /* device type (block or character device) */
    off_t           st_size;    /* total size, in bytes */
    blksize_t       st_blksize; /* blocksize for filesystem I/O */
    blkcnt_t        st_blocks;  /* number of blocks allocated */
    struct timespec st_atim;    /* time of last access */
    struct timespec st_mtim;    /* time of last modification */
    struct timespec st_ctim;    /* time of last inode change */
    ...
};
```

(The layout may be different on different architectures.) This structure uses a number of `typedef`'d types. Although they are all (typically) integer types, the use of specially defined types allows them to have different sizes on different systems. This keeps user-level code that uses them portable. Here is a fuller description of each field:

`st_dev`
: The device for a mounted filesystem. Each mounted filesystem has a unique value for `st_dev`. (Filesystems and mounting are discussed in Chapter 8, "Filesystems and Directory Walks," page 221.)

`st_ino`
: The file's inode number within the filesystem. The (`st_dev`, `st_ino`) pair *uniquely* identifies the file.

`st_mode`
: The file's type and its permissions encoded together in one field. We will shortly see how to extract this information.

`st_nlink`
: The number of hard links to the file (the link count). This can be zero if the file was unlinked after being opened.

`st_uid`
: The file's UID (owner number).

`st_gid`
: The file's GID (group number).

`st_rdev`
: The device type if the file is a block or character device. `st_rdev` encodes information about the device. We will shortly see how to extract this information. This field has no meaning if the file is not a block or character device.

`st_size`
: The logical size of the file. As mentioned in Section 4.5, "Random Access: Moving Around within a File," page 96, a file may have holes in it, in which case the size may not reflect the true amount of storage space that it occupies.

`st_blksize`
: The "block size" of the file. This represents the preferred size of a data block for I/O to or from the file. This is almost always larger than a physical disk sector. For the Linux `ext4` filesystem, this value is 4,096.

`st_blocks`
: The number of "blocks" used by the file. On Linux, this is in units of 512-byte blocks. On other systems, the size of a block may be different; check your local *stat*(2) manpage. (This number comes from the `DEV_BSIZE` constant in `<sys/param.h>`. This constant isn't standardized, but it is fairly widely used on Unix systems.)

: The number of blocks may be more than '`st_size / 512`'; besides the data blocks, a filesystem may use additional blocks to store the locations of the data blocks. This is particularly necessary for large files.

`st_atim`
: The file's access time—that is, the last time the file's data was read.

`st_mtim`
: The file's modification time—that is, the last time the file's data was written or truncated.

`st_ctim`
: The file's inode change time. This indicates the last time the file's metadata changed, such as the permissions or the owner.

The `struct timespec` type used for the `st_atim`, `st_mtim`, and `st_ctim` fields represents dates and times. The last three time-related values are sometimes termed *timestamps*. The `struct timespec` structure, and other time-related types, are defined in the `<time.h>` header file. POSIX says that it has at least the following fields:

```
struct timespec {
    ...
    time_t  tv_sec;   /* seconds */
    long    tv_nsec;  /* nanoseconds */
    ...
};
```

Briefly, the `time_t` type represents "seconds since the Epoch." The *Epoch* is the "beginning of time" for computer systems. GNU/Linux and Unix use midnight, January 1, 1970, UTC,[7] as the Epoch. Microsoft Windows systems use midnight, January 1, 1980 (local time, apparently), as the Epoch.

The original Unix (and POSIX) `struct stat` had the following timestamps:

```
    ...
    time_t      st_atime;     /* time of last access */
    time_t      st_mtime;     /* time of last modification */
    time_t      st_ctime;     /* time of last inode change */
    ...
```

For source code compatibility with older code, POSIX requires the following macros:

```
#define st_atime st_atim.tv_sec
#define st_mtime st_mtim.tv_sec
#define st_ctime st_ctim.tv_sec
```

Further discussion of how to use a `time_t` value is delayed until Section 6.1, "Times and Dates," page 155. Similar to `time_t`, the `uid_t` and `gid_t` types represent user and group ID numbers, which are discussed in Section 6.3, "User and Group Names," page 190. Most of the other types are not of general interest.

NOTE

The `st_ctim` field is *not* the file's "creation time"! There is no such thing in a Linux or Unix system. Some early documentation referred to the (original) `st_ctime` field as the creation time. This was a misguided effort to simplify the presentation of the file metadata.

[7] UTC is a language-independent acronym for Coordinated Universal Time. Older code (and sometimes older people) refers to this as "Greenwich Mean Time" (GMT), which is the time in Greenwich, England. When time zones came into widespread use, Greenwich was chosen as the location to which all other time zones are relative, either behind it or ahead of it.

5.4.3 Linux Only: Specifying Higher-Precision File Times

As we just saw, POSIX mandates nanosecond resolution on the file times. Standard conforming code would thus use something like `sbuf.st_mtim.tv_nsec` to get the nanoseconds part of the timestamp.

Before this standardization, the Linux kernel supplied three additional fields in the `struct stat` giving nanosecond resolution on the file times:

`st_atime_nsec`	The nanoseconds component of the file's access time.
`st_mtime_nsec`	The nanoseconds component of the file's modification time.
`st_ctime_nsec`	The nanoseconds component of the file's inode change time.

You can still use these fields, but doing so is not portable and not recommended. We mention them so that you'll know what they are if you encounter them in old code.

5.4.4 Determining File Type

Recall that the `st_mode` field encodes both the file's type and its permissions. `<sys/stat.h>` defines a number of macros that determine the file's type. In particular, these macros return true or false when applied to the `st_mode` field. The macros correspond to each of the file types described earlier. Assume that the following code has been executed:

```
struct stat stbuf;
char filename[PATH_MAX];    /* PATH_MAX is from <limits.h> */

... fill in filename with a file name ...
if (stat(filename, & stbuf) < 0) {
    /* handle error */
}
```

Once `stbuf` has been filled in by the system, the following macros can be called, being passed `stbuf.st_mode` as the argument:

`S_ISREG(stbuf.st_mode)`
: Returns true if `filename` is a regular file.

`S_ISDIR(stbuf.st_mode)`
: Returns true if `filename` is a directory.

`S_ISCHR(stbuf.st_mode)`
: Returns true if `filename` is a character device. Devices are shortly discussed in more detail.

`S_ISBLK(stbuf.st_mode)`
: Returns true if `filename` is a block device.

`S_ISFIFO(stbuf.st_mode)`
: Returns true if `filename` is a FIFO.

`S_ISLNK(stbuf.st_mode)`
: Returns true if `filename` is a symbolic link. (This could never return true if `stat()` or `fstat()` were used instead of `lstat()`.)

`S_ISSOCK(stbuf.st_mode)`
: Returns true if `filename` is a socket.

NOTE

On GNU/Linux, these macros return `1` for true and `0` for false. However, on other systems, it's possible that they return an arbitrary nonzero value for true, instead of `1`. (POSIX specifies only nonzero versus zero.) Thus, you should always use these macros as stand-alone tests instead of testing the return value:

```
if (S_ISREG(stbuf.st_mode)) ...                Correct
if (S_ISREG(stbuf.st_mode) == 1) ...           Incorrect
```

Along with the macros, `<sys/stat.h>` provides two sets of bitmasks. One set is for testing permission, and the other set is for testing the type of a file. We saw the permission masks in Section 4.6, "Creating Files," page 101, when we discussed the `mode_t` type and values for `open()` and `creat()`. The bitmasks, their values for GNU/Linux, and their meanings are described in Table 5.2.

Several of these masks serve to isolate the different sets of bits encoded in the `st_mode` field:

- `S_IFMT` represents bits 12–15, which are where the different types of files are encoded.
- `S_IRWXU` represents bits 6–8, which are the user's permission (read, write, execute for User).
- `S_IRWXG` represents bits 3–5, which are the group's permission (read, write, execute for Group).
- `S_IRWXO` represents bits 0–2, which are the "other" permission (read, write, execute for Other).

The permission and file-type bits are depicted graphically in Figure 5.3.

The file-type masks are standardized primarily for compatibility with older code; they should not be used directly, because such code is less readable than the corresponding macros.

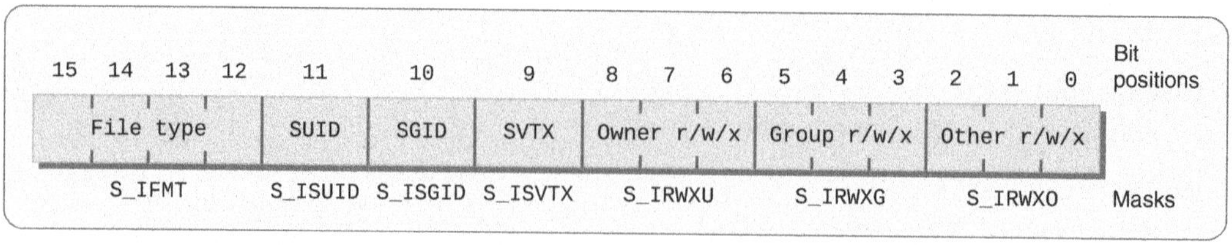

Figure 5.3: Permission and file-type bits

Table 5.2: POSIX file-type and permission bitmasks in <sys/stat.h>

Mask	Value	Meaning
S_IFMT	0170000	Bitmask for the file-type bitfields.
S_IFSOCK	0140000	Socket.
S_IFLNK	0120000	Symbolic link.
S_IFREG	0100000	Regular file.
S_IFBLK	0060000	Block device.
S_IFDIR	0040000	Directory.
S_IFCHR	0020000	Character device.
S_IFIFO	0010000	FIFO.
S_ISUID	0004000	Setuid bit.
S_ISGID	0002000	Setgid bit.
S_ISVTX	0001000	Sticky bit.
S_IRWXU	0000700	Mask for owner permissions.
S_IRUSR	0000400	Owner read permission.
S_IWUSR	0000200	Owner write permission.
S_IXUSR	0000100	Owner execute permission.
S_IRWXG	0000070	Mask for group permissions.
S_IRGRP	0000040	Group read permission.
S_IWGRP	0000020	Group write permission.
S_IXGRP	0000010	Group execute permission.
S_IRWXO	0000007	Mask for permissions for others.
S_IROTH	0000004	Other read permission.
S_IWOTH	0000002	Other write permission.
S_IXOTH	0000001	Other execute permission.

The macros are implemented, logically enough, with the masks, but that's irrelevant for user-level code.

The POSIX standard explicitly states that no new bitmasks will be standardized in the future and that tests for any additional kinds of file types that may be added will be available only as `S_IS`*xxx*`()` macros.

5.4.4.1 Device Information

Because it is meant to apply to non-Unix systems as well as Unix systems, the POSIX standard doesn't define the meaning for the `dev_t` type. However, it's worthwhile to know what's in a `dev_t`.

When `S_ISBLK(sbuf.st_mode)` or `S_ISCHR(sbuf.st_mode)` is true, then the device information is found in the `sbuf.st_rdev` field. Otherwise, this field does not contain any useful information.

Traditionally, Unix device files encode a *major* device number and a *minor* device number within the `dev_t` value. The major number distinguishes the device type, such as "disk drive" or "tape drive." Major numbers also distinguish among different types of devices, such as SSD disk versus USB disk. The minor number distinguishes the unit of that type, for example, the first disk or the second one. You can see these values with '`ls -l`':

```
$ ls -l /dev/sda*              Show numbers for first hard disk
brw-rw---- 1 root disk 8, 0 Dec  7 11:12 /dev/sda
brw-rw---- 1 root disk 8, 1 Dec  7 11:13 /dev/sda1

$ ls -l /dev/null              Show info for /dev/null, too
crw-rw-rw- 1 root root 1, 3 Dec  2 19:45 /dev/null
```

Instead of the file size, `ls` displays the major and minor numbers. In the case of the hard disk, `/dev/sda` represents the whole drive. `/dev/sda1` is the first partition within the drive. Were there additional partitions, they'd be numbered `/dev/sda2` and so on. They all share the same major device number (`8`) but have different minor device numbers.

Note that the disk devices are block devices, whereas `/dev/null` is a character device. Block devices and character devices are separate entities; even if a character device and a block device share the same major device number, they are not necessarily related.

The major and minor device numbers can be extracted from a `dev_t` value with the `major()` and `minor()` functions defined in `<sys/sysmacros.h>`:

```
#include <sys/types.h>                                    Common
#include <sys/sysmacros.h>

int major(dev_t dev);                         Major device number
int minor(dev_t dev);                         Minor device number
dev_t makedev(int major, int minor);          Create a dev_t value
```

(Some systems implement them as macros.)

The `makedev()` function goes the other way; it takes separate major and minor values and encodes them into a `dev_t` value. Its use is otherwise beyond the scope of this book; the morbidly curious should see *mknod*(2).

The following program, `ch-fileinfo-devnum.c`, shows how to use the `stat()` system call, the file-type test macros, and finally, the `major()` and `minor()` macros:

```
/* ch-fileinfo-devnum.c --- Demonstrate stat(), major(), minor(). */

#include <stdio.h>
#include <errno.h>
#include <stdlib.h>
#include <string.h>
#include <sys/types.h>
#include <sys/stat.h>
#include <sys/sysmacros.h>

int
main(int argc, char **argv)
{
```

```
    struct stat sbuf;
    char *devtype;

    if (argc != 2) {
        fprintf(stderr, "usage: %s path\n", argv[0]);
        exit(1);
    }

    if (stat(argv[1], & sbuf) < 0) {
        fprintf(stderr, "%s: stat: %s\n", argv[1], strerror(errno));
        exit(1);
    }

    if (S_ISCHR(sbuf.st_mode))
        devtype = "char";
    else if (S_ISBLK(sbuf.st_mode))
        devtype = "block";
    else {
        fprintf(stderr, "%s is not a block or character device\n", argv[1]);
        exit(1);
    }

    printf("%s: major: %d, minor: %d\n", devtype,
            major(sbuf.st_rdev), minor(sbuf.st_rdev));

    exit(0);
}
```

Here is what happens when the program is run:

```
$ ch-fileinfo-devnum /tmp                    Try a nondevice
/tmp is not a block or character device
$ ch-fileinfo-devnum /dev/null               Character device
char: major: 1, minor: 3
$ ch-fileinfo-devnum /dev/sda1               Block device
block: major: 8, minor: 1
```

Fortunately, the output agrees with that of `ls`, giving us confidence[8] that we have indeed written correct code.

Reproducing the output of `ls` is all fine and good, but is it really useful? The answer is yes. Any application that works with file hierarchies must be able to distinguish among all the different types of files. Consider an archiver such as `tar` or `cpio`. It would be disastrous if such a program treated a disk device file as a regular file, attempting to read it and store its contents in an archive! Or consider `find`, which can perform arbitrary actions based on the type and other attributes of files it encounters. (`find` is a complicated program; see *find*(1) if

[8]The technical term is *the warm fuzzies*.

you're not familiar with it.) Or even something as simple as a disk space accounting package has to distinguish regular files from everything else.

5.4.4.2 The V7 cat Revisited

In Section 4.4.4, "Example: Unix `cat`," page 94, we promised to return to the V7 `cat` program to review its use of the `stat()` system call. The first group of lines that used it were these:

```
31      fstat(fileno(stdout), &statb);
32      statb.st_mode &= S_IFMT;
33      if (statb.st_mode!=S_IFCHR && statb.st_mode!=S_IFBLK) {
34          dev = statb.st_dev;
35          ino = statb.st_ino;
36      }
```

This code should now make sense. Line 31 calls `fstat()` on the standard output to fill in the `statb` structure. Line 32 throws away all the information in `statb.st_mode` except the file type, by ANDing the mode with the `S_IFMT` mask. Line 33 checks that the file being used for standard output is *not* a device file. In that case, the program saves the device and inode numbers in `dev` and `ino`. These values are then checked for each input file in lines 50–56:

```
50          fstat(fileno(fi), &statb);
51          if (statb.st_dev==dev && statb.st_ino==ino) {
52              fprintf(stderr, "cat: input %s is output\n",
53                 fflg?"-": *argv);
54              fclose(fi);
55              continue;
56          }
```

If an input file's `st_dev` and `st_ino` values match those of the output file, then `cat` complains and continues to the next file named on the command line.

The check is done unconditionally, even though `dev` and `ino` are set only if the output is not a device file. This works out OK, because of how those variables are declared:

```
17      int dev, ino = -1;
```

Since `ino` is initialized to `-1`, no valid inode number will ever be equal to it.[9] The declaration on line 17 is bad style, initializing `ino` but not `dev`. This isn't a problem, since the test on line 51 requires that both the device and inode be equal. (A good compiler will complain that `dev` is used without being initialized.)

Note also that neither call to `fstat()` is checked for errors. This too is sloppy, although less so; it is unlikely that `fstat()` will fail on a valid file descriptor.

The test for input file equals output file is done only for nondevice files. This makes it possible to use `cat` to copy input from device files to themselves, such as with terminals:

```
$ tty                                    Print current terminal device name
/dev/pts/3
```

[9] This statement was true for V7; there are no such guarantees on modern systems.

```
$ cat /dev/pts/3 > /dev/pts/3          Copy keyboard input to screen
this is a line of text                 Type in a line
this is a line of text                 cat repeats it
```

5.4.5 Working with Symbolic Links

In general, symbolic links act like hard links; file operations such as `open()` and `stat()` apply to the pointed-to file instead of to the symbolic link itself. However, there are times when it really is necessary to work with the symbolic link instead of with the file the link points to.

For this reason, the `lstat()` system call exists. It behaves exactly like `stat()`, but if the file being checked happens to be a symbolic link, then the information returned applies to the symbolic link, and not to the pointed-to file. Specifically:

- `S_ISLNK(sbuf.st_mode)` will be true.
- `sbuf.st_size` is the number of bytes used by the name of the pointed-to file.

We already saw that the `symlink()` system call creates a symbolic link. But given an existing symbolic link, how can we retrieve the name of the file it points to? (`ls` obviously can, so we ought to be able to also.)

Opening the link with `open()` in order to read it with `read()` won't work; `open()` follows the link to the pointed-to file. Symbolic links thus necessitate an additional system call, named `readlink()`:

```
#include <unistd.h>                                    POSIX

int readlink(const char *path, char *buf, size_t bufsiz);
```

`readlink()` places the contents of the symbolic link named by `path` into the buffer pointed to by `buf`. No more than `bufsiz` characters are copied. The return value is the number of characters placed in `buf` or `-1` if an error occurred. `readlink()` does *not* supply the trailing zero byte.

Note that if the buffer passed in to `readlink()` is too small, you will lose information; the full name of the pointed-to file won't be available. To properly use `readlink()`, your code should do the following:

1. Use `lstat()` to verify that you have a symbolic link.
2. Make sure that your buffer to hold the link contents is at least '`sbuf.st_size + 1`' bytes big; the '`+ 1`' is for the trailing zero byte to turn the buffer into a usable C string.
3. Call `readlink()`. It doesn't hurt to verify that the returned value is the same as `sbuf.st_size`.
4. Assign `'\0'` to the byte after the contents of the link, to make it into a C string.

Code to do all that would look something like this:

```
/* Error checking omitted for brevity */
int count;
```

```
char linkfile[PATH_MAX], realfile[PATH_MAX];  /* PATH_MAX is in <limits.h> */
strut stat sbuf;

... fill in linkfile with path to symbolic link of interest ...
lstat(linkfile, & sbuf);                      Get stat information
if (! S_ISLNK(sbuf.st_mode))                  Check that it's a symlink
    /* not a symbolic link, handle it */
if (sbuf.st_size + 1 > PATH_MAX)              Check buffer size
    /* handle buffer size problems */

count = readlink(linkfile, realfile, PATH_MAX);   Read the link
if (count != sbuf.st_size)
    /* something weird going on, handle it */

realfile[count] = '\0';                       Make it into a C string
```

This example uses fixed-size buffers for simplicity of presentation. Real code would use `malloc()` to allocate a buffer of the correct size since the fixed-size arrays might be too small. Example code that does just this can be found in the file `lib/xreadlink.c` from the GNU Coreutils 5.0 distribution.[10] It reads the contents of a symbolic link into storage allocated by `malloc()`. We show here just the function; most of the file is boilerplate definitions. Line numbers are relative to the start of the file:

```
55  /* Call readlink to get the symbolic link value of FILENAME.
56     Return a pointer to that NUL-terminated string in malloc'd storage.
57     If readlink fails, return NULL (caller may use errno to diagnose).
58     If realloc fails, or if the link value is longer than SIZE_MAX :-),
59     give a diagnostic and exit.  */
60
61  char *
62  xreadlink (char const *filename)
63  {
64    /* The initial buffer size for the link value.  A power of 2
65       detects arithmetic overflow earlier, but is not required.  */
66    size_t buf_size = 128;
67
68    while (1)
69      {
70        char *buffer = xmalloc (buf_size);
71        ssize_t link_length = readlink (filename, buffer, buf_size);
72
73        if (link_length < 0)
74          {
75            int saved_errno = errno;
```

[10] The current Coreutils code is somewhat more complicated, obscuring the issue we want to demonstrate.

```
76             free (buffer);
77             errno = saved_errno;
78             return NULL;
79           }
80 
81         if ((size_t) link_length < buf_size)
82           {
83             buffer[link_length] = 0;
84             return buffer;
85           }
86 
87         free (buffer);
88         buf_size *= 2;
89         if (SSIZE_MAX < buf_size || (SIZE_MAX / 2 < SSIZE_MAX && buf_size == 0))
90           xalloc_die ();
91       }
92 }
```

The function body consists of an infinite loop (lines 68–91), broken at line 84, which returns the allocated buffer. The loop starts by allocating an initial buffer (line 70) and reading the link (line 71). Lines 73–79 handle the error case, saving and restoring `errno` so that it can be used correctly by the calling code.

Lines 81–85 handle the "success" case, in which the length of the link's contents is smaller than the buffer size. In this case, the terminating zero is supplied (line 83) and then the buffer returned (line 84), breaking the infinite loop. This ensures that the entire link contents have been placed into the buffer, since `readlink()` has no way to indicate "insufficient space in buffer."

Lines 87–88 free the buffer and double the buffer size for the next try at the top of the loop. Lines 89–90 handle the case in which the link's size is too big: `buf_size` is greater than `SSIZE_MAX`, or `SSIZE_MAX` is larger than the value that can be represented in a signed integer of the same size as used to hold `SIZE_MAX` and `buf_size` has wrapped around to zero. (These are unlikely conditions, but strange things do happen.) If either condition is true, the program dies with an error message. Otherwise, the function continues around to the top of the loop to make another try at allocating a buffer and reading the link.

Some further explanation: the '`SIZE_MAX / 2 < SSIZE_MAX`' condition is true only on systems on which '`SIZE_MAX < 2 * SSIZE_MAX`'; we don't know of any, but only on such a system can `buf_size` wrap around to zero. Since in practice this condition can't be true, the compiler can optimize away the whole expression, including the following '`buf_size == 0`' test.

After reading this code, you might ask, "Why not use `lstat()` to retrieve the size of the symbolic link, allocate a buffer of the right size with `malloc()`, and be done?" Well, there are a number of reasons:[11]

- `lstat()` is a system call—it's best to avoid the overhead of making it since the contents of most symbolic links will fit in the initial buffer size of 128.

[11] Thanks to Jim Meyering for explaining the issues.

- Calling `lstat()` introduces a race condition: the link could change between the execution of `lstat()` and `readlink()`, forcing the need to iterate anyway.
- Some systems don't properly fill in the `st_size` member for symbolic links. (Sad, but true.) In a similar fashion, as we see in Section 8.4.2, "Getting the Current Directory: `getcwd()`," page 248, Linux provides special symbolic links under `/proc` whose `st_size` is zero, but for which `readlink()` does return valid content.

Finally, when the buffer isn't big enough, `xreadlink()` uses `free()` and `malloc()` with a bigger size, instead of `realloc()`, to avoid the useless copying that `realloc()` does. (The comment on line 58 is thus out of date, since `realloc()` isn't being used; this is fixed in the post-5.0 version of the Coreutils.)

5.5 Avoiding Race Conditions: `openat()` and Friends

Arguably, this section belongs in Chapter 4, "Files and File I/O," page 79. It's here because it discusses system calls similar to just about all of the other system calls described in this chapter.

Many of the standard system calls we've presented so far are subject to race conditions, similar to what we described earlier in Section 5.1.4, "File Renaming," page 117, relating to file renaming. To solve this problem, and for other reasons, POSIX introduced a number of variants of the traditional system calls that accept a file descriptor open on the directory of interest, the name of the file in that directory upon which to perform the operation, and possibly additional information and/or flags to control the operation. Let's look at one:

```
#include <sys/types.h>                              POSIX
#include <sys/stat.h>
#include <fcntl.h>

int openat(int dir_fd, const char *pathname, int flags);
int openat(int dir_fd, const char *pathname, int flags, mode_t mode);
```

The "at" in the name means that the operation happens at the open directory given in the first argument. The parameters for `openat()` are as follows:

`dir_fd`
: A file descriptor open upon the directory of interest. You obtain such a file descriptor by using `open()` to open the directory for reading, by using `openat()` on the parent directory, or by using `dirfd()` on the `DIR *` returned by `opendir()`. `dir_fd` may be the special value `AT_FDCWD`, in which case the process's current working directory is used.

`pathname`
: The name of the file within the directory to open. If `pathname` is absolute, `dir_fd` is ignored. If `pathname` is relative, then it's taken to be relative to the directory referred to by `dir_fd`, not the process's current working directory.

Table 5.3: Additional *XXX*at() system calls

execveat()	fstatat()	mknodat()	unlinkat()
faccessat()	futimesat()	readlinkat()	utimensat()
fchmodat()	linkat()	renameat()	
fchownat()	mkdirat()	symlinkat()	

`flags`
: The bitwise-OR of the flags that may be used with `open()`. See Table 4.3, and also see Table 4.7.

`mode`
: The file permissions, as with `open()` (see Table 4.7).

The *open*(2) manpage points out that `dir_fd` provides a stable reference to the directory, even if the directory is later renamed or removed, and that it also prevents the containing filesystem from being dismounted, as does an open file. (Mounting and unmounting filesystems hasn't been discussed yet; see Chapter 8, "Filesystems and Directory Walks," page 221.)

While we're discussing opening files, it's worth mentioning that Linux provides two additional interesting flags:

`O_PATH`
: Open the directory, returning a file descriptor that may be used with any of the *XXX*`at()` system calls but isn't good for much else.

`O_TMPFILE`
: Open a file using an anonymous inode in the filesystem containing `dir_fd`'s directory. In this case, `pathname` is ignored. The file starts out unlinked, so to speak, and its data will be released when the last open file descriptor for it is closed. The *open*(2) manpage shows sample code that may be used to link the anonymous file into a directory, using `linkat()`.

Table 5.3 lists the additional *XXX*`at()` system calls. They all follow the pattern shown earlier for `openat()`, so we don't bother to describe them in detail, instead referring you to their respective manpages.

5.6 Changing Ownership, Permission, and Modification Times

Several system calls let you change file-related information—in particular, the owner and group of a file, the file's permissions, and the file's access and modification times.

5.6.1 Changing File Ownership: `chown()`, `fchown()`, and `lchown()`

File ownership and group are changed with three similar system calls:

```
#include <sys/types.h>                                    POSIX
#include <unistd.h>

int chown(const char *path, uid_t owner, gid_t group);
int fchown(int fd, uid_t owner, gid_t group);
int lchown(const char *path, uid_t owner, gid_t group);
```

`chown()` works on a pathname argument, `fchown()` works on an open file, and `lchown()` works on symbolic links instead of on the files pointed to by symbolic links. In all other respects, the three calls work identically, returning `0` on success and `-1` on error.

It is noteworthy that one system call changes both the owner and group of a file. To change only the owner or only the group, pass in a value of `-1` for the ID number that is to be left unchanged.

While you might think that you could pass in the corresponding value from a previously retrieved `struct stat` for the file or file descriptor, that method is more error prone. There's a race condition: the owner or group could have changed between the call to `stat()` and the call to `chown()`.

You might wonder, "Why be able to change ownership of a symbolic link? The permissions and ownership on them don't matter." But what happens if a user leaves but all their files are still needed? It's necessary to be able to change the ownership on *all* the person's files to someone else, including symbolic links.

GNU/Linux systems normally do not permit ordinary (non-`root`) users to change the ownership of ("give away") their files. Changing the group to one of the user's groups is allowed, of course. The restriction on changing owners follows BSD systems, which also have this prohibition. The primary reason is that allowing users to give away files can defeat disk accounting. Consider a scenario like this:

```
$ mkdir mywork                        Make a directory
$ chmod go-rwx mywork                 Set permissions to drwx------
$ cd mywork                           Go there
$ myprogram > large_data_file         Create a large file
$ chmod ugo+rw large_data_file        Set permissions to -rw-rw-rw-
$ chown otherguy large_data_file      Give file away to otherguy
```

In this example, `large_data_file` now belongs to user `otherguy`. The original user can continue to read and write the file, because of the permissions. But `otherguy` will be charged for the disk space it occupies. However, since it's in a directory that belongs to the original user, which cannot be accessed by `otherguy`, there is no way for `otherguy` to remove the file.

If you think about the context in which the BSD Unix systems developed, which were large time-sharing systems with multiple students and disk quotas, then these restrictions make sense. Although most modern desktop and laptop GNU/Linux systems have only one user, multiple users are still allowed, and, for example, system sharing within a family is totally reasonable.

Some legacy Unix systems do allow users to give away files. (Setuid and setgid files have the corresponding bit removed when the owner is changed.) This can be a particular problem when files are extracted from a `.tar` or `.cpio` archive; the extracted files end up belonging to the UID or GID encoded in the archive. On such systems, the `tar` and `cpio` programs have options that prevent this, but it's important to know that `chown()`'s behavior does vary across systems.

We will see in Section 6.3, "User and Group Names," page 190, how to relate user and group names to their corresponding numeric values.

5.6.2 Changing Permissions: `chmod()` and `fchmod()`

After all the discussion in Chapter 4, "Files and File I/O," page 79, and in this chapter, changing permissions is almost anticlimactic. It's done with one of two system calls, `chmod()` or `fchmod()`:

```
#include <sys/types.h>                                    POSIX
#include <sys/stat.h>

int chmod(const char *path, mode_t mode);
int fchmod(int fd, mode_t mode);
```

`chmod()` works on a pathname argument, and `fchmod()` works on an open file. (There is no `lchmod()` call in POSIX, since the system ignores the permission settings on symbolic links. Some systems do have such a call, though.) As with most other system calls, these return `0` on success and `-1` on failure. Only the file's owner or `root` can change a file's permissions.

The `mode` value is created in the same way as for `open()` and `creat()`, as discussed in Section 4.6, "Creating Files," page 101. See also Table 5.2, which lists the permission constants.

The system will not allow setting the setgid bit (`S_ISGID`) if the group of the file does not match the effective group ID of the process or one of its supplemental groups. (We have not yet discussed these issues in detail; see Section 11.1.1, "Real and Effective IDs," page 383.) Of course, this check does not apply to `root` or to code running as `root`.

5.6.3 Using `fchown()` and `fchmod()` for Security

The original Unix systems had only `chown()` and `chmod()` system calls. However, on heavily loaded systems, these system calls are subject to race conditions, by which an attacker could arrange to replace the file whose ownership or permissions were being changed with a different file.

However, once a file is opened, race conditions aren't an issue anymore. A program can use `stat()` on a pathname to obtain information about the file. If the information is what's expected, then after the file is opened, `fstat()` can verify that the file is the same (by comparing the `st_dev` and `st_ino` fields of the "before" and "after" `struct stat` structures).

Once the program knows that the files are the same, the ownership or permissions can then be changed with `fchown()` or `fchmod()`.

Extending this reasoning led to the later introduction of `openat()` and the various other *XXX*`at()` system calls (see Table 5.3).

5.6.4 Changing Timestamps: `utime()` and Successors

A number of system calls are standardized by POSIX for changing the access and modification times of a file. We begin the discussion by looking at the original Unix system calls, and then move on to the newer ones, which provide greater resolution in the timestamps that they use.

5.6.4.1 Early Unix: `utime()`

The original `struct stat` structure contained three fields of type `time_t`:

`st_atime`
: The time the file was last accessed (read).

`st_mtime`
: The time the file was last modified (written).

`st_ctime`
: The time the file's inode was last changed (for example, renamed).

We saw earlier that a `time_t` value represents time in "seconds since the Epoch" and that `time_t` values are sometimes referred to as *timestamps*. In Section 6.1, "Times and Dates," page 155, we look at how these values are obtained and how they're used. For now, it's enough to know what a `time_t` value is and that it represents seconds since the Epoch.

The `utime()` system call allows you to change a file's access and modification timestamps:

```
#include <sys/types.h>                                        Common
#include <utime.h>

int utime(const char *filename, struct utimbuf *buf);
```

A `struct utimbuf` looks like this:

```
struct utimbuf {
    time_t actime;  /* access time */
    time_t modtime; /* modification time */
};
```

If the call is successful, it returns `0`; otherwise, it returns `-1`. If `buf` is `NULL`, then the system sets both the access time and the modification time to the current time.

To change one time but not the other, you would use the original value from the `struct stat`. For example:

```
/* Error checking omitted for brevity */
struct stat sbuf;
struct utimbuf ut;
time_t now;
```

```
time(& now);                        Get current time of day, see next chapter
stat("/some/file", & sbuf);         Fill in sbuf
ut.actime = sbuf.st_atime;          Access time unchanged

ut.modtime = now - (24 * 60 * 60);  Set modtime to 24 hours ago

utime("/some/file", & ut);          Set the values
```

About now, you may be asking yourself, "Why would anyone want to change a file's access and modification times?" Good question.

To answer it, consider the case of a program that creates backup archives, such as `tar` or `cpio`. These programs have to read the contents of a file in order to archive them. Reading the file, of course, changes the file's access time.

However, that file might not have been read *by a human* in 10 years. Someone doing an '`ls -lu`', which displays the access time (instead of the default modification time), should see that the last time the file was read was 10 years ago. Thus, the backup program should save the original access and modification times, read the file in order to archive it, and then restore the original times with `utime()` (or better, with one of the additional calls we discuss shortly).

Similarly, consider the case of an archiving program *restoring* a file from an archive. The archive stores the file's original access and modification times. However, when a file is extracted from an archive to a newly created copy on disk, the new file has the current date and time of day for its access and modification times.

However, it's more useful if the newly created file *looks as if* it's the same age as the original file in the archive. Thus, the archiver needs to be able to set the access and modification times to those stored in the archive.

The `utime()` system call is no longer part of POSIX, but remains available in practice for compatibility with old code.

5.6.4.2 Microsecond Time Resolution: `utimes()`

Since modern systems provide clock granularity smaller than one second, over time additional functions were added for setting the timestamps with values of greater resolution than just one second.

The first of these is `utimes()` (note the final "s" in the name). This call gives you time resolution in microseconds:

```
#include <sys/time.h>                                            POSIX XSI

int utimes(const char *filename, const struct timeval tvp[2]);
```

The `tvp` argument should point to an array of two `struct timeval` structures; the values are used for the access and modification times, respectively. If `tvp` is `NULL`, then the system uses the current time of day. The `struct timeval` looks like this:

```
struct timeval {
    ...
    time_t        tv_sec;   /* seconds */
    suseconds_t   tv_usec;  /* microseconds */
    ...
};
```

POSIX marks this as a "legacy" function, meaning that it's standardized only to support old code and should not be used for new applications. The primary reason seems to be that there is no defined interface for *retrieving* file access and modification times that include the microseconds value; the original `struct stat` contained only `time_t` values, not `struct timeval` values, and the modern one contains `struct timespec` structures.

If you're thinking, "Gosh, there are so many time-related types!" you are correct. This is the result of evolution, as Unix systems moved from smaller systems to ever more powerful ones, with finer and finer clock resolutions.

5.6.4.3 Nanosecond Time Resolution: `futimens()` and `utimensat()`

Finally, we reach the current set of functions that work with timestamps of nanosecond resolution. We saw the definition of `struct timespec` earlier:

```
struct timespec {
    ...
    time_t  tv_sec;    /* seconds */
    long    tv_nsec;   /* nanoseconds */
    ...
};
```

The system calls we are about to describe use the newer model for specifying the file to be acted upon, whereby you pass a file descriptor open on the file, instead of the file name, or a file descriptor open on the directory containing the file (see Section 5.5, "Avoiding Race Conditions: `openat()` and Friends," page 144). The first call is `futimens()` ("file-utime-nanoseconds"):

```
#include <sys/stat.h>                                  POSIX

int futimens(int fd, const struct timespec times[2]);
```

The parameters are:

`fd`
: A file descriptor open on the file whose times are to be updated.

`const struct timespec times[2]`
: An array of `struct timespec` structures specifying the new time values. `times[0]` is used to update the access time, and `times[1]` is used for the modification time. Some special values may be used in the fields of the `struct timespec`, which we discuss momentarily. If `times` is `NULL` both values are set to the current time.

The next function works similarly, but provides additional control over the treatment of symbolic links. It's called `utimensat()` ("utime-nanosecond-at"):

```
#include <fcntl.h>                                    POSIX

int utimensat(int fd, const char *path,
              const struct timespec times[2], int flag);
```

The parameters are:

`fd`
: A file descriptor open on the directory containing the file whose times are to be updated. If `fd` has the special value `AT_FDCWD`, then the current directory is used.

`path`
: The name of the file within the given directory. An absolute pathname causes the value of `fd` to be ignored. A relative path is treated as relative to the current directory if `fd` is `AT_FDCWD`; otherwise it's relative to the directory upon which the file descriptor is open.

`const struct timespec times[2]`
: As described previously for `futimens()`.

`flag`
: This value should generally be set to zero. However, if the value is `AT_SYMLINK_NOFOLLOW` and the given file is a symbolic link, the system updates the times of the link, and *not* the times of the file pointed to by the link.

Two special values for the `tv_nsec` field of one or both of the `struct timespec` values modify the behavior of `futimens()` and `utimensat()`, as follows:

`UTIME_NOW`
: Set the relevant timestamp (access time or modified time) to the current time.

`UTIME_OMIT`
: Do not change the relevant timestamp.

When either of the special values are used, the corresponding `tv_sec` field is ignored.

5.7 Summary

- The file and directory hierarchy as seen by the user is one logical tree, rooted at `/`. It is made up of one or more storage partitions, each of which contains a filesystem. Within a filesystem, inodes store information about files (metadata), including the location of file data blocks.

- Directories make the association between file names and inodes. Conceptually, directory contents are just sequences of (inode, name) pairs. Each directory entry for a file is called a (hard) link, and files can have many links. Because they work only by inode number, hard links must all be on the same filesystem. Symbolic (soft) links are pointers to files or directories that work based on file name, not inode number, and thus are not restricted to being on the same filesystem.

- Hard links are created with link(), symbolic links are created with symlink(), links are removed with unlink(), and files are renamed (possibly being moved to another directory) with rename(). A file's data blocks are not reclaimed until the link count goes to zero and the last open file descriptor for the file is closed.

- Directories are created with mkdir() and removed with rmdir(); a directory must be empty (nothing left but . and ..) before it can be removed. The GNU/Linux version of the ISO C remove() function calls unlink() or rmdir() as appropriate.

- Directories are processed with opendir(), readdir(), rewinddir(), and closedir(). A struct dirent contains the inode number and the file's name. Maximally portable code uses only the file name in the d_name member. The BSD telldir() and seekdir() functions for saving and restoring the current position in a directory are widely available and even included in POSIX, but they are not as fully portable as the other directory processing functions. GNU/Linux and the BSDs provide file type information in the d_type member of the struct dirent.

- File metadata is retrieved with the stat() family of system calls; the struct stat structure contains all the information about a file *except* the file name. (Indeed, since a file may have many names or may even be completely unlinked, it's not possible to make the name available.)

- The S_IS*xxx*() macros in <sys/stat.h> make it possible to determine a file's type. The major() and minor() functions from <sys/sysmacros.h> make it possible to decode the dev_t values that represent block and character devices.

- Symbolic links can be checked for using lstat(), and the st_size field of the struct stat for a symbolic link returns the number of bytes needed to hold the name of the pointed-to file. The contents of a symbolic link are read with readlink(). Care must be taken to get the buffer size correct and to terminate the retrieved file name with a trailing zero byte so that it can be used as a C string.

- An additional suite of system calls work by being given a file descriptor open on a directory, the name of a file in that directory, and whatever additional information is needed for the given operation. These system calls offer protection against race conditions, at the cost of having less intuitive interfaces.

- Several miscellaneous system calls update other file information: the chown() family for the owner and group, the chmod() routines for the file permissions, and the utime() family to change file access and modification times.

Exercises

1. Write a routine '`const char *fmt_mode(mode_t mode)`'. The input is a `mode_t` value as provided by the `st_mode` field in the `struct stat`; that is, it contains both the permission bits and the file type.

   The output should be a 10-character string identical to the first field of output from '`ls -l`'. In other words, the first character identifies the file type, and the other nine characters identify the permissions.

   When the `S_ISUID` and `S_IXUSR` bits are set, use an `s` instead of an `x`; if only the `I_ISUID` bit is set, use an `S`. And similarly for the `S_ISGID` and `S_IXGRP` bits.

   If both the `S_ISVTX` and `S_IXOTH` bits are set, use `t`; for `S_ISVTX` alone, use `T`.

   For simplicity, you may use a `static` buffer whose contents are overwritten each time the routine is called.
2. Extend `ch-fileinfo-catdir.c` to call `stat()` on each file name found. Then print the inode number, the result of `fmt_mode()`, the link count, and the file's name.
3. Extend `ch-fileinfo-catdir.c` further such that if a file is a symbolic link, it will also print the name of the pointed-to file.
4. Add an option such that if a file name is that of a subdirectory, the program recursively enters the subdirectory and prints information about the subdirectory's files (and directories). Only one level of recursion is needed.
5. If you're not using a GNU/Linux system, run `ch-fileinfo-trymkdir` (see Section 5.2, "Creating and Removing Directories," page 121) on your system and compare the results to those we showed.
6. Write the `mkdir` program. See your local *mkdir*(1) manpage and implement all its options.
7. In the root directory, `/`, both the device and inode numbers for `.` and `..` are the same. Using this bit of information, write the `pwd` program.

   The program has to start by reading the contents of the parent directory to find the name of the current directory. It must then continue working its way up the filesystem hierarchy, until it reaches the root directory.

   Printing the directory name backward, from the current directory up to the root, is easy. How will your version of `pwd` manage to print the directory name in the correct way, from the root on down?
8. If you wrote `pwd` using recursion, write it again using iteration. If you used iteration, write it using recursion. Which is better? (Hint: consider very deeply nested directory trees.)
9. (Hard.) Read the *chmod*(1) manpage. Write code to parse the symbolic options argument, which allows adding, removing, and setting permissions based on user, group, other, and "all."

   Once you believe it works, write your own version of `chmod` that applies the permission specification to each file or directory named on the command line.

   Which function did you use—`chmod()`, or `open()` and `fchmod()`—and why?

Chapter 6

General Library Interfaces—Part 1

We saw in Chapter 5, "Directories and File Metadata," page 111, that directly reading a directory returns file names in the order in which they're kept in the directory. We also saw that the `struct stat` contains all the information about a file, except its name. However, some components of that structure are not directly usable; they're just numeric values.

This chapter presents the rest of the APIs needed to make full use of the `struct stat` component values. In order, we cover the following topics: `time_t` values for representing times and the time formatting functions; sorting and searching functions (for sorting file names, or any other data); the `uid_t` and `gid_t` types for representing users and groups and the functions that map them to and from the corresponding user and group names; and finally, a function to test whether a file descriptor represents a terminal.

POSIX systems have many more general-purpose APIs than just the ones in this chapter. We cover more of them later, in Chapter 13, "General Library Interfaces—Part 2," page 419, and in Chapter 16, "Extended Interfaces," page 557.

6.1 Times and Dates

Time values are kept in the type known as `time_t`. The ISO C standard guarantees that this is a numeric type but does not otherwise specify what it is (integer or floating-point), or the range or the precision of the values stored therein.

On GNU/Linux and Unix systems, `time_t` values represent "seconds since the Epoch." The *Epoch* is the beginning of recorded time, which is midnight, January 1, 1970, UTC. On most systems, a `time_t` is a C `long int`. For 32-bit systems, this means that the `time_t` "overflows" sometime on January 19, 2038. By then, we hope, everyone will be using 64-bit systems (or bigger!), where the `time_t` type is at least 64 bits big.

Various functions exist to retrieve the current time, compute the difference between two `time_t` values, convert `time_t` values into a more usable representation, and format both representations as character strings. Additionally, a date and time representation can be converted back into a `time_t`, and limited time-zone information is available.

A separate set of functions provides access to the current time with a higher resolution than one second. The functions work by providing two discrete values: the time as seconds since the Epoch, and the number of microseconds or nanoseconds within the current second. These functions are described later in the book, in Section 16.3.1 "Microsecond Times: `gettimeofday()`," page 567, and in Section 16.3.2, "Nanosecond Times: `clock_gettime()`," page 569.

The data structures were introduced briefly in Section 5.6.4, "Changing Timestamps: `utime()` and Successors," page 148.

6.1.1 Retrieving the Current Time: `time()` and `difftime()`

The `time()` system call retrieves the current date and time; `difftime()` computes the difference between two `time_t` values:

```
#include <time.h>                                          ISO C

time_t time(time_t *t);
double difftime(time_t time1, time_t time0);
```

`time()` returns the current time. If the `t` parameter is not `NULL`, then the value pointed to by `t` is also filled in with the current time. It returns `(time_t) -1` if there was an error, and `errno` is set.

Although ISO C doesn't specify what's in a `time_t` value, POSIX does indicate that it represents time in seconds. Thus, it's both common and portable to make this assumption. For example, to see if a time value represents something that is six months or more in the past, one might use code like this:

```
/* Error checking omitted for brevity */
time_t now, then, some_time;

time(& now);                                 Get current time
then = now - (6L * 31 * 24 * 60 * 60);       Approximately six months ago

... set some_time, for example, via stat() ...
if (some_time < then)
    /* more than 6 months in the past */
else
    /* less than 6 months in the past */
```

However, since strictly portable code may need to run on non-POSIX systems, the `difftime()` function exists to produce the difference between two times. The same test, using `difftime()`, would be written this way:

```
time_t now, some_time;
const double six_months = 6.0 * 31 * 24 * 60 * 60;

time(& now);                                 Get current time
... set some_time, for example, via stat() ...

if (difftime(now, some_time) >= six_months)
    /* more than 6 months in the past */
else
    /* less than 6 months in the past */
```

The return type of `difftime()` is a `double` because a `time_t` could possibly represent fractions of a second as well. On POSIX systems, it always represents whole seconds.

In each of the preceding examples, note the use of a typed constant to force the computation to be done with the right type of math: `6L` in the first instance for `long` integers; `6.0` in the second, for floating point.

6.1.2 Breaking Down Times: `gmtime()` and `localtime()`

In practice, the "seconds since the Epoch" form of a date and time isn't very useful except for simple comparisons. Computing the components of a time yourself, such as the month, day, year, and so on, is error prone, since the local time zone (possibly with daylight saving time) must be taken into account, leap years must be computed correctly, and so forth. Fortunately, two standard routines do this job for you:

ISO C

```
#include <time.h>

struct tm *gmtime(const time_t *timep);
struct tm *localtime(const time_t *timep);
```

`gmtime()` returns a pointer to a `struct tm` that represents UTC time. `localtime()` returns a pointer to a `struct tm` representing the local time; that is, it takes the current time zone and daylight saving time into account. In effect, this is "wall-clock time," the date and time as it would be displayed on a wall clock or on a wristwatch. (How this works is discussed later; see Section 6.1.6, "Getting Time-Zone Information," page 168.)

Both functions return a pointer to a `struct tm`, which looks like this:

```
struct tm {
    int     tm_sec;        /* seconds */
    int     tm_min;        /* minutes */
    int     tm_hour;       /* hours */
    int     tm_mday;       /* day of the month */
    int     tm_mon;        /* month */
    int     tm_year;       /* year */
    int     tm_wday;       /* day of the week */
    int     tm_yday;       /* day in the year */
    int     tm_isdst;      /* daylight saving time */
};
```

The `struct tm` is referred to as a *broken-down time*, since the `time_t` value is "broken down" into its component parts. The component parts, their ranges, and their meanings are shown in Table 6.1.

The ISO C standard presents most of these values as "*x* since *y*." For example, `tm_sec` is "seconds since the minute," `tm_mon` is "months since January," `tm_wday` is "days since Sunday," and so on. This helps to understand why all the values start at `0`. (The single exception, logically enough, is `tm_mday`, the day of the month, which ranges from 1–31.) Of course,

Table 6.1: Fields in the `struct tm`

Member	Range	Meaning
`tm_sec`	0–60	Second within a minute. Second 60 allows for leap seconds. (C90 had the range as 0–61.)
`tm_min`	0–59	Minute within an hour.
`tm_hour`	0–23	Hour within the day.
`tm_mday`	1–31	Day of the month.
`tm_mon`	0–11	Month of the year.
`tm_year`	0–*N*	Year, in years since 1900.
`tm_wday`	0–6	Day of week, Sunday = 0.
`tm_yday`	0–365	Day of year, January 1 = 0.
`tm_isdst`	< 0, 0, > 0	Daylight saving time flag.

having them start at zero is also practical; since C arrays are zero-based, it makes using these values as indices trivial:

```
static const char *const days[] = {                          Array of day names
    "Sunday", "Monday", "Tuesday", "Wednesday",
    "Thursday", "Friday", "Saturday",
};
time_t now;
struct tm *curtime;

time(& now);                                                 Get current time
curtime = gmtime(& now);                                     Break it down
printf("Day of the week: %s\n", days[curtime->tm_wday]);     Index and print
```

Both `gmtime()` and `localtime()` return a pointer to a `struct tm`. The pointer points to a `static struct tm` maintained by each routine, and it is likely that these `struct tm` structures are overwritten each time the routines are called. Thus, it's a good idea to make a *copy* of the returned `struct`. Reusing the previous example:

```
static const char *const days[] = { /* As before */ };
time_t now;
struct tm curtime;                                           Structure, not pointer

time(& now);                                                 Get current time
curtime = *gmtime(& now);                                    Break it down and copy data
printf("Day of the week: %s\n", days[curtime.tm_wday]);      Index and print, use . not ->
```

The `tm_isdst` field indicates whether or not daylight saving time (DST) is currently in effect. A value of `0` means DST is not in effect, a positive value means it is, and a negative value means that no DST information is available. (The C standard is purposely vague, indicating only zero, positive, or negative; this gives implementors the most freedom.)

6.1.3 Formatting Dates and Times

The examples in the previous section showed how the fields in a `struct tm` could be used to index arrays of character strings for printing informative date and time values. While you could write your own code to use such arrays for formatting dates and times, standard routines alleviate the work.

6.1.3.1 Simple Time Formatting: `asctime()` and `ctime()`

The first two standard routines, listed below, produce output in a fixed format:

```
#include <time.h>                                        ISO C

char *asctime(const struct tm *tm);
char *ctime(const time_t *timep);
```

As with `gmtime()` and `localtime()`, `asctime()` and `ctime()` return pointers to `static` buffers that are likely to be overwritten upon each call. Furthermore, these two routines return strings in the same format. They differ only in the kind of argument they accept. `asctime()` and `ctime()` should be used when all you need is simple date and time information:

```
#include <stdio.h>
#include <time.h>

int
main(void)
{
    time_t now;

    time(& now);
    printf("%s", ctime(& now));
}
```

When run, this program produces output of the form: '`Sun May 25 16:32:42 2025`'. The terminating newline *is* included in the result. To be more precise, the return value points to an array of 26 characters, as shown in Figure 6.1.

Much older Unix code relies on the fact that the values have a fixed position in the returned string. When using these routines, remember that they include a trailing newline. Thus, the

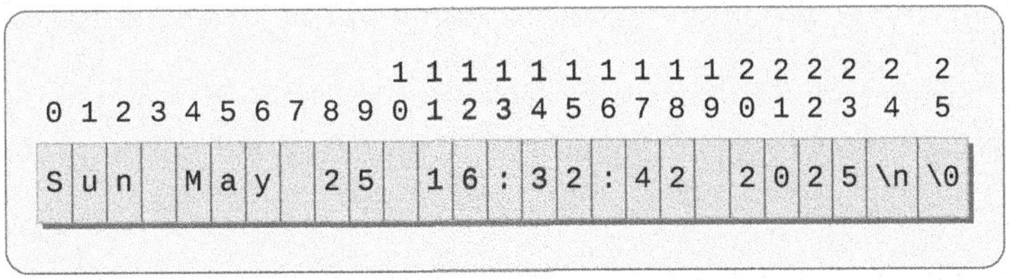

Figure 6.1: Return string from `ctime()` and `asctime()`

small example program uses a simple "%s" format string for printf(), and not "%s\n", as might be expected.

ctime() saves you the step of calling localtime(); it's essentially equivalent to

```
time_t now;
char *curtime;

time(& now);
curtime = asctime(localtime(& now));
```

6.1.3.2 Complex Time Formatting: strftime()

While asctime() and ctime() are often adequate, they are also limited:

- The output format is fixed. There's no way to rearrange the order of the elements.
- The output does not include time-zone information.
- The output uses abbreviated month and day names.
- The output assumes English names for the months and days.

For these reasons, C90 introduced the strftime() standard library routine:

```
#include <time.h>                                          ISO C

size_t strftime(char *s, size_t max, const char *format,
                const struct tm *tm);
```

strftime() is similar to sprintf(). The arguments are as follows:

char *s
: A buffer to hold the formatted string.

size_t max
: The size of the buffer.

const char *format
: The format string.

const struct tm *tm
: A struct tm pointer representing the broken-down time to be formatted.

The format string contains literal characters, intermixed with conversion specifiers that indicate what is to be placed into the string, such as the full weekday name, the hour according to a 24-hour or 12-hour clock, a.m. or p.m. designations, and so on. (Examples are coming shortly.)

If the entire string can be formatted within max characters, the return value is the number of characters placed in s, *not* including the terminating zero byte. Otherwise, the return value is `0`. In the latter case, the contents of `s` are "indeterminate." The following simple example gives the flavor of how `strftime()` is used:

```
#include <stdio.h>
#include <stdlib.h>
#include <time.h>

int
main(void)
{
    char buf[100];
    time_t now;
    struct tm *curtime;

    time(& now);
    curtime = localtime(& now);
    (void) strftime(buf, sizeof buf,
            "It is now %A, %B %d, %Y, %I:%M %p", curtime);

    printf("%s\n", buf);
    exit(0);
}
```

When run, this program prints something like:

```
It is now Sunday, May 25, 2025, 04:34 PM
```

Table 6.2 provides the full list of conversion specifiers, their possible alternative representations, and their meanings.

A *locale* is a way of describing the current location, taking into account such things as language, character set, and defaults for formatting dates, times, and monetary amounts. We deal with them in Chapter 15, "Internationalization and Localization," page 507. For now, it's enough to understand that the results from `strftime()` for the same format string can vary according to the current locale.

The versions starting with `%E` and `%O` are for "alternative representations." Some locales have multiple ways of representing the same thing; these specifiers provide access to the additional representations. If a particular locale does not support alternative representations, then `strftime()` uses the regular version.

Many Unix versions of `date` allow you to provide, on the command line, a format string that begins with a `+` character. `date` then formats the current date and time and prints it according to the format string:

```
$ date +'It is now %A, %B %d, %Y, %I:%M %p'
It is now Sunday, May 25, 2025, 04:35 PM
```

The output depends on the current locale (where in the world the system thinks you are; locales and the environment variables that control them are discussed later, in Section 15.2, "Locales

Table 6.2: `strftime()` conversion format specifiers

Specifier(s)	Meaning
`%a`	The locale's abbreviated weekday name.
`%A`	The locale's full weekday name.
`%b`, `%Ob`	The locale's abbreviated month name.
`%B`, `%OB`	The locale's full month name.
`%c`, `%Ec`	The locale's "appropriate" date and time representation.
`%C`, `%EC`	The century (`00`–`99`).
`%d`, `%Od`	The day of the month (`01`–`31`).
`%D`	Same as `%m/%d/%y`.
`%e`, `%Oe`	The day of the month. A single digit is preceded with a space (`1`–`31`).
`%F`	Same as `%Y-%m-%d` (ISO 8601 date format).
`%g`	The last two digits of week-based year (`00`–`99`).
`%G`	The ISO 8601 week-based year.
`%h`	Same as `%b`.
`%H`, `%OH`	The hour in a 24-hour clock (`00`–`23`).
`%I`, `%OI`	The hour in a 12-hour clock (`01`–`12`).
`%j`	The day of the year (`001`–`366`).
`%m`, `%Om`	The month as a number (`01`–`12`).
`%M`, `%OM`	The minute as a number (`00`–`59`).
`%n`	A newline character (`'\n'`).
`%p`	The locale's AM/PM designation.
`%r`	The locale's 12-hour clock time.
`%R`	Same as `%H:%M`.
`%S`, `%OS`	The second as a number (`00`–`60`).
`%t`	A tab character (`'\t'`).
`%T`	Same as `%H:%M:%S` (ISO 8601 time format).
`%u`, `%Ou`	ISO 8601 weekday number, Monday = 1 (`1`–`7`).
`%U`, `%OU`	Week number, first Sunday is first day of week 1 (`00`–`53`).
`%V`, `%OV`	ISO 8601 week number (`01`–`53`).
`%w`, `%Ow`	The weekday as a number, Sunday = 0 (`0`–`6`).
`%W`, `%OW`	Week number, first Monday is first day of week 1 (`00`–`53`).
`%x`, `%Ex`	The locale's "appropriate" date representation.
`%X`, `%EX`	The locale's "appropriate" time representation.
`%y`, `%Ey`, `%Oy`	The last two digits of the year (`00`–`99`).
`%Y`, `%EY`	The year as a number.
`%z`	Time zone offset from UTC, in the form `+hhmm` or `-hhmm`.
`%Z`	The locale's time zone, or no characters if no time-zone information is available.
`%%`	A single `%`.

and the C Library," page 508.) For example, by setting the environment variable `LC_ALL` to `it_IT.utf8` (Italy), we might get something like this:

```
$ LC_ALL=it_IT.utf8 date +'It is now %A, %B %d, %Y, %I:%M %p'
It is now domenica, maggio 25, 2025, 04:36
```

Table 6.3: "C" locale values for certain strftime() formats

Specifier	Meaning
%a	The first three characters of %A.
%A	One of Sunday, Monday, ..., Saturday.
%b	The first three characters of %B.
%B	One of January, February, ..., December.
%c	Same as %a %b %e %T %Y.
%p	One of AM or PM.
%r	Same as %I:%M:%S %p.
%x	Same as %m/%d/%y.
%X	Same as %T.
%Z	Implementation-defined.

Note that despite the %p in the format string, there is no a.m./p.m. indication. By setting LC_ALL to C, we can get the traditional Unix output:

```
$ LC_ALL=C date +'It is now %A, %B %d, %Y, %I:%M %p'
It is now Sunday, May 25, 2025, 04:35 PM
```

Many of strftime()'s specifiers come from such existing Unix date implementations. The %n and %t formats are not strictly necessary in C, since the tab and newline characters can be directly embedded in the string. However, in the context of a date format string on the command line, they make more sense. Thus they're included in the specification for strftime() as well.[1]

The ISO 8601 standard defines (among other things) how weeks are numbered within a year. According to this standard, weeks run Monday through Sunday, and Monday is day 1 of the week, not day 0. If the week in which January 1 comes out contains at least four days in the new year, then it is considered to be week 1. Otherwise, that week is the last week of the previous year, numbered 52 or 53. These rules are used for the computation of the %g, %G, and %V format specifiers. (While parochial Americans such as the author may find these rules strange, they are commonly used throughout Europe.)

Many of the format specifiers produce results that are specific to the current locale. In addition, several indicate that they produce the "appropriate" representation for the locale (for example, %x). The C standard defines the values for the "C" locale. These values are listed in Table 6.3.

In addition to the strftime() features mandated by the C standard, POSIX extends the format specifiers in a manner similar to what printf() allows. Between the % and the format letter, you may also provide:

- An optional flag. There are two possible values:

  0 Specify that the values should be padded with '0' characters.

  \+ Print a leading + for positive numeric values, or a - for negative ones.

[1] Modern shells provide a special type of string constant, $'...', wherein certain escape sequences are interpolated into them by the shell, including newline and tab. This makes %n and %t even less useful.

In our testing, GLIBC does not support either of these flags, but things may change in the future.

- A positive numeric field width. If the formatted value is smaller than the field's width, it is padded with the default padding character. On GLIBC systems, this is `'0'`.
- The optional `E` and `O` modifiers shown earlier.

It should be obvious that `strftime()` provides considerable flexibility and control over date- and time-related output, in much the same way as `printf()` and `sprintf()` do. Furthermore, `strftime()` cannot overflow its buffer, since it checks against the passed-in size parameter, making it a safer routine than is `sprintf()`.

As a simple example, consider the creation of program log files, when a new file is created every hour. The file name should embed the date and time of its creation in its name:

```
/* Error checking omitted for brevity */
char fname[PATH_MAX];       /* PATH_MAX is in <limits.h> */
time_t now;
struct tm *tm;
int fd;

time(& now);
tm = localtime(& now);
strftime(fname, sizeof fname, "/var/log/myapp.%Y-%m-%d-%H:%M", tm);
fd = creat(name, 0600);
...
```

The year-month-day-hour-minute format causes the file names to sort in the order they were created.

NOTE

Some time formats are more useful than others. For example, 12-hour times are ambiguous, as are any purely numeric date formats. (What does '`9/11`' mean? It depends on where you live.) Similarly, two-digit years are also a bad idea. Use `strftime()` judiciously.

6.1.4 Converting a Broken-Down Time to a `time_t`

Obtaining seconds-since-the-Epoch values from the system is easy; that's how date and times are stored in inodes and returned from `time()` and `stat()`. These values are also easy to compare for equality or by < and > for simple earlier-than/later-than tests.

However, dates entered by humans are not so easy to work with. For example, many versions of the `touch` command allow you to provide a date and time to which `touch` should set a file's modification or access time (with `utimensat()`, as described in Section 5.6.4, "Changing Timestamps: `utime()` and Successors," page 148).

Converting a date as entered by a person into a `time_t` value is difficult: leap years must be taken into account, time zones must be compensated for, and so on. Therefore, the C90 standard introduced the `mktime()` function:

```
#include <time.h>                                          ISO C

time_t mktime(struct tm *tm);
```

To use `mktime()`, fill in a `struct tm` with appropriate values: year, month, day, and so on. If you know whether daylight saving time was in effect for the given date, set the `tm_isdst` field appropriately: `0` for "no," and positive for "yes." Otherwise, use a negative value for "don't know." The `tm_wday` and `tm_yday` fields are ignored.

`mktime()` assumes that the `struct tm` represents a local time, not UTC. It returns a `time_t` value representing the passed-in date and time, or it returns `(time_t) -1` if the given date/time cannot be represented correctly. Upon a successful return, all the values in the `struct tm` are adjusted to be within the correct ranges, and `tm_wday` and `tm_yday` are set correctly as well. Here is a simple example:

```
/* ch-general1-echodate.c --- demonstrate mktime(). */

#include <stdio.h>
#include <stdlib.h>
#include <time.h>

int
main(void)
{
    struct tm tm;
    time_t then;

    printf("Enter a Date/time as YYYY/MM/DD HH:MM:SS : ");
    scanf("%d/%d/%d %d:%d:%d",
        & tm.tm_year, & tm.tm_mon, & tm.tm_mday,
        & tm.tm_hour, & tm.tm_min, & tm.tm_sec);

    /* Error checking on values omitted for brevity. */
    tm.tm_year -= 1900;
    tm.tm_mon--;

    tm.tm_isdst = -1;        /* Don't know about DST */

    then = mktime(& tm);

    printf("Got: %s", ctime(& then));
    exit(EXIT_SUCCESS);
}
```

Line 13 prompts for a date and time, and lines 14–16 read it in. (Production code should check the return value from `scanf()`. `mktime()` checks that the values it receives are within sane ranges.) Lines 19 and 20 compensate for the different basing of years and months, respectively. Line 24 indicates that we don't know whether the given date and time represent daylight saving time. Line 24 calls `mktime()`, and line 26 prints the result of the conversion. When compiled and run, we see that it works:

```
$ ch-general1-echodate
Enter a Date/time as YYYY/MM/DD HH:MM:SS : 2025/07/10 12:44:55
Got: Thu Jul 10 12:44:55 2025
```

Negative Times

In general, the `time_t` is a signed integer, making it possible to have "negative" times, or values representing times that occurred before the Epoch of January 1, 1970.

This presents a problem for `mktime()`, which can return `-1` upon an error. The C24 standard indicates how to distinguish the two cases:

> [on error] the function returns the value `(time_t)(-1)` and does not change the value of the `tm_wday` component of the structure.

By first setting `tm_wday` to a value that is out of range (less than zero or greater than six), and then checking if it changed, you can tell if the call to `mktime()` succeeded.[2] The *mktime*(3) manpage provides similar advice.

6.1.5 Parsing a Date and Time into a `struct tm`

With `strftime()`, we turn a `struct tm` into a human-readable string. POSIX provides an additional routine to go in the opposite direction: taking a string and turning it back into a `struct tm`. This lets you avoid the pain of manually parsing a date to get a `struct tm`. The routine is `strptime()`:

```
#define _XOPEN_SOURCE                                    GLIBC
#include <time.h>                                        POSIX XSI

char *strptime(const char *buf, const char *format, struct tm *tm);
```

The parameters are:

`const char *buf`
: The text of the date string to be parsed.

`const char *format`
: A format string describing the contents of `buf`.

[2]Thanks to Geoff Clare in `comp.lang.awk` for this tip.

`struct tm *tm`
: A pointer to a `struct tm` in which to place the parsed values.

Upon error the return value is `NULL`. Otherwise, the return value points to the first character that was not parsed. Here is a simple example program:

```
/* ch-general1-parsetime.c --- Adapted from POSIX strptime() description. */

#define _XOPEN_SOURCE       /* Needed on GLIBC, must be before all includes! */
#include <stdio.h>
#include <stdlib.h>
#include <errno.h>
#include <string.h>
#include <time.h>

int
main(int argc, char **argv)
{
    struct tm tm;
    time_t t;

    if (strptime("15 Dec 2025 18:07:53", "%d %b %Y %H:%M:%S", & tm) == NULL) {
        fprintf(stderr, "%s: strptime failed: %s\n", argv[0], strerror(errno));
        exit(EXIT_FAILURE);
    }

    printf("year: %d; month: %d; day: %d;\n",
        tm.tm_year + 1900, tm.tm_mon, tm.tm_mday);
    printf("hour: %d; minute: %d; second: %d\n",
        tm.tm_hour, tm.tm_min, tm.tm_sec);
    printf("week day: %d; year day: %d\n", tm.tm_wday, tm.tm_yday);

    /* Tell mktime() to determine if daylight saving time is in effect */
    tm.tm_isdst = -1;
    t = mktime(&tm);
    if (t == -1) {
        fprintf(stderr, "%s: mktime failed: %s\n", argv[0], strerror(errno));
        exit(EXIT_FAILURE);
    }
    printf("Seconds since the Epoch: %ld\n", (long) t);
    return EXIT_SUCCESS;
}
```

When run, it produces this output:

```
$ ch-general1-parsetime
year: 2025; month: 11; day: 15;
```

```
hour: 18; minute: 7; second: 53
week day: 1; year day: 348
Seconds since the Epoch: 1765814873
```

On GLIBC systems, in order to access the declaration of `strptime()`, you must define `_XOPEN_SOURCE` *before* including *any* standard header files.

The conversion specifiers available for use in `format` are purposely the same as those for `strftime()`; see Table 6.2. GLIBC provides an additional value, `%s`, which scans a seconds-since-the-Epoch value.

Additionally, `%a` and `%A` are equivalent to each other, as are `%b` and `%B`; `%n` and `%t` match any whitespace characters.

POSIX allows optional flags of `0` or `+` that are to be ignored, and an optional field width, neither of which are mentioned by the Linux *strptime*(3) manpage. The optional `E` and `O` modifiers are allowed.

6.1.6 Getting Time-Zone Information

Early Unix systems embedded time-zone information into the kernel when it was compiled. The rules for daylight saving time conversions were generally hard-coded, which was painful for users outside the United States or in places within the United States that didn't observe DST.

Modern systems have abstracted that information into binary files read by the C library when time-related functions are invoked. This technique avoids the need to recompile libraries and system executables when the rules in a particular location change and makes it much easier to update the rules.

The C language interface to time-zone information evolved across different Unix versions, both System V and Berkeley, until finally it was standardized by POSIX as follows:

```
#include <time.h>                                   POSIX

extern char *tzname[2];
extern long timezone;                               POSIX XSI
extern int daylight;                                POSIX XSI

void tzset(void);
```

The `tzset()` function examines the `TZ` environment variable to find time-zone and daylight saving time information.[3] If that variable isn't set, then `tzset()` uses an "implementation-defined default time zone," which is most likely the time zone of the machine you're running on.

After `tzset()` has been called, the local time-zone information is available in several variables:

[3]Although POSIX standardizes `TZ`'s format, it isn't all that interesting, so we haven't bothered to document it here. After all, it is `tzset()` that has to understand the format, not user-level code. Implementations can, and do, use formats that extend POSIX.

`extern char *tzname[2]`
: The standard and daylight saving time names for the time zone. For example, for U.S. locations in the Eastern time zone, the time-zone names are `"EST"` (Eastern Standard Time) and `"EDT"` (Eastern Daylight Time).

`extern long timezone`
: The difference, in seconds, between the current time zone and UTC. The standard does not explain how this difference works. In practice, negative values represent time zones *east* of (ahead of, or later than) UTC, and positive values represent time zones *west* of (behind, or earlier than) UTC. If you look at this value as "how much to change the local time to make it be the same as UTC," then the sign of the value makes sense.

`extern int daylight`
: This variable is zero if daylight saving time conversions should never be applied in the current time zone, and nonzero otherwise.

NOTE

The `daylight` variable does *not* indicate whether daylight saving time is currently in effect! Instead, it merely states whether the current time zone can even have daylight saving time.

The POSIX standard indicates that `ctime()`, `localtime()`, `mktime()`, and `strftime()` all act "as if" they call `tzset()`. This means that they need not actually call `tzset()`, but they must behave as if it had been called. (The wording is intended to provide a certain amount of flexibility for implementors while guaranteeing correct behavior for user-level code.)

In practice, this means that you will almost never have to call `tzset()` yourself. However, it's there if you need it.

Local Time: How Does It Know?

GNU/Linux systems store time-zone information in files and directories underneath `/usr/share/zoneinfo`:

```
$ cd /usr/share/zoneinfo
$ ls -FC
Africa/         America/        Antarctica/     Arctic/
Asia/           Atlantic/       Australia/      Brazil/
CET             CST6CDT         Canada/         Chile/
Cuba@           EET             EST             EST5EDT
Egypt@          Eire@           Etc/            Europe/
Factory         GB-Eire@        GB@             GMT+0@
GMT-0@          GMT0@           GMT@            Greenwich@
HST             Hongkong@       Iceland@        Indian/
Iran@           Israel@         Jamaica@        Japan@
Kwajalein@      Libya@          MET             MST
```

```
MST7MDT           Mexico/           NZ-CHAT@            NZ@
Navajo@           PRC@              PST8PDT             Pacific/
Poland@           Portugal@         ROC@                ROK@
Singapore@        Turkey@           UCT@                US/
UTC@              Universal@        W-SU@               WET
Zulu@             iso3166.tab       leap-seconds.list   leapseconds
localtime@        posix/            posixrules@         right/
tzdata.zi         zone.tab          zone1970.tab
```

Part of the process of installing a system is to choose the time zone. The correct time-zone data file is then placed in `/etc/localtime`:

```
$ file /etc/localtime
/etc/localtime: symbolic link to /usr/share/zoneinfo/Asia/Jerusalem
```

On our system, this is a symbolic link to a file in `/usr/share/zoneinfo`. On other systems, it may be a stand-alone copy of the time-zone file for the time zone. The advantage of using a separate copy is that everything still works if `/usr` isn't mounted.

The `TZ` environment variable, if set, overrides the default time zone:

```
$ date                                  Date and time in default time zone
Sun May 25 09:47:59 AM EDT 2025
$ export TZ=PST8PDT                     Change time zone to U.S. West Coast
$ date                                  Print date and time
Sun May 25 06:48:14 AM PDT 2025
```

6.1.6.1 BSD Systems Gotcha: `timezone()`, Not `timezone`

Instead of the POSIX `timezone` variable, several systems derived from 4.4 BSD provide a `timezone()` function:

```
#include <time.h>                                         BSD

char *timezone(int zone, int dst);
```

The `zone` argument is the number of *minutes* west of GMT, and `dst` is true if daylight saving time is in effect. The return value is a string giving the name of the indicated zone, or a value expressed relative to GMT. This function provides compatibility with the V7 function of the same name and behavior.

This function's existence makes portable use of the POSIX `timezone` variable difficult. Fortunately, we don't see a huge need for it: `strftime()` should be sufficient for all but the most unusual needs.

6.2 Sorting and Searching Functions

Sorting and searching are two fundamental operations for which a need arises continually in many applications. The C library provides a number of standard interfaces for performing these tasks. They are general purpose in nature, suitable for working with any kind of data, as opposed to being tuned for particular applications.

All the routines share a common theme: data is managed through `void *` pointers, and user-provided functions supply ordering. Note also that these APIs apply to *in-memory* data. Sorting and searching structures in files is considerably more involved and beyond the scope of an introductory text such as this one. (However, the `sort` command works well for text files; see the *sort*(1) manpage. Sorting binary files requires that a special-purpose program be written.)

Because no one algorithm works well for all applications, there are several different sets of library routines for maintaining searchable collections of data. This chapter covers only one simple interface for searching. A more advanced interface is described in Section 16.4, "Advanced Searching with Binary Trees," page 575. Furthermore, we purposely don't explain the underlying algorithms, since this is a book on APIs, not algorithms and data structures. What's important to understand is that you can treat the APIs as "black boxes" that do a particular job without needing to understand the details of *how* they do the job.

6.2.1 Sorting: `qsort()`

Sorting is accomplished with `qsort()`:

```
#include <stdlib.h>                                     ISO C

void qsort(void *base, size_t nmemb, size_t size,
           int (*compare)(const void *, const void *));
```

The name `qsort()` comes from C. A. R. Hoare's Quicksort algorithm, which was used in the initial Unix implementation. (Nothing in the POSIX standard dictates the use of this algorithm for `qsort()`. The GLIBC implementation uses a highly optimized combination of Quicksort and Insertion Sort.)

`qsort()` sorts arrays of arbitrary objects. It works by shuffling opaque chunks of memory from one spot within an array to another and relies on you, the programmer, to provide a comparison function that allows it to determine the ordering of one array element relative to another. The arguments are as follows:

`void *base`
: The address of the beginning of the array.

`size_t nmemb`
: The total number of elements in the array.

`size_t size`
: The size of each element in the array. The best way to obtain this value is with the C `sizeof` operator.

`int (*compare)(const void *, const void *)`
: A possibly scary declaration for a *function pointer*. It says that "`compare` points to a function that takes two '`const void *`' parameters, and returns an `int`."

Most of the work is in writing a proper comparison function. The return value should mimic that of `strcmp()`: less than zero if the first value is "less than" the second, zero if they are equal, and greater than zero if the first value is "greater than" the second. It is the comparison function that defines the meaning of "less than" and "greater than" for whatever it is you're sorting. For example, to compare two `double` values, we could use this function:

```
int
dcomp(const void *d1p, const void *d2p)
{
    const double *d1, *d2;

    d1 = (const double *) d1p;                    Cast pointers to right type
    d2 = (const double *) d2p;

    if (*d1 < *d2)                                Compare and return right value
        return -1;
    else if (*d1 > *d2)
        return 1;
    else if (*d1 == *d2)
        return 0
    else
        return -1;      /* NaN sorts before real numbers */
}
```

This shows the general boilerplate for a comparison function: convert the arguments from `void *` to pointers to the type being compared and then return a comparison value.

For floating-point values, a simple subtraction such as '`return *d1 - *d2`' doesn't work, particularly if one value is very small or if one or both values are special "not a number" or "infinity" values. Thus we have to do the comparison manually, including taking into account the not-a-number value (which doesn't even compare equal to itself!).

6.2.1.1 Example: Sorting Employees

For more complicated structures, a more involved function is necessary. For example, consider the following (rather trivial) `struct employee`:

```
struct employee {
    char lastname[30];
    char firstname[30];
```

```
    long emp_id;
    time_t start_date;
};
```

We might write a function to sort employees by last name, first name, and ID number:

```
int
emp_name_id_compare(const void *e1p, const void *e2p)
{
    const struct employee *e1, *e2;
    int last, first;

    e1 = (const struct employee *) e1p;                           Convert pointers
    e2 = (const struct employee *) e2p;

    if ((last = strcmp(e1->lastname, e2->lastname)) != 0)         Compare last names
        return last;                                              Last names differ

    /* same last name, check first name */
    if ((first = strcmp(e1->firstname, e2->firstname)) != 0)      Compare first names
        return first;                                             First names differ

    /* same first name, check ID numbers */
    if (e1->emp_id < e2->emp_id)                                  Compare employee ID
        return -1;
    else if (e1->emp_id == e2->emp_id)
        return 0;
    else
        return 1;
}
```

The logic here is straightforward, initially comparing on last names, then first names, and then using the employee ID number if the two names are the same. By using `strcmp()` on strings, we automatically get the right kind of negative/zero/positive value to return.

The employee ID comparison can't just use subtraction: suppose `long` is 64 bits and `int` is 32 bits, and the two values differ only in the upper 32 bits (say the lower 32 bits are zero). In such a case, the subtraction result would automatically be cast to `int`, throwing away the upper 32 bits and returning an incorrect value.

NOTE

We could have stopped with the comparison on first names, in which case all employees with the same last and first names would be grouped, but *without any other ordering*.

This point is important: `qsort()` does not guarantee a *stable* sort. A stable sort is one in which, if two elements compare equal based on some key value(s), they will maintain their original ordering, relative to each other, in the final sorted array. For example, consider three employees with the same first and last names and with employee numbers `17`, `42`, and `81`.

Their order in the original array might have been 42, 81, and 17 (meaning that employee 42 is at a lower index than employee 81, who, in turn, is at a lower index than employee 17). After sorting, the order might be 81, 42, and 17. If this is an issue, then the comparison routine must take *all* important key values into consideration. (Ours does.)

Simply by using a different function, we can sort employees by seniority:

```
int
emp_seniority_compare(const void *e1p, const void *e2p)
{
    const struct employee *e1, *e2;
    double diff;

    e1 = (const struct employee *) e1p;                Cast pointers to correct type
    e2 = (const struct employee *) e2p;

    diff = difftime(e1->start_date, e2->start_date);   Compare times
    if (diff < 0)
        return -1;
    else if (diff > 0)
        return 1;
    else
        return 0;
}
```

For maximum portability we have used `difftime()`, which returns the difference in seconds between two `time_t` values. For this specific case, a cast such as

```
return (int) difftime(e1->start_date, e2->start_date);
```

should do the trick, since `time_t` values are within reasonable ranges. Nevertheless, we instead use a full three-way `if` statement, just to be safe.

Here is a sample data file, listing nine U.S. presidents:

```
$ cat presdata.txt
Trump Donald 47 1737396000            Last name, First name, President number, Inauguration
Biden Joseph 46 1611165600
Trump Donald 45 1484935200
Obama Barack 44 1232474400
Bush George 43 980013600
Clinton William 42 727552800
Bush George 41 601322400
Reagan Ronald 40 348861600
Carter James 39 222631200
```

`ch-general1-sortemp.c` shows a simple program that reads this file into a `struct employee` array and then sorts it, using the two different comparison functions just presented:

```
/* ch-general1-sortemp.c --- Demonstrate qsort() with two comparison functions. */

#include <stdio.h>
#include <stdlib.h>
#include <string.h>
#include <time.h>

struct employee {
    char lastname[30];
    char firstname[30];
    long emp_id;
    time_t start_date;
};

/* emp_name_id_compare --- compare by name, then by ID */

int
emp_name_id_compare(const void *e1p, const void *e2p)
{
 ... as shown previously, omitted to save space ...
}

/* emp_seniority_compare --- compare by seniority */

int
emp_seniority_compare(const void *e1p, const void *e2p)
{
 ... as shown previously, omitted to save space ...
}

/* main --- demonstrate sorting */

int
main(void)
{
#define NPRES 20
    struct employee presidents[NPRES];
    int i, npres;
    char buf[BUFSIZ];

    /* Very simple code to read data: */
    for (npres = 0; npres < NPRES && fgets(buf, BUFSIZ, stdin) != NULL;
                npres++) {
        sscanf(buf, "%s %s %ld %ld\n",
                presidents[npres].lastname,
```

```
78                  presidents[npres].firstname,
79                  & presidents[npres].emp_id,
80                  & presidents[npres].start_date);
81      }
82
83      /* npres is now number of actual lines read. */
84
85      /* First, sort by name */
86      qsort(presidents, npres, sizeof(struct employee), emp_name_id_compare);
87
88      /* Print output */
89      printf("Sorted by name:\n");
90      for (i = 0; i < npres; i++)
91          printf("\t%s %s\t%ld\t%s",
92                  presidents[i].lastname,
93                  presidents[i].firstname,
94                  presidents[i].emp_id,
95                  ctime(& presidents[i].start_date));
96
97      /* Now, sort by seniority */
98      qsort(presidents, npres, sizeof(struct employee), emp_seniority_compare);
99
100     /* And print again */
101     printf("Sorted by seniority:\n");
102     for (i = 0; i < npres; i++)
103         printf("\t%s %s\t%ld\t%s",
104                 presidents[i].lastname,
105                 presidents[i].firstname,
106                 presidents[i].emp_id,
107                 ctime(& presidents[i].start_date));
108 }
```

Lines 74–81 read in the data. Note that *any* use of `scanf()` requires "well behaved" input data. If, for example, any name is more than 29 characters, there's a problem. In this case, we're safe, but production code must be considerably more careful.

Line 86 sorts the data by name and employee ID, and then lines 89–95 print the sorted data. Similarly, line 98 re-sorts the data, this time by seniority, with lines 101–107 printing the results. When compiled and run, the program produces the following results:

```
$ ch-general1-sortemp < presdata.txt
Sorted by name:
        Biden Joseph    46      Wed Jan 20 13:00:00 2021
        Bush George     41      Fri Jan 20 13:00:00 1989
        Bush George     43      Sat Jan 20 13:00:00 2001
        Carter James    39      Thu Jan 20 13:00:00 1977
        Clinton William 42      Wed Jan 20 13:00:00 1993
```

```
        Obama Barack    44      Tue Jan 20 13:00:00 2009
        Reagan Ronald   40      Tue Jan 20 13:00:00 1981
        Trump Donald    45      Fri Jan 20 13:00:00 2017
        Trump Donald    47      Mon Jan 20 13:00:00 2025
Sorted by seniority:
        Carter James    39      Thu Jan 20 13:00:00 1977
        Reagan Ronald   40      Tue Jan 20 13:00:00 1981
        Bush George     41      Fri Jan 20 13:00:00 1989
        Clinton William 42      Wed Jan 20 13:00:00 1993
        Bush George     43      Sat Jan 20 13:00:00 2001
        Obama Barack    44      Tue Jan 20 13:00:00 2009
        Trump Donald    45      Fri Jan 20 13:00:00 2017
        Biden Joseph    46      Wed Jan 20 13:00:00 2021
        Trump Donald    47      Mon Jan 20 13:00:00 2025
```

(We've used 1:00 p.m. as an approximation for the time when each president started working.)[4]

One point is worth mentioning: `qsort()` rearranges the data in the array. If each array element is a large structure, *a lot* of data will be copied back and forth as the array is sorted. It may pay instead to set up *a separate array of pointers*, each of which points at one element of the array, and then use `qsort()` to sort the pointer array, accessing the *unsorted* data through the *sorted* pointers.

The price paid is the extra memory to hold the pointers and modification of the comparison function to use an extra pointer indirection when comparing the structures. The benefit returned can be a considerable speedup, since only a four- or eight-byte pointer is moved around at each step, instead of a large structure. (Our `struct employee` is 68 bytes in size on a 32-bit system and 80 bytes in size on a 64-bit one. Swapping four-byte pointers moves 17 times less data than does swapping structures. Even swapping eight-byte pointers moves 10 times less data than does swapping structures.) For millions of in-memory structures, the difference can be significant, and this may be even more important if you're developing for an embedded system with very limited memory.

NOTE

If you're a C++ programmer, beware! `qsort()` may be dangerous to use with arrays of objects! `qsort()` does raw memory moves, copying bytes. It's completely unaware of C++ constructs such as copy constructors or `operator=()` functions. Instead, use one of the STL sorting functions, or use the separate-array-of-pointers technique.

6.2.1.2 Example: Sorting Directory Contents

In Section 5.3, "Reading Directories," page 123, we demonstrated that directory entries are returned in physical directory order. Most of the time, it's much more useful to have directory

[4]The output shown here is for U.S. Eastern Standard Time. You will get different results for the same program and data if you use a different time zone.

contents sorted in some fashion, such as by name or by modification time. Several routines make it easy to do this, using `qsort()` as the underlying sorting agent:

```
#include <dirent.h>                                            POSIX

int scandir(const char *dir, struct dirent ***namelist,
            int (*select)(const struct dirent *),
            int (*compare)(const struct dirent **, const struct dirent **));
int alphasort(const struct dirent **a, const struct dirent **b);

int versionsort(const struct dirent **a, const struct dirent **b);     GLIBC
```

The `scandir()` and `alphasort()` functions were first made available in 4.2 BSD. They have always been widely supported, and are now standardized by POSIX. `versionsort()` is a GNU extension.

`scandir()` reads the directory named by `dir`, creates an array of `struct dirent` pointers by using `malloc()`, and sets `*namelist` to point to the beginning of that array. Both the array of pointers and the pointed-to `struct dirent` structures are allocated with `malloc()`; it is up to the calling code to use `free()` to avoid memory leaks.

Use the `select` function pointer to choose entries of interest. When this value is `NULL`, all valid directory entries are included in the final array. Otherwise, `(*select)()` is called for each entry, and those entries for which it returns nonzero (true) are included in the array.

The `compare` function pointer compares two directory entries. It is passed to `qsort()` for use in sorting.

`alphasort()` compares file names lexicographically. It uses the `strcoll()` function for comparison. `strcoll()` is similar to `strcmp()` but takes locale-related sorting rules into consideration (see Section 15.2.3, "String Collation: `strcoll()` and `strxfrm()`," page 512).

`versionsort()` is a GNU extension, that uses the GNU `strverscmp()` function to compare file names (see *strverscmp*(3)). To make a long story short, this function understands common file name versioning conventions and compares appropriately.

`ch-general1-sortdir.c` shows a program similar to `ch-fileinfo-catdir.c`. However, it uses `scandir()` and `alphasort()` to do the work:

```
/* ch-general1-sortdir.c --- Demonstrate scandir(), alphasort(). */

#include <stdio.h>              /* for printf() etc. */
#include <errno.h>              /* for errno */
#include <stdlib.h>             /* for free() */
#include <string.h>             /* for strerror() */
#include <sys/types.h>          /* for system types */
#include <dirent.h>             /* for directory functions */

char *myname;
int process(const char *dir);

/* main --- loop over directory arguments */
```

```

int
main(int argc, char **argv)
{
    int i;
    int errs = 0;

    myname = argv[0];

    if (argc == 1)
        errs = process(".");    /* default to current directory */
    else
        for (i = 1; i < argc; i++)
            errs += process(argv[i]);

    return (errs != 0);
}

/* nodots --- ignore dot files, for use by scandir() */

int
nodots(const struct dirent *dp)
{
    return (dp->d_name[0] != '.');
}

/*
 * process --- do something with the directory, in this case,
 *             print inode/name pairs on standard output.
 *             Return 0 if all OK, 1 otherwise.
 */

int
process(const char *dir)
{
    DIR *dp;
    struct dirent **entries;
    int nents, i;

    nents = scandir(dir, & entries, nodots, alphasort);
    if (nents < 0) {
        fprintf(stderr, "%s: scandir failed: %s\n", myname,
                        strerror(errno));
        return 1;
    }
```

```
59
60      for (i = 0; i < nents; i++) {
61          printf("%8ld %s\n", entries[i]->d_ino, entries[i]->d_name);
62          free(entries[i]);
63      }
64
65      free(entries);
66
67      return 0;
68  }
```

The `main()` program (lines 1–30) follows the standard boilerplate we've used before. The `nodots()` function (lines 34–38) acts as the `select` parameter, choosing only file names that don't begin with a period.

The `process()` function (lines 46–68) is quite simple, with `scandir()` doing most of the work. Note how each element is released separately with `free()` (line 62) and how the entire array is also released (line 65).

When run, the directory contents do indeed come out in sorted order, without `.` and `..`:

```
$ ch-general1-sortdir                      Default action displays current directory
 9207429 00-preface.texi
 9208690 01-intro.texi
 9205291 02-cmdline.texi
 9207424 03-memory.texi
 9207611 04-fileio.texi
 9207616 05-fileinfo.texi
 9208272 06-general1.texi
...
```

6.2.2 Binary Searching: `bsearch()`

A *linear search* is pretty much what it sounds like: you start at the beginning, and check each element of the array being searched until you find what you need. For something simple like finding integers, this usually takes the form of a `for` loop. Consider this function:

```
/* ifind --- linear search, return index if found or -1 if not */

int
ifind(int x, const int array[], size_t nelems)
{
    size_t i;

    for (i = 0; i < nelems; i++)
        if (array[i] == x)  /* found it */
            return i;

    return -1;
}
```

The advantage to linear searching is that it's simple; it's easy to write the code correctly the first time. Furthermore, it always works. Even if elements are added to the end of the array or removed from the array, there's no need to sort the array.

The disadvantage to linear searching is that it's slow. On average, for an array containing `nelems` elements, a linear search for a random element does '`nelems / 2`' comparisons before finding the desired element. This becomes prohibitively expensive, even on modern high-performance systems, as `nelems` becomes large. Thus, you should only use linear searching on small arrays.

Unlike a linear search, binary searching requires that the input array already be sorted. The disadvantage here is that if elements are added, the array must be re-sorted before it can be searched. (When elements are removed, the rest of the array contents must still be shuffled down. This is not as expensive as re-sorting, but it can still involve a lot of data motion.)

The advantage to binary searching—and it's a significant one—is that binary searching is blindingly fast, requiring at most $\lfloor log_2(N) \rfloor + 1$ comparisons, where N is the number of elements in the array. The `bsearch()` function is declared as follows:

```
#include <stdlib.h>                                                  ISO C

void *bsearch(const void *key, const void *base, size_t nmemb,
              size_t size, int (*compare)(const void *, const void *));
```

The parameters and their purposes are similar to those of `qsort()`:

`const void *key`
: The object being searched for in the array.

`const void *base`
: The start of the array.

`size_t nmemb`
: The number of elements in the array.

`size_t size`
: The size of each element, obtained with `sizeof`.

`int (*compare)(const void *, const void *)`
: The comparison function. It must work the same way as the `qsort()` comparison function, returning negative/zero/positive according to whether the first parameter is less than/equal to/greater than the second one.

`bsearch()` returns `NULL` if the object is not found. Otherwise, it returns a pointer to the found object. If more than one array element matches `key`, it is unspecified which one is returned. Thus, as with `qsort()`, make sure that the comparison function accounts for all relevant parts of the searched data structure.

`ch-general1-searchemp.c` shows `bsearch()` in practice, extending the `struct employee` example used previously:

```
1  /* ch-general1-searchemp.c --- Demonstrate bsearch(). */
2
3  #include <stdio.h>
4  #include <errno.h>
5  #include <string.h>
6  #include <stdlib.h>
7  #include <time.h>
8
9  struct employee {
10     char lastname[30];
11     char firstname[30];
12     long emp_id;
13     time_t start_date;
14 };
15
16 /* emp_id_compare --- compare by ID */
17
18 int
19 emp_id_compare(const void *e1p, const void *e2p)
20 {
21     const struct employee *e1, *e2;
22
23     e1 = (const struct employee *) e1p;
24     e2 = (const struct employee *) e2p;
25
26     if (e1->emp_id < e2->emp_id)
27         return -1;
28     else if (e1->emp_id == e2->emp_id)
29         return 0;
30     else
31         return 1;
32 }
33
34 /* print_employee --- print an employee structure */
35
36 void
37 print_employee(const struct employee *emp)
38 {
39     printf("%s %s\t%ld\t%s", emp->lastname, emp->firstname,
40             emp->emp_id, ctime(& emp->start_date));
41 }
```

Lines 9–14 define the `struct employee`; it's the same as before. Lines 18–32 serve as the comparison function, for both `qsort()` and `bsearch()`. It compares on employee ID number only. Lines 36–41 define `print_employee()`, which is a convenience function for printing the structure, since this is done from multiple places. The code continues:

```
/* main --- demonstrate sorting */

int
main(int argc, char **argv)
{
#define NPRES 20
    struct employee presidents[NPRES];
    int i, npres;
    char buf[BUFSIZ];
    struct employee *the_pres;
    struct employee key;
    int id;
    FILE *fp;

    if (argc != 2) {
        fprintf(stderr, "usage: %s datafile\n", argv[0]);
        exit(1);
    }

    if ((fp = fopen(argv[1], "r")) == NULL) {
        fprintf(stderr, "%s: %s: could not open: %s\n", argv[0],
                        argv[1], strerror(errno));
        exit(1);
    }

    /* Very simple code to read data: */
    for (npres = 0; npres < NPRES && fgets(buf, BUFSIZ, fp) != NULL;
                npres++) {
        sscanf(buf, "%s %s %ld %ld",
                presidents[npres].lastname,
                presidents[npres].firstname,
                & presidents[npres].emp_id,
                & presidents[npres].start_date);
    }
    fclose(fp);

    /* npres is now number of actual lines read. */

    /* First, sort by id */
    qsort(presidents, npres, sizeof(struct employee), emp_id_compare);

    /* Print output */
    printf("Sorted by ID:\n");
    for (i = 0; i < npres; i++) {
        putchar('\t');
```

```
88             print_employee(& presidents[i]);
89         }
90
91         for (;;) {
92             printf("Enter ID number: ");
93             if (fgets(buf, BUFSIZ, stdin) == NULL)
94                     break;
95
96             sscanf(buf, "%d\n", & id);
97             key.emp_id = id;
98             the_pres = (struct employee *) bsearch(& key, presidents, npres,
99                             sizeof(struct employee), emp_id_compare);
100
101            if (the_pres != NULL) {
102                    printf("Found: ");
103                    print_employee(the_pres);
104            } else
105                    printf("Employee with ID %d not found!\n", id);
106        }
107
108        putchar('\n');  /* Print a newline on EOF. */
109
110        exit(0);
111    }
```

The `main()` function starts with argument checking (lines 57–60). It then reads the data from the named file (lines 68–77). Standard input cannot be used for the employee data, since that is reserved for prompting the user for the employee ID to search for.

Lines 82–89 sort and print the employees. The program then goes into a loop, starting on line 91. It prompts for an employee ID number, exiting the loop upon end-of-file. To search the array, we use the `struct employee` named `key`. It's enough to set just its `emp_id` field to the entered ID number; none of the other fields are used in the comparison (line 97).

If an entry is found with the matching key, `bsearch()` returns a pointer to it. Otherwise it returns `NULL`. The return is tested on line 101, and appropriate action is then taken. Finally, line 108 prints a newline character so that the system prompt will come out on a fresh line. Here's a transcript of what happens when the program is compiled and run:

```
$ ch-general1-searchemp presdata.txt                          Run the program
Sorted by ID:
        Carter James    39      Thu Jan 20 13:00:00 1977
        Reagan Ronald   40      Tue Jan 20 13:00:00 1981
        Bush George     41      Fri Jan 20 13:00:00 1989
        Clinton William 42      Wed Jan 20 13:00:00 1993
        Bush George     43      Sat Jan 20 13:00:00 2001
        Obama Barack    44      Tue Jan 20 13:00:00 2009
        Trump Donald    45      Fri Jan 20 13:00:00 2017
```

```
        Biden Joseph     46       Wed Jan 20 13:00:00 2021
        Trump Donald     47       Mon Jan 20 13:00:00 2025
Enter ID number: 45                                          Enter a valid number
Found: Trump Donald      45       Fri Jan 20 13:00:00 2017   It's found
Enter ID number: 29                                          Enter an invalid number
Employee with ID 29 not found!                               It's not found
Enter ID number: 40                                          Try another good one
Found: Reagan Ronald     40       Tue Jan 20 13:00:00 1981   This one is found too
Enter ID number: ^D                                          CTRL-D entered for EOF
$                                                            Ready for next command
```

Additional, more advanced APIs for searching data collections are described in Section 16.4, "Advanced Searching with Binary Trees," page 575.

6.2.2.1 Example: Sorting and Searching Together

Sorting data and searching it go together. We next present an example from real-world code, drawn this time from the current version of the original Unix `awk` program.[5] The code comes from that portion of `awk` that matches regular expressions.

By way of introduction, regular expression matching in `awk` uses a technique based on automata theory. In particular, it uses a Deterministic Finite Automaton, or DFA. The DFA matcher starts out in an initial state. Based on the input characters, it moves from one state to the next until it arrives at the terminating state or determines that it cannot do so. In the former case, the regular expression it represents has matched the input text; in the latter, it has not. Figure 6.2 shows the transitions among states for the regular expression '`(a|b)c`'.

State 1 is the initial state, and State 4 is the final state. The figure is very simplistic. From any given state, it may be possible to move to multiple following states, based on the current input character. This is termed a *state transition*.

In the early days of computing, when characters were always a single byte in size, the representation of a state transition was very simple. One could use a two-dimensional table,

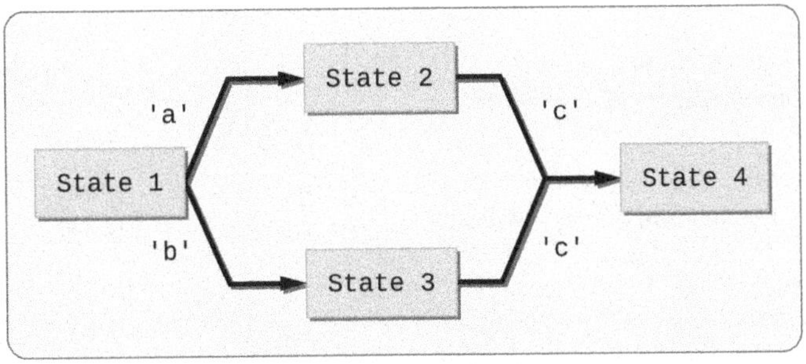

Figure 6.2: A very simple DFA

[5]See the code on GitHub (`https://github.com/onetrueawk/awk`) if you're interested.

where the row is indexed by the current state and the column is indexed by the current input character. The value stored in the table would indicate the next state to move to:

```
next_state = transition[current_state][current_char];
```

In such a representation, each row took up a maximum of 256 entries. And indeed, `awk` used such a representation:

```
...
if ((ns = f->gototab[s][*p]) != 0)
    s = ns;
...
```

Here, `f` is the DFA, `ns` is the next state, `s` is the current state, and `*p` is the current input character. `gototab` is short for "goto table": a table indicating which state to go to next.

The problem is that in today's world, characters are no longer just a single byte in size. In particular, the Unicode character set has code points (character values) that are normally represented with at least four bytes, and are encoded in files using one to four bytes. (There's more on this later in the book; see Section 15.4.2, "Multibyte Character Encodings," page 545.) There are well over a million valid Unicode code points—1,114,112 to be exact—thus it's not practical for each row in a transition table to have over a million entries.

To solve this problem, Brian Kernighan moved the goto table into a different structure, accessed via functions. The data structure for a `gototab` consisted of a "goto table entry":

```
typedef struct gtt { /* gototab entry */
    unsigned int ch;              The character of interest
    unsigned int state;           The state to move to
} gtt;
```

Initially, he left the size of each row at (approximately) 256 entries, and he used a linear search within the row to find the current input character, and from there return the next state. The function is named `get_gototab()`:

```
static int get_gototab(fa *f, int state, int ch) /* hide gototab implementation */
{
    int i;
    for (i = 0; i < f->gototab_len; i++) {
        if (f->gototab[state][i].ch == 0)
            break;
        if (f->gototab[state][i].ch == ch)
            return f->gototab[state][i].state;
    }
    return 0;
}
```

During the matching, if input characters are not found in the `gototab`, they and their next state are added to it.[6] This happens in `set_gototab()`:

---

[6]We don't understand why this is the case; the code is *very* opaque. We choose here to explain what the code does, without getting into why it works the way it does.

```
static int set_gototab(fa *f, int state, int ch, int val) /* hide gototab implementation */
{
    int i;
    for (i = 0; i < f->gototab_len; i++) {
        if (f->gototab[state][i].ch == 0 || f->gototab[state][i].ch == ch) {
            f->gototab[state][i].ch = ch;
            f->gototab[state][i].state = val;
            return val;
        }
    }
    overflo(__func__);
    return val; /* not used anywhere at the moment */
}
```

The new implementation worked, but if an input file contained many Unicode characters, `awk`'s matching became unacceptably slow, and it was possible to exceed the fixed limit on the number of entries.

Your author decided to see if these problems could be fixed without too much disruption in the code. This involved three changes:

- Dynamically growing the size of the `gototab` as needed.
- Looking up the entries in the `gototab` with a binary search.
- Keeping the entries sorted so that binary search would work.

First off, the structures got rearranged a little, in order to accommodate the dynamic sizing:

```
typedef struct gtte { /* gototab entry */
    unsigned int ch;
    unsigned int state;
} gtte;

typedef struct gtt {   /* gototab */
    size_t  allocated;
    size_t  inuse;
    gtte    *entries;
} gtt;
```

For both sorting and searching, we need a comparison function:

```
static int entry_cmp(const void *l, const void *r)
{
    const gtte *left, *right;

    left = (const gtte *) l;
    right = (const gtte *) r;

    return left->ch - right->ch;
}
```

Finding an entry uses a classic call to `bsearch()`:

```
static int get_gototab(fa *f, int state, int ch) /* hide gototab implementation */
{
    gtte key;
    gtte *item;

    key.ch = ch;
    key.state = 0;  /* irrelevant */
    item = bsearch(& key, f->gototab[state].entries,
            f->gototab[state].inuse, sizeof(gtte),
            entry_cmp);

    if (item == NULL)
        return 0;
    else
        return item->state;
}
```

Adding a new character and state is more complicated, because the list must be kept sorted.[7] In pseudocode, though, it's rather straightforward:

```
if the array is empty:
    add the character and state
    increment the count of entries in use
    return
else if the current character is greater than the last one in the array:
    // since it's greater, the array stays sorted
    grow the array if necessary
    add the character and state
    increment the count of entries in use
    return
else:
    binary search the list to see if we already have the current character
    if so, update the state and return

// At this point, the current character isn't in the list, so it must be added:
grow the array if necessary
add the character and state
increment the count of entries in use
sort the array
return
```

[7] There's potentially a lot of sorting happening here. Some versions of `qsort()` don't perform well on data that is almost sorted, as can happen in this case. The version in GLIBC doesn't have that problem.

With that introduction, here is the new version of `set_gototab()`:

```
static int set_gototab(fa *f, int state, int ch, int val) /* hide gototab implementation */
{
    if (f->gototab[state].inuse == 0) {
        f->gototab[state].entries[0].ch = ch;
        f->gototab[state].entries[0].state = val;
        f->gototab[state].inuse++;
        return val;
    } else if ((unsigned)ch > f->gototab[state].entries[f->gototab[state].inuse-1].ch) {
        // not seen yet, insert and return
        gtt *tab = & f->gototab[state];
        if (tab->inuse + 1 >= tab->allocated)
            resize_gototab(f, state);

        f->gototab[state].entries[f->gototab[state].inuse].ch = ch;
        f->gototab[state].entries[f->gototab[state].inuse].state = val;
        f->gototab[state].inuse++;
        return val;
    } else {
        // maybe we have it, maybe we don't
        gtte key;
        gtte *item;

        key.ch = ch;
        key.state = 0;  /* irrelevant */
        item = (gtte *) bsearch(& key, f->gototab[state].entries,
                f->gototab[state].inuse, sizeof(gtte),
                entry_cmp);

        if (item != NULL) {
            // we have it, update state and return
            item->state = val;
            return item->state;
        }
        // otherwise, fall through to insert and reallocate.
    }

    gtt *tab = & f->gototab[state];
    if (tab->inuse + 1 >= tab->allocated)
        resize_gototab(f, state);
    f->gototab[state].entries[tab->inuse].ch = ch;
    f->gototab[state].entries[tab->inuse].state = val;
    ++tab->inuse;
```

```
    qsort(f->gototab[state].entries,
        f->gototab[state].inuse, sizeof(gtte), entry_cmp);

    return val; /* not used anywhere at the moment */
}
```

The end result is that awk's regular expression matching is now both free of the previous fixed limit, and acceptably performant. Binary search saves the day!

We return to this suite of functions in Section 17.6.1.1, "Valgrind Example: gototab in the One True Awk," page 642.

6.3 User and Group Names

While the operating system works with user and group ID numbers for storage of file ownership and for permission checking, humans prefer to work with user and group *names*.

Early Unix systems kept the information that mapped names to ID numbers in simple text files, /etc/passwd and /etc/group. These files still exist on modern systems, and their format is unchanged from that of V7 Unix. However, they no longer tell the complete story. Large installations with many networked hosts keep the information in *network databases*: ways of storing the information on a small number of servers that are then accessed over the network.[8] However, this usage is *transparent* to most applications since access to the information is done through the same API as was used for retrieving the information from the text files. It is for this reason that POSIX standardizes only the APIs; the /etc/passwd and /etc/group files need not exist as such for a system to be POSIX compliant.

The APIs to the two databases are similar; most of our discussion focuses on the user database.

6.3.1 User Database

The traditional /etc/passwd format maintains one line per user. Each line has seven fields, each of which is separated from the next by a colon character:

```
$ grep arnold /etc/passwd
arnold:x:1000:1000:Arnold D. Robbins,,,:/home/arnold:/bin/bash
```

In order, the fields are as follows:

The user name
: This is what the user types to log in. It is also what shows up for 'ls -l' and in any other context that displays users.

[8]Common network databases include Sun Microsystems' Network Information Service (NIS) and NIS+, Kerberos (Hesiod), macOS DirectoryServices, and LDAP, the Lightweight Directory Access Protocol. BSD systems keep user information in on-disk databases and generate the /etc/passwd and /etc/group files automatically.

The password field

Once upon a time, this was the user's encrypted password. Today, this field is likely to be an `x` (as shown), meaning that the password information is held in a different file that isn't world-readable. This separation is a security measure; if the encrypted password isn't available to nonprivileged users, it is much harder to "crack."

The user ID number

This should be unique—one number per user.

The group ID number

This is the user's initial group ID number. As is discussed later, processes have multiple groups associated with them.

The user's real name

This is at least a first and last name. Some systems allow for comma-separated fields, for office location, phone number, and so on (again, as shown), but this is not standardized.

The login directory

This directory becomes the home directory for users when they log in (`$HOME`—the default for the `cd` command).

The login program

The program to run when the user logs in. This is usually a shell, but it need not be. If this field is left empty, the default is `/bin/sh`.

Access to the user database is through the routines declared in `<pwd.h>`:

```
#include <pwd.h>                                          POSIX

struct passwd *getpwnam(const char *name);
struct passwd *getpwuid(uid_t uid);

struct passwd *getpwent(void);                            POSIX XSI
void setpwent(void);
void endpwent(void);
```

The fields in the `struct passwd` used by the various API routines correspond directly to the fields in the password file:

```
struct passwd {
    char    *pw_name;       /* user name */
    char    *pw_passwd;     /* user password */
    uid_t   pw_uid;         /* user id */
    gid_t   pw_gid;         /* group id */
    char    *pw_gecos;      /* real name */
    char    *pw_dir;        /* home directory */
    char    *pw_shell;      /* shell program */
};
```

(The name `pw_gecos` is historical; when the early Unix systems were being developed, this field held the corresponding information for the user's account on the Bell Labs Honeywell systems running the GECOS operating system.)

The purpose of each routine is described in the following list:

`struct passwd *getpwent(void)`
: Return a pointer to an internal `static struct passwd` structure containing the "current" user's information. This routine reads through the entire password database one record at a time, returning a pointer to a structure for each user. The same pointer is returned each time; that is, the internal `struct passwd` is overwritten for each user's entry. When `getpwent()` reaches the end of the password database, it returns `NULL`. Thus it lets you step through the entire database, one user at a time. The order in which records are returned is undefined.

`void setpwent(void)`
: Reset the internal state such that the next call to `getpwent()` returns the first record in the password database.

`void endpwent(void)`
: "Close the database," so to speak, be it a simple file, network connection, or something else.

`struct passwd *getpwnam(const char *name)`
: Look up the user with a `pw_name` member equal to `name`, returning a pointer to a `static struct passwd` describing the user or `NULL` if the user is not found.

`struct passwd *getpwuid(uid_t uid)`
: Similarly, look up the user with the user ID number given by `uid`, returning a pointer to a `static struct passwd` describing the user or `NULL` if the user is not found.

`getpwuid()` is what's needed when you have a user ID number (such as from a `struct stat`) and you wish to print the corresponding user name. It's also useful if you want to look up your own information, such as home directory or login shell, based on the return value of `getuid()`. (`getuid()` is presented later, in Section 11.2, "Retrieving User and Group IDs," page 385.) `getpwnam()` converts a name to a user ID number, for example, if you wish to use `chown()` or `fchown()` on a file. In theory, both of these routines do a linear search through the password database to find the desired information. This is true in practice when a password file is used; however, behind-the-scenes databases (network or otherwise, as on BSD systems) tend to use more efficient methods of storage, so these calls are possibly not as expensive in such cases.[9]

`getpwent()` is useful when you need to go through the entire password database. For instance, you might wish to read it all into memory, sort it, and then search it quickly with `bsearch()`. This is very useful for avoiding the multiple linear searches inherent in looking things up one at a time with `getpwuid()` or `getpwnam()`.

---

[9]Unfortunately, if performance is an issue, there's no standard way to know how your library does things, and indeed, the way it works can vary at runtime! (See the *nsswitch.conf*(5) manpage on a GNU/Linux system.) On the other hand, the point of the API is, after all, to hide the details.

NOTE

The pointers returned by `getpwent()`, `getpwnam()`, and `getpwuid()` all point to internal `static` data. Thus, you should make a copy of their contents if you need to save the information.

Take a good look at the `struct passwd` definition. The members that represent character strings are pointers; they too point at internal `static` data, and if you're going to copy the structure, make sure to copy the data each member points to as well.

6.3.2 Group Database

The format of the `/etc/group` group database is similar to that of `/etc/passwd`, but with fewer fields:

```
$ grep arnold /etc/group | sort
adm:x:4:syslog,arnold,miriam
arnold:x:1000:
audio:x:29:pulse,arnold,miriam
cdrom:x:24:arnold,miriam,videos
dialout:x:20:miriam,arnold,videos
...
```

Again, there is one line per group, with fields separated by colons. The fields are as follows:

The group name
: This is the name of the group, as shown in '`ls -l`' or in any other context in which a group name is needed.

The group password
: This field is historical. It is no longer used.

The group ID number
: As with the user ID, this should be unique to each group.

The user list
: This is a comma-separated list of users who are members of the group.

In the previous example, we see that user `arnold` is a member of multiple groups. This membership is reflected in practice in what is termed the *group set*. Besides the main user ID and group ID number that processes have, the group set is a set of additional group ID numbers that each process carries around with it. The system checks all of these group ID numbers against a file's group ID number when performing permission checking. This subject is discussed in more detail in Chapter 11, "Permissions and User and Group ID Numbers," page 383.

The group database APIs are similar to those for the user database. The following functions are declared in `<grp.h>`:

```
#include <grp.h>                                          POSIX

struct group *getgrnam(const char *name);
struct group *getgrgid(gid_t gid);

struct group *getgrent(void);                             POSIX XSI
void setgrent(void);
void endgrent(void);
```

The `struct group` corresponds to the records in `/etc/group`:

```
struct group {
    char    *gr_name;       /* group name */
    char    *gr_passwd;     /* group password */
    gid_t   gr_gid;         /* group id */
    char    **gr_mem;       /* group members */
};
```

The `gr_mem` field bears some explanation. While declared as a pointer to a pointer (`char **`), it is best thought of as an array of strings (like `argv`). The last element in the array is set to `NULL`. When no members are listed, the first element in the array is `NULL`.

`ch-general1-groupinfo.c` demonstrates how to use the `struct group` and the `gr_mem` field. The program accepts a single user name on the command line and prints all group records in which that user name appears:

```
/* ch-general1-groupinfo.c --- Demonstrate getgrent() and struct group */

#include <stdio.h>
#include <stdlib.h>
#include <string.h>
#include <grp.h>

extern void print_group(const struct group *gr);

/* main --- print group lines for user named in argv[1] */

int
main(int argc, char **argv)
{
    struct group *gr;
    int i;

    if (argc != 2) {                                      Check arguments
        fprintf(stderr, "usage: %s user\n", argv[0]);
        exit(1);
    }

```

```
23      while ((gr = getgrent()) != NULL)                  Get each group record
24          for (i = 0; gr->gr_mem[i] != NULL; i++)        Look at each member
25              if (strcmp(gr->gr_mem[i], argv[1]) == 0)   If found the user ...
26                  print_group(gr);                       Print the record
27
28      endgrent();
29
30      exit(0);
31  }
```

The main() routine first does error checking (lines 18–21). The heart of the program is a nested loop. The outer loop (line 23) loops over all the group database records. The inner loop (line 24) loops over the members of the gr_mem array. If one of the members matches the name from the command line (line 25), then print_group() is called to print the record (line 26). Here is print_group():

```
33  /* print_group --- print a group record */
34
35  void
36  print_group(const struct group *gr)
37  {
38      int i;
39
40      printf("%s:%s:%ld:", gr->gr_name, gr->gr_passwd, (long) gr->gr_gid);
41
42      for (i = 0; gr->gr_mem[i] != NULL; i++) {
43          printf("%s", gr->gr_mem[i]);
44          if (gr->gr_mem[i+1] != NULL)
45              putchar(',');
46      }
47
48      putchar('\n');
49  }
```

The print_group() function (lines 35–49) is straightforward, with logic similar to that of main() for printing the member list. Group list members are comma separated; thus the loop body has to check that the *next* element in the array is not NULL before printing a comma. This code works correctly, even if there are no members in the group. However, for this program, we know there are members, or print_group() wouldn't have been called! Here's what happens when the program is run:

```
$ ch-general1-groupinfo arnold | sort
adm:x:4:syslog,arnold,miriam
audio:x:29:pulse,arnold,miriam
cdrom:x:24:arnold,miriam,videos
dialout:x:20:miriam,arnold,videos
...
```

Interestingly, the line 'arnold:x:1000:' is missing. This is because the group member list is empty, and our program examines only the members of that list.

6.4 Terminals: `isatty()`

The Linux/Unix standard input, standard output, standard error model discourages the special treatment of input and output devices. Programs generally should not need to know, or care, whether their output is a terminal, a file, a pipe, a network connection, a physical device, or whatever.

However, there are times when a program really does need to know what kind of a file a file descriptor is associated with. The `stat()` family of calls often provides enough information: regular file, directory, device, and so on. Sometimes, though, even that is not enough, and for interactive programs in particular, you may need to know if a file descriptor represents a tty.

A *tty* (short for Teletype, one of the early manufacturers of computer terminals) is any device that represents a terminal—that is, something that a human would use to interact with the computer. This may be either a hardware device, such as the keyboard and monitor of a personal computer, an old-fashioned video display terminal connected to a computer by a serial line or modem, or a software *pseudoterminal*, such as is used for windowing systems and network logins.

The discrimination can be made with `isatty()`:

```
#include <unistd.h>                                          POSIX

int isatty(int desc);
```

This function returns `1` if the file descriptor `desc` represents a terminal and `0` otherwise. According to POSIX, `isatty()` may set `errno` to indicate an error; thus you should set `errno` to `0` before calling `isatty()` and then check its value if the return is `0`. The POSIX standard also points out that `isatty()` returning `1` doesn't mean there's a human at the other end of the file descriptor!

One place where `isatty()` comes into use is in `ls`, in which the default is to print file names in columns if the standard output is a terminal and to print them one per line if not. Another is GNU `grep`'s `--color` option, which colorizes the matching text in the output if writing to a terminal.

There are a number of system calls and library functions for dealing specifically with terminals. We don't cover them in this book for reasons of space.

6.5 Suggested Reading

1. *Mastering Algorithms with C*, by Kyle Loudon. O'Reilly, 1999. ISBN-13: 978-1-56592-453-6.

   This book provides a practical, down-to-earth introduction to algorithms and data structures using C, covering hash tables, trees, sorting, and searching, among other things.

2. *The Art of Computer Programming*, vol. 3: *Sorting and Searching*, 2nd ed., by Donald E. Knuth. Addison-Wesley, 1998. ISBN-13: 978-0-201-89685-5.

   This book is usually cited as the final word on sorting and searching. Bear in mind that it is considerably denser and harder to read than the Loudon book.

3. The GTK project[10] consists of several libraries that work together. GTK is the underlying toolkit used by the GNU GNOME Project.[11] At the base of the library hierarchy is GLib, a library of fundamental types and data structures and functions for working with them. GLib includes facilities for all the basic operations we've covered so far in this book, and many more, including linked lists and hash tables. To get started, see GLib's online documentation.[12]

6.6 Summary

- Times are stored internally as `time_t` values, representing "seconds since the Epoch." The Epoch is midnight, January 1, 1970, UTC, for GNU/Linux and Unix systems. The current time is retrieved from the system by the `time()` system call, and `difftime()` returns the difference, in seconds, between two `time_t` values.
- The `struct tm` structure represents a "broken-down time," which is a much more usable representation of a date and time. `gmtime()` and `localtime()` convert `time_t` values into `struct tm` values, and `mktime()` goes in the opposite direction.
- `asctime()` and `ctime()` do simplistic formatting of time values, returning a pointer to a fixed-size, fixed-format `static` character string. `strftime()` provides much more flexible formatting, including locale-based values. The `strptime()` function parses a formatted date and time, filling in the members of a `struct tm`.
- Time-zone information is made available by a call to `tzset()`. Since the standard routines act as if they call `tzset()` automatically, it is rare to need to call this function directly.
- The standard routine for sorting arrays is `qsort()`. By using a user-provided comparison function and being told the number of array elements and their size, `qsort()` can sort any kind of data. This provides considerable flexibility.
- `scandir()` reads an entire directory into an array of `struct dirent`. User-provided functions can be used to select which entries to include and can provide ordering of elements within the array. `alphasort()` is a standard function for sorting directory entries by name; `scandir()` passes the comparison function straight through to `qsort()`.
- The `bsearch()` function works similarly to `qsort()`. It does fast binary searching. Use it if the cost of linear searching outweighs the cost of sorting your data. (An additional

[10] `https://www.gtk.org`

[11] `https://www.gnome.org`

[12] `https://docs.gtk.org/glib/`

API for searching data collections is described in Section 16.4, "Advanced Searching with Binary Trees," page 575.)

- The user and group databases may be kept in local disk files or may be made available over a network. The standard API purposely hides this distinction. Each database provides both linear scanning of the entire database and direct queries for a user/group name or user/group ID.
- Finally, for those times when `stat()` just isn't enough, `isatty()` can tell you whether or not an open file represents a terminal device.

Exercises

1. Write a simple version of the `date` command that accepts a format string on the command line and uses it to format and print the current time.
2. When a file is more than six months old, '`ls -l`' uses a simpler format for printing the modification time. The GNU version of `ls.c` uses this computation:

```
struct timespec six_months_ago;
     ...
/* Consider a time to be recent if it is within the past six months.
   A Gregorian year has 365.2425 * 24 * 60 * 60 == 31556952 seconds
   on the average.  Write this value as an integer constant to
   avoid floating point hassles.  */
six_months_ago.tv_sec = current_time.tv_sec - 31556952 / 2;
six_months_ago.tv_nsec = current_time.tv_nsec;
```

   Compare this to our example computation for computing the time six months in the past. What are the advantages and disadvantages of each method?

3. Write your own version of `strftime()`. Don't worry about locale differences; simply use the English names for the months and the days of the week. Be sure not to overflow the input buffer.

   Compare your version to the author's, available on GitHub.[13]

4. Write a simple version of the `touch` command that changes the modification time of the files named on the command line to the current time.
5. Add an option to your `touch` command that accepts a date and time specification on the command line and uses that value as the new modification time of the files named on the command line. Can you use `strptime()`?
6. Add another option to your version of `touch` that takes a file name and uses the modification time of the given file as the new modification time for the files named on the command line.

---

[13]`https://www.github.com/arnoldrobbins/strftime`

7. Enhance `ch-general1-sortemp.c` to sort a separate array of pointers that point into the array of employees.
8. Add options to `ch-general1-sortdir.c` to sort by inode number, modification time, access time, and size. Add a "reverse option" such that time-based sorts make the most *recent* file first and other criteria (size, inode) sort by largest value first.
9. Write a simple version of the `chown` command. Its usage should be

   `chown` *user*[`:` *group*] *files* ...

   Here, *user* and *group* are user and group names representing the new user and group for the named files. The *group* is optional; if present, it is separated from the *user* by a colon.

   To test your version on a GNU/Linux system, you will have to work as `root`. Do so carefully!
10. Enhance your `chown` to allow numeric user or group numbers, as well as names.
11. Write functions to copy user and group structures, including pointed-to data. Use `malloc()` to allocate storage as needed.
12. Write a specialized user-lookup library that reads the entire user database into a dynamically allocated array. Provide *fast* lookup of users, by both user ID number and name. Be sure to handle the case in which a requested user isn't found.
13. Do the same thing for the group database.
14. Enhance `ch-general1-groupinfo.c` to also examine the `gr_name` field of the `struct group`.
15. Write a `stat` program that prints the contents of the `struct stat` for each file named on the command line. It should print all the values in human-readable format: `time_t` values as dates and times, `uid_t` and `gid_t` values as the corresponding names (if available), and the contents of symbolic links. Print the `st_mode` field the same way that `ls` would.

    Compare your program to the GNU Coreutils `stat` program, both by comparing outputs and by looking at the source code.
16. Get a cup of coffee (or tea), sit down, and read the *stty*(1) manpage, which describes the myriad options and settings for terminals. When your head stops spinning, think about the history of terminal devices, from physical teletypes through video terminals and on to windowing systems. Which of the features that are still supported today are mostly irrelevant? Which are still necessary for day-to-day use?

Chapter 7

Putting It All Together: `ls`

The V7 `ls` command nicely ties together everything we've seen so far. It uses almost all of the APIs we've covered, touching on many aspects of Unix programming: memory allocation, file metadata, dates and times, user names, directory reading, and sorting.

7.1 V7 `ls` Options

In comparison to modern versions of `ls`, the V7 `ls` accepted only a handful of options, and the meaning of some of them is different for V7 than for current `ls`. The options are as follows:

`-a` Print all directory entries. Without this, don't print `.` (dot) and `..` (dot-dot). Interestingly enough, V7 `ls` ignores only `.` and `..`, while V1 through V6 ignore any file whose name begins with a period. This latter behavior is the default in modern versions of `ls`, as well.

`-c` Use the inode change time, instead of the modification time, with `-t` or `-l`.

`-d` For directory arguments, print information about the directory itself, not its contents.

`-f` "Force" each argument to be read as a directory, and print the name found in each slot. This option disables `-l`, `-r`, `-s`, and `-t`, and enables `-a`. (This option apparently existed for filesystem debugging and repair.)

`-g` For '`ls -l`', use the group name instead of the user name.

`-i` Print the inode number in the first column along with the file name or the long listing.

`-l` Provide the familiar long format output. Note, however, that V7 '`ls -l`' printed only the user name, not the user and group names together.

`-r` Reverse the sort order, be it alphabetic for file names or by time.

`-s` Print the size of the file in 512-byte blocks. The V7 *ls*(1) manpage states that *indirect blocks*—blocks used by the filesystem for locating the data blocks of large files—are also included in the computation, but, as we shall see, this statement was incorrect.

`-t` Sort the output by modification time, with most recent first, instead of by name.

`-u` Use the access time instead of the modification time with `-t` and/or `-l`.

The biggest differences between V7 `ls` and modern `ls` concern the `-a` option and the `-l` option. Modern systems omit all dot files unless `-a` is given, and they include both user and group names in the `-l` long listing. On modern systems, `-g` is taken to mean print only the group name, and `-o` means print only the user name. For what it's worth, GNU `ls` has almost 60 options!

7.2 V7 `ls` Code

The file `/usr/src/cmd/ls.c` in the V7 distribution contains the code.[1] It is all of 425 lines long:

```
/*
 * list file or directory
 */

#include <sys/param.h>
#include <sys/stat.h>
#include <sys/dir.h>
#include <stdio.h>

#define NFILES  1024
FILE    *pwdf, *dirf;
char    stdbuf[BUFSIZ];

```

Collects needed info

```
struct lbuf {
    union {
        char    lname[15];
        char    *namep;
    } ln;
    char    ltype;
    short   lnum;
    short   lflags;
    short   lnl;
    short   luid;
    short   lgid;
    long    lsize;
    long    lmtime;
};

int aflg, dflg, lflg, sflg, tflg, uflg, iflg, fflg, gflg, cflg;
int rflg    = 1;
long    year;
```

Global variables: auto init to 0

[1] A copy is included in the book's GitHub repository.

```
32 int flags;
33 int lastuid = -1;
34 char    tbuf[16];
35 long    tblocks;
36 int statreq;
37 struct  lbuf    *flist[NFILES];
38 struct  lbuf    **lastp = flist;
39 struct  lbuf    **firstp = flist;
40 char    *dotp   = ".";
41
42 char    *makename();
43 struct  lbuf *gstat();
44 char    *ctime();
45 long    nblock();
46
47 #define ISARG   0100000
```

*char *makename(char *dir, char *file);*
*struct lbuf *gstat(char *file, int argfl);*
*char *ctime(time_t *t);*
long nblock(long size);

The program starts with file inclusions (lines 5–8) and variable declarations. The `struct lbuf` (lines 14–27) encapsulates the parts of the `struct stat` that are of interest to `ls`. We see later how this structure is filled.

The variables `aflg`, `dflg`, and so on (lines 29 and 30) all indicate the presence of the corresponding option. This variable naming style is typical of V7 code. The `flist`, `lastp`, and `firstp` variables (lines 37–39) represent the files that `ls` reports information about. Note that `flist` is a fixed-size array, allowing no more than 1,024 files to be processed. We see shortly how all these variables are used.

After the variable declarations come function declarations (lines 42–45), and then the definition of `ISARG`, which distinguishes a file named on the command line from a file found when a directory is read. Here is the `main()` function:

```
49 main(argc, argv)                              int main(int argc, char **argv)
50 char *argv[];
51 {
52      int i;
53      register struct lbuf *ep, **ep1;          Variable and function declarations
54      register struct lbuf **slastp;
55      struct lbuf **epp;
56      struct lbuf lb;
57      char *t;
58      int compar();
59
60      setbuf(stdout, stdbuf);
61      time(&lb.lmtime);                         Get current time
62      year = lb.lmtime - 6L*30L*24L*60L*60L; /* 6 months ago */
```

`main()` starts by declaring variables and functions (lines 52–58), setting the buffer for standard output, retrieving the time of day (lines 60–61), and computing the seconds-since-the-Epoch value for approximately six months ago (line 62). Note that all the constants have the `L` suffix, indicating the use of `long` arithmetic. Next comes option parsing:

```
63      if (--argc > 0 && *argv[1] == '-') {
64          argv++;
65          while (*++*argv) switch (**argv) {        Parse options
66
67          case 'a':                                 All directory entries
68              aflg++;
69              continue;
70
71          case 's':                                 Size in blocks
72              sflg++;
73              statreq++;
74              continue;
75
76          case 'd':                                 Directory info, not contents
77              dflg++;
78              continue;
79
80          case 'g':                                 Group name instead of user name
81              gflg++;
82              continue;
83
84          case 'l':                                 Long listing
85              lflg++;
86              statreq++;
87              continue;
88
89          case 'r':                                 Reverse sort order
90              rflg = -1;
91              continue;
92
93          case 't':                                 Sort by time, not name
94              tflg++;
95              statreq++;
96              continue;
97
98          case 'u':                                 Access time, not modification time
99              uflg++;
100             continue;
101
102         case 'c':                                 Inode change time, not modification time
103             cflg++;
104             continue;
105
```

```
106         case 'i':                          Include inode number
107             iflg++;
108             continue;
109
110         case 'f':                          Force reading each arg as directory
111             fflg++;
112             continue;
113
114         default:                           Ignore unknown option letters
115             continue;
116         }
117         argc--;
118     }
```

Lines 63–118 parse the command-line options manually; `getopt()` hadn't been invented yet. The `statreq` variable is set to true when an option requires the use of the `stat()` system call.

Avoiding an unnecessary `stat()` call on each file is a big performance win. The `stat()` call was particularly expensive, because it could involve a disk seek to the inode location, a disk read to read the inode, and then a disk seek back to the location of the directory contents (in order to continue reading directory entries).

Modern systems have the inodes in groups, spread throughout a filesystem instead of clustered together at the front. This makes a noticeable performance improvement. Nevertheless, `stat()` calls are still not free; you should use them as needed, but not any more than that. The code continues:

```
119     if (fflg) {                            -f overrides -l, -s, -t, adds -a
120         aflg++;
121         lflg = 0;
122         sflg = 0;
123         tflg = 0;
124         statreq = 0;
125     }
126     if(lflg) {                             Open password or group file
127         t = "/etc/passwd";
128         if(gflg)
129             t = "/etc/group";
130         pwdf = fopen(t, "r");
131     }
132     if (argc==0) {                         Use current dir if no args
133         argc++;
134         argv = &dotp - 1;
135     }
```

Lines 119–125 handle the `-f` option, turning off `-l`, `-s`, `-t`, and `statreq`. Lines 126–131 handle `-l`, setting the file to be read for user or group information. Remember that the V7 `ls` shows only one or the other, not both.

If no arguments are left, lines 132–135 set up `argv` such that it points at a string representing the current directory. The assignment '`argv = &dotp - 1`' is valid, although unusual. The '`- 1`' compensates for the '`++argv`' on line 137. This avoids special case code for '`argc == 1`' in the main part of the program. Here is the rest of `main()`:

```
136         for (i=0; i < argc; i++) {                  Get info about each file
137             if ((ep = gstat(*++argv, 1))==NULL)
138                 continue;
139             ep->ln.namep = *argv;
140             ep->lflags |= ISARG;
141         }
142         qsort(firstp, lastp - firstp, sizeof *lastp, compar);
143         slastp = lastp;
144         for (epp=firstp; epp<slastp; epp++) {       Main code, see text
145             ep = *epp;
146             if (ep->ltype=='d' && dflg==0 || fflg) {
147                 if (argc>1)
148                     printf("\n%s:\n", ep->ln.namep);
149                 lastp = slastp;
150                 readdir(ep->ln.namep);
151                 if (fflg==0)
152                     qsort(slastp,lastp - slastp,sizeof *lastp,compar);
153                 if (lflg || sflg)
154                     printf("total %D\n", tblocks);
155                 for (ep1=slastp; ep1<lastp; ep1++)
156                     pentry(*ep1);
157             } else
158                 pentry(ep);
159         }
160         exit(0);
161     }                                               End of main()
```

Lines 136–141 loop over the arguments, gathering information about each one. The second argument to `gstat()` is a Boolean: true if the name is a command-line argument, false otherwise. Line 140 adds the `ISARG` flag to the `lflags` field for each command-line argument.

The `gstat()` function adds each new `struct lbuf` into the global `flist` array (line 137). It also updates the `lastp` global pointer to point into this array at the current last element.

Lines 142–143 sort the array, using `qsort()`, and save the current value of `lastp` in `slastp`. Lines 144–159 loop over each element in the array, printing file or directory info, as appropriate.

The code for directories deserves further explication:

`if (ep->ltype=='d' && dflg==0 || fflg) ...`

Line 146. If the file type is directory and if `-d` was not provided *or* if `-f` was, then `ls` has to read the directory instead of printing information about the directory itself.

`if (argc>1) printf("\n%s:\n", ep->ln.namep)`

Lines 147–148. Print the directory name and a colon if multiple files were named on the command line.

`lastp = slastp; readdir(ep->ln.namep)`

Lines 149–150. Reset `lastp` from `slastp`. The `flist` array acts as a two-level stack of file names. The command-line arguments are kept in `firstp` through `slastp - 1`. When `readdir()`[2] reads a directory, it puts the `struct lbuf` structures for the directory contents onto the stack, starting at `slastp` and going through `lastp`. This is illustrated in Figure 7.1.

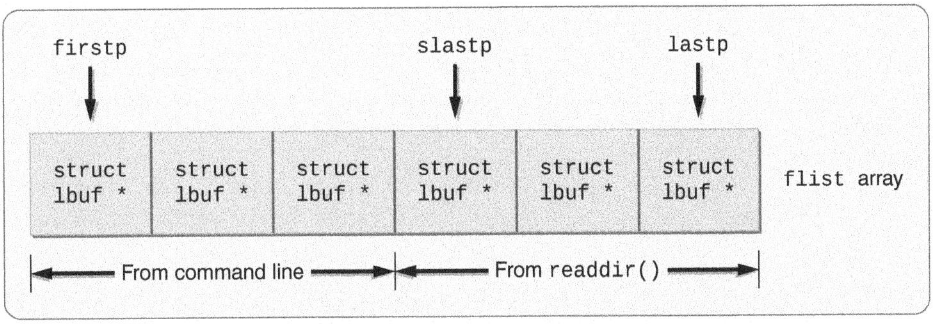

Figure 7.1: The `flist` array as a two-level stack

`if (fflg==0) qsort(slastp,lastp - slastp,sizeof *lastp,compar)`

Lines 151–152. Sort the subdirectory entries if `-f` is not in effect.

`if (lflg || sflg) printf("total %D\n", tblocks)`

Lines 153–154. Print the total number of blocks used by files in the directory, for `-l` or `-s`. This total is kept in the variable `tblocks`, which is reset for each directory. The `%D` format string for `printf()` is equivalent to `%ld` on modern systems; it means "print a long integer." (V7 also had `%ld`; see line 192.)

`for (ep1=slastp; ep1<lastp; ep1++) pentry(*ep1)`

Lines 155–156. Print the information about each file in the subdirectory. Note that the V7 `ls` descends only one level in a directory tree. It lacks the modern `-R` "recursive" option.

---

[2] This isn't the standard `readdir()` function presented earlier in Section 5.3.1, "Basic Directory Reading," page 124; that function hadn't been invented yet.

The `pentry()` routine prints information about a file:

```
163 pentry(ap)                                   void pentry(struct lbuf *ap)
164 struct lbuf *ap;
165 {
166     struct { char dminor, dmajor;};          Unused historical artifact from V6 ls
167     register t;
168     register struct lbuf *p;
169     register char *cp;
170
171     p = ap;
172     if (p->lnum == -1)
173         return;
174     if (iflg)
175         printf("%5u ", p->lnum);             Inode number
176     if (sflg)
177     printf("%4D ", nblock(p->lsize));        Size in blocks
```

Lines 172–173 check whether the `lnum` field is `-1`, and return if so. When '`p->lnum == -1`' is true, the `struct lbuf` is not valid. Otherwise, this field is the file's inode number.

Lines 174–175 print the inode number if `-i` is in effect. Lines 176–177 print the total number of blocks if `-s` is in effect. (As we see below, this number may not be accurate.)

Lines 178–197 handle the `-l` option:

```
178     if (lflg) {                              Long listing:
179         putchar(p->ltype);                   — File type
180         pmode(p->lflags);                    — Permissions
181         printf("%2d ", p->lnl);              — Link count
182         t = p->luid;
183         if(gflg)
184             t = p->lgid;
185         if (getname(t, tbuf)==0)
186             printf("%-6.6s", tbuf);          — User or group
187         else
188             printf("%-6d", t);
189         if (p->ltype=='b' || p->ltype=='c')  — Device: major and minor numbers
190             printf("%3d,%3d", major((int)p->lsize), minor((int)p->lsize));
191         else
192             printf("%7ld", p->lsize);        — Size in bytes
193         cp = ctime(&p->lmtime);
194         if(p->lmtime < year)                 — Modification time
195             printf(" %-7.7s %-4.4s ", cp+4, cp+20); else
196             printf(" %-12.12s ", cp+4);
197     }
198     if (p->lflags&ISARG)                     — File name
199         printf("%s\n", p->ln.namep);
```

```
200     else
201         printf("%.14s\n", p->ln.lname);
202 }
```

Lines 179–181 print the file's type, permissions, and number of links. Lines 182–184 set `t` to the user ID or the group ID, based on the `-g` option. Lines 185–188 retrieve the corresponding name and print it if available. Otherwise, the program prints the numeric value.

Lines 189–192 check whether the file is a block or character device. If it is, they print the major and minor device numbers, extracted with the `major()` and `minor()` macros. Otherwise, they print the file's size.

Lines 193–196 print the time of interest. If it's older than six months, the code prints the month, day, and year. Otherwise, it prints the month, day, and time (see Section 6.1.3.1, "Simple Time Formatting: `asctime()` and `ctime()`," page 159, for the format of `ctime()`'s result).

Finally, lines 198–201 print the file name. For a command-line argument, we know it's a zero-terminated string, and `%s` can be used. For a file read from a directory, it may not be zero-terminated, and thus an explicit precision, `%.14s`, must be used.

Next comes `getname()`:

```
204 getname(uid, buf)                          int getname(int uid, char buf[])
205 int uid;
206 char buf[];
207 {
208     int j, c, n, i;
209
210     if (uid==lastuid)                       Simple caching, see text
211         return(0);
212     if(pwdf == NULL)                        Safety check
213         return(-1);
214     rewind(pwdf);                           Start at front of file
215     lastuid = -1;
216     do {
217         i = 0;                              Index in buf array
218         j = 0;                              Counts fields in line
219         n = 0;                              Converts numeric value
220         while((c=fgetc(pwdf)) != '\n') {    Read lines
221             if (c==EOF)
222                 return(-1);
223             if (c==':') {                   Count fields
224                 j++;
225                 c = '0';
226             }
227             if (j==0)                       First field is name
228                 buf[i++] = c;
229             if (j==2)                       Third field is numeric ID
230                 n = n*10 + c - '0';
231         }
```

```
232         } while (n != uid);                    Keep searching until ID found
233         buf[i++] = '\0';
234         lastuid = uid;
235         return(0);
236 }
```

This function converts a user or group ID number into the corresponding name. It implements a simple caching scheme: if the passed-in `uid` is the same as the global variable `lastuid`, then the function returns `0`, for OK; the buffer will already contain the name (lines 210–211). `lastuid` is initialized to `-1` (line 33), so this test fails the first time `getname()` is called.

`pwdf` is already open on either `/etc/passwd` or `/etc/group` (see lines 126–130). The code here checks that the open succeeded and returns `-1` if it didn't (lines 212–213).

Surprisingly, `ls` does *not* use `getpwuid()` or `getgrgid()`. Instead, it takes advantage of the facts that the format of `/etc/passwd` and `/etc/group` is identical for the first three fields (name, password, numeric ID) and that both use a colon as separator.[3]

Lines 216–232 implement a linear search through the file. `j` counts the number of colons seen so far: zero for the name and two for the ID number. Thus, while scanning the line, it fills in both the name and the ID number.

Lines 233–235 terminate the `name` buffer, set the global `lastuid` to the found ID number, and return `0` for OK.

Next is `nblock()`:

```
238 long                                           long nblock(long size)
239 nblock(size)
240 long size;
241 {
242         return((size+511)>>9);
243 }
```

This function reports how many disk blocks the file uses. This calculation is based on the file's size as returned by `stat()`. The V7 block size was 512 bytes—the size of a physical disk sector.

The calculation on line 242 looks a bit scary. The '`>>9`' is a right-shift by nine bits. This divides by 512, to give the number of blocks. (On early hardware, a right-shift was much faster than division.) So far, so good. Now, a file of even one byte still takes up a whole disk block. However, '`1 / 512`' comes out as zero (integer division truncates), which is incorrect. This explains the '`size+511`'; by adding 511, the code ensures that the sum produces the correct number of blocks when it is divided by 512.

This calculation is only approximate, however. Very large files also have indirect blocks. Despite the claim in the V7 *ls*(1) manpage, this calculation does not account for indirect blocks.

Furthermore, consider the case of a file with large holes (created by seeking way past the end of the file with `lseek()`). Holes don't occupy disk blocks; however, this is not reflected

[3]Chet Ramey suggests that this code predates the `getpwuid()` and `getgrgid()` functions, and simply was never updated. We may never know the real reason.

in the size value. Thus, the calculation produced by `nblock()`, while usually correct, could produce results that are either smaller or larger than the real case.

For these reasons, the `st_blocks` member was added into the `struct stat` at 4.2 BSD, and then picked up for System V and POSIX. Moving on:

```
245 int m1[] = { 1, S_IREAD>>0, 'r', '-' };
246 int m2[] = { 1, S_IWRITE>>0, 'w', '-' };
247 int m3[] = { 2, S_ISUID, 's', S_IEXEC>>0, 'x', '-' };
248 int m4[] = { 1, S_IREAD>>3, 'r', '-' };
249 int m5[] = { 1, S_IWRITE>>3, 'w', '-' };
250 int m6[] = { 2, S_ISGID, 's', S_IEXEC>>3, 'x', '-' };
251 int m7[] = { 1, S_IREAD>>6, 'r', '-' };
252 int m8[] = { 1, S_IWRITE>>6, 'w', '-' };
253 int m9[] = { 2, S_ISVTX, 't', S_IEXEC>>6, 'x', '-' };
254
255 int *m[] = { m1, m2, m3, m4, m5, m6, m7, m8, m9};
256
257 pmode(aflag)                                  void pmode(int aflag)
258 {
259     register int **mp;
260
261     flags = aflag;
262     for (mp = &m[0]; mp < &m[sizeof(m)/sizeof(m[0])];)
263         select(*mp++);
264 }
265
266 select(pairp)                                 void select(register int *pairp)
267 register int *pairp;
268 {
269     register int n;
270
271     n = *pairp++;
272     while (--n>=0 && (flags&*pairp++)==0)
273         pairp++;
274     putchar(*pairp);
275 }
```

Lines 245–275 print the file's permissions. The code is compact and rather elegant; it requires careful study:

- Lines 245–253: The arrays `m1` through `m9` encode the permission bits to check for along with the corresponding characters to print. There is one array per character to print in the file permissions. The first element of each array is the number of (permission, character) pairs encoded in that particular array. The final element is the character to print in the event that none of the given permission bits are found.

Note also how the permissions are specified as '`I_READ>>0`', '`I_READ>>3`', '`I_READ>>6`', and so on. The individual constants for each bit (`S_IRUSR`, `S_IRGRP`, etc.) had not been invented yet. (See Table 4.5 in Section 4.6.1, "Specifying Initial File Permissions," page 101.)

- Line 255: The `m` array points to each of the `m1` through `m9` arrays.
- Lines 257–264: The `pmode()` function first sets the global variable `flags` to the passed-in parameter `aflag`. It then loops through the `m` array, passing each element to the `select()` function. The passed-in element represents one of the `m1` to `m9` arrays.
- Lines 266–275: The `select()` function understands the layout of each `m1` through `m9` array. `n` is the number of pairs in the array (the first element); line 271 sets it. Lines 272–273 look for permission bits, checking the global variable `flags` set previously on line 261.

Note the use of the `++` operator, both in the loop test and in the loop body. The effect is to skip over pairs in the array as long as the permission bit in the first element of the pair is not found in `flags`.

When the loop ends, *either* the permission bit has been found, in which case `pairp` points at the second element of the pair, which is the correct character to print, *or* it has not been found, in which case `pairp` points at the default character. In either case, line 274 prints the character that `pairp` points to.

As a side note, modern practice discourages the *coupling* of routines via global variables. But in a program as small as this, it probably doesn't matter so much.

A final point worth noting is that in C, character constants (such as `'x'`) have type `int`, not `char`.[4] So there's no problem putting such constants into an integer array; everything works correctly.

The code continues with the `makename()` function:

*char *makename(char *dir, char *file)*

```
277 char *
278 makename(dir, file)
279 char *dir, *file;
280 {
281     static char dfile[100];
282     register char *dp, *fp;
283     register int i;
284
285     dp = dfile;
286     fp = dir;
287     while (*fp)
288         *dp++ = *fp++;
289     *dp++ = '/';
290     fp = file;
```

[4]This is different in C++; there, character constants do have type `char`. This difference does not affect this particular code.

```
291     for (i=0; i<DIRSIZ; i++)
292         *dp++ = *fp++;
293     *dp = 0;
294     return(dfile);
295 }
```

This function's job is to concatenate a directory name and a file name, separated by a slash character, and produce a string. It does this in the `static` buffer `dfile` (line 281). Note that `dfile` is only 100 characters long and that no error checking is done.

The code itself is straightforward, copying characters one at a time. `makename()` is used by the `readdir()` function, which follows:

```
297 readdir(dir)                                            void readdir(char *dir)
298 char *dir;
299 {
300     static struct direct dentry;
301     register int j;
302     register struct lbuf *ep;
303
304     if ((dirf = fopen(dir, "r")) == NULL) {
305         printf("%s unreadable\n", dir);
306         return;
307     }
308     tblocks = 0;
309     for(;;) {
310         if (fread((char *)&dentry, sizeof(dentry), 1, dirf) != 1)
311             break;
312         if (dentry.d_ino==0
313          || aflg==0 && dentry.d_name[0]=='.' &&  (dentry.d_name[1]=='\0'
314             || dentry.d_name[1]=='.' && dentry.d_name[2]=='\0'))
315             continue;
316         ep = gstat(makename(dir, dentry.d_name), 0);
317         if (ep==NULL)
318             continue;
319         if (ep->lnum != -1)
320             ep->lnum = dentry.d_ino;
321         for (j=0; j<DIRSIZ; j++)
322             ep->ln.lname[j] = dentry.d_name[j];
323     }
324     fclose(dirf);
325 }
```

Lines 297–325 define the `readdir()` function, whose job is to read the contents of directories named on the command line.

Lines 304–307 open the directory for reading, returning if `fopen()` fails. (The error message on line 305 really should have gone to `stderr`.) Line 308 initializes the global variable `tblocks` to `0`. This was used earlier (lines 153–154) to print the total number of blocks used by files in a directory.

Lines 309–323 are a loop that reads directory entries and adds them to the `flist` array. Lines 310–311 read one entry, exiting the loop upon end-of-file.

Lines 312–315 skip uninteresting entries. If the inode number is zero, this slot isn't used. Otherwise, if `-a` was not given and the file name is either `.` or `..`, skip it.

Lines 316–318 call `gstat()` with the full name of the file, and a second argument of false, indicating that it's not from the command line. `gstat()` updates the global `lastp` pointer and the `flist` array. A `NULL` return value indicates some sort of failure.

Lines 319–322 save the inode number and name in the `struct lbuf`. If `ep->lnum` comes back from `gstat()` set to `-1`, it means that the `stat()` operation on the file failed. Finally, line 324 closes the directory.

The following function, `gstat()` (lines 327–398), is the core function for the operation of retrieving and storing file information:

```
327 struct lbuf *                                  struct lbuf *gstat(char *file, int argfl)
328 gstat(file, argfl)
329 char *file;
330 {
331     extern char *malloc();
332     struct stat statb;
333     register struct lbuf *rep;
334     static int nomocore;                       Auto init to zero (false)
335
336     if (nomocore)                              Ran out of memory earlier
337         return(NULL);
338     rep = (struct lbuf *)malloc(sizeof(struct lbuf));
339     if (rep==NULL) {
340         fprintf(stderr, "ls: out of memory\n");
341         nomocore = 1;
342         return(NULL);
343     }
344     if (lastp >= &flist[NFILES]) {             Check whether too many files given
345         static int msg;
346         lastp--;
347         if (msg==0) {
348             fprintf(stderr, "ls: too many files\n");
349             msg++;
350         }
351     }
352     *lastp++ = rep;                            Fill in information
353     rep->lflags = 0;
354     rep->lnum = 0;
355     rep->ltype = '-';                          Default file type
```

The static variable `nomocore` [*sic*] indicates that `malloc()` failed upon an earlier call. Since it's `static`, it's automatically initialized to `0` (that is, false). If it's true upon entry, `gstat()` just returns `NULL`. Otherwise, if `malloc()` fails, `ls` prints an error message, sets `nomocore` to true, and returns `NULL` (lines 334–343).

Lines 344–351 make sure that there is still room left in the `flist` array. If not, `ls` prints a message (but only once; note the use of the `static` variable `msg`), and then reuses the last slot in `flist`.

Line 352 makes the slot `lastp` points to point to the new `struct lbuf` (`rep`). This also updates `lastp`, which is used for sorting in `main()` (lines 142 and 152). Lines 353–355 set default values for the flags, inode number, and type fields in the `struct lbuf`. The function continues:

```
356         if (argfl || statreq) {
357             if (stat(file, &statb)<0) {                 stat() failed
358                 printf("%s not found\n", file);
359                 statb.st_ino = -1;
360                 statb.st_size = 0;
361                 statb.st_mode = 0;
362                 if (argfl) {
363                     lastp--;
364                     return(0);
365                 }
366             }
367             rep->lnum = statb.st_ino;                   stat() OK, copy info
368             rep->lsize = statb.st_size;
369             switch(statb.st_mode&S_IFMT) {
370
371             case S_IFDIR:
372                 rep->ltype = 'd';
373                 break;
374
375             case S_IFBLK:
376                 rep->ltype = 'b';
377                 rep->lsize = statb.st_rdev;
378                 break;
379
380             case S_IFCHR:
381                 rep->ltype = 'c';
382                 rep->lsize = statb.st_rdev;
383                 break;
384             }
385             rep->lflags = statb.st_mode & ~S_IFMT;
386             rep->luid = statb.st_uid;
387             rep->lgid = statb.st_gid;
388             rep->lnl = statb.st_nlink;
```

```
389         if(uflg)
390             rep->lmtime = statb.st_atime;
391         else if (cflg)
392             rep->lmtime = statb.st_ctime;
393         else
394             rep->lmtime = statb.st_mtime;
395         tblocks += nblock(statb.st_size);
396     }
397     return(rep);
398 }
```

Lines 356–396 handle the call to `stat()`. If this is a command-line argument or if `statreq` is true because of an option, the code fills in the `struct lbuf` as follows:

- Lines 357–366: Call `stat()`; if it fails, print an error message and set values as appropriate, and then return `NULL` (expressed as `0`). (The error message really should be sent to `stderr` with `fprintf()`, instead of using `printf()` to send it to `stdout`.)
- Lines 367–368: Set the inode number and size fields from the `struct stat` if the `stat()` succeeded.
- Lines 369–384: Handle the special cases of directory, block device, and character device. In all cases the code updates the `ltype` field. For devices, the `lsize` value is replaced with the `st_rdev` value.
- Lines 385–388: Fill in the `lflags`, `luid`, `lgid`, and `lnl` fields from the corresponding fields in the `struct stat`. Line 385 removes the file-type bits, leaving the 12 permissions bits (read/write/execute for user/group/other, and setuid, setgid, and save-text).
- Lines 389–394: Based on command-line options, use one of the three time fields from the `struct stat` for the `lmtime` field in the `struct lbuf`.
- Line 395: Update the global variable `tblocks` with the number of blocks in the file.

Next comes `compar()`, used for sorting with `qsort()`:

*int compar(struct lbuf **pp1, struct lbuf **pp2)*

```
400 compar(pp1, pp2)
401 struct lbuf **pp1, **pp2;
402 {
403     register struct lbuf *p1, *p2;
404 
405     p1 = *pp1;
406     p2 = *pp2;
407     if (dflg==0) {
408         if (p1->lflags&ISARG && p1->ltype=='d') {
409             if (!(p2->lflags&ISARG && p2->ltype=='d'))
410                 return(1);
411         } else {
412             if (p2->lflags&ISARG && p2->ltype=='d')
413                 return(-1);
414         }
415     }
```

```
416         if (tflg) {
417             if(p2->lmtime == p1->lmtime)
418                 return(0);
419             if(p2->lmtime > p1->lmtime)
420                 return(rflg);
421             return(-rflg);
422         }
423         return(rflg * strcmp(p1->lflags&ISARG? p1->ln.namep: p1->ln.lname,
424                     p2->lflags&ISARG? p2->ln.namep: p2->ln.lname));
425 }
```

This function is dense: there's a lot happening in little space. The first thing to remember is the meaning of the return value: a negative value means that the first file should sort to an earlier spot in the array than the second, zero means the files are equal, and a positive value means that the second file should sort to an earlier spot than the first.

The next thing to understand is that `ls` prints the contents of directories *after* it prints information about files. Thus the result of sorting should be that all directories *named on the command line* follow all files named on the command line.

Finally, the `rflg` variable helps implement the `-r` option, which reverses the sorting order. It is initialized to `1` (line 30). If `-r` is used, `rflg` is set to `-1` (lines 89–91).

The following pseudocode describes the logic of `compar()`; the line numbers in the left margin correspond to those of `ls.c`:

```
407 if ls has to read directories   # dflg == 0
408     if p1 is a command-line arg and p1 is a directory
409         if p2 is not a command-line arg and is not a directory
410             return 1    # first comes after second
            else
                fall through to time test
411     else
            # p1 is not a command-line directory
412         if p2 is a command-line arg and is a directory
413             return -1   # first comes before second
            else
414                 fall through to time test

416 if sorting is based on time   # tflg is true
        # compare times:
417     if p2's time is equal to p1's time
418         return 0
419     if p2's time > p1's time
420         return the value of rflg (positive or negative)
        # p2's time < p1's time
421     return opposite of rflg (negative or positive)

423 Multiply rflg by the result of strcmp()
424 on the two names and return the result
```

The arguments to `strcmp()` on lines 423–424 look messy. What's going on is that different members of the `ln` union in the `struct lbuf` must be used, depending on whether the file name is a command-line argument or was read from a directory.

7.3 Summary

- The V7 `ls` is a relatively small program, yet it touches on many of the fundamental aspects of Unix programming: file I/O, file metadata, directory contents, users and groups, time and date values, sorting, and dynamic memory management.
- The most notable external difference between V7 `ls` and modern `ls` is the treatment of the `-a` and `-l` options. The V7 version has many fewer options than do modern versions; a noticeable lack is the `-R` recursive option.
- The management of `flist` is a clean way to use the limited memory of the PDP-11 architecture yet still provide as much information as possible. The `struct lbuf` nicely abstracts the information of interest from the `struct stat`; this simplifies the code considerably. The code for printing the nine permission bits is compact and elegant.
- Some parts of `ls` use surprisingly small limits, such as the upper bound of `1024` on the number of files or the buffer size of `100` in `makename()`.

Exercises

1. Consider the `getname()` function. What happens if the requested ID number is `216` and the following two lines exist in `/etc/passwd`, in this order?

   ```
   joe:xyzzy:2160:10:Joe User:/usr/joe:/bin/sh
   jane:zzyxx:216:12:Jane User:/usr/jane:/bin/sh
   ```

2. Consider the `makename()` function. Could it use `sprintf()` to make the concatenated name? Why or why not?
3. Are lines 319–320 in `readdir()` really necessary?
4. Take the `stat` program you wrote for the exercises in "Exercises for Chapter 6," page 198. Add the `nblock()` function from the V7 `ls`, and print the results along with the `st_blocks` field from the `struct stat`. Add a visible marker when they're different.
5. How would you grade the V7 `ls` on its use of `malloc()`? (Hint: how often is `free()` called? Where should it be called?)
6. How would you grade the V7 `ls` for code clarity? (Hint: how many comments are there?)
7. Outline the steps you would take to adapt the V7 `ls` for modern systems.

8. In the book's GitHub code repository, in the `ch-07-ls` directory, you will find the code for both the V7 and V10 versions of **`ls.c`**. The latter is approximately 40% bigger (in terms of lines of code) that the former, representing 10.5 years of further Unix development. Review the V10 version and see what is the same, and what is new and different.
9. Outline the steps you would take to adapt the V10 `ls` for modern systems.

Chapter 8

Filesystems and Directory Walks

This chapter completes the discussion of Linux (and Unix) filesystems and directories. We first describe how a disk partition containing a filesystem is added to (and removed from) the logical filesystem namespace, such that in general a user need neither know nor care where a file is physically located. Along the way, we present the APIs for working with filesystems.

We then describe how to move around within the hierarchical file namespace, how to retrieve the full pathname of the current working directory, and how to easily process arbitrary directory hierarchies (trees), using the `fts()` suite of functions. Finally, we describe the specialized but important `chroot()` system call.

8.1 Mounting and Unmounting Filesystems

The unified hierarchical file namespace is a great strength of the Linux/Unix design. This section looks at how administrative files, commands, and the operating system cooperate to build the namespace from separate physical devices that contain file data and metadata.

8.1.1 Reviewing the Background

Chapter 5, "Directories and File Metadata," page 111, introduced inodes for file metadata and described how directory entries link file names to inodes. It also described partitions and filesystems, and you saw that hard links are restricted to working within a single filesystem because directories contain only inode numbers and inode numbers are not unique across the entire set of in-use filesystems.

Besides inodes and data blocks, filesystems also contain one or more copies of the *superblock*. This is a special disk block that describes the filesystem; its information is updated as the filesystem itself changes. For example, the superblock contains counts of free and used inodes, free and used blocks, and other information. It also includes a *magic number*: a unique special value in a special location that identifies the type of the filesystem. (We'll see how this is relevant, shortly.)

Making a partition that contains a filesystem available for use is called *mounting* the filesystem. Removing a filesystem from use is called, not surprisingly, *unmounting* the filesystem.

These two jobs are accomplished with the `mount` and `umount` [*sic*] programs, named for the corresponding system calls. Every Unix system's `mount()` system call has a different interface. Because mounting and unmounting are considered implementation issues, POSIX purposely does not standardize these system calls.

You mount a filesystem onto a directory; such a directory is referred to as the filesystem's *mount point*. By convention the directory should be empty, but nothing enforces this. However, if the mount point is not empty, all of its contents become *completely inaccessible* while a filesystem is mounted on it.[1]

The kernel maintains a unique number, known as the *device number*, that identifies each mounted partition. For this reason, it is the (device, inode) pair that together uniquely identifies a file; when the `struct stat` structures for two file names indicate that both numbers are the same, you can be sure that they do refer to the same file.

As mentioned earlier, user-level software places the inode structures and other metadata onto a disk partition, thereby creating the filesystem. This same software creates an initial root directory for the filesystem. Thus, we have to make a distinction between "the root directory named `/`," which is the topmost directory in the hierarchical file name namespace, and "the root directory of a filesystem," which is each filesystem's individual topmost directory. The `/` directory is also the "root directory" of the "root filesystem."

For reasons described in the sidebar "Root Inode Numbers," page 224, a filesystem's root directory *always* has inode number `2` (although this is not formally standardized). Since there can be multiple filesystems, each one's root directory has the same inode number, `2`. When resolving a pathname, the kernel knows where each filesystem is mounted and arranges for the mount point's name to refer to the root directory of the mounted filesystem. Furthermore, `..` (dot-dot) in the root of a mounted filesystem is made to refer to the parent directory of the mount point.

Figure 8.1 shows two filesystems: one for the root directory and one for `/usr`, before `/usr` is mounted. Figure 8.2 shows the situation after `/usr` is mounted.

The `/` directory, the root of the entire logical hierarchy, is special in an additional way: `/.` and `/..` refer to the same directory; this is not true of any other directory on the system. (Thus, after something like '`cd /../../../..`', you're still in `/`.) This behavior is implemented in a simple fashion: both `/.` and `/..` are hard links to the filesystem's root directory. (You can see this in both Figure 8.1 and Figure 8.2.) Every filesystem works this way, but the kernel treats `/` specially and does not treat as a special case the `..` directory for the filesystem mounted on `/`.

---

[1] GNU/Linux, Solaris, macOS, and the BSDs all provide for more specialized ways of mounting files and directories. This has advanced uses, which we don't otherwise discuss.

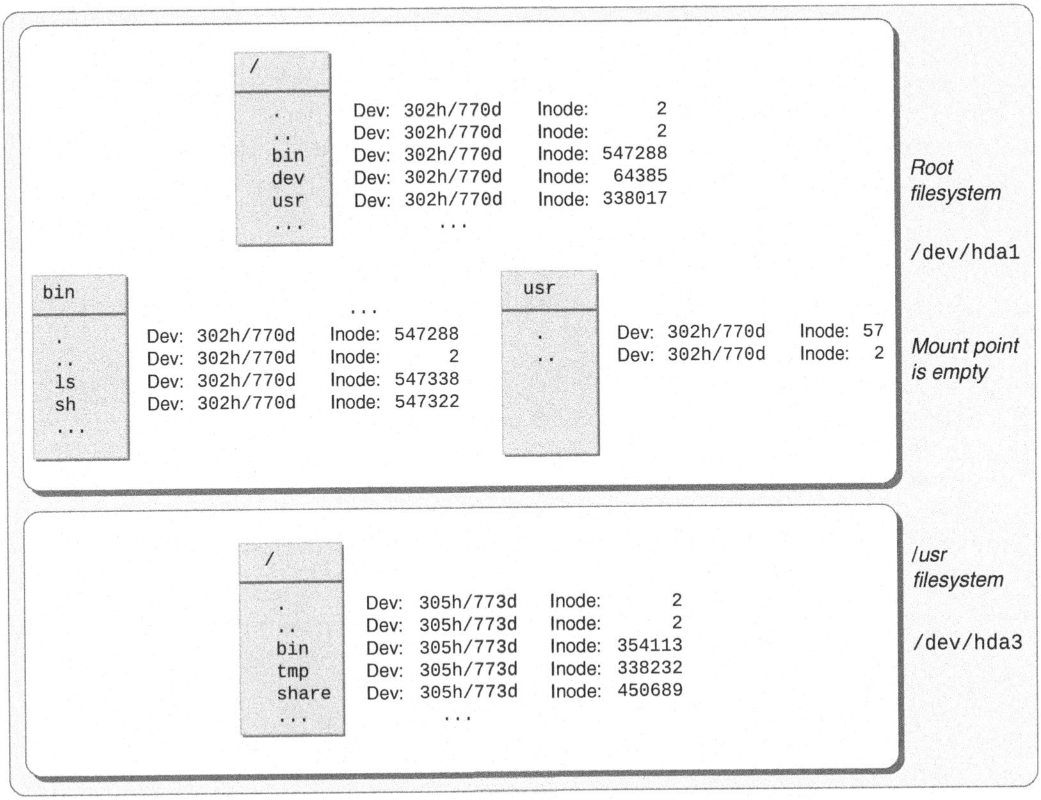

Figure 8.1: Separate filesystems, before mounting

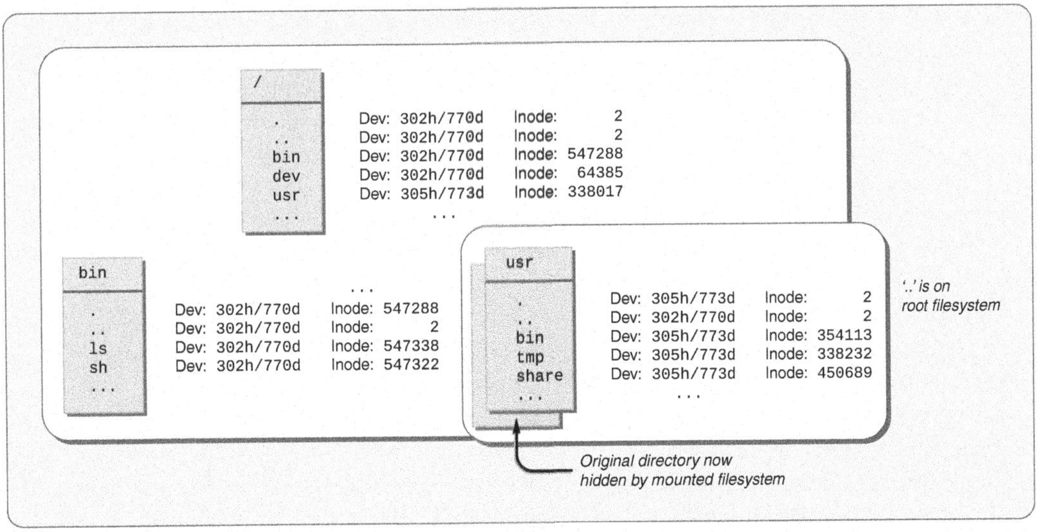

Figure 8.2: Separate filesystems, after mounting

Root Inode Numbers

The inode number for the root directory of a filesystem is always `2`. Why is that? The answer has to do with both technology and history.

As mentioned in Section 5.3, "Reading Directories," page 123, a directory entry with an inode number of zero indicates an unused, or empty, slot. So inode `0` cannot be used for a real file or directory.

OK, so what about inode `1`? Well, particularly in the 1970s and 1980s, disks were not as well made as they are now. When you bought a disk, it came with a (paper) list of *bad blocks*—known locations on the disk that were not usable. Each operating system had to have a way to keep track of those bad blocks and avoid using them.

Under Unix, you did this by creating a special-purpose file whose data blocks were the ones known to be bad. This file was attached on inode `1`, leaving inode `2` as the first inode usable for regular files or directories.

Modern disk drives have considerable built-in electronics and handle bad blocks on their own. Thus, technically, it would be feasible to use inode `1` for a file. However, since so much Unix software assumes that inode `2` is the inode for filesystem root directories, Linux follows this convention as well. (That said, Linux sometimes uses inode `1` for nonnative filesystems, such as `vfat` or `/proc`.)

8.1.2 Looking at Different Filesystem Types

Before we start, please note that the discussion in this section is specific to Linux. However, most modern Unix systems have similar features. We encourage you to explore your system's documentation.

Historically, V7 Unix supported only a single filesystem type; every partition's metadata and directory organization were structured the same way. 4.1 BSD used a filesystem with the same structure as that of V7, but with a 1,024-byte block size instead of a 512-byte one. 4.2 BSD introduced the "BSD Fast Filesystem," which dramatically changed the layout of inodes and data on disk and enabled the use of much larger block sizes. (In general, using larger contiguous blocks of data provides better throughput, especially for file reads.)

Through 4.3 BSD and System V Release 2 in the early and mid-1980s, Unix systems continued to support just one filesystem type. To switch a computer from one filesystem to another,[2] you had to first back up each filesystem to archival media (9-track tape), upgrade the system, and then restore the data.

In the mid-1980s, Sun Microsystems developed a kernel architecture that made it possible to use multiple filesystem architectures at the same time. This design was implemented for their SunOS operating system, primarily to support Sun's Network File System (NFS). However, as a consequence it was also possible to support multiple on-disk architectures. System V Release 3 used a similar architecture to support the Remote File System (RFS), but it continued to support only one on-disk architecture.[3] RFS was never widely used and is now only a historical footnote. (Even earlier than both of those, Research Unix had a "file system switch,"

[2] For example, consider upgrading a VAX 11/780 from 4.1 BSD to 4.2 BSD.

[3] System V Release 3 supported two different block sizes, 512 bytes and 1,024 bytes, but otherwise the disk organization was the same.

which allowed it to support both on-disk and network filesystems. By that time, however, the Unix world was no longer using systems from Bell Labs Research, and indeed, obtaining copies of the later Research Unix systems had become difficult.)

Sun's general design became popular and widely implemented in commercial Unix systems, including System V Release 4. Linux and BSD systems use a variant of this design to support multiple on-disk filesystem formats. In particular, it's common for all Unix variants on Intel x86 hardware to be able to mount MS-DOS/Windows FAT filesystems, including those supplying long file names, as well as ISO 9660–formatted DVDs and CD-ROMs.

Linux has multiple native (that is, on-disk) filesystems. The most popular is the `ext4` filesystem. *Many* more filesystem types are available, however. You can find information about most of them in the `/usr/src/linux/Documentation/filesystems/` directory if you have kernel source installed. (Note that the actual location may vary.) Table 8.1 lists a subset of the various filesystem names, with a brief description of each. The abbreviation "RW" means "read/write," and "RO" means "read-only."

Not all of these filesystems are supported by the `mount` command; see *mount*(8) for the list of those that are supported. See also `/proc/filesystems` and `/lib/modules/$(uname -r)/kernel/fs` for a complete list of the filesystems.

Journaling is a technique, pioneered in database systems, for improving the performance of file updates, in such a way that filesystem recovery in the event of a crash can be done both correctly and quickly. As of this writing, several different journaling filesystems are available. `ext4` is one such; it has the advantage of being upwardly compatible with existing `ext2` and `ext3` filesystems, and it's easy to convert a filesystem back and forth between `ext3` and `ext4`. (See *tune2fs*(8).) ReiserFS and XFS also have strong followings.

The `fat`, `msdos`, `umsdos`, and `vfat` filesystems all share common code. In general, you should use `vfat` to mount Windows FAT-32 (or other FAT-xx) partitions, and `umsdos` if you wish to use a FAT partition as the root filesystem for your GNU/Linux system.

The Coherent, Minix, original System V, and Xenix filesystems all have similar on-disk structures. The `sysv` filesystem type supports all of them; the names `coherent`, `minix`, `sysv`, and `xenix` are aliases for each other.

The BSD Fast Filesystem has evolved somewhat over the years. The `ufs` filesystem supports read/write operation for the version from 4.4 BSD, which is the basis for the three widely used BSD operating systems: FreeBSD, NetBSD, and OpenBSD. It also supports read/write operation for Sun's Solaris filesystem, for both SPARC and Intel x86 systems. The original BSD format and that from the NeXTStep operating system are supported read-only.

The "RO" designations in Table 8.1 mean that filesystems of those types can be mounted and read but files cannot be written on them or removed from them. (This may change with time; check your system's documentation.) For some, they are read-only because the underlying media are inherently read-only. For others, it's because the filesystem support is not fully developed.

8.1.3 Mounting Filesystems: `mount`

The `mount` command mounts filesystems, splicing their contents into the system file hierarchy at their mount points. Under GNU/Linux, it is somewhat complicated since it has to deal with all the known filesystem types and their options. Normally, only `root` can run `mount`, although it's possible to make exceptions for certain cases, as is discussed later in the chapter.

Table 8.1: Some of the supported Linux filesystems

Name	Support	Description
`9p`	RW	The Plan 9 from Bell Labs network file server protocol.
`adfs`	RW	The Acorn Advanced Disc Filing System.
`affs`	RO, RW	The Amiga Fast File System. Read-only versus read/write depends on the version of the filesystem.
`afs`	RW	The Andrew File System.
`autofs`	RW	Filesystem for interacting with the automounter daemon.
`bfs`	RW	SCO UnixWare Boot Filesystem.
`binfmt_misc`	RW	Special filesystem for running interpreters on compiled files (for example, Java files).
`btrfs`	RW	A high performance copy-on-write filesystem.
`cifs`	RW	Support for older versions of the Microsoft SMB protocol.
`ceph`	RW	A distributed filesystem.
`coda`	RW	An experimental distributed filesystem developed at Carnegie Mellon University.
`cramfs`	RO	A small filesystem for storing files in ROM.
`devpts`	RW	Special filesystem for pseudo-ttys.
`ecryptfs`	RW	A stacked cryptographic filesystem for Linux. See the eCryptfs website.[4]
`efivarfs`	RW	A filesystem for managing (U)EFI variables.
`erofs`	RO	The Enhanced Read-Only File System.
`ext2`	RW	The Second Extended Filesystem.
`ext3`	RW	The `ext2` filesystem with journaling.
`ext4`	RW	The `ext3` filesystem with a number of enhancements. This is the default GNU/Linux filesystem.
`f2fs`	RW	The Flash-Friendly File System.
`fuse`		Driver for user space filesystems.
`hfs`	RW	Apple Mac OS Hierarchical File System.
`hfsplus`	RW	The `hfs` filesystem with extensions.
`hpfs`	RW	The OS/2 High Performance File System.
`iso9660`	RO	The ISO 9660 CD-ROM filesystem. The Rock Ridge extensions are also supported, making a DVD or CD-ROM that uses them look like a normal (but read-only) filesystem.
`jffs2`	RW	Journaled Flash Filesystem 2 (for embedded systems).
`jfs`	RW	IBM's Journaled File System for Linux.
`nilfs2`	RW	A log-structured filesystem with continuous snap-shotting.
`ntfs`	RO	Support for Windows NTFS filesystem.
`ntfs3`	RW	More complete support for Windows NTFS filesystem.
`ocfs2`	RW	The Oracle Cluster File System (a distributed filesystem).
`overlayfs`	RW	A filesystem providing union directories.
`proc`	RW	Access to per-process and kernel information.
`qnx4`	RW	The QNX4 (a small, real-time operating system) filesystem.
`qnx6`	RW	The QNX6 filesystem.
`ramfs`	RW	A filesystem for creating RAM disks.
`reiserfs`	RW	An advanced journaling filesystem.

(continued)

[4] `https://launchpad.net/ecryptfs`

Table 8.1: Some of the supported Linux filesystems (*continued*)

Name	Support	Description
romfs	RO	A filesystem for creating simple read-only RAM disks.
rootfs	RW	A special version of the ramfs filesystem, for use during bootstrapping.
smbfs	RW	Client support for SMB filesystems (Windows file shares).
squashfs	RO	A popular compressed read-only filesystem.
sysv	RW	The System V Release 2, Xenix, Minix, and Coherent filesystems. coherent, minix, and xenix are aliases.
tmpfs	RW	A ramdisk filesystem, supporting dynamic growth.
ubifs	RW	Unsorted Block Images; a flash filesystem.
udf	RO	The UDF filesystem format used by DVD-ROMs.
ufs	RO, RW	The BSD Fast Filesystem; read/write for modern systems.
umsdos	RW	An extension to vfat making it look more like a Unix filesystem.
vboxsf	RW	A filesystem providing VirtualBox shared folders.
vfat	RW	All variants of MS-DOS/Windows FAT filesystems. msdos and fat are components.
virtiofs	RW	A filesystem providing paravirtualized guest access to the host system.
vxfs	RW	The Veritas VxFS journaling filesystem.
xfs	RW	A high-performance journaling filesystem developed by SGI for Linux. See the kernel documentation on XFS.[5]
zonefs	RW	A filesystem for zoned block devices (flash).

You specify the filesystem type with the -t option:

mount [*options*] *device mount-point*

For example (# is the root prompt):

```
# mount -t iso9660 /dev/dvd /mnt/dvd                Mount DVD
# mount -t vfat /dev/sdb1 /mnt/flash                Mount MS-DOS USB drive
# mount -t nfs files.example.com:/ /mnt/files       Mount NFS filesystem
```

You can use '-t auto' to force mount to guess the filesystem type. This usually works, although if you know for sure what kind of filesystem you have, it helps to supply the type and avoid the chance that mount will guess incorrectly. mount does this guessing by default, so '-t auto' isn't strictly necessary.

GNU/Linux systems provide a special kind of mounting by means of the *loopback* device. In this way, a filesystem image contained in a regular file can be mounted as if it were an actual disk device. This capability is very useful, for example, with CD-ROM or DVD images. It allows you to create an image and try it out, without having to burn it to a writable optical disk and mount the disk. The following example uses the Ubuntu MATE desktop 24.04.2 DVD image:

[5] https://docs.kernel.org/admin-guide/xfs.html

```
# ls -lh ubuntu-mate-24.04.2-desktop-amd64.iso                  Examine CD image file
-rw-rw-r-- 1 arnold arnold 4.1G Feb 18 12:54 ubuntu-mate-24.04.2-desktop-amd64.iso
# mkdir /mnt/dvd                                                Make a mount point
# mount -t iso9660 -o ro,loop \
>          ubuntu-mate-24.04.2-desktop-amd64.iso /mnt/dvd       Mount the image
# cd /mnt/dvd                                                   Go there
# ls                                                            Look at files
boot          casper  EFI      md5sum.txt  preseed
boot.catalog  dists   install  pool        ubuntu
# cd                                                            Change out
# umount /mnt/dvd                                               Unmount
```

Being able to mount an ISO 9660 image this way is particularly helpful when you are testing scripts that make CD/DVD images. You can create an image in a regular file, mount it, and verify that it's arranged correctly. Then, once you're sure it's correct, you can copy the image to a writable disk ("burn" the disk), or to a flash drive/disk-on-key.

8.1.4 Unmounting Filesystems: umount

The `umount` command unmounts a filesystem, removing its contents from the system file hierarchy. The usage is as follows:

`umount` *file-or-device*

The filesystem being unmounted must not be *busy*. This means that there aren't any processes with open files on the filesystem and that no process has a directory on the filesystem as its current working directory. Borrowing from the previous example:

```
$ sudo su -                                          Become root
[sudo] password for arnold:
# mount -t iso9660 -o ro,loop \                      Mount the DVD image
>      ubuntu-mate-24.04.2-desktop-amd64.iso /mnt/dvd
# cd /mnt/dvd                                        Go there
# umount /mnt/dvd                                    Attempt to unmount /mnt/dvd
umount: /mnt/dvd: target is busy.                    Doesn't work; it's still in use
# cd                                                 Change out of /mnt/dvd
# umount /mnt/dvd                                    Try to unmount /mnt/dvd again
#                                                    Silence is golden: unmount worked
```

8.2 Files for Filesystem Administration

The `/etc/fstab` file[6] lists filesystems that can be mounted. Most are automatically mounted when the system boots. The format is as follows:

device mount-point fs-type options dump-freq fsck-pass

---

[6]On GNU/Linux and most systems. Solaris and some systems based on System V Release 4 use `/etc/vfstab`, possibly with a different format.

(The *dump-freq* and *fsck-pass* are administrative features that aren't relevant to the current discussion.) When life was simpler, `/etc/fstab` might have looked something like this:

```
$ cat /etc/fstab
# device        mount-point    type      options                  freq passno
/dev/hda3       /              ext3      defaults                    1 1       Root filesystem
/dev/hda5       /d             ext3      defaults                    1 2
none            /dev/pts       devpts    gid=5,mode=620              0 0
none            /proc          proc      defaults                    0 0
none            /dev/shm       tmpfs     defaults                    0 0
# Windows partition:
/dev/hda1       /win           vfat      noauto,defaults,user,uid=2076,gid=10  0 0
/dev/hda3       swap           swap      defaults                    0 0
/dev/cdrom      /mnt/cdrom     iso9660   noauto,owner,ro             0 0       World mountable
/dev/fd0        /mnt/floppy    auto      noauto,owner                0 0       Floppy, same
```

Today, disks are often identified using a *universally unique identifier* (UUID). Fortunately, comments in `/etc/fstab` give some hint as to the associated actual device. For example, on our current system, the file looks like this:

```
$ cat /etc/fstab
# /etc/fstab: static file system information.
#
# Use 'blkid' to print the universally unique identifier for a
# device; this may be used with UUID= as a more robust way to name devices
# that works even if disks are added and removed. See fstab(5).
#
# <file system> <mount point>   <type>  <options>       <dump>  <pass>
# / was on /dev/nvme0n1p3 during installation
UUID=fb2e8411-852c-486e-9d6d-cf24d08d2039 /         ext4    errors=remount-ro 0    1
# /boot/efi was on /dev/nvme0n1p1 during installation
UUID=BCFA-8C70  /boot/efi       vfat    umask=0077      0       1
# /home was on /dev/nvme0n1p4 during installation
UUID=1af92cc0-14e8-4619-9983-55b9ca0a3a41 /home     ext4    defaults     0     2
```

Comments beginning with # are allowed. Discussion of the various options is provided shortly, in Section 8.2.1, "Using Mount Options," page 230.

This same file format is used for `/etc/mtab`, which is where `mount` writes information about filesystems as they are mounted; `umount` removes information from that file when a filesystem is unmounted:

```
$ cat /etc/mtab
sysfs /sys sysfs rw,nosuid,nodev,noexec,relatime 0 0
proc /proc proc rw,nosuid,nodev,noexec,relatime 0 0
udev /dev devtmpfs rw,nosuid,relatime,size=7958168k,nr_inodes=1989542,mode=755,inode64 0 0
devpts /dev/pts devpts rw,nosuid,noexec,relatime,gid=5,mode=620,ptmxmode=000 0 0
tmpfs /run tmpfs rw,nosuid,nodev,noexec,relatime,size=1604576k,mode=755,inode64 0 0
/dev/nvme0n1p3 / ext4 rw,relatime,errors=remount-ro 0 0
```

```
...
binfmt_misc /proc/sys/fs/binfmt_misc binfmt_misc rw,nosuid,nodev,noexec,relatime 0 0
/dev/nvme0n1p4 /home ext4 rw,relatime 0 0
...
```

In fact, `/etc/mtab` is a symbolic link to `/proc/self/mounts`, which is a special file provided by the kernel. On systems besides Linux, `/etc/mtab` is usually a real file.

8.2.1 Using Mount Options

The `mount` command supports options that control what operations the kernel will or will not allow for the filesystem. There are a fair number of these. Only two are really useful on the command line:

`ro`
: Mount the filesystem read-only. This is necessary for read-only media such as formatted CD-ROMs and DVDs. (Write-once CD and DVD media aren't part of this discussion.)

`loop`
: Use the loopback device for treating a regular file as a filesystem. We showed an example of this earlier (see Section 8.1.3, "Mounting Filesystems: `mount`," page 225).

Options are passed with the `-o` command-line option and can be grouped, separated by commas. For example, here is the command line used earlier:

```
mount -t iso9660 -o ro,loop ubuntu-mate-24.04.2-desktop-amd64.iso /mnt/dvd
```

The rest of the options are intended for use in `/etc/fstab` (although they can also be used on the command line). The following list provides the ones we think are most important for day-to-day use:

`auto`, `noauto`
: Filesystems marked `auto` are to be mounted when the system boots through '`mount -a`' (mount all filesystems). `noauto` filesystems must be mounted manually. Such filesystems still appear in `/etc/fstab` along with the other filesystems. (See, for example, the entry for `/win` in our early `/etc/fstab` file, shown previously.)

`defaults`
: Use the default options `rw`, `suid`, `dev`, `exec`, `auto`, `nouser`, and `async`. (`async` is an advanced option that increases I/O throughput.) The manpage notes that the true set of defaults depends on the filesystem type being mounted.

`dev`, `nodev`
: Allow (don't allow) the use of character or block device files on the filesystem.

`exec`, `noexec`
: Allow (don't allow) execution of binary executables on the filesystem.

`rw`
: Mount the filesystem read/write.

`suid`, `nosuid`
: Support (don't support) the setuid and setgid bits on executables on the filesystem.

`user`, `nouser`
: Allow (don't allow) any user to mount this filesystem. This is useful for CD-ROMs and DVDs; even if you're on a single-user workstation, it's convenient to not have to switch to `root` just to mount a disk. Only the user who mounted the filesystem can unmount it. `user` implies the `noexec`, `nosuid`, and `nodev` options.

The `nodev`, `noexec`, and `nosuid` options are particularly valuable for security on filesystems on removable media. Consider a student environment in which students are allowed to mount their own USB drives. It's trivial to craft a filesystem with a setuid-`root` shell or a world-writable device file for the hard disk that could let an enterprising user change permissions on system files. These options prevent such tricks, or at least make them more difficult.

Each filesystem has additional options specific to it. One important option for `ext4` is the `grpid` option. We defer discussion of this option until Section 11.4.1, "Default Group for New Files and Directories," page 391. The details for all supported filesystems can be found in the *mount*(8) manpage.

As a concrete example, reconsider the line for the Windows partition on a previous incarnation of our system:

```
# device    mount-point  type  options                                 freq passno
/dev/hda1   /win         vfat  noauto,defaults,user,uid=2076,gid=10    0 0
```

The `noauto` option prevents the Windows partition from being mounted at boot time. The `defaults` option is the same as `rw,suid,dev,exec,async`. The `user` option allows us to mount the filesystem without being `root`. The `uid=` and `gid=` options force the files in `/win` to belong to us as a regular user so that we don't need to be `root` when working on that partition.

8.2.2 Working with Mounted Filesystems: `getmntent()`

Any of `/etc/fstab`, `/etc/mtab`, and `/proc/self/mounts` can be read programmatically with the `getmntent()` suite of routines:

GLIBC

```
#include <stdio.h>
#include <mntent.h>

FILE *setmntent(const char *filename, const char *type);
struct mntent *getmntent(FILE *filep);
int addmntent(FILE *filep, const struct mntent *mnt);
int endmntent(FILE *filep);
char *hasmntopt(const struct mntent *mnt, const char *opt);
```

`setmntent()` opens the file containing mount point entries. The `filename` argument is the file to open. The `type` argument is like the second argument to `fopen()`, indicating read, write, or read/write access. (Consider the `mount` command, which has to add an entry to `/etc/mtab` for each filesystem it mounts, and `umount`, which has to remove one.)[7] The returned value of type `FILE *` is then used with the rest of the routines.

`getmntent()` reads through the file, returning a pointer to a `static struct mntent`, which is filled in with the appropriate values. This `static` storage is overwritten on each call. It returns `NULL` when there are no more entries. (This is similar to the routines for reading the password and group files; see Section 6.3, "User and Group Names," page 190.)

`addmntent()` is called to add more information to the end of the open file; it's intended for use by `mount`.

`endmntent()` closes the open file; call it when you're done processing. *Don't* just call `fclose()`; other internal data structures associated with the `FILE *` variable may need to be cleaned up.

`hasmntopt()` is a more specialized function. It scans the `struct mntent` passed as the first parameter for a mount option matching the second argument. If the option is found, it returns the address of the matching substring. Otherwise, it returns `NULL`.

The fields in the `struct mntent` correspond directly to the fields in the `/etc/fstab` file. It looks like this:

```
struct mntent {
   char *mnt_fsname;     /* Device or server for filesystem. */
   char *mnt_dir;        /* Directory mounted on. */
   char *mnt_type;       /* Type of filesystem: ext4, nfs, etc. */
   char *mnt_opts;       /* Comma-separated options for fs. */
   int mnt_freq;         /* Dump frequency (in days). */
   int mnt_passno;       /* Pass number for `fsck'. */
};
```

The normal paradigm for working with mounted filesystems is to write an outer loop that reads `/etc/mtab`, processing one `struct mntent` at a time. Our first example, `ch-mounting-mounted.c`, does exactly that:

```
/* ch-mounting-mounted.c --- print a list of mounted filesystems */

/* NOTE: GNU/Linux specific! */

#include <stdio.h>
#include <errno.h>
#include <mntent.h> /* for getmntent(), et al. */
#include <stdlib.h>
#include <string.h>
#include <unistd.h> /* for getopt() */

void process(const char *filename);
void print_mount(const struct mntent *fs);
```

[7] This statement no longer applies to GNU/Linux, where the kernel updates `/proc/self/mounts` and `/etc/mtab` is just a symbolic link to it.

```

char *myname;

/* main --- process options */

int
main(int argc, char **argv)
{
    int c;
    char *file = "/etc/mtab";   /* default file to read */

    myname = argv[0];
    while ((c = getopt(argc, argv, "f:")) != -1) {
        switch (c) {
        case 'f':
            file = optarg;
            break;
        default:
            fprintf(stderr, "usage: %s [-f fstab-file]\n", argv[0]);
            exit(1);
        }
    }

    process(file);
    return 0;
}

/* process --- read struct mntent structures from file */

void
process(const char *filename)
{
    FILE *fp;
    struct mntent *fs;

    fp = setmntent(filename, "r");
    if (fp == NULL) {
        fprintf(stderr, "%s: %s: could not open: %s\n",
            myname, filename, strerror(errno));
        exit(1);
    }

    while ((fs = getmntent(fp)) != NULL)
        print_mount(fs);

```

```
59         endmntent(fp);
60     }
61
62     /* print_mount --- print a single mount entry */
63
64     void
65     print_mount(const struct mntent *fs)
66     {
67         printf("%s %s %s %s %d %d\n",
68             fs->mnt_fsname,
69             fs->mnt_dir,
70             fs->mnt_type,
71             fs->mnt_opts,
72             fs->mnt_freq,
73             fs->mnt_passno);
74     }
```

Unlike most of the programs that we've seen up to now, this one is Linux specific. Many Unix systems have similar routines, but they're not guaranteed to be identical.

By default, `ch-mounting-mounted` reads `/etc/mtab`, printing the information about each mounted filesystem. The `-f` option allows you to specify a different file to read, such as `/etc/fstab`.

The `main()` function processes the command line (lines 26–35) and calls `process()` on the named file. (This program follows our standard boilerplate.)

`process()`, in turn, opens the file (line 49), and loops over each returned filesystem (lines 56–57). When done, it closes the file (line 59).

The `print_mount()` function prints the information in the `struct mntent`. The output ends up being much the same as that of '`cat /etc/mtab`':

```
$ ch-mounting-mounted                    Run the program
sysfs /sys sysfs rw,nosuid,nodev,noexec,relatime 0 0
proc /proc proc rw,nosuid,nodev,noexec,relatime 0 0
udev /dev devtmpfs rw,nosuid,relatime,size=7958160k,nr_inodes=1989540,mode=755,inode64 0 0
devpts /dev/pts devpts rw,nosuid,noexec,relatime,gid=5,mode=620,ptmxmode=000 0 0
tmpfs /run tmpfs rw,nosuid,nodev,noexec,relatime,size=1604576k,mode=755,inode64 0 0
/dev/nvme0n1p3 / ext4 rw,relatime,errors=remount-ro 0 0
...
/dev/nvme0n1p4 /home ext4 rw,relatime 0 0
...
```

8.3 Retrieving Per-Filesystem Information

Printing per-filesystem information is all fine and good, but it's not exciting. Once we know that a particular mount point represents a filesystem, we want information *about* the filesystem. This allows us to do things like print the information retrieved by `df` and '`df -i`':

```
$ df                                                         Show free/used space
Filesystem      1K-blocks      Used Available Use% Mounted on
tmpfs             1604576      2596   1601980   1% /run
/dev/nvme0n1p3   48898724  21549360  24832988  47% /
tmpfs             8022868         0   8022868   0% /dev/shm
tmpfs                5120         4      5116   1% /run/lock
efivarfs              438       270       164  63% /sys/firmware/efi/efivars
/dev/nvme0n1p4 428475584 200489096 206147692  50% /home
/dev/nvme0n1p1    1071104     79608    991496   8% /boot/efi
tmpfs             1604572       148   1604424   1% /run/user/1000

$ df -i                                                      Show free/used inodes
Filesystem        Inodes  IUsed    IFree IUse% Mounted on
tmpfs            2005717   1473  2004244    1% /run
/dev/nvme0n1p3   3129344 548065  2581279   18% /
tmpfs            2005717      1  2005716    1% /dev/shm
tmpfs            2005717      4  2005713    1% /run/lock
efivarfs               0      0        0     - /sys/firmware/efi/efivars
/dev/nvme0n1p4 27279360 785530 26493830    3% /home
/dev/nvme0n1p1         0      0        0     - /boot/efi
tmpfs             401143    145   400998    1% /run/user/1000
```

8.3.1 POSIX Style: `statvfs()` and `fstatvfs()`

Early Unix systems had only one kind of filesystem. For them, it was sufficient if `df` read the superblock of each mounted filesystem, extracted the relevant statistics, and formatted them nicely for printing. (The superblock was typically the second block in the filesystem; the first was the *boot block*, to hold bootstrapping code.)

However, in the modern world, such an approach would be untenable. POSIX provides two functions to access this information. The main function is called `statvfs()`. (The "vfs" part comes from the underlying SunOS technology, later used in System V Release 4, called a *virtual filesystem*.) There are two functions:

```
#include <sys/types.h>                                         POSIX
#include <sys/statvfs.h>

int statvfs(const char *path, struct statvfs *buf);
int fstatvfs(int fd, struct statvfs *buf);
```

`statvfs()` uses a pathname for any file; it returns information about the filesystem containing the file. `fstatvfs()` accepts an open file descriptor as its first argument; here, too, the information returned is about the filesystem containing the open file. The `struct statvfs` contains the following members:

```
struct statvfs {
    unsigned long int f_bsize;          Block size
    unsigned long int f_frsize;         Fragment size ("fundamental block size")
    fsblkcnt_t f_blocks;                Total number of blocks
    fsblkcnt_t f_bfree;                 Total number of free blocks
    fsblkcnt_t f_bavail;                Number of available blocks (≤ f_bfree)
    fsfilcnt_t f_files;                 Total number of inodes
    fsfilcnt_t f_ffree;                 Total number of free inodes
    fsfilcnt_t f_favail;                Number of available inodes (≤ f_files)
    unsigned long int f_fsid;           Filesystem ID
    unsigned long int f_flag;           Flags: ST_RDONLY and/or ST_NOSUID
    unsigned long int f_namemax;        Maximum file name length
};
```

The information it contains is enough to write `df`:

`unsigned long int f_bsize`
: The block size is the preferred size for doing I/O. The filesystem attempts to keep at least `f_bsize` bytes worth of data in contiguous sectors on disk. (A *sector* is the smallest amount of addressable data on the disk. Typically, a disk sector is 512 bytes.)

`unsigned long int f_frsize`
: Some filesystems (such as the BSD Fast Filesystem) distinguish between blocks and *fragments* of blocks. Small files whose total size is smaller than a block reside in some number of fragments. This avoids wasting disk space (at the admitted cost of more complexity in the kernel code). The fragment size is chosen at the time the filesystem is created.

`fsblkcnt_t f_blocks`
: The total number of blocks (in units of `f_bsize`) in the filesystem.

`fsblkcnt_t f_bfree`
: The total number of free blocks in the filesystem.

`fsblkcnt_t f_bavail`
: The number of blocks that may actually be used. Some filesystems reserve a percentage of the filesystem's blocks for use by the superuser, in case the filesystem fills up. Modern systems reserve around five percent, although this number can be changed by an administrator. (See *tune2fs*(8) on a GNU/Linux system, and *tunefs*(8) on Unix systems.)

`fsfilcnt_t f_files`
: The total number of inodes ("file serial numbers," in POSIX parlance) on the filesystem. This number is usually initialized and made permanent when the filesystem is created.

`fsfilcnt_t f_ffree`
: The total number of free inodes.

`fsfilcnt_t f_favail`
: The number of inodes that may actually be used. Some percentage of the inodes are reserved for the superuser, just as for blocks.

Table 8.2: GLIBC values for `f_flag`

Flag	POSIX	Meaning
`ST_MANDLOCK`		Enforce mandatory locking (see Section 16.2, "Locking Files," page 558).
`ST_NOATIME`		Don't update the access time field on each access.
`ST_NODEV`		Disallow access through device files.
`ST_NODIRATIME`		Don't update the access time field of directories.
`ST_NOEXEC`		Disallow execution of binaries.
`ST_NOSUID`	✓	Disallow the use of setuid and setgid bits.
`ST_RDONLY`	✓	Filesystem is read-only.
`ST_RELATIME`		Update atime relative to mtime/ctime; see *mount*(2).
`ST_SYNCHRONOUS`		All writes are synchronous (see Section 4.6.4, "Revisiting `open()`," page 104).

`unsigned long int f_fsid`
: The filesystem ID. POSIX doesn't specify what this represents, and it's apparently not used under Linux.

`unsigned long int f_flag`
: Flags giving information about the filesystem. POSIX specifies two: `ST_RDONLY`, for a read-only filesystem (such as a DVD or CD-ROM), and `ST_NOSUID`, which disallows the use of the setuid and setgid permission bits on executables. GNU/Linux systems provide additional flags; they are listed in Table 8.2.

`unsigned long int f_namemax`
: The maximum length of a file name. This refers to each individual component in a pathname—in other words, the maximum length for a directory entry. Programmatically, you would deal with this value using `pathconf()`, which is discussed in Section 12.2.3, "Filesystem Limitations: `pathconf()` and `fpathconf()`," page 409.

The `fsblkcnt_t` and `fsfilcnt_t` types are defined in `<sys/types.h>`. On modern systems they are a 64-bit type, since disks have gotten very large. The following program, `ch-mounting-statvfs.c`, shows how to use `statvfs()`:

```
/* ch-mounting-statvfs.c --- demonstrate statvfs */

/* NOTE: GNU/Linux specific! */

#include <stdio.h>
#include <errno.h>
#include <mntent.h> /* for getmntent(), et al. */
#include <stdlib.h>
#include <string.h>
#include <unistd.h> /* for getopt() */
#include <sys/types.h>
```

```
#include <sys/statvfs.h>

void process(const char *filename);
void do_statvfs(const struct mntent *fs);

int errors = 0;
char *myname;

/* main --- process options */

int
main(int argc, char **argv)
{
    int c;
    char *file = "/etc/mtab";   /* default file to read */

    myname = argv[0];
    while ((c = getopt(argc, argv, "f:")) != -1) {
        switch (c) {
        case 'f':
            file = optarg;
            break;
        default:
            fprintf(stderr, "usage: %s [-f fstab-file]\n", argv[0]);
            exit(1);
        }
    }

    process(file);
    return (errors != 0);
}

/* process --- read struct mntent structures from file */

void
process(const char *filename)
{
    FILE *fp;
    struct mntent *fs;

    fp = setmntent(filename, "r");
    if (fp == NULL) {
        fprintf(stderr, "%s: %s: could not open: %s\n",
            myname, filename, strerror(errno));
        exit(1);
    }
```

```
58
59      while ((fs = getmntent(fp)) != NULL)
60          do_statvfs(fs);
61
62      endmntent(fp);
63  }
```

Lines 1–63 are essentially the same as `ch-mounting-mounted.c`. `main()` handles the command line, and `process()` loops over each mounted filesystem. `do_statvfs()` does the real work, printing the `struct statvfs` for each interesting filesystem:

```
65  /* do_statvfs --- Use statvfs and print info */
66
67  void
68  do_statvfs(const struct mntent *fs)
69  {
70      struct statvfs vfs;
71
72      if (fs->mnt_fsname[0] != '/')   /* skip nonreal filesystems */
73          return;
74
75      if (statvfs(fs->mnt_dir, & vfs) != 0) {
76          fprintf(stderr, "%s: %s: statvfs failed: %s\n",
77              myname, fs->mnt_dir, strerror(errno));
78          errors++;
79          return;
80      }
81
82      printf("%s, mounted on %s:\n", fs->mnt_dir, fs->mnt_fsname);
83      printf("\tf_bsize: %ld\n",  (long) vfs.f_bsize);
84      printf("\tf_frsize: %ld\n", (long) vfs.f_frsize);
85      printf("\tf_blocks: %lu\n", (unsigned long) vfs.f_blocks);
86      printf("\tf_bfree: %lu\n",  (unsigned long) vfs.f_bfree);
87      printf("\tf_bavail: %lu\n", (unsigned long) vfs.f_bavail);
88      printf("\tf_files: %lu\n",  (unsigned long) vfs.f_files);
89      printf("\tf_ffree: %lu\n",  (unsigned long) vfs.f_ffree);
90      printf("\tf_favail: %lu\n", (unsigned long) vfs.f_favail);
91      printf("\tf_fsid: %#lx\n",  (unsigned long) vfs.f_fsid);
92
93      printf("\tf_flag: ");
94      if (vfs.f_flag == 0)
95          printf("(none)\n");
96      else {
97          if ((vfs.f_flag & ST_RDONLY) != 0)
98              printf("ST_RDONLY ");
99          if ((vfs.f_flag & ST_NOSUID) != 0)
```

```
100             printf("ST_NOSUID");
101         printf("\n");
102     }
103
104     printf("\tf_namemax: %ld\n", (long)vfs.f_namemax);
105 }
```

Lines 72–73 skip filesystems that are not based on a real disk device. This means that filesystems like `/proc` or `/dev/pts` are ignored. (Admittedly, this check is a heuristic, but it works: in `/etc/mtab` mounted devices are listed by the full device pathname—for example, `/dev/hda1`.) Line 75 calls `statvfs()` with appropriate error checking, and lines 82–104 print the information.

Lines 93–102 deal with *flags*: single bits of information that are or are not present. See the following subsection for a discussion of how flag bits are used in C code. Here is the output of `ch-mounting-statvfs`:

```
$ ch-mounting-statvfs                      Run the program
/, mounted on /dev/nvme0n1p3:              Results for ext4 filesystem
    f_bsize: 4096
    f_frsize: 4096
    f_blocks: 12224681
    f_bfree: 6836878
    f_bavail: 6207784
    f_files: 3129344
    f_ffree: 2581271
    f_favail: 2581271
    f_fsid: 0x5768a155354b4366
    f_flag:
    f_namemax: 255
...
/home, mounted on /dev/nvme0n1p4:
    f_bsize: 4096
    f_frsize: 4096
    f_blocks: 107118896
    f_bfree: 56999265
    f_bavail: 51539566
    f_files: 27279360
    f_ffree: 26493955
    f_favail: 26493955
    f_fsid: 0x587ce2de79797a83
    f_flag:
    f_namemax: 255
...
```

NOTE

Although POSIX specifies `statvfs()` and `fstatvfs()`, not all systems support them or support them correctly. Many systems (including Linux, as described shortly), have their own system calls that provide similar information. GNU `df` uses a library routine to acquire filesystem information; the source file for that routine is full of `#ifdefs` for a plethora of different systems. The current code prefers `statvfs()`, falling back to other mechanisms if it's not available.

8.3.1.1 A Programming Digression: Bit Flags

A common technique, applicable in many cases, is to have a set of *flag* values; when a flag is *set* (that is, true), a certain fact is true or a certain condition applies. Flag values are defined with either `#defined` symbolic constants or `enums`. In this chapter, the `fts()` API (described later) also uses flags. There are only two standard flags for the `struct statvfs` field `f_flag`:

```
#define ST_RDONLY      1      /* read-only filesystem */         Sample definitions
#define ST_NOSUID      2      /* setuid/setgid not allowed */
```

Flag values need to be powers of two. When there are many values, there are different ways of writing them. One way is to use a chain of << operators:

```
#define SYM1   (1<<0)
#define SYM2   (SYM1<<1)
#define SYM3   (SYM2<<1)
...
```

Another is to use hexadecimal values:

```
#define SYM1   0x01
#define SYM2   0x02
...
#define SYM14  0x0e
#define SYM15  0x0f
...
```

Instead of constants created with `#define`, it's also common to use `enum` values. The advantage of the latter is that such values print as themselves when using a debugger.

It is even likely that you will see `enums` combined with macros:

```
enum my_symbols {
    SYM1 = 0x01,
#define SYM1 SYM1
    SYM2 = 0x02,
#define SYM2 SYM2
...
    SYM14 = 0x0e,
#define SYM14 SYM14
    SYM15 = 0x0f,
#define SYM15 SYM15
};
```

(Remember that in C, if you define a macro to itself, the value is left alone and does not cause recursive expansion.) Why do this? It allows you to check if a value is defined via `#ifdef`, while still letting the symbolic values show up in a debugger.

Physically, each symbolic constant represents a different bit position within the `f_flag` value (and thus the requirement that they be powers of two). Logically, each value represents a separate bit of state information—that is, some fact or condition that is or isn't true for this particular instance of a `struct statvfs`.

Flags are set, tested, and cleared with the C bitwise operators. For example, `statvfs()` would set these flags, using the bitwise-OR operator:

```
int statvfs(const char *path, struct statvfs *vfs)
{
    ... fill in most of *vfs ...
    vfs->f_flag = 0;                        Make sure it starts out as zero
    if (filesystem is read-only)
        vfs->f_flag |= ST_RDONLY;           Add the ST_RDONLY flag
    if (filesystem disallows setuid)
        vfs->f_flag |= ST_NOSUID;           Add the ST_NOSUID flag
    ... rest of routine ...
}
```

The bitwise-AND operator tests whether a flag is set, and a combination of the bitwise-AND and COMPLEMENT operators clears one or more flags:

```
if ((vfs.f_flag & ST_RDONLY) != 0)          True if ST_RDONLY flag is set

vfs.f_flag &= ~(ST_RDONLY|ST_NOSUID);       Clear both flags
```

The bitwise operators are daunting if you've not used them before. However, the example code just shown represents common C idioms. Study each operation carefully; perhaps draw yourself a few pictures showing how these operators work. Once you understand them, you can train yourself to recognize these operators as *high-level operations for managing flag values* instead of treating them as *low-level bit manipulations*.

The reason to use flag values is that they provide considerable savings in data space. The single `unsigned long` field lets you store at least 32 separate bits of information. GLIBC (as of this writing) defines 13 different flags for the `f_flag` field.[8] If you used a separate `char` field for each flag, that would use 13 bytes instead of just the four used by the `unsigned long`. If you had 32 flags, that would be 32 bytes instead of just four!

8.3.2 Linux Style: `statfs()` and `fstatfs()`

The `statfs()` and `fstatfs()` system calls are Linux specific. Their declarations are as follows:

```
#include <sys/types.h>                                          GLIBC
#include <sys/vfs.h>
```

[8] See `/usr/include/bits/statvfs.h` on a GNU/Linux system. Three of them are not documented in the *statvfs*(3) manpage.

```
int statfs(const char *path, struct statfs *buf);
int fstatfs(int fd, struct statfs *buf);
```

As with `statvfs()` and `fstatvfs()`, the two versions work on a file name or an open file descriptor, respectively. The `struct statfs` looks like this:

```
struct statfs {
   __fsword_t f_type;     /* Type of filesystem (see below) */
   __fsword_t f_bsize;    /* Optimal transfer block size */
   fsblkcnt_t f_blocks;   /* Total data blocks in filesystem */
   fsblkcnt_t f_bfree;    /* Free blocks in filesystem */
   fsblkcnt_t f_bavail;   /* Free blocks available to
                             unprivileged user */
   fsfilcnt_t f_files;    /* Total inodes in filesystem */
   fsfilcnt_t f_ffree;    /* Free inodes in filesystem */
   fsid_t     f_fsid;     /* Filesystem ID */
   __fsword_t f_namelen;  /* Maximum length of filenames */
   __fsword_t f_frsize;   /* Fragment size (since Linux 2.6) */
   __fsword_t f_flags;    /* Mount flags of filesystem
                             (since Linux 2.6.36) */
   __fsword_t f_spare[xxx];
                          /* Padding bytes reserved for future use */
};
```

The fields are analogous to those in the `struct statvfs`. In GLIBC, the POSIX `statvfs()` and `fstatvfs()` functions are wrappers around `statfs()` and `fstatfs()`, respectively, copying the values from one kind of `struct` to the other.

The advantage to using `statfs()` or `fstatfs()` is that they are system calls. The kernel returns the information directly. The main disadvantage to using these calls is that they are Linux specific.

One field in the `struct statfs` deserves special note. This is the `f_type` field, which indicates the type of the filesystem. The value is the filesystem's magic number, extracted from the superblock. The *statfs*(2) manpage provides a list of commonly used filesystems and their magic numbers, which we use in `ch-mounting-statfs.c`. (Alas, there is no separate `#include` file.) There are 84(!) different filesystem types listed; we've omitted most of them in the book to save space, but the code in the book's GitHub repository is complete:

```
/* ch-mounting-statfs.c --- demonstrate Linux statfs */

/* NOTE: GNU/Linux specific! */

#include <stdio.h>
#include <errno.h>
#include <mntent.h> /* for getmntent(), et al. */
#include <stdlib.h>
#include <string.h>
```

```
#include <unistd.h> /* for getopt() */
#include <sys/types.h>
#include <sys/vfs.h>

/* Defines taken from statfs(2) man page: */
#define ADFS_SUPER_MAGIC      0xadf5
#define AFFS_SUPER_MAGIC      0xadff
#define AFS_SUPER_MAGIC       0x5346414f
#define ANON_INODE_FS_MAGIC   0x09041934 /* Anonymous inode FS */
...
#define XENFS_SUPER_MAGIC     0xabba1974
#define XENIX_SUPER_MAGIC     0x012ff7b4
#define XFS_SUPER_MAGIC       0x58465342
#define _XIAFS_SUPER_MAGIC    0x012fd16d /* Linux 2.0 and earlier */

void process(const char *filename);
void do_statfs(const struct mntent *fs);

int errors = 0;
char *myname;
...           main() and process() omitted to save space, see text
/* type2str --- convert fs type to printable string, from statfs(2) */

const
char *type2str(long type)
{
    static struct fsname {
        long type;
        const char *name;
    } table[] = {
        { ADFS_SUPER_MAGIC, "ADFS_SUPER_MAGIC"  },
        { AFFS_SUPER_MAGIC, "AFFS_SUPER_MAGIC"  },
        { AFS_SUPER_MAGIC, "AFS_SUPER_MAGIC"  },
        { ANON_INODE_FS_MAGIC, "ANON_INODE_FS_MAGIC"  },
...
        { XENIX_SUPER_MAGIC, "XENIX_SUPER_MAGIC"  },
        { XFS_SUPER_MAGIC, "XFS_SUPER_MAGIC"  },
        { _XIAFS_SUPER_MAGIC, "_XIAFS_SUPER_MAGIC"  },
        { 0, NULL },
    };
    static char unknown[100];
    int i;

    for (i = 0; table[i].type != 0; i++)
        if (table[i].type == type)
            return table[i].name;
```

```
252
253         sprintf(unknown, "unknown type: %#lx", type);
254         return unknown;
255     }
256
257     /* do_statfs --- Use statfs and print info */
258
259     void
260     do_statfs(const struct mntent *fs)
261     {
262         struct statfs vfs;
263
264         if (fs->mnt_fsname[0] != '/')    /* skip nonreal filesystems */
265             return;
266
267         if (statfs(fs->mnt_dir, & vfs) != 0) {
268             fprintf(stderr, "%s: %s: statfs failed: %s\n",
269                 myname, fs->mnt_dir, strerror(errno));
270             errors++;
271             return;
272         }
273
274         printf("%s, mounted on %s:\n", fs->mnt_dir, fs->mnt_fsname);
275
276         printf("\tf_type: %s\n", type2str(vfs.f_type));
277         printf("\tf_bsize: %ld\n", vfs.f_bsize);
278         printf("\tf_blocks: %ld\n", vfs.f_blocks);
279         printf("\tf_bfree: %ld\n", vfs.f_bfree);
280         printf("\tf_bavail: %ld\n", vfs.f_bavail);
281         printf("\tf_files: %ld\n", vfs.f_files);
282         printf("\tf_ffree: %ld\n", vfs.f_ffree);
283         printf("\tf_namelen: %ld\n", vfs.f_namelen);
284         printf("\tf_frsize: %ld\n", vfs.f_frsize);
285         printf("\tf_flags: %#lx\n", vfs.f_flags);
286     }
```

To save space, we've omitted `main()`, which is unchanged from the other programs presented earlier, and we've also omitted `process()`, which now calls `do_statfs()` instead of `do_statvfs()`.

Lines 14–98 contain the list of filesystem magic numbers from the *statfs*(2) manpage. Although the numbers could be retrieved from kernel source code header files, such retrieval is painful (we tried), and the presentation here is easier to follow. Lines 151–255 define `type2str()`, which converts the magic number to a printable string. It does a simple linear search on a table of (value, string) pairs. In the (unlikely) event that the magic number isn't in the table, `types2str()` creates an "unknown type" message and returns that (lines 253–254).

`do_statfs()` (lines 259–286) prints the information from the `struct statfs`. The `f_fsid` member is omitted since `fsid_t` is an opaque type. The code is straightforward; line 276 uses `type2str()` to print the filesystem type. As for the similar program using `statvfs()`, this function ignores filesystems that aren't on local devices (lines 264–265). Here is the output on our system:

```
$ ch-mounting-statfs                          Run the program
/, mounted on /dev/nvme0n1p3:                 Results for ext4 filesystem
    f_type: EXT2_SUPER_MAGIC
    f_bsize: 4096
    f_blocks: 12224681
    f_bfree: 6833922
    f_bavail: 6204828
    f_files: 3129344
    f_ffree: 2581271
    f_namelen: 255
    f_frsize: 4096
    f_flags: 0x1020
...
/home, mounted on /dev/nvme0n1p4:
    f_type: EXT2_SUPER_MAGIC
    f_bsize: 4096
    f_blocks: 107118896
    f_bfree: 56989695
    f_bavail: 51529996
    f_files: 27279360
    f_ffree: 26492809
    f_namelen: 255
    f_frsize: 4096
    f_flags: 0x1020
/boot/efi, mounted on /dev/nvme0n1p1:         Results for vfat filesystem
    f_type: MSDOS_SUPER_MAGIC
    f_bsize: 4096
    f_blocks: 267776
    f_bfree: 247874
    f_bavail: 247874
    f_files: 0
    f_ffree: 0
    f_namelen: 1530
    f_frsize: 4096
    f_flags: 0x1020
```

In conclusion, whether to use `statvfs()` or `statfs()` in your own code depends on your requirements. If you have `statvfs()`, using it keeps your code portable.

8.4 Moving Around in the File Hierarchy

Several system calls and standard library functions let you change your current directory and determine the full pathname of the current directory. More complicated functions let you perform arbitrary actions for every filesystem object in a directory hierarchy.

8.4.1 Changing Directory: `chdir()` and `fchdir()`

In Section 1.2, "The Linux/Unix Process Model," page 7, we said:

> The current working directory is the one to which relative pathnames (those that don't start with a `/`) are relative. This is the directory you are "in" after you issue a '`cd` *`someplace`*' command to the shell.

Each process has a current working directory. Each new process inherits its current directory from the process that started it (its parent). Two functions let you change to another directory:

```
#include <unistd.h>

int chdir(const char *path);                                 POSIX
int fchdir(int fd);
```

The `chdir()` function takes a string naming a directory, whereas `fchdir()` expects a file descriptor that was opened on a directory with `open()`.[9] Both return `0` on success and `-1` on error (with `errno` set appropriately). Typically, if `open()` on a directory succeeded, then `fchdir()` will also succeed, unless someone changed the permissions on the directory between the calls.

These functions are almost trivial to use. The following program, `ch-mounting-chdir.c`, demonstrates both functions. It also demonstrates that `fchdir()` can fail if the permissions on the open directory don't include search (execute) permission:

```
/* ch-mounting-chdir.c --- demonstrate chdir() and fchdir().
                           Error checking omitted for brevity */

#include <stdio.h>
#include <fcntl.h>
#include <unistd.h>
#include <sys/types.h>
#include <sys/stat.h>

int
main(void)
```

[9]On GNU/Linux and BSD systems, you can apply the `dirfd()` function to a `DIR *` pointer to obtain the underlying file descriptor; see the GNU/Linux *dirfd*(3) manpage.

```
12 {
13     int fd;
14     struct stat sbuf;
15
16     fd = open(".", O_RDONLY);    /* open directory for reading */
17     fstat(fd, & sbuf);           /* obtain info, need original permissions */
18     int junk = chdir("..");      /* 'cd ..' */
19     fchmod(fd, 0);               /* zap permissions on original directory */
20
21     if (fchdir(fd) < 0)          /* try to 'cd' back, should fail */
22         perror("fchdir back");
23
24     fchmod(fd, sbuf.st_mode & 07777);   /* restore original permissions */
25     close(fd);          /* all done */
26
27     return 0;
28 }
```

Line 16 opens the current directory. Line 17 calls `fstat()` on the open directory so that we have a copy of its permissions. Line 18 uses `chdir()` to move up a level in the file hierarchy. (Without the assignment to `junk` variable on line 18 we would get a compiler warning about the result being unused. We use this technique throughout the book whenever it's necessary.) Line 19 does the dirty work, turning off *all* permissions on the original directory.

Lines 21–22 attempt to change back to the original directory. It is expected to fail, since the current permissions don't allow it. Line 24 restores the original permissions. The '`sbuf.st_mode & 07777`' retrieves the low-order 12 permission bits; these are the regular 9 `rwxrwxrwx` bits, and the setuid, setgid, and "sticky" bits, which we discuss in Chapter 11, "Permissions and User and Group ID Numbers," page 383. Finally, line 25 cleans up by closing the open file descriptor. Here's what happens when the program runs:

```
$ ls -ld .                                              Show current permissions
drwxrwxr-x 4 arnold arnold 4096 Jan 17 21:24 .
$ ch-mounting-chdir
fchdir back: Permission denied                          Fails as expected
$ ls -ld .                                              Look at permissions again
drwxrwxr-x 4 arnold arnold 4096 Jan 17 21:24 .          Everything is back as it was
```

8.4.2 Getting the Current Directory: `getcwd()`

The aptly named `getcwd()` function retrieves the absolute pathname of the current working directory:

```
#include <unistd.h>                                     POSIX

char *getcwd(char *buf, size_t size);
```

The function fills in `buf` with the pathname; it expects `buf` to have `size` bytes. Upon success, it returns its first argument. Otherwise, if it needs more than `size` bytes, it returns

NULL and sets errno to ERANGE. The intent is that if ERANGE happens, you should try to allocate a larger buffer (with malloc() or realloc()) and try again.

Chet Ramey points out that a better alternative is to use pathconf(".", _PC_PATH_MAX) to get the buffer size for getcwd(). See Section 12.2.3, "Filesystem Limitations: pathconf() and fpathconf()," page 409, for more information.

If any of the directory components leading to the current directory are not readable or searchable, then getcwd() can fail and errno will be EACCES. The following simple program demonstrates its use:

```
/* ch-mounting-getcwd.c --- demonstrate getcwd().
                            Error checking omitted for brevity */

#include <stdio.h>
#include <fcntl.h>
#include <limits.h>
#include <unistd.h>
#include <sys/types.h>
#include <sys/stat.h>

int
main(void)
{
    char buf[PATH_MAX];
    char *cp;

    cp = getcwd(buf, sizeof(buf));
    printf("Current dir: %s\n", buf);

    printf("Changing to ..\n");
    int junk = chdir("..");          /* 'cd ..' */

    cp = getcwd(buf, sizeof(buf));
    printf("Current dir is now: %s\n", buf);

    return 0;
}
```

This simple program prints the current directory, changes to the parent directory, and then prints the new current directory. (cp isn't really needed here, but in a real program it would be used for error checking.) When run, it produces the following output:

```
$ ch-mounting-getcwd
Current dir: /home/arnold/work/prenhall/progex1-2e/code/ch-08-mounting
Changing to ..
Current dir is now: /home/arnold/work/prenhall/progex1-2e/code
```

Formally, if the `buf` argument is `NULL`, the behavior of `getcwd()` is undefined. In this case, the GLIBC version of `getcwd()` will call `malloc()` for you, allocating a buffer of size `size`. Going even further out of its way to be helpful, if `size` is `0`, then the buffer it allocates will be "big enough" to hold the returned pathname. In either case, you should call `free()` on the returned pointer when you're done with the buffer.

The GLIBC behavior is helpful, but it's not portable. For code that has to work across platforms, you can write a replacement function that provides the same functionality while having your replacement function call `getcwd()` directly if on a GLIBC system.

GNU/Linux systems provide the file `/proc/self/cwd`. This file is a symbolic link to the current directory:

```
$ cd /tmp                        Change directory someplace
$ ls -l /proc/self/cwd           Look at the file
lrwxrwxrwx 1 arnold arnold 0 Jan 17 21:31 /proc/self/cwd -> /tmp
$ cd                             Change to home directory
$ ls -l /proc/self/cwd           Look at it again
lrwxrwxrwx 1 arnold arnold 0 Jan 17 21:31 /proc/self/cwd -> /home/arnold
```

This is convenient at the shell level but presents a problem at the programmatic level. In particular, the size of the file is zero! (This is because it's a file in `/proc`, which the kernel fakes; it's not a real file living on disk.)

Why is the zero size a problem? If you remember from Section 5.4.5, "Working with Symbolic Links," page 141, `lstat()` on a symbolic link returns the number of characters in the name of the linked-to file in the `st_size` field of the `struct stat`. This number can then be used to allocate a buffer of the appropriate size for use with `readlink()`. That won't work here, since the size is zero. You have to use (or allocate) a buffer that you guess is big enough. However, since `readlink()` does not fill in any more characters than you provide, *you can't tell* whether the buffer is big enough; `readlink()` does not fail when there isn't enough room. (See the Coreutils `xreadlink()` function in Section 5.4.5, "Working with Symbolic Links," page 141, which solves the problem.)

In addition to `getcwd()`, GLIBC has several other nonportable routines. These save you the trouble of managing buffers and provide compatibility with older BSD systems. For the details, see *getcwd*(3).

8.4.3 Processing a File Hierarchy: `fts_open()` and Friends

A common programming task is to process entire directory hierarchies, doing something for every file and every directory and subdirectory in an entire tree. Consider, for example, `du`, which prints disk usage information; '`chown -R`', which recursively changes ownership; or the `find` program, which finds files matching certain criteria.

At this point, you know enough to write your own code to manually open and read directories, call `stat()` (or `lstat()`) for each entry, and recursively process subdirectories. However, such code is challenging to get right: it's possible to run out of file descriptors if you leave parent directories open while processing subdirectories; you have to decide whether to process symbolic links as themselves or as the files they point to; you have to be able to deal with directories that aren't readable or searchable; and so on. It's also painful to have to write the same code over and over again if you need it for multiple applications.

8.4.3.1 The `nftw()` Interface

To obviate the problems, System V introduced the `ftw()` ("file tree walk") function. `ftw()` did all the work to "walk" a file tree (hierarchy). You supplied it with a pointer to a function, and it called the function for every file object it encountered. Your function could then process each filesystem object as it saw fit.

Over time, it became clear that the `ftw()` interface didn't quite do the full job; for example, originally it didn't support symbolic links.[10] For this reason, `nftw()` ("new `ftw()`" [*sic*]) was added to the X/Open Portability Guide; it's now part of POSIX. Here's the prototype:

```
#include <ftw.h>                                   POSIX XSI

int nftw(const char *dir,                          Starting point
         int (*fn)(const char *file,               Function pointer to
                   const struct stat *sb,          function of four arguments
                   int flag, struct FTW *s),
         int nopenfd, int flags);                  Max open fds, flags
```

And here are the arguments:

`const char *dir`
: A string naming the starting point of the hierarchy to process.

`int (*fn)(const char *file, const struct stat *sb, int flag, struct FTW *s)`
: A pointer to a function with the given arguments. This function is called for every object in the hierarchy.

`int nopenfd`
: To avoid running out of file descriptors, `nftw()` keeps no more than `nopenfd` directories open simultaneously. This does *not* prevent `nftw()` from processing hierarchies that are more than `nopenfd` levels deep, but smaller values for `nopenfd` mean that `nftw()` has to do more work.

`flags`
: A set of flags, bitwise-OR'd, that direct how `nftw()` should process the hierarchy.

Jim Meyering, the maintainer of the GNU Coreutils, notes that the `nftw()` design isn't perfect, due to its recursive nature. (It calls itself recursively when processing subdirectories.) If a directory hierarchy gets really deep, in the 20,000–40,000 level range(!), `nftw()` can run out of stack space, killing the program. There are other problems related to `nftw()`'s design

---

[10] In the past, POSIX standardized the `ftw()` interface to support existing code, but it no longer does so. GNU/Linux and commercial Unix systems continue to supply it. However, since it's underpowered, we don't otherwise discuss it. See *ftw*(3) if you're interested.

as well. Because of this, versions of the GNU Coreutils after 5.0 switched to the `fts()` suite of routines, which we're about to dive into. For that reason we're not going to cover `nftw()` any more in this book. (However, `ch-mounting-nftw.c` is available in the book's code repository if you wish to see how to use it.)

8.4.3.2 Processing a File Tree Stream

Instead of talking about `nftw()`, we now describe a suite of routines that process files and directories in a "stream." That is, user code runs a `while` loop, retrieving and processing file objects one at a time, and avoiding the problems inherent in recursion. The `fts()` suite was introduced with 4.4 BSD. It is widely available, but surprisingly, it is not standardized by POSIX:

```
#include <sys/types.h>                          Common
#include <sys/stat.h>
#include <fts.h>

FTS *fts_open(char *const *path_argv, int options,
              int (*compar)(const FTSENT **, const FTSENT **));
FTSENT *fts_read(FTS *ftsp);
FTSENT *fts_children(FTS *ftsp, int instr);
int fts_set(FTS *ftsp, FTSENT *f, int instr);
int fts_close(FTS *ftsp);
```

The design is similar to that of the `opendir()` suite. You "open" a stream of file objects with `fts_open()`, and read one object at a time with `fts_read()`. When you're done, you close the stream with `fts_close()`. `fts_read()` may change the current directory during the traversal. This is a performance optimization that you can disable.

The full suite is powerful but complicated. Thus we will go through it one function at a time. The first is `fts_open()`:

`FTS *fts_open(char *const *path_argv, int options, int (*compar)(const FTSENT **, const FTSENT **))`

Open a file stream. Return a non-`NULL` pointer to an opaque `FTS` object upon success, or return `NULL` upon failure. This pointer is then used with the other routines in this suite. The arguments are:

`path_argv`
: An `argv`-style array of pointers to characters. Each string is a directory that should be traversed.

`options`
: The bitwise-OR of a number of flags that tell `fts_read()` how to process the hierarchy. We describe the flags shortly.

`int (*compar)(const FTSENT **, const FTSENT **)`
: A pointer to a function that may be used to order the traversal. For example, you may wish to order it alphabetically, or by file age, or by file size, or by any other

criteria. From the manpage: "If the `compar()` argument is `NULL`, the directory traversal order is in the order listed in `path_argv` for the root paths, and in the order listed in the directory for everything else."

Here are the possible option flags for use with the `options` parameter. You *must* supply one of either `FTS_LOGICAL` or `FTS_PHYSICAL`:

`FTS_COMFOLLOW`
: If any of the directories named in `path_argv` is a symbolic link, follow the link. That is, use the link's target. This is done even if `FTS_LOGICAL` is not supplied.

`FTS_LOGICAL`
: Return information about the target of a symbolic link, instead of information about the link itself. This option is mutually exclusive with `FTS_PHYSICAL`.

`FTS_NOCHDIR`
: Don't change directory during the file hierarchy traversal. Normally, `fts_read()` may change directories during the traversal, which improves performance. This option disables that behavior.

`FTS_NOSTAT`
: Don't retrieve the `stat()` information for the current file. This can improve performance if you don't need that information.

`FTS_PHYSICAL`
: Return information about symbolic links, instead of about the files they point to. It is likely that this option will be of the most use to you. This option is mutually exclusive with `FTS_LOGICAL`.

`FTS_SEEDOT`
: Return information about the `.` and `..` entries in a directory. Normally, these entries are skipped.

`FTS_XDEV`
: Don't cross filesystem boundaries. That is, don't move into a different mounted filesystem if such should be encountered.

The next function, and the one you are most likely to use, is `fts_read()`:

`FTSENT *fts_read(FTS *ftsp)`
: Return a pointer to an `FTSENT` structure describing the next file in the hierarchy described by `ftsp`.

The `FTSENT` structure looks like this:

```
typedef struct _ftsent {
   unsigned short  fts_info;     /* flags for FTSENT structure */
   char           *fts_accpath;  /* access path */
```

```
    char            *fts_path;      /* root path */
    short            fts_pathlen;   /* strlen(fts_path) +
                                       strlen(fts_name) */
    char            *fts_name;      /* filename */
    short            fts_namelen;   /* strlen(fts_name) */
    short            fts_level;     /* depth (-1 to N) */
    int              fts_errno;     /* file errno */
    long             fts_number;    /* local numeric value */
    void            *fts_pointer;   /* local address value */
    struct _ftsent  *fts_parent;    /* parent directory */
    struct _ftsent  *fts_link;      /* next file structure */
    struct _ftsent  *fts_cycle;     /* cycle structure */
    struct stat     *fts_statp;     /* stat(2) information */
} FTSENT;
```

There may be other fields intended for private use. The fields and their purposes are as follows:

`unsigned short fts_info`
: Flags describing the type of file and other information. See Table 8.3.

`char *fts_accpath`
: The path to the file relative to the current directory.

`char *fts_path`
: The path to the file relative to the root of the traversal, i.e., the respective string in `path_argv`.

`short fts_pathlen`
: The manpage says '`/* strlen(fts_path) + strlen(fts_name) */`', but it seems to actually be the length of `fts_path`, which includes the file name.

`char *fts_name`
: The name of the file.

`short fts_namelen`
: The length of `fts_name`.

`short fts_level`
: The depth of the traversal for the current item. The root of the traversal is any directory in `path_argv`; the level of a root is zero. The parent of a root is at level −1. Levels above zero are descendants of the root directories.

`int fts_errno`
: The value of `errno` if a problem occurred getting information about this file.

`long fts_number`
`void *fts_pointer`
: These two fields are for use by the application. They are initialized to zero and `NULL`, respectively.

`struct _ftsent *fts_parent`
A pointer to the `FTSENT` structure for the parent directory containing this file.

`struct _ftsent *fts_link`
A pointer to the next `FTSENT` structure in the linked list returned by `fts_children()` (see further on). The list is `NULL`-terminated.

`struct _ftsent *fts_cycle`
If there is a cycle in the tree structure, this field points to the other `FTSENT` structure in the hierarchy that references this file. Cycles generally do not occur; see the manpage for cases in which they can.

`struct stat *fts_statp`
A pointer to a `struct stat` describing this file.

Table 8.3 describes the possible values for the `fts_info` field.

The description of the `FTS_D` and `FTS_DP` values needs some explanation. When traversing a directory tree, `fts_read()` visits a directory *twice*: once on its way down the tree, and again on its way back up, after visiting all of a directory's children. The first is referred to in computer science as a *preorder* visit (thus `FTS_D`), and the second is called a *postorder* visit (`FTS_DP`).

The next routine is `fts_children()`:

`FTSENT *fts_children(FTS *ftsp, int instr)`
Create a linked list of `FTSENT` structures describing the children of the most recently returned directory from `fts_read()`.

Table 8.3: Possible values for the `fts_info` field

`FTS_D`	A directory being visited in preorder.
`FTS_DC`	A directory that causes a cycle.
`FTS_DEFAULT`	An `FTSENT` structure for a file type not described by one of the other values in this table.
`FTS_DNR`	An unreadable directory. `fts_errno` will describe the error.
`FTS_DOT`	A file named `.` or `..` that was not included `path_argv`. These will only show up if `FTS_SEEDOT` was supplied to `fts_open()`.
`FTS_DP`	A directory being visited in postorder. All of the other information in the `FTSENT` structure will be identical to what it was during the preorder visit.
`FTS_ERR`	An error occurred. `fts_errno` will describe the error.
`FTS_F`	A regular file.
`FTS_NS`	A file for which no `stat()` information was available. `fts_errno` will describe the error.
`FTS_NSOK`	A file for which no `stat()` information was requested. This can happen when using `fts_children()`.
`FTS_SL`	A symbolic link.
`FTS_SLNONE`	A symbolic link with a nonexistent target. In this case, the `struct stat` pointed to by the `fts_statp` field describes the symbolic link itself.

In the special case that `fts_read()` has not yet been called, the linked list contains the children of the directory specified in the `path_argv` argument to `fts_open()`.

The `instr` ("instruction") parameter should be either zero or `FTS_NAMEONLY`, the latter indicating that only the names of the directory's children are needed.

The next routine is a little complicated:

`int fts_set(FTS *ftsp, FTSENT *f, int instr)`
Specify further processing of the file pointed to by `f` in the stream pointed to by `ftsp`, based on the value of `instr`. The value may be one of the following:

`0`
Do nothing.

`FTS_AGAIN`
Revisit the file. The next call to `fts_read()` returns this file, updating the `fts_stat` and `fts_info` fields. This can be used only on the most recently returned file from `fts_read()`. The typical use is upon the postorder visit of a directory, causing the directory and its children to be visited again.

`FTS_FOLLOW`
This can be used only when the referenced file is a symbolic link. It causes the next entry from `fts_read()` to refer to the file referenced by the link. Only the `fts_info` and `fts_statp` fields are updated. If the target of the link does not exist, the `fts_info` field is set to `FTS_SLNONE`.

`FTS_SKIP`
Do not visit any children of this file. The file may be one that was returned by either `fts_read()` or `fts_children()`.

The final routine is the simplest:

`int fts_close(FTS *ftsp)`
Close the stream referred to by `ftsp` and restore the current directory to the one from which `fts_read()` started. Return `0` upon success or `-1` upon failure.

Let's tie all this together with an example program. `ch-mounting-fts.c` processes the files and directories named on the command line, running `fts_read()` on them. The function that processes each file prints the file name and type with indentation, showing the hierarchical position of each file. For a change, we show the results first, and then we show and discuss the program:

```
$ pwd                                              Where we are
/home/arnold/work/prenhall/progex1-2e
$ code/ch-08-mounting/ch-mounting-fts code         Walk the code directory
code (directory preorder visit)                    Top-level directory
    fts_accpath: code
    fts_path: code
```

```
    fts_pathlen: 4
    fts_namelen: 4
    ... Lots of output ...
    ch-06-general1 (directory preorder visit)     Subdirectories one level indented
        fts_accpath: ch-06-general1
        fts_path: code/ch-06-general1
        fts_pathlen: 19
        fts_namelen: 14
        ch-general1-sortemp.c (file)              Files in subdirs two levels indented
            fts_accpath: ch-general1-sortemp.c
            fts_path: code/ch-06-general1/ch-general1-sortemp.c
            fts_pathlen: 41
            fts_namelen: 21
...
code (directory postorder visit)
    fts_accpath: code
    fts_path: code
    fts_pathlen: 4
    fts_namelen: 4
Starting dir: /home/arnold/work/prenhall/progex1-2e
Finishing dir: /home/arnold/work/prenhall/progex1-2e
```

Here's the program itself:

```
/* ch-mounting-fts.c --- demonstrate fts() */

#include <stdio.h>
#include <errno.h>
#include <getopt.h>
#include <fts.h>     /* gets <sys/types.h> and <sys/stat.h> for us */
#include <limits.h>     /* for PATH_MAX */
#include <stdbool.h>
#include <stdlib.h>
#include <string.h>
#include <unistd.h> /* for getcwd() */

extern bool process_ent(FTSENT *fent);

/* usage --- print message and die */

void
usage(const char *name)
{
    fprintf(stderr, "usage: %s [-CLcdsx] directory ...\n", name);
    exit(1);
}
```

```

/* main --- run fts_*() on each command-line argument */

int
main(int argc, char **argv)
{
    int i, c;
    int errors = 0;
    int flags = FTS_PHYSICAL;
    char start[PATH_MAX], finish[PATH_MAX];

    while ((c = getopt(argc, argv, "CLcdsx")) != -1) {
        switch (c) {
        case 'C':
            flags |= FTS_COMFOLLOW;
            break;
        case 'L':
            flags &= ~FTS_PHYSICAL;
            flags |= FTS_LOGICAL;
            break;
        case 'c':
            flags |= FTS_NOCHDIR;
            break;
        case 'd':
            flags |= FTS_SEEDOT;
            break;
        case 's':
            flags |= FTS_NOSTAT;
            break;
        case 'x':
            flags |= FTS_XDEV;
            break;
        default:
            usage(argv[0]);
            break;
        }
    }

    if (optind == argc)
        usage(argv[0]);

    char *junk = getcwd(start, sizeof start);

    FTS *fstream;
    FTSENT *fent;
```

```
68
69     if ((fstream = fts_open(argv + optind, flags, NULL)) == NULL) {
70         fprintf(stderr, "%s: from %s: cannot fts_open: %s\n",
71                 argv[0], argv[optind], strerror(errno));
72         exit(1);
73     }
74
75     while ((fent = fts_read(fstream)) != NULL) {
76         if (! process_ent(fent)) {
77             fprintf(stderr, "error occurred, bailing out\n");
78             fts_close(fstream);
79             exit(1);
80         }
81     }
82
83     fts_close(fstream);
84
85     junk = getcwd(finish, sizeof finish);
86     printf("Starting dir: %s\n", start);
87     printf("Finishing dir: %s\n", finish);
88
89     exit(0);
90 }
```

Lines 3–11 include header files. Line 31 sets the default behavior to `FTS_PHYSICAL`. Lines 35–59 process options. The options `FTS_PHYSICAL` and `FTS_LOGICAL` are mutually exclusive, so we ensure that only one is set.

Line 64 saves the starting directory for later use, using **`getcwd()`**.

Lines 69–73 open the stream on the rest of the command-line arguments. If this fails, we exit with a message and an error.

Lines 75–81 process files using a simple `while` loop. If an error occurs, we close the stream (line 78) and exit.

Finally, lines 85–87 are reached at the end of processing. The program closes the stream, prints out the starting and ending directories (they should be the same), and exits successfully.

The function of real interest is `process_ent()`, which processes each file. It uses the basic template for processing `FTSENT` structures, which is a `switch` statement on the `fts_info` value. The `print_entry()` function is a helper routine to print out the information relevant to all files:

```
92 /* print_entry --- print the rest of the FTSENT */
93
94 void
95 print_entry(FTSENT *fent, int level)
96 {
97     printf("%*sfts_accpath: %s\n", level, "", fent->fts_accpath);
98     printf("%*sfts_path: %s\n", level, "", fent->fts_path);
99     printf("%*sfts_pathlen: %d\n", level, "", fent->fts_pathlen);
```

```
    printf("%*sfts_namelen: %d\n", level, "", fent->fts_namelen);
    if (fent->fts_errno != 0)
        printf("%*sfts_path: %s\n", level, "", strerror(fent->fts_errno));

}

/* process_ent --- print out each file at the right level */

bool
process_ent(FTSENT *fent)
{
    bool retval = true;
    const char *name = fent->fts_name;
    int level = fent->fts_level <= 0 ? 0 : fent->fts_level;

    printf("%*s", level * 4, "");   /* indent over */

    switch (fent->fts_info) {
    case FTS_F:
        printf("%s (file)\n", name);
        break;
    case FTS_D:
        printf("%s (directory preorder visit)\n", name);
        break;
    case FTS_DC:
        printf("%s (directory cycle)\n", name);
        break;
    case FTS_DP:
        printf("%s (directory postorder visit)\n", name);
        break;
    case FTS_DNR:
        printf("%s (unreadable directory)\n", name);
        break;
    case FTS_DOT:
        printf("%s (dot or dot-dot)\n", name);
        break;
    case FTS_ERR:
        printf("%s (error: %s)\n", name, strerror(fent->fts_errno));
        retval = false;
        break;
    case FTS_SL:
        printf("%s (symbolic link)\n", name);
        break;
    case FTS_SLNONE:
        printf("%s (symbolic link, no target)\n", name);
        break;
```

```
146     case FTS_NS:
147         printf("%s (stat failed): %s\n", name, strerror(errno));
148         retval = false;
149         break;
150     case FTS_NSOK:
151         printf("%s (stat not requested): %s\n", name, strerror(errno));
152         break;
153     case FTS_DEFAULT:
154         printf("%s (default) [?]\n", name);
155         retval = false;
156         break;
157     default:
158         printf("%s: unknown fts_info value %d: can't happen!\n",
159                 name, fent->fts_info);
160         retval = false;
161         break;
162     }
163     if (retval)
164         print_entry(fent, (level + 1) * 4);
165
166     return retval;
167 }
```

Line 115 indents the right amount of spaces, using a nice trick. Using `%*s`, `printf()` takes the field width from the first argument. This is computed dynamically as '`level * 4`', where `level` is derived from `fent->fts_level`. The string to be printed is `""`, the null string. The end result is that `printf()` produces the right amount of space for us, without our having to run a loop. The same trick is used again, on line 164.

Lines 117–162 are the `switch` statement. In this case, it doesn't do anything terribly interesting except print the file's name and its type (file, directory, etc.). Then lines 163–164 print the rest of the information if there was no error.

Although this program doesn't use the `struct stat`, it should be clear that you could do anything you need to when processing `FTSENT` structures.

8.5 Processing a File Hierarchy: GNU du

The version of `du` in the GNU Coreutils uses the `fts()` suite to traverse one or more file hierarchies, gathering and producing statistics concerning the amount of disk space used. It has a large number of options that control its behavior with respect to symbolic links, output format of numbers, and so on. This makes the code harder to decipher than a simpler version would be. (However, we're not going to let that stop us.) Here is a summary of du's options, which will be helpful shortly when we look at the code:

```
$ du --help
Usage: du [OPTION]... [FILE]...
  or:  du [OPTION]... --files0-from=F
Summarize disk usage of the set of FILEs, recursively for directories.

Mandatory arguments to long options are mandatory for short options too.
  -0, --null            end each output line with NUL, not newline
  -a, --all             write counts for all files, not just directories
      --apparent-size   print apparent sizes, rather than disk usage; although
                          the apparent size is usually smaller, it may be
                          larger due to holes in ('sparse') files, internal
                          fragmentation, indirect blocks, and the like
  -B, --block-size=SIZE  scale sizes by SIZE before printing them; e.g.,
                           '-BM' prints sizes in units of 1,048,576 bytes;
                           see SIZE format below
  -b, --bytes           equivalent to '--apparent-size --block-size=1'
  -c, --total           produce a grand total
  -D, --dereference-args  dereference only symlinks that are listed on the
                          command line
  -d, --max-depth=N     print the total for a directory (or file, with --all)
                          only if it is N or fewer levels below the command
                          line argument;  --max-depth=0 is the same as
                          --summarize
      --files0-from=F   summarize disk usage of the
                          NUL-terminated file names specified in file F;
                          if F is -, then read names from standard input
  -H                    equivalent to --dereference-args (-D)
  -h, --human-readable  print sizes in human readable format (e.g., 1K 234M 2G)
      --inodes          list inode usage information instead of block usage
  -k                    like --block-size=1K
  -L, --dereference     dereference all symbolic links
  -l, --count-links     count sizes many times if hard linked
  -m                    like --block-size=1M
  -P, --no-dereference  don't follow any symbolic links (this is the default)
  -S, --separate-dirs   for directories do not include size of subdirectories
      --si              like -h, but use powers of 1000 not 1024
  -s, --summarize       display only a total for each argument
  -t, --threshold=SIZE  exclude entries smaller than SIZE if positive,
                          or entries greater than SIZE if negative
      --time            show time of the last modification of any file in the
                          directory, or any of its subdirectories
      --time=WORD       show time as WORD instead of modification time:
                          atime, access, use, ctime or status
```

```
      --time-style=STYLE  show times using STYLE, which can be:
                            full-iso, long-iso, iso, or +FORMAT;
                            FORMAT is interpreted like in 'date'
  -X, --exclude-from=FILE  exclude files that match any pattern in FILE
      --exclude=PATTERN    exclude files that match PATTERN
  -x, --one-file-system    skip directories on different file systems
      --help     display this help and exit
      --version  output version information and exit

Display values are in units of the first available SIZE from --block-size,
and the DU_BLOCK_SIZE, BLOCK_SIZE and BLOCKSIZE environment variables.
Otherwise, units default to 1024 bytes (or 512 if POSIXLY_CORRECT is set).

The SIZE argument is an integer and optional unit (example: 10K is 10*1024).
Units are K,M,G,T,P,E,Z,Y (powers of 1024) or KB,MB,... (powers of 1000).
Binary prefixes can be used, too: KiB=K, MiB=M, and so on.

GNU coreutils online help: <https://www.gnu.org/software/coreutils/>
Full documentation <https://www.gnu.org/software/coreutils/du>
or available locally via: info '(coreutils) du invocation'
```

As du processes files and directories, it collects information in a `struct duinfo`:

```
/* Define a class for collecting directory information. */
struct duinfo
{
  /* Size of files in directory.  */
  uintmax_t size;

  /* Number of inodes in directory.  */
  uintmax_t inodes;

  /* Latest timestamp found.  If tmax.tv_sec == TYPE_MINIMUM (time_t)
     && tmax.tv_nsec < 0, no timestamp has been found.  */
  struct timespec tmax;
};
```

These structures, in turn, are collected in a `struct dulevel`, one per level of the file hierarchy:

```
/* A structure for per-directory level information.  */
struct dulevel
{
  /* Entries in this directory.  */
  struct duinfo ent;

  /* Total for subdirectories.  */
```

```
126     struct duinfo subdir;
127   };
```

Here is the `process_file()` function from `du.c`. Line numbers are relative to the start of the function:

```
1   /* This function is called once for every file system object that fts
2      encounters.  fts does a depth-first traversal.  This function knows
3      that and accumulates per-directory totals based on changes in
4      the depth of the current entry.  It returns true on success.  */
5
6   static bool
7   process_file (FTS *fts, FTSENT *ent)
8   {
9     bool ok = true;
10    struct duinfo dui;
11    struct duinfo dui_to_print;
12    size_t level;
13    static size_t n_alloc;
14    /* First element of the structure contains:
15       The sum of the sizes of all entries in the single directory
16       at the corresponding level.  Although this does include the sizes
17       corresponding to each subdirectory, it does not include the size of
18       any file in a subdirectory. Also corresponding last modified date.
19       Second element of the structure contains:
20       The sum of the sizes of all entries in the hierarchy at or below the
21       directory at the specified level.  */
22    static struct dulevel *dulvl;
23
24    char const *file = ent->fts_path;
25    const struct stat *sb = ent->fts_statp;
26    int info = ent->fts_info;
```

This function does a lot since it has to implement most of `du`'s options. It starts by assigning values from the `FTSENT` entry to local variables whose names are easier to read. Then, based on the value of `info`, it decides what to do:

```
28    if (info == FTS_DNR)                                    Directory not readable
29      {
30        /* An error occurred, but the size is known, so count it.  */
31        error (0, ent->fts_errno, _("cannot read directory %s"), quoteaf (file));
32        ok = false;
33      }
34    else if (info != FTS_DP)                                NOT the postorder visit of a directory
35      {
36        bool excluded = excluded_file_name (exclude, file);
37        if (! excluded)                                     Not --exclude
```

```
    {
      /* Make the stat buffer *SB valid, or fail noisily.  */

      if (info == FTS_NSOK)                       No stat(2) information requested
        {
          fts_set (fts, ent, FTS_AGAIN);          Try again
          MAYBE_UNUSED FTSENT const *e = fts_read (fts);
          affirm (e == ent);
          info = ent->fts_info;
        }

      if (info == FTS_NS || info == FTS_SLNONE)   No information available
        {
          error (0, ent->fts_errno, _("cannot access %s"), quoteaf (file));
          return false;
        }

      /* The --one-file-system (-x) option cannot exclude anything
         specified on the command-line.  By definition, it can exclude
         a file or directory only when its device number is different
         from that of its just-processed parent directory, and du does
         not process the parent of a command-line argument.  */
      if (fts->fts_options & FTS_XDEV             -x requested
          && FTS_ROOTLEVEL < ent->fts_level       In a subtree
          && fts->fts_dev != sb->st_dev)          Not the same device
        excluded = true;
    }
```

The first set of checks handles error cases, either returning early, or setting `excluded` to `true`.

To keep track of links, du maintains a hash table of already seen (device, inode) pairs:[11]

```
  if (excluded
      || (! opt_count_all
          && (hash_all || (! S_ISDIR (sb->st_mode) && 1 < sb->st_nlink))
          && ! hash_ins (di_files, sb->st_ino, sb->st_dev)))
    {
      /* If ignoring a directory in preorder, skip its children.
         Ignore the next fts_read output too, as it's a postorder
         visit to the same directory.  */
      if (info == FTS_D)
        {
          fts_set (fts, ent, FTS_SKIP);
          MAYBE_UNUSED FTSENT const *e = fts_read (fts);
```

[11] A hash table is a data structure that allows quick retrieval of stored information; the details are beyond the scope of this book. Hash tables are used to implement Python dictionaries and `java.util.Hashtables` in Java.

```
              affirm (e == ent);
            }

          return true;
        }
```

The condition in the `if` statement is a complicated one. It tests if:

(1) this file should be excluded (ignored) OR
(2a) we are *not* counting hard links multiple times AND
(2b) [1] we have to check every file to only count hard links once AND
(2b) [2] the file is not a directory and it has multiple links AND
(2c) the file is already being tracked

If all that is true, return. Additionally, in the case of a directory, tell `fts_read()` not to return a postorder visit. Wow!

The following code deals with files that we do want to process:

```
      switch (info)
        {
        case FTS_D:                        Directory, preorder visit
          return true;

        case FTS_ERR:                      Something went wrong
          /* An error occurred, but the size is known, so count it.  */
          error (0, ent->fts_errno, "%s", quotef (file));
          ok = false;
          break;

        case FTS_DC:                       Directory with cycles
          /* If not following symlinks and not a (bind) mount point.  */
          if (cycle_warning_required (fts, ent)
              && ! mount_point_in_fts_cycle (ent))
            {
              emit_cycle_warning (file);
              return false;
            }
          return true;
        }
    }

  duinfo_set (&dui,                        Set the size of the file
              (apparent_size
               ? (usable_st_size (sb) ? MAX (0, sb->st_size) : 0)
               : (uintmax_t) ST_NBLOCKS (*sb) * ST_NBLOCKSIZE),
              (time_type == time_mtime ? get_stat_mtime (sb)
```

```
112                 : time_type == time_atime ? get_stat_atime (sb)
113                 : get_stat_ctime (sb)));
```

After finding a file to be handled, the size is computed according to either the size in the `struct stat` or the number of disk blocks (lines 108–110). This decision is based on the `apparent_size` variable, which is set if the `--apparent-size` option is used. The particular timestamp to use is also set (lines 111–113), based on the `--time-style` option. Continuing on:

```
115   level = ent->fts_level;
116   dui_to_print = dui;
117
118   if (n_alloc == 0)
119     {
120       n_alloc = level + 10;
121       dulvl = xcalloc (n_alloc, sizeof *dulvl);
122     }
```

Line 115 sets the current level. Line 116 sets `dui_to_print` to `dui`; this variable may be updated depending on whether it has to include the sizes of any children. Although `dui` could have been reused, the separate variable makes the code easier to read.

Lines 118–122 manage the dynamic memory used to hold file size statistics. `n_alloc` is a `static` variable (line 13) that is zero the first time `process_file()` is called. In this case, `calloc()` is called (through a wrapper macro on line 121; this was discussed in Section 3.2.1.8, "Example: Reading Arbitrarily Long Lines," page 65). The rest of the time, `n_alloc` is nonzero, and `realloc()` is used (again, through a wrapper macro—see lines 136–140):

```
123   else
124     {
125       if (level == prev_level)
126         {
127           /* This is usually the most common case.  Do nothing.  */
128         }
129       else if (level > prev_level)
130         {
131           /* Descending the hierarchy.
132              Clear the accumulators for *all* levels between prev_level
133              and the current one.  The depth may change dramatically,
134              e.g., from 1 to 10.  */
135
136           if (n_alloc <= level)
137             {
138               dulvl = xnrealloc (dulvl, level, 2 * sizeof *dulvl);
139               n_alloc = level * 2;
140             }
141
142           for (size_t i = prev_level + 1; i <= level; i++)
```

```
143             {
144               duinfo_init (&dulvl[i].ent);
145               duinfo_init (&dulvl[i].subdir);
146             }
147         }
148       else /* level < prev_level */
149         {
150           /* Ascending the hierarchy.
151              Process a directory only after all entries in that
152              directory have been processed.  When the depth decreases,
153              propagate sums from the children (prev_level) to the parent.
154              Here, the current level is always one smaller than the
155              previous one.  */
156           affirm (level == prev_level - 1);
157           duinfo_add (&dui_to_print, &dulvl[prev_level].ent);
158           if (!opt_separate_dirs)
159             duinfo_add (&dui_to_print, &dulvl[prev_level].subdir);
160           duinfo_add (&dulvl[level].subdir, &dulvl[prev_level].ent);
161           duinfo_add (&dulvl[level].subdir, &dulvl[prev_level].subdir);
162         }
163     }
```

Lines 125–162 compare the current level to the previous one. There are three possible cases:

The levels are the same.
In this case, there's no need to worry about child statistics (lines 126–128).

The current level is higher than the previous level.
In this case, we've gone down the hierarchy, and the statistics must be reset (lines 130–147). The term "accumulator" in the comment is apt: each element accumulates the total disk space used at that level. (In the early days of computing, CPU registers were often termed "accumulators.")

The current level is lower than the previous level.
In this case, we've finished processing all the children in a directory and have just moved back up to the parent directory (lines 150–162). The code updates the totals, including `dui_to_print`.

```
165   prev_level = level;
166
167   /* Let the size of a directory entry contribute to the total for the
168      containing directory, unless --separate-dirs (-S) is specified.  */
169   if (! (opt_separate_dirs && IS_DIR_TYPE (info)))
170     duinfo_add (&dulvl[level].ent, &dui);
171
```

```
172    /* Even if this directory is unreadable or we can't chdir into it,
173       do let its size contribute to the total. */
174    duinfo_add (&tot_dui, &dui);
175
176    if ((IS_DIR_TYPE (info) && level <= max_depth)
177        || (opt_all && level <= max_depth)
178        || level == 0)
179      {
180        /* Print or elide this entry according to the --threshold option.  */
181        uintmax_t v = opt_inodes ? dui_to_print.inodes : dui_to_print.size;
182        if (opt_threshold < 0
183            ? v <= -opt_threshold
184            : v >= opt_threshold)
185          print_size (&dui_to_print, file);
186      }
187
188    return ok;
189  }
```

Line 165 sets the `static` variable `prev_level` so that it'll have the correct values for a subsequent call to `process_file()`, ensuring that all the previous code works correctly.

Lines 167–174 adjust statistics on the basis of options and the file type. The comments and code are fairly straightforward. Lines 176–186 decide to print the information based on the type of the file, the current level, the setting of the `--max-depth` option, and the setting of the `--threshold` option.

Whew! That's a lot of code. We find this to be on the upper end of the complexity spectrum, at least as far as what can be easily presented in a book of this nature. However, it demonstrates that real-world code is often complex. The best way to manage such complexity is with clearly named variables and detailed comments. `du.c` is good in that respect; we were able to extract the code and examine it fairly easily, without having to show all 735 lines of the program!

8.6 Changing the Root Directory: `chroot()`

The current working directory, set with `chdir()` or `fchdir()` (see Section 8.4.1, "Changing Directory: `chdir()` and `fchdir()`," page 247), is an attribute of the process, just like the set of open files. It is also inherited by new processes.

Less well known is that every process also has a *current root directory*. It is this directory to which the pathname `/` refers. Most of the time, a process's root and the system root directories are identical. However, the superuser can change the root directory, with the (you guessed it) `chroot()` system call:

```
#include <unistd.h>                                        Common

int chroot(const char *path);
```

The return value is `0` upon success and `-1` upon error.

As the GNU/Linux *chroot*(2) manpage points out, changing the root directory does not change the current directory; programs that must make sure that they stay underneath the new root directory must also execute `chdir()` afterward:

```
if (chroot("/new/root") < 0)          Set new root directory
    /* handle error */

if (chdir("/some/dir") < 0)           Pathnames now relative to new root
    /* handle error */
```

The `chroot()` system call is used most often for *daemons*—background programs that must run in a special contained environment. For example, consider an Internet FTP daemon that allows anonymous FTP (connection by anyone, from anywhere, without a regular user name and password). Obviously, such a connection should not be able to see all the files on the whole system. Instead, the FTP daemon does a `chroot()` to a special directory with just enough structure to allow it to function (for example, its own `/bin/ls` for listing files, its own copy of the C runtime library if it's shared, and possibly its own copy of `/etc/passwd` and `/etc/group` to show a limited set of user and group names).

POSIX doesn't standardize this system call, although GNU/Linux and all Unix systems support it. (It's been around since V7.) It is specialized, but when you need it, it's very handy.

8.7 Summary

- Filesystems are collections of free, inode, metadata, and data blocks, organized in a specific fashion. Filesystems correspond one-to-one with the (physical or logical) partitions in which they are made. Each filesystem has its own root directory; by convention, the root directory always has inode number `2`.
- The `mount` command mounts a filesystem, grafting it onto the logical hierarchical file namespace. The `umount` command detaches a filesystem. The kernel arranges for `/.` and `/..` to be the same; the root directory of the entire namespace is its own parent. In all other cases, the kernel arranges for `..` in the root of a mounted filesystem to point to the parent directory of the mount point.
- Modern Unix systems support multiple types of filesystems. In particular, Oracle's (originally from Sun Microsystems) Network File System (NFS) is universally supported, as is the ISO 9660 standard format for DVDs and CD-ROMs, and MS-DOS FAT partitions are supported on all Unix systems that run on Intel x86 hardware. To our knowledge, Linux supports the largest number of different filesystems—well over 80! Many are specialized, but many others are for general use, including multiple different journaling filesystems.
- The `/etc/fstab` file lists each system's partitions, their mount points, and any relevant mount options. `/etc/mtab` lists those filesystems that are currently mounted, as

does `/proc/self/mounts` on GNU/Linux systems. (On GNU/Linux, `/etc/mtab` is a symbolic link to `/proc/self/mounts`.) The `loop` option to `mount` is particularly useful under GNU/Linux for mounting filesystem images contained in regular files, such as DVD or CD-ROM images. Other options are useful for security and for mounting foreign filesystems, such as Windows `vfat` and NTFS filesystems.

- The `/etc/fstab`-format files can be read with the `getmntent()` suite of routines. The GNU/Linux format is shared with several other commercial Unix variants, most notably Solaris.
- The `statvfs()` and `fstatvfs()` functions are standardized by POSIX for retrieving filesystem information, such as the number of free and used disk blocks, the number of free and used inodes, and so on. Linux has its own system calls for retrieving similar information: `statfs()` and `fstatfs()`.
- `chdir()` and `fchdir()` let a process change its current directory. `getcwd()` retrieves the absolute pathname of the current directory. These three functions are straightforward to use.
- The `fts()` suite of functions centralize the task of "walking a file tree"—that is, visiting every filesystem object (file, device, symbolic link, directory) in an entire directory hierarchy. Different flags control its behavior. `FTSENT` structures are read in a simple loop; user-level code can then process these structures as necessary. The `FTSENT` structure includes each file's name, a `struct stat` for the file, the file's type, and information about the file's name and level in the hierarchy. GNU `du` uses the `fts()` suite to do its job.
- Finally, the `chroot()` system call changes a process's current root directory. This is a specialized but important facility, which is particularly useful for certain daemon-style programs.

Exercises

1. Examine the *mount*(2) manpage under GNU/Linux and on as many other different Unix systems as you have access to. How do the system calls differ?
2. Enhance `ch-mounting-statvfs.c` to take an option giving an open integer file descriptor; it should use `fstatvfs()` to retrieve filesystem information.
3. Enhance `ch-mounting-statvfs.c` to not ignore NFS-mounted filesystems. Such filesystems have a device of the form `server.example.com:/big/disk`.
4. Modify `ch-mounting-statfs.c` (the one that uses the Linux-specific `statfs()` call) to produce output that looks like that from `df`.
5. Add a `-i` option to the program you wrote for the previous exercise to produce output like that of '`df -i`'.

6. Using `opendir()`, `readdir()`, `stat()` or `fstat()`, `dirfd()`, and `fchdir()`, write your own version of `getcwd()`. How will you compute the total size the buffer needs to be? How will you move through the directory hierarchy?
7. Enhance your version of `getcwd()` to allocate a buffer for the caller if the first argument is `NULL`.
8. Can you use `fts_read()` to write `getcwd()`? If not, why not?
9. Using `fts_read()`, write your own version of `chown` that accepts a `-R` option to recursively process entire directory trees. Make sure that without `-R`, '`chown` *`user directory`*' does *not* recurse. How will you test it?
10. The `nftw()` function provides a different way to process directory hierarchies. In particular, it processes subdirectories using recursion. It is standardized by POSIX and is available in GLIBC.

    Read the *nftw*(3) manpage. (It may help you to print it and have it handy.) Rewrite your private version of `chown` to use `nftw()`.
11. Look at the *find*(1) manpage. If you were to try to write `find` from scratch, which file tree suite would you prefer, `nftw()` or `fts()`? Why?

Part II

Processes, Networking, and Internationalization

Chapter 9

Process Management and Pipes

As we said in Chapter 1, "Introduction," page 3, if you were to summarize Unix (and thus Linux) in three words, those words would have to be "files and processes." Now that we've seen how to work with files and directories, it's time to look at the rest of the story: processes. In particular, we examine how processes are created and managed, how they interact with open files, and how they can communicate with each other. Subsequent chapters examine signals—a coarse way for one process (or the kernel) to let another know that some event has occurred—permission checking, resource limitations, and per-user and per-process resource limits.

In this chapter the picture begins to get more complicated. In particular, to be fairly complete, we must mention things that aren't covered until later in the chapter or later in the book. In such cases, we provide forward references, but you should be able to get the gist of each section without looking ahead.

9.1 Process Creation and Management

Unlike many predecessor and successor operating systems, process creation in Unix was intended to be (and is) cheap. Furthermore, Unix separated the idea of "create a new process" from that of "run a given program in a process." This was an elegant design decision, one that simplifies many operations.

9.1.1 Creating a Process: `fork()`

The first step in starting a new program is calling `fork()`:

```
#include <sys/types.h>                                    POSIX
#include <unistd.h>

pid_t fork(void);
```

Using `fork()` is simple. Before the call, one process, which we term the *parent*, is running. When `fork()` returns, there are two processes: the parent and the *child*.

Here is the key: *the two processes both run the same program.* The two processes can distinguish themselves based on the return value from `fork()`:

Negative
: If there is an error, `fork()` returns `-1`, and no new process is created. The original process continues running.

Zero

In the child, `fork()` returns `0`.

Positive

In the parent, `fork()` returns the positive process identification number (PID) of the child.

Boilerplate code for creating a child process looks like this:

```
pid_t child;

if ((child = fork()) < 0)
    /* handle error */
else if (child == 0)
    /* this is the new process */
else
    /* this is the original parent process */
```

The `pid_t` is a signed integer type for holding PID values. It is most likely a plain `int`, but it makes code more self-documenting and should be used instead of `int`.

In Unix parlance, besides being the name of a system call, the word "fork" is both a verb and a noun. We might say that "one process forks another," and that "after the fork, two processes are running." (Think "fork in a road" and not "fork, knife, and spoon.")

9.1.1.1 After the `fork()`: Shared and Distinct Attributes

The child "inherits" identical copies of a large number of attributes from the parent. Many of these attributes are specialized and irrelevant here. Thus, the following list is purposely incomplete. The following attributes are the relevant ones:

- The environment; see Section 2.4, "The Environment," page 37.
- All open files and open directories; see Section 4.4.1, "Understanding File Descriptors," page 87, and Section 5.3.1, "Basic Directory Reading," page 124. (This doesn't include files marked close-on-fork, as described later in this chapter; see Section 9.4.3.1, "The Close-on-Exec and Close-on-Fork Flags," page 316.)
- The umask setting; see Section 4.6.2, "Controlling Default Permissions with `umask()`," page 102.
- The current working directory; see Section 8.4.1, "Changing Directory: `chdir()` and `fchdir()`," page 247.
- The root directory; see Section 8.6, "Changing the Root Directory: `chroot()`," page 269.
- The current priority, a.k.a. "nice value." We discuss this shortly; see Section 9.1.3, "Setting Process Priority: `nice()`," page 282.
- The controlling terminal. This is the terminal device (physical console or terminal-emulator window) that is allowed to send signals to a process (such as CTRL-Z to stop running jobs). This is discussed in Section 9.2.1, "Job Control Overview," page 300.

- The process signal mask and all current signal dispositions (not discussed yet; see Chapter 10, "Signals," page 333).
- The real, effective, and saved set-user and set-group IDs and the supplemental group set (not discussed yet; see Chapter 11, "Permissions and User and Group ID Numbers," page 383).
- Resource limits. These are discussed in Chapter 12, "Resource Limits," page 405.
- Shared memory segments and System V IPC message descriptors. (We don't describe these features in this book.)

Besides the `fork()` return value, the two processes differ in the following ways:

- Each one has a unique process ID and parent process ID (PID and PPID). These are described in Section 9.1.2, "Identifying a Process: `getpid()` and `getppid()`," page 279.
- The child's PID will not equal that of any existing process group ID (see Section 9.2, "Process Groups," page 300).
- The accumulated CPU times for the child process and its future children are initialized to zero. (This makes sense; after all, it is a brand-new process.)
- Any signals that were pending in the parent are cleared in the child, as are any pending alarms or timers. (We haven't covered these topics yet; see Chapter 10 "Signals," page 333, and Section 16.3.3, "Interval Timers: `setitimer()` and `getitimer()`," page 570.)
- File locks held by the parent are not duplicated in the child (also not discussed yet; see Section 16.2, "Locking Files," page 558).

9.1.1.2 File Descriptor Sharing

The attributes that the child inherits from the parent are all set to the same values they had in the parent at the time of the `fork()`. From then on, though, the two processes proceed on their merry ways, (mostly) independent of each other. For example, if the child changes directory, the parent's directory is not affected. Similarly, if the child changes its environment, the parent's environment is *not* changed.

Open files are a significant exception to this rule. Open file descriptors are *shared*, and an action by one process on a shared file descriptor affects the state of the file for the other process as well. This is best understood after study of Figure 9.1.

The figure displays the kernel's internal data structures. The key data structure is the *file table*. Each element refers to an open file. Besides other bookkeeping data, the file table maintains the current position (read/write offset) in the file. This is adjusted either automatically each time a file is read or written, or directly with `lseek()` (see Section 4.5, "Random Access: Moving Around within a File," page 96).

The file descriptor returned by `open()` or `creat()` acts as an index into a per-process array of pointers into the file table. This per-process array won't be any larger than the value returned by `getdtablesize()` (see Section 4.4.1, "Understanding File Descriptors," page 87).

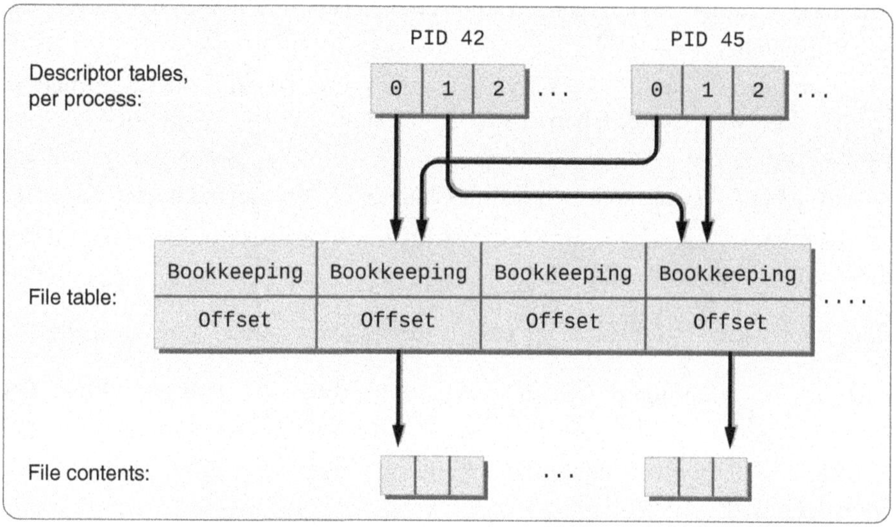

Figure 9.1: File descriptor sharing

Figure 9.1 shows two processes sharing standard input and standard output; for each process, file descriptors `0` and `1` point to the same respective entries in the file table. Thus, when process 45 (the child) does a `read()`, the shared offset is updated; the next time process 42 (the parent) does a `read()`, it starts at the position where process 45's `read()` finished.

This can be seen easily at the shell level:

```
$ cat data                                          Show demo data file contents
line 1
line 2
line 3
line 4
$ ls -l test1 ; cat test1                           Mode and contents of test program
-rwxrwxr-x 1 arnold arnold 82 Jan 25 14:52 test1
#! /bin/sh
read line ; echo p: $line                           Read a line in parent shell, print it
( read line ; echo c: $line )                       Read a line in child shell, print it
read line ; echo p: $line                           Read a line in parent shell, print it
$ test1 < data                                      Run the program
p: line 1                                           Parent starts at beginning
c: line 2                                           Child picks up where parent left off
p: line 3                                           Parent picks up where child left off
```

The first executable line of `test1` reads a line from standard input, changing the offset in the file. The second line of `test1` runs the commands enclosed between the parentheses in a *subshell*. This is a separate shell process created—you guessed it—with `fork()`. The child subshell inherits standard input from the parent, including the current file offset. This process reads a line and updates the *shared* offset into the file. When the third line, back in the parent shell, reads the file, it starts where the child left off.

Although the `read` command is built into the shell, things work the same way with external commands. Some early Unix systems had a `line` command that read one line of input (one character at a time!) for use within shell scripts; if the file offset weren't shared, it would be impossible to use such a command in a loop.

File descriptor sharing and inheritance play a pivotal role in shell I/O redirection; the system calls and their semantics make the shell-level primitives straightforward to implement in C, as we see later in the chapter.

9.1.1.3 File Descriptor Sharing and `close()`

The fact that multiple file descriptors can point at the same open file has an important consequence: *a file is not closed until all its file descriptors are closed.* (This was also discussed earlier, in Section 5.1.5.2, "Removing Open Files," page 118, where we described how you could unlink an open file, but still continue to use it.)

We see later in this chapter that multiple descriptors for the same file can exist not only across processes but even within the same process; this rule is particularly important for working with pipes.

If you need to know if two descriptors are open on the same file, you can use `fstat()` (see Section 5.4.2, "Retrieving File Information," page 131) on the two descriptors with two different `struct stat` structures. If the corresponding `st_dev` and `st_ino` fields are equal, they're the same file.

We complete the discussion of file descriptor manipulation and the file descriptor table later in the chapter.

9.1.2 Identifying a Process: `getpid()` and `getppid()`

Each process has a unique process ID number (the PID). Two system calls provide the current PID and the PID of the parent process:

```
#include <sys/types.h>                                    POSIX
#include <unistd.h>

pid_t getpid(void);
pid_t getppid(void);
```

The functions are about as simple as they come:

`pid_t getpid(void)`
: Return the PID of the current process.

`pid_t getppid(void)`
: Return the parent's PID.

PID values are unique; by definition, there cannot be two running processes with the same PID. PIDs usually increase in value, in that a child process generally has a higher PID than its parent. On many systems, however, PID values *wrap around*; when the system maximum value for PIDs is exceeded, the next process created will have the lowest unused PID number. (Nothing in POSIX requires this behavior, and some systems assign unused PID numbers randomly.) In short, you shouldn't assume that a given PID value won't be reused later.

If the parent dies or exits, the child is given a new parent, `init`. In this case, the new parent PID will be `1`, which is `init`'s PID. Such a child is termed an *orphan*. The following program, `ch-processes-reparent.c`, demonstrates this. This is also the first example we've seen of `fork()` in action:

```
/* ch-processes-reparent.c --- show that getppid() can change values */

#include <stdio.h>
#include <errno.h>
#include <stdlib.h>
#include <string.h>
#include <sys/types.h>
#include <unistd.h>

/* main --- do the work */

int
main(int argc, char **argv)
{
    pid_t pid, old_ppid, new_ppid;
    pid_t child, parent;

    parent = getpid();      /* before fork() */

    if ((child = fork()) < 0) {
        fprintf(stderr, "%s: fork of child failed: %s\n",
            argv[0], strerror(errno));
        exit(1);
    } else if (child == 0) {
        old_ppid = getppid();
        sleep(2);       /* see Chapter 10 */
        new_ppid = getppid();
    } else {
        sleep(1);
        exit(0);        /* parent exits after fork() */
    }

    /* only the child executes this */
    printf("Original parent: %d\n", parent);
    printf("Child: %d\n", getpid());
```

```
36      printf("Child's old ppid: %d\n", old_ppid);
37      printf("Child's new ppid: %d\n", new_ppid);
38
39      exit(0);
40  }
```

Line 18 retrieves the PID of the initial process, using `getpid()`. Lines 20–23 fork the child, checking for an error return.

Lines 24–27 are executed by the child: line 25 retrieves the PPID, line 26 suspends the process for two seconds (see Section 10.8.1, "Alarm Clocks: `sleep()`, `alarm()`, and `SIGALRM`," page 363, for information about `sleep()`), and then line 27 retrieves the PPID again.

Lines 28–31 run in the parent. Line 29 delays the parent for one second, giving the child enough time to make the first `getppid()` call. Line 30 then exits the parent.

Lines 34–37 print the values. Note that the `parent` variable, which was set before the fork, still maintains its value in the child. After forking, the two processes have identical but independent copies of their address spaces. Here's what happens when the program runs:

```
$ ch-processes-reparent              Run the program
$ Original parent: 6582              Program finishes: shell prompts and child prints
Child: 6583
Child's old ppid: 6582
Child's new ppid: 1                  Parent is now init
```

Remember that the two programs execute *in parallel*. This is depicted graphically in Figure 9.2.

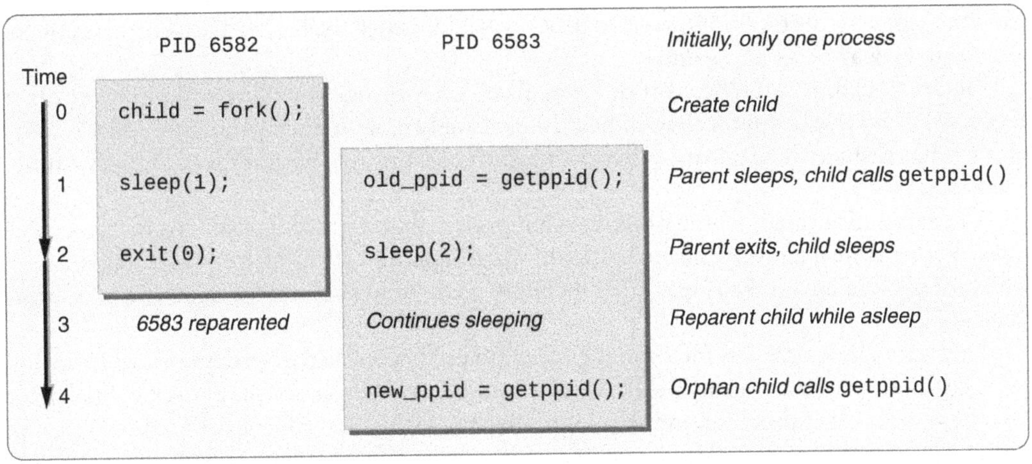

Figure 9.2: Two processes running in parallel after forking

NOTE

The use of `sleep()` to have one process outlive another works most of the time. However, occasionally it fails, leading to hard-to-reproduce and hard-to-find bugs. To guarantee correct behavior, use explicit synchronization with `wait()` or `waitpid()`, which are described further on in the chapter (see Section 9.1.6.1, "Using POSIX Functions: `wait()`, `waitpid()`, and `waitid()`," page 294). (There are other ways to synchronize, but `wait()` and `waitpid()` make for the clearest code.)

9.1.3 Setting Process Priority: `nice()`

As processes run, the kernel dynamically changes each process's *priority*. As in life, higher-priority items get attention before lower-priority ones. In brief, each process is allotted a small amount of time in which to run, called its *time slice*. When the time slice finishes, if the current process is still the one with the highest priority, it is allowed to continue running.

Linux, like Unix, provides *preemptive multitasking*. This means that the kernel can preempt a process (pause it) if it's time to let another process run. Processes that have been running a lot (for example, compute-intensive processes) have their priority lowered at the end of their time slice, to let other processes have a chance at the processor. Similarly, processes that have been idle while waiting for I/O (such as an interactive text editor) are given a higher priority so that they can respond to the I/O when it happens. In short, the kernel makes sure that all processes, averaged over time, get their "fair share" of the CPU. Raising and lowering priorities are part of this process.

Designing a good process scheduler for the kernel is an art; the nitty-gritty details are beyond the scope of this book. However, a process can influence the kernel's priority assignment algorithm by way of its *nice value*.

The nice value is an indication of "how nice" the process is willing to be toward other processes. Thus, higher nice values indicate increasingly more patient processes—that is, ones that are increasingly nice toward others, lowering their priority with respect to that of other processes.

A negative nice value, on the other hand, indicates that a process wishes to be "less nice" toward others. Such a process is more selfish, wanting more CPU time for itself.[1] Fortunately, while users can increase their nice value (be more nice), only `root` can decrease the nice value (be less nice).

The nice value is only one factor in the equation used by the kernel to compute the priority; the nice value is not the priority itself, which varies over time, based on the process's behavior and the state of other processes in the system. To change the nice value, use the `nice()` system call:

```
#include <unistd.h>                                    POSIX XSI

int nice(int inc);
```

[1] Such processes often display childlike behavior.

The default nice value is `0`. The allowed range for nice values is `-20` to `19`. This takes some getting used to. The more negative the value, the higher the process's priority: `-20` is the highest priority (least nice), and `19` is the lowest priority (most nice).

The `inc` argument is the increment by which to change the nice value. Use '`nice(0)`' to retrieve the current value without changing it. If the result of '`current_nice_value + inc`' would be outside the range `-20` to `19`, the system forces the result to be inside the range.

The return value is the new nice value, or `-1` if there was an error. Since `-1` is also a valid nice value, when calling `nice()` you must explicitly set `errno` to zero first, and then check it afterward to see if there was a problem:

```
int niceval;
int inc = /* whatever */;

errno = 0;
if ((niceval = nice(inc)) < 0 && errno != 0) {
    fprintf(stderr, "nice(%d) failed: %s\n", inc, strerror(errno));
    /* other recovery */
}
```

This example can fail if `inc` has a negative value and the process is not running as `root`.

9.1.3.1 POSIX versus Reality

The nice value range of `-20` to `19` that Linux uses is historical; it dates back at least as far as V7. POSIX expresses the situation in more indirect language, which allows for implementation flexibility while maintaining historical compatibility. It also makes the standard harder to read and understand, but then, that's why you're reading this book. So, here's how POSIX describes it.

First, the *process's nice value* as maintained by the system ranges from `0` to '`(2 * NZERO) -1`'. The constant `NZERO` is defined in `<limits.h>` and must be at least `20`. This gives us the range 0–39.

Second, as we described, the sum of the current nice value and the `incr` increment is forced into this range.

Finally, the return value from `nice()` is the process nice value *minus* `NZERO`. With an `NZERO` value of `20`, this gives us the original `-20` to `19` range that we initially described.

The upshot is that `nice()`'s return value actually ranges from '`-NZERO`' to '`NZERO-1`', and it's best to write your code in terms of that symbolic constant. However, practically speaking, you're unlikely to find a system in which `NZERO` is not `20`.

9.1.4 Starting New Programs: The `exec()` Family

Once a new process is running (through `fork()`), the next step is to start a different program running in the process. There are multiple functions that serve different purposes:

```
#include <unistd.h>                                        POSIX

int execve(const char *filename, char *const argv[],      System call
           char *const envp[]);
```

```
int fexecve(int fd, char *const argv[],                      Also a system call
            char *const envp[]);

int execl(const char *path, const char *arg, ...);            Wrappers
int execlp(const char *file, const char *arg, ...);
int execle(const char *path, const char *arg, ..., char *const envp[]);
int execv(const char *path, char *const argv[]);
int execvp(const char *file, char *const argv[]);
```

We refer to these functions as the "`exec()` family." There is no function named `exec()`; instead we use this function name to mean any of the above listed functions. As with `fork()`, "exec" is used in Unix parlance as a verb, meaning to execute (run) a program, and as a noun.

9.1.4.1 The `execve()` System Call

The simplest function to explain is `execve()`. It is also the main underlying system call (most of the others are wrapper functions, as is explained shortly):

`int execve(const char *filename, char *const argv[], char *const envp[])`

> `filename` is the name of the program to execute. It may be a full or relative pathname. The file must be in an executable format that the kernel understands. Modern systems uses the ELF (Extensible Linking Format) executable format. GNU/Linux understands ELF and several others. Interpreted scripts can be executed with `execve()` if they use the '`#!`' special first line that names the interpreter to use. (Scripts that don't start with '`#!`' will fail.) Section 1.1.3, "Executable Files," page 6, provides an example use of '`#!`'.
>
> `argv` is a standard C argument list—an array of character pointers to argument strings, *including the value to use for* `argv[0]`, terminated with a `NULL` pointer.
>
> `envp` is the environment to use for the new process, with the same layout as the `environ` global variable (see Section 2.4, "The Environment," page 37). In the new program, this environment becomes the initial value of `environ`.

A call to `exec()` should not return. If it does, there was a problem. Most commonly, either the requested program doesn't exist, or it exists but isn't executable (`ENOENT` and `EACCES` for `errno`, respectively). Many more things can go wrong; see the *execve*(2) manpage.

Assuming that the call succeeds, the current contents of the process's address space are thrown away. (The kernel does arrange to save the `argv` and `envp` data in a safe place first.) The kernel loads the executable code for the new program, along with any global and `static` variables. Next, the kernel initializes the environment with that passed to `execve()`, and then it calls the new program's `main()` routine with the `argv` array passed to `execve()`. It counts the number of arguments and passes that value to `main()` in `argc`.

At that point, the new program is running. It doesn't know (and can't find out) what program was running in the process before it. Note that the process ID *does not change*. Many other attributes remain in place across the exec; we cover this in more detail shortly.

In a loose analogy, `exec()` is to a process what life roles are to a person. At different times during the day, a single person might function as parent, spouse, friend, student, worker, store customer, and so on. Yet it is the same underlying person performing the different roles. So too, the process—its PID, open files, current directory, etc.—doesn't change, while the particular job it's doing—the program run with `exec()`—can.

9.1.4.2 Specifying the Executable via File Descriptor: `fexecve()`

The `fexecve()` system call is relatively new; it was introduced in the 2018 POSIX standard. It is similar to `execve()`, except that the file to execute is specified via an open file descriptor:

`int fexecve(int fd, char *const argv[], char *const envp[])`
: `fd` is a valid file descriptor open on the file to execute. It must have been opened read-only, with `O_RDONLY`, or on GNU/Linux, with `O_PATH`. Here too, the file must be in an executable format that the kernel understands. `argv` and `envp` are the same as for `execve()`.

The file descriptor can be for any open file, even one that was inherited from a parent. But, in general, you should be careful about which file descriptor you pass to `fexecve()`. To avoid executing arbitrary (and thus possibly malicious) code, it's best to pass it a file descriptor that you opened yourself.

POSIX specifies that you can open a file only for execution by using the `O_EXEC` flag; on GNU/Linux you should use `O_PATH` instead. See Table 4.8, in Section 4.6.4, "Revisiting `open()`," page 104.

9.1.4.3 Wrapper Functions: `execl()` et al.

Five additional functions, acting as wrappers, provide more convenient interfaces to `execve()`. The first group all take a list of arguments, each one passed as an explicit function parameter:

`int execl(const char *path, const char *arg, ...)`
: The first argument, `path`, is the pathname of the file to execute. Subsequent arguments, starting with `arg`, are the individual elements to be placed in `argv`. As before, `argv[0]` must be explicitly included. You must pass a terminating `NULL` pointer as the final argument so that `execl()` can tell where the argument list ends. The new program inherits whatever environment is in the current program's `environ` variable.

`int execlp(const char *file, const char *arg, ...)`
: This function is like `execl()`, but it simulates the shell's command searching mechanism, looking for `file` in each directory named in the `PATH` environment variable. If `file` contains a `/` character, this search is not done. If `PATH` isn't present in the environment, `execlp()` uses a default path. On GNU/Linux, the default is `"/bin:/usr/bin"`, but it may be different on other systems. (Note that as there is no leading or trailing colon in this default search path, the current directory is *not* searched.)

  Furthermore, if the file is found and has execute permission but cannot be exec'd because it isn't in a known executable format, `execlp()` assumes that the program is a shell script, and execs the shell with the file name as an argument.

Table 9.1: Alphabetical `exec()` family summary

Function	Path search	Uses environ	Purpose
`execl()`		✓	Execute argument list.
`execle()`			Execute argument list with environment.
`execlp()`	✓	✓	Execute argument list by `PATH` search.
`execv()`		✓	Execute with `argv`.
`execve()`			Execute with `argv` and environment (system call).
`execvp()`	✓	✓	Execute with `argv` by `PATH` search.
`fexecve()`			Execute with `argv` and environment (system call).

`int execle(const char *path, const char *arg, ..., char *const envp[])`
This function is also like `execl()`, but it accepts an additional argument, `envp`, which becomes the new program's environment. As with `execl()`, you must supply the terminating `NULL` pointer to end the argument list, before `envp`.

The second group of wrapper functions accepts an `argv`-style array:

`int execv(const char *path, char *const argv[])`
This function is like `execve()`, but the new program inherits whatever environment is in the current program's `environ` variable.

`int execvp(const char *file, char *const argv[])`
This function is like `execv()`, but it does the same `PATH` search that `execlp()` does. It also does the same falling back to execing the shell if the found file cannot be executed directly.

Table 9.1 summarizes the seven `exec()` functions.

The `execlp()` and `execvp()` functions' behavior is intended to mimic that of the shell; in particular, the fallback to running the shell if the file isn't an executable is what the shell does. We recommend avoiding these two functions unless you know that the `PATH` environment variable contains a reasonable list of directories.

9.1.4.4 Program Names and `argv[0]`

Until now, we have always treated `argv[0]` as the program name. We know that it may or may not contain a `/` character, depending on how the program is invoked; if it does, then that's usually a good clue as to the pathname used to invoke the program.

However, as should be clear by now, `argv[0]` being the file name is *only a convention*. There's nothing stopping you from passing an arbitrary string to the exec'd program for `argv[0]`. The following program, `ch-processes-run.c`, demonstrates passing an arbitrary string:

```
/* ch-processes-run.c --- run a program with a different name and any arguments */

#include <stdio.h>
#include <errno.h>
```

```
5  #include <stdlib.h>
6  #include <string.h>
7  #include <unistd.h>
8
9  /* main --- adjust argv and run named program */
10
11 int
12 main(int argc, char **argv)
13 {
14     char *path;
15
16     if (argc < 3) {
17         fprintf(stderr, "usage: %s path arg0 [ arg ... ]\n", argv[0]);
18         exit(1);
19     }
20
21     path = argv[1];
22
23     execv(path, argv + 2);  /* skip argv[0] and argv[1] */
24
25     fprintf(stderr, "%s: execv() failed: %s\n", argv[0],
26         strerror(errno));
27     exit(1);
28 }
```

The first argument is the pathname of the program to run and the second is the new name for the program (which most utilities ignore, other than for error messages); any other arguments are passed on to the program being exec'd.

Lines 16–19 do error checking. Line 21 saves the path in `path`. Line 23 does the exec; if lines 25–27 run, it's because there was a problem. Here's what happens when we run the program:

```
$ ch-processes-run /bin/grep whoami foo                  Run grep
a line                                                   Input line doesn't match
a line with foo in it                                    Input line that does match
a line with foo in it                                    It's printed
^D                                                       EOF

$ ch-processes-run nonexistent-program foo bar           Demonstrate failure
ch-processes-run: execv() failed: No such file or directory
```

This next example is a bit bizarre: we have `ch-processes-run` run *itself*, passing '`foo`' as the program name. Since there aren't enough arguments for the second run, it prints the usage message and exits:

```
$ ch-processes-run ./ch-processes-run foo
usage: foo path arg0 [ arg ... ]
```

While not very useful, `ch-processes-run` clearly shows that `argv[0]` need not have any relationship to the file that is actually run.

In System III (circa 1980), the `cp`, `ln`, and `mv` commands were one executable file, with three links by those names in `/bin`. The program would examine `argv[0]` and decide what it should do. This saved a modest amount of disk space, at the expense of complicating the source code and forcing the program to choose a default action if invoked by an unrecognized name. (Some current commercial Unix systems continue this practice!)

Without stating an explicit reason, the *GNU Coding Standards* recommends that a program *not* base its behavior on its name. One reason we see is that administrators often install the GNU version of a utility alongside the standard ones on commercial Unix systems, using a `g` prefix: `gmake`, `gawk`, and so on. If such programs expect only the standard names, they'll fail when run with a different name.

Also, disk space is cheap today; if two almost identical programs can be built from the same source code, it's better to do it that way, using `#ifdef` or what-have-you.

9.1.4.5 Attributes Inherited across `exec()`

As with `fork()`, a number of attributes remain in place after a program does an exec:

- All open files and open directories; see Section 4.4.1, "Understanding File Descriptors," page 87, and Section 5.3.1, "Basic Directory Reading," page 124. (This doesn't include files marked close-on-exec, as described later in the chapter; see Section 9.4.3.1, "The Close-on-Exec and Close-on-Fork Flags," page 316.) POSIX requires that open directory streams (created via `opendir()`; see Section 5.3.1, "Basic Directory Reading," page 124) not remain open.
- The umask setting; see Section 4.6.2, "Controlling Default Permissions with `umask()`," page 102.
- The current working directory; see Section 8.4.1, "Changing Directory: `chdir()` and `fchdir()`," page 247.
- The root directory; see Section 8.6, "Changing the Root Directory: `chroot()`," page 269.
- The current nice value.
- The process ID and parent process ID.
- The process group ID; see Section 9.2, "Process Groups," page 300.
- The session ID and the controlling terminal; for both, see Section 9.2.1, "Job Control Overview," page 300.
- The process signal mask and any pending signals, as well as any unexpired alarms or timers (discussed later; see Chapter 10, "Signals," page 333).
- The real user ID and group IDs and the supplemental group set. The effective user and group IDs (and thus the saved set-user and set-group IDs) can be set by the setuid and setgid bits on the file being exec'd. (None of this has been discussed yet; see Chapter 11, "Permissions and User and Group ID Numbers," page 383).
- File locks (also discussed later; see Section 16.2, "Locking Files," page 558).

- Accumulated CPU times for the process and its children.
- File size and resource limits (also discussed later; see Chapter 12, "Resource Limits," page 405).

After an exec, signal disposition changes; see Section 10.9, "Signals across `fork()` and `exec()`," page 378, for more information.

By default, all open files remain open and available after the exec. This is how programs inherit standard input, output, and error: they're in place when the program starts up.

Most of the time when you fork and exec a separate program, you don't want it to inherit anything but file descriptors `0`, `1`, and `2`. In this case, you can manually close all other open files in the child, after the fork but before the exec. (To do that, you can use a loop based on `getdtablesize()`; see Section 4.4.1, "Understanding File Descriptors," page 87.) Alternatively, you can mark a file descriptor to be automatically closed by the system upon either a fork or an exec; this latter option is discussed later in the chapter (see Section 9.4.3.1, "The Close-on-Exec and Close-on-Fork Flags," page 316).

9.1.5 Terminating a Process

Process termination involves two steps: the process exits, passing an exit status to the system, and the parent process recovers the information.

9.1.5.1 Defining Process Exit Status

The *exit status* (also known variously as the *exit value*, the *return code*, or the *return value*) is an eight-bit value that the parent can recover when the child exits (in Unix parlance, "when the child dies"). By convention, an exit status of `0` means that the program ran with no problems. Any nonzero exit status indicates some sort of failure; the program determines the values to use and their meanings, if any. (For example, `grep` uses `0` to mean that it matched the pattern at least once, `1` to mean that it did not match the pattern at all, and `2` to mean that an error occurred.) This exit status is available at the shell level (for Bourne-style shells) in the special variable `$?`.

The C standard defines two constants, which are all you should use for strict portability to non-POSIX systems:

`EXIT_SUCCESS`
: The program exited with no problems. Zero can also be used to mean success.

`EXIT_FAILURE`
: The program had some kind of problem.

In practice, using only these values is rather constraining. Instead, you should pick a small set of return codes, document their meanings, and use them (for example, `1` for command-line option and argument errors, `2` for I/O errors, `3` for bad data errors, and so on). For readability, it pays to use `#define`d constants or an `enum` for them. Having too large a list of errors makes using them cumbersome; most of the time the invoking program (or user) cares only about zero versus nonzero.

When the binary success/failure distinction is adequate, the pedantic programmer uses `EXIT_SUCCESS` and `EXIT_FAILURE`. Our own style is more idiomatic, using the explicit constants `0` or `1` with `return` and `exit()`. This is so common that it is learned early on and quickly becomes second nature. However, you should make your own decision for your projects.

NOTE

Only the least-significant eight bits of the value are available to the parent process. Thus, you should use values in the range 0–255. As we'll see shortly, `126` and `127` have a conventional meaning (above and beyond plain "unsuccessful"), to which your programs should adhere.

Since only the least-significant eight bits matter, you should *never* use a negative exit status. When the last eight bits are retrieved from small negative numbers, they become large positive values! (For example, –1 becomes 255, and –5 becomes 251.) We have seen C programming books that get this wrong—don't be misled.

9.1.5.2 Returning from `main()`

A program can terminate voluntarily in one of two ways: by using one of the functions described in the next section or by returning from `main()`. (A third, more drastic way is described later, in Section 13.4, "Committing Suicide: `abort()`," page 434.) In the latter case, you should use an explicit return value instead of falling off the end of the function:

```
/* Good: */
int main(int argc, char **argv)
{
    /* code here */
    return 0;
}
```

```
/* Bad: */
int main(int argc, char **argv)
{
    /* code here */
    /* ?? What does main() return ?? */
}
```

The 1999 C standard indicates that when `main()` returns by falling off the end, the behavior is as if it had returned `0`. (This is also true for C++; however, the 1990 C standard leaves this case purposely undefined.) In all cases, it's poor practice to rely on this behavior; one day you may be programming for a system with meager C runtime support or for an embedded system, or somewhere else where it makes a difference. (In general, falling off the end of any non-`void` function is a bad idea; it can only lead to buggy code. And your compiler may not warn you about it!)

The value returned from `main()` is automatically passed back to the system, from which the parent can recover it later. We describe how in Section 9.1.6.1, "Using POSIX Functions: `wait()`, `waitpid()`, and `waitid()`," page 294.

9.1.5.3 Exiting Functions

The other way to voluntarily terminate a program is by calling an exit function. The C standard defines the following functions:

```
#include <stdlib.h>                                    ISO C

void exit(int status);
```

```
void _Exit(int status);
int atexit(void (*function)(void));
```

The functions work as follows:

`void exit(int status)`
: This function terminates the program. `status` is passed to the system for recovery by the parent. Before the program exits, `exit()` calls all functions registered with `atexit()`, flushes and closes all open `<stdio.h> FILE *` streams, and removes any temporary files created with `tmpfile()` (see Section 13.3.2, "Creating and Opening Temporary Files (Good)," page 430). When the process exits, the kernel closes any remaining open file descriptors (network sockets, files and directories opened by `open()` or `creat()`, or inherited file descriptors), frees up its address space, and releases any other resources it may have been using. `exit()` never returns.

`void _Exit(int status)`
: This function is essentially identical to the POSIX `_exit()` function; we delay discussion of it for a short while.

`int atexit(void (*function)(void))`
: `function` is a pointer to a callback function to be called at program exit. `exit()` invokes the callback function before it closes files and terminates. The idea is that an application can provide one or more cleanup functions to be run before finally shutting down. Providing a function is called *registering* it.

  `atexit()` returns `0` on success or `-1` on error, and sets `errno` appropriately.

The following program does no useful work, but it does demonstrate how `atexit()` works:

```
/* ch-processes-atexit.c --- demonstrate atexit().
                             Error checking omitted for brevity. */

#include <stdio.h>
#include <stdlib.h>

/*
 * The callback functions here just answer roll call.
 * In a real application, they would do more.
 */

void callback1(void) { printf("callback1 called\n"); }
void callback2(void) { printf("callback2 called\n"); }
void callback3(void) { printf("callback3 called\n"); }

/* main --- register functions and then exit */

int
main(int argc, char **argv)
```

```
{
    printf("registering callback1\n");  atexit(callback1);
    printf("registering callback2\n");  atexit(callback2);
    printf("registering callback3\n");  atexit(callback3);

    printf("exiting now\n");
    exit(EXIT_SUCCESS);
}
```

Here's what happens when it's run:

```
$ ch-processes-atexit
registering callback1                Main program runs
registering callback2
registering callback3
exiting now
callback3 called                     Callback functions run in reverse order
callback2 called
callback1 called
```

As the example demonstrates, functions registered with `atexit()` run in the reverse order in which they were registered, with the most recent one first. (This is also termed *last-in first-out*, abbreviated as LIFO.)

POSIX also defines the `_exit()` function. Unlike `exit()`, which invokes callback functions and does `<stdio.h>` cleanup, `_exit()` is the "die immediately" function:

```
#include <unistd.h>                                              POSIX

void _exit(int status);
```

The `status` is given to the system, just as for `exit()`, but the process terminates immediately. The kernel still does the usual cleanup: all open file descriptors are closed, the memory used by the address space is released, and any other resources the process was using are also released.

In practice, the ISO C `_Exit()` function is identical to `_exit()`. The C standard says it's implementation defined as to whether `_Exit()` calls functions registered with `atexit()` and closes open files. For GLIBC systems, it does not, behaving like `_exit()`.

The time to use `_exit()` is when an exec fails in a forked child. In this case, you *don't* want to use regular `exit()`, since that flushes any buffered data held by `FILE *` streams. When the parent later flushes its copies of the buffers, the buffered data ends up being written *twice*; obviously this is not good.

For example, suppose you wish to run a shell command and do the fork and exec yourself. Such code would look like this:

```
const char shellcommand[] = "...";
pid_t child;
```

```
if ((child = fork()) == 0) {  /* child */
    execl("/bin/sh", "sh", "-c", shellcommand, NULL);
    _exit(errno == ENOENT ? 127 : 126);
}
/* parent continues */
```

The `errno` test and exit values follow conventions used by the POSIX shell. If a requested program doesn't exist (`ENOENT`—no entry for it in a directory), then the exit value is `127`. Otherwise, the file exists but couldn't be exec'd for some other reason, so the exit status is `126`. It's a good idea to follow this convention in your own programs too.

Briefly, to make good use of `exit()` and `atexit()`, you should do the following:

- Define a small set of exit status values that your program will use to communicate information to its caller. Use `#define`d constants or an `enum` for them in your code.
- Document these values in your program's documentation!
- Decide if having callback functions for use with `atexit()` makes sense. If it does, register them in `main()` at the appropriate point—for example, after parsing options, and after initializing whatever data structures the callback functions are supposed to clean up. Remember that the functions are called in LIFO (last-in first-out) order.
- Use `exit()` everywhere to exit from the program whenever something goes wrong and exiting is the correct action to take. Use the error codes that you defined and documented.
- An exception is `main()`, for which you can use `return` if you wish. Our own style is generally to use `exit()` when there are problems and '`return 0`' (or '`return EXIT_SUCCESS`') at the end of `main()` if everything has gone well.
- Use `_exit()` or `_Exit()` in a child process if `exec()` fails.

9.1.6 Recovering a Child's Exit Status

When a process dies, the normal course of action is for the kernel to release all its resources. The kernel does retain the dead process's exit status, as well as information about the resources it used during its lifetime, and the PID continues to be counted as being in use. Such a dead process is termed a *zombie*.

The parent process, be it the original parent or `init`, can recover the child's exit status. Or, by use of BSD functions that aren't standardized by POSIX, the exit status together with the resource usage information can be recovered. Status recovery is done by waiting for the process to die; this is also known as *reaping* the process.[2]

There is considerable interaction between the mechanisms that wait for children to die and the signal mechanisms we haven't described yet. Which one to describe first is a bit of a chicken-and-egg problem; we've chosen to talk about the child-waiting mechanisms first, and Chapter 10, "Signals," page 333, provides the full story on signals.

---

[2] We are not making this up. The terminology is indeed rather morbid, but such was the original Unix designers' sense of humor.

For now, it's enough to understand that a signal is a way to notify a process that some event has occurred. Processes can generate signals that get sent to themselves, or signals can be sent externally by other processes or by a user at a terminal. For example, CTRL-C sends an "interrupt" signal, and CTRL-Z sends a job control "stop" signal.

By default, many signals, such as the interrupt signal, cause the receiving process to die. Others, such as the job control signals, cause it to change state. The child-waiting mechanisms can determine whether a process suffered death-by-signal and, if so, which signal it was. The same is true for processes stopping and, on some systems, when a process continues.

9.1.6.1 Using POSIX Functions: `wait()`, `waitpid()`, and `waitid()`

The original V7 system call was `wait()`. The newer POSIX call, based on BSD functionality, is `waitpid()`. The newest POSIX call, `waitid()`, is more general than the others. The function declarations are:

```
#include <sys/types.h>                                        POSIX
#include <sys/wait.h>

pid_t wait(int *status);
pid_t waitpid(pid_t pid, int *status, int options);
int waitid(idtype_t idtype, id_t id, siginfo_t *infop, int options);
```

`wait()` waits for *any* child process to die; the information as to how it died is returned in `*status`. (We discuss how to interpret `*status` shortly.) The return value is the PID of the process that died or `-1` if an error occurred.

If there is no child process, `wait()` returns `-1` with `errno` set to `ECHILD` (no child process). Otherwise, it waits for the first child to die or for a signal to come in.

The `waitpid()` function lets you wait for a specific child process to exit. It provides considerable flexibility and is preferred over `wait()`. It too returns the PID of the process that died or `-1` if an error occurred. The arguments are as follows:

`pid_t pid`

The value specifies which child to wait for, both by real `pid` and by process group. The `pid` value has the following meanings:

`pid` < −1	Wait for any child process with a process group ID equal to the absolute value of `pid`.
`pid` = −1	Wait for any child process. This is the way `wait()` works.
`pid` = 0	Wait for any child process with a process group ID equal to that of the parent process's process group.
`pid` > 0	Wait for the specific process with the PID equal to `pid`.

`int *status`

This is the same as for `wait()`. <sys/wait.h> defines various macros that interpret the value in `*status`, which we describe soon.

`int options`
This should be either `0` or the bitwise-OR of one or more of the following flags:

`WNOHANG`
If no child has exited, return immediately. That way you can check periodically to see if any children have died. (Such periodic checking is known as *polling* for an event.)

`WUNTRACED`
Return information about a child process that has stopped but that hasn't exited yet (for example, with job control).

`WCONTINUED`
Return information about a child process that has continued if the status of the child has not been reported since it changed. This too is for job control. (This is an XSI extension; POSIX doesn't require it for systems that don't implement the XSI extensions.)

Multiple macros work on the filled-in `*status` value to determine what happened. They tend to come in pairs: one macro to determine if something occurred, and if that macro is true, one or more macros that retrieve the details. The macros are as follows:

`WIFEXITED(status)`
This macro is nonzero (true) if the process exited (as opposed to changing state).

`WEXITSTATUS(status)`
This macro gives the exit status; it equals the least-significant eight bits of the value passed to `exit()` or returned from `main()`. You should use this macro only if `WIFEXITED(status)` is true.

`WIFSIGNALED(status)`
This macro is nonzero if the process suffered death-by-signal.

`WTERMSIG(status)`
This macro provides the signal number that terminated the process. You should use this macro only if `WIFSIGNALED(status)` is true.

`WIFSTOPPED(status)`
This macro is nonzero if the process was stopped.

`WSTOPSIG(status)`
This macro provides the signal number that stopped the process. (Several signals can stop a process.) You should use this macro only if `WIFSTOPPED(status)` is true. Job control signals are discussed in Section 10.8.2, "Job Control Signals," page 365.

`WIFCONTINUED(status)`
This macro is nonzero if the process was continued. There is no corresponding `WCONTSIG()` macro, since only one signal can cause a process to continue. (This is an XSI extension.)

Table 9.2: Possible values for `idtype`

Constant	Linux only	Meaning
`P_PID`		Wait for the child denoted by `(pid_t) id`.
`P_PGID`		Wait for any child with a process group ID equal to `(pid_t) id`.
`P_PIDFD`	✓	Wait for the child referred to by the PID file descriptor in `id`.[3]
`P_ALL`		Wait for any child; `id` is ignored.

`WCOREDUMP(status)`

This macro is nonzero if the process dumped core. A *core dump* is the memory image of a running process created when the process terminates. It is intended for use later for debugging. Certain signals terminate a process and produce a core dump automatically.

Unix systems named the file `core`, placing it in the current directory of the program that died (assuming that the process had write permission there). On GNU/Linux the story is much more complicated. We delay discussion of how to get a core dump file until Section 17.3.1, "Getting a `core` File," page 594.

Note that this macro is nonstandard. GNU/Linux, Solaris, and BSD systems support it, but some legacy Unix systems do not. Thus, if you wish to use it, bracket such use inside '`#ifdef WCOREDUMP ... #endif`'.

Finally, the newest function defined by POSIX is `waitid()`. It is more flexible than the others, in that it can return information about a child process's change of state, instead of just waiting for a child to die. Its arguments are:

`idtype_t idtype`

This describes the child process to be waited for. The value of `idtype` should be one of the values in Table 9.2.

`id_t id`

Specifies the process ID or process group ID of a child to wait for.

`siginfo_t *infop`

Information related to the process is filled into this structure. We delay discussion of the contents of a `siginfo_t` until Section 10.6.4, "Catching Signals: `sigaction()`," page 353.

`int options`

The bitwise-OR of one or more of the following flags:

`WCONTINUED`	Wait for a child that has resumed due to job control.
`WEXITED`	Wait for a child that has exited.
`WNOHANG`	Return immediately if there are no children to wait for.
`WNOWAIT`	Just retrieve information; the child can be waited for again, later.
`WSTOPPED`	Wait for a child that has stopped due to job control.

[3] This is extremely specialized and not otherwise covered; see *pidfd_open*(2) for more information.

The return value is `0` if information was retrieved or `WNOHANG` was used. Otherwise `-1` is returned upon an error.

Most programs don't care *why* a child process died; they merely care *that* it died, perhaps noting if it exited successfully or not. The GNU Coreutils `install` program demonstrates such straightforward use of `fork()`, `execlp()`, and `waitpid()`. The `-s` option causes `install` to run the `strip` program on the binary executable being installed. (`strip` removes debugging and other information from an executable file. This can save considerable space, relatively speaking. On modern systems with multi-terabyte disk drives, it's rarely necessary to strip executables upon installation. An example was shown earlier, in Section 3.1, "Linux/Unix Address Space," page 51.) Here is the `strip()` function from `install.c`:

```
/* Strip the symbol table from the file NAME.
   We could dig the magic number out of the file first to
   determine whether to strip it, but the header files and
   magic numbers vary so much from system to system that making
   it portable would be very difficult.  Not worth the effort. */

static bool
strip (char const *name)
{
  int status;
  bool ok = false;
  pid_t pid = fork ();

  switch (pid)
    {
    case -1:
      error (0, errno, _("fork system call failed"));
      break;
    case 0:          /* Child. */
      {
        char const *safe_name = name;
        if (name && *name == '-')
          safe_name = file_name_concat (".", name, nullptr);
        execlp (strip_program, strip_program, safe_name, nullptr);
        error (EXIT_FAILURE, errno, _("cannot run %s"),
               quoteaf (strip_program));
      }
    default:             /* Parent. */
      if (waitpid (pid, &status, 0) < 0)
        error (0, errno, _("waiting for strip"));
      else if (! WIFEXITED (status) || WEXITSTATUS (status))
        error (0, 0, _("strip process terminated abnormally"));
      else
        ok = true;      /* strip succeeded */
```

```
518         break;
519     }
520     return ok;
521 }
```

Line 495 calls `fork()`. The `switch` statement then takes the correct action for error return (lines 499–501), child process (lines 502–510), and parent process (lines 511–519). (As an aside, what's happening on lines 505–506, and why?)

Line 512 uses `waitpid()` to wait for the specific PID of the forked child. `status` is then checked for an error exit using `WIFEXITED()` and `WEXITSTATUS()` (lines 514–515).

From the description and code presented so far, it may appear that parent programs must choose a specific point to wait for any child processes to die, possibly polling in a loop, waiting for all children. In Section 10.8.3, "Parental Supervision: Three Different Strategies," page 366, we'll see that this is not necessarily the case. Rather, signals provide a range of mechanisms for managing parent notification when a child process dies.

9.1.6.2 Using BSD Functions: `wait3()` and `wait4()`

The BSD `wait3()` and `wait4()` system calls are useful if you're interested in the resources used by a child process. They are nonstandard (meaning they're not part of POSIX) but are widely available, including on GNU/Linux. The declarations are as follows:

Common

```
#include <sys/types.h>
#include <sys/time.h>
#include <sys/resource.h>
#include <sys/wait.h>

pid_t wait3(int *status, int options, struct rusage *rusage);
pid_t wait4(pid_t pid, int *status, int options, struct rusage *rusage);
```

The `status` variable is the same as for `wait()` and `waitpid()`. All the macros described earlier (`WIFEXITED()`, `WEXITSTATUS()`, etc.) can also be used with it.

The `options` value is also the same as for `waitpid()`: either `0` or the bitwise-OR of one or both of `WNOHANG` and `WUNTRACED`.

`wait3()` behaves like `wait()`, retrieving information about the first available zombie child, and `wait4()` is like `waitpid()`, retrieving information about a particular process. Both return the PID of the reaped child, `-1` on error, or `0` if no process is available and `WNOHANG` was used. The `pid` argument can take on the same values as the `pid` argument for `waitpid()`.

The added value of `wait3()` and `wait4()` over `wait()` and `waitpid()` is the `struct rusage` pointer. If not `NULL`, the system fills it in with information about the process. This structure is described in POSIX and in the *getrusage*(2) manpage:

```
struct rusage {
    struct timeval ru_utime; /* user time used */
    struct timeval ru_stime; /* system time used */
    long   ru_maxrss;        /* maximum resident set size */
    long   ru_ixrss;         /* integral shared memory size */
```

```
    long    ru_idrss;         /* integral unshared data size */
    long    ru_isrss;         /* integral unshared stack size */
    long    ru_minflt;        /* page reclaims */
    long    ru_majflt;        /* page faults */
    long    ru_nswap;         /* swaps */
    long    ru_inblock;       /* block input operations */
    long    ru_oublock;       /* block output operations */
    long    ru_msgsnd;        /* messages sent */
    long    ru_msgrcv;        /* messages received */
    long    ru_nsignals;      /* signals received */
    long    ru_nvcsw;         /* voluntary context switches */
    long    ru_nivcsw;        /* involuntary context switches */
};
```

Pure BSD systems (4.3 Reno and later) support all of the fields. Table 9.3 describes the availability of the various fields in the `struct rusage` for POSIX and GNU/Linux.

Only the fields marked "POSIX" are defined by the standard. The other fields named in the table are maintained by the Linux kernel. However, you may want to double-check the *getrusage*(2) manpage.

The fields of most interest are `ru_utime` and `ru_stime`, the user and system CPU times, respectively. (User CPU time is time spent executing user-level code. System CPU time is time spent in the kernel on behalf of the process.)

These two fields use a `struct timeval`, which maintains time values down to microsecond intervals. See Section 5.6.4.2, "Microsecond Time Resolution: `utimes()`," page 149, for more information on this structure.

In 4.2 and 4.3 BSD, the `status` argument to `wait()` and `wait3()` was a `union wait`. It fit into an `int` and provided access to the same information as `WIFEXITED()` and the other modern macros do, but through the `union`'s members. Not all members were valid in all situations. The members and their uses are described in Table 9.4.

Table 9.3: Availability of `struct rusage` fields

Field	POSIX	GNU/Linux
`ru_utime`	✓	✓
`ru_stime`	✓	✓
`ru_maxrss`		✓
`ru_minflt`		✓
`ru_majflt`		✓
`ru_inblock`		✓
`ru_oublock`		✓
`ru_nvcsw`		✓
`ru_nivcsw`		✓

Table 9.4: The 4.2 and 4.3 BSD `union wait`

POSIX macro	Union member	Usage	Meaning
`WIFEXITED()`	`w_termsig`	`w.w_termsig == 0`	True if normal exit.
`WEXITSTATUS()`	`w_retcode`	`code = w.w_retcode`	Exit status if not by signal.
`WIFSIGNALED()`	`w_termsig`	`w.w_termsig != 0`	True if death-by-signal.
`WTERMSIG()`	`w_termsig`	`sig = w.w_termsig`	Signal that caused termination.
`WIFSTOPPED()`	`w_stopval`	`w.w_stopval == WSTOPPED`	True if stopped.
`WSTOPSIG()`	`w_stopsig`	`sig = w.w_stopsig`	Signal that caused stopping.
`WCOREDUMP()`	`w_coredump`	`w.w_coredump != 0`	True if child dumped core.

POSIX doesn't standardize the `union wait`, and 4.4 BSD doesn't document it, instead using the POSIX macros. Earlier versions of GLIBC jumped through several hoops to make old code using it continue to work. Current versions no longer support it. We describe it here primarily so that you'll recognize it if you see it; new code should use the macros described in Section 9.1.6.1, "Using POSIX Functions: `wait()`, `waitpid()`, and `waitid()`," page 294.

9.2 Process Groups

A *process group* is a group of related processes that should be treated together for job control purposes. Processes with the same process group ID are members of the process group, and the process whose PID is the same as the process group ID is the *process group leader*. New processes inherit the process group ID of their parent process.

We have already seen that `waitpid()` and `waitid()` allow you to wait for any process in a given process group. In Section 10.6.7, "Sending Signals: `kill()` and `killpg()`," page 358, we'll also see that you can send a signal to all the processes in a particular process group as well. (Permission checking always applies; you can't send a signal to a process you don't own.)

9.2.1 Job Control Overview

Job control is an involved topic, one that we've chosen not to delve into for this book. However, here's a quick conceptual overview.

The terminal device (physical or otherwise) with a user working at it is called the *controlling terminal*.

A *session* is a collection of process groups associated with the controlling terminal. There is only one session per terminal, with multiple process groups in the session. One process is designated the *session leader*; this is normally a shell that can do job control, such as Bash, `mksh`, `zsh`, or `ksh93`.[4] We refer to such a shell as a *job control shell*.

Each job started by a job control shell, be it a single program or a pipeline, receives a separate process group identifier. That way, the shell can manipulate the job as a single entity, although it may have multiple processes.

[4] `csh` and `tcsh` can be included in this category too, but we prefer Bourne-style shells.

The controlling terminal also has a process group identifier associated with it. When a user types a special character such as CTRL-C for "interrupt" or CTRL-Z for "stop," the kernel sends the given signal to the processes in the terminal's process group.

The process group whose process group ID is the same as that of the controlling terminal is allowed to read from and write to the terminal. This is called the *foreground process group.* It also receives the keyboard-generated signals. Any other process groups in the session are *background process groups* and cannot read from or write to the terminal; they receive special signals that stop them if they try.

Jobs move in and out of the foreground, *not* by a change to an attribute of the job but rather by a change to the controlling terminal's process group. It is the job control shell that makes this change, and if the new process group was stopped, the shell continues it by sending a "continue" signal to all members of the process group.

In days of yore, users often used serial terminals connected to modems to dial in to centralized minicomputer Unix systems. When the user closed the connection (hung up the phone), the serial line detected the disconnection and the kernel sent a "hangup" signal to all processes connected to the terminal.

This concept remains: if a hangup occurs, the kernel sends the hangup signal to the foreground process group. (Serial hardware does still exist and is still in use, so you can get a physical hangup. And you get a hangup signal when you close the window of a terminal emulator instead of exiting the shell.) If the session leader exits, the same thing happens.

An *orphaned process group* is one where, for every process in the group, that process's parent is also in the group or is in a different session. (This can happen if a job control shell exits with background jobs running.) Running processes in an orphaned process group are allowed to run to completion. If there are any already stopped processes in an orphaned process group when it becomes orphaned, the kernel sends those processes a hangup signal and then a continue signal. This causes them to wake up so that they can exit instead of remaining stopped forever.

9.2.2 Process Group Identification: `getpgrp()` and `getpgid()`

For compatibility with older systems, POSIX provides multiple ways to retrieve process group information:

```
#include <unistd.h>                                    POSIX

pid_t getpgrp(void);
pid_t getpgid(pid_t pid);
```

The `getpgrp()` function returns the current process's process group ID. `getpgid()` returns the process group ID of the given process `pid`. A `pid` of `0` means "the current process's process group." Thus '`getpgid(0)`' is the same as '`getpgrp()`'. For general programming, `getpgrp()` should be used.

9.2.3 Process Group Setting: `setpgid()` and `setpgrp()`

Two functions set the process group:

```
#include <unistd.h>

int setpgid(pid_t pid, pid_t pgid);                    POSIX
int setpgrp(void);                                     Common
```

The `setpgrp()` function is simple: it sets the process group ID to be the same as the process ID. Doing so creates a new process group in the same session, and the calling process becomes the process group leader. It was once standardized by POSIX but no longer is; nonetheless, it remains available.

The `setpgid()` function is intended for job control use. It allows one process to set the process group of another. A process may change only its own process group ID or the process group ID of a child process, and then only if that child process has not yet done an exec. Job control shells make this call after the fork, in *both* the parent and the child. For one of them the call succeeds, and the process group ID is changed. (Otherwise, there's no way to guarantee the ordering, such that the parent could change the child's process group ID before the child execs. If the parent's call succeeds first, it can move on to the next task, such as manipulating other jobs or the terminal.)

With `setpgid()`, `pgid` must be an existing process group that is part of the current session, effectively joining `pid` to that process group. Otherwise, `pgid` must be equal to `pid`, creating a new process group.

There are some special case values for both `pid` and `pgid`:

`pid` = 0
: In this case, `setpgid()` changes the process group of the calling process to `pgid`. It's equivalent to '`setpgid(getpid(), pgid)`'.

`pgid` = 0
: This sets the process group ID for the given process to be the same as its PID. Thus, '`setpgid(pid, 0)`' is the same as '`setpgid(pid, pid)`'. This causes the process with PID `pid` to become a process group leader.

In all cases, session leaders are special; their PID, process group ID, and session ID values are all identical, and the process group ID of a session leader cannot be changed. (Session IDs are set with `setsid()` and retrieved with `getsid()`. These are specialized calls; see the *setsid*(2) and *getsid*(2) manpages.)

9.3 Basic Interprocess Communication: Pipes and FIFOs

Interprocess communication (IPC) is what it sounds like: a way for two separate processes to communicate. The oldest IPC mechanism on Unix systems is the *pipe*, a one-way communication channel. Data written into one end of the channel comes out the other end.

9.3.1 Pipes

Pipes manifest themselves as regular file descriptors. Without going to special lengths, you can't tell if a file descriptor is a file or a pipe. This is a feature; programs that read standard input and write standard output don't have to know or care that they may be communicating with another process. Should you need to know, the canonical way to check is to attempt '`lseek(fd, 0L, SEEK_CUR)`' on the file descriptor; this call attempts to seek zero bytes from the current position—that is, it's a do-nothing operation.[5] This operation fails for pipes and does no damage for other files.

9.3.1.1 Creating Pipes

The `pipe()` system call creates a pipe:

```
#include <unistd.h>                                          POSIX

int pipe(int filedes[2]);
```

The argument value is the address of a two-element integer array. `pipe()` returns `0` upon success and `-1` if there was an error.

If the call was successful, the process now has two additional open file descriptors. The value in `filedes[0]` is the *read end* of the pipe, and `filedes[1]` is the *write end*. (A handy mnemonic device is that the read end uses index `0`, analogous to standard input being file descriptor `0`, and the write end uses index `1`, analogous to standard output being file descriptor `1`.)

As mentioned, data written into the write end is read from the read end. When you're done with a pipe, you close both ends with a call to `close()`. The following simple program, `ch-processes-pipedemo.c`, demonstrates pipes by creating one, writing data to it, and then reading the data back from it:

```
/* ch-processes-pipedemo.c --- demonstrate I/O with a pipe. */

#include <stdio.h>
#include <errno.h>
#include <stdlib.h>
#include <string.h>
#include <unistd.h>

/* main --- create a pipe, write to it, and read from it. */

int
main(int argc, char **argv)
{
    static const char mesg[] = "Don't Panic!";  /* a famous message */
    char buf[BUFSIZ];
    ssize_t rcount, wcount;
    int pipefd[2];
```

[5] Such an operation is often referred to as a *no-op*, short for "no operation."

```
18      size_t len;
19
20      if (pipe(pipefd) < 0) {
21          fprintf(stderr, "%s: pipe failed: %s\n", argv[0],
22              strerror(errno));
23          exit(EXIT_FAILURE);
24      }
25
26      printf("Read end = fd %d, write end = fd %d\n",
27          pipefd[0], pipefd[1]);
28
29      len = strlen(mesg);
30      if ((wcount = write(pipefd[1], mesg, len)) != len) {
31          fprintf(stderr, "%s: write failed: %s\n", argv[0],
32              strerror(errno));
33          exit(EXIT_FAILURE);
34      }
35
36      if ((rcount = read(pipefd[0], buf, BUFSIZ)) != wcount) {
37          fprintf(stderr, "%s: read failed: %s\n", argv[0],
38              strerror(errno));
39          exit(EXIT_FAILURE);
40      }
41
42      buf[rcount] = '\0';
43
44      printf("Read <%s> from pipe\n", buf);
45      (void) close(pipefd[0]);
46      (void) close(pipefd[1]);
47
48      return EXIT_SUCCESS;
49  }
```

Lines 14–18 declare local variables; of most interest is `mesg`, which is the text that will traverse the pipe.

Lines 20–24 create the pipe, with error checking; lines 26–27 print the values of the new file descriptors (just to prove that they won't be `0`, `1`, or `2`).

Line 29 gets the length of the message, to use with `write()`. Lines 30–34 write the message down the pipe, again with error checking.

Lines 36–40 read the contents of the pipe, again with error checking.

Line 42 supplies a terminating zero byte, so that the read data can be used as a regular string. Line 44 prints the data, and lines 45–46 close both ends of the pipe. Here's what happens when the program runs:

```
$ ch-processes-pipedemo
Read end = fd 3, write end = fd 4
Read <Don't Panic!> from pipe
```

This program doesn't do anything useful, but it does demonstrate the basics. Note that there are no calls to `open()` or `creat()` and that the program isn't using its three inherited file descriptors. Yet the `write()` and `read()` succeed, proving that the file descriptors are valid and that data that goes into the pipe does come out of it.[6]

Pipes have only so much room in them, a fact we discuss in the next section. This means that had the message been too big, our program wouldn't have worked; the `write()` would have blocked, waiting for someone to empty the pipe.

Like other file descriptors, those for a pipe are inherited by a child after a fork and, if not closed, are still available after an exec. We see shortly how to make use of this fact and do something interesting with pipes.

9.3.1.2 Pipe Buffering

Pipes *buffer* their data, meaning that data written to the pipe is held by the kernel until it is read. However, a pipe can hold only so much written but not yet read data. We can call the writing process the *producer*, and the reading process the *consumer.* How does the system manage full and empty pipes?

When the pipe is full, the system automatically *blocks* the producer the next time it attempts to `write()` data into the pipe. Once the pipe empties out, the system copies the data into the pipe and then allows the `write()` system call to return to the producer.

Similarly, if the pipe is empty, the consumer blocks in the `read()` until there is more data in the pipe to be read. (The blocking behavior can be turned off; this is discussed in Section 9.4.3.5, "Nonblocking I/O for Pipes and FIFOs," page 320.)

When the producer does a `close()` on the pipe's write end, the consumer can successfully read any data still buffered in the pipe. After that, further calls to `read()` return `0`, indicating end-of-file.

Conversely, if the consumer closes the read end, a `write()` to the write end fails—drastically. In particular, the kernel sends the producer a "broken pipe" signal, whose default action is to terminate the process.

Our favorite analogy for pipes is that of a husband and wife washing and drying dishes together. One spouse washes the dishes, placing the clean but wet plates into a dish drainer by the sink. The other spouse takes the dishes from the drainer and dries them. The dish washer is the producer, the dish drainer is the pipe, and the dish dryer is the consumer.[7]

If the drying spouse is faster than the washing one, the drainer becomes empty, and the dryer has to wait until more dishes are available. Conversely, if the washing spouse is faster, then the drainer becomes full, and the washer has to wait until it empties out before putting more clean dishes into it. This is depicted in Figure 9.3.

---

[6] We're sure you weren't worried. After all, you probably use pipelines from the shell dozens of times a day.

[7] What they ate for dinner is left unspecified.

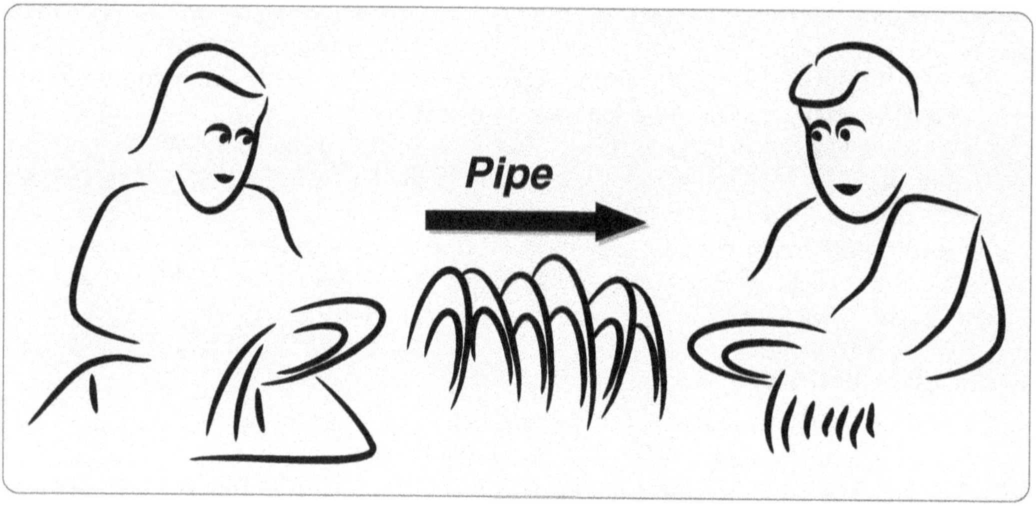

Figure 9.3: Synchronization of pipe processes

We saw that `ch-processes-pipedemo.c` both wrote to and read from a pipe in a single process. This was for demonstration purposes. Doing this in practice can lead to a deadlock situation if you write too much to a pipe before trying to read from it.[8]

9.3.2 FIFOs

With traditional pipes, the only way for two separate programs to have access to the same pipe is through file descriptor inheritance. This means that the processes must be the children of a common parent, or one process must be an ancestor of the other.

This can be a severe limitation. Many system services run as *daemons*, disconnected long-running processes. There needs to be an easy way to send data to such processes (and possibly receive data from them). Files are inappropriate for this; synchronization is difficult or impossible, and pipes can't be created to do the job, since there are no common ancestors.

To solve this problem, System III invented the notion of a FIFO. A *FIFO*, or *named pipe*, is a file in the filesystem that acts like a pipe.[9] In other words, one process opens the FIFO for writing, while another opens it for reading. Data then written to the FIFO is read by the reader. The data is buffered by the kernel, not stored on disk.

Consider a line printer spooler. The spooler daemon controls the physical printers, creating print jobs that print one by one. To add a job to the queue, user-level line-printer software has to communicate with the spooler daemon. One way to do this is for the spooler to create a FIFO with a well-known file name. The user software can then open the FIFO, write a request to it, and close it. The spooler sits in a loop, reading requests from the FIFO and processing them.

---

[8]A *deadlock* is a situation in which two parties want the same resource, and each one is waiting for the other to release it. Here, there's only the one party; if too much data is written to the pipe, the `write()` never returns, because no one is available to read from the pipe in order to empty it out.

[9]FIFO is an acronym for "first-in first-out." This is the way pipes work.

The `mkfifo()` function creates FIFO files:

```
#include <sys/types.h>                                   POSIX
#include <sys/stat.h>

int mkfifo(const char *pathname, mode_t mode);
```

The `pathname` argument is the name of the FIFO file to create, and `mode` is the permissions to give it, analogous to the second argument to `creat()` or the third argument to `open()` (see Section 4.6, "Creating Files," page 101). FIFO files are removed like any other file, with `remove()` or `unlink()` (see Section 5.1.5, "File Removal," page 118).

The GNU/Linux *mkfifo*(3) manpage points out that the FIFO must be open for both reading and writing at the same time, before I/O can be done: "Opening a FIFO for reading normally blocks until some other process opens the same FIFO for writing, and vice versa." Once a FIFO file is opened, it acts like a regular pipe; that is, it's just another file descriptor.

The `mkfifo` command brings this system call to the command level. This makes it easy to show a FIFO file in action:

```
$ mkfifo afifo                              Create a FIFO file
$ ls -l afifo                               Show type and permissions, note leading 'p'
prw-rw-r-- 1 arnold arnold 0 Jan 31 21:08 afifo
$ cat < afifo &                             Start a reader in the background
[1] 22100
$ echo It was a Blustery Day > afifo        Send data to the FIFO
It was a Blustery Day                       cat prints the data
[1]+  Done                    cat < afifo   cat exits
$                                           Shell prompts for next command
```

9.4 File Descriptor Management

At this point, the pieces of the puzzle are almost complete. `fork()` and `exec()` create processes and run programs in them. `pipe()` creates a pipe that can be used for IPC. What's still missing is a way to move the pipe's file descriptors into place as standard output and standard input for a pipeline's producer and consumer.

The `dup()` and `dup2()` system calls, together with `close()`, let you move (well, copy) an open file descriptor to another number. The `fcntl()` system call lets you do the same thing and manipulate several important attributes of open files.

9.4.1 Duplicating Open Files: `dup()` and `dup2()`

Two system calls create a copy of an open file descriptor:

```
#include <unistd.h>                                      POSIX

int dup(int oldfd);
int dup2(int oldfd, int newfd);
```

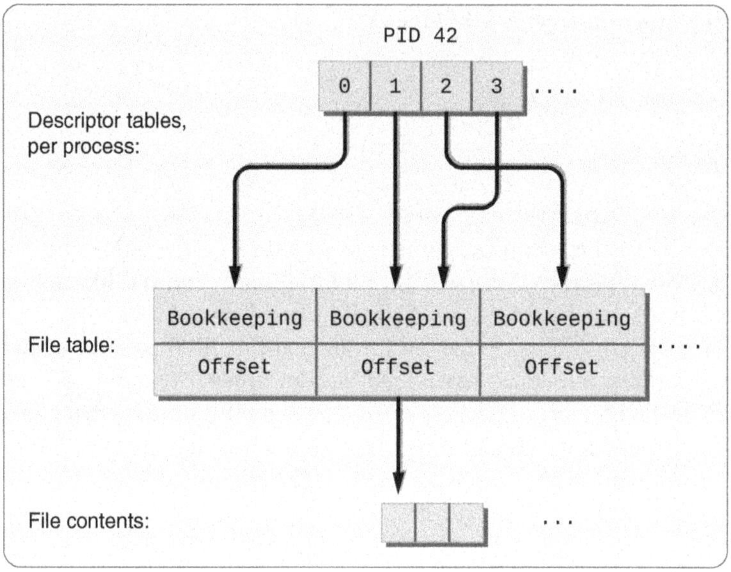

Figure 9.4: File descriptor sharing after '`dup2(1, 3)`'

The functions are as follows:

`int dup(int oldfd)`
: Returns the lowest unused file descriptor value; it is a copy of `oldfd`. `dup()` returns a nonnegative integer on success or `-1` on failure.

`int dup2(int oldfd, int newfd)`
: Makes `newfd` be a copy of `oldfd`; if `newfd` is open, it's closed first, as if by `close()`. `dup2()` returns the new descriptor or `-1` if there was a problem.

Remember Figure 9.1, in which two processes shared pointers to the same file entry in the kernel's file table? Well, `dup()` and `dup2()` create the same situation within a single process—see Figure 9.4.

In this figure, the process executed '`dup2(1, 3)`' to make file descriptor `3` a copy of standard output, file descriptor `1`. Exactly as described before, the two descriptors share the file offset for the open file.

In Section 4.4.2, "Opening and Closing Files," page 88, we mentioned that `open()` *always* returns the lowest unused integer file descriptor value for the file being opened, and the same is true of `creat()`. In fact, almost all system calls that return new file descriptors follow this rule, not just `open()` and `creat()`. (`dup2()` is an exception since it provides a way to get a particular new file descriptor, even if it's not the lowest unused one.)

Given the "return lowest unused number" rule combined with `dup()`, it's now easy to move a pipe's file descriptors into place as standard input and output. Assuming that the current process is a shell and that it needs to fork two children to set up a simple two-stage pipeline, here are the steps:

1. Create the pipe with `pipe()`. This must be done first so that the two children can inherit the open file descriptors.
2. Fork what we'll call the "left-hand child." This is the one whose standard output goes down the pipe. In this child, do the following:

   a. Use '`close(pipefd[0])`' since the read end of the pipe isn't needed in the left-hand child.
   b. Use '`close(1)`' to close the original standard output.
   c. Use '`dup(pipefd[1])`' to copy the write end of the pipe to file descriptor `1`.
   d. Use '`close(pipefd[1])`' since we don't need two copies of the open descriptor.
   e. Exec the program to be run.

3. Fork what we'll call the "right-hand child." This is the one whose standard input comes from the pipe. The steps in this child are the mirror image of those in the left-hand child:

   a. Use '`close(pipefd[1])`' since the write end of the pipe isn't needed in the right-hand child.
   b. Use '`close(0)`' to close the original standard input.
   c. Use '`dup(pipefd[0])`' to copy the read end of the pipe to file descriptor `0`.
   d. Use '`close(pipefd[0])`' since we don't need two copies of the open descriptor.
   e. Exec the program to be run.

4. In the parent, close both ends of the pipe: '`close(pipefd[0]); close(pipefd[1])`'.
5. Finally, use `wait()` (or a variant) in the parent to wait for both children to finish.

Note how important it is to close the unused copies of the pipe's file descriptors. As we pointed out earlier, a file isn't closed until the last open file descriptor for it is closed. This is true even though multiple processes share the file descriptors. Closing unused file descriptors matters because the process reading from the pipe won't get an end-of-file indication until *all* the copies of the write end have been closed.

In our case, after the two children are forked, there are three processes: the parent and the two children, each of which has copies of the two pipe file descriptors. The parent closes both ends since it doesn't need the pipe. The left-hand child is writing down the pipe, so it has to close the read end. The right-hand child is reading from the pipe, so it has to close the write end. This leaves exactly one copy of each file descriptor open.

When the left-hand child finishes, it exits. The system then closes all of its file descriptors. When that happens, the right-hand child finally receives the end-of-file notification, and it too can then finish up and exit.

The following program, `ch-processes-pipeline.c`, creates the equivalent of the following shell pipeline:

```
$ echo hi there | sed s/hi/hello/g
hello there
```

Here's the program:

```
/* ch-processes-pipeline.c --- fork two processes into their own pipeline.
                               Minimal error checking for brevity. */

#include <stdio.h>
#include <errno.h>
#include <stdlib.h>
#include <sys/types.h>
#include <sys/wait.h>
#include <unistd.h>

int pipefd[2];

extern void left_child(void), right_child(void);

/* main --- fork children, wait for them to finish */

int
main(int argc, char **argv)
{
    pid_t left_pid, right_pid;
    pid_t ret;
    int status;

    if (pipe(pipefd) < 0) {     /* create pipe, very first thing */
        perror("pipe");
        exit(EXIT_FAILURE);
    }

    if ((left_pid = fork()) < 0) {  /* fork left-hand child */
        perror("fork");
        exit(EXIT_FAILURE);
    } else if (left_pid == 0)
        left_child();

    if ((right_pid = fork()) < 0) { /* fork right-hand child */
        perror("fork");
        exit(EXIT_FAILURE);
    } else if (right_pid == 0)
        right_child();
```

```
40
41      close(pipefd[0]);       /* close parent's copy of pipe */
42      close(pipefd[1]);
43
44      while ((ret = wait(& status)) > 0) {    /* wait for children */
45          if (ret == left_pid)
46              printf("left child terminated, status: %x\n", status);
47          else if (ret == right_pid)
48              printf("right child terminated, status: %x\n", status);
49          else
50              printf("yow! unknown child %d terminated, status %x\n",
51                  ret, status);
52      }
53
54      return EXIT_SUCCESS;
55  }
```

Lines 24–27 create the pipe. This has to be done first.

Lines 29–33 create the left-hand child, and lines 35–39 create the right-hand child. In both instances, the parent continues a linear execution path through `main()` while the child calls the appropriate function to manipulate file descriptors and do the exec.

Lines 41–42 close the parent's copy of the pipe.

Lines 44–52 loop, reaping children, until `wait()` returns an error. The code continues:

```
57  /* left_child --- do the work for the left child */
58
59  void
60  left_child(void)
61  {
62      static char *left_argv[]  = { "echo", "hi", "there", NULL };
63
64      close(pipefd[0]);
65      close(1);
66      int junk = dup(pipefd[1]);
67      close(pipefd[1]);
68
69      execvp("echo", left_argv);
70      _exit(errno == ENOENT ? 127 : 126);
71  }
72
73  /* right_child --- do the work for the right child */
74
75  void
76  right_child(void)
77  {
78      static char *right_argv[] = { "sed", "s/hi/hello/g", NULL };
```

```
79
80        close(pipefd[1]);
81        close(0);
82        int junk = dup(pipefd[0]);
83        close(pipefd[0]);
84
85        execvp("sed", right_argv);
86        _exit(errno == ENOENT ? 127 : 126);
87 }
```

Lines 57–71 are the code for the left-hand child. The procedure follows the steps given above to close the unneeded end of the pipe, close the original standard output, `dup()` the pipe's write end to `1`, and then close the original write end. At that point, line 69 calls `execvp()`, and if it fails, line 70 calls `_exit()`. (Remember that line 70 is never executed if `execvp()` succeeds.)

Lines 73–87 do the similar steps for the right-hand child.

In both functions (lines 66 and 82), the result of `dup()` is assigned to a junk variable, since on current systems the compiler warns if the return value from `dup()` is not used. In a production program, we should be checking the return value for failure. Instead, we are (rather cavalierly) relying on it to return the lowest available file descriptor number, `1` or `0`, respectively.

Here's what happens when the program runs:

```
$ ch-processes-pipeline                  Run the program
left child terminated, status: 0         Left child finishes before output(!)
hello there                              Output from right child
right child terminated, status: 0
$ ch-processes-pipeline                  Run the program again
hello there                              Output from right child and ...
right child terminated, status: 0        Right child finishes before left one
left child terminated, status: 0
```

Note that the order in which the children finish isn't deterministic. It depends on the system load and many other factors that can influence process scheduling. You should be careful to avoid making ordering assumptions when you write code that creates multiple processes, particularly the code that calls one of the `wait()` family of functions.

The whole process is illustrated in Figure 9.5.

Figure 9.5-A depicts the situation after the parent has created the pipe (lines 24–27) and the two children (lines 29–39).

Figure 9.5-B shows the situation after the parent has closed the pipe (lines 41–42) and started to wait for the children (lines 44–52). Each child has moved the pipe into place as standard output (left child, lines 64–67) and standard input (right child, lines 80–83).

Finally, Figure 9.5-C depicts the situation after the children have closed off the original pipe (lines 64 and 80) and called `execvp()` (lines 69 and 85).

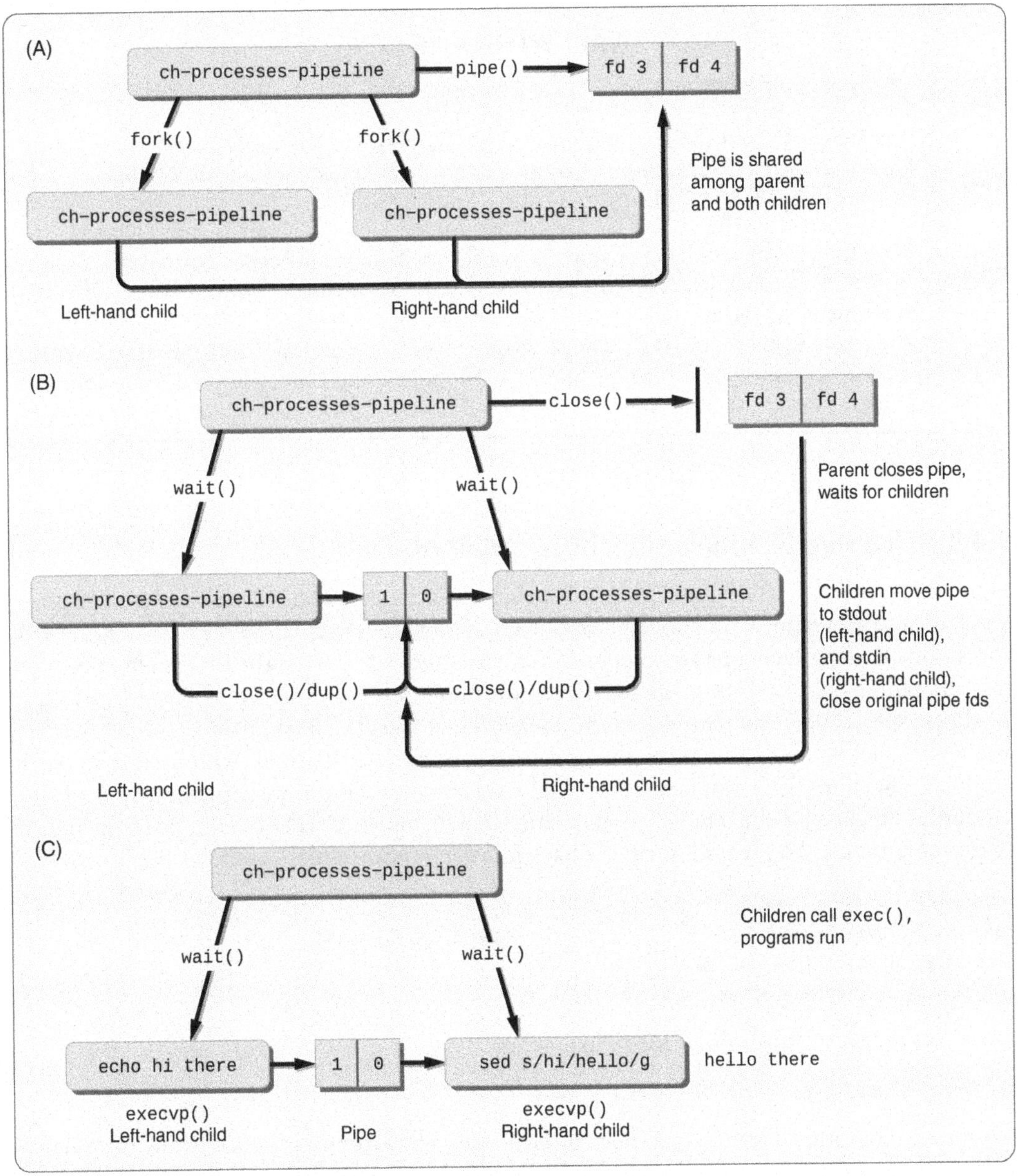

Figure 9.5: Parent creating a pipeline

> **dup() versus dup2()**
>
> Chet Ramey notes the following:
>
> > [For step] 2(c): you should always use `dup2()` rather than rely on fd `1` being the lowest-numbered file descriptor. A script may have closed fd `0`. Same with 3(c), but only for completeness.
>
> Chet writes from his perspective as maintainer of the shell. In `ch-processes-pipeline.c`, we didn't close fd `0`, so using `dup()` directly is perfectly safe, and it clearly illustrates the canonical steps for setting up a pipeline.
>
> However, using `dup2(pipefd[1], 1)` instead of '`close(1); dup(pipefd[1])`' guarantees that the pipe file descriptor will become the new fd `1`. In short, using `dup2()` in production code is the right idea.

9.4.2 Creating Nonlinear Pipelines: `/dev/fd/XX`

Many modern Unix systems, including GNU/Linux, support special files in the `/dev/fd` directory.[10] These files represent open file descriptors, with names such as `/dev/fd/0`, `/dev/fd/1`, and so on. Passing such a name to `open()` returns a new file descriptor that is effectively the same as calling `dup()` on the given file descriptor number.

These special files find their use at the shell level: at least the Bash, `ksh88` (some versions), and `ksh93` shells supply a feature called *process substitution* that makes it possible to create *nonlinear* pipelines. The notation at the shell level is '`<( ... )`' for input pipelines, and '`>( ... )`' for output pipelines. For example, suppose you wish to apply the `diff` command to the output of two commands. You would normally have to use temporary files:

```
command1 > /tmp/out.$$.1
command2 > /tmp/out.$$.2
diff /tmp/out.$$.1 /tmp/out.$$.2
rm /tmp/out.$$.1 /tmp/out.$$.2
```

With process substitution, it looks like this:

```
diff <(command1) <(command2)
```

No messy temporary files to remember to clean up. For example, the following commands show that on our system, `/bin` is a symbolic link to `/usr/bin`:

```
$ cd /bin
$ diff <(pwd) <(/bin/pwd)
1c1
< /bin
---
> /usr/bin
```

---

[10] On GNU/Linux systems, `/dev/fd` is a symbolic link to `/proc/self/fd`, but since `/dev/fd` is the common place for these special files, that's what you should use in your code.

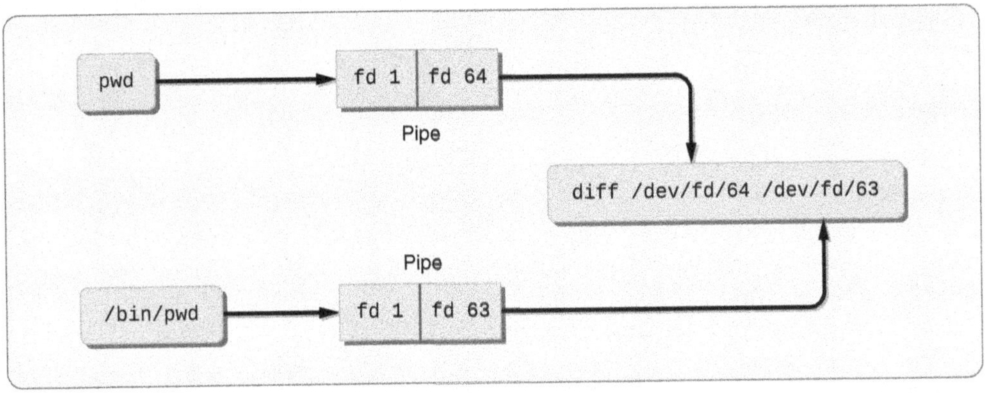

Figure 9.6: Process substitution

The plain `pwd` is the one built into the shell: it prints the current logical pathname as managed by the shell with `cd`. The `/bin/pwd` program does a physical filesystem walk to print the pathname.

How does process substitution work? The shell creates the subsidiary commands.[11] ('`pwd`' and '`/bin/pwd`') Each one's output is connected to a pipe, with the read end open on a new file descriptor for the main process ('`diff`'). The shell then passes *the names of files in* `/dev/fd` to the main process as the command-line argument. We can see this by turning on execution tracing in the shell:

```
$ set -x                              Turn on execution tracing
$ diff <(pwd) <(/bin/pwd)             Run command
++ pwd                                Shell trace: subsidiary program
+ diff /dev/fd/63 /dev/fd/62          Shell trace: main program, note arguments
++ /bin/pwd                           Shell trace: subsidiary program
1c1                                   Output from diff
< /bin
---
> /usr/bin
```

This is illustrated in Figure 9.6.

If your system has `/dev/fd`, you may be able to take advantage of this facility as well. Do be careful, though, to document what you're doing. The file descriptor manipulation at the C level is considerably less transparent than the corresponding shell notations!

As a side note, the Bash shell uses FIFOs if `/dev/fd` isn't available. So if Bash is your shell, you can use process substitution on any POSIX-compliant system.

9.4.3 Managing File Attributes: `fcntl()`

The `fcntl()` ("file control") system call provides control over miscellaneous attributes of either the file descriptor itself or the underlying open file. The GNU/Linux *fcntl*(2) manpage describes it this way:

[11] Although we've shown simple commands, arbitrary pipelines are allowed.

```
#include <unistd.h>                                         POSIX
#include <fcntl.h>

int fcntl(int fd, int cmd, ... /* arg */ );
```

In other words, it takes at least two arguments; based on the second argument, it may take additional arguments.

This system call is also used for applying and removing file locks. However, file locking is a large topic in its own right; we delay discussion until Section 16.2, "Locking Files," page 558.

9.4.3.1 The Close-on-Exec and Close-on-Fork Flags

After a `fork()` and before an `exec()`, you should make sure that the new program inherits only the open files it needs. You don't want a child process messing with the parent's open files unless it's supposed to. On the flip side, if a parent has lots of files open, that will artificially limit the number of new files the child can open. (See the sidebar "A Close-on-Exec War Story from `gawk`," page 318.)

Organizationally, this behavior may present a problem. The part of your program that starts a new child shouldn't particularly need access to the other part(s) of your program that manipulates open files. And a loop like the following is painful, since there may not be any additional open files:

```
int j;

for (j = getdtablesize(); j >= 3; j--)    /* close all but 0, 1, 2 */
    (void) close(j);
```

The solution is the *close-on-exec flag*. This is an attribute of the *file descriptor itself*, not the underlying open file. When this flag is set, the system automatically closes the file when the process does an exec. By setting this flag as soon as you open a file, you don't have to worry about any child processes accidentally inheriting it. (The Bash shell automatically sets this flag for all file descriptors it opens for its own use.)

For most of the time that Unix, GNU/Linux, and POSIX have existed, the only way to set the close-on-exec flag was with `fcntl()`, which is what we're about to discuss. But we note that more recently, you can also set the flag when you open the file by using the `O_CLOEXEC` flag to `open()` (see Section 4.6.4, "Revisiting `open()`," page 104).

Getting back to `fcntl()`, the `cmd` argument has two values related to the file descriptor flags:

`F_GETFD`
: Retrieve the file descriptor flags. The return value is the setting of all the file descriptor flags or `-1` on error.

`F_SETFD`
: Set the file descriptor flags to the value in `arg` (the third argument). The return value is `0` on success or `-1` on error.

For many years, only one file descriptor flag was defined: `FD_CLOEXEC`. This symbolic constant is a POSIX invention,[12] and most code uses a straight `1` or `0`:

```
if (fcntl(fd, F_SETFD, 1) < 0) ...   /* try to set close-on-exec, handle any errors */

if (fcntl(fd, F_GETFD) == 1) ...     /* close-on-exec flag is already set */
```

However, the POSIX definition allows for additional flags, and thus the correct way to write such code is along these lines:

```
int fd;
long fd_flags;

if ((fd_flags = fcntl(fd, F_GETFD)) < 0)        Retrieve flags
    /* handle error */

fd_flags |= FD_CLOEXEC;                         Add close-on-exec flag
if (fcntl(fd, F_SETFD, fd_flags) < 0)           Set flags
    /* handle error */
```

The 2024 POSIX standard introduces an additional flag, `FD_CLOFORK`. A file descriptor marked with this flag in the parent is closed in the child after a call to `fork()`. It parallels the close-on-exec flag in that it can also be set with `open()` using `O_CLOFORK`, and in many other aspects, as we're about to see.

To enable setting the close-on-exec and close-on-fork flags at the same time as a file descriptor comes into being, POSIX added a number of system calls and flags for the system calls. In other words, file descriptor creation (via `open()` or `dup()`) and setting the flag(s) become a single *atomic* operation. This is important in threaded programs, where one thread might be opening a file, and before it could set one of the flags, another thread would do a fork or exec, "leaking" open file descriptors into the new process or program. (Yet another instance of a race condition.)

Bearing this in mind makes it easier to understand why the various flags and `fcntl()` commands that we're about to see exist and make sense.

NOTE

The close-on-exec and close-on-fork flags are a property of the *descriptor*, not the underlying *file*. Thus, the new descriptor returned by `dup()` or `dup2()` (or by `fcntl()` with `F_DUPD`, as we're about to see) does *not* inherit the close-on-exec or close-on-fork settings of the original descriptor. If you want them set for the new file descriptor also, you must remember to do it yourself, or when you create the descriptor.

This behavior makes sense: if you've just called `dup()`, copying one end of a pipe to `0` or `1`, you don't want the system to close it for you as soon as the process does an exec!

---

[12]The POSIX standard purposely does not give it a value. However, for old code to continue to work, the only value any implementation could sensibly use is `1`.

A Close-on-Exec War Story from gawk

Within the awk language, I/O statements use a redirection notation similar to that of the shell. This includes one-way pipes to and from subprocesses:

```
print "something brilliant" > "/some/file"              Output to file
getline my_record < "/some/other/file                   Input from file

print "more words of wisdom" | "a_reader process"       Output to subprocess
"a_writer process" | getline some_input                 Input from subprocess
```

The awk interpreter has an open file descriptor for all file redirections, and for the pipe notations that create a subprocess, the awk interpreter creates a pipe and then does a fork and exec of a shell to run the command as given by the string.

Now, on modern systems, part of the C runtime startup code (that runs before `main()` is called) needs to temporarily open files in order to manage the use of shared libraries. This means that there *must* be at least a few unused file descriptors available to a brand-new program after an exec, or else the program just won't run.

One day, a user reported that when the awk program had the maximum number of files open, any child process that it tried to fork and exec for a pipeline would fail to start!

You can probably guess what was happening. The child shell inherited all the open file descriptors that gawk itself was using for its redirections. We modified gawk to set the close-on-exec flag for all file and pipe redirections, and that fixed the problem.

9.4.3.2 Duplicating a File Descriptor and Setting Flags Atomically

The 2024 POSIX standard introduces an additional system call, `dup3()`:

```
#include <unistd.h>                                   POSIX

int dup3(int fildes, int fildes2, int flags);
```

This call is like `dup2()`. However, it accepts a third argument that specifies the file descriptor flags. Passing `FD_CLOEXEC` lets you create the new file descriptor and mark it close-on-exec in one action. You may instead pass in `FD_CLOFORK`, or bitwise-OR both flags together. GNU/Linux has had the `dup3()` call for a long time; POSIX apparently picked it up from there.

As we discussed earlier, the point of `dup3()` is to create the file descriptor and set the flag(s) atomically, avoiding any race conditions in threaded code.

9.4.3.3 File Descriptor Duplication

When `fcntl()`'s `cmd` argument is `F_DUPFD`, the behavior is similar, but not quite identical, to `dup2()`. In this case, `arg` is a file descriptor representing the *lowest acceptable value* for the new file descriptor:

```
int new_fd = fcntl(old_fd, F_DUPFD, 7);         Return value is between 7 and maximum, or failure

int new_fd = dup2(old_fd, 7);                   Return value is 7, or failure
```

You can simulate the behavior of `dup()`, which returns the lowest free file descriptor, by using '`fcntl(old_fd, F_DUPFD, 0)`'.

If you remember that file descriptors are just indexes into an internal table, understanding how this function works should be clear. The third argument merely provides the index at which the kernel should start its search for an unused file descriptor.

Whether to use `fcntl()` with `F_DUPFD` or one of the `dup()` functions in your own code is largely a matter of taste. All four APIs are part of POSIX and are widely supported. We have a mild preference for `dup()` and `dup2()` since those are more specific in their action, and thus are more self-documenting. But because all of them are pretty simple, this reasoning may not convince you.

POSIX provides some additional commands:

`F_DUPFD_CLOEXEC`
: This duplicates the file descriptor and sets the close-on-exec flag all in one go. GNU/Linux supports this command.

`F_DUPFD_CLOFORK`
: This is like `F_DUPFD_CLOEXEC`, but it sets the close-on-fork flag instead. This command was introduced in the 2024 POSIX standard.

Again, the point of both of these commands is to atomically create the descriptor and set the given flag. Unlike with `dup3()`, you must choose one or the other.

9.4.3.4 Manipulation of File Status Flags and Access Modes

In Section 4.6.4, "Revisiting `open()`," page 104, we provided the full list of `O_`*xx* flags that `open()` accepts. We can break these down by function, classifying them as described in Table 9.5.

Besides setting the various flags initially with `open()`, you can use `fcntl()` to retrieve the current settings, as well as to change them. This is done with the `F_GETFL` and `F_SETFL` values for `cmd`, respectively. For example, you might use these commands to change the setting of the nonblocking flag, `O_NONBLOCK`, like so:

```
int fd_flags;

if ((fd_flags = fcntl(fd, F_GETFL)) < 0)
    /* handle error */
```

Table 9.5: `O_`*xx* flags for `open()`, `creat()`, and `fcntl()`

Category	Functions	Flags
File access	`open()`, `fcntl()`	`O_RDONLY`, `O_RDWR`, `O_WRONLY`
File creation	`open()`	`O_CREAT`, `O_EXCL`, `O_NOCTTY`, `O_TRUNC`
File status	`open()`, `fcntl()`	`O_APPEND`, `O_DSYNC`, `O_NONBLOCK`, `O_RSYNC`, `O_SYNC`

```
if ((fd_flags & O_NONBLOCK) != 0) {              /* Nonblocking flag is set */
    fd_flags &= ~O_NONBLOCK;                     /* Clear it */
    if (fcntl(fd, F_SETFL, fd_flags) != 0)       /* Give kernel new value */
        /* handle error */
}
```

Besides the modes themselves, the `O_ACCMODE` symbolic constant is a *mask* you can use to retrieve the file access modes from the return value:

```
fd_flags = fcntl(fd, F_GETFL);

switch (fd_flags & O_ACCMODE) {
case O_RDONLY:
    ... action for read-only ...
    break;
case O_WRONLY:
    ... action for write-only ...
    break;
case O_RDWR:
    ... action for read/write ...
    break;
}
```

POSIX requires that `O_RDONLY`, `O_RDWR`, and `O_WRONLY` be bitwise distinct; thus, code such as that just shown is guaranteed to work and is an easy way to determine how an arbitrary file descriptor was opened.

By using `F_SETFL`, you can change these modes as well, although permission checking still applies. According to the GNU/Linux *fcntl*(2) manpage, you may change only the `O_APPEND`, `O_ASYNC`, `O_DIRECT`, `O_NOATIME`, and `O_NONBLOCK` flags. You cannot change the `O_DSYNC` and `O_SYNC` flags.

9.4.3.5 Nonblocking I/O for Pipes and FIFOs

Earlier, we used the metaphor of two people washing and drying dishes, and using a dish drainer to describe the way a pipe works: when the drainer fills up, the dish washer stops, and when it empties out, the dish dryer stops. This is *blocking* behavior: the producer or consumer blocks in the call to `write()` or `read()`, waiting either for more room in the pipe or for more data to come into it.

In the real world, a human being waiting for the dish drainer to empty out or fill up would not just stand by, immobile.[13] Rather, the idle one would go and find some other kitchen task to do (such as sweeping up all the kids' crumbs on the floor) until the dish drainer was ready again.

In Unix/POSIX parlance, this concept is termed *nonblocking I/O*. That is, the requested I/O either completes or returns an error value indicating no data (for the reader) or no room

---

[13] Well, we're ignoring the idea that two spouses might want to talk and enjoy each other's company.

(for the writer). Nonblocking I/O applies to pipes and FIFOs, not to regular disk files. It can also apply to certain devices, such as terminals (which are beyond the scope of this book), and to network connections.

The `O_NONBLOCK` flag can be used with `open()` to specify nonblocking I/O, and it can be set or cleared with `fcntl()`. For `open()` and `read()`, nonblocking I/O is straightforward.

Opening a FIFO with `O_NONBLOCK` set or clear displays the following behavior:

`open("/fifo/file", O_RDONLY, mode)`
: Blocks until the FIFO is opened for writing.

`open("/fifo/file", O_RDONLY|O_NONBLOCK, mode)`
: Opens the file, returning immediately.

`open("/fifo/file", O_WRONLY, mode)`
: Blocks until the FIFO is opened for reading.

`open("/fifo/file", O_WRONLY|O_NONBLOCK, mode)`
: If the FIFO has been opened for reading, opens the FIFO and returns immediately. Otherwise, returns an error (return value of `-1` and `errno` set to `ENXIO`).

As described for regular pipes, a `read()` of a FIFO that is no longer open for writing returns end-of-file (a return value of `0`). The `O_NONBLOCK` flag is irrelevant in this case. Things get more interesting for an *empty* pipe or FIFO—one that is still open for writing but has no data in it:

`read(fd, buf, count)`, and `O_NONBLOCK` clear
: The `read()` blocks until more data comes into the pipe or FIFO.

`read(fd, buf, count)`, and `O_NONBLOCK` set
: The `read()` returns `-1` immediately, with `errno` set to `EAGAIN`.

Finally, `write()` behavior is more complicated. To discuss it, we have to first introduce the concept of an *atomic write*. An atomic write is one in which all the requested data is written together, without being interleaved with data from other writes. POSIX defines the constant `PIPE_BUF` in `<limits.h>`. Writes of amounts less than or equal to `PIPE_BUF` bytes to a pipe or FIFO either succeed or block, according to the details we get into shortly. The minimum value for `PIPE_BUF` is `_POSIX_PIPE_BUF`, which is `512`. `PIPE_BUF` itself can be larger; current GLIBC systems define it to be `4096`, but in any case you should use the symbolic constant and not expect `PIPE_BUF` to be the same value across different systems.

In all cases, for pipes and FIFOs, a `write()` appends data to the end of the pipe. This derives from the fact that pipes don't have file offsets: they aren't seekable.

Also in all cases, as mentioned, writes of up to `PIPE_BUF` are atomic: the data is not interleaved with the data from other writes. Data from a write of more than `PIPE_BUF` bytes can be interleaved with the data from other writes *on arbitrary boundaries*. This last means that you *cannot* expect every `PIPE_BUF` subchunk of a large amount of data to be written atomically. The `O_NONBLOCK` setting does not affect this rule.

As with `read()`, when `O_NONBLOCK` is not set, `write()` blocks until all the data is written.

Things are most complicated with `O_NONBLOCK` set. For a pipe or FIFO, the behavior is as follows:

	space ≥ nbytes	**space < nbytes**
`nbytes` ≤ `PIPE_BUF`	`write()` succeeds	`write()` returns `-1`/`EAGAIN`
	space > 0	**space = 0**
`nbytes` > `PIPE_BUF`	`write()` writes what it can	`write()` returns `-1`/`EAGAIN`

For nonpipe and non-FIFO files to which `O_NONBLOCK` can be applied, the behavior is as follows:

space > 0 `write()` writes what it can.

space = 0 `write()` returns `-1`/`EAGAIN`.

Although there is a bewildering array of behavior changes based on pipe/nonpipe, `O_NONBLOCK` set or clear, the space available in the pipe, and the size of the attempted write, the rules are intended to make programming straightforward:

- End-of-file is always distinguishable: `read()` returns zero bytes.
- If no data is available to be read, `read()` either succeeds or returns a "nothing to read" indication: `-1` and `EAGAIN`, which means "try again later."
- If there's no room to write data, `write()` either blocks until it can succeed (`O_NONBLOCK` clear) or fails with a "no room right now" error: `EAGAIN`.
- When there's room, as much data will be written as can be, so that eventually all the data can be written out.

In summary, if you intend to use nonblocking I/O, any code that uses `write()` has to be able to handle a short write, where less than the requested amount is successfully written. Robust code should be written this way anyway: even for a regular file, it's possible that a disk could become full and that a `write()` will only partially succeed.

Furthermore, you should be prepared to handle `EAGAIN`, understanding that in this case `write()` failing isn't necessarily a fatal error. The same is true of code that uses nonblocking I/O for reading: recognize that `EAGAIN` isn't fatal here either. (It may pay, though, to count such occurrences, giving up after too many.)

Nonblocking I/O does complicate your life, no doubt about it. But for many applications, it's a necessity that lets you get your job done. Consider the print spooler again. The spooler daemon can't afford to sit in a blocking `read()` on the FIFO file to which incoming jobs are submitted. It has to be able to monitor running jobs as well and possibly periodically check the status of the printer devices (for example, to make sure they have paper or aren't jammed).

Table 9.6: `fcntl()` summary

cmd value	arg value	Returns
`F_DUPFD`	Lowest new descriptor	Duplicate of the `fd` argument.
`F_DUPFD_CLOEXEC`	Lowest new descriptor	Duplicate of the `fd` argument, with close-on-exec set.
`F_DUPFD_CLOFORK`	Lowest new descriptor	Duplicate of the `fd` argument, with close-on-fork set. New in the 2024 POSIX standard.
`F_GETFD`		Retrieve file descriptor flags (close-on-exec, close-on-fork).
`F_SETFD`	New flag value	Set file descriptor flags (close-on-exec, close-on-fork).
`F_GETFL`		Retrieve flags on underlying file.
`F_SETFL`	New flag value	Set flags on underlying file.

9.4.3.6 `fcntl()` Summary

The `fcntl()` system call is summarized in Table 9.6.

The file creation, status, and access flags are copied when a file descriptor is duplicated. The close-on-exec and close-on-fork flags are not.

9.5 Example: Two-Way Pipes in gawk

A *two-way pipe* connects two processes bidirectionally. Typically, for at least one of the processes, both standard input and standard output are set up on pipes to the other process. The Korn shell (`ksh`) introduced two-way pipes at the language level, with what it terms a *coprocess*:

```
database engine command and arguments |&        Start coprocess in background
print -p "database command"                     Write to coprocess
read -p db_response                             Read from coprocess
```

Here, *database engine* represents any back-end program that can be driven by a front end, in this case the `ksh` script. *database engine* has standard input and standard output connected to the shell by way of two separate one-way pipes.[14] This is illustrated in Figure 9.7.

In standard `awk`, pipes to or from subprocesses are one-way: there's no way to send data to a program and read a response back from it—you have to use a temporary file. GNU `awk` (`gawk`) borrows the '`|&`' notation from `ksh` to extend the `awk` language:

```
print "a command" |& "database engine"           Start coprocess, write to it
"database engine" |& getline db_response         Read from coprocess
```

[14] There is only one default coprocess (accessible with '`read -p`' and '`print -p`') at a time. Shell scripts can use the `exec` command with a special redirection notation to move the coprocess's file descriptors to specific numbers. Once this is done, another coprocess can be started. Bash has a considerably more sophisticated coprocess mechanism, but with different syntax.

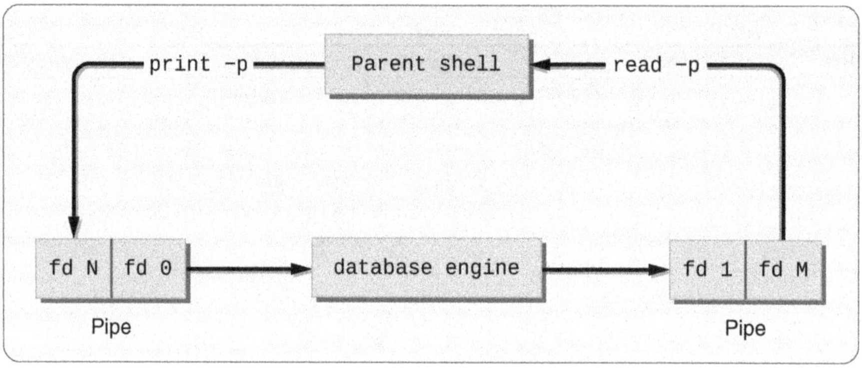

Figure 9.7: Korn shell coprocess

`gawk` also uses the '`|&`' notation for TCP/IP sockets (see Chapter 14, "Sockets and Basic Networking," page 473). The following code from `io.c` in the `gawk` 5.3.0 distribution is the part of the `two_way_open()` function that sets up a simple coprocess: it creates two pipes, forks the child process, and does all the file descriptor manipulation. We have omitted a number of irrelevant pieces of code (this function is bigger than it should be):

```
static int
two_way_open(const char *str, struct redirect *rp, int extfd)
{
    ...
    /* case 4: two way pipe to a child process */
    {
    int ptoc[2], ctop[2];
    int pid;
    int save_errno;
    ...
    if (pipe(ptoc) < 0)
        return false;   /* errno set, diagnostic from caller */

    if (pipe(ctop) < 0) {
        save_errno = errno;
        close(ptoc[0]);
        close(ptoc[1]);
        errno = save_errno;
        return false;
    }
```

The first step is to create the two pipes. `ptoc` is "parent to child," and `ctop` is "child to parent." Bear in mind as you read the code that index `0` is the read end and index `1` is the write end.

Lines 2367–2368 create the first pipe, `ptoc`. Lines 2370–2376 create the second one, closing the first one if this fails. This is important. Failure to close an open but unused pipe leads to *file descriptor leaks*. Like memory, file descriptors are a finite resource, and once you run out of them, they're gone.[15] The same is true of open files: make sure that all your error-handling code always closes any open files or pipes that you won't need when a failure happens.

`save_errno` saves the `errno` values as set by `pipe()`, on the off chance that `close()` might fail (line 2371). `errno` is then restored on line 2374. The code continues:

```
2452    if ((pid = fork()) < 0) {
2453        save_errno = errno;
2454        close(ptoc[0]); close(ptoc[1]);
2455        close(ctop[0]); close(ctop[1]);
2456        errno = save_errno;
2457        return false;
2458    }
```

Lines 2452–2458 fork the child, this time closing both pipes if `fork()` failed. Here too, the original `errno` value is saved and restored for later use in producing a diagnostic.

Lines 2460–2478 handle the child's code, with appropriate error checking and messages at each step:

```
2460    if (pid == 0) { /* child */
2461        if (close(1) == -1)
2462            fatal(_("close of stdout in child failed: %s"),
2463                strerror(errno));
2464        if (dup(ctop[1]) != 1)
2465            fatal(_("moving pipe to stdout in child failed (dup: %s)"), strerror(errno));
2466        if (close(0) == -1)
2467            fatal(_("close of stdin in child failed: %s"),
2468                strerror(errno));
2469        if (dup(ptoc[0]) != 0)
2470            fatal(_("moving pipe to stdin in child failed (dup: %s)"), strerror(errno));
2471        if (   close(ptoc[0]) == -1 || close(ptoc[1]) == -1
2472            || close(ctop[0]) == -1 || close(ctop[1]) == -1)
2473            fatal(_("close of pipe failed: %s"), strerror(errno));
2474        /* stderr does NOT get dup'ed onto child's stdout */
2475        set_sigpipe_to_default();
2476        execl("/bin/sh", "sh", "-c", str, NULL);
2477        _exit(errno == ENOENT ? 127 : 126);
2478    }
```

Line 2461 closes standard output. Line 2464 copies the child-to-parent pipe write end to `1`. Line 2466 closes standard input, and line 2469 copies the parent-to-child read end to `0`. If this all works, the child's standard input and output are now in place, connected to the parent.

---

[15] Well, you can close them, obviously. But if you don't know they're open, then they're lost just as effectively as memory through a memory leak.

(Hmmm ... this code could probably benefit from Chet Ramey's advice to use `dup2()` instead of `close()` plus `dup()`.)

Lines 2471–2478 close all four original pipe file descriptors since they're no longer needed. Line 2474 reminds us that standard error remains in place. This is the best decision, since the user will see errors from the coprocess. An `awk` program that must capture standard error can use the '`2>&1`' shell notation in the command to redirect the coprocess's standard error or send it to a separate file.

Finally, lines 2476–2477 attempt to run `execl()` on the shell and exit appropriately if that fails. Next comes the parent's code:

```
2481        /* parent */
            ...
2486        rp->pid = pid;
2487        rp->iop = iop_alloc(ctop[0], str, 0);
2488        find_input_parser(rp->iop);
2489        iop_finish(rp->iop);
2490        if (! rp->iop->valid) {
2491            if (! do_traditional && rp->iop->errcode != 0)
2492                update_ERRNO_int(rp->iop->errcode);
2493            iop_close(rp->iop);
2494            rp->iop = NULL;
2495            (void) close(ctop[1]);
2496            (void) close(ptoc[0]);
2497            (void) close(ptoc[1]);
2498            (void) kill(pid, SIGKILL);
2499
2500            return false;
2501        }
```

The first step in the parent is to manage the input end from the coprocess. The `rp` pointer points to a `struct redirect`, which maintains a field to hold the child's PID, a `FILE *` for output, and an `IOBUF *` pointer named `iop`. The `IOBUF` is a `gawk` internal data structure for doing input. It in turn keeps a copy of the underlying file descriptor.

Line 2486 saves the process ID value. Line 2487 allocates a new `IOBUF` for the given file descriptor and command string. The third argument here is zero; it's used to initialize an internal copy of `errno`.

If the allocation fails, lines 2490–2501 clean up by setting `gawk`'s `ERRNO` variable, closing the `*iop` structure, closing the pipes, and sending a "kill" signal to the child process to cause it to terminate. (The `kill()` function is described in Section 10.6.7, "Sending Signals: `kill()` and `killpg()`," page 358.) The next lines are analogous:

```
2502        rp->output.fp = fdopen(ptoc[1], binmode("w"));
2503        rp->output.mode = "w";
2504        rp->output.name = str;
2505        if (rp->output.fp == NULL) {
2506            iop_close(rp->iop);
2507            rp->iop = NULL;
2508            (void) close(ctop[0]);
```

```
2509            (void) close(ctop[1]);
2510            (void) close(ptoc[0]);
2511            (void) close(ptoc[1]);
2512            (void) kill(pid, SIGKILL);
2513
2514            return false;
2515        }
```

Lines 2502–2515 set up the parent's output to the child, saving the file descriptor for the parent-to-child pipe write end in a `FILE *` by means of `fdopen()`. If this fails, lines 2505–2515 take the same action as before: closing all the pipe descriptors and sending a signal to the child.

From this point on, the write end of the parent-to-child pipe, and the read end of the child-to-parent pipe are held down in the larger structures: the `FILE *` and `IOBUF`, respectively. They are closed automatically by the regular routines that close these structures. However, two tasks remain:

```
2520        os_close_on_exec(ctop[0], str, "pipe", "from");
2521        os_close_on_exec(ptoc[1], str, "pipe", "from");
2522
2523        (void) close(ptoc[0]);
2524        (void) close(ctop[1]);
            ...
2527        return true;
2528        }
```

Lines 2520–2521 set the close-on-exec flag for the two descriptors that will remain open. `os_close_on_exec()` is a simple wrapper routine that does the job on Unix- and POSIX-compatible systems but does nothing on systems that don't have a close-on-exec flag. This buries the portability issue in a single place and avoids lots of messy `#ifdef`s throughout the code here and elsewhere in `io.c`. (Line 2521 should indicate that the pipe is `"to"` the child process. We have since fixed this.)

Finally, lines 2523–2524 close the ends of the pipes that the parent doesn't need, and line 2527 returns `true`, for success.

9.6 Suggested Reading

Job control is complicated, involving process groups, sessions, the wait mechanisms, signals, and manipulation of the terminal's process group. As such, we've chosen not to get into the details. However, you may wish to look at these books:

1. *Advanced Programming in the UNIX Environment*, 3rd ed., by W. Richard Stevens and Stephen A. Rago. Addison-Wesley, 2013. ISBN-13: 978-0-321-63773-4.

This book is both complete and thorough, covering elementary and advanced Unix programming. It does an excellent job of covering process groups, sessions, job control, and signals.

2. *The Design and Implementation of the FreeBSD Operating System*, 2nd ed., by Marshall Kirk McKusick, George V. Neville-Neil, and Robert N. M. Watson. Addison-Wesley, 2015. ISBN-13: 978-0-321-96897-5.

   This book gives a good overview of the same material, including a discussion of kernel data structures.

9.7 Summary

- New processes are created with `fork()`. After a fork, both processes run the same code, the only difference being the return value: `0` in the child and a positive PID number in the parent. The child process inherits copies of almost all the parent's attributes, of which the open files are perhaps the most important.
- Inherited shared file descriptors make possible much of the higher-level Unix semantics and elegant shell control structures. This is one of the most fundamental parts of the original Unix design. Because of descriptor sharing, a file isn't really closed until the last open file descriptor is closed. This particularly affects pipes, but it also affects the release of disk blocks for unlinked but still open files.
- The `getpid()` and `getppid()` calls return the current and parent process ID numbers, respectively. A process whose parent dies is reparented to the special `init` process, PID `1`. Thus, it's possible for the PPID to change, and applications should be prepared for this.
- The `nice()` system call lets you adjust your process's priority. The nicer you are to other processes, the lower your priority, and vice versa. Only the superuser can be less nice to other processes. On modern systems, especially single-user ones, there's no real reason to change the nice value.
- The `exec()` system calls start a new program running in an existing process. Seven different versions of the call provide flexibility in the setup of argument and environment lists, at the cost of initial confusion as to which one is best to use. Two variants simulate the shell's path-searching mechanism and fall back to the use of the shell to interpret the file in case it isn't a binary executable; these variants should be used with care.
- The new program's value for `argv[0]` normally comes from the file name being executed, but this is only convention. As with `fork()`, a significant but not identical set of attributes is inherited across an exec. Other attributes are reset to reasonable default values.
- The standard exit values `EXIT_SUCCESS` and `EXIT_FAILURE` should be used for utmost portability. If defining your own exit codes, document them, and don't define too many.

- The atexit() function registers callback functions to run in LIFO order when a program terminates. The exit(), _exit(), and _Exit() functions all terminate the program, passing an exit status back to the parent. exit() cleans up open FILE * streams and runs functions registered with atexit(). The other two functions exit immediately and should be used only when an exec has failed in a forked child. Returning from main() is like calling exit() with the given return value. In C99 and C++, falling off the end of main() is the same as 'exit(0)' but is bad practice.
- wait(), waitpid() and waitid() are the POSIX functions for recovering a child's exit status. Various macros let you determine whether the child exited normally and determine its exit status if so, or whether the child suffered death-by-signal and which signal committed the crime if so. With specific options, waitpid() and waitid() also provide information about children that haven't died but have changed state.
- GNU/Linux and most Unix systems support the BSD wait3() and wait4() functions. The BSD functions provide a struct rusage, allowing access to CPU time information, which can be handy. If waitpid() or waitid() will suffice, though, they are the most portable ways to go.
- Process groups are part of the larger job control mechanism, which includes signals, sessions, and manipulation of the terminal's state. getpgrp() returns the current process's process group ID, and getpgid() returns the PGID of a specific process. Similarly, setpgrp() sets the current process's PGID to its PID, making it a process group leader; setpgid() lets a parent process set the PGID of a child that hasn't yet exec'd.
- Pipes and FIFOs provide a one-way communications channel between two processes. Pipes must be set up by a common ancestor, whereas a FIFO can be used by any two processes. Pipes are created with pipe(), and FIFO files are created with mkfifo(). Pipes and FIFOs buffer their data, stopping the producer or consumer as the pipe fills up or empties out.
- dup() and dup2() create copies of open file descriptors. In combination with close(), they enable pipe file descriptors to be put in place as standard input and output for pipelines. For pipes to work correctly, all copies of unused ends of the pipes must be closed before execing the target program(s). /dev/fd can be used to create nonlinear pipelines, as demonstrated by the Bash and Korn shells' process substitution capability.
- dup3() atomically duplicates a file descriptor and sets any requested flags. This helps avoid race conditions in threaded code.
- fcntl() is a catchall function for doing miscellaneous jobs. It manages attributes of both the file descriptor itself and the open file underlying the descriptor. In this chapter, we saw that fcntl() is used for the following:
  - Duplicating a file descriptor, simulating dup(), and almost simulating dup2() and dup3().
  - Retrieving and setting the close-on-exec and close-on-fork flags. The close-on-exec flag is possibly the more important one. Neither flag is copied by a dup() action; they should be explicitly set on any file descriptors that should not remain open

after a fork or an exec (depending on your program's logic). In practice, setting at least the close-on-exec flag should be done for most file descriptors.

— Retrieving and setting flags controlling the underlying file. Of these, `O_NONBLOCK` is perhaps the most useful, at least for FIFOs and pipes. It is definitely the most complicated flag.

Exercises

1. Write a program that prints as much information as possible about the current process: PID, PPID, open files, current directory, nice value, and so on. How can you tell which files are open? If multiple file descriptors reference the same file, so indicate. (Again, how can you tell?)

2. How do you think `atexit()` stores the pointers to the callback functions? Implement `atexit()`, keeping the GNU "no arbitrary limits" principle in mind. Sketch an outline (pseudocode) for `exit()`. What information (`<stdio.h>` library internals) are you missing, the absence of which prevents you from writing `exit()`?

3. The `xargs` program is designed to run a command and arguments multiple times, when there would be too many arguments to pass directly on the command line. It does this by reading lines from standard input, treating each line as a separate argument for the named command, and bundling arguments until there are just enough to still be below the system maximum. For example:

   ```
   $ grep ARG_MAX /usr/include/*.h /usr/include/*/*.h     Command line
   bash: /bin/grep: Argument list too long                Shell's error message

   $ find /usr/include -name '*.h' | xargs grep ARG_MAX  find and xargs works
   /usr/include/sys/param.h:#define        NCARGS          ARG_MAX
   ...
   ```

   The constant `ARG_MAX` in `<limits.h>` represents the combined total memory used by the environment and the command-line arguments. The POSIX standard doesn't say whether this includes the pointer arrays or just the strings themselves.

   Write a simple version of `xargs` that works as described. Don't forget the environment when calculating how much space you have. Be sure to manage your memory carefully.

4. The layout of the `status` value filled in by `wait()` and `waitpid()` isn't defined by POSIX. Historically, though, it's a 16-bit value that looks as shown in Figure 9.8.

   - A nonzero value in bits 0–6 indicates death-by-signal.
   - All 1-bits in the signal field indicates that the child process stopped. In this case, bits 8–15 contain the signal number that caused the process to stop.

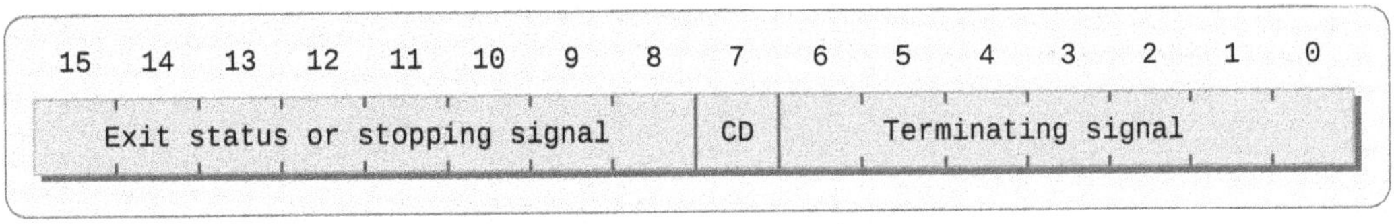

Figure 9.8: Layout of status value from `wait()`

- A 1-bit in bit 7 indicates death with core dump.
- If bits 0–7 are zero, the process exited normally. In this case, bits 8–15 are the exit status.

Given this information, write the POSIX `WIFEXITED()` et al. macros.

5. Remembering that `dup2()` closes the requested file descriptor first, implement `dup2()` using `close()` and `fcntl()`. How will you handle the case that `fcntl()` returns a value lower than the one requested?

6. Does your system have a `/dev/fd` directory? If so, how is it implemented?

7. Write a new version of `ch-processes-pipeline.c` that forks only one process. After forking, the parent should rearrange its file descriptors and exec one of the new programs itself.

8. Write a new version of `ch-processes-pipeline.c` that creates FIFOs and sets up the pipeline. What additional steps are necessary both for setup and for cleanup?

9. (Hard.) How can you tell if your process ever called `chroot()`? Write a program that checks and prints a message indicating yes or no. Can your program be fooled? If so, how?

10. Does your system have a `/proc` directory? If so, what kind of per-process information does it make available?

Chapter 10

Signals

This chapter covers the ins and outs of signals, an important but complicated part of the GNU/Linux API.

10.1 Introduction

A *signal* is an indication that some event has happened—for example, an attempt to reference a memory address that isn't part of your program's address space, or a user pressing CTRL-C to stop your program (called *generating an interrupt*).

Your program can tell only that a particular signal has happened at least once. Generally, you can't tell if the same signal has happened multiple times. You can distinguish one signal from another and control the way in which your program reacts to different signals.

Signal handling mechanisms have evolved over time. As is the case with almost all such mechanisms, both the original and the newer APIs are standardized and available. However, of the fundamental APIs, signal handling displays possibly the broadest change; there's a lot to get a handle on to be able to use the most capable APIs. As a result, this is perhaps the most difficult chapter in the book. We'll do our best to make a coherent presentation, but it'll help if you work your way through this chapter more carefully than usual.

Unlike most of the chapters in this book, our presentation here is historical, covering the APIs as they evolved, *including some APIs that you should never use in new code.* We do this because it simplifies the presentation, making it straightforward to understand why the POSIX `sigaction()` API supports all the facilities that it does.

10.2 Signal Actions

Every signal (we provide a full list shortly) has a default *action* associated with it. POSIX terms this the signal's *disposition.* This action is what the kernel does for the process when a particular signal arrives. The default actions vary:

Termination
: The process is terminated.

Ignored
: The signal is ignored. The program is never aware that anything happened.

Core dump
: The process is terminated, and the kernel creates a `core` file containing the image of the running program at the time the signal arrived. The core dump can be used later with a debugger for examination of the state of the program (see Chapter 17, "Debugging," page 591).

  Traditional Unix systems name the file `core`, placing it in the current directory of the process that died, and it's up to you to save any `core` files for later reexamination if there's a chance that more will be created in the same directory.

  On GNU/Linux the story is much more complicated; we delay discussion until Section 17.3.1, "Getting a `core` File," page 594.

Stopped
: The process is stopped. It may be continued later. (If you've used shell job control with CTRL-Z, `fg`, and `bg`, you understand stopping a process.)

10.3 Standard C Signals: `signal()` and `raise()`

The ISO C standard defines the original V7 signal management API and an invented API for sending signals. You should use these APIs for programs that have to work on non-POSIX systems, or for cases in which the functionality they provide is adequate.

10.3.1 The `signal()` Function

You change a signal's action with the `signal()` function. You can change the action to one of "ignore this signal," "restore the system's default action for this signal," or "call my function with the signal number as a parameter when the signal occurs."

A function you provide to deal with the signal is called a *signal handler* (or just a *handler*), and putting a handler in place is arranging to *catch the signal.*

With that introduction, let's proceed to the APIs. The `<signal.h>` header file provides macro definitions for supported signals and declares the signal management function provided by Standard C:

```
#include <signal.h>                                    ISO C

void (*signal(int signum, void (*func)(int)))(int);
```

This declaration for `signal()` is almost impossible to read. Thus, the GNU/Linux *signal*(2) manpage defines it this way:

```
typedef void (*sighandler_t)(int);

sighandler_t signal(int signum, sighandler_t handler);
```

Now it's more intelligible. The type `sighandler_t` is a pointer to a function returning `void`, which accepts a single integer argument. This integer is the number of the arriving signal.

The `signal()` function accepts a signal number as its first parameter and a pointer to a function (the new handler) as its second argument. If not a function pointer, the second argument may be either `SIG_DFL`, which means "restore the default action," or `SIG_IGN`, which means "ignore the signal."

`signal()` changes the action for `signum` and returns the previous action. (This allows you to later restore the previous action if you so desire.) The return value may also be `SIG_ERR`, which indicates that something went wrong. (Some signals can't be caught or ignored; supplying a signal handler for them, or an invalid `signum`, generates this error return.) Table 10.1 lists the signals available under GNU/Linux, their numeric values, each one's default action, the formal standard or modern operating system that defines them, and each one's meaning. Items marked "former POSIX" used to be included in the POSIX standard but no longer are. Nonetheless, they remain available.

Older versions of the Bourne shell (`/bin/sh`) associated *traps*, which are shell-level signal handlers, directly with signal numbers. (Modern shells still support this.) Thus, the well-rounded Unix programmer needed to know not only the signal names for use from C code but also the corresponding signal numbers! POSIX requires the `trap` command to understand symbolic signal names (without the '`SIG`' prefix), so this is no longer necessary. However (mostly against our better judgment), we have provided the numbers in the interest of completeness and because you may one day have to deal with a pre-POSIX shell script or ancient C code that uses signal numbers directly.

NOTE

For many of the signals, especially from `16` on up, the association between signal number and signal name isn't necessarily the same across platforms! Check your system header files and manpages. Table 10.1 is correct for most GNU/Linux systems.

Some systems also define other signals, such as `SIGEMT`, `SIGLOST`, and `SIGINFO`. The GNU/Linux *signal*(7) manpage provides a complete listing; if your program needs to handle signals not supported by GNU/Linux, the way to do it is with an `#ifdef`:

```
#ifdef SIGLOST
... handle SIGLOST here ...
#endif
```

With the exception of `SIGSTKFLT`, the signals listed in Table 10.1 are widely available and don't need to be bracketed with `#ifdef`.

`SIGKILL` and `SIGSTOP` cannot be caught or ignored (or blocked, as described later in the chapter). They always perform the default action listed in Table 10.1.

Table 10.1: GNU/Linux signals

Name	Value	Default	Source	Meaning
SIGHUP	1	Term	POSIX	Hangup.
SIGINT	2	Term	ISO C	Interrupt.
SIGQUIT	3	Core	POSIX	Quit.
SIGILL	4	Core	ISO C	Illegal instruction.
SIGTRAP	5	Core	POSIX	Trace trap.
SIGABRT	6	Core	ISO C	Abort.
SIGIOT	6	Core	BSD	IOT trap.[1]
SIGBUS	7	Core	POSIX	Bus error.
SIGFPE	8	Core	ISO C	Floating-point exception.
SIGKILL	9	Term	POSIX	Kill, unblockable.
SIGUSR1	10	Term	POSIX	User-defined signal 1.
SIGSEGV	11	Core	ISO C	Segmentation violation.
SIGUSR2	12	Term	POSIX	User-defined signal 2.
SIGPIPE	13	Term	POSIX	Broken pipe.
SIGALRM	14	Term	POSIX	Alarm clock.
SIGTERM	15	Term	ISO C	Termination.
SIGSTKFLT	16	Term	Linux	Stack fault on a processor (unused).
SIGCHLD	17	Ignore	POSIX	Child process status changed.
SIGCLD	17	Ignore	System V	Same as `SIGCHLD` (for compatibility only).
SIGCONT	18		POSIX	Continue if stopped.
SIGSTOP	19	Stop	POSIX	Stop, unblockable.
SIGTSTP	20	Stop	POSIX	Keyboard stop.
SIGTTIN	21	Stop	POSIX	Background read from tty.
SIGTTOU	22	Stop	POSIX	Background write to tty.
SIGURG	23	Ignore	POSIX	Urgent condition on socket.
SIGXCPU	24	Core	POSIX	CPU limit exceeded.
SIGXFSZ	25	Core	POSIX	File size limit exceeded.
SIGVTALRM	26	Term	POSIX	Virtual alarm clock. (XSI)
SIGPROF	27	Term	former POSIX	Profiling alarm clock.
SIGWINCH	28	Ignore	BSD	Window size change.
SIGIO	29	Term	BSD	I/O now possible.
SIGPOLL	29	Term	former POSIX	Pollable event occurred; same as `SIGIO`. (XSI)
SIGPWR	30	Term	System V	Power failure restart.
SIGSYS	31	Core	POSIX	Bad system call.

Key: **Core**: terminate the process and produce a `core` file.
Ignore: ignore the signal.
Stop: stop the process.
Term: terminate the process.

You can use '`kill -l`' to see a list of supported signals. From one of our GNU/Linux systems:

[1] This is the same as `SIGABRT`. It's provided for historical compatibility.

```
$ kill -l                    Letter l, not digit 1
 1) SIGHUP       2) SIGINT       3) SIGQUIT      4) SIGILL       5) SIGTRAP
 6) SIGABRT      7) SIGBUS       8) SIGFPE       9) SIGKILL     10) SIGUSR1
11) SIGSEGV     12) SIGUSR2     13) SIGPIPE     14) SIGALRM     15) SIGTERM
16) SIGSTKFLT   17) SIGCHLD     18) SIGCONT     19) SIGSTOP     20) SIGTSTP
21) SIGTTIN     22) SIGTTOU     23) SIGURG      24) SIGXCPU     25) SIGXFSZ
26) SIGVTALRM   27) SIGPROF     28) SIGWINCH    29) SIGIO       30) SIGPWR
31) SIGSYS      34) SIGRTMIN    35) SIGRTMIN+1  36) SIGRTMIN+2  37) SIGRTMIN+3
38) SIGRTMIN+4  39) SIGRTMIN+5  40) SIGRTMIN+6  41) SIGRTMIN+7  42) SIGRTMIN+8
43) SIGRTMIN+9  44) SIGRTMIN+10 45) SIGRTMIN+11 46) SIGRTMIN+12 47) SIGRTMIN+13
48) SIGRTMIN+14 49) SIGRTMIN+15 50) SIGRTMAX-14 51) SIGRTMAX-13 52) SIGRTMAX-12
53) SIGRTMAX-11 54) SIGRTMAX-10 55) SIGRTMAX-9  56) SIGRTMAX-8  57) SIGRTMAX-7
58) SIGRTMAX-6  59) SIGRTMAX-5  60) SIGRTMAX-4  61) SIGRTMAX-3  62) SIGRTMAX-2
63) SIGRTMAX-1  64) SIGRTMAX
```

The `SIGRTxxx` signals are real-time signals, an advanced topic that we don't cover. On Gnu/Linux they range from `34`–`64`. Other systems use other ranges.

10.3.2 Sending Signals Programmatically: `raise()`

Besides being generated externally, a program can send itself a signal directly, using the Standard C function `raise()`:

```
#include <signal.h>                                         ISO C

int raise(int sig);
```

This function sends the signal `sig` to the calling process. (This action has its uses; we show an example shortly.)

Because `raise()` is defined by Standard C, it is the most portable way for a process to send itself a signal. There are other ways, which we discuss further on in the chapter.

10.4 Signal Handlers in Action

Much of the complication and variation shows up once a signal handler is in place, as it is invoked, and after it returns.

10.4.1 Traditional Systems

After putting a signal handler in place, your program proceeds on its merry way. Things don't get interesting until a signal comes in (for example, the user pressed CTRL-C to interrupt your program, or a call to `raise()` was made).

Upon receipt of the signal, the kernel stops the process wherever it may be. It then simulates a procedure call to the signal handler, passing it the signal number as its sole argument. The kernel arranges things such that a normal return from the signal handler function (either through `return` or by falling off the end of the function) returns to the point in the program at which the signal happened.

Once a signal has been handled, what happens the next time the same signal comes in? Does the handler remain in place? Or is the signal's action reset to its default? The answer, for historical reasons, is "it depends." In particular, the C standard leaves it as implementation defined.

In practice, V7 and traditional System V systems, such as Solaris, reset the signal's action to the default.

Let's see a simple signal handler in action under Solaris. The following program, `ch-signals-catchint.c`, catches `SIGINT`. You normally generate this signal by typing CTRL-C at the keyboard:

```
/* ch-signals-catchint.c --- catch a SIGINT, at least once. */

#include <signal.h>
#include <string.h>
#include <unistd.h>

/* handler --- simple signal handler. */

void
handler(int signum)
{
    char buf[200], *cp;
    int offset;

    /* Jump through hoops to avoid fprintf(). */
    strcpy(buf, "handler: caught signal ");
    cp = buf + strlen(buf); /* cp points at terminating '\0' */
    if (signum > 100)   /* unlikely */
        offset = 3;
    else if (signum > 10)
        offset = 2;
    else
        offset = 1;
    cp += offset;

    *cp-- = '\0';        /* terminate string */
    while (signum > 0) {    /* work backwards, filling in digits */
        *cp-- = (signum % 10) + '0';
        signum /= 10;
    }
    strcat(buf, "\n");
    int junk = write(2, buf, strlen(buf));
}
```

```
34
35  /* main --- set up signal handling and go into infinite loop */
36
37  int
38  main(void)
39  {
40      (void) signal(SIGINT, handler);
41
42      for (;;)
43          pause();    /* wait for a signal, see later in the chapter */
44
45      return 0;
46  }
```

Lines 9–33 define the signal handling function (cleverly named `handler()`). All this function does is print the caught signal's number and return. It does a lot of manual labor to generate the message, since `fprintf()` is not "safe" for calling from within a signal handler. (This is described shortly, in Section 10.4.6, "Additional Caveats," page 346.) As we've seen earlier in the book, we assign the return value of `write()` to a junk variable in order to avoid a compiler warning.

The `main()` function sets up the signal handler (line 40) and then goes into an infinite loop (lines 42–43). Here's what happens when it's run:

```
$ ssh solaris.example.com                       Log in to a handy Solaris system
Last login: Sat Feb  3 07:03:59 2024 from A.B.C.D
Oracle Solaris 11.4.54.138.1                       Assembled January 2023
Oracle Corporation      SunOS 5.11      11.4    October 2019
$ cc ch-signals-catchint.c                      Compile the program
$ a.out                                         Run it
^Chandler: caught signal 2                      Type ^C, handler is called
^C                                              Try again, but this time ...
$                                               The program dies
```

Because V7 and other traditional systems reset the signal's action to the default, when you wish to receive the signal again in the future, the handler function should immediately reinstall itself:

```
void
handler(int signum)
{
    char buf[200], *cp;
    int offset;

    (void) signal(signum, handler);        /* reinstall handler */

    ... rest of function as before ...
}
```

10.4.2 BSD and GNU/Linux

4.2 BSD changed the way `signal()` worked.[2] On BSD systems, the signal handler remains in place after the handler returns. GNU/Linux systems follow the BSD behavior. Here's what happens under GNU/Linux:

```
$ ch-signals-catchint                          Run the program
^Chandler: caught signal 2                     Type ^C, handler is called
^Chandler: caught signal 2                     And again ...
^Chandler: caught signal 2                     And again!
^Chandler: caught signal 2                     Help!
^Chandler: caught signal 2                     How do we stop this?!
^\Quit (core dumped)                           ^\, generate SIGQUIT. Whew
```

On a BSD or GNU/Linux system, a signal handler doesn't need the extra '`signal(signum, handler)`' call to reinstall the handler. However, the extra call also doesn't hurt anything, since it maintains the status quo.

In fact, for a while, POSIX provided a `bsd_signal()` function, which is identical to `signal()`, except that it guarantees that the signal handler stays installed:

```
#include <signal.h>

void (*bsd_signal(int sig, void (*func)(int)))(int);
```

However, this function was removed from more recent versions of the standard, even though it is still available on GNU/Linux. As we'll see, the POSIX `sigaction()` API provides enough facilities to let you write a workalike version, should you need to.

An additional change made in 4.2 BSD was that the signal that caused a handler to be invoked was blocked during the execution of the handler. Signal blocking is discussed further on in this chapter.

10.4.3 Ignoring Signals

More practically, when a signal handler is invoked, it usually means that the program should finish up and exit. It would be annoying if most programs, upon receipt of a `SIGINT`, printed a message and continued; the point of the signal is that they should stop!

For example, consider the `sort` program. `sort` may have created any number of temporary files for use in intermediate stages of the sorting process. Upon receipt of a `SIGINT`, `sort` should remove the temporary files and then exit. Here is a simplified version of the signal handler from the GNU Coreutils `sort.c`:

---

[2] They did this with the best of intentions: the original semantics made it hard to write reliable code, or to write reasonable networking or job control code. Nonetheless, it would have been better to use a new name, such as `signal2()`. Changing the semantics of a defined interface always creates trouble, leading to confusion, and making code portability difficult, if not impossible. While especially true for operating system designers, *anyone* designing a general-purpose library should keep this lesson in mind.

```
/* Handle interrupts and hangups. */         Simplified for presentation

static void
sighandler (int sig)
{
  signal (sig, SIG_IGN);                      Ignore this signal from now on
  cleanup ();                                 Clean up after ourselves
  signal (sig, SIG_DFL);                      Restore default action
  raise (sig);                                Now resend the signal
}
```

Setting the action to `SIG_IGN` ensures that any further `SIGINT` signals that come in won't affect the cleanup action in progress. Once `cleanup()` is done, resetting the action to `SIG_DFL` allows the system to dump core if the signal that came in would do so. Calling `raise()` regenerates the signal. The regenerated signal then invokes the default action, which most likely terminates the program. (We show the full `sort.c` signal handler later in this chapter.)

10.4.4 Restartable System Calls

The `EINTR` value for `errno` (see Section 4.3, "Determining What Went Wrong," page 81) indicates that a system call was interrupted. While a large number of system calls can fail with this error value, the two most important ones are `read()` and `write()`. Consider the following code:

```
void handler(int signal) { /* handle signals */ }

int
main(int argc, char **argv)
{
    signal(SIGINT, handler);
    ...
    while ((count = read(fd, buf, sizeof buf)) > 0) {
        /* process the buffer */
    }
    if (count == 0)
        /* end of file, clean up etc. */
    else if (count == -1)
        /* failure */
    ...
}
```

Suppose that the system has successfully read (and filled in) part of the buffer when a `SIGINT` occurs. The `read()` system call has not yet returned from the kernel to the program, but the kernel decides that it can deliver the signal. `handler()` is called, runs, and returns into the middle of the `read()`. What does `read()` return?

In days of yore (V7, and earlier System V systems), `read()` would return `-1` and set `errno` to `EINTR`. There was *no way to tell* that data had been transferred. In this case, V7 and System

V act as if nothing happened: no data is transferred to or from the user's buffer, and the file offset isn't changed.

4.2 BSD changed this. There were two cases:

Slow devices
: A "slow device" is essentially a terminal or almost anything but a regular file. In this case, `read()` could fail with `EINTR` *only* if no data was transferred when the signal arrived. Otherwise, the system call would be *restarted*, and `read()` would return normally.

Regular files
: The system call would be restarted. In this case, `read()` would return normally; the return value would be either as many bytes as were requested or the number of bytes that were actually readable (such as when reading close to the end of the file).

The BSD behavior is clearly valuable; you can always tell how much data you've read.

The POSIX behavior is similar but not identical to the original BSD behavior. POSIX indicates that `read()`[3] fails with `EINTR` only if a signal occurred before any data was transferred. Although POSIX doesn't say anything about "slow devices," in practice this condition occurs only on such devices.

Otherwise, if a signal interrupts a partially successful `read()`, the return is the number of bytes read so far. For this reason (as well as being able to handle short files), you should always check the return value from `read()` and never assume that it read the full number of bytes requested. (The POSIX `sigaction()` API, described later, allows you to get the behavior of BSD restartable system calls if you want it.)

10.4.4.1 Example: GNU Coreutils `safe_read()` and `safe_write()`

The GNU Coreutils use two routines, `safe_read()` and `safe_write()`, to handle the `EINTR` case on traditional systems. The code is complicated a bit by the fact that the same file, by means of `#include` and macros, implements both functions. (Doing it this way avoids duplicating code, at some cost in readability.) From `lib/safe-read.c` in the Coreutils distribution:

```
/* An interface to read and write that retries after interrupts.

   Copyright (C) 1993-1994, 1998, 2002-2006, 2009-2023 Free Software
   Foundation, Inc.
```

... lots of boilerplate stuff omitted ...

```
#include <config.h>

/* Specification.  */
#ifdef SAFE_WRITE
# include "safe-write.h"
#else
# include "safe-read.h"
```

---

[3]Although we are describing `read()`, the rules apply to all system calls that can fail with `EINTR`, such as those of the `wait()` family.

```
26 #endif
   ... more boilerplate stuff omitted ...
42 #ifdef SAFE_WRITE
43 # define safe_rw safe_write
44 # define rw write
45 #else
46 # define safe_rw safe_read
47 # define rw read
48 # undef const
49 # define const /* empty */
50 #endif
51
52 /* Read(write) up to COUNT bytes at BUF from(to) descriptor FD, retrying if
53    interrupted.  Return the actual number of bytes read(written), zero for EOF,
54    or SAFE_READ_ERROR(SAFE_WRITE_ERROR) upon error.  */
55 size_t
56 safe_rw (int fd, void const *buf, size_t count)
57 {
58   for (;;)
59     {
60       ssize_t result = rw (fd, buf, count);
61
62       if (0 <= result)
63         return result;
64       else if (IS_EINTR (errno))
65         continue;
66       else if (errno == EINVAL && SYS_BUFSIZE_MAX < count)
67         count = SYS_BUFSIZE_MAX;
68       else
69         return result;
70     }
71 }
```

Lines 42–49 handle the definitions, creating `safe_read()` and `safe_write()`, as appropriate (see `safe_write.c`, below).

Lines 58–70 are the actual loop, performing the operation repeatedly, as long as it fails with `EINTR`. The `IS_EINTR()` macro isn't shown, but it handles the case for systems on which `EINTR` isn't defined. (There must be at least one out there or the code wouldn't bother setting up the macro; it was probably done for a Unix or POSIX emulation on top of a non-Unix system.) Lines 66–67 make sure that we don't request more bytes than the system can handle; `SYS_BUFSIZE_MAX` is a macro set up by the Coreutils configuration process.

Here is `safe_write.c`:

```
/* An interface to write that retries after interrupts.
   Copyright (C) 2002, 2009-2023 Free Software Foundation, Inc.
```

... lots of boilerplate stuff omitted ...

```
16
17 #define SAFE_WRITE
18 #include "safe-read.c"
```

The `#define` on line 17 defines `SAFE_WRITE`; this ties in to lines 21–26 and 42–50 in `safe-read.c`.

10.4.4.2 GLIBC Only: `TEMP_FAILURE_RETRY()`

The GLIBC `<unistd.h>` file defines a macro, `TEMP_FAILURE_RETRY()`, that you can use to encapsulate any system call that can fail and set `errno` to `EINTR`. Its "declaration" is as follows:

```
#include <unistd.h>                                          GLIBC

long int TEMP_FAILURE_RETRY(expression);
```

Here is the macro's definition:

```
/* Evaluate EXPRESSION, and repeat as long as it returns -1 with `errno'
   set to EINTR.  */

# define TEMP_FAILURE_RETRY(expression) \
  (__extension__                                          \
    ({ long int __result;                                 \
       do __result = (long int) (expression);             \
       while (__result == -1L && errno == EINTR);         \
       __result; }))
```

The macro uses a GCC extension to the C language (as marked by the `__extension__` keyword) that allows brace-enclosed statements inside parentheses to return a value, thus acting like a simple expression.

Using this macro, we might rewrite `safe_read()` as follows:

```
size_t
safe_read(int fd, void const *buf, size_t count)
{
    ssize_t result;

    result = TEMP_FAILURE_RETRY(read(fd, buf, count));

    return (size_t) result;
}
```

10.4.5 Race Conditions and `sig_atomic_t` (ISO C)

So far, handling one signal at a time looks straightforward: install a signal handler in `main()`, and (optionally) have the signal handler reinstall itself (or set the action to `SIG_IGN`) as the first thing it does.

What happens, though, if *two* identical signals come in, one right after the other? In particular, what if your system resets the signal's action to the default, and the second signal comes in *after* the signal handler is called but *before* it can reinstall itself?

Or, what if you have older code using `bsd_signal()`, so the handler stays installed, but the second signal is different from the first one? Usually, the first signal handler needs to complete its job before the second one runs, and every signal handler shouldn't have to temporarily ignore all other possible signals!

Both of these are race conditions. One workaround for these problems is to make signal handlers as simple as possible. You can do this by creating flag variables that indicate that a signal occurred. The signal handler sets the variable to true and returns. Then the main logic checks the flag variable at strategic points:

```
bool sig_int_flag = false;          /* signal handler sets to true */
                                    bool is not the correct type; see text

void
int_handler(int signum)
{
    sig_int_flag = true;
}

int
main(int argc, char **argv)
{
    bsd_signal(SIGINT, int_handler);
    ... program proceeds on ...
    if (sig_int_flag) {
        /* SIGINT occurred, handle it */
    }
    ... rest of logic ...
}
```

(Note that this strategy *reduces* the window of vulnerability but does not eliminate it.)

Standard C introduces a special type—`sig_atomic_t`—for use with such flag variables. The idea behind the name is that assignments to variables of this type are *atomic*: that is, they happen in one indivisible action. For example, on most machines, assignment to an `int` value happens atomically, whereas a structure assignment is likely to be done either by copying all the bytes with a (compiler-generated) loop, or by issuing a "block move" instruction that can be interrupted. Since assignment to a `sig_atomic_t` value is atomic, once started, it completes before another signal can come in and interrupt it.

Having a special type is only part of the story. `sig_atomic_t` variables should also be declared `volatile`:

```
volatile sig_atomic_t sig_int_flag = 0;  /* signal handler sets to true (nonzero) */
... rest of code as before ...
```

The `volatile` keyword tells the compiler that the variable can be changed externally, behind the compiler's back, so to speak. This keeps the compiler from doing optimizations that might otherwise affect the code's correctness.

Structuring an application exclusively around `sig_atomic_t` variables is not reliable. The correct way to deal with signals is shown later, in Section 10.7, "Signals for Interprocess Communication," page 360.

10.4.6 Additional Caveats

The POSIX standard provides several caveats for signal handlers:

- It is undefined what happens when handlers for `SIGBUS`, `SIGFPE`, `SIGILL`, `SIGSEGV`, or any other signals that represent "computation exceptions" return.
- If a handler was invoked as a result of calls to `abort()`, `raise()`, or `kill()`, the handler cannot call `raise()`. (`abort()` is described in Section 13.4, "Committing Suicide: `abort()`," page 434, and `kill()` is described later in this chapter.) The `sigaction()` API, with the three-argument signal handler described later, makes it possible to tell if this is the case.
- Signal handlers can only call the functions in Table 10.2. In particular, they should avoid <stdio.h> functions. The problem is that an interrupt may come in while a <stdio.h> function is running, when the internal state of the library is in the middle of being updated. Further calls to <stdio.h> functions could corrupt the internal state.

The list in Table 10.2 comes from Section 2.4 of the *System Interfaces* volume of the 2024 POSIX standard, titled *Signal Concepts*. Many if not most of these functions are advanced APIs not otherwise covered in this book.

10.4.7 Our Story So Far, Episode I

Previously, on Avatar ...
— Avatar: The Last Airbender

Signals are a complicated topic, and it's about to get more confusing. So let's pause for a moment, take a step back, and summarize what we've discussed so far:

- Signals are an indication that some external event has occurred.
- `raise()` is the ISO C function for sending signals *to the current process*. We have yet to describe how to send signals to other processes.
- `signal()` controls the disposition of a signal—that is, the process's reaction to the signal when it comes in. The signal may be left set to the system default, ignored, or caught.
- A handler function runs when a signal is caught. Here is where complexity starts to rear its ugly head:

Table 10.2: Functions that can be called from a signal handler

_Exit()	lseek()	stpcpy()
_Fork()	lstat()	stpncpy()
_exit()	memccpy()	strcat()
abort()	memchr()	strchr()
accept()	memcmp()	strcmp()
accept4()	memcpy()	strcpy()
access()	memmove()	strcspn()
aio_error()	memset()	strlcat()
aio_return()	mkdir()	strlcpy()
aio_suspend()	mkdirat()	strlen()
alarm()	mkfifo()	strncat()
be16toh()	mkfifoat()	strncmp()
be32toh()	mknod()	strncpy()
be64toh()	mknodat()	strnlen()
bind()	ntohl()	strpbrk()
cfgetispeed()	ntohs()	strrchr()
cfgetospeed()	open()	strspn()
cfsetispeed()	openat()	strstr()
cfsetospeed()	pause()	strtok_r()
chdir()	pipe()	symlink()
chmod()	pipe2()	symlinkat()
chown()	poll()	tcdrain()
clock_gettime()	posix_close()	tcflow()
close()	ppoll()	tcflush()
connect()	pread()	tcgetattr()
creat()	pselect()	tcgetpgrp()
dup()	pthread_kill()	tcgetwinsize()
dup2()	pthread_self()	tcsendbreak()
dup3()	pthread_setcancelstate()	tcsetattr()
execl()	pthread_sigmask()	tcsetpgrp()
execle()	pwrite()	tcsetwinsize()
execv()	quick_exit()	time()
execve()	raise()	timer_getoverrun()
faccessat()	read()	timer_gettime()
fchdir()	readlink()	timer_settime()
fchmod()	readlinkat()	times()
fchmodat()	readv()	umask()
fchown()	recv()	uname()
fchownat()	recvfrom()	unlink()
fcntl()	recvmsg()	unlinkat()
fdatasync()	rename()	utimensat()
fexecve()	renameat()	utimes()
ffs()	rmdir()	va_arg()
fstat()	select()	va_copy()
fstatat()	sem_post()	va_end()
fsync()	send()	va_start()

(continued)

Table 10.2: Functions that can be called from a signal handler *(continued)*

`ftruncate()`	`sendmsg()`	`wait()`
`futimens()`	`sendto()`	`waitid()`
`getegid()`	`setegid()`	`waitpid()`
`geteuid()`	`seteuid()`	`wcpcpy()`
`getgid()`	`setgid()`	`wcpncpy()`
`getgroups()`	`setpgid()`	`wcscat()`
`getpeername()`	`setregid()`	`wcschr()`
`getpgrp()`	`setresgid()`	`wcscmp()`
`getpid()`	`setresuid()`	`wcscpy()`
`getppid()`	`setreuid()`	`wcscspn()`
`getresgid()`	`setsid()`	`wcslcat()`
`getresuid()`	`setsockopt()`	`wcslcpy()`
`getsockname()`	`setuid()`	`wcslen()`
`getsockopt()`	`shutdown()`	`wcsncat()`
`getuid()`	`sig2str()`	`wcsncmp()`
`htobe16()`	`sigaction()`	`wcsncpy()`
`htobe32()`	`sigaddset()`	`wcsnlen()`
`htobe64()`	`sigdelset()`	`wcspbrk()`
`htole16()`	`sigemptyset()`	`wcsrchr()`
`htole32()`	`sigfillset()`	`wcsspn()`
`htole64()`	`sigismember()`	`wcsstr()`
`htonl()`	`siglongjmp()`	`wcstok()`
`htons()`	`signal()`	`wmemchr()`
`kill()`	`sigpending()`	`wmemcmp()`
`killpg()`	`sigprocmask()`	`wmemcpy()`
`le16toh()`	`sigqueue()`	`wmemmove()`
`le32toh()`	`sigsuspend()`	`wmemset()`
`le64toh()`	`sleep()`	`write()`
`link()`	`sockatmark()`	`writev()`
`linkat()`	`socket()`	
`listen()`	`socketpair()`	
`longjmp()`	`stat()`	

– ISO C leaves as unspecified whether signal disposition is restored to its default before the handler runs or whether the disposition remains in place. The former is the behavior of V7 and modern System V systems such as Solaris. The latter is the BSD behavior also found on GNU/Linux.

– What happens when a system call is interrupted by a signal also varies along the traditional versus BSD line. Traditional systems return `-1` with `errno` set to `EINTR`. BSD systems restart the system call after the handler returns. The GLIBC `TEMP_FAILURE_RETRY()` macro can help you write code to handle system calls that return `-1` with `errno` set to `EINTR`.

POSIX requires that a system call that has partially completed return a success value indicating how much succeeded. A system call that hasn't started yet is restarted.

- The `signal()` mechanism provides fertile ground for growing race conditions. The ISO C `sig_atomic_t` data type helps with this situation but doesn't solve it, and the mechanism as defined can't be made safe from race conditions.
- A number of additional caveats apply, and in particular, only a subset of the standard library functions can be *safely* called from within a signal handler.

Despite the problems, for simple programs, the `signal()` interface is often adequate, and it is still widely used.

10.5 The System V Release 3 Signal APIs: `sigset()` et al.

4.0 BSD (circa 1980) introduced additional APIs to provide "reliable" signals.[4] In particular, it became possible to *block* signals. In other words, a program could tell the kernel, "Hang on to these particular signals for the next little while, and then deliver them to me when I'm ready to take them." A big advantage is that this feature simplifies signal handlers, which automatically run with their own signal blocked (to avoid the two-signals-in-a-row problem) and possibly with others blocked as well.

System V Release 3 (circa 1984) picked up these APIs and popularized them; in most Unix-related documentation and books, you'll probably see these APIs referred to as being from System V Release 3. The functions are as follows:

```
#include <signal.h>                                 Deprecated

int sighold(int sig);                               Add sig to process signal mask
int sigrelse(int sig);                              Remove sig from process signal mask

int sigignore(int sig);                             Short for sigset(sig, SIG_IGN)
int sigpause(int sig);                              Suspend process, allow sig to come in
void (*sigset(int sig, void (*disp)(int)))(int);    sighandler_t sigset(int sig, sighandler_t disp);
```

These functions are no longer included in POSIX. However, their behavior may be described in terms of each process's *process signal mask*. The process signal mask tracks which signals (if any) a process currently has blocked. This is described in more detail in Section 10.6.2, "Signal Sets: `sigset_t` and Related Functions," page 351. In the System V Release 3 API there is no way to retrieve or modify the process signal mask as a whole. The functions work as follows:

`int sighold(int sig)`
: Adds `sig` to the list of blocked processes (the process signal mask).

[4] The APIs required linking with a separate library, `-ljobs`, in order to be used.

`int sigrelse(int sig)`
: Removes (releases) `sig` from the process signal mask.

`int sigignore(int sig)`
: Ignores `sig`. This is a convenience function.

`int sigpause(int sig)`
: Removes `sig` from the process signal mask, and then suspends the process until a signal comes in (see Section 10.7, "Signals for Interprocess Communication," page 360).

`sighandler_t sigset(int sig, sighandler_t disp)`
: Is a replacement for `signal()`. (We've used the GNU/Linux manpage notation here to make the declaration easier to read.)

For `sigset()`, the `handler` argument can be `SIG_DFL`, `SIG_IGN`, or a function pointer, just as for `signal()`. However, it may also be `SIG_HOLD`. In this case, `sig` is added to the process's process signal mask, but its associated action is otherwise unchanged. (In other words, if it had a handler, the handler is still in place; if it was the default action, that has not changed.)

When `sigset()` is used to install a signal handler and the signal comes in, the kernel first adds the signal to the process signal mask, blocking any additional receipt of that signal. The handler runs, and when it returns, the kernel restores the process signal mask to what it was before the handler ran. (In the POSIX model, if a signal handler changes the signal mask, that change is overridden by the restoration of the previous mask when the handler returns.)

`sighold()` and `sigrelse()` may be used together to bracket so-called *critical sections* of code: chunks of code that should not be interrupted by particular signals so that no data structures are corrupted by code from a signal handler.

NOTE

These interfaces used to be standardized for compatibility with old code. And they may even still be available on your system. However, the `sigaction()` APIs described shortly let you do everything that these APIs do, and more. You should not use these APIs in new programs. Instead, use `sigaction()`.

10.6 POSIX Signals

The POSIX API is based on the `sigvec()` API from 4.2 and 4.3 BSD. With minor changes, this API was able to subsume the functionality of both the V7 and System V Release 3 APIs. POSIX made these changes and renamed the API `sigaction()`. Because the `sigvec()` interface was not widely used, we don't describe it. Instead, this section describes only `sigaction()`, which is what you should use anyway. (Indeed, the 4.4 BSD manuals from 1994 mark `sigvec()` as obsolete, pointing the reader to `sigaction()`.)

10.6.1 Uncovering the Problem

What's wrong with the System V Release 3 APIs? After all, they provide signal blocking, so signals aren't lost and any given signal can be handled reliably.

The answer is that the API works with only *one signal at a time*. Programs generally handle more than one signal. And when you're in the middle of handling one signal, you don't want to have to worry about handling another one. (Suppose you've just answered your office phone when your cell phone starts ringing: you'd prefer to have the phone system tell your caller you're on another line and you'll be there shortly, rather than having to do it yourself.)

With the `sigset()` API, each signal handler would have to temporarily block *all* the other signals, do its job, and then unblock them. The problem is that in the interval between any two calls to `sighold()`, a not-yet-blocked signal could come up. The scenario is once again rife with race conditions.

The solution is to make it possible to work with groups of signals atomically—that is, with one system call. You effect this by working with signal sets and the process signal mask.

10.6.2 Signal Sets: `sigset_t` and Related Functions

The *process signal mask* is a list of signals that a process currently has blocked. The strength of the POSIX API is that the process signal mask can be manipulated atomically, as a whole.

The process signal mask is represented programmatically with a *signal set*. This is the `sigset_t` type. Conceptually, it's just a bitmask, with `0` and `1` values in the mask representing a particular signal's absence or presence in the mask:

```
/* Signal mask manipulated directly.  DO NOT DO THIS! */
int mask = (1 << SIGHUP) | (1 << SIGINT);     /* bitmask for SIGHUP and SIGINT */
```

However, because a system can have more signals than can be held in a single `int` or `long`, and because heavy use of the bitwise operators is hard to read, several APIs exist to manipulate signal sets:

```
#include <signal.h>                                                    POSIX

int sigemptyset(sigset_t *set);
int sigfillset(sigset_t *set);
int sigaddset(sigset_t *set, int signum);
int sigdelset(sigset_t *set, int signum);
int sigismember(const sigset_t *set, int signum);
```

The functions are as follows:

`int sigemptyset(sigset_t *set)`
: Empty out a signal set. Upon return, `*set` has no signals in it. Return `0` on success or `-1` on error.

`int sigfillset(sigset_t *set)`
: Completely fill in a signal set. Upon return, `*set` contains all the signals defined by the system. Return `0` on success or `-1` on error.

`int sigaddset(sigset_t *set, int signum)`
Add `signum` to the process signal mask in `*set`. Return `0` on success or `-1` on error.

`int sigdelset(sigset_t *set, int signum)`
Remove `signum` from the process signal mask in `*set`. Return `0` on success or `-1` on error.

`int sigismember(const sigset_t *set, int signum)`
Return true/false if `signum` is or isn't present in `*set`.

You must always call one of `sigemptyset()` or `sigfillset()` before doing anything else with a `sigset_t` variable. Both interfaces exist because sometimes you want to start out with an empty set and then just work with one or two signals, and other times you want to work with all signals, possibly taking away one or two.

10.6.3 Managing the Signal Mask: `sigprocmask()` et al.

The process signal mask starts out empty—initially, no signals are blocked. (This is a simplification; see Section 10.9, "Signals across `fork()` and `exec()`," page 378.) Three functions let you work directly with the process signal mask:

```
#include <signal.h>                                         POSIX

int sigprocmask(int how, const sigset_t *set, sigset_t *oldset);
int sigpending(sigset_t *set);
int sigsuspend(const sigset_t *set);
```

The functions are as follows:

`int sigprocmask(int how, const sigset_t *set, sigset_t *oldset)`
If `oldset` is not `NULL`, retrieve the current process signal mask and place it in `*oldset`. Update the process signal mask according to the contents of `set` and the value of `how`, which must be one of the following:

`SIG_BLOCK`	Merge the signals in `*set` with the current process signal mask. The new mask is the union of the current mask and `*set`.
`SIG_UNBLOCK`	Remove the signals in `*set` from the process signal mask. It is not a problem if `*set` contains a signal that is not currently in the process signal mask.
`SIG_SETMASK`	Replace the process signal mask with the contents of `*set`.

If `set` is `NULL` and `oldset` isn't, the value of `how` isn't important. This combination retrieves the current process signal mask without changing it.

`int sigpending(sigset_t *set)`
This function lets you see which signals are *pending*; that is, `*set` is filled in with those signals that have been sent but haven't yet been delivered since they're blocked.

`int sigsuspend(const sigset_t *set)`
: This function *temporarily* replaces the process's process signal mask with `*set` and then suspends the process until a signal is received. By definition, only a signal not in `*set` can cause the function to return (see Section 10.7, "Signals for Interprocess Communication," page 360).

10.6.4 Catching Signals: `sigaction()`

Finally, we're ready to look at the `sigaction()` function. This function is complicated, and we intentionally omit many details that are only for advanced uses. The POSIX standard and the *sigaction*(2) manpage provide full details, although you must carefully read both to fully absorb everything. Here is its declaration:

```
#include <signal.h>                                         POSIX

int sigaction(int signum,
              const struct sigaction *act,
              struct sigaction *oldact);
```

The arguments are as follows:

`int signum`
: The signal of interest, as with the other signal handling functions.

`const struct sigaction *act`
: The new handler specification for signal `signum`.

`struct sigaction *oldact`
: The current handler specification. If not `NULL`, the system fills in `*oldact` before installing `*act`. `act` can be `NULL`, in which case `*oldact` is filled in, but nothing else changes.

Thus, `sigaction()` both sets the new handler and retrieves the old one, in one shot. The `struct sigaction` looks like this:

```
/* NOTE: Order in struct may vary. There may be other fields too! */
struct sigaction {
    sigset_t sa_mask;                                    Additional signals to block
    int sa_flags;                                        Control behavior
    void (*sa_handler)(int);                             May be union with sa_sigaction
    void (*sa_sigaction)(int, siginfo_t *, void *);      May be union with sa_handler
}
```

The fields are as follows:

`sigset_t sa_mask`
: A set of *additional* signals to block when the signal handler function runs. Thus, when the handler is invoked, the total set of blocked signals is the union of those in the process signal mask, those in `act->sa_mask`, and, if `SA_NODEFER` is clear, `signum`.

`int sa_flags`
Flags that control the kernel's handling of the signal. See the discussion further on.

`void (*sa_handler)(int)`
A pointer to a "traditional" handler function. It has the same *signature* (return type and parameter list) as the handler functions for `signal()`, `bsd_signal()`, and `sigset()`.

`void (*sa_sigaction)(int, siginfo_t *, void *)`
A pointer to a "new style" handler function. The function takes three arguments, as described shortly.

Which of `act->sa_handler` and `act->sa_sigaction` is used depends on the `SA_SIGINFO` flag in `act->sa_flags`. When present, `act->sa_sigaction` is used; otherwise, `act->sa_handler` is used. Both POSIX and the GNU/Linux manpage point out that these two fields may overlap in storage (that is, be part of a `union`). Thus, you should *never* use both fields in the same `struct sigaction`.

The `sa_flags` field is the bitwise-OR of one or more of the flag values listed in Table 10.3.

When the `SA_SIGINFO` flag is set in `act->sa_flags`, then the `act->sa_sigaction` field is a pointer to a function declared as follows:

```
void
action_handler(int sig, siginfo_t *info, void *context)
{
    /* handler body here */
}
```

The `siginfo_t` structure provides a wealth of information about the signal:

```
/* POSIX definition.  Actual contents likely to vary across systems. */
typedef struct {
    int si_signo;             /* signal number */
    int si_errno;             /* <errno.h> value if an error */
    int si_code;              /* signal code; see text */
    pid_t si_pid;             /* process ID of process that sent signal */
    uid_t si_uid;             /* real UID of sending process */
    void *si_addr;            /* address of instruction that faulted */
    int si_status;            /* exit value, may include death-by-signal */
    long si_band;             /* band event for SIGPOLL/SIGIO */
    union sigval si_value;    /* signal value (advanced) */
} siginfo_t;
```

The `si_signo`, `si_code`, and `si_value` fields are available for all signals. The other fields can be members of a `union` and thus should be used only for the signals for which they're defined. There may also be other fields in the `siginfo_t` structure.

Almost all the fields are for advanced uses. The full details are in the POSIX standard and in the *sigaction*(2) manpage. However, we can describe a straightforward use of the `si_code` field.

Table 10.3: Flag values for sa_flags

Flag	Meaning
SA_NOCLDSTOP	This flag is meaningful only for SIGCHLD. When set, the parent does not receive the signal when a child process is stopped by SIGSTOP, SIGTSTP, SIGTTIN, or SIGTTOU. These signals are discussed later, in Section 10.8.2, "Job Control Signals," page 365.
SA_NOCLDWAIT	This flag is meaningful only for SIGCHLD. Its behavior is complicated. We delay explanation until later in the chapter; see Section 10.8.3, "Parental Supervision: Three Different Strategies," page 366.
SA_NODEFER	Normally, the given signal is blocked while the signal handler runs. When this flag is set, the given signal is not blocked while the signal handler runs. SA_NODEFER is the official POSIX name of the flag (which you should use).
SA_NOMASK	An alternative, nonstandard name for SA_NODEFER.[5]
SA_SIGINFO	The signal handler takes three arguments. As mentioned, with this flag set, the sa_sigaction field should be used instead of sa_handler. According to Ulrich Drepper, one of the authors of GLIBC, this option should always be used with the realtime signals, SIGRTMIN ... SIGRTMAX.
SA_ONSTACK	This is an advanced feature. Signal handlers can be called, using user-provided memory as an "alternative signal stack." Such memory is given to the kernel for this use with sigaltstack() (see *sigaltstack*(2)). This feature is not otherwise described in this book.
SA_RESETHAND	This flag provides the V7 behavior: the signal's action is reset to its default when the handler is called. SA_RESETHAND is the official POSIX name of the flag (which you should use).
SA_ONESHOT	An alternative, nonstandard name for SA_RESETHAND.
SA_RESTART	This flag provides BSD semantics: system calls that can fail with EINTR, and that receive this signal, are restarted.

For SIGBUS, SIGCHLD, SIGFPE, SIGILL, SIGPOLL, SIGSEGV, and SIGTRAP, the si_code field can take on any of a set of predefined values specific to each signal, indicating the cause of the signal. Frankly, the details are a bit overwhelming; everyday code doesn't really need to deal with them (although we'll look at the values for SIGCHLD later on). For all other signals, the si_code member has one of the values in Table 10.4.

In particular, the SI_USER value is useful; it allows a signal handler to tell if the signal was sent by raise() or kill() (described later). You can use this information to avoid calling raise() or kill() a second time.

The third argument to a three-argument signal handler, void *context, is an advanced feature, and is not otherwise discussed.

---

[5] As far as we could determine, the names SA_NOMASK and SA_ONESHOT are specific to GNU/Linux. If anyone knows differently, please inform us!

Table 10.4: Signal origin values for `si_code`

Value	GLIBC only	Meaning
`SI_ASYNCIO`		Asynchronous I/O completed (advanced).
`SI_KERNEL`	✓	Kernel sent the signal.
`SI_MESGQ`		Message queue state changed (advanced).
`SI_QUEUE`		Signal sent from `sigqueue()` (advanced).
`SI_SIGIO`	✓	A `SIGIO` was queued (advanced).
`SI_TIMER`		A timer expired.
`SI_TKILL`	✓	Signal sent to a thread by `tgkill()` (advanced).
`SI_USER`		Signal sent by `kill()`. `raise()`, and `abort()` are allowed to produce this too but are not required to.

Finally, to see `sigaction()` in use, let's examine the full text of the signal handler for `sort.c`:

```
/* Use SA_NOCLDSTOP as a proxy for whether the sigaction machinery is
   present.  */
...
/* Handle interrupts and hangups. */

static void
sighandler (int sig)
{
  if (! SA_NOCLDSTOP)                        On non-POSIX style system ...
    signal (sig, SIG_IGN);                   — Set action to ignore

  cleanup ();                                Run cleanup code

  signal (sig, SIG_DFL);                     Set action to default
  raise (sig);                               Resend the signal
}
```

Here is the code in `main()` that puts the handler in place:

```
#if SA_NOCLDSTOP                                     On a POSIX system ...
    struct sigaction act;

    sigemptyset (&caught_signals);                   — Initialize the set
    for (i = 0; i < nsigs; i++)                      — For all signals
      {
        sigaction (sig[i], nullptr, &act);           — Get handler for the signal
        if (act.sa_handler != SIG_IGN)               — If it's not ignored ...
          sigaddset (&caught_signals, sig[i]);       — Add it to set of caught signals
      }
```

```
4362
4363     act.sa_handler = sighandler;                      — Signal handling function
4364     act.sa_mask = caught_signals;                     — Set process signal mask for handler
4365     act.sa_flags = 0;                                 — No special flags
4366
4367     for (i = 0; i < nsigs; i++)                       — For all signals
4368       if (sigismember (&caught_signals, sig[i]))      — If it's being caught ...
4369         sigaction (sig[i], &act, nullptr);            — Use our handler for it
4370 #else
4371     for (i = 0; i < nsigs; i++)                       On older system, for all signals ...
4372       if (signal (sig[i], SIG_IGN) != SIG_IGN)        — If not ignoring the signal ...
4373         {
4374           signal (sig[i], sighandler);                — Use our handler for it
4375           siginterrupt (sig[i], 1);                   — Allow signals to interrupt
4376         }                                               system calls
4377 #endif
```

Of interest are lines 4356–4361 and 4371–4376, which show the correct way to check whether a signal is being ignored and to install a handler only if it's not.

NOTE

The `sigaction()` API and the `signal()` API should not be used together for the same signal. Although POSIX goes to great lengths to make it possible to use `signal()` initially, retrieve a `struct sigaction` representing the disposition from `signal()`, and restore it, doing so is still a bad idea. Code will be easier to read, write, and understand if you use one API or the other, exclusively.

10.6.5 Retrieving Pending Signals: `sigpending()`

The `sigpending()` system call, described earlier, lets you retrieve the set of signals that are pending—that is, those that have come in, but are not yet delivered because they were blocked:

```
#include <signal.h>                                      POSIX

int sigpending(sigset_t *set);
```

Besides unblocking the pending signals so that they get delivered, you may choose to ignore them. Setting the action for a pending signal to `SIG_IGN` causes the pending signal to be discarded (even if it was blocked). Similarly, for those signals for which the default action is to ignore the signal, setting the action to `SIG_DFL` causes such a pending signal to also be discarded.

10.6.6 Making Functions Interruptible: `siginterrupt()`

As a convenience, the `siginterrupt()` function can be used to make functions interruptible for a particular signal or to make them restartable, depending on the value of the second argument. The declaration is:

```
#include <signal.h>                                        Deprecated

int siginterrupt(int sig, int flag);
```

This function too has been removed from the POSIX standard, but is still available on GNU/Linux. The behavior of `siginterrupt()` is equivalent to the following code:

```
int
siginterrupt(int sig, int flag)
{
    int ret;
    struct sigaction act;

    (void) sigaction(sig, NULL, &act);     Retrieve old setting

    if (flag)                               If flag is true ...
        act.sa_flags &= ~SA_RESTART;        Disable restarting
    else                                    Otherwise ...
        act.sa_flags |= SA_RESTART;         Enable restarting

    ret = sigaction(sig, &act, NULL);      Put new setting in place
    return ret;                             Return result
}
```

The return value is `0` on success or `-1` on error.

10.6.7 Sending Signals: `kill()` and `killpg()`

The traditional Unix function for sending a signal is named `kill()`. The name is something of a misnomer; all it does is send a signal. (Often the result is that the signal's recipient dies, but that need not be true. However, it's way too late now to change the name.) The `killpg()` function sends a signal to a specific process group. The declarations are:

```
#include <sys/types.h>                                    POSIX
#include <signal.h>

int kill(pid_t pid, int sig);
int killpg(int pgrp, int sig);                            POSIX XSI
```

The `sig` argument is either a signal name or `0`. In the latter case, no signal is sent, but the kernel still performs error checking. In particular, this is the correct way to verify that a given process or process group exists, as well as to verify that you have permission to send signals to the process or process group. `kill()` and `killpg()` return `0` on success and `-1` on error; `errno` then indicates the problem.

The rules for the pid value are a bit complicated:

pid > 0 — pid is a process number, and the signal is sent to that process.

pid = 0 — The signal is sent to every process in the sending process's process group.

pid = −1 — The signal is sent to every process on the system except for any special system processes. Permission checking still applies. On GNU/Linux systems, only the init process (PID 1) is excluded, but other systems may have other special processes.

pid < −1 — The signal is sent to the process group represented by the absolute value of pid. Thus, you can send a signal to an entire process group, duplicating killpg()'s functionality. This nonorthogonality provides historical compatibility.

The meanings of pid for kill() are similar to those of waitpid() (see Section 9.1.6.1, "Using POSIX Functions: wait(), waitpid(), and waitid()," page 294).

The Standard C function raise() is essentially equivalent to

```
int
raise(int sig)
{
    return kill(getpid(), sig);
}
```

The C standards committee chose the name raise() because C also has to work in non-Unix environments, and kill() was considered specific to Unix. It was also a good opportunity to use a more descriptive name for the function.

killpg() sends a signal to a process group. As long as the pgrp value is greater than 1, it is equivalent to 'kill(-pgrp, sig)'. POSIX states that if pid is less than or equal to 1, the behavior is undefined. However, the GNU/Linux *killpg*(2) manpage states that if pgrp is 0, the signal is sent to the sending process's process group. (This is the same as kill().)

As you might imagine, you cannot send signals to arbitrary processes (unless you are the superuser, root). For ordinary users, the real or effective UID of the sending process must match the real user ID or saved set-user ID of the receiving process; otherwise the attempt to send the signal will fail. (The different UIDs are described in Section 11.1.1, "Real and Effective IDs," page 383.)

However, SIGCONT is a special case: as long as the receiving process is a member of the same session as the sender, the signal will go through. (Sessions were described briefly in Section 9.2.1, "Job Control Overview," page 300.) This special rule allows a job control shell to continue a stopped descendant process, even if that stopped process is running with a different user ID.

10.6.8 Our Story So Far, Episode II

The System V Release 3 APIs were intended to remedy the various problems presented by the original V7 signal APIs. The notion of signal blocking, in particular, is an important additional concept.

However, those APIs didn't go far enough, since they worked on only one signal at a time, leaving wide open plenty of windows through which undesired signals could arrive. The POSIX APIs, by working *atomically* on multiple signals (the process signal mask, represented programmatically by the `sigset_t` type), solves this problem, closing the windows.

The first set of functions we examined manipulate `sigset_t` values: `sigfillset()`, `sigemptyset()`, `sigaddset()`, `sigdelset()`, and `sigismember()`.

The next set works with the process signal mask: `sigprocmask()` sets and retrieves the process signal mask, `sigpending()` retrieves the set of pending signals, and `sigsuspend()` puts a process to sleep, temporarily replacing the process signal mask with the one in its parameter.

The POSIX `sigaction()` API is (severely) complicated by the need to supply

- Backward-compatible behavior: `SA_RESETHAND` and `SA_RESTART` in the `sa_flags` field.
- A choice as to whether or not the received signal is also blocked: `SA_NODEFER` for `sa_flags`.
- The ability to have two different kinds of signal handlers: one-argument or three-argument.
- A choice of behaviors for managing `SIGCHLD`: `SA_NOCLDSTOP` and `SA_NOCLDWAIT` for `sa_flags`.

The `siginterrupt()` function is a convenience API for enabling or disabling restartable system calls for a given signal.

Finally, `kill()` and `killpg()` can be used to send signals, not just to the current process but to other processes as well (permissions permitting, of course).

10.7 Signals for Interprocess Communication

> *THIS IS A TERRIBLE IDEA! SIGNALS ARE NOT MEANT FOR THIS! Just say* NO.
>
> — Geoff Collyer

One of the primary mechanisms for interprocess communication (IPC) is the pipe, which is described in Section 9.3, "Basic Interprocess Communication: Pipes and FIFOs," page 302. It is possible to use signals for very simple IPC as well.[6] Doing so is rather clumsy; the recipient can tell only that a particular signal came in. While the `sigaction()` API does allow the recipient to learn the PID and owner of the process that sent the signal, such information usually isn't terribly helpful.

[6] Our thanks to Ulrich Drepper for helping us understand the issues involved.

NOTE

As the opening quote indicates, using signals for IPC is almost always a bad idea. We recommend avoiding it if possible. But our goal is to teach you how to use the Linux/Unix facilities, including their negative points, leaving it to you to make an informed decision about what to use.

Signals as IPC may sometimes be the only choice for many programs. In particular, pipes are not an option if two communicating programs were not started by a common parent, and FIFO files may not be an option if one of the communicating programs works only with standard input and output. (One instance in which signals are commonly used is with certain system daemon programs, such as `xinetd`, which accepts several signals advising that it should reread its control file, do a consistency check, and so on.)

The typical high-level structure of a signal-based application looks like this:

```
for (;;) {
    Wait for signal

    Process signal
}
```

The original V7 interface to wait for a signal is `pause()`:

```
#include <unistd.h>                                    POSIX

int pause(void);
```

`pause()` suspends a process; it returns only after a signal has been delivered and the signal handler has returned. `pause()`, by definition, is useful only with caught signals—ignored signals are ignored when they come in, and signals with a default action that terminates the process (with or without a `core` file) still do so.

The problem with the high-level application structure just described is the *Process signal* part. When that code is running, you don't want to have to handle another signal; you want to finish processing the current signal before going on to the next one. One solution is to structure the signal handler to set a flag and check for that flag within the main loop:

```
volatile sig_atomic_t signal_waiting = 0;  /* true if undealt-with signals */

void
handler(int sig)
{
    signal_waiting = 1;
    Set up any other data indicating which signal
}
```

In the mainline code, check the flag:

```
for (;;) {
    if (! signal_waiting) {        If another signal came in
        pause();                   This code is skipped
        signal_waiting = 1;
    }

    Determine which signal came in
    signal_waiting = 0;
    Process the signal
}
```

Unfortunately, this code is rife with race conditions:

```
for (;;) {
    if (! signal_waiting) {
            <----------------------- Signal could arrive here, after condition checked!
        pause();                     pause() would be called anyway
        signal_waiting = 1;
    }

    Determine which signal came in     <---- A signal here could overwrite global data
    signal_waiting = 0;
    Process the signal                 <---- Same here, especially if multiple signals
}
```

The solution is to keep the signal of interest blocked at all times, *except* when waiting for it to arrive. For example, suppose `SIGINT` is the signal of interest:

```
void
handler(int sig)
{
    /* sig is automatically blocked with sigaction() */
    Set any global data about this signal
}

int
main(int argc, char **argv)
{
    sigset_t set;
    struct sigaction act;

    ... usual setup, process options, etc. ...

    sigemptyset(& set);                    Initialize set to empty
    sigaddset(& set, SIGINT);              Add SIGINT to set
    sigprocmask(SIG_BLOCK, & set, NULL);   Block it
```

```
    act.sa_mask = set;                        Set up handler
    act.sa_handler = handler;
    act.sa_flags = 0;
    sigaction(sig, & act, NULL);              Install it

    ...                                       Possibly install separate handlers
    ...                                       For other signals

    sigemptyset(& set);                       Reset to empty, allows SIGINT to arrive

    for (;;) {
        sigsuspend(& set);                    Wait for SIGINT to arrive

        Process signal                        SIGINT is again blocked here
    }

    ... any other code ...
    return 0;
}
```

The key to this working is that `sigsuspend()` *temporarily* replaces the process signal mask with the one passed in as its argument. This allows `SIGINT` to arrive. Once it does, it's handled; the signal handler returns and then `sigsuspend()` returns as well. By the time `sigsuspend()` returns, the original process signal mask is back in place.

You can easily extend this paradigm to multiple signals by blocking all signals of interest during `main()` and during the signal handlers, and unblocking them only in the call to `sigsuspend()`.

Given all this, you should not use `pause()` in new code. `pause()` is standardized by POSIX primarily to support old code. Rather, if you need to structure your application to use signals for IPC, use the `sigsuspend()` and `sigaction()` APIs exclusively.

NOTE

The preceding example code presumes that the process signal mask starts out empty. Production code should instead work with whatever signal mask is in place when the program starts.

10.8 Important Special-Purpose Signals

Several signals serve special purposes. We describe the most important ones here.

10.8.1 Alarm Clocks: `sleep()`, `alarm()`, and `SIGALRM`

It is often necessary to write programs of the form

```
while (some condition isn't true) {
    wait for a while
}
```

This need comes up frequently in shell scripting, for example, to wait until a particular user has logged in:

```
until who | grep '^arnold' > /dev/null
do
    sleep 10
done
```

Two mechanisms, one lower level and one higher level, let a running process know when a given number of seconds have passed.

10.8.1.1 Harder but with More Control: `alarm()` and `SIGALRM`

The most basic building block is the `alarm()` system call:

```
#include <unistd.h>                                    POSIX

unsigned int alarm(unsigned int seconds);
```

After `alarm()` returns, the program keeps running. However, when `seconds` seconds have elapsed, the kernel sends a `SIGALRM` to the process. The default action is to terminate the process, but most likely you will instead have installed a signal handler for `SIGALRM`.

The return value is either `0` or, if a previous alarm had been set, the number of seconds remaining before it would have gone off. However, there is only one such alarm for a process; the previous alarm is canceled and the new one is put in place.

The advantage here is that with your own handler in place, you can do anything you wish when the signal comes in. The disadvantage is that you have to be prepared to work in multiple contexts: that of the mainline program and that of the signal handler.

10.8.1.2 Simple and Easy: `sleep()`

An easier way to wait a fixed amount of time is with `sleep()`:

```
#include <unistd.h>                                    POSIX

unsigned int sleep(unsigned int seconds);
```

The return value is `0` if the process slept for the full amount of time. Otherwise, the return value is the remaining time left to sleep. This latter return value can occur if a signal came in while the process was napping.

NOTE

The `sleep()` function is often implemented with a combination of `signal()`, `alarm()`, and `pause()`. This approach makes it dangerous to mix `sleep()` with your own calls to `alarm()`

(or to the `setitimer()` advanced function, described in Section 16.3.3, "Interval Timers: `setitimer()` and `getitimer()`," page 570). To learn about the `nanosleep()` function now, see Section 16.3.4, "More Exact Pauses: `nanosleep()`," page 573.

10.8.2 Job Control Signals

Several signals are used to implement *job control*—the ability to start and stop jobs and move them to and from the background and foreground. At the user level, you have undoubtedly done this: using CTRL-Z to stop a job, using `bg` to put a stopped job into the background, and occasionally using `fg` to move a background or stopped job into the foreground.

Section 9.2.1, "Job Control Overview," page 300, describes generally how job control works. This section completes the overview by describing the job control signals, since you may occasionally wish to catch them directly:

`SIGTSTP`
: This signal effects a "terminal stop." It is the signal the kernel sends to the process when the user at the terminal (or window emulating a terminal) types a particular key. Normally, this is CTRL-Z, just as CTRL-C normally sends a `SIGINT`.

  The default action for `SIGTSTP` is to stop (suspend) the process. However, you can catch this signal, just like any other. It is a good idea to do so if your program changes the state of the terminal. For example, consider the `vim` or Emacs screen editors, which put the terminal into character-at-a-time mode. Upon receipt of `SIGTSTP`, they should restore the terminal to its normal line-at-a-time mode and then suspend themselves.

`SIGSTOP`
: This signal also stops a process, but it cannot be caught, blocked, or ignored. It can be used manually (with the `kill` command) as a last resort, or programmatically. For example, the `SIGTSTP` handler just discussed, after restoring the terminal's state, could then use '`raise(SIGSTOP)`' to stop the process.

`SIGTTIN`
`SIGTTOU`
: These signals were defined earlier as "background read from tty" and "background write to tty." A *tty* is a terminal device. On job control systems, processes running in the background are blocked from reading from or writing to the terminal. When a process attempts either operation, the kernel sends it the appropriate signal. For both of them, the default action is to stop the process. You may catch these signals if you wish, but there is rarely a reason to do so.

`SIGCONT`
: This signal continues a stopped process. It is ignored if the process is running. You can catch it if you wish, but again, for most programs there's little reason to do so. Continuing our example, the `SIGCONT` handler for a screen editor should put the terminal back into character-at-a-time mode and arrange to redraw the screen before returning.

When a process is stopped, any other signals sent to it become pending. The exception to this is `SIGKILL`, which is always delivered to the process and which cannot be caught, blocked, or ignored. Assuming that signals besides `SIGKILL` have been sent, upon receipt of a `SIGCONT`, the pending signals are delivered and the process then continues execution after they've been handled.

Finally, we must note that there is actually quite a lot to understand if you wish to manage job control and your terminal settings (like, if you're writing a screen editor). Unfortunately, it's all beyond the scope of this book.

10.8.3 Parental Supervision: Three Different Strategies

As described in Section 9.1.1, "Creating a Process: `fork()`," page 275, one side effect of calling `fork()` is the creation of parent-child relationships among processes. A parent process can wait for one or more of its children to die and recover the child's exit status using one of the `wait()` family of system calls.

Dead child processes that haven't been waited for are termed *zombies*. Normally, every time a child process dies, the kernel sends a `SIGCHLD` signal to the parent process.[7] The default action is to ignore this signal. In this case, zombie processes accrue until the parent does a `wait()` or until the parent itself dies. In the latter case, the zombie children are reparented to the `init` system process (PID 1), which reaps them as part of its normal work. Similarly, active children are also reparented to `init` and will be reaped when they exit.

`SIGCHLD` is used for more than death-of-children notification. Any time a child is stopped (by one of the job control signals discussed earlier), `SIGCHLD` is also sent to the parent. The POSIX standard indicates that `SIGCHLD` "may be sent" when a child is continued as well; apparently there are differences among historical Unix systems.

A combination of flags for the `sa_flags` field in the `struct sigaction` and the use of `SIG_IGN` as the action for `SIGCHLD` allows you to change the way the kernel deals with children stopping, continuing, or dying.

As with signals in general, the interfaces and mechanisms described here are complicated because they have evolved over time.

10.8.3.1 Poor Parenting: Ignoring Children Completely

The simplest thing you can do is to change the action for `SIGCHLD` to `SIG_IGN`. In this case, children that terminate do not become zombies. Instead, their exit status is thrown away, and they are removed from the system entirely. Another option that produces the same effect is use of the `SA_NOCLDWAIT` flag. In code:

```
/* Old style: */                    /* New style: */
                                    struct sigaction sa;
                                    sa.sa_handler = SIG_IGN;
signal(SIGCHLD, SIG_IGN);           sa.sa_flags = SA_NOCLDWAIT;
                                    sigemptyset(& sa.sa_mask);
                                    sigaction(SIGCHLD, & sa, NULL);
```

[7] Historically, BSD systems used the name `SIGCHLD`, and this is what POSIX uses. System V had a similar signal named `SIGCLD`. GNU/Linux `#define`s the latter to be the former—see Table 10.1.

10.8.3.2 Permissive Parenting: Supervising Minimally

Alternatively, you may only care about child termination and not be interested in simple state changes (stopped or continued). In this case, use the `SA_NOCLDSTOP` flag, and set up a signal handler that calls `wait()` (or one of its siblings) to reap the process.

In general, you *cannot* expect to get one `SIGCHLD` per child that dies. You should treat `SIGCHLD` as meaning "at least one child has died" and be prepared to reap as many children as possible whenever you process `SIGCHLD`.

The following program, `ch-signals-reap1.c`, blocks `SIGCHLD` until it's ready to recover the children:

```
1  /* ch-signals-reap1.c --- demonstrate SIGCHLD management, using a loop */
2
3  #include <stdio.h>
4  #include <errno.h>
5  #include <signal.h>
6  #include <string.h>
7  #include <unistd.h>
8  #include <sys/types.h>
9  #include <sys/wait.h>
10
11 #define MAX_KIDS    42
12 #define NOT_USED    -1
13
14 pid_t kids[MAX_KIDS];
15 size_t nkids = 0;
```

The `kids` array tracks the process IDs of children processes. If an element is `NOT_USED`, then it doesn't represent an unreaped child. (Lines 93–94, below, initialize it.) `nkids` indicates how many values in `kids` should be checked.

Because signal handlers should not call any member of the `printf()` family, we provide a simple "helper" function, `format_num()`, to turn a decimal signal or PID number into a string. This is primitive, but it works:

```
17 /* format_num --- helper function since can't use [sf]printf() */
18
19 const char *
20 format_num(int num)
21 {
22 #define NUMSIZ  30
23     static char buf[NUMSIZ];
24     int i;
25
26     if (num <= 0) {
27         strcpy(buf, "0");
28         return buf;
29     }
```

```

    i = NUMSIZ - 1;
    buf[i--] = '\0';

    /* Generate digits backwards into string. */
    do {
        buf[i--] = (num % 10) + '0';
        num /= 10;
    } while (num > 0);

    return & buf[i+1];
}
```

Here is the signal handling function:

```
/* childhandler --- catch SIGCHLD, reap all available children */

void
childhandler(int sig)
{
    int status, ret;
    int i;
    char buf[100];
    static const char entered[] = "Entered childhandler\n";
    static const char exited[] = "Exited childhandler\n";

    int junk = write(1, entered, strlen(entered));
    for (i = 0; i < nkids; i++) {
        if (kids[i] == NOT_USED)
            continue;

    retry:
        if ((ret = waitpid(kids[i], & status, WNOHANG)) == kids[i]) {
            strcpy(buf, "\treaped process ");
            strcat(buf, format_num(ret));
            strcat(buf, "\n");
            junk = write(1, buf, strlen(buf));
            kids[i] = NOT_USED;
        } else if (ret == 0) {
            strcpy(buf, "\tpid ");
            strcat(buf, format_num(kids[i]));
            strcat(buf, " not available yet\n");
            junk = write(1, buf, strlen(buf));
        } else if (ret == -1 && errno == EINTR) {
            junk = write(1, "\tretrying\n", 10);
            goto retry;
```

```
74         } else {
75             strcpy(buf, "\twaitpid() failed: ");
76             strcat(buf, strerror(errno));
77             strcat(buf, "\n");
78             junk = write(1, buf, strlen(buf));
79         }
80     }
81     junk = write(1, exited, strlen(exited));
82 }
```

Lines 54 and 81 print "entered" and "exited" messages, so that we can clearly see when the signal handler is invoked. Other messages start with a leading tab character.

The main part of the signal handler is a large loop (lines 55–80). Lines 56–57 check for `NOT_USED` and continue the loop if the current slot isn't in use.

Line 60 calls `waitpid()` on the PID in the current element of `kids`. We supply the `WNOHANG` option, which causes `waitpid()` to return immediately if the requested child isn't available. This call is necessary since it's possible that not all of the children have exited.

Based on the return value, the code takes the appropriate action. Lines 60–65 handle the case in which the child is found by printing a message and marking the appropriate slot in `kids` as `NOT_USED`.

Lines 66–70 handle the case in which the requested child is not available. The return value is `0` in this case, so we print a message and keep going.

Lines 71–73 handle the case in which the system call was interrupted. In this case, a `goto` back to the `waitpid()` call is the cleanest way to handle things. (Since `main()` causes all signals to be blocked when the signal handler runs [line 100], this interruption shouldn't happen. But this example shows you how to deal with all the cases.)

Lines 74–79 handle any other error, printing an appropriate error message. The code continues:

```
84 /* main --- set up child-related information and signals, create children */
85
86 int
87 main(int argc, char **argv)
88 {
89     struct sigaction sa;
90     sigset_t childset, emptyset;
91     int i;
92
93     for (i = 0; i < nkids; i++)
94         kids[i] = NOT_USED;
95
96     sigemptyset(& emptyset);
97
98     sa.sa_flags = SA_NOCLDSTOP;
99     sa.sa_handler = childhandler;
100    sigfillset(& sa.sa_mask);   /* block everything when handler runs */
```

```
101         sigaction(SIGCHLD, & sa, NULL);
102
103         sigemptyset(& childset);
104         sigaddset(& childset, SIGCHLD);
105
106         sigprocmask(SIG_SETMASK, & childset, NULL); /* block it in main code */
107
108         for (nkids = 0; nkids < 5; nkids++) {
109             if ((kids[nkids] = fork()) == 0) {
110                 sleep(3);
111                 _exit(0);
112             }
113         }
114
115         sleep(5);   /* give the kids a chance to terminate */
116
117         printf("waiting for signal\n");
118         sigsuspend(& emptyset);
119
120         return 0;
121     }
```

Lines 93–94 initialize `kids`. Line 96 initializes `emptyset`. Lines 98–101 set up and install the signal handler for `SIGCHLD`. Note the use of `SA_NOCLDSTOP` on line 98, while line 100 blocks all signals when the handler is running.

Lines 103–104 create a signal set representing just `SIGCHLD`, and line 106 installs it as the process signal mask for the program.

Lines 108–113 create five child processes, each of which sleeps for three seconds. Along the way, it updates the `kids` array and `nkids` variable.

Line 115 then gives the children a chance to terminate by sleeping longer than they did. (This doesn't *guarantee* that the children will terminate, but the chances are pretty good.)

Finally, lines 117–118 print a message and then pause, replacing the process signal mask that blocks `SIGCHLD` with an empty one. This allows the `SIGCHLD` signal to come through, in turn causing the signal handler to run. Here's what happens:

```
$ ch-signals-reap1                              Run the program
waiting for signal
Entered childhandler
    reaped process 70395
    reaped process 70396
    reaped process 70397
    reaped process 70398
    reaped process 70399
Exited childhandler
```

The signal handler reaps all of the children in one go.

The following program, `ch-signals-reap2.c` is similar to `ch-signals-reap1.c`. The difference is that it allows `SIGCHLD` to arrive at any time. This behavior increases the chance of receiving more than one `SIGCHLD` but does *not* guarantee it. As a result, the signal handler still has to be prepared to reap multiple children in a loop:

```
/* ch-signals-reap2.c --- demonstrate SIGCHLD management, one signal per child */

 ... unchanged code omitted ...

pid_t kids[MAX_KIDS];
size_t nkids = 0;
size_t kidsleft = 0;                /* <<< Added */

 ... unchanged code for format_num() omitted ...

/* childhandler --- catch SIGCHLD, reap all available children */

void
childhandler(int sig)
{
    int status, ret;
    int i;
    char buf[100];
    static const char entered[] = "Entered childhandler\n";
    static const char exited[] = "Exited childhandler\n";

    int junk = write(1, entered, strlen(entered));
    for (i = 0; i < nkids; i++) {
        if (kids[i] == NOT_USED)
            continue;

    retry:
        if ((ret = waitpid(kids[i], & status, WNOHANG)) == kids[i]) {
            strcpy(buf, "\treaped process ");
            strcat(buf, format_num(ret));
            strcat(buf, "\n");
            junk = write(1, buf, strlen(buf));
            kids[i] = NOT_USED;
            kidsleft--;         /* <<< Added */
        } else if (ret == 0) {
 ... unchanged code omitted ...
    junk = write(1, exited, strlen(exited));
}
```

This is identical to the previous version, except we have a new variable, `kidsleft`, indicating how many unreaped children there are. Lines 15 and 67 flag the new code. `main()` is modified as follows:

```
86  /* main --- set up child-related information and signals, create children */
87
88  int
89  main(int argc, char **argv)
90  {
     ... unchanged code omitted ...
104
105     sigemptyset(& childset);
106     sigaddset(& childset, SIGCHLD);
107
108 /*  sigprocmask(SIG_SETMASK, & childset, NULL); /* block it in main code */
109
110     for (nkids = 0; nkids < 5; nkids++) {
111         if ((kids[nkids] = fork()) == 0) {
112             sleep(3);
113             _exit(0);
114         }
115         kidsleft++;     /* <<< Added */
116     }
117
118 /*  sleep(5);   /* give the kids a chance to terminate */
119
120     while (kidsleft > 0) {      /* <<< Added */
121         printf("waiting for signals\n");
122         sigsuspend(& emptyset);
123     }                /* <<< Added */
124
125     return 0;
126 }
```

Here, too, the code is almost identical. Lines 108 and 118 are commented out from the earlier version, and lines 115, 120, and 123 were added. The program receives one signal for more than one child:

```
$ ch-signals-reap2                              Run the program
waiting for signals
Entered childhandler
    reaped process 70432                        Reaped four children
    reaped process 70433
    reaped process 70434
    reaped process 70435
    pid 70436 not available yet                 But one isn't ready yet
```

```
Exited childhandler
Entered childhandler
    pid 70436 not available yet                    Still not ready
Exited childhandler
waiting for signals
Entered childhandler
    reaped process 70436                           Reaped the last one
Exited childhandler
```

NOTE

The code for `ch-signals-reap2.c` has one important flaw—a race condition. Take another look at lines 110–116 in `ch-signals-reap2.c`. What happens if a `SIGCHLD` comes in while this code is running? It's possible for the `kids` array and `nkids` and `kidsleft` variables to become corrupted: the main code adds in a new process, but the signal handler takes one away.

This piece of code is an excellent example of a critical section; it must run uninterrupted. The correct way to manage this code is to bracket it with calls that first block and then unblock `SIGCHLD`.

10.8.3.3 Strict Parental Control

The `siginfo_t` structure and three-argument signal catcher make it possible to learn what happened to a child. For `SIGCHLD`, the `si_code` field of the `siginfo_t` indicates the reason the signal was sent (child stopped, continued, exited, etc.). Table 10.5 presents the full list of values. All of these are defined in the POSIX standard.

The following program, `ch-signals-status.c`, demonstrates the use of the `siginfo_t` structure:

Table 10.5: `si_code` values for `SIGCHLD`

Value	Meaning
`CLD_CONTINUED`	A stopped child has been continued. Some systems send `SIGCHLD` to a parent process when their child is sent `SIGCONT`. Some don't. Linux does.
`CLD_DUMPED`	Child terminated abnormally and dumped core.
`CLD_EXITED`	Child exited normally.
`CLD_KILLED`	Child was killed by a signal.
`CLD_STOPPED`	The child process was stopped.
`CLD_TRAPPED`	A child process being traced has stopped. (This condition occurs if a program is being traced—either from a debugger or for real-time monitoring. In any case, you're not likely to see it in run-of-the-mill situations.)

```
1  /* ch-signals-status.c --- demonstrate SIGCHLD management, use 3 argument handler */
2
3  #include <stdio.h>
4  #include <errno.h>
5  #include <signal.h>
6  #include <string.h>
7  #include <stdlib.h>
8  #include <unistd.h>
9  #include <sys/types.h>
10 #include <sys/wait.h>
11
12 void manage(siginfo_t *si);
13
```

... unchanged code for format_num() omitted ...

Lines 3–10 include standard header files, line 12 declares `manage()`, which deals with the child's status changes; the `format_num()` function is unchanged from before. Here is the signal handling function:

```
40 /* childhandler --- catch SIGCHLD, reap just one child */
41
42 void
43 childhandler(int sig, siginfo_t *si, void *context)
44 {
45     int status, ret;
46     int i;
47     char buf[100];
48     static const char entered[] = "Entered childhandler\n";
49     static const char exited[] = "Exited childhandler\n";
50
51     int junk = write(1, entered, strlen(entered));
52 retry:
53     if ((ret = waitpid(si->si_pid, & status, WNOHANG)) == si->si_pid) {
54         strcpy(buf, "\treaped process ");
55         strcat(buf, format_num(si->si_pid));
56         strcat(buf, "\n");
57         junk = write(1, buf, strlen(buf));
58         manage(si);          /* deal with what happened to it */
59     } else if (ret > 0) {
60         strcpy(buf, "\treaped unexpected pid ");
61         strcat(buf, format_num(ret));
62         strcat(buf, "\n");
63         junk = write(1, buf, strlen(buf));
64         goto retry;      /* why not? */
65     } else if (ret == 0) {
66         strcpy(buf, "\tpid ");
```

```
67          strcat(buf, format_num(si->si_pid));
68          strcat(buf, " changed status\n");
69          junk = write(1, buf, strlen(buf));
70          manage(si);          /* deal with what happened to it */
71      } else if (ret == -1 && errno == EINTR) {
72          junk = write(1, "\tretrying\n", 10);
73          goto retry;
74      } else {
75          strcpy(buf, "\twaitpid() failed: ");
76          strcat(buf, strerror(errno));
77          strcat(buf, "\n");
78          junk = write(1, buf, strlen(buf));
79      }
80
81      junk = write(1, exited, strlen(exited));
82  }
```

The signal handler is similar to those shown earlier. Note the argument list (line 43), and that there is no loop.

Lines 53–58 handle process termination, including calling `manage()` to print the status.

Lines 59–64 handle the case of an unexpected child dying. This case shouldn't happen, since this signal handler is passed information specific to a particular child process.

Lines 65–70 are what interest us: the return value is `0` for status changes. `manage()` deals with the details (line 70).

Lines 71–73 handle interrupts, and lines 74–79 deal with errors.

The `child()` function handles the child's behavior, taking actions of the sort to cause the parent to be notified:[8]

```
84  /* child --- what to do in the child */
85
86  void
87  child(void)
88  {
89      raise(SIGCONT);      /* should be ignored */
90      raise(SIGSTOP);      /* go to sleep, parent wakes us back up */
91      printf("\t---> child restarted <---\n");
92      exit(42);            /* normal exit, let parent get value */
93  }
```

Line 89 sends `SIGCONT`, which might cause the parent to get a `CLD_CONTINUED` event. Line 90 sends a `SIGSTOP`, which stops the process (the signal is uncatchable) and causes a `CLD_STOPPED` event for the parent. Once the parent restarts the child, the child prints a message to show it's active again and then exits with a distinguished exit status.

[8] Perhaps `child_at_school()` would be a better function name.

The `main()` function sets everything up:

```
95  /* main --- set up child-related information and signals, create child */
96
97  int
98  main(int argc, char **argv)
99  {
100     pid_t kid;
101     struct sigaction sa;
102     sigset_t childset, emptyset;
103
104     sigemptyset(& emptyset);
105
106     sa.sa_flags = SA_SIGINFO;
107     sa.sa_sigaction = childhandler;
108     sigfillset(& sa.sa_mask);   /* block everything when handler runs */
109     sigaction(SIGCHLD, & sa, NULL);
110
111     sigemptyset(& childset);
112     sigaddset(& childset, SIGCHLD);
113
114     sigprocmask(SIG_SETMASK, & childset, NULL); /* block it in main code */
115
116     if ((kid = fork()) == 0)
117         child();
118
119     /* parent executes here */
120     for (;;) {
121         printf("waiting for signals\n");
122         sigsuspend(& emptyset);
123     }
124
125     return 0;
126 }
```

Lines 106–109 put the handler in place. Line 106 sets the `SA_SIGINFO` flag so that the three-argument handler is used. Lines 111–114 block `SIGCHLD`.

Line 116 creates the child process. Lines 120–123 continue in the parent, using `sigsuspend()` to wait for signals to come in.

Through the `manage()` function, the parent deals with the status change in the child. `manage()` is called when the status changes and when the child has exited:

```
/* manage --- deal with different things that could happen to child */

void manage(siginfo_t *si)
{
```

```
132     char buf[100];
133     int junk;
134
135     switch (si->si_code) {
136     case CLD_STOPPED:
137         junk = write(1, "\tchild stopped, restarting\n", 27);
138         kill(si->si_pid, SIGCONT);
139         break;
140
141     case CLD_CONTINUED:
142         junk = write(1, "\tchild continued\n", 17);
143         break;
144
145     case CLD_EXITED:
146         strcpy(buf, "\tchild exited with status ");
147         strcat(buf, format_num(si->si_status));
148         strcat(buf, "\n");
149         junk = write(1, buf, strlen(buf));
150         exit(0);    /* we're done */
151         break;
152 153     case CLD_DUMPED:
154         junk = write(1, "\tchild dumped\n", 14);
155         break;
156
157     case CLD_KILLED:
158         junk = write(1, "\tchild killed\n", 14);
159         break;
160
161     case CLD_TRAPPED:
162         junk = write(1, "\tchild trapped\n", 15);
163         break;
164     }
165 }
```

Lines 136–139 handle the case in which the child stopped; the parent restarts the child by sending `SIGCONT`.

Lines 141–143 print a notification that the child continued. The POSIX standard lists `CLD_CONTINUED` as an XSI extension, so on some systems it may not occur. GNU/Linux does support it.

Lines 145–151 handle the case in which the child exits, printing the exit status. For this program, the parent is done too, so the code exits, although in a larger program, that's not the right action to take.

The other cases are more specialized. In the event of `CLD_KILLED`, the `status` value filled in by `waitpid()` would be useful in determining more details.

Here is what happens when it runs:

```
$ ch-signals-status                              Run the program
waiting for signals
Entered childhandler                             Signal handler entered
        pid 72018 changed status
        child stopped, restarting                Handler takes action
Exited childhandler
waiting for signals
Entered childhandler
        pid 72018 changed status
        child continued                          Child was continued
Exited childhandler
waiting for signals
        ---> child restarted <---                From the child
Entered childhandler
        reaped process 72018                     Parent's handler reaps child
        child exited with status 42
```

Unfortunately, because there is no way to guarantee the delivery of one `SIGCHLD` per process, your program has to be prepared to recover multiple children at one shot.

10.9 Signals across `fork()` and `exec()`

When a program calls `fork()`, the signal situation in the child is almost identical to that of the parent. Installed handlers remain in place, blocked signals remain blocked, and so on. However, any signals pending for the parent are cleared for the child, including time left as set by `alarm()`. This is straightforward, and it makes sense.

When a process calls one of the `exec()` functions, the disposition in the new program is as follows:

- Signals set to their default action stay set to their default.
- Any caught signals are reset to their default action.
- Signals that are ignored stay ignored. `SIGCHLD` is a special case. If `SIGCHLD` is ignored before the exec, it may stay ignored after it. Alternatively, it may be reset to the default action. (This allows a program that ignores `SIGCHLD` to fork and exec a shell, which needs to be able to handle `SIGCHLD` in order to do its job.) What actually happens is purposely unspecified by POSIX. The GNU/Linux *execve*(2) manpage says that if `SIGCHLD` is being ignored, it remains that way.
- Signals that are blocked before the exec remain blocked after it. In other words, the new program inherits the process's existing process signal mask.
- Any pending signals (those that have arrived but that were blocked) are cleared. The new program won't get them.

- The time remaining for an `alarm()` remains in place. (In other words, if a process sets an alarm and then calls `exec()` directly, the new image will eventually get the `SIGALRM`. If it does a `fork()` first, the parent keeps the alarm setting, while the child, which does the exec, does not.)

NOTE

Many, if not most, programs assume that signal actions are initialized to their defaults and that no signals are blocked. Thus, particularly if you didn't write the program being run with `exec()`, it's a good idea to unblock all signals before doing the exec.

10.10 Summary

Our story so far, Episode III.
— Arnold Robbins

- Signal handling interfaces have evolved from being simple but prone to race conditions, to being complicated but reliable. Unfortunately, the multiplicity of interfaces makes them harder to learn than many other Linux/Unix APIs.
- Each signal has an action associated with it. The action is one of the following: ignore the signal; perform the system default action; or call a user-provided handler. The system default action, in turn, is one of the following: ignore the signal; kill the process; kill the process and dump core; stop the process; or continue the process if stopped.
- `signal()` and `raise()` are standardized by ISO C. `signal()` manages actions for particular signals; `raise()` sends a signal to the current process. Whether signal handlers stay installed upon invocation or are reset to their default values is up to the implementation. `signal()` and `raise()` are the simplest interfaces, and they suffice for many applications.
- Earlier versions of POSIX defined the `bsd_signal()` function, which is like `signal()` but guarantees that the handler stays installed. It has since been removed from the standard, although GLIBC still supports it.
- What happens after a signal handler returns varies according to the type of system. Traditional systems (V7, Solaris, and likely others) reset signal dispositions to their default. On those systems, interrupted system calls return `-1`, setting `errno` to `EINTR`. BSD systems leave the handler installed and return `-1` with `errno` set to `EINTR` only when no data was transferred; otherwise, they restart the system call.
- GNU/Linux follows POSIX, which is similar but not identical to BSD. If no data was transferred, the system call returns `-1`/`EINTR`. Otherwise, it returns a count of the amount

of data transferred. The BSD "always restart" behavior is available in the `sigaction()` interface but is not the default.

- Signal handlers used with `signal()` are prone to race conditions. Variables of type `volatile sig_atomic_t` should be used exclusively inside signal handlers. (For expositional purposes, we did not follow this rule in some of our examples.) Similarly, only the functions in Table 10.2 are safe to call from within a signal handler.
- The System V Release 3 signal API (lifted from 4.0 BSD) was an initial attempt at reliable signals. Don't use it in new code.
- The POSIX API has multiple components:

  - The process signal mask, which contains the currently blocked signals.
  - The `sigset_t` type to represent signal masks, and the `sigfillset()`, `sigemptyset()`, `sigaddset()`, `sigdelset()`, and `sigismember()` functions for working with it.
  - The `sigprocmask()` function to set and retrieve the process signal mask.
  - The `sigpending()` function to retrieve the set of pending signals.
  - The `sigaction()` API and `struct sigaction` in all their glory.

  These facilities together use signal blocking and the process signal mask to provide reliable signals. Furthermore, through various flags, it's possible to get restartable system calls and a more capable signal handler that receives more information about the reason for a particular signal (the `siginfo_t` structure).

- `kill()` and `killpg()` are the POSIX mechanisms for sending signals. These differ from `raise()` in two ways: (1) one process may send a signal to another process or to an entire process group (permissions permitting, of course); and (2) sending signal `0` does not send anything but does do the checking. Thus, these functions provide a way to verify the existence of a particular process or process group, along with the ability to send it (them) a signal.
- Signals can be used as an IPC mechanism, although such use is a poor way to structure your application and is prone to race conditions. If someone holds a gun to your head to make you work that way, use careful signal blocking and the `sigaction()` interface to do it correctly.
- `SIGALRM` and the `alarm()` system call provide a low-level mechanism for notification after a certain number of seconds have passed. `pause()` suspends a process until any signal comes in. `sleep()` uses these to put a process to sleep for a given amount of time; `sleep()` and `alarm()` should not be used together. `pause()` itself opens up race conditions; signal blocking and `sigsuspend()` should be used instead.
- Job control signals implement job control for shells. Most of the time you should leave them set to their default, but it's good to know that occasionally it makes sense to catch them.

- Catching `SIGCHLD` lets a parent know what its children processes are doing. Using '`signal(SIGCHLD, SIG_IGN)`' (or `sigaction()` with `SA_NOCLDWAIT`) ignores children altogether. Using `sigaction()` with `SA_NOCLDSTOP` provides notification only about termination. In the latter case, whether or not `SIGCHLD` is blocked, signal handlers for `SIGCHLD` should be prepared to reap multiple children at once. Finally, using `sigaction()` without `SA_NOCLDSTOP` with a three-argument signal handler gives you the reason for receipt for the signal. (Whew!)
- After a `fork()`, signal disposition in the child remains the same, except that pending signals and alarms are cleared. After an exec, it's a little more complicated—essentially everything that can be left alone is; anything else is reset to its defaults.

Exercises

1. Implement `bsd_signal()` by using `sigaction()`.
2. If you're not running GNU/Linux, run `ch-signals-catchint` on your system. Is your system traditional or BSD?
3. Implement the System V Release 3 functions `sighold()`, `sigrelse()`, `sigignore()`, `sigpause()`, and `sigset()` by using `sigaction()` and the other related functions in the POSIX API.
4. Practice your bit-bashing skills. Assuming that there is no signal `0` and that there are no more than 31 signals, provide a `typedef` for `sigset_t` and write `sigemptyset()`, `sigfillset()`, `sigaddset()`, `sigdelset()`, and `sigismember()`.
5. Practice your bit-bashing skills some more. Repeat the previous exercise, this time assuming that the highest signal is `84`.
6. Now that you've done the previous two exercises, find `sigemptyset()` et al. in your `<signal.h>` header file. (You may have to search for them; they could be in files `#included` by `<signal.h>`.) Are they macros or functions?
7. In Section 10.7, "Signals for Interprocess Communication," page 360, we mentioned that production code should work with the initial process signal mask, adding signals to be blocked and removing them except in the call to `sigsuspend()`. Rewrite the example, using the appropriate calls to do this.
8. In Section 2.4, "The Environment," page 37, we showed the options accepted by the `env` command:

```
$ env --help
Usage: env [OPTION]... [-] [NAME=VALUE]... [COMMAND [ARG]...]
Set each NAME to VALUE in the environment and run COMMAND.

Mandatory arguments to long options are mandatory for short options too.
  -i, --ignore-environment  start with an empty environment
```

```
  -0, --null           end each output line with NUL, not newline
  -u, --unset=NAME     remove variable from the environment
  -C, --chdir=DIR      change working directory to DIR
  -S, --split-string=S  process and split S into separate arguments;
                        used to pass multiple arguments on shebang lines
      --block-signal[=SIG]    block delivery of SIG signal(s) to COMMAND
      --default-signal[=SIG]  reset handling of SIG signal(s) to the default
      --ignore-signal[=SIG]   set handling of SIG signal(s) to do nothing
      --list-signal-handling  list non default signal handling to stderr
  -v, --debug          print verbose information for each processing step
      --help     display this help and exit
      --version  output version information and exit

A mere - implies -i.  If no COMMAND, print the resulting environment.

SIG may be a signal name like 'PIPE', or a signal number like '13'.
Without SIG, all known signals are included.  Multiple signals can be
comma-separated.  An empty SIG argument is a no-op.

Exit status:
  125  if the env command itself fails
  126  if COMMAND is found but cannot be invoked
  127  if COMMAND cannot be found
  -    the exit status of COMMAND otherwise

GNU coreutils online help: <https://www.gnu.org/software/coreutils/>
Full documentation <https://www.gnu.org/software/coreutils/env>
or available locally via: info '(coreutils) env invocation'
```

The signal-related options should now make much more sense to you. Review the code in the Coreutils `env.c` that implements the signal handling.

9. Write your own version of the `kill` command. The interface should be

   `kill` [`-s` *signal-name*] *pid* ...

   Without a specific signal, the program should send `SIGTERM`.

10. Why do you think modern shells such as Bash and `ksh93` have `kill` as a built-in command?

11. (Hard). Implement `sleep()`, using `alarm()`, `signal()`, and `pause()`. What if a signal handler for `SIGALRM` is already in place?

12. Experiment with `ch-signals-reap1.c`, changing the amount of time each child sleeps and arranging to call `sigsuspend()` enough times to reap all the children.

13. See if you can get `ch-signals-reap2.c` to corrupt the information in `kids`, `nkids`, and `kidsleft`. Now add blocking/unblocking around the critical section and see if it makes a difference.

Chapter 11

Permissions and User and Group ID Numbers

Linux, following Unix, is a *multiuser system*. Unlike many early operating systems for personal computers, in which there is only one user and whoever is physically in front of the computer has complete control, Linux and Unix separate files and processes by the owners and groups to which they belong. In this chapter, we examine permission checking and look at the APIs for retrieving and setting the owner and group identifiers.

11.1 Checking Permissions

As we saw in Section 5.4.2, "Retrieving File Information," page 131, the filesystem stores a file's user identifier and group identifier as numeric values; these are the types `uid_t` and `gid_t`, respectively. For brevity, we use the abbreviations UID and GID for "user identifier" and "group identifier."

Every process has several user and group identifiers associated with it. As a simplification, one particular UID and GID are used for permission checking; when the UID of a process matches the UID of a file, the file's user permission bits dictate what the process can do with the file. If they don't match, the system checks the GID of the process against the GID of the file, if those match, the group permissions apply; otherwise the "other" permissions apply.

Besides files, the UID controls how one process can affect another by sending it a signal. Signals are described in Chapter 10, "Signals," page 333.

Finally, the superuser, `root`, is a special case. `root` is identified by a UID of `0`. When a process has UID `0`, the kernel lets it do whatever it wants to: read, write, or remove files, send signals to arbitrary processes, and so on. (POSIX is more obtuse about this, referring to processes with "appropriate privilege." This language in turn has filtered down into the GNU/Linux manpages and the GLIBC online Info manual. Some operating systems do separate privilege by user, and Linux is moving in this direction as well. Nevertheless, in current practice, "appropriate privilege" just means processes with UID `0`.)

11.1.1 Real and Effective IDs

UID and GID numbers are like personal identification. Sometimes you need to carry more than one bit of identification around with you. For instance, you may have a driver's license or national government identity card.[1] In addition, your university or company may have issued you an identification card. Such is the case with processes too; they carry multiple UID and GID numbers around with them, as follows:

Real user ID
: The UID of the user that forked the process.

Effective user ID
: The UID used for most permission checking. Most of the time, the effective and real UIDs are the same. The effective UID can be different from the real one at startup if the *setuid* bit of the executable program's file is set and the file is owned by someone other than the user running the program (more details soon).

Saved set-user ID
: The original effective UID at program startup (after the exec). This plays a role in permission checking when a process needs to swap its real and effective UIDs back and forth. This concept came from System V.

Real group ID
: The GID of the user that created the process, analogous to the real UID.

Effective group ID
: The GID used for permission checking, analogous to the effective UID.

Saved set-group ID
: The original effective GID at program startup, analogous to the saved set-user ID.

Supplemental group set
: 4.2 BSD introduced the idea of a *group set*. Besides the real and effective GIDs, each process has some set of additional groups to which it *simultaneously* belongs. Thus, when permission checking is done for a file's group permissions, the kernel not only checks the effective GID but also checks all of the GIDs in the group set.

Any process can retrieve all of these values. A regular (non-superuser) process can switch its real and effective user and group IDs back and forth. A `root` process (one with an effective UID of `0`) can also set the values however it needs to (although this can be a one-way operation).

11.1.2 Setuid and Setgid Bits

The *setuid* and *setgid* bits[2] in the file permissions cause a process to acquire an effective UID or GID that is different from the real one. These bits are applied manually to a file with the `chmod` command:

---

[1] Although the United States doesn't have official identity cards, many countries do.

[2] Dennis Ritchie, the inventor of C and a cocreator of Unix, received a patent for the setuid bit: *Protection of Data File Contents*, US patent number 4,135,240. A copy is included in the file `Documents/US4135240.pdf` in the book's GitHub repository. AT&T assigned the patent to the public, allowing anyone to use its technology.

```
$ chmod u+s myprogram                 Add setuid bit
$ chmod g+s myprogram                 Add setgid bit
$ ls -l myprogram
-rwsr-sr-x 1 arnold arnold 35120 Feb  8 21:00 myprogram
```

The s character where an x character usually appears indicates the presence of the setuid/setgid bits.

As mentioned in Section 8.2.1, "Using Mount Options," page 230, the `nosuid` option to `mount` for a filesystem prevents the kernel from honoring both the setuid and setgid bits. This is a security feature; for example, a user with a home GNU/Linux system might handcraft a USB flash drive with a copy of the shell executable made setuid to `root`. But if the GNU/Linux system in the office or the lab will only mount such filesystems with the `nosuid` option, then running this shell won't provide `root` access.[3]

The canonical (and probably overused) motivating example of a setuid program is a game program. Suppose you've written a really cool game, and you wish to allow users on the system to play it. The game keeps a score file, listing the highest scores.

If you're not the system administrator, you can't create a separate group of just those users who are allowed to play the game and thus write to the score file. But if you make the file world-writable so that anyone can play the game, then anyone can also cheat and put any name at the top.

However, by making the game program setuid to yourself, users running the game have your UID as their effective UID. The game program can then open and update the score file as needed, but arbitrary users can't come along and edit it. You also open yourself up to most of the dangers of setuid programming; for example, if the game program has a hole that can be exploited to produce a shell running as you, *all* your files are available for deletion or change. This is a justifiably scary thought.

The same logic applies to setgid programs, although in practice setgid programs are much less used than setuid ones. This is too bad; many things that are done with setuid `root` programs could easily be done with setgid programs or programs that are setuid to a regular user instead.[4]

11.2 Retrieving User and Group IDs

Getting the UID and GID information from the system is straightforward. The functions are as follows:

```
#include <unistd.h>                                     POSIX

uid_t getuid(void);                       Real and effective UID
uid_t geteuid(void);
```

[3]Security for GNU/Linux and Unix systems is a deep topic in and of itself. This is just an example; see Section 11.8, "Suggested Reading," page 400, for more.

[4]One program designed for this purpose is GNU `userv` (`https://ftp.gnu.org/gnu/userv/`).

```
gid_t getgid(void);                          Real and effective GID
gid_t getegid(void);

int getgroups(int size, gid_t list[]);       Supplemental group list
```

The functions are:

`uid_t getuid(void)`
: Return the real UID.

`uid_t geteuid(void)`
: Return the effective UID.

`gid_t getgid(void)`
: Return the real GID.

`gid_t getegid(void)`
: Return the effective GID.

`int getgroups(int size, gid_t list[])`
: Fill in up to `size` elements of `list` from the process's supplemental group set. The return value is the number of elements filled in or `-1` if there's an error. It is implementation defined whether the effective GID is also included in the set.

  On POSIX-compliant systems, you can pass in a `size` value of zero; in this case, `getgroups()` returns the number of groups in the process's group set. You can then use that value to dynamically allocate an array that's big enough. (You can also use '`sysconf(_SC_NGROUPS_MAX)`' to get the value. This is discussed in Section 12.2, "System Limits: `sysconf()`, `pathconf()`, and `fpathconf()`," page 405.)

  On non-POSIX systems, the constant `NGROUPS_MAX` defines the maximum necessary size for the `list` array. This constant can be found in `<limits.h>` on modern systems or in `<sys/param.h>` on older ones. We present an example shortly.

You may have noticed that there are no calls to get the saved set-user ID or saved set-group ID values. These are just the original values of the effective UID and effective GID. Thus, you can use code like this at program startup to obtain the six values:

```
uid_t ruid, euid, saved_uid;
gid_t rgid, egid, saved_gid;

int
main(int argc, char **argv)
{
    ruid = getuid();
    euid = saved_uid = geteuid();

    rgid = getgid();
```

```
    egid = saved_gid = getegid();

    ... rest of program ...
}
```

Here is an example of retrieving the group set. As an extension, gawk provides awk-level access to the real and effective UID and GID values and the supplemental group set. To do this, it has to retrieve the group set. The following function is from `main.c` in the gawk 5.3.0 distribution:

```
1453 /* init_groupset --- initialize groupset */
1454
1455 static void
1456 init_groupset()
1457 {
1458 #if defined(HAVE_GETGROUPS) && defined(NGROUPS_MAX) && NGROUPS_MAX > 0
1459 #ifdef GETGROUPS_NOT_STANDARD
1460     /* For systems that aren't standards conformant, use old way. */
1461     ngroups = NGROUPS_MAX;
1462 #else
1463     /*
1464      * If called with 0 for both args, return value is
1465      * total number of groups.
1466      */
1467     ngroups = getgroups(0, NULL);
1468 #endif
1469     /* If an error or no groups, just give up and get on with life. */
1470     if (ngroups <= 0)
1471         return;
1472
1473     /* fill in groups */
1474     emalloc(groupset, GETGROUPS_T *, ngroups * sizeof(GETGROUPS_T), "init_groupset");
1475
1476     ngroups = getgroups(ngroups, groupset);
1477     /* same thing here, give up but keep going */
1478     if (ngroups == -1) {
1479         efree(groupset);
1480         ngroups = 0;
1481         groupset = NULL;
1482     }
1483 #endif
1484 }
```

The `ngroups` and `groupset` variables are global; their declarations aren't shown. The `GETGROUPS_T` macro (line 1474) is the type to use for the second argument; it's `gid_t` on a POSIX system, `int` otherwise.

Lines 1458 and 1483 bracket the entire function body; on ancient systems that don't have group sets at all, the function has an empty body.

Lines 1459–1461 handle non-POSIX systems; `GETGROUPS_NOT_STANDARD` is defined by the configuration mechanism before the program is compiled. In this case, the code uses `NGROUPS_MAX`, as described earlier.

Lines 1462–1468 are for POSIX systems, using a `size` parameter of zero to retrieve the number of groups.

Lines 1469–1471 do error checking. If the return value was less than or equal to `0`, there aren't any supplemental groups, so `init_groupset()` merely returns early.

Finally, line 1474 uses `malloc()` (through an error-checking wrapper macro—see Section 3.2.1.8, "Example: Reading Arbitrarily Long Lines," page 65) to allocate an array that's large enough. Line 1476 then fills in the array. Lines 1478–1482 handle failure, should that happen.

11.3 Checking as the Real User: `access()`

Most of the time, the effective and real UID and GID values are the same. Thus, it doesn't matter that file permission checking is performed against the effective ID and not the real one.

However, when writing a setuid or setgid application, you sometimes want to check whether a file operation that's OK for the effective UID and GID is also OK for the *real* UID and GID. This is the job of the `access()` function:

```
#include <unistd.h>                                    POSIX

int access(const char *path, int amode);
```

The `path` argument is the pathname of the file to check the real UID and GID against. `amode` is the bitwise-OR of one or more of the following values:

- `R_OK` The real UID/GID can read the file.
- `W_OK` The real UID/GID can write the file.
- `X_OK` The real UID/GID can execute the file—or, if a directory, search through the directory.
- `F_OK` Check whether the file exists.

Each component in the pathname is checked, and on some implementations, when checking for `root`, `access()` might act as if `X_OK` is true, even if no execute bits are set in the file's permissions. (Strange but true; in this case, forewarned is forearmed.) Linux doesn't have this problem.

If `path` is a symbolic link, `access()` checks the file that the symbolic link points to.

The return value is `0` if the operation is permitted to the real UID and GID, or it's `-1` otherwise. Thus, if `access()` returns `-1`, a setuid program can deny access to a file that the effective UID/GID would otherwise be able to work with:

```
if (access("/some/special/file", R_OK|W_OK) < 0) {
    fprintf(stderr, "Sorry: /some/special/file: %s\n", strerror(errno));
    exit(1);
}
```

For example, the `stdbuf` command allows you to control the buffering of programs that use `<stdio.h>` for input and output. It does this by placing special values in the environment, arranging to load a special shared library, and then doing an exec of the desired program. To find the shared library, it checks in several places, including using `access()` to check the directories named in `$PATH`:

```
static void
set_program_path (char const *arg)
{
  if (strchr (arg, '/'))        /* Use absolute or relative paths directly.  */
    {
      program_path = dir_name (arg);
    }
  else
    {
      char *path = xreadlink ("/proc/self/exe");
      if (path)
        program_path = dir_name (path);
      else if ((path = getenv ("PATH")))
        {
          char *dir;
          path = xstrdup (path);
          for (dir = strtok (path, ":"); dir != nullptr;
               dir = strtok (nullptr, ":"))
            {
              char *candidate = file_name_concat (dir, arg, nullptr);
              if (access (candidate, X_OK) == 0)
                {
                  program_path = dir_name (candidate);
                  free (candidate);
                  break;
                }
              free (candidate);
            }
        }
      free (path);
    }
}
```

Lines 147–163 are the search of `$PATH`. The loop on lines 151–162 tries to find the full name of the program to exec in each directory in `$PATH`. Line 155 uses `access()` to check if the given file exists and is executable.

NOTE

While using `access()` before opening (or execing) a file is proper practice, a race condition exists: the file being checked could be swapped out in between the check with `access()` and the call to `open()`. Careful programming is required, such as checking owner and permission with `stat()` and `fstat()` before and after the calls to `access()` and `open()`.

To get around the race condition problem, POSIX mandates the `faccessat()` system call:

```
#include <unistd.h>                                            POSIX
#include <fcntl.h>

int faccessat(int fd, const char *path, int amode, int flag);
```

Like `access()`, `faccessat()` defaults to checking the permissions based on the real UID and GID. The arguments are:

`int fd`
: A file descriptor open on the directory from where the lookup of `path` will start. This can be `AT_FDCWD`, in which case, the process's current working directory is used.

`const char *path`
: The pathname of the file to check. Absolute pathnames ignore the value of `fd`. Otherwise, the lookup is relative to the directory on which `fd` is open.

`int amode`
: The bitwise-OR of one or more `R_OK`, `W_OK`, `X_OK`, or `F_OK`, as for `access()`.

`int flag`
: Either zero, or the bitwise-OR of one or more of the following:

  `AT_EACCESS`
  : Check permissions based on the effective UID and GID.

  `AT_SYMLINK_NOFOLLOW`
  : If `path` refers to a symbolic link, do the check on the link itself, instead of on the file to which the link refers. Note that this flag is Linux-specific.

GLIBC provides two additional functions named `euidaccess()` and `eaccess()` that work like `access()` but that check according to the effective UID, GID, and group set. Given the `AT_EACCESS` flag for `faccessat()`, there's no need to use these two functions in new code.

11.4 Setting Extra Permission Bits for Directories

The setgid and "sticky" bits each have special meaning when applied to directories.

11.4.1 Default Group for New Files and Directories

In the original Unix system, when `open()` or `creat()` created a new file, the file received the effective UID and GID of the process creating it.

V7, BSD through 4.1 BSD, and System V through Release 3 all treated directories like files. However, with the addition of the supplemental group set in 4.2 BSD, the way new directories were created changed: new directories inherited the group of the parent directory. Furthermore, new files also inherited the group ID of the parent directory and *not* the effective GID of the creating process.

The idea behind having multiple groups and directories that work this way is to facilitate group cooperation. Each organizational project using a system would have a separate group assigned to it. The top-level directory for each project would be in that project's group, and files for the project would all have group read and write (and if necessary, execute) permission. In addition, new files automatically get the group of the parent directory. By being simultaneously in multiple groups (the group set), a user could move among projects at will with a simple `cd` command, and all files and directories would maintain their correct group.

What happens on modern systems? Well, this is another of the few cases where it's possible to have our cake and eat it too. SunOS 4.0 invented a mechanism that was included in System V Release 4; it is used today by at least Solaris and GNU/Linux. These systems give meaning to the setgid bit on the parent directory of the new file or directory, as follows:

Setgid bit on parent directory clear
: New files and directories receive the creating process's effective GID.

Setgid bit on parent directory set
: New files and directories receive the parent directory's GID. New directories also inherit the setgid bit being on.

(Until SunOS 4.0, the setgid bit on a directory had no defined meaning.) The following session shows the setgid bit in action:

```
$ cd /tmp                                               Move to /tmp
$ ls -ld .                                              Check its permissions
drwxrwxrwt 16 root root 40960 Feb 12 09:09 .
$ id                                                    Check out current groups
uid=1000(arnold) gid=1000(arnold) groups=1000(arnold),4(adm),20(dialout),...
$ mkdir d1 ; ls -ld d1                                  Make a new directory
drwxrwxr-x 2 arnold arnold 4096 Feb 12 09:09 d1         Effective group ID inherited
$ chgrp adm d1                                          Change the group
$ chmod g+s d1                                          Add setgid bit
$ ls -ld d1                                             Verify change
```

```
drwxrwsr-x 2 arnold adm 4096 Feb 12 09:09 d1
$ cd d1                                          Change into it
$ echo this should have group adm on it > f1     Create a new file
$ ls -l f1                                       Check permissions
-rw-rw-r-- 1 arnold adm 33 Feb 12 09:10 f1       Inherited from parent
$ mkdir d2                                       Make a directory
$ ls -ld d2                                      Check permissions
drwxrwsr-x 2 arnold adm 4096 Feb 12 09:10 d2     Group and setgid inherited
```

The `ext2`, `ext3`, and `ext4` filesystems for GNU/Linux work as just shown. In addition, they support special mount options, `grpid` and `bsdgroups`, that make the "use parent directory group" semantics the default. (The two names mean the same thing.) In other words, when these mount options are used, parent directories need not have their setgid bits set.

The opposite mount options are `nogrpid` and `sysvgroups`. This is the default behavior; however, the setgid bit is still honored if it's present. (Here, too, the two names mean the same thing.)

POSIX specifies that new files and directories inherit either the effective GID of the creating process or the group of the parent directory. However, implementations have to provide a way to make new directories inherit the group of the parent directory. Furthermore, the standard recommends that applications not rely on one behavior or the other, but in cases where it matters, applications should use `chown()` to force the ownership of the new file or directory's group to the desired GID.

11.4.2 Directories and the Sticky Bit

Sherman, set the wayback machine for 1976.
— Mr. Peabody

The *sticky bit* originated in the PDP-11 versions of Unix and was applied to regular executable files.[5] This bit was applied to programs that were expected to be heavily used, such as the shell and the editor. When a program had this bit set, the kernel would keep a copy of the program's executable code on the swap device, from which it could be quickly loaded into memory for reuse. (Loading from the filesystem took longer: the image on the swap device was stored in contiguous disk blocks, whereas the image in the filesystem might be spread all over the disk.) The executable images "stuck" to the swap device, hence the name.

Thus, even if the program was not currently in use, it was expected that it would be in use again shortly when another user went to run it, so it would be loaded quickly.

Modern systems have considerably faster disk and memory hardware than the PDP-11s of yore. They also use a technique called *demand paging* to load into memory only those parts of an executable program that are being executed. Thus the sticky bit on a regular executable file serves no purpose today, and indeed it has no effect.

[5]Images come to mind of happy youthful programs, their faces and hands covered in chocolate.

However, in Section 1.1.2, “Directories and File Names,” page 5, we mentioned that the sticky bit on an otherwise writable directory prevents file removal from that directory, or file renaming within it, by anyone except the file’s owner, or `root`. Here is an example:

```
$ ls -ld /tmp                                                   Show /tmp's permissions
drwxrwxrwt 16 root root 40960 Feb 12 09:21 /tmp
$ cd /tmp                                                       Change there
$ echo this is my file > arnolds-file                           Create a file
$ ls -l arnolds-file                                            Show its permissions
-rw-rw-r-- 1 arnold arnold 16 Feb 12 09:22 arnolds-file
$ su - miriam                                                   Change to another user
Password:
$ cd /tmp                                                       Change to /tmp
$ rm arnolds-file                                               Attempt to remove file
rm: remove write-protected regular file 'arnolds-file'? y       rm is cautious
rm: cannot remove 'arnolds-file': Operation not permitted       Kernel disallows removal
```

The primary purpose of this feature is exactly for directories such as `/tmp`, where multiple users wish to place their files. On the one hand, the directory needs to be world-writable so that anyone can create files in it. On the other hand, once it’s world-writable, any user can remove any other user’s files! The directory sticky bit solves this problem nicely. Use ‘`chmod +t`’ to add the sticky bit to a file or directory:

```
$ mkdir mytmp                                                   Create directory
$ chmod a+wxt mytmp                                             Add all-write, sticky bits
$ ls -ld mytmp                                                  Verify result
drwxrwxrwt 2 arnold arnold 4096 Feb 12 09:26 mytmp
```

Finally, note that with the permissions in this example, the directory’s owner can also remove files, even if they don’t belong to him.

11.5 Setting Real and Effective IDs

Things get interesting once a process has to change its UID and GID values. Setting the group set is straightforward. Changing real and effective UID and GID values around is more involved.

11.5.1 Changing the Group Set

The `setgroups()` function installs a new group set:

```
#include <sys/types.h>                                          Common
#include <unistd.h>
#include <grp.h>

int setgroups(size_t size, const gid_t *list);
```

The `size` parameter indicates how many items there are in the `list` array. The return value is `0` if all went well, `-1` with `errno` set otherwise.

Unlike the functions for manipulating the real and effective UID and GID values, this function may be called only by a process running as `root`. This is one example of what POSIX terms a *privileged operation*; as such it's not formally standardized by POSIX.

`setgroups()` is used by any program that does a login to a system, such as `/usr/bin/login` for console logins or `/usr/bin/sshd` for remote logins with `ssh`.[6]

The GNU/Linux *setgroups*(2) manpage points out that a process can drop all of its groups with

```
setgroups(0, NULL);
```

11.5.2 Changing the Real and Effective IDs

Running with two different user IDs presents a challenge to the application programmer. There are things that a program may need to do when working with the effective UID, and other things that it may need to do when using the real UID.

For example, before Unix systems had job control, many programs provided *shell escapes*—that is, a way to run a command or interactive shell from within the current program. The `ed` editor is a good example of this: typing a command line beginning with `!` ran the rest of the line as a shell command. Typing '`!sh`' gave you an interactive shell. (This still works—try it!) Suppose the hypothetical game program described earlier also provides a shell escape: the shell should be run as the real user, *not* the effective one. Otherwise, it again becomes trivial for the game player to directly edit the score file or do lots more worse things!

Thus, there is a clear need to be able to change the effective UID to be the real UID. Furthermore, it's helpful to be able to switch the effective UID *back* to what it was originally. (This is the reason for having a saved set-user ID in the first place; it becomes possible to regain the original privileges that the process had when it started out.)

As with many Unix APIs, different systems solved the problem in different ways, sometimes by using the same API but with different semantics and sometimes by introducing different APIs. Delving into the historic details is only good for producing headaches, so we don't bother. Instead, we look at what POSIX provides and how each API works. Furthermore, our discussion focuses on the real and effective UID values; the GID values work analogously, so we don't bother to repeat the details for those system calls. The functions are as follows:

```
#include <sys/types.h>                                  POSIX
#include <unistd.h>

int seteuid(uid_t euid);                   Set effective ID
int setegid(gid_t egid);
```

[6]On many GNU/Linux systems, `/bin` is a symbolic link to `/usr/bin`; if `/bin` is a real directory, it's likely that `login` and `sshd` live there.

```
int setuid(uid_t uid);                     Set effective ID; if root, set all
int setgid(gid_t gid);

int setreuid(uid_t ruid, uid_t euid);      BSD compatibility, set both
int setregid(gid_t rgid, gid_t egid);
```

There are three sets of functions. The first two were created by POSIX:

`int seteuid(uid_t euid)`
: This function sets only the effective UID. A regular (non-`root`) user can only set the ID to one of the real, effective, or saved set-user ID values. Applications that will switch the effective UID around should use this function exclusively.

  A process with an effective UID of zero can set the effective UID to any value. Since it is also possible to set the effective UID to the saved set-user ID, the process can regain its `root` privileges with another call to `seteuid()`.

`int setegid(gid_t egid)`
: This function does for the effective group ID what `seteuid()` does for the effective user ID.

The next set of functions offers the original Unix API for changing the real and effective UID and GID. Under the POSIX model, these functions are what a setuid-`root` program should use to make a *permanent* change of real and effective UID:

`int setuid(uid_t uid)`
: For a regular user, this function also sets only the effective UID. As with `seteuid()`, the effective UID may be set to any of the current real, effective, or saved set-user ID values. The change is not permanent; the effective UID can be changed to another value (from the same source set) with a subsequent call.

  However, for `root`, this function sets *all three* of the real, effective, and saved set-user IDs to the given value. Furthermore, the change is permanent; the IDs cannot be changed back. (This makes sense: once the saved set-user ID is changed, there isn't a different ID to change back to.)

`int setgid(gid_t gid)`
: This function does for the effective group ID what `setuid()` does for the effective user ID. The same distinction between regular users and `root` applies.

NOTE

The ability to change the group ID hinges on the *effective user ID*. An effective GID of `0` has no special privileges.

Finally, POSIX provides two functions from 4.2 BSD for historical compatibility. It is best not to use these in new code. However, since you may see older code that does use these functions, we describe them here:

`int setreuid(uid_t ruid, uid_t euid)`
: This function sets the real and effective UIDs to the given values. A value of `-1` for `ruid` or `euid` leaves the respective ID unchanged. (This is similar to `chown()`; see Section 5.6.1, "Changing File Ownership: `chown()`, `fchown()`, and `lchown()`," page 146.)

  `root` is allowed to set both the real and the effective ID to any value. According to POSIX, non-`root` users may change only the effective ID; it is "unspecified" what happens if a regular user attempts to change the real UID. However, the GNU/Linux *setreuid*(2) manpage spells out the Linux behavior: the real UID may be set to either the real or the effective UID, and the effective UID may be set to any of the real, effective, or saved set-user IDs. (For other systems, see the *setreuid*(2) manpage.)

`int setregid(gid_t rgid, gid_t egid)`
: This function does for the real and effective group IDs what `setreuid()` does for the real and effective user ID. The same distinction between regular users and `root` applies.

The saved set-user ID didn't exist in the BSD model, so the idea behind `setreuid()` and `setregid()` was to make it simple to swap the real and effective IDs:

```
setreuid(geteuid(), getuid());  /* swap real and effective */
```

However, given POSIX's adoption of the saved set-user ID model and the `seteuid()` and `setegid()` functions, the BSD functions should not be used in new code. Even the 4.4 BSD documentation marks these functions as obsolete, recommending `seteuid()`/`setuid()` and `setegid()`/`setgid()` instead.

11.5.3 Using the Setuid and Setgid Bits

There are important cases in which a program running as `root` must *irrevocably* change all three of the real, effective, and saved set-user IDs to that of a regular user. The most obvious is the `login` program, which you use every time you log in to a GNU/Linux or Unix system (either directly or remotely).[7] There is a hierarchy of programs, as outlined in Figure 11.1.

The code for `login` is too complicated to be shown here, since it deals with a number of tasks that aren't relevant to the current discussion. But we can outline the steps that happen at login time, as follows:

1. `init` is the primordial process. It has PID `1`. All other processes are descended from it. The kernel handcrafts process `1` at boot time and runs `init` in it. It runs with both the real and the effective UID set to zero (that is, as `root`).
2. `init` reads `/etc/inittab`, which, among other things, tells `init` on which hardware devices it should start a `getty` process. For each such device (such as the console, serial terminals, or virtual consoles on a GNU/Linux system), `init` forks a new process.

[7] These days, you likely use a graphical program to log in, but the principles and mechanisms are the same. If you switch to a Linux virtual console and log in, you'll be using the same suite of programs described here.

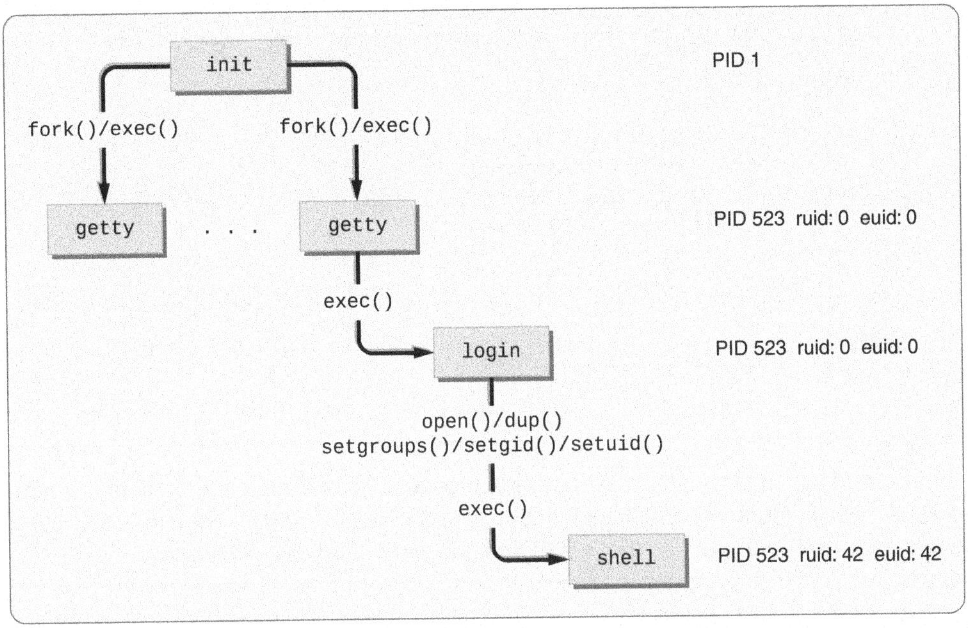

Figure 11.1: From `init` to `getty` to `login` to shell

This new process then uses `exec()` to run `getty` ("get tty," that is, a terminal). This command may have a different name, such as `agetty`. The program opens the device, resets its state, and prints the '`login:`' prompt.

3. Upon reading a login name, `getty` execs `login`. The `login` program looks up the user name in the password file, prompts for a password, and verifies the password. If they match, the login process continues.
4. `login` changes to the user's home directory, sets up the initial environment, and then sets up the initial set of open files. It closes all file descriptors, opens the terminal, and uses `dup()` to copy the terminal's file descriptor to `0`, `1`, and `2`. This is where the already opened standard input, output, and error file descriptors come from.
5. `login` then uses `setgroups()` to set the supplemental group set, `setgid()` to set the real, effective, and saved set-group IDs to those of the user, and finally `setuid()` to set all three of the real, effective, and saved set-user IDs to those of the logging-in user. Note that the call to `setuid()` must come *last* so that the other two calls will succeed.
6. Finally, `login` execs the user's login shell. Bourne-style shells then read at least `/etc/profile` and `$HOME/.profile`, if those files exist. They may read other startup files, as well. Finally, the shell prints a prompt.

Note how one process changes its nature from system process to user process. Each child of `init` starts out as a copy of `init`. By using `exec()`, the same process does different jobs. By calling `setuid()` to change from `root` to a regular user, the process finally goes directly to work for the user. When you exit the shell (by CTRL-D or `exit`), the process simply dies. `init` then restarts the cycle, spawning a fresh `getty`, which prints a fresh '`login:`' prompt.

Table 11.1: API summary for setting real and effective IDs

Function	Sets	Permanent	Regular user	Root
`seteuid()`	E	No	From R, E, S	Any value
`setegid()`	E	No	From R, E, S	Any value
`setuid()`	Root: R, E, S Other: E	Root: yes Other: no	From R, E	Any value
`setgid()`	Root: R, E, S Other: E	Root: yes Other: no	From R, E	Any value
`setreuid()`	E, may set R	No	From R, E	Any value
`setregid()`	E, may set R	No	From R, E	Any value

NOTE

Open files remain open and usable, even after a process has changed any or all of its UIDs or GIDs. Thus, setuid programs should open any necessary files up front, change their IDs to those of the real user, and continue with the rest of their job without any extra privilege.

Table 11.1 summarizes the six standard functions for manipulating UID and GID values.

11.6 Working with All Three IDs: `getresuid()` and `setresuid()` (Linux)

Linux provides additional system calls by which you can work directly with the real, effective, and saved user and group IDs:

```
#define _GNU_SOURCE                                    Linux
#include <sys/types.h>
#include <unistd.h>

int getresuid(uid_t *ruid, uid_t *euid, uid_t *suid);
int getresgid(gid_t *rgid, gid_t *egid, gid_t *sgid);

int setresuid(uid_t ruid, uid_t euid, uid_t suid);
int setresgid(gid_t rgid, gid_t egid, gid_t sgid);
```

The functions are as follows:

`int getresuid(uid_t *ruid, uid_t *euid, uid_t *suid)`
: Retrieve the real, effective, and saved set-user ID values. The return value is `0` on success or `-1` if an error, with `errno` indicating the problem.

`int getresgid(gid_t *rgid, gid_t *egid, gid_t *sgid)`
: Retrieve the real, effective, and saved set-group ID values. The return value is `0` on success or `-1` if an error, with `errno` indicating the problem.

`int setresuid(uid_t ruid, uid_t euid, uid_t suid)`
: Set the real, effective, and saved set-user ID values, respectively. When a parameter value is `-1`, the corresponding UID is left unchanged.

  When the process is running as `root`, the parameters can be any arbitrary values. (However, using a nonzero value for `euid` causes a permanent, irrevocable loss of `root` privilege.) Otherwise, the parameters must be one of the current real, effective, or saved set-user ID values.

`int setresgid(gid_t rgid, gid_t egid, gid_t sgid)`
: Set the real, effective, and saved set-group ID values, respectively. When a parameter value is `-1`, the corresponding GID is left unchanged.

The `setresuid()` and `setresgid()` functions are particularly valuable because the semantics are clearly defined. A programmer knows exactly what the effect of the call will be.

Furthermore, the calls are "all or nothing" operations: they either succeed completely, making the desired change, or fail completely, leaving the current situation as it was. This improves reliability since, again, it's possible to be sure of exactly what happened.

11.7 Crossing a Security Minefield: Setuid `root`

Real minefields are difficult but not impossible to cross. However, it's not something to attempt lightly, without training or experience.

So, too, writing programs that run setuid to `root` is a difficult task. There are many, many issues to be aware of, and almost anything can have unexpected security consequences. Such an endeavor should be undertaken carefully.

In particular, it pays to read up on Linux/Unix security issues and to invest time in learning how to write setuid `root` programs. If you dive straight into such a challenge having read this book and nothing else, rest assured that your system will be broken into, *easily and immediately*. It's unlikely that either you or your customers will be happy.

Here are a few guiding principles:

- Do as little as possible as `root`. Use your superpowers sparingly, only where they're absolutely needed.
- Design your program properly. Compartmentalize your program so that all of the `root` operations can be done up front, with the rest of the program running as a regular user.
- When changing or dropping privileges, use the Linux-specific `setresuid()` system call if you have it. Otherwise, use `seteuid()`. Use `setuid()` only when you want the change to be permanent.

- Change from `root` to regular user in the proper order: set the group set and GID values first, and then the UID values.
- Be especially careful with `fork()` and `exec()`; the real and effective UIDs are not changed across them unless you explicitly change them.
- Consider using setgid permissions and a special group for your application. If that will work, it'll save you much headache.
- Consider throwing out the inherited environment. If you must keep some environment variables around, keep as few as possible. Be sure to provide reasonable values for the `PATH` and `IFS` environment variables.
- Avoid `execlp()` and `execvp()`, which depend on the value of the `PATH` environment variable (although this is less problematic if you've reset `PATH` yourself).

These are just a few of the many tactics for traversing a danger zone notable for pitfalls, booby traps, and landmines. See the next section for pointers to other sources of information.

11.8 Suggested Reading

Unix (and thus GNU/Linux) security is a topic that requires knowledge and experience to handle properly. It has gotten only harder in the Internet Age, not easier. The first three items here are considered "classics."

1. *Practical UNIX and Internet Security*, 3rd ed., by Simson Garfinkel, Gene Spafford, and Alan Schwartz. O'Reilly, 2003. ISBN-13: 978-0-596-00323-4.

   This is the standard book on Unix security.

2. *Building Secure Software: How to Avoid Security Problems the Right Way*, by John Viega and Gary McGraw. Addison-Wesley, 2001. ISBN-13: 978-0-201-72152-2.

   This is a good book on writing secure software, and it includes how to deal with setuid issues. It assumes you are familiar with the basic Linux/Unix APIs; by the time you finish reading our book, you should be ready to read *Building Secure Software*.

3. "Setuid Demystified" by Hao Chen, David Wagner, and Drew Dean. *Proceedings of the 11th USENIX Security Symposium*, August 5–9, 2002. `http://www.cs.berkeley.edu/~daw/papers/setuid-usenix02.pdf`.

   Garfinkel, Spafford, and Schwartz recommend reading this paper "before you even think about writing code that tries to save and restore privileges." We most heartily agree with them.

This next group of books focuses on secure coding.

4. *Secure Coding in C and C++*, 2nd ed., by Robert C. Seacord. Addison-Wesley, 2013. ISBN-13: 978-0-321-82213-0.

5. *Secure Coding: Principles and Practices*, by Mark G. Graff and Kenneth R. van Wyk. O'Reilly, 2003. ISBN-13: 978-0-596-00242-8.

6. *Writing Secure Code*, 2nd ed., by Michael Howard and David LeBlanc. Microsoft Press, 2003. ISBN-13: 978-0-7356-1722-3.

7. *Secure Programming HOWTO: Creating Secure Software*, edition v3.72, by David A. Wheeler. Published by the author, 2015. Available for free from `https://dwheeler.com/secure-programs/`.

   This comprehensive book covers many aspects of secure programming in C and C++, as well as other languages. Thanks to Nelson H. F. Beebe for making us aware of this resource.

The following texts are more general in scope, focussing on the Internet and secure software design.

8. *Computer Security and the Internet: Tools and Jewels from Malware to Bitcoin*, 2nd ed., by Paul C. van Oorschot. Springer, 2021. ISBN-13: 978-3-030-83410-4.

9. *Thinking Security: Stopping Next Year's Hackers* by Steven M. Bellovin. Addison-Wesley, 2016. ISBN-13: 978-0-13-427754-7.

10. *Security Engineering: A Guide to Building Dependable Distributed Systems*, third edition, by Ross Anderson. Wiley, 2020. ISBN-10: 1-119-64278-7, ISBN-13: 978-1-119-64278-7.

11. *Designing Secure Software: A Guide for Developers* by Loren Kohnfelder. No Starch Press, 2021. ISBN-13: 978-1-7185-0192-8.

12. *Building Secure and Reliable Systems: Best Practices for Designing, Implementing, and Maintaining Systems*, by Heather Adkins, Betsy Beyer, Paul Blankinship, Piotr Lewandowski, Ana Oprea, and Adam Stubblefield. O'Reilly, 2020. ISBN-13: 978-1-4920-8312-2.

13. *Secure by Design*, by Dan Bergh Johnsson, Daniel Deogun, and Daniel Sawano. Manning, 2019. ISBN-13: 978-1-61729-435-8.

11.9 Summary

- The use of user and group ID values (UIDs and GIDs) to identify files and processes is what makes Linux and Unix into multiuser systems. Processes carry both real and effective UID and GID values, as well as a supplemental group set. It is generally the effective UID that determines how one process might affect another, and the effective UID, GID, and group set that are checked against a file's permissions. A user with an effective UID of zero, known as `root` or the *superuser*, is allowed to do what they like; the system doesn't apply permission checks to such a user.

- The saved set-user ID and saved set-group ID concepts came from System V and have been adopted by POSIX with full support in GNU/Linux. Having these separate ID values makes it possible to easily and correctly swap real and effective UIDs (and GIDs) as necessary.
- Setuid and setgid programs create processes in which the effective and real IDs differ. The programs are marked as such with additional bits in the file permissions. The setuid and setgid bits must be added to a file after it is created.
- `getuid()` and `geteuid()` retrieve the real and effective UID values, respectively, and `getgid()` and `getegid()` retrieve the real and effective GID values, respectively. `getgroups()` retrieves the supplemental group set and in a POSIX environment, can query the system as to how many members the group set contains.
- The group set is changed with `setgroups()`. This function isn't standardized by POSIX, but it exists on all modern Unix systems. Only `root` may use it.
- The `access()` function does file permission checking as the *real* user, making it possible for setuid programs to check the real user's permissions. Note that, often, examining the information as retrieved by `stat()` may not provide the full picture, given that the file may reside on a nonnative or network filesystem.
- The `faccessat()` function is similar to `access()`, but also gives you the option to check based on the effective UID and GID values. On GNU/LINUX, you have the additional option of not following symbolic links.
- The setgid and sticky bits, when applied to directories, introduce extra semantics. When a directory has its setgid bit on, new files in that directory inherit the directory's group. New directories do also, and they automatically inherit the setting of the setgid bit. Without the setgid bit, new files and directories receive the effective GID of the creating process. The sticky bit on otherwise writable directories restricts file removal to the file's owner, the directory's owner, and `root`.
- Changing UIDs and GIDs is considerably involved. The semantics of various system calls have changed over the years. New applications that will change only their effective UID/GID should use `seteuid()` and `setegid()`. Non-`root` applications can also set their effective IDs with `setuid()` and `setgid()`. The `setreuid()` and `setregid()` calls from BSD were intended for swapping the UID and GID values; their use in new programs is discouraged.
- Applications running as `root` can permanently change the real, effective, and saved ID values with `setuid()` and `setgid()`. One example of this is `login`, which has to change from a system program running as `root` to a nonprivileged login shell running as a regular user.
- The Linux `setresuid()` and `setresgid()` functions should be used when they're available, since they provide the cleanest and most reliable behavior.
- Writing setuid-`root` applications is not a task for a novice. If you need to do such a thing, read up on security issues first; the sources cited previously are excellent.

Exercises

1. Write a simple version of the `id` command. Its action is to print the user and group IDs, with the group names, to standard output. When the effective and real IDs are different, both are printed. For example:

   ```
   $ id
   uid=1000(arnold) gid=1000(arnold) groups=1000(arnold),4(adm),20(dialout),21(fax),...
   ```

   Its usage is:

   ```
   id [ user ]
   id -G [ -nr ] [ user ]
   id -g [ -nr ] [ user ]
   id -u [ -nr ] [ user ]
   ```

   With *user*, that user's information is displayed; otherwise, `id` prints the invoking user's information. The options are as follows:

`-G`	Print all the group values as numeric values only, no names.
`-n`	Print the name only, no numeric values. Applies to user and group values.
`-g`	Print just the effective GID.
`-r`	Print the real ID instead of the effective ID.
`-u`	Print just the effective UID.

2. Write a simple program, named `sume`, that is setuid to yourself. It should prompt for a password (see *getpass*(3)), which for the purposes of this exercise, can be hardwired into the program's source code. If the person running the program correctly enters the password, `sume` should exec a shell. Get another user to help you test it.
3. How do you feel about making `sume` available to your friends? To your fellow students or coworkers? To every user on your system?
4. Using `faccessat()`, write your own version of `euidaccess()`. Consider the different ways you might write the function, and the advantages and disadvantages of these different ways. How did you do it? Why did you choose the way you did?

Chapter 12

Resource Limits

This chapter covers resource limits. Although today's systems are much (much!) larger than the original Unix systems (and even the early GNU/Linux systems), nothing is in infinite supply. Memory is limited, disks are limited, and even file sizes have an ultimate limit.

12.1 Introduction

Any system has two kinds of limits. First, there are limits imposed by the operating system itself that apply to all users and all processes. Some of these limits are static (they never change), while others can be dynamic.

An example of a static limit is the maximum number of supplemental group IDs that a process may have (see Section 11.2, "Retrieving User and Group IDs," page 385). An example of a dynamic limit is the maximum length of a file name in a directory entry, which can vary based on the type of filesystem in which the directory resides (see Section 8.1.2, "Looking at Different Filesystem Types," page 224).

Next, there are per-process and per-user limits, such as the maximum number of open files, or the maximum number of simultaneous processes a user may have running. POSIX systems provide functions for querying the values of all these kinds of limits.

POSIX also provides for *options*—facilities that may or may not be supported on a given system.

12.2 System Limits: `sysconf()`, `pathconf()`, and `fpathconf()`

Two header files and three functions provide access to information about system limits.

12.2.1 How It Works

First off, your program should include `<limits.h>` and `<unistd.h>`. The next thing to understand is that for each limit, there are two defined constants. The first is used to check at compile time if a limit is specified, and if so, it provides a minimum value for the limit. The second constant is used in a call to one of `sysconf()`, `pathconf()`, or `fpathconf()` to find the actual limit value at runtime.

12.2.2 System Configuration Constants: `sysconf()`

`sysconf()` tells us about system configuration constants:

```
#include <limits.h>                    POSIX
#include <unistd.h>

int sysconf(int name);
```

Let's look at an example. `NGROUPS_MAX` and `_SC_NGROUPS_MAX` tell us how many supplemental group IDs a process may have. The following program checks both the compile-time and runtime values and prints them:

```
1  /* ch-limits-ngroups.c --- determine how many group IDs we may have */
2
3  #include <stdio.h>
4  #include <errno.h>
5  #include <stdlib.h>
6  #include <string.h>
7  #include <limits.h>
8  #include <unistd.h>
9
10 int
11 main(int argc, char **argv)
12 {
13     int compile_time_ngroups = 0;
14     int run_time_ngroups = 0;
15 #ifdef NGROUPS_MAX
16     compile_time_ngroups = NGROUPS_MAX;
17
18     run_time_ngroups = sysconf(_SC_NGROUPS_MAX);
19     if (run_time_ngroups < 0) {
20         fprintf(stderr, "%s: could not get runtime information: %s\n",
21                 argv[0], strerror(errno));
22         exit(EXIT_FAILURE);
23     }
24 #endif
25     printf("compile_time_ngroups = %d, run_time_ngroups = %d\n",
26             compile_time_ngroups, run_time_ngroups);
27
28     exit(EXIT_SUCCESS);
29 }
```

The code to do the checking is bracketed with `#ifdef` and `#endif` (lines 15–24). If `NGROUPS_MAX` is not defined, we know that the number of supplemental groups is zero. If it is defined, we set `compile_time_ngroups` to it (line 16). Line 18 checks the runtime value by

Table 12.1: Important POSIX configuration constants

Variable name	Parameter name	Meaning
ARG_MAX	_SC_ARG_MAX	Maximum length of arguments to exec().
CHILD_MAX	_SC_CHILD_MAX	Maximum simultaneous processes per user ID.
HOST_NAME_MAX	_SC_HOST_NAME_MAX	Maximum length of a hostname.
LOGIN_NAME_MAX	_SC_LOGIN_NAME_MAX	Maximum length of a user name.
NGROUPS_MAX	_SC_NGROUPS_MAX	Maximum number of supplemental group IDs.
OPEN_MAX	_SC_OPEN_MAX	Maximum number of open files per process.
RE_DUP_MAX	_SC_RE_DUP_MAX	Maximum number of repeated occurrences in a basic regular expression.
TZNAME_MAX	_SC_TZNAME_MAX	Maximum length of a time-zone name.
_POSIX_VERSION	_SC_VERSION	The year and month when the POSIX.1 standard was approved in the form *YYYYMM*L. This is the version of the POSIX standard to which the system claims conformance. It's important, since different versions of the standard have different APIs and behavior.

calling `sysconf()` and lines 19–23 handle an error return. Finally, lines 25–26 print the two values. Here is the result on our system:

```
$ ch-limits-ngroups
compile_time_ngroups = 65536, run_time_ngroups = 65536
```

(Wow! That's a lot of possible groups!)

Table 12.1 lists some of the important system configuration constants and what they represent.

The return value is not as simple as in most cases, as follows:

An error occurred
: The return value will be `-1` and `errno` will be set to indicate the problem.

The value requested was a limit, but that limit is indeterminate
: In this case, the return value is `-1` but `errno` is unchanged. To distinguish this case from the previous one, you should set `errno` to zero before calling `sysconf()`.

The value requested represents an option
: A positive value indicates that the option is supported. Otherwise `-1` is returned. (We discuss options shortly.)

Anything else
: Any other return value is the actual value of the limit requested. It will not be smaller than the value of the corresponding compile-time constant.

12.2.2.1 POSIX Options

`sysconf()` can also be used to determine if optional features are available. For example, we can test if we can use FORTRAN and C on our system:

```c
/* ch-limits-langdev.c --- can we use FORTRAN and C on this system? */

#include <stdio.h>
#include <errno.h>
#include <stdlib.h>
#include <string.h>
#include <limits.h>
#include <unistd.h>

int
main(int argc, char **argv)
{
#ifdef _POSIX2_FORT_DEV
    long fortran = sysconf(_SC_2_FORT_DEV);

    printf("_POSIX2_FORT_DEV defined ...\n");
    printf("sysconf replies about _SC_2_FORT_DEV: %ld\n", fortran);
#else
    printf("No FORTRAN available, sorry\n");
#endif
#ifdef _POSIX2_C_DEV
    long c_dev = sysconf(_SC_2_C_DEV);

    printf("_POSIX2_C_DEV defined ...\n");
    printf("sysconf replies about _SC_2_C_DEV: %ld\n", c_dev);
#else
    printf("No C available, sorry (really?!?)\n");
#endif
    exit(EXIT_SUCCESS);
}
```

This code is pretty straightforward. Let's see what happens when we compile and run it:

```
$ cc ch-limits-langdev.c -o ch-limits-langdev          Compile it
$ ch-limits-langdev                                    Run it
No FORTRAN available, sorry                            Not surprising
_POSIX2_C_DEV defined ...                              Whew! C is available
sysconf replies about _SC_2_C_DEV: 200809
```

Clearly, these tests are less useful in practice than one might otherwise think. In particular, it's nice to know that the system thinks we can compile C programs, but if something wasn't working right, we would have noticed much earlier on that we could not![1]

[1] Basically, it's a chicken-and-egg problem.

Using #ifdef for Feature Tests

The POSIX standard expects you to bracket your runtime tests with compile-time '#ifdef ... #endif' tests. We've shown our code that way, since that's the pedantic way to do it.

Practically speaking, however, particularly on GLIBC systems, we don't think that the #ifdefs are necessary, and it's OK to just write the runtime tests.

Therefore, you should think carefully about your portability needs. If your code may need to run on a less run-of-the-mill system (such as, say, OpenVMS), you may want to use the #ifdef tests. Otherwise, you probably don't need to.

12.2.3 Filesystem Limitations: pathconf() and fpathconf()

pathconf() and fpathconf() tell us about filesystem limits:

```
#include <limits.h>                                   POSIX
#include <unistd.h>

long fpathconf(int fd, int name);
long pathconf(const char *path, int name);
```

The two functions work in the same way; fpathconf() is used for an open file descriptor, and pathconf() is used for a file name. These functions are similar to sysconf(), in that there are both a compile-time constant and a runtime parameter name that can be checked for each defined limit.

For example, we can check on the maximum number of bytes that can be written atomically to a pipe. This program is a straightforward modification of ch-limits-ngroups.c, shown earlier:

```
/* ch-limits-pipebuf.c --- how many bytes can be written atomically? */

#include <stdio.h>
#include <errno.h>
#include <stdlib.h>
#include <string.h>
#include <limits.h>
#include <unistd.h>

int
main(int argc, char **argv)
{
    int compile_time_size = 0;
    long run_time_size = 0;
#ifdef _POSIX_PIPE_BUF
    compile_time_size = _POSIX_PIPE_BUF;

```

```
    run_time_size = pathconf(".", _PC_PIPE_BUF);
    if (run_time_size < 0) {
        fprintf(stderr, "%s: could not get runtime information: %s\n",
                argv[0], strerror(errno));
        exit(EXIT_FAILURE);
    }
#endif
    printf("compile_time_size = %d, run_time_size = %ld\n",
            compile_time_size, run_time_size);

    exit(EXIT_SUCCESS);
}
```

For the case of pipes, the returned value is the maximum number of bytes that can be written atomically to a FIFO file (see Section 9.3.2, "FIFOs," page 306), were we to create such a file in the directory named by the `path` argument. (In this case, we just used dot, the current directory.) For `fpathconf()`, the `fd` argument should be a file descriptor representing a pipe.

Here's what happens when we run it:

```
$ ch-limits-pipebuf
compile_time_size = 512, run_time_size = 4096
```

Table 12.2 lists some of the more useful parameters you can test for relating to files and paths.

Additional values relate to limits on inputs from terminals; see *fpathconf*(3) for the details.

The return value from `fpathconf()` and `pathconf()` works the same as for `sysconf()`; see the previous section.

Table 12.2: Important POSIX path configuration constants

Variable name	Parameter name	Meaning
`_POSIX_CHOWN_RESTRICTED`	`_PC_CHOWN_RESTRICTED`	Root privileges are needed to give away ownership of a file.
`_POSIX_LINK_MAX`	`_PC_LINK_MAX`	Maximum number of hard links to a file.
`_POSIX_NAME_MAX`	`_PC_NAME_MAX`	Maximum length of a file name that can be created in the given directory.
`_POSIX_NO_TRUNC`	`_PC_NO_TRUNC`	True if accessing file names longer than `_POSIX_NAME_MAX` returns an error.
`_POSIX_PATH_MAX`	`_PC_PATH_MAX`	Maximum length of a relative pathname starting from the given directory.
`_POSIX_PIPE_BUF`	`_PC_PIPE_BUF`	Maximum number of bytes that can be written atomically to a pipe or FIFO.

12.3 Getting Configuration String Variables: `confstr()`

A configuration variable is a string of some sort that either provides useful information, indicates how to compile your program in a certain way, or provides environment settings to use in certain cases. (This is a vague description; more details to follow shortly.) The `confstr()` function provides access to the values of defined configuration variables:

```
#include <unistd.h>                                    POSIX

size_t confstr(int name, char *buffer, size_t len);
```

Most of the configuration variables relate to the flags needed to compile your C programs in different ways: mainly with either 32-bit pointers or 64-bit pointers. They're not of general interest, so we won't describe them in detail. Four of the configuration variables are more interesting:

`_CS_PATH`
: The value to use for `PATH` in order to access POSIX-compliant utilities. This is normally `"/bin:/usr/bin"`.

`_CS_V7_ENV`
: The environment variable and value to use in order to cause utilities to behave in a POSIX-compliant fashion. On GNU/Linux systems this is generally `POSIXLY_CORRECT=1`.

`_CS_GNU_LIBC_VERSION`
: On GLIBC systems, this is the value of the GLIBC version.

`_CS_GNU_LIBPTHREAD_VERSION`
: On GLIBC systems, this is the value of the `lpthread` library version. For example, '`NPTL 2.39`'. NTPL is the "Native POSIX Threading Library," which GLIBC has been using for two decades or so.

The `V7` in `_CS_V7_ENV` does *not* relate to Version 7 Unix. Rather, it relates to the seventh edition of the POSIX standard, which is from 2018. On systems following the 2024 standard, this (and the other variables we're about to see) use `V8` in their name.

The following program, `ch-limits-confstr.c`, retrieves and prints the values of the POSIX-standard configuration values, as well as the two GLIBC-specific values just mentioned:

```
/* ch-limits-confstr.c --- demonstrate the confstr(3) API */

#include <stdio.h>
#include <errno.h>
#include <stdlib.h>
#include <string.h>
#include <limits.h>
#include <unistd.h>

```

```
struct config_var {
    int value;
    const char *name;
} config_vars[] = {
    // Using _CS_POSIX_V7_xxx instead of _CS_POSIX_V8_xxx because the
    // 2024 POSIX standard is too new as of this writing. See the text.
    { _CS_PATH, "_CS_PATH" },
    { _CS_POSIX_V7_ILP32_OFF32_CFLAGS, "_CS_POSIX_V7_ILP32_OFF32_CFLAGS" },
    { _CS_POSIX_V7_ILP32_OFF32_LDFLAGS, "_CS_POSIX_V7_ILP32_OFF32_LDFLAGS" },
    { _CS_POSIX_V7_ILP32_OFF32_LIBS, "_CS_POSIX_V7_ILP32_OFF32_LIBS" },
    { _CS_POSIX_V7_ILP32_OFFBIG_CFLAGS, "_CS_POSIX_V7_ILP32_OFFBIG_CFLAGS" },
    { _CS_POSIX_V7_ILP32_OFFBIG_LDFLAGS, "_CS_POSIX_V7_ILP32_OFFBIG_LDFLAGS" },
    { _CS_POSIX_V7_ILP32_OFFBIG_LIBS, "_CS_POSIX_V7_ILP32_OFFBIG_LIBS" },
    { _CS_POSIX_V7_LP64_OFF64_CFLAGS, "_CS_POSIX_V7_LP64_OFF64_CFLAGS" },
    { _CS_POSIX_V7_LP64_OFF64_LDFLAGS, "_CS_POSIX_V7_LP64_OFF64_LDFLAGS" },
    { _CS_POSIX_V7_LP64_OFF64_LIBS, "_CS_POSIX_V7_LP64_OFF64_LIBS" },
    { _CS_POSIX_V7_LPBIG_OFFBIG_CFLAGS, "_CS_POSIX_V7_LPBIG_OFFBIG_CFLAGS" },
    { _CS_POSIX_V7_LPBIG_OFFBIG_LDFLAGS, "_CS_POSIX_V7_LPBIG_OFFBIG_LDFLAGS" },
    { _CS_POSIX_V7_LPBIG_OFFBIG_LIBS, "_CS_POSIX_V7_LPBIG_OFFBIG_LIBS" },
//  { _CS_POSIX_V7_THREADS_CFLAGS, "_CS_POSIX_V7_THREADS_CFLAGS" },     // not in our GLIBC
//  { _CS_POSIX_V7_THREADS_LDFLAGS, "_CS_POSIX_V7_THREADS_LDFLAGS" },
    { _CS_POSIX_V7_WIDTH_RESTRICTED_ENVS, "_CS_POSIX_V7_WIDTH_RESTRICTED_ENVS" },
    { _CS_V7_ENV, "_CS_V7_ENV" },
    { _CS_GNU_LIBC_VERSION, "_CS_GNU_LIBC_VERSION" },
    { _CS_GNU_LIBPTHREAD_VERSION, "_CS_GNU_LIBPTHREAD_VERSION" },
    { -1, NULL },
};

int
main(int argc, char **argv)
{
    char *buf = NULL;
    size_t n;
    int i;

    for (i = 0; config_vars[i].name != NULL; i++) {
        if (buf != NULL)
            free(buf);

        n = confstr(config_vars[i].value, NULL, 0);
        buf = malloc(n);
        if (buf == NULL) {
            fprintf(stderr, "%s: could not allocate memory: %s\n",
                    argv[0], strerror(errno));
            exit(EXIT_FAILURE);
        }
```

```
56          confstr(config_vars[i].value, buf, n);
57          printf("%s = %s\n", config_vars[i].name, buf);
58      }
59      if (buf != NULL)
60          free(buf);
61
62      exit(EXIT_SUCCESS);
63  }
```

Lines 10–13 define a `struct` to hold the defined constant and string name of each defined configuration variable. Lines 13–36 define an array of these, with all the values filled in. Note the comments on lines 14–15 about the use of `V7` values instead of `V8` values.

Lines 45–58 loop through the table, retrieving each value in turn and printing out the result. Lines 29–30 are commented out since those values are not available on our system; leaving them in causes a compilation error. When run, here is the output:

```
$ ch-limits-confstr
_CS_PATH = /bin:/usr/bin
_CS_POSIX_V7_ILP32_OFF32_CFLAGS =
_CS_POSIX_V7_ILP32_OFF32_LDFLAGS =
_CS_POSIX_V7_ILP32_OFF32_LIBS =
_CS_POSIX_V7_ILP32_OFFBIG_CFLAGS =
_CS_POSIX_V7_ILP32_OFFBIG_LDFLAGS =
_CS_POSIX_V7_ILP32_OFFBIG_LIBS =
_CS_POSIX_V7_LP64_OFF64_CFLAGS = -m64
_CS_POSIX_V7_LP64_OFF64_LDFLAGS = -m64
_CS_POSIX_V7_LP64_OFF64_LIBS =
_CS_POSIX_V7_LPBIG_OFFBIG_CFLAGS =
_CS_POSIX_V7_LPBIG_OFFBIG_LDFLAGS =
_CS_POSIX_V7_LPBIG_OFFBIG_LIBS =
_CS_POSIX_V7_WIDTH_RESTRICTED_ENVS = POSIX_V7_LP64_OFF64
_CS_V7_ENV = POSIXLY_CORRECT=1
_CS_GNU_LIBC_VERSION = glibc 2.39
_CS_GNU_LIBPTHREAD_VERSION = NPTL 2.39
```

12.4 Basic Process Limits: `ulimit()`

You may be familiar with the `ulimit` command in the shell. This command retrieves and/or sets certain system limits. The name derives from the *ulimit*(2) system call. This call is considered obsolete as of the POSIX 2008 standard, and is no longer present in the 2024 standard. However, it's widely implemented, and you may come across old code that uses it. Since it's obsolete, we discuss it only briefly, and don't bother to show sample code using it:

```
#include <ulimit.h>                                    Common

long ulimit(int cmd);                        Retrieve limit
long ulimit(int cmd, newlimit);              Set limit
```

Here, `cmd` indicates the limit you're interested in retrieving or setting. If setting a limit, you must provide a second argument providing the new value of the limit.

When System V first introduced this call, the manpage for it simply listed numeric values for `cmd`. Thankfully, these days there are symbolic constants defined for `cmd`:

`UL_GETFSIZE` (1)
: Return the limit on the size of a file, in units of 512 bytes.

`UL_SETFSIZE` (2)
: Set the limit on the size of a file. This is also in units of 512 bytes.

`UL_GMEMLIM` (3)
: Return the maximum possible address of the data segment (the heap; see Section 3.1, "Linux/Unix Address Space," page 51). This is not implemented for GNU/Linux, and no symbolic constant is provided.

`UL_GDESLIM` (4)
: Return the maximum number of files that the current process can have open. This is implemented on GNU/Linux, but GLIBC does *not* provide the symbolic constant.

12.5 Hard and Soft Limits: `getrlimit()` and `setrlimit()`

When BSD Unix was being developed, systems were much, much smaller than they are today,[2] and they also were shared among many simultaneous users. Control of resources was very important on such systems, particularly (but not exclusively) in academic environments. Therefore, the BSD developers created a facility that is considerably more sophisticated than `ulimit()`.

First, they defined a number of limits, such as CPU, memory, file size, and so on. Second, they introduced the concepts of *soft limits* and *hard limits*. Normally, the soft limit is what's enforced by the kernel. Regular (non-superuser) processes can raise and lower a resource's soft limit, up to the value of the hard limit. Such processes can also (irreversibly) lower their hard limits. Superuser processes can do what they like with the limits.

Changed limits are inherited by any subsequent processes that may be started from the process that changed the limits.

One system call retrieves limits, and the other sets them:

```
#include <sys/resource.h>                         POSIX

int getrlimit(int resource, struct rlimit *rlp);
int setrlimit(int resource, const struct rlimit *rlp);
```

[2] Although physically, they were much, much larger!

The standard values for `resource` are as follows:

Limit	Meaning
RLIMIT_AS	The maximum size of a process's address space.
RLIMIT_CORE	Maximum size of a core file in bytes (see Section 17.3.1, "Getting a `core` File," page 594). A limit of zero prevents creating core files.
RLIMIT_CPU	The maximum amount of CPU time, in seconds, that a process can use.
RLIMIT_DATA	The maximum size of a process's data segment.
RLIMIT_FSIZE	The maximum size of a file that a process can create, in bytes.
RLIMIT_NOFILE	The maximum number of files that a process may have open at once.
RLIMIT_STACK	The maximum size of the initial thread's stack. (We don't discuss threads in this book.)

GNU/Linux provides a number of additional resources:

Limit	Meaning
RLIMIT_LOCKS	The maximum number of *flock*(2) and *fcntl*(2) locks that a process may have. This applies to older kernel versions (2.4.0 to 2.4.24).
RLIMIT_MEMLOCK	The maximum number of bytes that a process may lock into physical memory.
RLIMIT_MSGQUEUE	The maximum number of bytes that may be allocated for POSIX message queues.
RLIMIT_NICE	The "ceiling to which the process's nice value can be raised."
RLIMIT_NPROC	The maximum number of simultaneous threads that the process's real user ID may have running.
RLIMIT_RSS	The maximum number of bytes in the process's resident set (bytes of virtual memory resident in physical memory).
RLIMIT_RTPRIO	The ceiling on the process's real-time priority (an advanced feature).
RLIMIT_RTTIME	The maximum number of microseconds a real-time-scheduled process may run before making a system call (also advanced).
RLIMIT_SIGPENDING	The maximum number of signals that may be queued for the real user ID of the calling process.

A `struct rlimit` looks like this:

```
struct rlimit {
    rlim_t rlim_cur;  /* Soft limit */
    rlim_t rlim_max;  /* Hard limit (ceiling for rlim_cur) */
};
```

The `rlim_t` type is an integer type of appropriate size for your system.

A special limit value, `RLIM_INFINITY`, indicates that the particular limit is, in effect, unlimited. This value is supposed to be larger than any possible actual limit.

The following program, `ch-limits-showlimits.c`, prints out the soft and hard limits for the POSIX-standard limits:

```
/* ch-limits-showlimits.c --- show the current limits */

#include <stdio.h>
#include <errno.h>
#include <stdlib.h>
#include <string.h>
#include <limits.h>
#include <unistd.h>
#include <sys/resource.h>

struct limit_var {
    int value;
    const char *name;
} limit_vars[] = {
    { RLIMIT_AS, "RLIMIT_AS" },
    { RLIMIT_CORE, "RLIMIT_CORE" },
    { RLIMIT_CPU, "RLIMIT_CPU" },
    { RLIMIT_DATA, "RLIMIT_DATA" },
    { RLIMIT_FSIZE, "RLIMIT_FSIZE" },
    { RLIMIT_NOFILE, "RLIMIT_NOFILE" },
    { RLIMIT_STACK, "RLIMIT_STACK" },
    { -1, NULL },
};

int
main(int argc, char **argv)
{
    int i;
    struct rlimit limits;

    for (i = 0; limit_vars[i].name != NULL; i++) {
        if (getrlimit(limit_vars[i].value, & limits) < 0) {
            fprintf(stderr, "%s: could not get limit for %s: %s\n",
                    argv[0], limit_vars[i].name,
                    strerror(errno));
            continue;
        }
        printf("%s: soft limit: %lu, hard limit: %lu\n",
                limit_vars[i].name, limits.rlim_cur, limits.rlim_max);
    }

    exit(EXIT_SUCCESS);
}
```

When run on our system, we see the following:

```
$ ch-limits-showlimits
RLIMIT_AS: soft limit: 18446744073709551615, hard limit: 18446744073709551615
RLIMIT_CORE: soft limit: 18446744073709551615, hard limit: 18446744073709551615
RLIMIT_CPU: soft limit: 18446744073709551615, hard limit: 18446744073709551615
RLIMIT_DATA: soft limit: 18446744073709551615, hard limit: 18446744073709551615
RLIMIT_FSIZE: soft limit: 18446744073709551615, hard limit: 18446744073709551615
RLIMIT_NOFILE: soft limit: 1024, hard limit: 1048576
RLIMIT_STACK: soft limit: 8388608, hard limit: 18446744073709551615
```

Setting limits is straightforward. You fill in a `struct rlimit` with the requested soft and hard limits, and pass a pointer to it to `setrlimit()`:

```
int resource = RLIMIT_xxx;            The limit you wish to change
struct rlimit limit;
limit.rlim_cur = ...                  The new limit values
limit.rlim_max = ...

if (setrlimit(resource, & limit) < 0) {
    fprintf(stderr, "Could not set new limit: %s\n",
        strerror(errno));
    ...
}
...
```

12.6 Summary

- Although programs should strive to meet the "no arbitrary limits" GNU principle, in practice any system always has some physical limits. Particularly on embedded systems, it pays to be aware of them.
- Some limits are static and unchanging. Others are dynamic, depending on a process's current situation. There are also per-process and per-user limits.
- `sysconf()`, `pathconf()`, and `fpathconf()` provide access to the various limits, with both compile-time checks (`#ifdef`) and runtime checks. Checks for optional features let you determine if those features are or are not available.
- `confstr()` returns string values for configuration variables, items that provide useful information or control over the environment. Only a few of these are really useful for day-to-day work.
- `ulimit()` was the original System V system call for getting and setting certain per-process limits. It's been considered obsolete for many years, but its legacy lives on in the name of the related shell built-in command, `ulimit`.

- The BSD calls `getrlimit()` and `setrlimit()` define a broader range of limits than `ulimit()` did and also use the concepts of soft and hard limits. These are what you should use in your own programs.

Exercises

1. Take a look at the *getconf*(1) manpage. Review the *sysconf*(3), *pathconf*(3), and *confstr*(3) manpages. Write your own version of `getconf`.
2. The source for `getconf` for most GNU/Linux systems comes with the GLIBC source code. A copy is included in the book's GitHub repository. Review it. How does it compare to your version?
3. Enhance `ch-limits-showlimits.c` to print large values in a more user-friendly fashion, such as kilobytes, megabytes, and gigabytes.
4. Write a program that lets you change the soft and hard limits. Does changing a limit work even though your program is not built into the shell? You can check by comparing the output of the shell's `ulimit` command before and after running your program.
5. (Hard, or at least time consuming.) Install a system simulator such as SimH[3] on your system. Bring up 4.3 BSD on a simulated DEC VAX 11/780. Explore the limits available to you. You may need to use the `csh` shell with its built-in `limit` command to do so, or you can write a simple C program. For the latter, be aware that the default compiler `cc` is for K&R C, not ANSI/ISO C.

---

[3] `https://simh.trailing-edge.com/`

Chapter 13

General Library Interfaces—Part 2

Chapter 6, "General Library Interfaces—Part 1," page 155, presented the first set of general-purpose library APIs. In a sense, those APIs support working with the fundamental objects that Linux and Unix systems manage: the time of day, users and groups for files, and sorting and searching.

This chapter is more eclectic; the APIs covered here are not particularly related to each other. However, all are useful for day-to-day Linux/Unix programming. Our presentation moves from simpler, more general APIs to more complicated and more specialized ones.

13.1 Assertion Statements: `assert()`

An *assertion* is a statement you make about the state of your program at certain points in time during its execution. The use of assertions for programming was originally developed by C. A. R. Hoare.[1] The general idea is part of "program verification": as you design and develop a program, you can show that it's correct by making carefully reasoned statements about the effects of your program's code. Often, such statements are made about *invariants*—facts about the program's state that are supposed to remain true throughout the execution of a chunk of code.

Assertions are particularly useful for describing two kinds of invariants, *preconditions* and *postconditions*; these are conditions that must hold true before or after, respectively, the execution of a code segment. A simple example of preconditions and postconditions is linear search:

```
/* lsearch --- return index in array of value, or -1 if not found */

int
lsearch(int *array, size_t size, int value)
{
    size_t i;

    /* precondition: array != NULL */
    /* precondition: size > 0 */
    for (i = 0; i < size; i++)
        if (array[i] == value)
```

[1] In his 1981 ACM Turing Award lecture, however, Dr. Hoare states that Alan Turing himself promoted this idea.

```
            return i;

    /* postcondition: i == size */

    return -1;
}
```

This example states the conditions using comments. But wouldn't it be better to be able to test the conditions by using code? This is the job of the `assert()` macro:

```
#include <assert.h>                                         ISO C

void assert(scalar expression);
```

When the *scalar expression* is false, the `assert()` macro prints a diagnostic message and exits the program (with the `abort()` function; see Section 13.4, "Committing Suicide: `abort()`," page 434). `ch-general2-assert.c` provides the `lsearch()` function again, this time with assertions and a `main()` function:

```
/* ch-general2-assert.c --- demonstrate assertions */

#include <stdio.h>
#include <assert.h>

/* lsearch --- return index in array of value, or -1 if not found */

int
lsearch(int *array, size_t size, int value)
{
    size_t i;

    assert(array != NULL);
    assert(size > 0);
    for (i = 0; i < size; i++)
        if (array[i] == value)
            return i;

    assert(i == size);

    return -1;
}

/* main --- test out assertions */

int
main(void)
```

```
28 {
29 #define NELEMS  4
30     static int array[NELEMS] = { 1, 17, 42, 91 };
31     int index;
32
33     index = lsearch(array, NELEMS, 21);
34     assert(index == -1);
35
36     index = lsearch(array, NELEMS, 17);
37     assert(index == 1);
38
39     index = lsearch(NULL, NELEMS, 10);  /* won't return */
40
41     printf("index = %d\n", index);
42
43     return 0;
44 }
```

When compiled and run, the assertion on line 13 "fires":

```
$ ch-general2-assert                                    Run the program
ch-general2-assert: ch-general2-assert.c:13: lsearch: Assertion `array != NULL' failed.
Aborted (core dumped)
```

The message from `assert()` varies from system to system. For GLIBC on GNU/Linux, the message includes the program name, the source code file name and line number, the function name, and then the text of the failed assertion.

The '`Aborted (core dumped)`' message means that `ch-general2-assert` created a `core` file—that is, a snapshot of the process's address space right before it died.[2] This file can be used later, with a debugger; see Section 17.3, "GDB Basics," page 593. Core file creation is a purposeful side effect of `assert()`; the assumption is that something went drastically wrong, and you'll want to examine the program with a debugger to determine what.

You can disable assertions by compiling your program with the command-line option '`-DNDEBUG`'. When this macro is defined before `<assert.h>` is included, the `assert()` macro expands into code that does nothing. For example:

```
$ cc -DNDEBUG=1 ch-general2-assert.c -o ch-general2-assert     Compile with -DNDEBUG
$ ch-general2-assert                                           Run it
Segmentation fault (core dumped)                               What happened?
```

Here, we got a real core dump! We know that assertions were disabled; there's no "failed assertion" message. So what happened? Consider line 16 of `lsearch()`, when called from line 39 of `main()`. In this case, the `array` variable is `NULL`. Accessing memory through a `NULL` pointer is an error. (Technically, the various standards leave as "undefined" what happens

[2]The exact location of this file varies across GNU/Linux systems. Discussion of where to find it is delayed until Section 17.3.1, "Getting a `core` File," page 594.

when you dereference a `NULL` pointer. Most modern systems do what GNU/Linux does: they kill the process by sending it a `SIGSEGV` signal; this in turn produces a core dump. This process is described in Chapter 10, "Signals," page 333.)

This case raises an important point about assertions. Frequently, programmers mistakenly use assertions *instead of* runtime error checking. In our case, the test for '`array != NULL`' should be a runtime check:

```
if (array == NULL)
    return -1;
```

The test for '`size > 0`' (line 14) is less problematic; if `size` is `0`, the loop never executes and `lsearch()` (correctly) returns `-1`. (In truth, this assertion isn't needed because the code correctly handles the case in which '`size == 0`'. It can never be true that '`size < 0`', since the type of `size` is `size_t`, which is an `unsigned` type.)

The logic behind turning off assertions is that the extra checking can slow program performance and thus they should be disabled for the production version of a program. C. A. R. Hoare made this observation, however:

> Finally, it is absurd to make elaborate security checks on debugging runs, when no trust is put in the results, and then remove them in production runs, when an erroneous result could be expensive or disastrous. What would we think of a sailing enthusiast who wears his lifejacket when training on dry land, but takes it off as soon as he goes to sea?[3]

Given these sentiments, our recommendation is to use assertions thoughtfully. First, for any given assertion, consider whether it should instead be a runtime check. Second, place your assertions carefully so that you won't mind leaving assertion checking enabled, even in the production version of your program.

Finally, we'll note the following, from the "BUGS" section of the GNU/Linux *assert*(3) manpage:

> `assert()` is implemented as a macro; if the expression tested has side-effects, program behavior will be different depending on whether `NDEBUG` is defined. This may create Heisenbugs which go away when debugging is turned on.

Heisenberg's famous uncertainty principle from physics indicates that the more precisely you can determine a particle's velocity, the less precisely you can determine its position, and vice versa. In layman's terms, it states that the mere act of observing the particle affects it.

A similar phenomenon unrelated to particle physics occurs in programming: the act of compiling a program for debugging, or running a program with debugging enabled, can change the program's behavior. In particular, the original bug can disappear. Such a bug is known colloquially as a *heisenbug*.

[3]From *Hints on Programming Language Design*. See Section 13.9, "Suggested Reading," page 467, for the full citation.

The manpage is warning us against putting expressions with side effects into `assert()` calls:

```
assert(*p++ == '\n');
```

The side effect here is that the `p` pointer is incremented as part of the test. When `NDEBUG` is defined, the expression argument *disappears* from the source code; it's never executed. This can lead to an unexpected failure. However, as soon as assertions are reenabled in preparation for debugging, things start working again! Such problems are painful to track down.

13.2 Low-Level Memory: The memXXX() Functions

Several functions provide low-level services for working with arbitrary blocks of memory. Their names all start with the prefix '`mem`':

```
#include <string.h>                                              ISO C

void *memset(void *buf, int val, size_t count);
void *memcpy(void *dest, const void *src, size_t count);
void *memmove(void *dest, const void *src, size_t count);
void *memccpy(void *dest, const void *src, int val, size_t count);
int memcmp(const void *buf1, const void *buf2, size_t count);
void *memchr(const void *buf, int val, size_t count);
```

13.2.1 Setting Memory: memset()

The `memset()` function copies the value `val` (treated as an `unsigned char`) into the first `count` bytes of `buf`. It is particularly useful for zeroing out blocks of dynamic memory:

```
void *p = malloc(count);
if (p != NULL)
    memset(p, 0, count);
```

However, `memset()` can be used on any kind of memory, not just dynamic memory. The return value is the first argument: `buf`.

13.2.2 Copying Memory: memcpy(), memmove(), and memccpy()

Three functions copy one block of memory to another. The first two differ in their handling of *overlapping* memory areas; the third one copies memory but stops upon seeing a particular value:

`void *memcpy(void *dest, const void *src, size_t count)`
: This is the simplest function. It copies `count` bytes from `src` to `dest`. It does not handle overlapping memory areas. It returns `dest`.

```
struct xyz { ... } data[8];
memcpy( & data[3], data, sizeof(data[0]) * 4);
```

versus

```
memmove(& data[3], data, sizeof(data[0]) * 4);
```

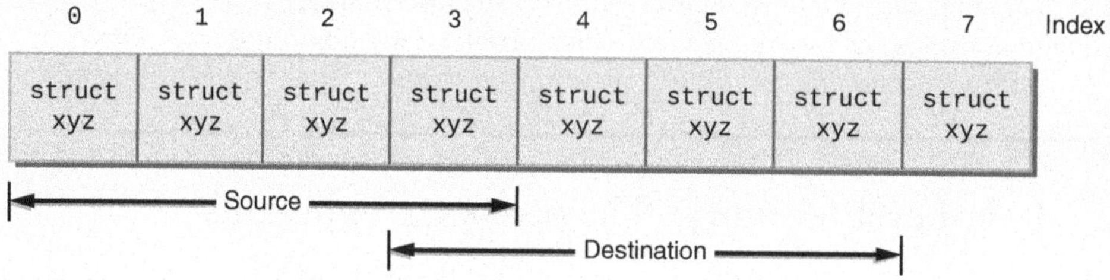

Figure 13.1: Overlapping copies

`void *memmove(void *dest, const void *src, size_t count)`
: Similar to `memcpy()`, this also copies `count` bytes from `src` to `dest`. However, it does handle overlapping memory areas. It returns `dest`.

`void *memccpy(void *dest, const void *src, int val, size_t count)`
: This copies bytes from `src` to `dest`, stopping *either* after copying `val` into `dest` *or* after copying `count` bytes. If it found `val`, it returns a pointer to the position in `dest` just beyond where `val` was placed. Otherwise, it returns `NULL`.

Now, what's the issue with overlapping memory? Consider Figure 13.1.

The goal is to copy the four instances of `struct xyz` in `data[0]` through `data[3]` into `data[3]` through `data[6]`. `data[3]` is the problem here; a byte-by-byte copy moving forward in memory from `data[0]` will clobber `data[3]` before it can be safely copied into `data[6]`! (It's also possible to come up with a scenario in which a backward copy through memory destroys overlapping data.)

The `memcpy()` function was the original System V API for copying blocks of memory; its behavior for overlapping blocks of memory wasn't particularly defined one way or the other. For the 1990 C standard, the committee felt that this lack of defined behavior was a problem; thus they invented `memmove()`. For historical compatibility, `memcpy()` was left alone, with the behavior for overlapping memory specifically stated as undefined, and `memmove()` was invented to provide a routine that would correctly deal with problem cases.

Which one should you use in your own code? For a library function that has no knowledge of the memory areas being passed into it, you should use `memmove()`. That way, you're guaranteed that there won't be any problems with overlapping areas. For application-level code that "knows" that two areas don't overlap, it's safe to use `memcpy()`.

For both memcpy() and memmove() (as for strcpy()), the destination buffer is the first argument and the source is the second one. To remember this, note that the order is the same as for an assignment statement:

```
dest = src;
```

(The manpages on many systems don't help, providing the prototype as 'void *memcpy(void *buf1, void *buf2, size_t n)' and relying on the prose to explain which is which. Fortunately, the GNU/Linux manpage uses better names.)

13.2.3 Comparing Memory Blocks: memcmp()

The memcmp() function compares count bytes from two arbitrary buffers of data. Its return value is like strcmp(): negative, zero, or positive if the first buffer is less than, equal to, or greater than the second one.

You may be wondering, "Why not use strcmp() for such comparisons?" The difference between the two functions is that memcmp() doesn't care about zero bytes (the '\0' string terminator). Thus, memcmp() is the function to use when you need to compare arbitrary binary data.

Another advantage to memcmp() is that it's quite likely faster than the typical C implementation:

```
/* memcmp --- example C implementation, NOT for real use */

int
memcmp(const void *buf1, const void *buf2, size_t count)
{
    const unsigned char *cp1 = (const unsigned char *) buf1;
    const unsigned char *cp2 = (const unsigned char *) buf2;
    int diff;

    while (count-- != 0) {
        diff = *cp1++ - *cp2++;
        if (diff != 0)
            return diff;
    }

    return 0;
}
```

The speed can be due to special "block memory compare" instructions that many architectures support or to comparisons in units larger than bytes. (This latter operation is tricky and is best left to the library's author.)

For these reasons, you should *always* use your library's version of memcmp() instead of rolling your own. Chances are excellent that the library author knows the machine better than you do.

13.2.4 Searching for a Byte Value: `memchr()`

The `memchr()` function is similar to the `strchr()` function: it returns the location of a particular value within an arbitrary buffer. As with `memcmp()` versus `strcmp()`, the principal reason to use `memchr()` is that you can have arbitrary binary data.

Normally, GNU `sort` sorts lines. However, with the `-z` option, it expects "lines" to be zero-terminated strings. To that end, it uses `memchr()` to find the line terminator inside each input buffer that it reads:

```
      /* Find and record each line in the just-read input.  */
      while ((p = memchr (ptr, eol, ptrlim - ptr)))
        {
...
```

The `eol` variable will be either `'\n'` or zero.

13.3 Temporary Files

A *temporary file* is exactly what it sounds like: a file that, while a program runs, holds data that isn't needed once the program exits. An excellent example is the `sort` program. `sort` reads standard input if no files are named on the command line or if you use '`-`' as the file name. Yet `sort` has to read *all* of its input data before it can output the sorted results. (Think about this a bit and you'll see that it's true.) While standard input is being read, the data must be stored somewhere until `sort` can sort it; this is the perfect use for a temporary file. `sort` also uses temporary files for storing intermediate sorted results.

Amazingly, there are *seven* different standard functions for creating temporary objects (files or directories). Three of them work by creating strings representing (supposedly) unique file names. As we'll see, these should generally be avoided. The others work by creating and opening the temporary object; these functions are preferred.

13.3.1 Generating Temporary File Names (Bad)

There are three functions whose purpose is to create the *name* of a unique, nonexistent file. Once you have such a file name, you can use it to create a temporary file. Since the name is unique, you're "guaranteed" exclusive use of the file. Here are the function declarations:

```
#include <stdio.h>

char *tmpnam(char *s);                                    ISO C
char *tempnam(const char *dir, const char *pfx);          Common
char *mktemp(char *template);                             ISO C
```

The functions all provide different variations of the same theme: they fill in or create a buffer with the path of a unique temporary file name. The file is unique in that the created name doesn't exist as of the time the functions create the name and return it. The functions work as follows:

char *tmpnam(char *s)
: Generates a unique file name. If s is not NULL, it should be at least L_tmpnam bytes in size, and the unique name is copied into it. If s is NULL, the name is generated in an internal static buffer that can be overwritten on subsequent calls. The directory prefix of the path will be P_tmpdir. Both P_tmpdir and L_tmpnam are defined in <stdio.h>.

char *tempnam(const char *dir, const char *pfx)
: Like tmpnam(), but lets you specify the directory prefix. If dir is NULL, P_tmpdir is used. The pfx argument, if not NULL, specifies up to five characters to use as the leading characters of the file name.

: tempnam() allocates storage for the file names it generates. This storage can be released later with free().

char *mktemp(char *template)
: Generates a unique file name based on a template. The last six characters of template must be 'XXXXXX'; these characters are replaced with a unique suffix. The result is different each time it's called.

NOTE

The template argument to mktemp() is overwritten in place. Thus it should *not* be a string constant. Many pre–Standard C compilers put string constants into the data segment, along with regular global variables. Although defined as constants in the source code, they were *writable*; thus, code like the following was not uncommon:

```
/* Old-style code: don't do this. */
char *tfile = mktemp("/tmp/myprogXXXXXX");
... use tfile ...
```

On modern systems, such code will likely fail; string constants nowadays find themselves in read-only segments of memory.

Using these functions is quite straightforward. The file ch-general2-mktemp.c demonstrates mktemp(); changes to use the other functions are not difficult:

```
/* ch-general2-mktemp.c --- demonstrate naive use of mktemp().
                            Error checking omitted for brevity */

#include <stdio.h>
#include <fcntl.h>  /* for open flags */
#include <limits.h> /* for PATH_MAX */
#include <stdlib.h>
#include <string.h>
#include <unistd.h>

```

```
11 /* main --- demonstrate mktemp() */
12
13 int
14 main(void)
15 {
16     static const char template[] = "/tmp/myfileXXXXXX";
17     char fname[PATH_MAX];
18     static char mesg[] =
19         "Here's lookin' at you, kid!\n";    /* beats "hello, world" */
20     int fd;
21
22     strcpy(fname, template);
23     mktemp(fname);
24
25     /* RACE CONDITION WINDOW OPENS */
26
27     printf("Filename is %s\n", fname);
28
29     /* RACE CONDITION WINDOW LASTS TO HERE */
30
31     fd = open(fname, O_CREAT|O_RDWR|O_TRUNC, 0600);
32     ssize_t junk = write(fd, mesg, strlen(mesg));
33     close(fd);
34
35     /* unlink(fname); */
36
37     return 0;
38 }
```

The `template` variable (line 16) defines the file name template; the '`XXXXXX`' will be replaced with a unique value. Line 22 copies the template into `fname`, which isn't `const`: it can be modified. Line 23 calls `mktemp()` to generate the file name, and line 27 prints it so we can see what it is. (We explain the comments on lines 25 and 29 shortly.)

Line 31 opens the file, creating it if necessary. Line 32 writes the message in `mesg`, and line 33 closes the file. (Once again, we use a `junk` variable to avoid compiler warnings.) In a program in which the file should be removed when we're done with it, line 35 would not be commented out. (Sometimes, a temporary file should not be unlinked—for example, if the file will be renamed once it's completely written.) We've commented it out so that we can run this program and look at the file afterward. Here's what happens when the program runs:

```
$ ch-general2-mktemp                         Run the program
Filename is /tmp/myfileOwMi4K                File name printed
$ cat /tmp/myfileOwMi4K
Here's lookin' at you, kid!                  Contents are what we expect
$ ls -l /tmp/myfileOwMi4K                    So are owner and permissions
-rw------- 1 arnold arnold 28 Feb 16 15:50 /tmp/myfileOwMi4K
```

```
$ rm  /tmp/myfileOwMi4K                               Remove it
$ ch-general2-mktemp                                  Is same file name reused?
Filename is /tmp/myfileW6roou                         No. That's good
$ cat /tmp/myfileW6roou                               Check contents again
Here's lookin' at you, kid!
$ ls -l /tmp/myfileW6roou                             Check owner and permissions again
-rw------- 1 arnold arnold 28 Feb 16 15:50 /tmp/myfileW6roou
```

Everything seems to be working fine. `mktemp()` gives back a unique name, `ch-general2-mktemp` creates the file with the right permissions, and the contents are as expected. So what's the problem with all these functions?

Historically, `mktemp()` used a simple, *predictable* algorithm to generate the replacement characters for the '`XXXXXX`' in the template. Furthermore, the interval between the time the file name is *generated* and the time the file itself is *created* produces a race condition.

How? Well, Linux and Unix systems use *time slicing*, a technique that shares the processor among all the executing processes. This means that, although a program *appears* to be running all the time, in actuality there are times when processes are *sleeping*—that is, waiting to run on the processor.

Now, consider a professor's program for tracking student grades. Both the professor and a malicious student are using a heavily loaded, multiuser system at the same time. The professor's program uses `mktemp()` to create temporary files, and the student, having in the past watched the grading program create and remove temporary files, has figured out the algorithm that `mktemp()` uses. (The GLIBC version doesn't have this problem, but not all systems use GLIBC!) Figure 13.2 illustrates the race condition and how the student takes advantage of it.

Here's what happened:

1. The grading program uses `mktemp()` to generate a file name. Upon return from `mktemp()`, the race condition window is now open (line 25 in `ch-general2-mktemp.c`).
2. The kernel stops the grader so that other programs on the system can run. This happens before the call to `open()`.

   While the grader is stopped, the student creates the file with the same name `mktemp()` returned to the grader program. (Remember, the algorithm was easy to figure out.) The

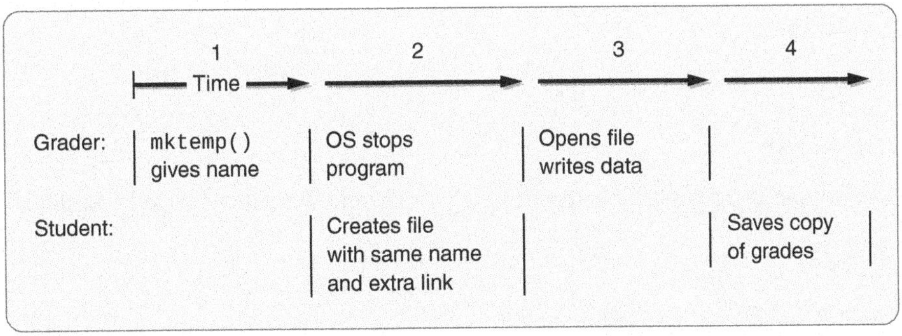

Figure 13.2: Race condition with `mktemp()`

student creates the file with an extra link to it, so that when the grading program unlinks the file, it will still be available for perusal.

3. The grader program now opens the file and writes data to it. The student created the file with `-rw-rw-rw-` permissions, so this isn't a problem.
4. When the grader program is finished, it unlinks the temporary file. However, the student still has a copy and may have a profit opportunity to sell classmates their grades in advance.

Our example is simplistic; besides just stealing the grade data, a clever (if immoral) student might be able to *change* the data in place (if the file is writable). If the professor doesn't double-check their program's results, no one would be the wiser.

NOTE

We do not recommend doing any of this! If you are a student, *don't try any of this*. First and foremost, it is unethical. Second, it's likely to get you kicked out of school. Third, your professors are probably not so naive as to have used `mktemp()` to code their programs. The example is for illustration only!

For the reasons given, and others, all three functions described in this section should never be used. (Well, actually, there may be times when `mktemp()` is your only option; we talk about that in the next section.) They exist in POSIX and/or in GLIBC only to support old programs that were written before the dangers of these routines were understood. To this end, GNU/Linux systems generate a warning at link time:

```
$ cc ch-general2-mktemp.c -o ch-general2-mktemp
/bin/ld: /tmp/cckEiz1G.o: in function `main':
ch-general2-mktemp.c:(.text+0x4b): warning: the use of `mktemp' is dangerous,
better use `mkstemp' or `mkdtemp'
```

(We cover `mkstemp()` and `mkdtemp()` in the next subsection.)

13.3.2 Creating and Opening Temporary Files (Good)

There are four functions that don't have race condition problems. One is intended for use with the `<stdio.h>` library:

```
#include <stdio.h>                                    ISO C

FILE *tmpfile(void);
```

The second and third functions are for use with the file-descriptor-based system calls:

```
#include <stdlib.h>                                   POSIX

int mkstemp(char *template);
int mkostemp(char *template, int flag);
```

The fourth function makes a uniquely named directory:

```
#include <stdlib.h>                                          POSIX

char *mkdtemp(char *template);
```

`tmpfile()` returns a `FILE *` value representing a unique, open temporary file. The file is opened in `"w+b"` mode. The `w+` means "open for reading and writing, truncate the file first," and the `b` means binary mode, not text mode. (There's no difference on a GNU/Linux or Unix system, but there is on other systems.) The file is automatically deleted when the file pointer is closed; there is no way to get to the file's name to save its contents. The program in `ch-general2-tmpfile.c` demonstrates `tmpfile()`:

```
/* ch-general2-tmpfile.c --- demonstrate tmpfile().
                             Error checking omitted for brevity */

#include <stdio.h>

int
main(void)
{
    static char mesg[] =
        "Here's lookin' at you, kid!";  /* beats "hello, world" */
    FILE *fp;
    char buf[BUFSIZ];

    fp = tmpfile();                 /* Get temp file */
    fprintf(fp, "%s", mesg);        /* Write to it */
    fflush(fp);                     /* Force it out */

    rewind(fp);                     /* Move to front */
    char *junk;
    junk = fgets(buf, sizeof buf, fp);  /* Read contents */

    printf("Got back <%s>\n", buf);     /* Print retrieved data */

    fclose(fp);                     /* Close file, goes away */
    return 0;                       /* All done */
}
```

The returned `FILE *` value is no different from any other `FILE *` returned by `fopen()`. When run, the results are what's expected:

```
$ ch-general2-tmpfile
Got back <Here's lookin' at you, kid!>
```

We saw earlier that the GLIBC authors recommend the use of `mkstemp()` function:

```
$ cc ch-general2-mktemp.c -o ch-general2-mktemp
/bin/ld: /tmp/cckEiz1G.o: in function `main':
ch-general2-mktemp.c:(.text+0x4b): warning: the use of `mktemp' is dangerous,
better use `mkstemp' or `mkdtemp'
```

This function is similar to `mktemp()` in that it takes a file name ending in '`XXXXXX`' and replaces those characters with a unique suffix to create a unique file name. However, it goes one step further. It *creates and opens the file*. The file is created with mode `0600` (that is, `-rw-------`). Thus, only the user running the program can access the file.

Furthermore—and this is what makes `mkstemp()` more secure—the file is created using the `O_EXCL` flag, which guarantees that the file doesn't exist and keeps anyone else from opening the file.

`mkostemp()` is just like `mkstemp()`, except that you can pass in additional flags to be passed on to `open()`. It's new in the 2024 POSIX standard.

The return value from either function is an open file descriptor that can be used for reading and writing. The pathname now stored in the buffer passed to `mkstemp()` should be used to remove the file when you're done. This is all demonstrated in `ch-general2-mkstemp.c`, which is a straightforward modification of `ch-general2-tmpfile.c`:

```
/* ch-general2-mkstemp.c --- demonstrate mkstemp().
                              Error checking omitted for brevity */

#include <stdio.h>
#include <fcntl.h>  /* for open flags */
#include <limits.h> /* for PATH_MAX */
#include <stdlib.h>
#include <string.h>
#include <unistd.h>

/* main --- create a temporary file and test it out */

int
main(void)
{
    static const char template[] = "/tmp/myfileXXXXXX";
    char fname[PATH_MAX];
    static char mesg[] =
        "Here's lookin' at you, kid!\n";    /* beats "hello, world" */
    int fd;
    char buf[BUFSIZ];
    int n;

    strcpy(fname, template);            /* Copy template */
    fd = mkstemp(fname);                /* Create and open temp file */
    printf("Filename is %s\n", fname);  /* Print it for information */
```

```
    ssize_t junk;
    junk = write(fd, mesg, strlen(mesg));   /* Write something to file */

    lseek(fd, 0L, SEEK_SET);                /* Rewind to front */
    n = read(fd, buf, sizeof(buf));         /* Read data back; NOT '\0' terminated! */
    printf("Got back: %.*s", n, buf);       /* Print it out for verification */

    close(fd);                              /* Close file */
    unlink(fname);                          /* Remove it */

    return 0;
}
```

When run, the results are as expected:

```
$ ch-general2-mkstemp
Filename is /tmp/myfileNNOIHm
Got back: Here's lookin' at you, kid!
```

Finally, the `mkdtemp()` function makes a directory with a unique name, returning the pathname as the result. Its usage is straightforward, so we won't bore you with an example program.

Now, remember we said that there are times when you may have no choice but to use `mktemp()`? This is the case when you need to create a temporary object that isn't a regular file or directory, such as a FIFO. A possible alternative is to use `mkdtemp()` to create a temporary directory and then create your objects inside that directory. (Thanks to Chet Ramey for this.)

13.3.3 Using the `TMPDIR` Environment Variable

Many standard utilities pay attention to the `TMPDIR` environment variable, using the directory it names as the place in which to put their temporary files. If `TMPDIR` isn't set, then the default directory for temporary files is usually `/tmp`, although most modern systems have a `/var/tmp` directory as well. `/tmp` is usually cleared of all files and directories by administrative shell scripts at system startup.

This variable dates from when systems were considerably smaller than they are today. The idea is that `/tmp` may not be big enough for some needs, and if there is a filesystem with more space somewhere else, setting `TMPDIR` to point to a directory on it lets a program make use of that space.

So if you have a need for temporary files, you should check the `TMPDIR` environment variable and use it if it's set. Otherwise, fall back to putting your temporary files in `/tmp`. Using `TMPDIR` for your own programs is straightforward. We offer the following outline:

```
const char template[] = "myprog.XXXXXX";
char *tmpdir, *tfile;
size_t count;
int fd;
```

```
if ((tmpdir = getenv("TMPDIR")) == NULL)                Use TMPDIR value if there
    tmpdir = "/tmp";                                     Otherwise, default to /tmp

count = strlen(tmpdir) + strlen(template) + 2;          Compute size of file name
tfile = (char *) malloc(count);                          Allocate space for it
if (tfile == NULL)                                       Check for error
    /* recover */

snprintf(tfile, count, "%s/%s", tmpdir, template);       Create final template
fd = mkstemp(tfile);                                     Create and open file
... use tempfile via fd ...
close(fd);                                               Clean up
unlink(tfile);
free(tfile);
```

Depending on your application's needs, you may wish to unlink the file immediately after opening it instead of doing so as part of the cleanup.

13.4 Committing Suicide: `abort()`

There are times when a program just can't continue. Generally, the best thing to do is to generate an error message and call `exit()`. However, particularly for errors that are likely to be programming problems, it's helpful not just to exit but also to produce a core dump, which saves the state of the running program in a file for later examination with a debugger. This is the job of the `abort()` function:

```
#include <stdlib.h>                                        ISO C

void abort(void);
```

The `abort()` function sends a `SIGABRT` signal to the process itself. This happens even if `SIGABRT` is blocked or ignored. The normal action for `SIGABRT`, which is to produce a core dump, then takes place.

An example of `abort()` in action is the `assert()` macro described at the beginning of this chapter. When `assert()` finds that its expression is false, it prints an error message and then calls `abort()` to dump core.

According to the C standard, it is implementation defined whether or not `abort()` does any cleanup actions. The GLIBC version does not do any cleanup. As well, nothing is done for open files that use the file-descriptor-based system calls. (Nothing needs to be done if all that are open are files or pipes. Network connections—discussed later in Chapter 14, "Sockets and Basic Networking," page 473—are also closed by the system, but not closing them yourself is poor practice.)

13.5 Nonlocal Gotos

Go directly to jail. Do not pass GO. Do not collect $200.
— Monopoly

You undoubtedly know what a `goto` is: a transfer of control flow to a label somewhere else within the current function. `goto` statements, when used sparingly, can contribute to the readability and correctness of a function. (For example, when all error checks use a `goto` to a label at the end of a function, such as `clean_up`, the code at that label then cleans things up [closing files, etc.] and returns.) When used poorly, `goto` statements can lead to so-called spaghetti code, the logic of which becomes impossible to follow.

The `goto` statement is constrained by the C language to jump to a label within the current function. Many languages in the Algol family, such as Pascal, allow a `goto` to "jump out" of a nested function into an earlier calling function. In C, however, there is no way, within the syntax of the language itself, to jump to a location in a different function, even a calling one. Such a jump is termed a *nonlocal goto*.

Why is a nonlocal goto useful? Consider an interactive program that reads commands and processes them. Suppose the user starts a long-running task, gets frustrated or changes their mind about doing the task, and then presses CTRL-C to generate a `SIGINT` signal. When the signal handler runs, it can jump back to the start of the main read-commands-and-process-them loop. The `ed` line editor provides a straightforward example of this:

```
$ ed -p '> ' sayings                        Start ed, use `> ' as prompt
sayings: No such file or directory
> a                                         Append text
Hello, world
Don't panic
^C                                          Generate SIGINT
?                                           The "one size fits all" error message
> 1,$p                                      ed returns to command loop
Hello, world                                '1,$p' prints all the lines
Don't panic
> w                                         Save file
25
> q                                         All done
```

Internally, `ed` sets up a return point before the command loop, and the signal handler then does a nonlocal goto back to the return point.

13.5.1 Using Standard Functions: `setjmp()` and `longjmp()`

Nonlocal gotos are accomplished with the `setjmp()` and `longjmp()` functions. These functions come in two flavors. The traditional routines are defined by the ISO C standard:

```
#include <setjmp.h>                                      ISO C

int setjmp(jmp_buf env);
void longjmp(jmp_buf env, int val);
```

The `jmp_buf` type is `typedef`'d in `<setjmp.h>`. `setjmp()` saves the current "environment" in `env`. `env` is typically a global or file-level `static` variable so that it can be used from a called function. This environment includes whatever information is necessary for jumping to the location at which `setjmp()` is called. The contents of a `jmp_buf` are by nature machine dependent; thus, `jmp_buf` is an opaque type—something you use without knowing what's inside it.

`setjmp()` returns `0` when it is called to save the current environment in a `jmp_buf`. It returns nonzero when a nonlocal jump is made using the environment:

```
jmp_buf command_loop;              At global level
... then in main() ...
if (setjmp(command_loop) == 0)     State saved OK, proceed on
    ;
else                               We get here via nonlocal goto
    printf("?\n");                 ed's famous message
... now start the command loop ...
```

`longjmp()` makes the jump. The first parameter is a `jmp_buf` that must have been initialized by `setjmp()`. The second is an integer *nonzero* value that `setjmp()` returns in the original environment. This is so that code such as that just shown can distinguish between setting the environment and arriving by way of a nonlocal jump.

The C standard states that even if `longjmp()` is called with a second argument of `0`, `setjmp()` still returns nonzero. In such a case, it instead returns `1`.

The ability to pass an integer value and have that come back from the return of `setjmp()` is useful; it lets user-level code distinguish the reason for the jump. For instance, earlier versions of `gawk` used this capability to handle the `break` and `continue` statements inside loops. (The `awk` language is deliberately similar to C in its syntax for loops, with `while`, `do-while`, and `for` loops, and `break` and `continue`.) The use of `setjmp()` looks like this (from `eval.c` in the `gawk` 3.1.8 distribution):

```
	case Node_K_while:
		PUSH_BINDING(loop_tag_stack, loop_tag, loop_tag_valid);

		stable_tree = tree;
		while (eval_condition(stable_tree->lnode)) {
			INCREMENT(stable_tree->exec_count);
			switch (setjmp(loop_tag)) {
			case 0:	/* normal non-jump */
				(void) interpret(stable_tree->rnode);
				break;
			case TAG_CONTINUE:	/* continue statement */
```

```
673                 break;
674             case TAG_BREAK: /* break statement */
675                 RESTORE_BINDING(loop_tag_stack, loop_tag, loop_tag_valid);
676                 return 1;
677             default:
678                 cant_happen();
679             }
680         }
681         RESTORE_BINDING(loop_tag_stack, loop_tag, loop_tag_valid);
682         break;
```

This code fragment represents a `while` loop. Line 663 manages nested loops by means of a stack of saved `jmp_buf` variables. Lines 666–680 run the `while` loop (using a C `while` loop!). Line 666 tests the loop's condition. If it's true, line 668 does a `switch` on the `setjmp()` return value. If it's `0` (lines 669–671), then line 670 runs the statement's body. However, when `setjmp()` returns either `TAG_CONTINUE` or `TAG_BREAK`, the `switch` statement handles them appropriately (lines 672–673 and 674–676, respectively).

An `awk`-level `break` statement passes `TAG_BREAK` to `longjmp()`, and the `awk`-level `continue` passes `TAG_CONTINUE`. Again, from `eval.c`, with some irrelevant details omitted:

```
case Node_K_break:
    INCREMENT(tree->exec_count);
    ...
        longjmp(loop_tag, TAG_BREAK);
    break;

case Node_K_continue:
    INCREMENT(tree->exec_count);
    ...
        longjmp(loop_tag, TAG_CONTINUE);
    break;
```

You can think of `setjmp()` as placing the label, and `longjmp()` as the `goto`, with the extra advantage of being able to tell where the code "came from" (by the return value).

(As a side issue, `gawk` no longer works the way just shown, but the older code makes our point very clearly.)

13.5.2 Handling Signal Masks: `sigsetjmp()` and `siglongjmp()`

For historical reasons that would most likely bore you to tears, the 1999 C standard is silent about the effect of `setjmp()` and `longjmp()` on the state of a process's signals, and POSIX states explicitly that their effect on the process signal mask (see Section 10.6, "POSIX Signals," page 350) is undefined.

In other words, if a program changes its process signal mask between the first call to `setjmp()` and a call to `longjmp()`, what is the state of the process signal mask after the `longjmp()`? Is it the mask in effect when `setjmp()` was first called? Or is it the current mask? POSIX says explicitly, "there's no way to know."

To make handling of the process signal mask explicit, POSIX introduced two additional functions and one `typedef`:

```
#include <setjmp.h>                                    POSIX

int sigsetjmp(sigjmp_buf env, int savesigs);      Note: sigjmp_buf, not jmp_buf!
void siglongjmp(sigjmp_buf env, int val);
```

The main difference is the `savesigs` argument to `sigsetjmp()`. If nonzero, then the current set of blocked signals is saved in `env`, along with the rest of the environment that would be saved by `setjmp()`. A `siglongjmp()` with an `env` where `savesigs` was true restores the saved process signal mask.

NOTE

POSIX is also clear that if `savesigs` is zero (false), it's *undefined* whether the process signal mask is saved and restored, just like `setjmp()`/`longjmp()`. This in turn implies that if you're going to use '`sigsetjmp(env, 0)`', you may as well not bother: the whole point is to have control over saving and restoring the process signal mask!

13.5.3 Observing Important Caveats

There are multiple technical caveats to be aware of when using `setjmp()` and `longjmp()`.

First, because the environment saving and restoring can be messy, machine-dependent tasks, `setjmp()` and `longjmp()` are allowed to be macros.

Second, the C standard limits the use of `setjmp()` to the following situations:

- As the sole controlling expression of a loop or condition statement (`if`, `switch`).
- As one operand of a comparison expression (==, <, etc.), with the other operand as an integer constant. The comparison expression can be the sole controlling expression of a loop or condition statement.
- As the operand of the unary `!` operator, with the resulting expression being the sole controlling expression of a loop or condition statement.
- As the entire expression of an expression statement, possibly cast to `void`. For example:

  ```
  (void) setjmp(buf);
  ```

Third, if you wish to change a local variable in the function that calls `setjmp()`, *after* the call, and you want that variable to maintain its most recently assigned value after a `longjmp()`, you must declare the variable to be `volatile`. Otherwise, any non-`volatile` local variables changed after `setjmp()` was initially called have indeterminate values. (Note that the `jmp_buf` variable itself need not be declared `volatile`.) For example:

```
1  /* ch-general2-setjmp.c --- demonstrate setjmp()/longjmp() and volatile. */
2
3  #include <stdio.h>
4  #include <setjmp.h>
5
6  jmp_buf env;
7
8  /* comeback --- do a longjmp */
9
10 void
11 comeback(void)
12 {
13     longjmp(env, 1);
14     printf("This line is never printed\n");
15 }
16
17 /* main --- call setjmp, fiddle with vars, print values */
18
19 int
20 main(void)
21 {
22     int i = 5;
23     volatile int j = 6;
24
25     if (setjmp(env) == 0) {     /* first time */
26         i++;
27         j++;
28         printf("first time: i = %d, j = %d\n", i, j);
29         comeback();
30     } else                  /* second time */
31         printf("second time: i = %d, j = %d\n", i, j);
32
33     return 0;
34 }
```

In this example, only `j` (line 23) is guaranteed to maintain its value for the second call to `printf()`. The value of `i` (line 22), according to the 1999 C standard, is indeterminate. It may be `6`, it may be `5`, or it may even be something else! Here is what we get on our system:

```
$ ch-general2-setjmp
first time: i = 6, j = 7
second time: i = 5, j = 7
```

Fourth, as described in Section 13.5.2, "Handling Signal Masks: `sigsetjmp()` and `siglongjmp()`," page 437, the 1999 C standard makes no statement about the effect, if any, of `setjmp()` and `longjmp()` on the state of the program's signals. If that's important, you have to use `sigsetjmp()` and `siglongjmp()` instead.

Fifth, these routines provide amazing potential for memory leaks! Consider a program in which `main()` calls `setjmp()` and then calls several nested functions, each of which allocates dynamic memory with `malloc()`. If the most deeply nested function does a `longjmp()` back into `main()`, the pointers to the dynamic memory are lost. Consider `ch-general2-memleak.c`:

```
/* ch-general2-memleak.c --- demonstrate memory leaks with setjmp()/longjmp(). */

#include <stdio.h>
#include <malloc.h>     /* for definition of ptrdiff_t on GLIBC */
#include <setjmp.h>
#include <unistd.h>

/*
 * Run this on a Solaris or other traditional Unix system.
 * GLIBC malloc() doesn't use sbrk!
 */

jmp_buf env;

void f1(void), f2(void);

/* main --- leak memory with setjmp() and longjmp() */

int
main(void)
{
    char *start_break;
    char *current_break;
    ptrdiff_t diff;

    start_break = sbrk((ptrdiff_t) 0);

    if (setjmp(env) == 0)       /* first time */
        printf("setjmp called\n");

    current_break = sbrk((ptrdiff_t) 0);

    diff = current_break - start_break;
    printf("memsize = %ld\n", (long) diff);

    f1();

    return 0;
}

/* f1 --- allocate some memory, make a nested call */
```

```
42
43  void
44  f1(void)
45  {
46      char *p = malloc(1024 * 1024);
47
48      f2();
49  }
50
51  /* f2 --- allocate some memory, make longjmp */
52
53  void
54  f2(void)
55  {
56      char *p = malloc(1024 * 1024);
57
58      longjmp(env, 1);
59  }
```

This program sets up an infinite loop, using `setjmp()` and `longjmp()`. Line 26 uses `sbrk()` (see Section 3.2.3, "System Calls: `brk()` and `sbrk()`," page 72) to find the current start of the heap, and then line 28 calls `setjmp()`. Line 31 gets the current start of the heap; this location changes each time through since the code is entered repeatedly by `longjmp()`. Lines 33–34 compute how much memory has been allocated and print the amount. Here's what happens when it runs:

```
$ ch-general2-memleak                    Run the program
setjmp called
memsize = 0
memsize = 2113536
memsize = 4210688
memsize = 6307840
memsize = 8404992
memsize = 10502144
memsize = 12599296
memsize = 14696448
...
```

The program leaks memory like a sieve. It runs until interrupted from the keyboard or until it runs out of memory (at which point it produces a massive core dump).

Functions `f1()` and `f2()` each allocate memory, and `f2()` does the `longjmp()` back to `main()` (line 58). Once that happens, the *local* pointers (lines 46 and 56) to the allocated memory are gone! Such memory leaks can be difficult to track down because they are often for small amounts of memory, and as such, they can go unnoticed literally for years.[4]

[4] We once had such a leak in `gawk`. Fortunately, it's fixed.

This code is clearly pathological, but it's intended to illustrate our point: `setjmp()` and `longjmp()` can lead to hard-to-find memory leaks. Suppose that `f1()` called `free()` correctly *after* the call and supposed return from `f2()`. It would then be far from obvious that the memory would never be freed. In a larger, more realistic program, in which `longjmp()` might be called only by an `if`, such a leak becomes even harder to find.

In the presence of `setjmp()` and `longjmp()`, dynamic memory must thus be managed by global variables, and you must have code that detects entry with `longjmp()` (by checking the `setjmp()` return value). Such code should then clean up any dynamically allocated memory that's no longer needed. In a large program, you should probably create a set of dedicated functions and data structures for managing dynamic memory, instead of doing things inline upon return via `longjmp()`.

(By the way, we ran this program on a Solaris system. GLIBC's `malloc()` doesn't use `sbrk()`. Nonetheless, the point being made remains valid.)

The sixth caveat is that `longjmp()` and `siglongjmp()` should not be used from any functions registered with `atexit()` (see Section 9.1.5.3, "Exiting Functions," page 290).

Seventh, `setjmp()` and `longjmp()` can be costly operations on machines with lots of registers.

Given all of these issues, you should take a hard look at your program's design. If you don't need to use `setjmp()` and `longjmp()`, then you're probably better off not doing so. However, if their use is the best way to structure your program, then go ahead and use them, but do so carefully.

13.6 Pseudorandom Numbers

Many applications need sequences of random numbers. For example, game programs that simulate rolling a die, dealing cards, or turning the wheels on a slot machine need to be able to pick one of a set of possible values at random. (Consider the `fortune` program, which has a large collection of pithy sayings; it prints a different one "at random" each time it's called.) Many cryptographic algorithms also require "high quality" random numbers. This section describes different ways to get sequences of random numbers.

NOTE

The nature of randomness, the generation of random numbers, and the "quality" of random numbers are all broad topics and beyond the scope of this book. We provide an introduction to the available APIs, but that's about all we can do. See Section 13.9, "Suggested Reading," page 467, for sources of more detailed information.

Computers, by design, are *deterministic*. The same calculation, with the same inputs, should produce the same outputs, every time. Thus, they are not good at generating truly random numbers—that is, sequences of numbers in which each number in the sequence is completely independent of the number (or numbers) that came before it. Instead, the kinds of numbers usually dealt with at the programmatic level are called *pseudorandom* numbers. That is, within any given sequence, the numbers appear to be independent of each other, but the sequence as a whole is repeatable. (This repeatability can be an asset; it provides determinism for the program as a whole.)

Many methods of producing pseudorandom number sequences work by performing the same calculation each time on a starting, or *seed*, value. The stored seed value is then updated for use next time. APIs provide a way to specify a new seed. Each initial seed produces the same sequence of pseudorandom numbers, although different seeds (should) produce different sequences.

13.6.1 Standard C: `rand()` and `srand()`

Standard C defines two related functions for pseudorandom numbers:

```
#include <stdlib.h>                                          ISO C

int rand(void);
void srand(unsigned int seed);
```

`rand()` returns a pseudorandom number between `0` and `RAND_MAX` (inclusive, as far as we can tell from the C99 standard) each time it's called. The constant `RAND_MAX` must be at least 32,767; it can be larger.

`srand()` seeds the random number generator with `seed`. If `srand()` is never called by the application, `rand()` behaves as if the initial seed were `1`.

The following program, `ch-general2-rand.c`, uses `rand()` to print die faces:

```
/* ch-general2-rand.c --- generate die rolls, using rand(). */

#include <stdio.h>
#include <stdlib.h>

const char *die_faces[] = { /* ASCII graphics rule! */
    "       ",
    "   *   ",  /* 1 */
    "       ",

    "       ",
    " *   * ",  /* 2 */
    "       ",

    "       ",
    " * * * ",  /* 3 */
    "       ",

    " *   * ",
    "       ",  /* 4 */
```

```
21         " *   * ",
22
23         " *   * ",
24         "   *   ",   /* 5 */
25         " *   * ",
26
27         " * * * ",
28         "       ",   /* 6 */
29         " * * * ",
30 };
31
32 /* main --- print N different die faces */
33
34 int
35 main(int argc, char **argv)
36 {
37     int nfaces;
38     int i, j, k;
39
40     if (argc != 2) {
41         fprintf(stderr, "usage: %s number-die-faces\n", argv[0]);
42         exit(EXIT_FAILURE);
43     }
44
45     nfaces = atoi(argv[1]);
46
47     if (nfaces <= 0) {
48         fprintf(stderr, "usage: %s number-die-faces\n", argv[0]);
49         fprintf(stderr, "\tUse a positive number!\n");
50         exit(EXIT_FAILURE);
51     }
52
53     for (i = 1; i <= nfaces; i++) {
54         j = rand() % 6;     /* force to range 0 <= j <= 5 */
55         printf("+-------+\n");
56         for (k = 0; k < 3; k++)
57             printf("|%s|\n", die_faces[(j * 3) + k]);
58         printf("+-------+\n\n");
59     }
60
61     return EXIT_SUCCESS;
62 }
```

This program uses simple ASCII graphics to print out the semblance of a die face. You call it with the number of die faces to print. This is computed on line 45 with `atoi()`. (In general, `atoi()` should be avoided for production code since it does no error or overflow checking, nor does it do any input validation.)

The key line is line 54, which converts the `rand()` return value into a number between zero and five, using the remainder operator, `%`. The value '`j * 3`' acts a starting index into the `die_faces` array for the three strings that make up each die's face. Lines 55 and 58 print out surrounding top and bottom lines, and the loop on lines 56 and 57 prints the face itself. When run, it produces output like the following:

```
$ ch-general2-rand 2          Print two dice
+-------+
|       |
| *   * |
|       |
+-------+

+-------+
| *   * |
|   *   |
| *   * |
+-------+
```

The `rand()` interface dates back to V7 and the PDP-11. In particular, on many older systems the result is only a 16-bit number, which severely limits the range of numbers that can be returned. Furthermore, the algorithm it used is considered "weak" by modern standards. (The GLIBC version of `rand()` doesn't have these problems, but portable code needs to be written with the awareness that `rand()` isn't the best API to use.)

`ch-general2-rand.c` uses a simple technique to obtain a value within a certain range: the `%` operator. This technique uses the low bits of the returned value (just as in decimal division, where the remainder of dividing by 10 or 100 uses the lowest one or two decimal digits). It turns out that the historical `rand()` generator did a better job of producing random values in the middle and higher-order bits than in the lower bits. Thus, if you must use `rand()`, try to avoid the lower bits.

The GNU/Linux *rand*(3) manpage formerly cited *Numerical Recipes in C* which recommends this technique:[5]

```
j = 1+(int) (10.0*rand()/(RAND_MAX+1.0));  /* for a number between 1 and 10 */
```

13.6.2 POSIX Functions: `random()` and `srandom()`

4.3 BSD introduced `random()` and its partner functions. These functions use a much better random number generator, which returns at least a 31-bit value. They are now an XSI extension standardized by POSIX:

```
#include <stdlib.h>                                  POSIX XSI

long random(void);
void srandom(unsigned int seed);
char *initstate(unsigned int seed, char *state, size_t n);
char *setstate(char *state);
```

[5] See Section 13.9, "Suggested Reading," page 467, for the full citation.

The first two functions correspond closely to `rand()` and `srand()` and can be used similarly. However, instead of a single seed value producing the sequence of pseudorandom numbers, these functions use a seed value along with a *state array*: an array of bytes that holds state information for calculating the pseudorandom numbers. The last two functions let you manage the state array:

`long random(void)`
: Returns a number between 0 and $2^{31}-1$. (POSIX is explicit that the range is 0 to $2^{31}-1$.)

`void srandom(unsigned int seed)`
: Sets the seed. If `srandom()` is never called, the default seed is `1`.

`char *initstate(unsigned int seed, char *state, size_t n)`
: Initializes the `state` array with information for use in generating random numbers. `seed` is the seed value to use, as for `srandom()`, and `n` is the number of bytes in the `state` array.

  `n` should be one of the values `8`, `32`, `64`, `128`, or `256`. Larger values produce better sequences of random numbers. Values less than `8` cause `random()` to use a simple random number generator similar to that of `rand()`. Values larger than `8` that are not equal to a value in the list are rounded down to the nearest appropriate value.

`char *setstate(char *state)`
: Sets the internal state to the `state` array, which must have been initialized by `initstate()`. This lets you switch back and forth between different states at will, providing multiple random number generators.

If `initstate()` and `setstate()` are never called, `random()` uses an internal state array of size 128 and acts as if the initial seed is `1`.

The `state` array is opaque; you initialize it with `initstate()` and pass it to the `random()` function with `setstate()`, but you don't otherwise need to look inside it. If you use `initstate()` and `setstate()`, you don't have to also call `srandom()`, since the seed is included in the state information. `ch-general2-random.c` uses these routines instead of `rand()`. It also uses a common technique, which is to seed the random number generator with the time of day, added to the PID:

```
/* ch-general2-random.c --- generate die rolls, using random(). */

#include <stdio.h>
#include <stdlib.h>
#include <sys/types.h>
#include <time.h>
#include <unistd.h>

const char *die_faces[] = { /* ASCII graphics rule! */
        ... as before ...
};

/* main --- print N different die faces */
```

```

int
main(int argc, char **argv)
{
    int nfaces;
    int i, j, k;
    char state[256];
    time_t now;

    ... check args, compute nfaces, as before ...

    (void) time(& now); /* seed with time of day and PID */
    (void) initstate((unsigned int) (now + getpid()), state, sizeof state);
    (void) setstate(state);

    for (i = 1; i <= nfaces; i++) {
        j = random() % 6;        /* force to range 0 <= j <= 5 */
        printf("+-------+\n");
        for (k = 0; k < 3; k++)
            printf("|%s|\n", die_faces[(j * 3) + k]);
        printf("+-------+\n\n");
    }

    return EXIT_SUCCESS;
}
```

Including the PID as part of the seed value guarantees that you'll get different results, even when two programs are started within the same second.

Because it produces a higher-quality sequence of random numbers, `random()` is preferred over `rand()`, and GNU/Linux and all modern Unix systems support it.

13.6.3 The `/dev/random` and `/dev/urandom` Special Files

Both `rand()` and `srandom()` are pseudorandom number generators. Their output, for the same seed, is a reproducible sequence of numbers. Some applications, such as cryptography, require their random numbers to be (more) truly random. To this end, the Linux kernel, as well as various BSD and commercial Unix systems, provide special device files that provide access to an "entropy pool" of random bits that the kernel collects from physical devices and other sources. There are two device files:

`/dev/urandom`
: Reads from this file wait until there is enough random data in the kernel's entropy pool before returning the requested amount of data. The process doesn't block (that is, it does not give up the CPU).

`/dev/random`
: Reads from this file return random bytes only within the estimated number of bits of fresh noise in the entropy pool. If there aren't enough bits, the process reading data may block until more are available.

  `/dev/random` is considered to be a legacy interface, and you should almost always use `/dev/urandom`. See the *random*(4) manpage for times when you might still want to use `/dev/random`.

If you're going to be writing high-quality cryptographic algorithms, you should read up on cryptography and randomness first; don't rely on the cursory presentation here! Here's our die rolling program once more, this time using `/dev/urandom`:

```
/* ch-general2-devrandom.c --- generate die rolls, using /dev/urandom. */

#include <stdio.h>
#include <fcntl.h>
#include <stdlib.h>
#include <unistd.h>

const char *die_faces[] = { /* ASCII graphics rule! */
        ... as before ...
};

/* myrandom --- return data from /dev/urandom as unsigned long */

unsigned long
myrandom(void)
{
    static int fd = -1;
    unsigned long data;

    if (fd == -1)
        fd = open("/dev/urandom", O_RDONLY);

    if (fd == -1 || read(fd, & data, sizeof data) <= 0)
        return random();    /* fall back */

    return data;
}

/* main --- print N different die faces */

int
main(int argc, char **argv)
{
    int nfaces;
```

```
57      int i, j, k;
58
        ... check args, compute nfaces, as before ...
71
72      for (i = 1; i <= nfaces; i++) {
73          j = myrandom() % 6;       /* force to range 0 <= j <= 5 */
74          printf("+-------+\n");
75          for (k = 0; k < 3; k++)
76              printf("|%s|\n", die_faces[(j * 3) + k]);
77          printf("+-------+\n");
78          putchar('\n');
79      }
80
81      return EXIT_SUCCESS;
82  }
```

Lines 36–49 provide a function-call interface to `/dev/urandom`, reading an `unsigned long`'s worth of data each time. The cost is one file descriptor that remains open throughout the program's life.

13.6.4 Using `getrandom()` Instead of `/dev/urandom`

Finally, we briefly present the `getrandom()` system call; it is available on GNU/Linux, as well as on some BSD systems, such as NetBSD and FreeBSD:

```
#include <sys/random.h>                         Linux and others

ssize_t getrandom(void *buf, size_t buflen, unsigned int flags);
```

The arguments are:

`void *buf`
: A pointer to a buffer into which `getrandom()` will place random bytes of data. The default is to bring data from the same source as used for `/dev/urandom`.

`size_t buflen`
: The size of `buf`.

`unsigned int flags`
: Either `0`, or the bitwise-OR of one or more of these flags:

  `GRND_RANDOM`
  : Bring data from the same source as `/dev/random`, instead of from `/dev/urandom`.

  `GRND_NONBLOCK`
  : If not enough data is available, don't block. Instead return `-1` with `errno` set to `EAGAIN`.

Upon success, `getrandom()` returns the number of bytes placed into `buf`. This may be less than `buflen`, for example, if the call was interrupted by a signal.

The example program, `ch-general2-getrandom.c`, differs from the previous one only in the `myrandom()` function:

```
/* myrandom --- return data from getrandom() as unsigned long */

unsigned long
myrandom(void)
{
    unsigned long data;
    if (getrandom(& data, sizeof(data), 0) != sizeof(data))
        return random();    /* fall back */

    return data;
}
```

13.6.5 Cryptographically Secure Random Numbers

Three functions available on GNU/Linux, macOS, and several of the BSD systems provide "cryptographically secure" random numbers:

```
#include <stdlib.h>

uint32_t arc4random(void);
uint32_t arc4random_uniform(uint32_t upper_bound);
void arc4random_buf(void *buf, size_t n);
```

Linux, macOS, BSDs

They work as follows:

`arc4random()`
: Returns a uniformly distributed 32-bit integer value.

`arc4random_uniform(uint32_t upper_bound)`
: Returns a uniformly distributed 32-bit integer value less than `upper_bound`.

`arc4random_buf(void *buf, size_t n)`
: Places `n` bytes of pseudorandom data into `buf`.

13.7 Metacharacter Expansions

Three function sets of increasing complexity provide the ability to match shell wildcard patterns. Many programs need such library functions. One example is `find`: '`find . -name '*.c' -print`'. Another is the `--exclude` option in many programs that accepts a wildcard pattern of files to exclude from some action or other. This section looks at each set of functions in turn.

13.7.1 Simple Pattern Matching: `fnmatch()`

We start with the `fnmatch()` ("file name match") function:

```
#include <fnmatch.h>                                    POSIX

int fnmatch(const char *pattern, const char *string, int flags);
```

This function matches `string` against `pattern`, which is a regular shell wildcard pattern. The `flags` value (described shortly) modifies the function's behavior. The return value is `0` if `string` matches `pattern`, `FNM_NOMATCH` if it doesn't, and a nonzero value if an error occurred. Unfortunately, POSIX doesn't define any specific errors; thus, you can tell that *something* went wrong, but not what.

The `flags` variable is the bitwise-OR of one or more of the flags listed in Table 13.1.

The Korn shell (`ksh`) introduced an extended pattern matching notation that brings the full power of extended regular expressions to shell wildcard matching. With the `FNM_EXTMATCH` flag, `fnmatch()` supports these patterns as well. The extended patterns are described in terms of a *pattern-list*, which is one more patterns separated by '`|`':

`?(`*`pattern-list`*`)`
: Match zero or one occurrences of any of the patterns in *pattern-list*.

`*(`*`patterns-list`*`)`
: Match zero or more occurrences of any of the patterns in *pattern-list*.

Table 13.1: Flag values for `fnmatch()`

Flag name	GLIBC only	Meaning
`FNM_CASEFOLD`	✓	Do case-insensitive matching.
`FNM_EXTMATCH`	✓	Support extended patterns as introduced by `ksh`. See further in the text.
`FNM_FILE_NAME`	✓	This is a GNU synonym for `FNM_PATHNAME`.
`FNM_LEADING DIR`	✓	This is a flag for internal use by GLIBC; don't use it in your programs. See *fnmatch*(3) for the details.
`FNM_NOESCAPE`		Backslash is an ordinary character, not an escape character.
`FNM_PATHNAME`		Slash in `string` must match slash in `pattern`; it cannot be matched by `*`, `?`, or '`[...]`'.
`FNM_PERIOD`		A leading period in `string` is matched only if `pattern` also has a leading period. The period must be the first character in `string`. However, if `FNM_PATHNAME` is also set, a period following a slash is treated as a leading period.

`+(patterns-list)`
: Match one or more occurrences of any of the patterns in *pattern-list.*

`@(patterns-list)`
: Match exactly one occurrence of any of the patterns in *pattern-list.*

`!(pattern-list)`
: Match anything that does not match any of the patterns in *pattern-list.*

`fnmatch()` works with strings from any source; strings to be matched need not be actual file names. In practice, though, you would use `fnmatch()` from code that reads directory entries with `readdir()` (see Section 5.3.1, "Basic Directory Reading," page 124):

```
struct dirent dp;
DIR *dir;
char pattern[100];
... fill pattern, open directory, check for errors ...
while ((dp = readdir(dir)) != NULL) {
    if (fnmatch(pattern, dir->d_name, FNM_PERIOD) == 0)
        /* file name matches pattern */
    else
        continue;    /* doesn't match */
}
```

GNU `ls` uses `fnmatch()` to implement its `--ignore` option. You can provide multiple patterns to ignore (with multiple options). `ls` tests each file name against all the patterns. It does this with the `patterns_match()` function in `ls.c`:

```
/* Return true if one of the PATTERNS matches FILE.  */

static bool
patterns_match (struct ignore_pattern const *patterns, char const *file)
{
  struct ignore_pattern const *p;
  for (p = patterns; p; p = p->next)
    if (fnmatch (p->pattern, file, FNM_PERIOD) == 0)
      return true;
  return false;
}
```

NOTE

`fnmatch()` can be an expensive function if it's used in a locale that uses a multibyte character set. We discuss multibyte character sets in Section 15.4, "Can You Spell That for Me, Please?," page 540.

13.7.2 File Name Expansion: `glob()` and `globfree()`

The `glob()` and `globfree()` functions are more elaborate than `fnmatch()`:

```
#include <glob.h>                                          POSIX

int glob(const char *pattern, int flags,
         int (*errfunc)(const char *epath, int eerrno),
         glob_t *pglob);
void globfree(glob_t *pglob);
```

The `glob()` function does directory scanning and wildcard matching, returning a list of all pathnames that match the `pattern`. Wildcards can be included at multiple points in the pathname, not just for the last component (for example, '`/usr/*/*.so`'). The arguments are as follows:

`const char *pattern`
: The pattern to expand.

`int flags`
: Flags that control `glob()`'s behavior, described shortly.

`int (*errfunc)(const char *epath, int eerrno)`
: A pointer to a function to use for reporting errors. This value may be `NULL`. If it's not, and if `(*errfunc)()` returns nonzero or if `GLOB_ERR` is set in `flags`, then `glob()` stops processing.

  The arguments to `(*errfunc)()` are the pathname that caused a problem and the value of `errno` set by `opendir()`, `readdir()`, or `stat()`.

`glob_t *pglob`
: A pointer to a `glob_t` structure used to hold the results.

The `glob_t` structure holds the list of pathnames that `glob()` produces:

```
typedef struct {                                           POSIX
    size_t gl_pathc;        Count of paths matched so far
    char **gl_pathv;        List of matched pathnames
    size_t gl_offs;         Slots to reserve in gl_pathv
} glob_t;
```

`size_t gl_pathc`
: The number of paths that were matched.

`char **gl_pathv`
: An array of matched pathnames. `gl_pathv[gl_pathc]` is always `NULL`.

`size_t gl_offs`
: "Reserved slots" in `gl_pathv`. The idea is to reserve slots *at the front* of `gl_pathv` for the application to fill in later, such as with a command name and options. The list can then be passed directly to `execv()` or `execvp()` (see Section 9.1.4, "Starting New Programs:

Table 13.2: Flags for `glob()`

Flag name	Meaning
`GLOB_APPEND`	Append current call's results to those of a previous call.
`GLOB_DOOFFS`	Reserve `gl_offs` spots at the front of `gl_pathv`.
`GLOB_ERR`	Return early when an error is encountered.
`GLOB_MARK`	Append a `/` character to the end of each pathname that is a directory.
`GLOB_NOCHECK`	If the pattern doesn't match any file name, return it unchanged.
`GLOB_NOESCAPE`	Treat backslash as a literal character. This makes it impossible to escape wildcard metacharacters.
`GLOB_NOSORT`	Don't sort the results; the default is to sort them.

The `exec()` Family," page 283). Reserved slots are set to `NULL`. For all this to work, `GLOB_DOOFFS` must be set in `flags`.

Table 13.2 lists the standard flags for `glob()`.

The GLIBC version of the `glob_t` structure contains additional members:

```
typedef struct {                                          GLIBC
/* POSIX components: */
    size_t gl_pathc;                                      Count of paths matched so far
    char **gl_pathv;                                      List of matched pathnames
    size_t gl_offs;                                       Slots to reserve in gl_pathv

/* GLIBC components: */
    int gl_flags;                                         Copy of flags, additional GLIBC flags
    void (*gl_closedir)(DIR *);                           Private version of closedir()
    struct dirent *(*gl_readdir)(DIR *);                  Private version of readdir()
    DIR *(*gl_opendir)(const char *);                     Private version of opendir()
    int (*gl_lstat)(const char *, struct stat *);         Private version of lstat()
    int (*gl_stat)(const char *, struct stat *);          Private version of stat()
} glob_t;
```

The members are as follows:

`int gl_flags`
: Copy of `flags`. Also includes `GLOB_MAGCHAR` if `pattern` included any metacharacters.

`void (*gl_closedir)(DIR *)`
: Pointer to alternative version of `closedir()`.

`struct dirent *(*gl_readdir)(DIR *)`
: Pointer to alternative version of `readdir()`.

`DIR *(*gl_opendir)(const char *)`
: Pointer to alternative version of `opendir()`.

`int (*gl_lstat)(const char *, struct stat *)`
: Pointer to alternative version of `lstat()`.

`int (*gl_stat)(const char *, struct stat *)`
: Pointer to alternative version of `stat()`.

The pointers to private versions of the standard functions are mainly for use in implementing GLIBC; it is highly unlikely that you will ever need to use them. Because GLIBC provides the `gl_flags` field and additional flag values, the manpage and Info manual document the rest of the GLIBC `glob_t` structure. Table 13.3 lists the additional flags.

The `GLOB_ONLYDIR` flag serves as a *hint* to the implementation that the caller is interested only in directories. Its primary use is by other functions within GLIBC, and a caller still has to be prepared to handle nondirectory files. You should not use it in your programs.

`glob()` can be called more than once: the first call should *not* have the `GLOB_APPEND` flag set, and all subsequent calls *must* have it set. You cannot change `gl_offs` between calls, and if you modify any values in `gl_pathv` or `gl_pathc`, you must restore them before making a subsequent call to `glob()`.

The ability to call `glob()` multiple times allows you to build up the results in a single list. This is quite useful; it approaches the power of the shell's wildcard expansion facility, but at the C programming level.

`glob()` returns `0` if there were no problems or one of the values in Table 13.4 if there were.

Table 13.3: Additional GLIBC flags for `glob()`

Flag name	Meaning
`GLOB_ALTDIRFUNC`	Use alternative functions for directory access (see text).
`GLOB_BRACE`	Perform `csh`- and Bash-style brace expansions.
`GLOB_MAGCHAR`	Set in `gl_flags` if metacharacters were found.
`GLOB_NOMAGIC`	Return the pattern if it doesn't contain metacharacters.
`GLOB_ONLYDIR`	If possible, only match directories. See text.
`GLOB_PERIOD`	Allow metacharacters like * and ? to match a leading period.
`GLOB_TILDE`	Do shell-style tilde expansions.
`GLOB_TILDE_CHECK`	Like `GLOB_TILDE`, but if there are problems with the named home directory, return `GLOB_NOMATCH` instead of placing `pattern` into the list.

Table 13.4: `glob()` return values

Constant	Meaning
`GLOB_ABORTED`	Scanning stopped early because `GLOB_ERR` was set or because `(*errfunc)()` returned nonzero.
`GLOB_NOMATCH`	No file names matched `pattern`, and `GLOB_NOCHECK` was not set in the flags.
`GLOB_NOSPACE`	There was a problem allocating dynamic memory.

`globfree()` releases all the memory that `glob()` dynamically allocated. The following program, `ch-general2-glob.c`, demonstrates `glob()`:

```
/* ch-general2-glob.c --- demonstrate glob(). */

#include <stdio.h>
#include <errno.h>
#include <glob.h>
#include <stdlib.h>
#include <string.h>

const char *myname;

/* globerr --- print error message for glob() */

int
globerr(const char *path, int eerrno)
{
    fprintf(stderr, "%s: %s: %s\n", myname, path, strerror(eerrno));
    return 0;   /* let glob() keep going */
}

/* main --- expand command-line wildcards and print results */

int
main(int argc, char **argv)
{
    int i;
    int flags = 0;
    glob_t results;
    int ret;

    if (argc == 1) {
        fprintf(stderr, "usage: %s wildcard ...\n", argv[0]);
        exit(EXIT_FAILURE);
    }

    myname = argv[0];   /* for globerr() */

    for (i = 1; i < argc; i++) {
        flags |= (i > 1 ? GLOB_APPEND : 0);
        ret = glob(argv[i], flags, globerr, & results);
        if (ret != 0) {
            fprintf(stderr, "%s: problem with %s (%s), stopping early\n",
                myname, argv[i],
        /* ugly: */ (ret == GLOB_ABORTED ? "filesystem problem" :
                 ret == GLOB_NOMATCH ? "no match of pattern" :
```

```
45                  ret == GLOB_NOSPACE ? "no dynamic memory" :
46                  "unknown problem"));
47              break;
48          }
49      }
50
51      for (i = 0; i < results.gl_pathc; i++)
52          printf("%s\n", results.gl_pathv[i]);
53
54      globfree(& results);
55      return EXIT_SUCCESS;
56  }
```

Line 9 defines `myname`, which points to the program's name; this variable is for error messages from `globerr()`, defined on lines 13–18.

Lines 37–49 are the heart of the program. They loop over the patterns given on the command line, calling `glob()` on each one to append its results to the list. Most of the loop is error handling (lines 40–48). Lines 51–52 print the resulting list, and lines 54–55 clean up and return.

Lines 43–46 aren't pretty—a separate function that converts the integer constant to a string should be used; we've done it this way primarily to save space. Code like this is tolerable in a small program, but a larger program should use a function.

If you think about all the work going on under the hood (opening and reading directories, matching patterns, dynamic allocation to grow the list, sorting the list), you can start to appreciate how much `glob()` does for you! Here are some results:

```
$ ch-general2-glob '/usr/lib/lib*.so' '../../bookfiles/*.texi'
/usr/lib/libImageProcessor-x86_64.so
/usr/lib/libImageProcessor.so
/usr/lib/libhpdiscovery.so
/usr/lib/libhpip.so
/usr/lib/libhpipp.so
/usr/lib/libhpmud.so
../../bookfiles/00-preface.texi
../../bookfiles/01-intro.texi
../../bookfiles/02-cmdline.texi
...
```

Note that we have to quote the arguments to keep the shell from doing the expansion!

Globbing? What's That?

In days of yore, circa V6 Unix, the shell used a separate program to perform wildcard expansion behind the scenes. This program was named `/etc/glob`, and according to the V6 source code, the name "glob" is short for "global."[6]

[6]See `/usr/source/s1/glob.c` in the V6 distribution.

> The verb "to glob" thus passed into the Unix lexicon, with the meaning "to perform wildcard expansion." This in turn gives us the function names `glob()` and `globfree()`. The usually understated sense of humor that occasionally peeked through from the Unix manual therefore lives on, formally enshrined in the POSIX standard. (Can you imagine anyone at IBM, in the 1970s or 1980s, naming a system routine `glob()`?)

13.7.3 Shell Word Expansion: `wordexp()` and `wordfree()`

Many members of the POSIX committee felt that `glob()` didn't do enough; they wanted a library routine capable of doing everything the shell can do: tilde expansion ('`echo ~arnold`'), shell variable expansion ('`echo $HOME`'), and command substitution ('`echo $(cd ; pwd)`'). Many others felt that `glob()` wasn't the right function for this purpose. To "satisfy" everyone, POSIX supplies an additional two functions that do everything:

```
#include <wordexp.h>                                        POSIX

int wordexp(const char *words,
            wordexp_t *pwordexp,
            int flags);
void wordfree(wordexp_t *wordexp);
```

These functions work similarly to `glob()` and `globfree()`, but on a `wordexp_t` structure:

```
typedef struct {
    size_t we_wordc;           Count of words matched
    char **we_wordv;           List of expanded words
    size_t we_offs;            Slots to reserve in we_wordv
} wordexp_t;
```

The members are completely analogous to those of the `glob_t` described earlier; we won't repeat the whole description here.

As with `glob()`, several flags control `wordexp()`'s behavior. The flags are listed in Table 13.5.

The return value is `0` if everything went well, or one of the values in Table 13.6 if not.

We leave it to you as an exercise (see later) to modify `ch-general2-glob.c` to use `wordexp()` and `wordfree()`. Here's our version in action:

```
$ ch-general2-wordexp 'echo $HOME'              Shell variable expansion
echo
/home/arnold
$ ch-general2-wordexp 'echo $HOME/*.gz'         Variables and wildcards
echo
/home/arnold/48000.wav.gz
```

Table 13.5: Flags for `wordexp()`

Constant	Meaning
`WRDE_APPEND`	Append current call's results to those of a previous call.
`WRDE_DOOFFS`	Reserve `we_offs` spots at the front of `we_wordv`.
`WRDE_NOCMD`	Don't allow command substitution.
`WRDE_REUSE`	Reuse the storage already pointed to by `we_wordv`.
`WRDE_SHOWERR`	Don't be silent about errors during expansion.
`WRDE_UNDEF`	Cause undefined shell variables to produce an error.

Table 13.6: `wordexp()` error return values

Constant	Meaning
`WRDE_BADCHAR`	A metacharacter (one of newline, '|', &, ;, <, >, (,), {, or }) appeared in an invalid location.
`WRDE_BADVAL`	A variable was undefined and `WRDE_UNDEF` is set.
`WRDE_CMDSUB`	Command substitution was attempted and `WRDE_NOCMD` was set.
`WRDE_NOSPACE`	There was a problem allocating dynamic memory.
`WRDE_SYNTAX`	There was a shell syntax error.

```
/home/arnold/ipmasq-HOWTO.tar.gz
/home/arnold/rc.firewall-examples.tar.gz
$ ch-general2-wordexp 'echo ~arnold'                 Tilde expansion
echo
/home/arnold
$ ch-general2-wordexp 'echo ~arnold/.p*'             Tilde and wildcards
echo
/home/arnold/.postitnotes
/home/arnold/.procmailrc
/home/arnold/.profile
$ ch-general2-wordexp "echo '~arnold/.p*'"           Quoting works
echo
~arnold/.p*
```

13.8 Regular Expressions

A *regular expression* is a way to describe patterns of text to be matched. If you've used GNU/Linux or Unix for any time at all, you're undoubtedly familiar with regular expressions: they are a fundamental part of the Unix programmer's toolbox. They are integral to such everyday programs as `grep`, `sed`, `awk`, Perl, and the `ed`, `vi`, `vim`, and Emacs editors. Shell wildcards are also regular expressions, although in a more limited form than provided by other utilities. If you're not at all familiar with regular expressions, we suggest you take a detour to some of the books or URLs named in Section 13.9, "Suggested Reading," page 467.

POSIX defines two flavors of regular expressions: *basic* and *extended*. Programs such as `grep`, `sed`, and the `ed` line editor use basic regular expressions. Programs such as '`grep -E`' and `awk` use extended regular expressions. The following functions give you the ability to use either flavor in your programs:

```
#include <sys/types.h>                                    POSIX
#include <regex.h>

int regcomp(regex_t *preg,
            const char *regex,
            int cflags);
int regexec(const regex_t *preg,
            const char *string,
            size_t nmatch,
            regmatch_t pmatch[],
            int eflags);
size_t regerror(int errcode,
                const regex_t *preg,
                char *errbuf,
                size_t errbuf_size);
void regfree(regex_t *preg);
```

To do regular expression matching, you must first *compile* a string version of the regular expression. Compilation converts the regular expression into an internal form. The compiled form is then *executed* against a string to see whether it matches the original regular expression. The functions are as follows:

`int regcomp(regex_t *preg, const char *regex, int cflags)`
: Compiles the regular expression `regex` into the internal form, storing it in the `regex_t` structure pointed to by `preg`. `cflags` controls how the compilation is done; its value is either `0` or the bitwise-OR of one or more of the flags in Table 13.7.

`int regexec(const regex_t *preg, const char *string, size_t nmatch, regmatch_t pmatch[], int eflags)`
: Executes the compiled regular expression in `*preg` against the string `string`. `eflags` controls how the execution is done; its value is either `0` or the bitwise-OR of one or more of the flags in Table 13.8. We discuss the other arguments shortly.

`size_t regerror(int errcode, const regex_t *preg, char *errbuf, size_t errbuf_size)`
: Converts an error returned by either `regcomp()` or `regexec()` into a string that can be printed for a human to read.

`void regfree(regex_t *preg)`
: Frees dynamic memory used by the compiled regular expression in `*preg`.

Table 13.7: Flags for `regcomp()`

Constant	Meaning
`REG_EXTENDED`	Use extended regular expressions. The default is basic regular expressions.
`REG_ICASE`	Matches with `regexec()` ignore case.
`REG_NEWLINE`	Operators that can match any character *don't* match newline.
`REG_NOSUB`	Subpattern start and end information isn't needed (see text).

Table 13.8: Flags for `regexec()`

Constant	Meaning
`REG_NOTBOL`	Don't allow the `^` (beginning of line) operator to match.
`REG_NOTEOL`	Don't allow the `$` (end of line) operator to match.

The `<regex.h>` header file defines a number of flags. Some are for use with `regcomp()`; others are for use with `regexec()`. However, they all start with the prefix '`REG_`'. Table 13.7 lists the flags for regular expression compilation with `regcomp()`.

The flags for regular expression matching with `regexec()` are given in Table 13.8.

The `REG_NEWLINE`, `REG_NOTBOL` and `REG_NOTEOL` flags interact with each other. It's a little complicated, so we take it one step at a time:

- When `REG_NEWLINE` is not included in `cflags`, the newline character acts like an ordinary character. The '`.`' (match any character) metacharacter can match it, as can complemented character lists ('`[^...]`'). Also, `$` does not match immediately before an embedded newline, and `^` does not match immediately after one.
- When `REG_NOTBOL` is set in `eflags`, the `^` operator does not match the beginning of the string. This is useful when the `string` parameter is the address of a character in the middle of the text being matched.
- Similarly, when `REG_NOTEOL` is set in `eflags`, the `$` operator does not match the end of the string.
- When `REG_NEWLINE` is included in `cflags`, then:
  - Newline is not matched by '`.`' or by a complemented character list.
  - The `^` operator always matches immediately following an embedded newline, no matter the setting of `REG_NOTBOL`.
  - The `$` operator always matches immediately before an embedded newline, no matter the setting of `REG_NOTEOL`.

When you're doing line-at-a-time I/O, such as by `grep`, you can leave `REG_NEWLINE` out of `cflags`. If you have multiple lines in a buffer and want to treat each one as a separate string, with `^` and `$` matching within them, then you should include `REG_NEWLINE`.

The `regex_t` structure is mostly opaque. It has one member that user-level code can examine; the rest is for internal use by the regular expression routines:

```
typedef struct {
    ... internal stuff here ...
    size_t re_nsub;
    ... internal stuff here ...
} regex_t;
```

The `regmatch_t` structure has at least two members for use by user-level code:

```
typedef struct {
    ... possible internal stuff here ...
    regoff_t rm_so;          Byte offset to start of substring
    regoff_t rm_eo;          Byte offset to first character after substring end
    ... possible internal stuff here ...
} regmatch_t;
```

Both the `re_nsub` field and the `regmatch_t` structure are for *subexpression matching*. Consider an extended regular expression such as:

```
[[:space:]]+([[:digit:]]+)[[:space:]]+([[:alpha:]])+
```

The two parenthesized subexpressions can each match one or more characters. Furthermore, the text matching each subexpression can start and end at arbitrary positions within the string.

`regcomp()` sets the `re_nsub` field to the number of parenthesized subexpressions in the regular expression. `regexec()` fills in the `pmatch` array of `regmatch_t` structures with the start and ending byte offsets of the text that matched the corresponding subexpressions. Taken together, this data allows you to do text substitution—deletion of matched text or replacement of matched text with other text, just as in your favorite text editor.

`pmatch[0]` describes the portion of `string` that matched the entire regular expression. `pmatch[1]` through `pmatch[preg->re_nsub]` describe the portions that matched each parenthesized subexpression. (Thus, subexpressions are numbered from 1.) Unused elements in the `pmatch` array have their `rm_so` and `rm_eo` elements set to `-1`.

`regexec()` fills in no more than `nmatch - 1` elements of `pmatch`; you should thus ensure that there are at least as many elements (plus 1) as in `preg->re_nsub`.

Finally, the `REG_NOSUB` flag for `regcomp()` indicates that starting and ending information isn't necessary. You should use this flag when you don't need the information; it can potentially improve the performance of `regexec()`, making a significant difference.

In other words, if all you need to know is "did it match?" then include `REG_NOSUB`. However, if you also need to know "where is the matching text?" then omit it.

Finally, both `regcomp()` and `regexec()` return `0` if they were successful or a specific error code if not. The error codes are listed in Table 13.9.

To demonstrate the regular expression routines, `ch-general2-grep.c` provides a basic reimplementation of the standard `grep` program, which searches files for a pattern. Our version uses basic regular expressions by default. It accepts a `-E` option to use extended regular expressions instead and a `-i` option to ignore case. Like the real `grep`, if no files are provided

Table 13.9: Error codes for `regcomp()` and `regexec()`

Constant	Meaning
`REG_BADBR`	The contents of '`\{...\}`' are invalid.
`REG_BADPAT`	The regular expression is invalid.
`REG_BADRPT`	A ?, +, or * is not preceded by valid regular expression.
`REG_EBRACE`	Braces ('`\{...\}`') are not balanced correctly.
`REG_EBRACK`	Square brackets ('`[...]`') are not balanced correctly.
`REG_ECOLLATE`	The pattern used an invalid collating element.
`REG_ECTYPE`	The pattern used an invalid character class.
`REG_EESCAPE`	The pattern has a trailing \ character.
`REG_EPAREN`	Grouping parentheses ('`(...)`' or '`\(...\)`') are not balanced correctly.
`REG_ERANGE`	The endpoint in a range expression is invalid.
`REG_ESPACE`	The function ran out of memory.
`REG_ESUBREG`	The digit in '`\digit`' is invalid.
`REG_NOMATCH`	`regexec()` did not match the string to the pattern.

on the command line, our `grep` reads standard input, and also as in the real `grep`, a file name of '`-`' can be used to mean standard input. (This technique is useful for searching standard input along with other files.) Here's the program:

```
1  /* ch-general2-grep.c --- Simple version of grep using POSIX R.E. functions. */
2
3  #include <stdio.h>
4  #include <errno.h>
5  #include <regex.h>
6  #include <stdbool.h>
7  #include <stdlib.h>
8  #include <string.h>
9  #include <unistd.h>
10 #include <sys/types.h>
11
12 const char *myname;            /* for error messages */
13 bool ignore_case = false;      /* -i option: ignore case */
14 bool extended = false;         /* -E option: use extended RE's */
15 int errors = 0;                /* number of errors */
16
17 regex_t pattern;               /* pattern to match */
18
19 void compile_pattern(const char *pat);
20 void process(const char *name, FILE *fp);
21 void usage(void);
```

Lines 12–17 declare the program's global variables. The first set (lines 12–15) are for options and error messages. Line 17 declares `pattern`, which holds the compiled pattern. Lines 19–21 declare the program's other functions.

`main()` starts off with argument parsing:

```
23  /* main --- process options, open files */
24
25  int
26  main(int argc, char **argv)
27  {
28      int c;
29      int i;
30      FILE *fp;
31
32      myname = argv[0];
33      while ((c = getopt(argc, argv, ":iE")) != -1) {
34          switch (c) {
35          case 'i':
36              ignore_case = true;
37              break;
38          case 'E':
39              extended = true;
40              break;
41          case '?':
42              usage();
43              break;
44          }
45      }
46
47      if (optind == argc)     /* sanity check */
48          usage();
49
50      compile_pattern(argv[optind]);  /* compile the pattern */
51      if (errors)         /* compile failed */
52          return EXIT_FAILURE;
53      else
54          optind++;
```

Line 32 sets `myname`, and lines 33–48 parse the options. Lines 50–54 compile the regular expression, placing the results into `pattern`. `compile_pattern()` increments `errors` if there was a problem. (Coupling the functions by means of a global variable like this is generally considered bad form. It's OK for a small program such as this one, but such coupling can become a problem in larger programs.) If there was no problem, line 54 increments `optind` so that the remaining arguments are the files to be processed.

The rest of `main()` processes the files named on the command line:

```
56      if (optind == argc)     /* no files, default to stdin */
57          process("standard input", stdin);
58      else {
```

```
59         /* loop over files */
60         for (i = optind; i < argc; i++) {
61             if (strcmp(argv[i], "-") == 0)
62                 process("standard input", stdin);
63             else if ((fp = fopen(argv[i], "r")) != NULL) {
64                 process(argv[i], fp);
65                 fclose(fp);
66             } else {
67                 fprintf(stderr, "%s: %s: could not open: %s\n",
68                     argv[0], argv[i], strerror(errno));
69                 errors++;
70             }
71         }
72     }
73
74     regfree(& pattern);
75     return errors != 0 ? EXIT_FAILURE : EXIT_SUCCESS;
76 }
```

Lines 56–72 process the files, searching for lines that match the pattern. Lines 56–57 handle the case in which no files are provided: the program reads standard input. Otherwise, lines 60–71 loop over the files. Line 61 handles the special casing of '-' to mean standard input, lines 63–65 handle regular files, and lines 66–70 handle problems.

The `compile_pattern()` function compiles the pattern for use during pattern matching:

```
/* compile_pattern --- compile the pattern */

void
compile_pattern(const char *pat)
{
    int flags = REG_NOSUB;  /* don't need where-matched info */
    int ret;
#define MSGBUFSIZE  512 /* arbitrary */
    char error[MSGBUFSIZE];

    if (ignore_case)
        flags |= REG_ICASE;
    if (extended)
        flags |= REG_EXTENDED;

    ret = regcomp(& pattern, pat, flags);
    if (ret != 0) {
        (void) regerror(ret, & pattern, error, sizeof error);
        fprintf(stderr, "%s: pattern `%s': %s\n", myname, pat, error);
        errors++;
    }
}
```

Lines 78–99 define the `compile_pattern()` function. It first sets `flags` to `REG_NOSUB` since all we need to know is "did a line match?" and not "where in the line is the matching text?".

Lines 88–91 add additional flags in accordance with the command-line options. Line 93 compiles the pattern, and lines 94–98 report any problems. (Although we used a fixed-size buffer for `regerror()`, you can instead pass it a fourth argument of `0`. In this case, it returns the number of bytes needed to hold the error string.)

Lines 101–125 define `process()`, which reads an input file and does the regular expression match:

```
101 /* process --- read lines of text and match against the pattern */
102
103 void
104 process(const char *name, FILE *fp)
105 {
106     char *buf = NULL;
107     size_t size = 0;
108     char error[MSGBUFSIZE];
109     int ret;
110
111     while (getline(& buf, &size, fp) != -1) {
112         ret = regexec(& pattern, buf, 0, NULL, 0);
113         if (ret != 0) {
114             if (ret != REG_NOMATCH) {
115                 (void) regerror(ret, & pattern, error, sizeof error);
116                 fprintf(stderr, "%s: file %s: %s\n", myname, name, error);
117                 free(buf);
118                 errors++;
119                 return;
120             }
121         } else
122             printf("%s: %s", name, buf);    /* print matching lines */
123     }
124     free(buf);
125 }
```

The outer loop (lines 111–123) reads input lines. We use `getline()` (see Section 3.2.1.9, "Reading Entire Lines: `getline()` and `getdelim()`," page 70) to avoid line-length problems. Line 112 calls `regexec()`. A nonzero return indicates either failure to match or some other error. Thus, lines 114–120 check for `REG_NOMATCH` and print an error only if some *other* problem occurred—failure to match isn't an error.

If the return value was `0`, the line matched the pattern and thus line 122 prints the file name and matching line.

Finally, the `usage()` function prints a usage message and exits. It's called when invalid options are provided or if no pattern is provided (lines 41–43 and 47–48):

```
/* usage --- print usage message and exit */

void
usage(void)
{
    fprintf(stderr, "usage: %s [-i] [-E] pattern [ files ... ]\n", myname);
    exit(EXIT_FAILURE);
}
```

That's it! A modest yet useful version of `grep`, in under 140 lines of code.

13.9 Suggested Reading

1. *Programming Pearls*, 2nd ed., by Jon Bentley. Addison-Wesley, 2000. ISBN-13: 978-0-201-65788-3.

   Program design with assertions is one of the fundamental themes in the book.

2. *Hints on Programming Language Design* by C. A. R. Hoare. Stanford University Computer Science Technical Report CS-73-403,[7] December, 1973.

3. *Building Secure Software: How to Avoid Security Problems the Right Way*, by John Viega and Gary McGraw. Addison-Wesley, Reading, Massachusetts, USA, 2001. ISBN-13: 978-0-201-72152-2.

   Race conditions are only one of many issues to worry about when you are writing secure software. Random numbers are another. This book covers both, among other things. (We mentioned it in Chapter 11.)

4. *The Art of Computer Programming*, vol. 2, *Seminumerical Algorithms*, 3rd ed., by Donald E. Knuth. Addison-Wesley, 1998. ISBN-13: 978-0-201-89684-8. See also the book's website.[8]

   This is the classic reference on random number generation.

5. *Random Number Generation and Monte Carlo Methods*, 2nd ed., by James E. Gentle. Springer, 2003. ISBN-13: 978-0-387-00178-4.

   This book has wide coverage of the methods for generating and testing pseudorandom numbers. While it still requires background in mathematics and statistics, the level is not as high as that of Knuth's book. (Thanks to Nelson H. F. Beebe for the pointer to this reference.)

6. *Numerical Recipes in C: The Art of Scientific Computing*, 2nd ed., by William H. Press, Brian P. Flannery, Saul A. Teukolsky, and William T. Vetterling. Cambridge University Press, 1993. ISBN-13: 978-0-521-43108-8. There is a newer edition.

---

[7] `http://i.stanford.edu/pub/cstr/reports/cs/tr/73/403/CS-TR-73-403.pdf`

[8] `https://www-cs-faculty.stanford.edu/~knuth/taocp.html`

7. *sed & awk*, 2nd ed., by Dale Dougherty and Arnold Robbins. O'Reilly, 1997. ISBN-13: 978-1-56592-225-9.

   This book gently introduces regular expressions and text processing, starting with `grep` before moving on to the more powerful `sed` and `awk` tools.

8. *Mastering Regular Expressions*, 3rd ed., by Jeffrey E. F. Friedl. O'Reilly, 2006. ISBN-13: 978-0-59652-812-6.

   Regular expressions are an important part of Unix. For learning how to chop, slice, and dice text using regular expressions, we recommend this book.

9. The online manual for GNU `grep` also explains regular expressions. On a GNU/Linux system, you can use '`info grep`' to look at the local copy. Or use a web browser to read the GNU Project's online documentation for `grep`.[9]

13.10 Summary

- Assertions provide a way to make statements about the expected state of a program. They are a useful design and debugging tool and should generally be left in production code. Be careful, however, not to confuse assertions with runtime checks for possible failure conditions.
- The `mem`*`XXX`*`()` functions provide analogues to the better-known `str`*`XXX`*`()` functions. Their greatest value is that they can work on binary data; zero bytes are no different from other bytes. Of particular note is `memcpy()` versus `memmove()` and the handling of overlapping copies.
- Temporary files are useful in many applications. The `tmpfile()`, `mkstemp()`, and `mkdtemp()` APIs are the preferred way to create temporary files and directories while avoiding race conditions and their security implications. Many programs use the `TMPDIR` environment variable to specify the location for their temporary files, with a meaningful default (usually `/tmp`) if that variable isn't defined. This is a good convention, one you should adopt for your own programs.
- The `abort()` function sends a `SIGABRT` to the calling process. The effect is to kill the process and (hopefully) create a core dump, presumably for debugging.
- `setjmp()` and `longjmp()` provide a nonlocal goto. This is a powerful facility that must be used with care. `sigsetjmp()` and `siglongjmp()` can save and restore the process signal mask when a program does a nonlocal jump. The problems with nonlocal gotos sometimes outweigh their benefits; thus, use these routines only if there isn't a better way to structure your application.
- Random numbers are useful in a variety of applications. Most software uses pseudorandom numbers—sequences of numbers that appear random but that can be reproduced

[9] `https://www.gnu.org/software/grep/doc/grep.html`

by starting with the same seed each time. `rand()` and `srand()` are the original API, standardized by the C language. On many systems, `rand()` uses a subpar algorithm. `random()` and `srandom()` use a better algorithm, are included in the POSIX standard, and are preferred over `rand()` and `srand()`. Use the `/dev/urandom` and `/dev/random` special files (a) if they're available and (b) if you need high-quality random numbers.

On GNU/Linux systems, `getrandom()` provides the easiest way to get truly random numbers. The `arc4random()`, `arc4random_uniform()`, and `arc4random_buf()` functions provide cryptographically secure random numbers.

- Three APIs provide increasingly powerful facilities for metacharacter expansion (wildcarding):
  - `fnmatch()` is the simplest, returning true/false as a given string does or doesn't match a shell wildcard pattern.
  - `glob()` works its way through the filesystem, returning a list of pathnames that match a given wildcard. When the standard `glob()` functionality is all that's needed, it should be used. While the GLIBC version of `glob()` has some extensions, portable programs needing the extra power should use `wordexp()` instead. (Programs that will run only on GNU/Linux systems should feel free to use the full power of the GLIBC `glob()`.)
  - `wordexp()` not only does what `glob()` does, but it also does full shell word expansion, including tilde expansion, shell variable expansion, and command substitution.
- The `regcomp()` and `regexec()` functions give you access to POSIX basic and extended regular expressions. By using one or the other, you can make your program behave identically to the standard utilities, making it much easier for people familiar with GNU/Linux and Unix to use your program.

Exercises

1. Use `read()` and `memcmp()` to write a simple version of the `cmp` program that compares two files. Your version need not support any options.
2. Use the `<stdio.h>` `getc()` macro and direct comparison of each read character to write another version of `cmp` that compares two files. Compare the performance of this version against the one you wrote for the previous exercise.
3. (Medium.) Consider the `<stdio.h>` `fgets()` and `getline()` functions. Would `memcpy()` be useful for implementing them? Sketch a possible implementation of `fgets()` using it.
4. (Hard.) Download the source for GLIBC using Git: '`git clone git://sourceware.org/git/glibc.git`'. Find the source to the GLIBC version of `memcmp()`. Examine the code, and explain it.

5. Test your memory. How does `tmpfile()` arrange for the file to be deleted when the file pointer is closed?
6. Using `mkstemp()` and `fdopen()` and any other functions or system calls you think necessary, write your own version of `tmpfile()`. Test it too.
7. Review the *linkat*(2) and *openat*(2) manpages. Write a program that creates a temporary file with `tmpfile()` and populates it with some data. Use `fileno()`, `openat()`, and `linkat()` to give the temporary file a real path, before closing the file. Did it work?
8. Describe the advantages and disadvantages of using `unlink()` on the file name created by `mkstemp()` immediately after `mkstemp()` returns.
9. Write your own version of `mkstemp()`, using `mktemp()` and `open()`. How can you make the same guarantees about uniqueness that `mkstemp()` does?
10. Programs using `mkstemp()` should arrange to clean up the file when they exit. (Assume that the file is not immediately unlinked after opening, for whatever reason.) This includes the case in which a terminating signal could arrive. So, as part of a signal catcher, the file should be removed. How do you do this?
11. (Hard.) Even with the first-cut signal handling cleanup, there's still a race condition. There's a small window between the time `mkstemp()` creates the temporary file and the time its name is returned and recorded (for use by the signal handling function) in a variable. If an uncaught signal is delivered in that window, the program dies and leaves behind the temporary file. How do you close that window? (Thanks to Jim Meyering.)
12. Try compiling and running `ch-general2-setjmp.c` on as many different systems with as many different compilers as you have access to. Try compiling with and without different levels of optimizations. What variations in behavior, if any, did you see?
13. Look at the file `/usr/src/libc/gen/sleep.c` in the V7 Unix source distribution. (A copy is included in the book's GitHub repository.) It implements the `sleep()` function described in Section 10.8.1, "Alarm Clocks: `sleep()`, `alarm()`, and `SIGALRM`," page 363. Print it, and annotate it in the style of our examples to explain how it works.
14. On a GNU/Linux or System V Unix system, look at the *lrand48*(3) manpage. Does this interface look easier or harder to use than `random()`?
15. Take `ch-mounting-fts.c` from Section 8.4.3.2, "Processing a File Tree Stream," page 252, and add a `--exclude=`*`pat`* option. Files matching the pattern should not be printed.
16. (Hard.) Why would GLIBC need pointers to private versions of the standard directory and `stat()` calls? Can't it just call them directly?
17. Modify `ch-general2-glob.c` to use the `wordexp()` API. Experiment with it by doing some of the extra things it provides. Be sure to quote your command-line arguments so that `wordexp()` is really doing all the work!
18. The standard `grep` prints the file name only when more than one file is provided on the command line. Make `ch-general2-grep.c` perform the same way.
19. Look at the *grep*(1) manpage. Add the standard `-e`, `-q`, and `-v` options to `ch-general2-grep.c`.

20. Write a simple substitution program:

    `subst [-g]` *pattern replacement* [*files* ...]

    It should read lines of text from the named *files* or from standard input if no files are given. It should search each line for a match of *pattern*. If it finds one, it should replace it with *replacement*.

    With `-g`, it should replace not just the first match but *all* matches on the line.

21. Enhance the `subst` program from the previous exercise such that an `&` in the *replacement* text is replaced with the input text that matched the pattern.

Chapter 14

Sockets and Basic Networking

This chapter provides a *very* basic introduction to networking and interprocess communication with sockets.

14.1 Introduction, with a Little Bit of History

The *socket* abstraction for networking and interprocess communication (IPC) was introduced to the Unix world in 1983 with the release of 4.2 BSD. The system included support for the Internet Protocol Suite, named after two of the primary protocols: Transmission Control Protocol and Internet Protocol, or TCP/IP.

Today, networking is ubiquitous; our cell phones and laptops connect seamlessly and transparently to millions of server systems over the worldwide Internet, all built upon TCP/IP. But underneath the nice graphic displays on those phones and in the web browsers, everything still happens with sockets.

At the time of 4.2 BSD's release, there were many networking protocols in the computing world; most were vendor specific, intended for communication among systems all from the same vendor, such as IBM, DEC, or Prime.[1] Some, however, competed with TCP/IP to become the standard for *internetworking*—enabling disparate computing systems to communicate with each other. The most notable of these was the ISO suite of protocols. However, those "wars" are long over, and today TCP/IP is dominant.

This history still shows itself in the design of the socket API. Because there were many networking suites at the time, the API is general; it was intended to be usable with many different kinds of networks, such that once a connection was created, software could then use any connection in the same way. Just as `read()` reads bytes from an open file descriptor, no matter what the input source is, so too should networking code be able to read bytes from a network connection, no matter whether that network is running TCP/IP, the ISO protocols, or even AppleTalk.

This chapter looks at the very basics of socket programming. After more than 40 years of development, you can do much more with sockets than what we cover here, particularly on GNU/Linux systems. We hope that you will explore further on your own.

[1] Prime (now defunct) was a minicomputer vendor who at the time had an advanced networking facility.

14.2 Networking Technologies

There are multiple ways to move data from one place to another. They are easy to understand based on analogies to the real world. There are two basic paradigms:

Datagrams

Datagrams are self-contained units of data sent from a source to a destination. The analogy in the real world is a letter mailed from your home to that of a friend in another part of your city or country or somewhere else in the world. The outside of the envelope has your address (the sender) and that of your friend (the recipient). Inside the envelope is your letter, which is the actual data of interest.

Suppose you have *a lot* of information to send your friend, so that you break up your missive into multiple pages, putting a few pages at a time into separate envelopes. You number the envelopes, so that your friend will know the order in which to read the letters. Even if you mail those letters all on the same day, they may arrive at your friend's home over several days, in any order; some may not even arrive at all.

In networking, datagrams work in the same way. Each datagram has the source and destination addresses in it, along with its data. Multiple datagrams may arrive in any order, be dropped, or (unlike real letters) be duplicated.

Virtual circuits

A virtual circuit is a two-way communications channel, in which data is sent in order, without loss. The analogy in the real world is a telephone call from a phone in your home to a phone in your friend's home, wherever that may be. Once the connection is made, you and your friend can both talk (two-way, or *duplex*), and (usually) without any noise or loss.[2]

In networking, particularly TCP/IP networking, a virtual circuit is often referred to as a *stream*, since data flows from one place to another. Stream connections provide full duplex communication, without data loss or data duplication.

14.3 Internet Building Blocks

With those ideas out of the way, there are a few more basics that should be presented. The first thing to know is that the basic protocol is IP (Internet Protocol). IP is a datagram protocol, where each *packet* (chunk of data) is self-contained, and packets may be lost, duplicated, or delivered out of order. The other protocols are built on top of IP. IP provides the fundamental idea of an *address*, a unique identifier (a number) that identifies a particular system. More on that shortly.

[2]Telephone service often isn't as good as it used to be, for various reasons. Nonetheless, the analogy remains valid.

The second important idea is that of a *port.* A port identifies a unique *service* on a particular system. For example, one might connect to the same system using a web browser (HTTP, port 80), the file transfer protocol (FTP, port 21), or `ssh` (the Secure Shell, port 22).

The real-world analogy for a port would be something like calling the office of a company. The office will have a single phone number, and then you might be prompted for the *extension* of the person you wish to reach within the company (sales, service, accounting, etc.).

Some ports are *privileged,* meaning that only programs running as `root` may act as servers on these ports. On POSIX systems, ports below 1024 are privileged.

The TCP protocol provides stream communications on top of IP; it also provides ports. The UDP protocol is a datagram protocol also built on top of IP; its primary contribution over that of IP is that it too provides ports.

We note here that the nitty-gritty details of how TCP/IP networking works are very much beyond our scope. See Section 14.11, "Suggested Reading," page 502, for a list of excellent books should you be interested in a deep dive.

14.3.1 IPv4 Addresses

IPv4 addresses are 32 bits in size. They are represented in *dotted decimal* notation, something like `142.250.75.100`, where the value of each byte in the address is given in decimal, separated by periods. Most of the world still uses IPv4, although there are places where only IPv6 is available.

IP addresses have a *network part* and a *host part.* The network part identifies the network (such as that of a company, `example.com`), and the host part identifies a unique host within the network. Some number of the high bits are for the network, the rest are for the host, and the quantity defining which is which varies from network to network.

Unfortunately, you can't tell by looking at a random IP address which bits are the network part and which are the host part. Fortunately, for most end uses it doesn't matter.

Some IP addresses are defined to have special meanings. The most common example is `127.0.0.1`, for the *local host.* When you connect to this address, you are talking to yourself. Similarly, IP addresses that start with `192.168` are reserved for local networks that sit behind routers (such as may be the case if you have an Internet connection with Wi-Fi); these addresses don't represent systems that are reachable on the Internet. (Again, we're only scratching the surface here; there are many more details.)

14.3.2 IPv6 Addresses

IPv6 became an Internet standard in July 2017; however, it was under development for many years before that. IPv6 offers 128-bit addresses. They are written using hexadecimal values separated by colons—for example, `2a00:1450:4028:800::2004`. The double-colon indicates that the intervening bytes of the address are all zero.

In this chapter we focus mainly on IPv4 networking, but we will mention some things that are relevant for IPv6.

What Happened to IPv5?

Quoting from Wikipedia:[3]

> The Internet Stream Protocol (ST) is a family of experimental protocols first defined in Internet Experiment Note IEN-119 in 1979, and later substantially revised in RFC 1190 (ST-II) and RFC 1819 (ST2+). The protocol uses the version number 5 in the version field of the Internet Protocol header, but was never known as IPv5. The successor to IPv4 was thus named IPv6 to eliminate any possible confusion about the actual protocol in use.

14.3.3 Addresses and Interfaces

An additional clarification is needed. An IP address actually identifies a machine's networking *interface*, the bit of hardware connected to a particular physical network. Early on, most machines had only one interface, although some machines had more than one and could act as *routers* between networks. Today, multiple interfaces are much more common, as exemplified by a laptop having both an Ethernet port and a Wi-Fi adaptor, or by the Wi-Fi and cellular networking abilities of modern cell phones. Fortunately, all this is generally transparent to us as end users.

When used by a server program, the special address `0.0.0.0` means that the server should accept connections on all of a machine's interfaces. It has other meanings in other contexts, which we don't discuss.

14.3.4 Network Byte Order

Computers of different architectures use different byte orders, referred to as *big endian* (where the most significant byte is stored first) and *little endian* (where the most significant byte is stored last). This has been the case for decades. The difference is depicted in Figure 14.1.

Quoting from `techtarget.com`:[4]

> Big-endian and little-endian derive from Jonathan Swift's *Gulliver's Travels*, in which the Big Endians were a political faction that broke their eggs at the large end, or "the primitive way." They rebelled against the Lilliputian King, who required his subjects, the Little Endians, to break their eggs at the small end.

Different endianness raises a conundrum. If two machines of different architecture are supposed to share data, which order should they use? The architects of the Internet chose big-endian as the *network byte order*. Before sending binary data, systems must convert it from their native byte order to network byte order, and do the reverse upon receiving such data.

[3] `https://en.wikipedia.org/wiki/Internet_Stream_Protocol`

[4] `https://www.techtarget.com/searchnetworking/definition/big-endian-and-little-endian`

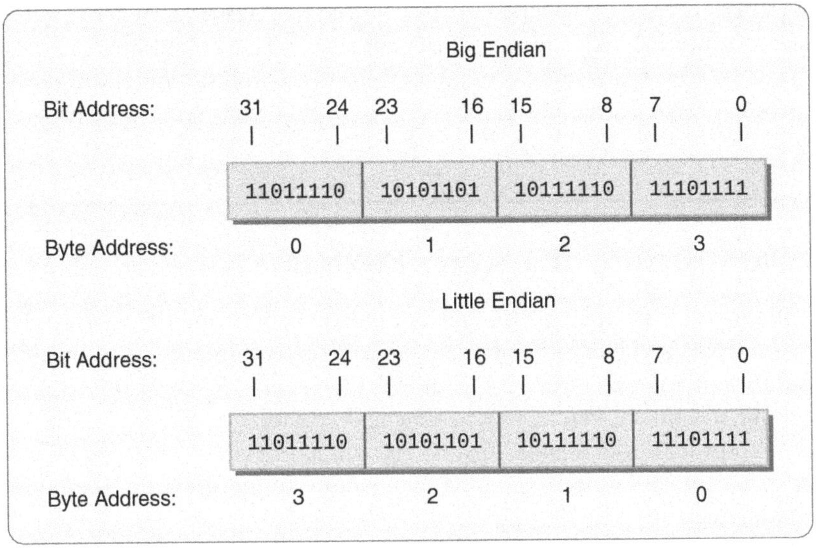

Figure 14.1: Byte endianness

Here are the standard routines to do these conversions:

```
#include <arpa/inet.h>                              POSIX

uint32_t htonl(uint32_t hostlong);                  Host to network long (32 bits)
uint16_t htons(uint16_t hostshort);                 Host to network short (16 bits)
uint32_t ntohl(uint32_t netlong);                   Network to host long (32 bits)
uint16_t ntohs(uint16_t netshort);                  Network to host short (16 bits)
```

On big-endian machines, these functions are no-ops; they simply return the original value as is. We will see some uses shortly.

14.4 Networking and Client/Server

It takes two to tango.
—Al Hoffman and Dick Manning, authors of the song "Takes Two to Tango"

In any conversation, there are two participants. In networking, we define one as the *client*, and the other as the *server*. As an analogy, consider a drive-in window at a bank. The teller is the server who is always available,[5] waiting for a customer to drive up. The customer is the client, initiating the conversation upon arrival and making a request ("I'd like to deposit this cash into my account").

[5] At least during banking hours.

For networking programs, the server is always running,[6] waiting for someone to connect to it and make a request (think website). The client is the one who initiates the conversation, connecting to the server and issuing a request (think web browser, once you enter [or click on] a URL). Upon receiving a request, the server responds, and then the two-way conversation continues.

14.5 Basic Structure of a Server Program

A bank teller in the real world can service only one customer at a time. If there is only one teller but there are multiple customers, the first customer is served, and the others wait (patiently, we hope) until the teller is free.

In networking, it works differently. When a client connects to a server, the server accepts the connection and then forks a child process to handle the client. The original server can then go back to accepting connections. The flow is thus an infinite loop, something like the following pseudocode:

```
setup_initial_socket();
setup_process_as_server();
for (;;) {
    int new_fd = start_the_conversation();
    pid_t pid = fork();
    if (pid < 0)
        handle_error();
    else if (pid == 0) {
        // new_fd inherited across the fork
        do_the_actual_work(new_fd);
        exit(EXIT_SUCCESS);
    } else {
        close(new_fd);
        // continue around in the loop
    }
}
```

In the following subsections, we present the socket routines that implement the steps above, ending with sample code from the 4.2 BSD `ftpd` daemon.

14.5.1 Creating a Socket: `socket()`

The first thing to do is create a socket with the `socket()` system call:

```
#include <sys/types.h>                          POSIX
#include <sys/socket.h>

int socket(int domain, int type, int protocol);
```

[6] This is not strictly true, which we discuss later in the chapter.

Table 14.1: The most useful address families

Family	Purpose	Manpage
`AF_UNIX`	On machine IPC	*unix*(7)
`AF_INET`	IPv4 Internet Protocols	*ip*(7)
`AF_INET6`	IPv6 Internet Protocols	*ipv6*(7)

The arguments are as follows:

`int domain`
: This indicates what kind of networking or IPC you wish to use. It essentially selects the protocol suite to use, as there are many more besides just TCP/IP. This is often referred to as the *address family*; this name is reflected in the `AF_` prefix used with the values provided for this parameter (see Table 14.1).

`int type`
: This indicates the type of the connection. The two main choices are for datagrams or virtual circuits, but there are other options. Table 14.2 presents the available values for `type`.

`int protocol`
: Within the chosen address family, there may be more than one protocol that provides the requested type of socket. In that case, the `protocol` parameter provides the designated choice. If there's only one, you can use `0` for this parameter. We'll offer a little more on this later.

GNU/Linux systems offer over 20 different choices for the address family (see *socket*(2)). Only a few of them are needed for regular use. Table 14.1 describes those that are. Borrowing from the *socket*(2) manpage, we provide a reference to the separate manpage for each family.

You may see very old code that uses constants like `PF_INET` and `PF_UNIX`, where the `PF_` prefix stands for "protocol family." This usage is obsolete, and the *socket*(2) manpage points out that the standards use only the `AF_` prefix.

The `type` parameter provides the communication semantics. The valid types are provided in Table 14.2.

Of the socket types presented in Table 14.2, only the first two, `SOCK_STREAM` and `SOCK_DGRAM`, are widely used; the others are much more specialized.

GNU/Linux, and the 2024 POSIX standard, let you bitwise-OR the `type` parameter with one of the following values (see Section 4.6.4, "Revisiting `open()`," page 104, and Section 9.4.3.1, "The Close-on-Exec and Close-on-Fork Flags," page 316, for information about the related file descriptor flags):

`SOCK_CLOEXEC`
: Set the `FD_CLOEXEC` flag on the returned file descriptor.

Table 14.2: Socket types

Type	Semantics
`SOCK_STREAM`	Reliable, ordered two-way byte streams.
`SOCK_DGRAM`	Datagrams. Delivery is not guaranteed, and messages have a maximum length.
`SOCK_SEQPACKET`	Datagrams, but delivery is guaranteed, in order. Communications are two-way, and messages have a maximum length. Entire packets must be read each time.
`SOCK_RAW`	Raw network protocol access. In TCP/IP, these are IP packets.
`SOCK_RDM`	Reliable datagrams. Delivery is guaranteed; ordering is not.

`SOCK_CLOFORK`
: Set the `FD_CLOFORK` flag on the returned file descriptor. As of this writing, `SOCK_CLOFORK` is still very new, but you can expect it to be supported in GNU/Linux before long.

`SOCK_NONBLOCK`
: Set the `O_NONBLOCK` flag on the returned file descriptor.

The `protocol` argument is usually `0`, but the formal way to get the correct value is via one of the following functions:

```
#include <netdb.h>                          POSIX

struct protoent *getprotoent(void);
struct protoent *getprotobyname(const char *name);
struct protoent *getprotobynumber(int proto);
void setprotoent(int stayopen);
void endprotoent(void);
```

`setprotoent()`, `getprotoent()`, and `endprotoent()` are similar to the functions for the password and group databases (see Section 6.3.1 "User Database," page 190, and Section 6.3.2, "Group Database," page 193); they walk through the entire list of possible protocols, one at a time.

`getprotobyname()` and `getprotobynumber()` look up a protocol by (you guessed it) name or number, respectively. Along with `getprotoent()`, they return a pointer to a `struct protoent`, which looks like this:

```
struct protoent {
    char *p_name;           Official name of the protocol
    char **p_aliases;       List of additional names, NULL terminated
    int p_proto;            Protocol number
};
```

For TCP/IP, additional symbolic constants let you avoid calling `getprotobyname()`:

Constant	Meaning
`IPPROTO_TCP`	A TCP socket.
`IPPROTO_UDP`	A UDP socket.
`IPPROTO_RAW`	A "raw" (IP) socket.

It's finally time to create a socket—in particular, a TCP stream socket:

```
int sockfd;

sockfd = socket(AF_INET, SOCK_STREAM, IPPROTO_TCP);
if (sockfd < 0) {
    fprintf(stderr, "%s: socket failed: %s\n", argv[0], strerror(errno));
    exit(EXIT_FAILURE);
}
```

`socket()` returns a valid file descriptor upon success. Upon error, it returns `-1` and sets `errno`.

The newly created socket exists, but in a vacuum. It is not yet usable for anything. For the next step, read on.

14.5.2 Associating the Socket with an Address: `bind()`

The `bind()` system call associates an address with a newly created socket:

```
#include <sys/types.h>                    POSIX
#include <sys/socket.h>

int bind(int sockfd, const struct sockaddr *addr, socklen_t addrlen);
```

Here, `sockfd` is the socket's file descriptor, `addr` represents the address to bind to the socket, and `addrlen` is the size of the structure pointed to by `addr`.

Remember we said that sockets could be used for different types of networks? And we saw that IPv4 and IPv6 have different address sizes. So practically speaking, depending on what kind of networking we're doing, we pass in different structures and cast the address of those structures to '`(const struct sockaddr *)`'. The `struct sockaddr` looks like this:

```
struct sockaddr {
    sa_family_t sa_family;
    char        sa_data[14];
};
```

Every socket address structure has an identical `sa_family` member at the front of it indicating the address family (as used when the socket was created).

For IPv4, the data structures look like this:

```
struct sockaddr_in {
    sa_family_t    sin_family; /* address family: AF_INET */
    in_port_t      sin_port;   /* port in network byte order */
    struct in_addr sin_addr;   /* Internet address */
};
```

```
/* Internet address. */
struct in_addr {
    uint32_t       s_addr;     /* address in network byte order */
};
```

Let's say we want to listen on the localhost address, on port 4242, for incoming connections. We can use `inet_ntoa()` (see *inet_ntoa*(3)) for that:

```
struct sockaddr_in local_addr;

local_addr.sin_family = AF_INET;
local_addr.sin_port = htons(4242);
inet_ntoa("127.0.0.1", & local_addr.sin_addr);        Error checking omitted for brevity

if (bind(sockfd, (const struct sockaddr *) & local_addr, sizeof(local_addr)) < 0) {
    fprintf(stderr, "failed to bind socket: %s\n", strerror(errno));
    exit(EXIT_FAILURE);
}
```

Our socket is now associated with an address.

14.5.3 Waiting for a Connection: `listen()`

Now that the socket has an address, like a receptionist waiting for the phone to ring, the next step is to tell the system that we want to wait for someone to try to reach us. This is done with the `listen()` system call:

```
#include <sys/types.h>                          POSIX
#include <sys/socket.h>

int listen(int sockfd, int backlog);
```

This system call defines the socket as one that will be used to accept incoming connections (termed a *passive* socket in the manpage).

Consider a web server. Many clients may try to connect to the same server on port 443 (for HTTPS). A server can handle only one incoming connection at a time. Thus it's desirable that incoming connections be queued up, to await their turn to be answered by the server.

That is the purpose of the `backlog` parameter; it indicates how many incoming connections can wait in line for the server. If the queue is full, additional incoming connections are refused.

`listen()` returns zero upon success, or `-1` upon error, setting `errno`:

```
#define BACKLOG 42

if (listen(sockfd, BACKLOG) < 0) {
    fprintf(stderr, "failed to listen on socket: %s\n", strerror(errno));
    exit(EXIT_FAILURE);
}
```

14.5.4 Starting a Conversation: accept()

What happens when the phone rings and it's answered? In the real world, the line is tied up until the conversation ends. In the networking world, our analogies finally break down, and things work differently.[7]

The `accept()` system call accepts an incoming connection, allowing a conversation to begin. It returns a new file descriptor that should be used for the conversation, allowing the main server flow to go back to listening for connections.

Let's look again at the outline of the flow from Section 14.5, "Basic Structure of a Server Program," page 478:

```
setup_initial_socket();                        This is done with socket() and bind()
setup_process_as_server();                     This is done with listen()
for (;;) {
    int new_fd = start_the_conversation();     This is done with accept()
    pid_t pid = fork();
    if (pid < 0)
        handle_error();
    else if (pid == 0) {
        // new_fd inherited across the fork    Aha! Conversations happen in the child processes
        do_the_actual_work(new_fd);
        exit(EXIT_SUCCESS);
    } else {
        close(new_fd);                         The parent just waits for connections
        // continue around in the loop
    }
}
```

Here is the declaration of `accept()`:

```
#include <sys/types.h>                      POSIX
#include <sys/socket.h>

int accept(int sockfd, struct sockaddr *addr,
          socklen_t *addrlen);
int accept4(int socket, struct sockaddr *address,
           socklen_t *address_len, int flag);
```

Hmmm, what are the parameters `addr` and `addrlen` for? Like caller ID in a phone system, the network knows the IP address and port from which the connection was made. That information is used to fill in information about the *peer*—the client system that initiated the connection. This information can be logged (for example), validated to make sure the connection is from an allowed system, or used in any other way our application may see fit. If we don't care who is connecting to us, we may pass `NULL` as the value of `addr`.

[7] Well, the analogies haven't been exactly one-to-one up to this point anyway, but we hope that they help.

As with `bind()`, we must use a structure of the correct type for the kind of networking we're doing. `addrlen` should contain the size of the structure being passed in. Upon return, it is filled in with the actual size of the peer's address. If there's a mismatch, the data in `*addr` will be truncated. Here is a call:

```
struct sockaddr_in peer_addr;
socklen_t peer_addr_size = sizeof(peer_addr);

if (accept(new_fd, (struct sockaddr *) & peer_addr, & peer_addr_size) < 0) {
    fprintf(stderr, "could not accept new connection: %s\n", strerror(errno));
    exit(EXIT_FAILURE);
}
```

The `accept4()` function entered POSIX in 2024 by way of Linux. The additional `flag` argument should be the bitwise-OR of one or more of `SOCK_CLOEXEC`, `SOCK_CLOFORK`, and `SOCK_NONBLOCK`, with the same meaning as for `socket()`.

14.5.5 Running the Application: `read()/write()`

At this point, the control flow divides. The server forks a child that handles the conversation, and the parent goes back to waiting for incoming connections:

```
...
pid_t pid;

if ((pid = fork()) < 0) {
    handle error
} else if (pid == 0) {
    process(new_fd, & peer_addr);
} else {
    close(new_fd);
    // continue around in the loop
}
...

/* process --- run a conversation */

void
process(int fd, struct sockaddr_in *peer)
{
    // get peer info in native byte order, if we want it
    int32_t peer_ip = ntohl(peer->sin_addr.s_addr);
    int peer_port = ntohs(peer->sin_port);

    ... application-specific code here ...
}
```

Basically, up to this point, everything has been setup; it's almost boilerplate code. We now have to write the code that is application specific. If implementing a defined protocol, or designing a new one of our own, this is the time to do it.

How? With good old `read()` and `write()`. The file descriptor is a two-way channel to the client on the other end. `read()` returns what they send to you, and `write()` sends your response over the network back to them.

14.5.6 Cleaning Up: `close()` and `shutdown()`

As always, when done reading and writing data, we should close our file descriptors. This frees up resources within the operating system and ensures robustness.

Although the socket file descriptor is created using different calls than file descriptors for files and devices, once it's open it acts like a regular file descriptor. In particular, you can close it using the regular `close()` system call (see Section 4.4.2, "Opening and Closing Files," page 88).

Sockets, being two-way connections, have some additional flexibility. We can end one side of the communication while leaving the other side available, should we choose to do so. This is done with the `shutdown()` system call:

```
#include <sys/socket.h>                    POSIX

int shutdown(int sockfd, int how);
```

The value for `how` is one of the following symbolic constants:

`SHUT_RD`	Disable reading from the socket.
`SHUT_WR`	Disable writing to the socket.
`SHUT_RDWR`	Disable reading and writing.

Apparently, using `SHUT_RDWR` disables all communication but doesn't actually close the socket.

As usual, zero is returned upon success. Upon error, `-1` is returned, and `errno` indicates the error.

14.5.7 Identifying the Ends of a Connection

There are times when a function or some other bit of code is handed a socket file descriptor that it didn't open. For example, such a descriptor may be inherited across an exec, or passed as an `int fd` parameter to a function.

In such a case, you don't know anything about the connection, such as your IP address and port, or that of the system on the other end. There are two routines you can use to get that information, if you want it:

```
#include <sys/socket.h>                    POSIX

int getsockname(int sockfd, struct sockaddr *addr, socklen_t *addrlen);
int getpeername(int sockfd, struct sockaddr *addr, socklen_t *addrlen);
```

`getsockname()` retrieves the address and port information for the local end of the connection. `getpeername()` retrieves the address and port information for the remote end.

The `addr` and `addrlen` parameters are like those for `accept()`; you pass in a pointer to a `struct sockaddr_in` for `addr`. `*addrlen` should contain the size of the structure passed in and is set to the number of bytes that were actually copied out upon return.

These two routines may be used to verify that a file descriptor is indeed a socket, although you can also do that using `fstat()`.

14.5.8 Example Server Code: `ftpd`

Finding a simple example of a pure server is not so easy these days; many servers need to work with multiple open files and/or devices (such as terminals) and/or sockets. So, in order to present an example from real code, we've reached way into the past, and we present here the FTP server from 4.2 BSD, which goes through all the setup we've shown until now.

In 4.2 BSD the FTP server, called `ftpd`, ran as a *daemon*—a process that is always running in the background. Thus the code does a lot of things unique to daemons, such as setting up signals properly and dealing with its inherited file descriptors. These are not of interest to us, so those bits are omitted. Line numbers are relative to the start of the file:

```
5   /*
6    * FTP server.
7    */
8   #include <sys/param.h>
9   #include <sys/stat.h>
10  #include <sys/ioctl.h>
11  #include <sys/socket.h>
...
42  struct  sockaddr_in ctrl_addr;                  Relevant address structures
43  struct  sockaddr_in data_source;
44  struct  sockaddr_in data_dest;
45  struct  sockaddr_in his_addr;
...
77  int lostconn();                                 Signal handlers
78  int reapchild();
...
81  main(argc, argv)                                int main(int argc, char **argv)
82      int argc;
83      char *argv[];
84  {
85      int ctrl, s, options = 0;
86      char *cp;
87
88      sp = getservbyname("ftp", "tcp");           Get service protocol and port
89      if (sp == 0) {
90          fprintf(stderr, "ftpd: ftp/tcp: unknown service\n");
91          exit(1);
92      }
```

```
    ctrl_addr.sin_port = sp->s_port;                              Start setting up address info
    data_source.sin_port = htons(ntohs(sp->s_port) - 1);
    signal(SIGPIPE, lostconn);
...
    while ((s = socket(AF_INET, SOCK_STREAM, 0)) < 0) {           Create socket
        perror("ftpd: socket");
        sleep(5);
    }
...
    while (bind(s, &ctrl_addr, sizeof (ctrl_addr), 0) < 0) {      Bind it to our address
        perror("ftpd: bind");
        sleep(5);
    }
    signal(SIGCHLD, reapchild);
    listen(s, 10);                                                Mark as listening
    for (;;) {
        int hisaddrlen = sizeof (his_addr);

        ctrl = accept(s, &his_addr, &hisaddrlen, 0);              Accept the connection
        if (ctrl < 0) {                                           Error handling
            if (errno == EINTR)
                continue;
            perror("ftpd: accept");
            continue;
        }
        if (fork() == 0) {                                        Fork child
            signal (SIGCHLD, SIG_IGN);
            dolog(&his_addr);
            close(s);                                             Close the original
            dup2(ctrl, 0), close(ctrl), dup2(0, 1);               Move new socket to stdin/stdout
            /* do telnet option negotiation here */               Left over copy/paste :-)
...
            (void) getsockname(0, &ctrl_addr, sizeof (ctrl_addr));
            gethostname(hostname, sizeof (hostname));
            reply(220, "%s FTP server (%s) ready.",               Send "I'm ready" message
                hostname, version);
            for (;;) {                                            Read/reply loop
                setjmp(errcatch);
                yyparse();                                        Work done here
            }
        }
        close(ctrl);                                              In the parent, close new socket
    }
}
```

Lines 8–11 are the basic socket includes; there are more which we've omitted. Lines 42–45 declare the `sockaddr_in` structures (a little more about them, shortly). Lines 77–78 declare the signal handlers.

The main program starts out by retrieving the service information—that is, the protocol and port to use, via *getservbyname*(3) (lines 88–92). The service information is kept in the file `/etc/services`. See the manpage; it's straightforward.

Next, the program sets up the ports. FTP is unusual, in that two ports are defined for it—one for control (commands), and the other for data:

```
$ grep -w ftp /etc/services
ftp-data        20/tcp
ftp             21/tcp
...
```

Line 94 sets the data port to be one less than the control port by converting the control port value to a native `short` and then subtracting one.

Now we get to the nitty-gritty. Lines 143–146 create the socket. Lines 152–155 bind it to our address (`ctrl_addr`). Line 156 handles reaping child processes by setting up a signal handler. Line 157 marks the socket as listening via `listen()`.

Lines 158–193 are the server's infinite loop. Line 161 calls `accept()`, and lines 162–167 handle any error, simply by retrying. Lines 168–191 fork the child to handle the conversation; line 192 in the parent closes the new socket file descriptor returned by `accept()`.

Within the child, line 169 ignores `SIGCHLD` for itself. Line 170 logs the new connection. Line 171 closes the parent's original socket—an important action that we didn't mention earlier. (Modern code could set the `FD_CLOFORK` flag after the socket is created, or use the `SOCK_CLOFORK` flag in the call to `socket()`.) Line 172 moves the new socket onto file descriptors `0` and `1`, standard input and standard output. This allows the "do the work" code to simply work with them as it would in any other program.

Line 173 is amusing; apparently it's left over from a copy/paste from the TELNET server code.[8] Lines 185–186 send a "ready" message to the client. Lines 187–190 run an infinite loop to read commands and execute them. Eventually, one of them will be "quit," causing the child server process to exit.

14.6 Basic Structure of a Client Program

In the previous section, we covered most of the details for basic creation and usage of sockets. Now we'll take a look at the client side of the picture: how to create and use a client socket.

[8] TELNET is a protocol for interactive remote login. It's no longer used much, as all of its traffic is sent as clear text, allowing for possible snooping by bad guys.

14.6.1 Creating a Socket: `socket()`

The first part is easy. Creating a client socket is the same as creating one for a server—you call `socket()`:

```
int sockfd;

sockfd = socket(AF_UNIX, SOCK_STREAM, IPPROTO_TCP);
if (sockfd < 0) {
    fprintf(stderr, "%s: socket failed: %s\n", argv[0], strerror(errno));
    exit(EXIT_FAILURE);
}
```

As before, the socket now exists, but in a vacuum; it is not yet usable for anything.

14.6.2 Making the Call: `connect()`

A client connects to a server using the `connect()` system call:

POSIX

```
#include <sys/types.h>
#include <sys/socket.h>

int connect(int sockfd, const struct sockaddr *addr, socklen_t addrlen);
```

By now, the `addr` and `addrlen` parameters should be familiar. You fill in a `struct sockaddr_in` with the address family, address, and port of the system to which you wish to connect:

```
socklen_t socklen;
struct sockaddr_in server_addr;
... fill it in ...
socklen = sizeof(server_addr);

if (connect(sockfd, & server_addr, socklen) < 0) {
    fprintf(stderr, "could not connect: %s\n", strerror(errno));
    exit(EXIT_FAILURE);
}
```

Once the socket is connected, communications are the same as for the server side; you receive data with `read()` and send it with `write()`.

When done, you can shut down one or both ends with `shutdown()`, or more likely, just close the socket with `close()`.

14.6.3 Example Client Code: `ftp`

Let's take a look at the 4.4 BSD FTP client, `ftp`. From the file `ftp.c`, the `hookup()` function does all the socket work. Line numbers are relative to the beginning of the file. It starts with header includes and global variable declarations:

Includes

```
38 #include <sys/param.h>
39 #include <sys/stat.h>
```

```
#include <sys/ioctl.h>
#include <sys/socket.h>
#include <sys/time.h>
#include <sys/file.h>
...
struct  sockaddr_in hisctladdr;
struct  sockaddr_in data_addr;
int data = -1;
int abrtflag = 0;
int ptflag = 0;
struct  sockaddr_in myctladdr;
```

Address structures

The first step is to get the address of the server. The code checks first for an IP address. If that fails, it looks up the server by name. This is done with a function called `gethostbyname()`. The function still exists but has been obsoleted (see "Exercises," page 504, for some more information):

*char *hookup(char *host, int port)*

```
char *
hookup(host, port)
    char *host;
    int port;
{
    register struct hostent *hp = 0;
    int s, len, tos;
    static char hostnamebuf[80];

    bzero((char *)&hisctladdr, sizeof (hisctladdr));
    hisctladdr.sin_addr.s_addr = inet_addr(host);
    if (hisctladdr.sin_addr.s_addr != -1) {
        hisctladdr.sin_family = AF_INET;
        (void) strncpy(hostnamebuf, host, sizeof(hostnamebuf));
    } else {
        hp = gethostbyname(host);
        if (hp == NULL) {
            fprintf(stderr, "ftp: %s: ", host);
            herror((char *)NULL);
            code = -1;
            return((char *) 0);
        }
        hisctladdr.sin_family = hp->h_addrtype;
        bcopy(hp->h_addr_list[0],
            (caddr_t)&hisctladdr.sin_addr, hp->h_length);
        (void) strncpy(hostnamebuf, hp->h_name, sizeof(hostnamebuf));
    }
```

Like memset(ptr, 0, count)
See if it's an IP address
Look up the server by name

The next step is to set up the socket:

```
105     hostname = hostnamebuf;
106     s = socket(hisctladdr.sin_family, SOCK_STREAM, 0);
107     if (s < 0) {
108         perror("ftp: socket");
109         code = -1;
110         return (0);
111     }
112     hisctladdr.sin_port = port;
113     while (connect(s, (struct sockaddr *)&hisctladdr, sizeof (hisctladdr)) < 0) {
114         if (hp && hp->h_addr_list[1]) {
115             int oerrno = errno;
116             extern char *inet_ntoa();
117
118             fprintf(stderr, "ftp: connect to address %s: ",
119                 inet_ntoa(hisctladdr.sin_addr));
120             errno = oerrno;
121             perror((char *) 0);
122             hp->h_addr_list++;
123             bcopy(hp->h_addr_list[0],
124                  (caddr_t)&hisctladdr.sin_addr, hp->h_length);
125             fprintf(stdout, "Trying %s...\n",
126                 inet_ntoa(hisctladdr.sin_addr));
127             (void) close(s);
128             s = socket(hisctladdr.sin_family, SOCK_STREAM, 0);
129             if (s < 0) {
130                 perror("ftp: socket");
131                 code = -1;
132                 return (0);
133             }
134             continue;
135         }
```

The code creates the socket with `socket()`. It then enters a loop, attempting to connect to all of the server's possible addresses with `connect()`. (The `bcopy()` function is like `memcpy()`, but argument order is reversed; the first argument is the source, and the second one is the destination.) Note lines 127–128. If the `connect()` fails, the socket is closed and a new one is created.

Next, the code retrieves the address and port information for the local side, using `getsockname()`:

```
140     len = sizeof (myctladdr);
141     if (getsockname(s, (struct sockaddr *)&myctladdr, &len) < 0) {
142         perror("ftp: getsockname");
143         code = -1;
144         goto bad;
145     }
```

Finally, the socket file descriptor is moved into `FILE *` objects for use with Standard I/O library functions (compare the direct use of the file descriptor twice with the FTP server's use of `dup2()`):

*Move to use of FILE * objects*

```
    cin = fdopen(s, "r");
    cout = fdopen(s, "w");
    if (cin == NULL || cout == NULL) {
        fprintf(stderr, "ftp: fdopen failed.\n");
        if (cin)
            (void) fclose(cin);
        if (cout)
            (void) fclose(cout);
        code = -1;
        goto bad;
    }
    if (verbose)
        printf("Connected to %s.\n", hostname);
    if (getreply(0) > 2) {  /* read startup message from server */
...
        goto bad;
    }
...
    return (hostname);
bad:
    (void) close(s);
    return ((char *)0);
}
```

14.7 Specialized Send and Receive Functions

Six additional system calls may be used in place of `read()` and `write()` for socket communication. They are more specialized, each serving different purposes. Here are their declarations:

POSIX

```
#include <sys/types.h>
#include <sys/socket.h>

ssize_t send(int sockfd, const void *buf, size_t len, int flags);
ssize_t sendto(int sockfd, const void *buf, size_t len, int flags,
               const struct sockaddr *dest_addr, socklen_t addrlen);
ssize_t sendmsg(int sockfd, const struct msghdr *msg, int flags);

ssize_t recv(int sockfd, void *buf, size_t len, int flags);
ssize_t recvfrom(int sockfd, void *buf, size_t len, int flags,
                 struct sockaddr *src_addr, socklen_t *addrlen);
ssize_t recvmsg(int sockfd, struct msghdr *msg, int flags);
```

Here is a short summary of what each one does, and then we explain in more detail:

`send()`	Write data, as modified by `flags`.
`sendto()`	Write data to the given remote address, as modified by `flags`.
`sendmsg()`	Write data scatter/gather, as specified by `*msg` and `flags`.
`recv()`	Read data, as modified by `flags`.
`recvfrom()`	Read data from the given remote address, as modified by `flags`.
`recvmsg()`	Read data scatter/gather, as specified by `*msg` and `flags`.

For `send()`, `recv()`, `sendto()`, and `recvfrom()`, the `buf` and `len` arguments are the same as for `read()` and `write()`. The functions return the number of bytes actually read or written, or `-1` upon error.

The `sendmsg()` and `recvmsg()` system calls are for very advanced and complicated uses. As this is just an introduction to networking, we don't cover them further.

14.7.1 Using `send()` and `recv()`

Let's start with `send()` and `recv()`. If `flags` is zero, they are completely identical to `write()` and `read()`. The socket must be in the connected state; we address this shortly. Quoting from the standard, for `send()`, `flags` is the bitwise-OR of one or more of the following:

`MSG_EOR`
: Terminates a record (if supported by the protocol).

`MSG_OOB`
: Sends out-of-band data on sockets that support out-of-band communications. The significance and semantics of out-of-band data are protocol specific.

`MSG_NOSIGNAL`
: Requests not to send the `SIGPIPE` signal if an attempt to send is made on a stream-oriented socket that is no longer connected. The `EPIPE` error shall still be returned.

Quoting again from the standard, for `recv()`, `flags` is the bitwise-OR of one or more of the following:

`MSG_PEEK`
: Peeks at an incoming message. The data is treated as unread and the next `recv()` or similar function shall still return this data.

`MSG_OOB`
: Requests out-of-band data. The significance and semantics of out-of-band data are protocol specific.

`MSG_WAITALL`
: On `SOCK_STREAM` sockets, this requests that the function block until the full amount of data can be returned. The function may return the smaller amount of data if the socket is a message-based socket, if a signal is caught, if the connection is terminated, if `MSG_PEEK` was specified, or if an error is pending for the socket.

Out-of-band data is an advanced topic that we don't cover; see the resources in Section 14.11, "Suggested Reading," page 502.

As a general statement, `send()` and `recv()` are specialized mainly for datagram sockets (see the next section). For stream sockets, you'll be better off using `read()` and `write()`.

14.7.2 Connectionless Communication: UDP Sockets

Up to now, we've been describing stream communication with TCP, whereby the connection is established and remains open for the length of the conversation. Such sockets are, by definition, in the *connected* state.

UDP communication is connectionless: each chunk of data sent is unrelated to what was sent before it or what may be sent after it. Although most regular applications use TCP, a number of important Internet services use UDP—most notably, the Domain Name Service (DNS).

UDP sockets are created with `socket()`, as follows:

```
int sockfd;

sockfd = socket(AF_INET, SOCK_DGRAM, IPPROTO_UDP);
if (sockfd < 0) {
    fprintf(stderr, "%s: socket failed: %s\n", argv[0], strerror(errno));
    exit(EXIT_FAILURE);
}
```

You then have two ways to proceed for sending data. One option is to connect the socket to a particular destination with `connect()`, as shown earlier (see Section 14.6.2, "Making the Call: `connect()`," page 489). Doing so puts the UDP socket into the connected state, allowing you to use `write()`/`read()` and/or `send()`/`recv()`.

Or you can specify the address to use each time you want to send or receive. In this case, you would use `sendto()` and `recvfrom()`. For these functions, the `flag` values are the same as for `send()` and `recv()`, and the pointers to `struct sockaddr` in reality would point to appropriately filled-in `struct sockaddr_in` structures.

If you initially used `connect()` on a UDP socket with one address, and then supply a different address with `sendto()` or `recvfrom()`, the supplied address overrides the original one.

14.8 Handling Multiple Open Connections: `select()`

In the original 4.2 BSD system, there were multiple network daemons similar to `ftpd`. Most of the time they were idle, waiting for incoming network connections from clients. See Figure 14.2.

Experience showed that doing things this way was problematic. Each daemon, even while idle, took up resources in the system, such as some amount of memory, as well as occupying resources within the operating system (process information, open files, and so on).

To solve this problem, the BSD developers created `inetd`, a "super server." `inetd` works by opening multiple sockets, one for each protocol to be served, as listed in its configuration file.

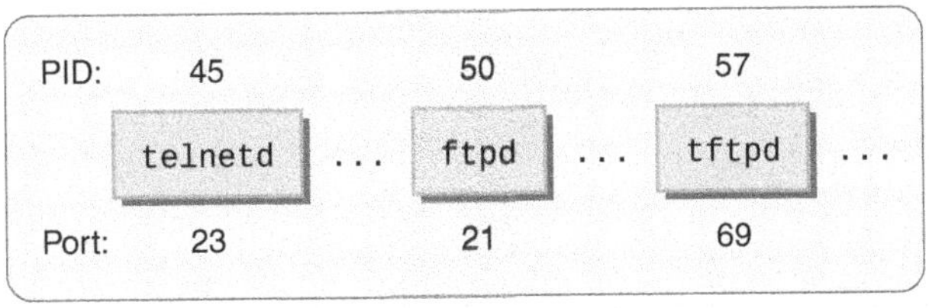

Figure 14.2: Multiple network daemons

Along with the service (such as `ftp` or `telnet`), the configuration file gives the name of the server program to run, the user to run it as, and other information. (Some GNU/Linux systems use a newer version of `inetd` called `xinetd`. On others, the functionality is subsumed by a program called `systemd`. But the idea remains the same.)

When a connection comes in on a particular service's open socket, `inetd` accepts the connection with `accept()`, and forks a child server process. In the child, it moves the new socket to standard input, standard output, and standard error, and then execs the server process. The server process is written (or was rewritten) to expect the socket to already be available on file descriptors zero, one, and two. A few services are provided directly by functions built into `inetd`.

The magic system call that makes `inetd` possible is `select()`, which lets a process monitor multiple open file descriptors simultaneously:

```
#include <sys/select.h>                          POSIX

int select(int nfds, fd_set *readfds, fd_set *writefds,
           fd_set *exceptfds, struct timeval *timeout);

void FD_CLR(int fd, fd_set *set);
int  FD_ISSET(int fd, fd_set *set);
void FD_SET(int fd, fd_set *set);
void FD_ZERO(fd_set *set);
```

When called, `select()` waits until at least one file descriptor becomes "ready" for a given operation, such as a read or write. It uses a data type called an `fd_set` to mark the file descriptor or descriptors that have become available. We describe `fd_sets` and how to work with them shortly.

The arguments to `select()` are as follows:

`int nfds`

The total number of open file descriptors to monitor. Since file descriptor values start at zero, this should be the value of the largest open file descriptor, plus one. If a program doesn't close any file descriptors after opening them, this can be the value of the most recently opened file descriptor, plus one.

There is a limit on the number of open file descriptors `select()` can monitor, as discussed shortly.

`fd_set *readfds`
: The set of file descriptors that are ready for reading.

`fd_set *writefds`
: The set of file descriptors that are ready for writing.

`fd_set *exceptfds`
: The set of file descriptors where an "exceptional condition" has occurred. This is an advanced use case that we don't discuss further.

`struct timeval *timeout`
: If no file descriptor becomes available within the amount of time as specified by `*timeout`, then `select()` returns `-1`. If `timeout` is `NULL`, then `select()` waits until something changes. (The `struct timeval` was introduced in Section 5.6.4.2, "Microsecond Time Resolution: `utimes()`," page 149.)

`select()` works with a data type called an `fd_set`. This is essentially a bitmap, indexed by file descriptor value. A number of functions (which were originally macros) provide operations on `fd_set`s:

`void FD_CLR(int fd, fd_set *set);`
: Remove (clear) `fd` from the set.

`int FD_ISSET(int fd, fd_set *set);`
: Check if `fd` is "in" the set.

`void FD_SET(int fd, fd_set *set);`
: Place `fd` into the set.

`void FD_ZERO(fd_set *set);`
: Clear out (initialize, or reinitialize) the contents of `*set`.

An `fd_set` can hold file descriptor values up to `FD_SETSIZE`.

Although we've presented `select()` as though it was introduced later "just" for use in `inetd`, that is not in fact the case. `select()` works on socket file descriptors, on file descriptors open on regular files (which are always "ready"), and on those for open terminal devices. It was introduced in 4.2 BSD along with the rest of the socket-related system calls.

14.8.1 Example Code: 4.4 BSD `inetd`

Here are selected lines from the 4.4 BSD version of `inetd.c`. The program starts with file includes, macro definitions, and variable, structure, and function declarations. We've omitted the includes and structure declarations to save space. The full code is available in the book's Github repository:

...   *Includes omitted to save space*

```
#define TOOMANY     40      /* don't start more than TOOMANY */
#define CNT_INTVL   60      /* servers in CNT_INTVL sec. */
```

```
#define RETRYTIME   (60*10)     /* retry after bind or server fail */

#define SIGBLOCK    (sigmask(SIGCHLD)|sigmask(SIGHUP)|sigmask(SIGALRM))

extern  int errno;

void    config(), reapchild(), retry();
char    *index();
char    *malloc();

int debug = 0;
int nsock, maxsock;
fd_set  allsock;
int options;
int timingout;
struct  servent *sp;
...
int echo_stream(), discard_stream(), machtime_stream();
int daytime_stream(), chargen_stream();
int echo_dg(), discard_dg(), machtime_dg(), daytime_dg(), chargen_dg();
...
char    *CONFIG = _PATH_INETDCONF;
char    **Argv;
char    *LastArg;
```

Functions for built-in services

The first thing to do is to parse the command-line options:

*int main(int argc, char **argv, char **envp)*

```
main(argc, argv, envp)
    int argc;
    char *argv[], *envp[];
{
    extern char *optarg;
    extern int optind;
    register struct servtab *sep;
    register struct passwd *pwd;
    register int tmpint;
    struct sigvec sv;
    int ch, pid, dofork;
    char buf[50];

    Argv = argv;
    if (envp == 0 || *envp == 0)
        envp = argv;
    while (*envp)
        envp++;
    LastArg = envp[-1] + strlen(envp[-1]);
```

```
194
195     while ((ch = getopt(argc, argv, "d")) != EOF)          Option parsing
196         switch(ch) {
197         case 'd':
198             debug = 1;
199             options |= SO_DEBUG;
200             break;
201         case '?':
202         default:
203             fprintf(stderr, "usage: inetd [-d]");
204             exit(1);
205         }
206     argc -= optind;
207     argv += optind;
208
209     if (argc > 0)
210         CONFIG = argv[0];
211     if (debug == 0)
212         daemon(0, 0);
```

The next step is to initialize logging (see *syslog*(3)) and to set up signal handling. The code uses the `sigvec()` API, mentioned in Section 10.6, "POSIX Signals," page 350; it's essentially the same as the modern `sigaction()` API:

```
213     openlog("inetd", LOG_PID | LOG_NOWAIT, LOG_DAEMON);
214     bzero((char *)&sv, sizeof(sv));
215     sv.sv_mask = SIGBLOCK;
216     sv.sv_handler = retry;
217     sigvec(SIGALRM, &sv, (struct sigvec *)0);
218     config();                                          Read config file, open sockets
219     sv.sv_handler = config;
220     sigvec(SIGHUP, &sv, (struct sigvec *)0);           Reread config upon SIGHUP
221     sv.sv_handler = reapchild;
222     sigvec(SIGCHLD, &sv, (struct sigvec *)0);
```

Buried in the signal code are three important lines: lines 218–220. The call to `config()` on line 218 reads the configuration file and opens all the sockets listed in it. Lines 219 and 220 set `config()` as the function to call upon receipt of `SIGHUP`, which is how an administrator notifies `inetd` that the configuration file has changed.

`inetd` now enters an infinite loop, waiting for one of the open sockets to become ready:

```
234     for (;;) {
235         int n, ctrl;
236         fd_set readable;
...
244         readable = allsock;
245         if ((n = select(maxsock + 1, &readable, (fd_set *)0,    Call select()
```

```
            (fd_set *)0, (struct timeval *)0)) <= 0) {
            if (n < 0 && errno != EINTR)
                syslog(LOG_WARNING, "select: %m\n");
            sleep(1);
            continue;                                        On error, retry
        }
        for (sep = servtab; n && sep; sep = sep->se_next)    Loop over services
            if (sep->se_fd != -1 && FD_ISSET(sep->se_fd, &readable)) {    Found a ready socket
                n--;
                if (debug)
                    fprintf(stderr, "someone wants %s\n",
                    sep->se_service);
                if (sep->se_socktype == SOCK_STREAM) {
                    ctrl = accept(sep->se_fd, (struct sockaddr *)0,    Accept the connection
                        (int *)0);
...
                } else
                    ctrl = sep->se_fd;                       UDP socket
```

`ctrl` is now the socket to use for actual communication. The next step is to decide whether it's necessary to fork a child. If so, there is error-checking code to notice if the daemon process is failing to run. If not, `fork()` is called:

```
                (void) sigblock(SIGBLOCK);
                pid = 0;
                dofork = (sep->se_bi == 0 || sep->se_bi->bi_fork);
                if (dofork) {
...     Error code for failing server omitted
                    pid = fork();
                }
                if (pid < 0) {
                    syslog(LOG_ERR, "fork: %m");
                    if (sep->se_socktype == SOCK_STREAM)
                        close(ctrl);
                    sigsetmask(0L);
                    sleep(1);
                    continue;
                }
```

After forking a child and checking for error, the parent continues by checking if it needs to wait for the child server to finish. If so, it removes the socket's file descriptor from the set it will check upon the next call to `select()`:

```
                if (pid && sep->se_wait) {
                    sep->se_wait = pid;
                    if (sep->se_fd >= 0) {
                        FD_CLR(sep->se_fd, &allsock);
```

```
316                 nsock--;
317             }
318         }
319         sigsetmask(0L);
```

The child closes all the other open file descriptors:

```
320         if (pid == 0) {
321             if (debug && dofork)
322                 setsid();
323             if (dofork)
324                 for (tmpint = maxsock; --tmpint > 2; )
325                     if (tmpint != ctrl)
326                         close(tmpint);
```

The next step is to see if the service is handled internally by `inetd` itself (lines 327–328). If not, then the socket's file descriptor is moved to standard input, standard output, and standard error:

```
327             if (sep->se_bi)
328                 (*sep->se_bi->bi_fn)(ctrl, sep);
329             else {
330                 if (debug)
331                     fprintf(stderr, "%d execl %s\n",
332                         getpid(), sep->se_server);
333                 dup2(ctrl, 0);
334                 close(ctrl);
335                 dup2(0, 1);
336                 dup2(0, 2);
```

The next step is to change the user and group IDs to those of the user specified in the configuration file (lines 337–349) before doing the `execv()` on line 350:

```
337                 if ((pwd = getpwnam(sep->se_user)) == NULL) {
338                     syslog(LOG_ERR,
339                         "getpwnam: %s: No such user",
340                         sep->se_user);
341                     if (sep->se_socktype != SOCK_STREAM)
342                         recv(0, buf, sizeof (buf), 0);
343                     _exit(1);
344                 }
345                 if (pwd->pw_uid) {
346                     (void) setgid((gid_t)pwd->pw_gid);
347                     initgroups(pwd->pw_name, pwd->pw_gid);
348                     (void) setuid((uid_t)pwd->pw_uid);
349                 }
350                 execv(sep->se_server, sep->se_argv);
```

Finally, there is error handling if the `execv()` fails:

```
                        if (sep->se_socktype != SOCK_STREAM)
                            recv(0, buf, sizeof (buf), 0);
                        syslog(LOG_ERR, "execv %s: %m", sep->se_server);
                        _exit(1);
                    }
                }
                if (sep->se_socktype == SOCK_STREAM)
                    close(ctrl);
            }
    }
}
```

14.9 `pselect()`: A Smarter Version of `select()`

You may have noticed that `inetd` does a fair amount of messing around with signals—setting up a signal mask, and blocking and unblocking signals. There are thus race conditions involved in using `select()`, and for that reason the `pselect()` call was added later on:

```
#include <sys/select.h>                                    POSIX

int pselect(int nfds, fd_set *readfds, fd_set *writefds,
            fd_set *exceptfds, const struct timespec *timeout,
            const sigset_t *sigmask);
```

The manpage succinctly outlines the differences with `select()`, so we'll just quote it:

> The operation of `select()` and `pselect()` is identical, other than these three differences:
>
> - `select()` uses a timeout that is a `struct timeval` (with seconds and microseconds), while `pselect()` uses a `struct timespec` (with seconds and nanoseconds).
> - `select()` may update the `timeout` argument to indicate how much time was left. `pselect()` does not change this argument.
> - `select()` has no `sigmask` argument, and behaves as `pselect()` called with [a] `NULL` `sigmask`.
>
> `sigmask` is a pointer to a signal mask (see *sigprocmask*(2)); if it is not `NULL`, then `pselect()` first replaces the current signal mask by the one pointed to by `sigmask`, then does the "select" function, and then restores the original signal mask. (If `sigmask` is `NULL`, the signal mask is not modified during the `pselect()` call.)

And that's that.

14.10 Unix-Domain Sockets

In Section 9.3.2, "FIFOs," page 306, we introduced a file type called a named pipe. It's a file in the filesystem that can be opened by two unrelated processes and provides for communication between them.

At the time that the socket API was being designed and developed, the BSD developers did not have named pipes; they hadn't been invented yet. However, the need for something like named pipes was clear, and they chose to solve the problem in a different fashion: the so-called Unix domain socket.

Unix domain sockets use the `AF_UNIX` address family. A synonym is `AF_LOCAL`. On GNU/Linux, such sockets may be stream sockets, datagram sockets, or sequenced packet sockets (see Table 14.2).

A Unix domain socket's address is represented by a `struct sockaddr_un`:

```
struct sockaddr_un {
    sa_family_t sun_family;             /* AF_UNIX */
    char        sun_path[108];          /* Pathname */
};
```

The `sun_path` element is the pathname in the filesystem of the socket. It should be NUL-terminated.

The flow for use of a Unix domain socket is otherwise similar to that of a regular TCP/IP socket; you create the socket and "bind" it into the filesystem with `socket()` and `bind()`:

```
int sockfd = socket(AF_UNIX, SOCK_STREAM, 0);    // error checking omitted
struct sockaddr_un mysock = {
    AF_UNIX,
    "/tmp/mysock"
};
bind(sockfd, & mysock, sizeof(mysock));          // error checking omitted
```

Connections then proceed with `listen()`, `accept()`, and `connect()`, as usual.

As this chapter is long enough already, we will not trouble you with an example. Unix domain sockets can do a lot more than we've described here. For (much) more information, see the *unix*(7) manpage.

14.11 Suggested Reading

The following books by the late Richard Stevens are considered classics for network programming. The first one describes how to do network programming. The other books get into the details of how the protocol stack itself is implemented in the BSD family of operating systems:

1. *Unix Network Programming: The Sockets Networking API*, vol. 1, 3rd ed., by W. Richard Stevens, Bill Fenner, and Andrew M. Rudoff. Addison-Wesley, 2003. ISBN-13: 978-0-131-41155-5.
2. *TCP/IP Illustrated*, vol. 1, *The Protocols*, 2nd ed., by Kevin R. Fall and W. Richard Stevens. Addison-Wesley, 2011. ISBN-13: 978-0-321-33631-6.
3. *TCP/IP Illustrated*, vol. 2, *The Implementation*, by Gary R. Wright and W. Richard Stevens. Addison-Wesley, 1995. ISBN-13: 978-0-201-63354-2.
4. *TCP/IP Illustrated*, vol. 3, *TCP for Transactions, HTTP, NNTP, and the Unix Domain Protocols*, by W. Richard Stevens. Addison-Wesley, 1996. ISBN-13: 978-0-201-63495-2.

The following books by Douglas Comer are also classics, as evidenced by the fact that many have had multiple editions. The first book is a general introduction to networking. The next two describe TCP/IP implementation, and the final one describes socket programming. Comer is an excellent author; his books are well worth reading:

5. *Computer Networks and Internets*, 6th ed., by Douglas E. Comer. Pearson, 2015. ISBN-13: 978-0-13-358793-7.
6. *Internetworking with TCP/IP*, vol. 1, *Principles, Protocol, and Architecture*, 6th ed., by Douglas E. Comer. Pearson, 2014. ISBN-13: 978-0-13-608530-0.
7. *Internetworking with TCP/IP*, vol. 2, *Design, Implementation, and Internals*, 3rd ed., by Douglas E. Comer and David L. Stevens. Pearson, 1998. ISBN-13: 978-13-973843-2.
8. *Internetworking with TCP/IP*, vol. 3, *Client-Server Programming and Applications, Linux/POSIX Sockets Version*, by Douglas E. Comer and David L. Stevens. Pearson, 2000. ISBN-13: 978-0-13-032071-1.

Finally, see the Wikipedia article on IPv6[9] for information about IPv6.

14.12 Summary

- The socket API entered the world in 1983 with the release of 4.2 BSD. It quickly became the standard mechanism for networking and is the basis upon which rests all of today's Internet.
- The two main types of network communications are *streams* (analogous to a telephone call) and *datagrams* (analogous to postal letters). The socket API supports these and more, as well as multiple network protocol suites. The TCP/IP protocol suite is the primary one in use today.

[9] `https://en.wikipedia.org/wiki/IPv6`

- The `AF_INET` and `AF_INET6` address families provide IP networking. The `AF_UNIX` address family provides interprocess communication on the local system via the filesystem.
- The IP protocol uses 32-bit (IPv4) or 128-bit (IPv6) addresses. IPv4 has been in use for decades. IPv6 is in use in some parts of the world and may eventually displace IPv4 entirely.
    - TCP provides stream networking over IP and *ports*; a port is a 16-bit number designating particular services on a server.
    - UDP provides datagram networking over IP and ports.
- There are details to keep track of when doing network programming, such as the different types of address structures to use, and network versus host byte ordering.
- The participants in a networked conversation are designated the *client* and the *server*. Servers await incoming connections. Clients initiate connections to servers. The code flow is different depending on what kind of application you're developing.
- The socket system calls may be summarized as follows:

System call	**Purpose**
`socket()`	Create a new socket.
`bind()`	Bind a socket to an address.
`listen()`	Wait for an incoming connection (server).
`accept()`	Accept a connection onto a new socket (server).
`connect()`	Connect to an address (client).
`shutdown()`	Close one or both ends of connection.
`send()`	Send data on a socket (usually for UDP).
`sendto()`	Like `send()`, but with a provided address.
`recv()`	Received data from a socket (usually for UDP).
`recvfrom()`	Like `recv()`, but with a provided address.
`select()`	Wait for one or more file descriptors to become "ready."
`pselect()`	Like `select()`, with atomic signal masking.

Exercises

1. Start by reading RFC 862.[10] Write a simple server that reads whatever a client sends to it and echoes it back to the client. Choose a nonprivileged port such as `4242` for your program. Print the input on `stderr` for debugging purposes. You can test it by using '`telnet localhost 4242`'. (You may need to install `telnet` before you can use it. Since it uses a protocol where data is sent in the clear, many modern systems no longer install it by default. This is particularly true of macOS.)

[10] `https://www.rfc-editor.org/rfc/rfc862`

2. Per RFC 862, port `7` is reserved for echo servers:

```
$ grep echo /etc/services
echo          7/tcp
echo          7/udp
echo          4/ddp              # AppleTalk Echo Protocol
```

   What happens if you try '`telnet localhost echo`' on your system?

3. Write a client for your echo server and test it, running the server in a shell in one window, and the client in another.

4. In Section 14.5, "Basic Structure of a Server Program," page 478, we mentioned that `gethostbyname()` is now considered obsolete. Its replacement is a function named `getaddrinfo()`. Look at the *getaddrinfo*(3) manpage. Read it carefully, although feel free to skip the GLIBC-specific parts.

   Write a program using `getaddrinfo()` that looks up one or more hosts and prints out all the returned information in human-readable form.

5. The *netcat* program, `nc`, is intended to be like `cat`, but for networking. Take a look at the *nc*(1) manpage to get a feel for how it works.

   `nc` has *many* bells and whistles. Write a simple version that can be used to create arbitrary servers (TCP or UDP) and clients. Test it by running it as a server in one window and as a client in another, connecting to your server.

6. Review the *poll*(2) and *epoll*(2) manpages. Think about the advantages and disadvantages of these interfaces over `select()`'s interface.

7. Write two programs, a "server" and a "client" that use a FIFO to communicate. Something simple, similar to the echo server from the first exercise, will do.

   Now rewrite it to use Unix domain sockets.

   Which version do you like better, and why?

8. FIFOs have a big advantage in day-to-day use over Unix domain sockets. What is it? (Hint: think about programs written in higher-level languages than C.)

Chapter 15

Internationalization and Localization

Early computing systems generally used English for their output (prompts, error messages) and input (responses to queries, such as "yes" and "no"). This was true of Unix systems, even into the mid-1980s. In the late 1980s, beginning with the first ISO standard for C and continuing with the POSIX standards of the 1990s and the current POSIX standard, facilities were developed to make it possible for programs to work in multiple languages, without a requirement to maintain multiple versions of the same program. This chapter describes how modern programs should deal with multiple-language issues.

15.1 Introduction

The central concept is the *locale*, the place in which a program is run. Locales encapsulate information about the following: the local character set; how to display date and time information; how to format and display monetary amounts; and how to format and display numeric values (with or without a thousands separator, what character to use as the decimal point, and so on).

Internationalization is the process of writing (or modifying) a program so that it can function in multiple locales. *Localization* is the process of tailoring an internationalized program for a specific locale. These terms are often abbreviated *i18n* and *l10n*, respectively. (The numeric values indicate how many characters appear in the middle of the word, and these abbreviations bear a minor visual resemblance to the full terms. They're also considerably easier to type.) Another term that appears frequently is *native language support*, abbreviated *NLS*; NLS refers to the programmatic support for doing i18n and l10n.

Additionally, some people use the term *globalization* (abbreviated *g10n*) to mean the process of preparing all possible localizations for an internationalized program—in other words, making the program ready for global use.

NLS facilities exist at two levels. The first level is the C library. It provides information about the locale; routines to handle much of the low-level detail work for formatting date/time, numeric, and monetary values; and routines for locale-correct regular expression matching and character classification and comparison. The library facilities appear in the C and POSIX standards. Additionally, the 2024 POSIX standard includes some of the command-line utilities for handling translations of program messages.

At the application level, GNU `gettext` provides commands and a library for localizing a program—that is, making all output messages available in one or more natural languages. GNU `gettext` is based on a design originally done by Sun Microsystems for Solaris;[1] however, it was implemented from scratch and now provides extensions to the original Solaris `gettext`. GNU `gettext` is a de facto standard for program localization, particularly in the GNU world.

In addition to locales and `gettext`, Standard C provides facilities for working with multiple character sets and their *encodings*—ways to represent large character sets with fewer bytes than just using the character values directly.

15.2 Locales and the C Library

You control locale-specific behavior by setting environment variables to describe which locale(s) to use for particular kinds of information. The number of available locales offered by any particular operating system ranges from fewer than ten on some commercial Unix systems to hundreds of locales on GNU/Linux systems. ('`locale -a`' prints the full list of available locales. Each GNU/Linux distribution has a mechanism to install additional locales, should they be needed.)

Two locales, `"C"` and `"POSIX"`, are guaranteed to exist. They act as the default locale, providing a seven-bit ASCII environment whose behavior is the same as traditional, non-locale-aware Unix systems. Otherwise, locales specify a language and country and, optionally, character set information. For example, `"fr_FR"` is for French in France using the system's default character set, and `"fr_FR.utf8"` uses the UTF-8 character encoding for the Unicode character set.

More details on locale names can be found in the GNU/Linux *setlocale*(3) manpage. Typically, GNU/Linux distributions set the default locale for a system when it's installed, based on the language chosen by the installer, and users don't need to worry about it anymore.

15.2.1 Locale Categories and Environment Variables

The `<locale.h>` header file defines the locale functions and structures. Locale *categories* define the kinds of information about which a program will be locale aware. The categories are available as a set of symbolic constants. They are listed in Table 15.1.

These categories are the ones defined by the various standards. Some systems may support additional categories, such `LC_TELEPHONE` or `LC_ADDRESS`. However, these are not standardized; any program that needs to use them but that still needs to be portable should use `#ifdef` to enclose the relevant sections.

By default, C programs and the C library act as if they are in the `"C"` or `"POSIX"` locale, to provide compatibility with historical systems and behavior. However, by calling `setlocale()` (as described in the next section), a program can enable locale awareness. Once a program

[1] An earlier design, known as `catgets()`, exists. Although this design is standardized by POSIX, it is much harder to use, and we don't recommend it.

Table 15.1: ISO C locale category constants defined in `<locale.h>`

`LC_ALL`	This category includes all possible locale information. This consists of the rest of the items in this table.
`LC_COLLATE`	The category for string collation (discussed shortly) and regular expression ranges.
`LC_CTYPE`	The category for classifying characters (uppercase, lowercase, etc.). This affects regular expression matching and the `is`*XXX*`()` functions in `<ctype.h>`. It is also the category used for character encoding, whether or not the character set contains multibyte characters.
`LC_MESSAGES`	The category for locale-specific messages. This category comes into play with GNU `gettext`, discussed later in the chapter. (This one is not mentioned in the C standard.)
`LC_MONETARY`	The category for formatting monetary information, such as the local and international symbols for the local currency (for example, `$` versus `USD` for U.S. dollars), how to format negative values, and so on.
`LC_NUMERIC`	The category for formatting numeric values. Some programmers choose to set this separately from the other values, in order to force '`.`' to be the decimal point, instead of what might be specified in the locale (some locales use a comma).
`LC_TIME`	The category for formatting dates and times.

does this, the user can, by setting environment variables, enable and disable the degree of locale functionality that the program will have.

The environment variables have the same names as the locale categories listed in Table 15.1. Thus, the command

```
export LC_NUMERIC=en_DK.utf8 LC_TIME=C
```

specifies that numbers should be printed according to the `"en_DK.utf8"` (English in Denmark) locale, but that date and time values should be printed according to the regular `"C"` locale. (This example merely illustrates that you *can* specify different locales for different categories; it's not necessarily something that you *should* do.)

The environment variable `LC_ALL` overrides all other `LC_`*xxx* variables. If `LC_ALL` isn't set, then the library looks for the specific variables (`LC_CTYPE`, `LC_MONETARY`, and so on). Finally, if none of those is set, the library looks for the variable `LANG`. Here is a small demonstration that prints a number and the time of day. We show the code for `ch-i18n-locale-demo` shortly:

```
$ unset LC_ALL LANG                              Remove default variables
$ ch-i18n-locale-demo                            Print a number, current date, time
1.234 = 1.234
It is now: Thu May  8 18:10:34 2025
$ export LC_NUMERIC=en_DK.utf8 LC_TIME=C         European numbers, default date, time
$ ch-i18n-locale-demo                            Print a number, current date, time
```

```
1.234 = 1,234
It is now: Thu May  8 18:10:55 2025
$ export LC_NUMERIC=it_IT.utf8 LC_TIME=it_IT.utf8      Italian numbers, date, time
$ ch-i18n-locale-demo                                   Print a number, current date, time
1.234 = 1,234
It is now: gio 8 mag 2025, 18:13:44
$ export LC_ALL=C                                       Set overriding variable
$ ch-i18n-locale-demo                                   Print a number, current date, time
1.234 = 1.234
It is now: Thu May  8 18:14:09 2025
```

Almost all GNU versions of the standard Unix utilities are locale aware. Thus, particularly on GNU/Linux systems, setting these variables gives you control over the system's behavior.

15.2.2 Setting the Locale: `setlocale()`

As mentioned, if you do nothing, C programs and the C library act as if they're in the `"C"` locale. The `setlocale()` function enables locale awareness:

```
#include <locale.h>                                                 ISO C

char *setlocale(int category, const char *locale);
```

The `category` argument is one of the locale categories described in Table 15.1. The `locale` argument is a string naming the locale to use for that category. When `locale` is the empty string (`""`), `setlocale()` inspects the appropriate environment variables.

If `locale` is `NULL`, the locale information is not changed. Instead, the function returns a string representing the current locale for the given category.

Because each category can be set individually, the application's author decides how locale aware the program will be. For example, if `main()` *only* does this:

```
setlocale(LC_TIME, "");         /* Be locale aware for time, but that's it. */
```

then no matter what other `LC_`*xxx* variables are set in the environment, only the time and date functions obey the locale. All others act as if the program is still in the `"C"` locale. Similarly, the call

```
setlocale(LC_TIME, "it_IT.utf8");    /* For the time, we're always in Italy. */
```

overrides the `LC_TIME` environment variable (as well as `LC_ALL`), forcing the program to be Italian for time/date computations. (Although Italy may be a great place to be, programs are better off using `""` so that they work correctly everywhere; this example is here just to explain *how* `setlocale()` works.)

You can call `setlocale()` individually for each category, but the simplest thing to do is to set everything in one fell swoop:

```
/* When in Rome, do as the Romans do, for *everything*. :-) */
setlocale(LC_ALL, "");
```

`setlocale()`'s return value is the current setting of the locale. This is either a string value passed in from an earlier call or an *opaque* value representing the locale in use at startup. This same value can then later be passed back to `setlocale()`. For later use, the return value should be copied into local storage since it is a pointer to internal data:

```
char *initial_locale;

initial_locale = strdup(setlocale(LC_ALL, ""));   /* save copy */
...
(void) setlocale(LC_ALL, initial_locale);         /* restore it */
```

Here, we've saved a copy by using the `strdup()` function (see Section 3.2.2, "String Copying: `strdup()`," page 71).

Once you, as a program author, call `setlocale()` with a `category` argument of either `LC_CTYPE` or `LC_ALL`, be aware that you will likely have to deal with multibyte character issues, as discussed later in this chapter.

Here is the code for `ch-i18n-locale-demo.c` that we ran earlier:

```
/* ch-i18n-locale-demo.c --- demonstrate different locale formatting */

#include <stdio.h>
#include <locale.h>
#include <stdlib.h>
#include <time.h>

/* main --- set the locale, show some differences */

int
main(int argc, char **argv)
{
    char buf[BUFSIZ];
    time_t now;

    setlocale(LC_ALL, "");
    printf("1.234 = %g\n", 1.234);

    time(& now);
    struct tm *the_time = localtime(& now);
    strftime(buf, sizeof buf, "%c", the_time);
    printf("It is now: %s\n", buf);

    return EXIT_SUCCESS;
}
```

Finally, some older versions of GLIBC store the return value of `setlocale()` in memory allocated by `malloc()`. If you don't save the return value in a global or `static` variable or in a variable local to `main()`, then technically that becomes a memory leak, which might be reported by tools such as Valgrind (to be discussed later in the book; see Section 17.6.1, "Valgrind: A Versatile Tool," page 634). You don't really need to worry about such a leak, but if you get a bug report related to it, at least you'll know what's happening.

15.2.3 String Collation: `strcoll()` and `strxfrm()`

The familiar `strcmp()` function compares two strings, returning a negative, zero, or positive value if the first string is less than, equal to, or greater than the second one. This comparison is based on the numeric values of characters in the machine's character set. Because of this, `strcmp()`'s result *never varies*.

However, in a locale-aware world, simple numeric comparison isn't enough. Each locale defines the *collating sequence* for characters within it—in other words, the relative order of characters within the locale. For example, in simple seven-bit ASCII, the characters `A` and `a` have the decimal numeric values 65 and 97, respectively. Thus, in the fragment

```
int i = strcmp("A", "a");
```

`i` has a negative value. However, in the `"en_US.UTF-8"` locale, `A` comes *after* `a`, not before it. Thus, using `strcmp()` for applications that need to be locale aware is a bad idea; we might say it returns a locale-ignorant answer.

The `strcoll()` (string collate) function exists to compare strings in a locale-aware fashion:

```
#include <string.h>                                                  ISO C

int strcoll(const char *s1, const char *s2);
```

Its return value is the same negative/zero/positive as `strcmp()`. The following program, `ch-i18n-compare.c`, interactively demonstrates the difference:

```
/* ch-i18n-compare.c --- demonstrate strcmp() versus strcoll() */

#include <stdio.h>
#include <stdlib.h>
#include <locale.h>
#include <string.h>

int
main(void)
{
#define STRBUFSIZE  1024
    char locale[STRBUFSIZE], curloc[STRBUFSIZE];
    char left[STRBUFSIZE], right[STRBUFSIZE];
    char buf[BUFSIZ];
    int count;

    setlocale(LC_ALL, "");                  /* set to env locale */
    strcpy(curloc, setlocale(LC_ALL, NULL));    /* save it */

```

```
20     printf("--> "); fflush(stdout);
21     while (fgets(buf, sizeof buf, stdin) != NULL) {
22         locale[0] = '\0';
23         count = sscanf(buf, "%s %s %s", left, right, locale);
24         if (count < 2)
25             break;
26 
27         if (*locale) {
28             setlocale(LC_ALL, locale);
29             strcpy(curloc, locale);
30         }
31 
32         printf("%s: strcmp(\"%s\", \"%s\") is %d\n", curloc, left,
33                 right, strcmp(left, right));
34         printf("%s: strcoll(\"%s\", \"%s\") is %d\n", curloc, left,
35                 right, strcoll(left, right));
36 
37         printf("\n--> "); fflush(stdout);
38     }
39 
40     exit(EXIT_SUCCESS);
41 }
```

The program starts out with whatever locale is set in the environment. It reads input lines, which consist of two words to compare and, optionally, a locale to use for the comparison. If the locale is given, that becomes the locale for subsequent entries.

The `curloc` array saves the current locale for printing results; `left` and `right` are the left- and right-hand words to compare (lines 13–14). The main part of the program is a loop (lines 21–38) that reads lines and does the work. Lines 23–25 split up the input line. `locale` is initialized to the empty string, in case a third value isn't provided.

Lines 27–30 set the new locale, if there is one. Lines 32–35 print the comparison results, and line 37 prompts for more input. Here's a demonstration:

```
$ ch-i18n-compare                              Run the program
--> ABC abc C                                  Enter two words, use "C" locale
C: strcmp("ABC", "abc") is -32
C: strcoll("ABC", "abc") is -32                Identical results in "C" locale

--> ABC abc en_US.utf8                         Same words, "en_US.utf8" locale
en_US.utf8: strcmp("ABC", "abc") is -32
en_US.utf8: strcoll("ABC", "abc") is 5         Different value

--> junk JUNK                                  New words
en_US.utf8: strcmp("junk", "JUNK") is 32       Previous locale used
en_US.utf8: strcoll("junk", "JUNK") is -5
```

This program clearly demonstrates the difference between `strcmp()` and `strcoll()`. Since `strcmp()` works in accordance with the numeric character values, it always returns the same result. `strcoll()` understands collation issues, and its result varies according to the locale. We see that in the `en_US.utf8` locale, the uppercase letters come after the lowercase ones.

NOTE

Locale-specific string collation is also an issue in regular-expression matching. Regular expressions allow character ranges within bracket expressions, such as '`[a-z]`' or '`["-/]`'. The exact meaning of such a construct (the characters numerically between the start and end points, inclusive) is defined only for the `"C"` and `"POSIX"` locales.

For non-ASCII locales, a range such as '`[a-z]`' can also match uppercase letters, not just lowercase ones!

The most portable long-term solution is to use POSIX character classes, such as '`[[:lower:]]`' and '`[[:punct:]]`'. If you find yourself needing to use range expressions on systems that are locale aware and on older systems that are not, but without having to change your program, the solution is to use brute force and list each character individually within the brackets. It isn't pretty, but it works.

There is some progress being made in the GNU world with respect to having ranges behave rationally. For more information, see the discussion of ranges in the GNU `awk` manual.[2]

Locale-based collation is potentially expensive. If you expect to be doing lots of comparisons, where at least one of the strings will not change or where string values will be compared against each other multiple times (such as in sorting a list), then you should consider using the `strxfrm()` function to convert your strings to versions that can be used with `strcmp()`. The `strxfrm()` function is declared as follows:

```
#include <string.h>                                          ISO C

size_t strxfrm(char *dest, const char *src, size_t n);
```

The idea is that `strxfrm()` transforms the first `n` characters of `src`, placing them into `dest`. The return value is the number of bytes necessary to hold the transformed characters. If this is more than `n`, then the contents of `dest` are "unspecified."

The POSIX standard explicitly allows `n` to be zero and `dest` to be `NULL`. In this case, `strxfrm()` returns the size of the array needed to hold the transformed version of `src` (not including the final `'\0'` character). Presumably, this value would then be used with `malloc()` for creating the `dest` array or for checking the size against a predefined array bound. (When doing this `src` must have a terminating zero byte, obviously.) This fragment illustrates how to use `strxfrm()`:

```
#define STRBUFSIZE ...
char s1[STRBUFSIZE], s2[STRBUFSIZE];          Original strings
char s1x[STRBUFSIZE], s2x[STRBUFSIZE];        Transformed copies
size_t len1, len2;
int cmp;
```

---

[2] `https://www.gnu.org/software/gawk/manual/html_node/Ranges-and-Locales.html`

```
... fill in s1 and s2 ...
len1 = strlen(s1);
len2 = strlen(s2);

if (strxfrm(s1x, s1, len1) >= STRBUFSIZE || strxfrm(s2x, s2, len2) >= STRBUFSIZE)
    /* too big, recover */

cmp = strcmp(s1x, s2x);
if (cmp == 0)
    /* equal */
else if (cmp < 0)
    /* s1 < s2 */
else
    /* s1 > s2 */
```

For one-time comparisons, it is probably faster to use `strcoll()` directly. But if strings will be compared multiple times, then using `strxfrm()` once and `strcmp()` on the transformed values will be faster.

There are no locale-aware collation functions that correspond to `strncmp()` or `strcasecmp()`.

15.2.4 Low-Level Numeric and Monetary Formatting: `localeconv()`

Correctly formatting numeric and monetary values requires a fair amount of low-level information. Said information is available in the `struct lconv`, which is retrieved with the `localeconv()` function:

```
#include <locale.h>                                          ISO C

struct lconv *localeconv(void);
```

Similarly to the `ctime()` function, this function returns a pointer to internal `static` data. You should make a copy of the returned data, since subsequent calls could return different values if the locale has been changed. Here is the `struct lconv` (condensed slightly), direct from GLIBC's `<locale.h>`:

```
struct lconv {
  /* Numeric (non-monetary) information.  */
  char *decimal_point;          /* Decimal point character.  */
  char *thousands_sep;          /* Thousands separator.  */
  /* Each element is the number of digits in each group;
     elements with higher indices are farther left.
     An element with value CHAR_MAX means that no further grouping is done.
     An element with value 0 means that the previous element is used
     for all groups farther left.  */
  char *grouping;
```

```
    /* Monetary information.  */
    /* First three chars are a currency symbol from ISO 4217.
       Fourth char is the separator.  Fifth char is '\0'.  */
    char *int_curr_symbol;
    char *currency_symbol;        /* Local currency symbol.  */
    char *mon_decimal_point;      /* Decimal point character.  */
    char *mon_thousands_sep;      /* Thousands separator.  */
    char *mon_grouping;           /* Like 'grouping' element (above).  */
    char *positive_sign;          /* Sign for positive values.  */
    char *negative_sign;          /* Sign for negative values.  */
    char int_frac_digits;         /* Int'l fractional digits.  */
    char frac_digits;             /* Local fractional digits.  */
    /* 1 if currency_symbol precedes a positive value, 0 if succeeds.  */
    char p_cs_precedes;
    /* 1 iff a space separates currency_symbol from a positive value.  */
    char p_sep_by_space;
    /* 1 if currency_symbol precedes a negative value, 0 if succeeds.  */
    char n_cs_precedes;
    /* 1 iff a space separates currency_symbol from a negative value.  */
    char n_sep_by_space;
    /* Positive and negative sign positions:
       0 Parentheses surround the quantity and currency_symbol.
       1 The sign string precedes the quantity and currency_symbol.
       2 The sign string follows the quantity and currency_symbol.
       3 The sign string immediately precedes the currency_symbol.
       4 The sign string immediately follows the currency_symbol.  */
    char p_sign_posn;
    char n_sign_posn;
    /* 1 if int_curr_symbol precedes a positive value, 0 if succeeds.  */
    char int_p_cs_precedes;
    /* 1 iff a space separates int_curr_symbol from a positive value.  */
    char int_p_sep_by_space;
    /* 1 if int_curr_symbol precedes a negative value, 0 if succeeds.  */
    char int_n_cs_precedes;
    /* 1 iff a space separates int_curr_symbol from a negative value.  */
    char int_n_sep_by_space;
    /* Positive and negative sign positions:
       0 Parentheses surround the quantity and int_curr_symbol.
       1 The sign string precedes the quantity and int_curr_symbol.
       2 The sign string follows the quantity and int_curr_symbol.
       3 The sign string immediately precedes the int_curr_symbol.
       4 The sign string immediately follows the int_curr_symbol.  */
    char int_p_sign_posn;
    char int_n_sign_posn;
};
```

The comments make it fairly clear what's going on. Let's look at the first several fields in the `struct lconv`:

`decimal_point`
: The decimal point character to use. In the United States and other English-speaking countries, it's a period, but many countries use a comma.

`thousands_sep`
: The character to separate each three digits in a value.

`grouping`
: An array of single-byte integer values. Each element indicates how many digits to group. As the comment says, `CHAR_MAX` means no further grouping should be done, and `0` means reuse the last element. (We show some sample code later in the chapter.)

`int_curr_symbol`
: This is the international symbol for the local currency—for example, `"USD"` for U.S. dollars.

`currency_symbol`
: This is the local symbol for the local currency—for example, `$` for U.S. dollars.

`mon_decimal_point`
`mon_thousands_sep`
`mon_grouping`
: These correspond to the earlier fields, providing the same information but for monetary amounts.

Most of the rest of the values are not useful for day-to-day programming. The following program, `ch-i18n-lconv.c`, prints some of these values, to give you a feel for what kind of information is available:

```
/* ch-i18n-lconv.c --- show some of the components of the struct lconv */

#include <stdio.h>
#include <stdlib.h>
#include <limits.h>
#include <locale.h>

int
main(void)
{
    struct lconv l;
    int i;

    setlocale(LC_ALL, "");
    l = *localeconv();
```

```
    printf("decimal_point = [%s]\n", l.decimal_point);
    printf("thousands_sep = [%s]\n", l.thousands_sep);

    for (i = 0; l.grouping[i] != 0 && l.grouping[i] != CHAR_MAX; i++)
        printf("grouping[%d] = [%d]\n", i, l.grouping[i]);

    printf("int_curr_symbol = [%s]\n", l.int_curr_symbol);
    printf("currency_symbol = [%s]\n", l.currency_symbol);
    printf("mon_decimal_point = [%s]\n", l.mon_decimal_point);
    printf("mon_thousands_sep = [%s]\n", l.mon_thousands_sep);
    printf("positive_sign = [%s]\n", l.positive_sign);
    printf("negative_sign = [%s]\n", l.negative_sign);

    return EXIT_SUCCESS;
}
```

When run with different locales, we unsurprisingly get different results:

```
$ LC_ALL=en_US.utf8 ch-i18n-lconv      Results for the United States
decimal_point = [.]
thousands_sep = [,]
grouping[0] = [3]
grouping[1] = [3]
int_curr_symbol = [USD ]
currency_symbol = [$]
mon_decimal_point = [.]
mon_thousands_sep = [,]
positive_sign = []
negative_sign = [-]

$ LC_ALL=it_IT.utf8 ch-i18n-lconv      Results for Italy
decimal_point = [,]
thousands_sep = [.]
grouping[0] = [3]
grouping[1] = [3]
int_curr_symbol = [EUR ]
currency_symbol = [€]
mon_decimal_point = [,]
mon_thousands_sep = [.]
positive_sign = []
negative_sign = [-]
```

Note how the values for `int_curr_symbol` in both locales include a trailing space character that acts to separate the symbol from the following monetary value.

15.2.5 High-Level Numeric and Monetary Formatting: `strfmon()` and `printf()`

After looking at all the fields in the `struct lconv`, you may be wondering, "Do I *really* have to figure out how to use all that information just to format a monetary value?" Fortunately, the answer is no.[3] The `strfmon()` function does all the work for you:

```
#include <monetary.h>                                        POSIX

ssize_t strfmon(char *s, size_t max, const char *format, ...);
```

This routine is much like `strftime()` (see Section 6.1.3.2, "Complex Time Formatting: `strftime()`," page 160), using `format` to copy literal characters and formatted numeric values into `s`, placing no more than `max` characters into it. The following simple program, `ch-i18n-strfmon.c`, demonstrates how `strfmon()` works:

```
/* ch-i18n-strfmon.c --- demonstrate strfmon() */

#include <stdio.h>
#include <stdlib.h>
#include <locale.h>
#include <monetary.h>

int
main(void)
{
    char buf[BUFSIZ];
    double val = 1234.567;

    setlocale(LC_ALL, "");
    strfmon(buf, sizeof buf, "You owe me %n (%i)\n", val, val);

    fputs(buf, stdout);
    return EXIT_SUCCESS;
}
```

When run in two different locales, it produces this output:

```
$ LC_ALL=en_US.utf8 ch-i18n-strfmon          In the United States
You owe me $1,234.57 (USD 1,234.57)
$ LC_ALL=fr_FR.utf8 ch-i18n-strfmon          In France
You owe me 1 234,57 € (1 234,57 EUR)
```

[3] We're as happy as you are, since we don't have to provide example code that uses this, er, full-featured `struct`.

As you can see, `strfmon()` is like `strftime()`, copying regular characters unchanged into the destination buffer and formatting arguments according to its own formatting specifications. There are only three:

`%n`	Print the national (that is, local) form of the currency value.
`%i`	Print the international form of the currency value.
`%%`	Print a literal `%` character.

The values to be formatted must be of type `double` (although with a prototype in scope, variables of other numeric types will be converted to `double` appropriately). We see the difference between `%n` and `%i` in the `"en_US.utf8"` locale: `%n` uses a `$` character, whereas `%i` uses `USD`, which stands for "U.S. dollar."

Flexibility—and thus a certain amount of complexity—comes along with many of the APIs that were developed for POSIX, and `strfmon()` is no exception. As with `printf()`, several optional items that can appear between the `%` and the `i` or `n` provide increased control. The full forms are as follows:

`%[`*flags*`][`*field width*`][#`*left-prec*`][.` *right-prec*`]i`
`%[`*flags*`][`*field width*`][#`*left-prec*`][.` *right-prec*`]n`
`%%` *No flag, field width, etc. allowed*

The flags are listed in Table 15.2.

The field width is a decimal digit string, providing a minimum width. The default is to use as many characters as necessary based on the rest of the specification. Values smaller than the field width are padded with spaces on the left (or on the right, if the '`-`' flag was given).

The left precision consists of a `#` character and a decimal digit string. It indicates the minimum number of digits to appear to the left of the decimal point character;[4] if the converted

Table 15.2: Flags for `strfmon()`

Flag	Meaning
`=`*c*	Use the single-byte character *c* for the numeric fill character, for use with the left precision. The default fill character is a space. A common alternative fill character is `0`.
`^`	Disable the use of the grouping character (for example, a comma in the United States).
`(`	Enclose negative amounts in parentheses. Mutually exclusive with the `+` flag.
`+`	Handle positive/negative values normally. Use the locale's positive and negative signs. Mutually exclusive with the `(` flag.
`!`	Do not include the currency symbol. This flag is useful if you wish to use `strfmon()` to get more flexible formatting of regular numbers than what `sprintf()` provides.
`-`	Left-justify the result. The default is right justification. This flag has no effect without a field width.

[4] The technical term used in the standards is *radix point*, since numbers in different bases may have fractional parts as well. However, for monetary values, it seems pretty safe to use the term *decimal point*.

value is smaller than this, the result is padded with the numeric fill character. The default is a space, but the = flag can be used to change it. Grouping characters are not included in the count.

Finally, the right precision consists of a '.' character and a decimal digit string. This indicates how many digits to round the value to before it is formatted. The default is provided by the `frac_digits` and `int_frac_digits` fields in the `struct lconv`. If this value is `0`, no decimal point character is printed.

`strfmon()` returns the number of characters placed into the buffer, not including the terminating zero byte. If there's not enough room, it returns `-1` and sets `errno` to `E2BIG`.

Besides `strfmon()`, POSIX (but *not* ISO C) provides a special flag—the single-quote character, `'`—for the `printf()` formats `%i`, `%d`, `%u`, `%f`, `%F`, `%g`, and `%G`. In locales that supply a thousands separator, this flag adds the locale's thousands separator. The following simple program, `ch-i18n-quoteflag.c`, demonstrates the output:

```
/* ch-i18n-quoteflag.c --- demonstrate printf's quote flag */

#include <stdio.h>
#include <stdlib.h>
#include <locale.h>

int
main(void)
{
    setlocale(LC_ALL, "");      /* Have to do this, or it won't work */
    printf("%'d\n", 1234567);
    return EXIT_SUCCESS;
}
```

Here's what happens for two different locales, one that does not supply a thousands-separator and one that does:

```
$ LC_ALL=C ch-i18n-quoteflag                 Traditional environment, no separator
1234567
$ LC_ALL=en_US.utf8 ch-i18n-quoteflag        English in United States locale, has separator
1,234,567
```

The `'` flag is supported on at least GNU/Linux, Solaris, macOS, FreeBSD, and NetBSD. Double-check your system's *printf*(3) manpage.

15.2.6 Example: Formatting Numeric Values in gawk

`gawk` implements its own version of the `printf()` and `sprintf()` functions. For full locale awareness, `gawk` must support the `'` flag, as in C. The following fragment, from the file `builtin.c` in `gawk` 5.3.0, shows how `gawk` uses the `struct lconv` for numeric formatting:

```
case 'd':
case 'i':
```

```
 3      ...
 4  #if defined(HAVE_LOCALE_H)
 5      quote_flag = (quote_flag && loc.thousands_sep[0] != 0);
 6  #endif
 7      ...
 8      ii = jj = 0;
 9      do {
10          PREPEND(*chp);
11          chp--; i--;
12  #if defined(HAVE_LOCALE_H)
13          if (quote_flag && loc.grouping[ii] && ++jj == loc.grouping[ii]) {
14              if (i) {    /* only add if more digits coming */
15                  int k;
16                  const char *ts = loc.thousands_sep;
17
18                  for (k = strlen(ts) - 1; k >= 0; k--) {
19                      PREPEND(ts[k]);
20                  }
21              }
22              if (loc.grouping[ii+1] == 0)
23                  jj = 0;     /* keep using current val in loc.grouping[ii] */
24              else if (loc.grouping[ii+1] == CHAR_MAX)
25                  quote_flag = false;
26              else {
27                  ii++;
28                  jj = 0;
29              }
30          }
31  #endif
32      } while (i > 0);
```

(The line numbers are relative to the start of the fragment.) Some parts of the code that aren't relevant to the discussion have been omitted to make it easier to focus on the parts that are important.

The integer value to be formatted is first formatted normally into a separate buffer. The character pointer `chp` is set to point at the last character in this buffer. This code is not shown.

The variable `loc`, used in lines 16–19, is a `struct lconv`. It's initialized in `main()`. Of interest to us here are `loc.thousands_sep`, which is the thousands-separator character, and `loc.grouping`, which is an array describing how many digits between separators. A zero element means "use the value in the previous element for all subsequent digits," and a value of `CHAR_MAX` means "stop inserting thousands separators."

With that introduction, let's look at the code. `ii` and `jj` keep track of the position in `loc.grouping` and the number of digits in the current group that have been converted, respectively.[5]

[5] We probably should have chosen more descriptive names than just `ii` and `jj`. Since the code that uses them is short, our lack of imagination is not a significant problem.

`quote_flag` is true when a `'` character has been seen in a conversion specification. Lines 4–6 verify that the locale has a thousands-separator character; if not, then there's no need to try to format the value with it.

The `do-while` loop generates digit characters in reverse, filling in a buffer from the back end toward the front end. The current digit is added to the buffer on line 10.

Lines 12–31 are what interest us. The work is done only on a system that supports locales, as indicated by the presence of the `<locale.h>` header file. The symbolic constant `HAVE_LOCALE_H` will be true on such a system.[6]

When the condition on line 13 is true, it's time to add in a thousands-separator character. This condition can be read in English as "if grouping is requested, *and* the current position in `loc.grouping` indicates an amount for grouping, *and* the current count of digits equals the grouping amount." If this condition is true, lines 14–20 add the thousands-separator character. In case there is more than one character in the thousands separator, it is worked through, backward, to be added to the buffer.

Once the current position in `loc.grouping` has been used, lines 22–29 look ahead at the value in the next position. If it's `0`, then the current position's value should continue to be used. We specify this by resetting `jj` to `0` (line 23). On the other hand, if the next position is `CHAR_MAX`, no more grouping should be done, and line 25 turns it off entirely by setting `quote_flag` to false. Otherwise, the next value is a grouping value, so line 27 increments `ii`, and line 28 resets `jj` to `0`.

This is low-level, detailed code. However, once you understand how the information in the `struct lconv` is presented, the code is straightforward to read (and it was straightforward to write).

15.2.7 Formatting Date and Time Values: `ctime()` and `strftime()`

Section 6.1, "Times and Dates," page 155, described the functions for retrieving and formatting time and date values. The `strftime()` function is also locale aware if `setlocale()` has been called appropriately. The following simple program, `ch-i18n-times.c`, demonstrates this:

```
/* ch-i18n-times.c --- demonstrate locale-based times */

#include <stdio.h>
#include <stdlib.h>
#include <locale.h>
#include <time.h>

int
main(void)
{
    char buf[100];
    time_t now;
    struct tm *curtime;
```

[6]This is set by the Autoconf and Automake machinery. Autoconf and Automake are powerful software suites that make it possible to support a wide range of Unix systems in a systematic fashion.

```
    setlocale(LC_ALL, "");
    time(& now);
    curtime = localtime(& now);
    (void) strftime(buf, sizeof buf,
            "It is now %A, %B %d, %Y, %I:%M %p", curtime);

    printf("%s\n", buf);

    printf("ctime() says: %s", ctime(& now));

    exit(EXIT_SUCCESS);
}
```

When the program is run, we see that the `strftime()` results indeed vary, while the `ctime()` results do not:

```
$ LC_ALL=en_US.utf8 ch-i18n-times                    Time in the United States
It is now Tuesday, May 27, 2025, 02:23 PM
ctime() says: Tue May 27 14:23:07 2025

$ LC_ALL=fr_FR.utf8 ch-i18n-times                    Time in France
It is now mardi, mai 27, 2025, 02:23
ctime() says: Tue May 27 14:23:21 2025
```

The reason for the lack of variation is that `ctime()` and `asctime()` (on which `ctime()` is based) are legacy interfaces; they exist to support old code. `strftime()`, being a newer interface (developed initially for C90), is free to be locale aware.

15.2.8 Other Locale Information: `nl_langinfo()`

Although we said earlier that the `catgets()` API is hard to use, one part of that API is generally useful: `nl_langinfo()`. It provides additional locale-related information, above and beyond that which is available from the `struct lconv`:

```
#include <langinfo.h>                                          POSIX

char *nl_langinfo(nl_item item);
```

The `nl_item` type is most likely an `int` or an `enum`. The `item` parameter is one of the symbolic constants defined in `<langinfo.h>`. The return value is a string that can be used as needed, either directly or as a format string for `strftime()`.

The available information comes from several locale categories. Table 15.3 lists the item constants, the corresponding locale category, and the item's meaning.

An *era* is a particular time in history. As it relates to dates and times, it makes the most sense in countries ruled by emperors or dynasties.[7]

---

[7] Although Americans often refer to the eras of particular presidents, these are not a formal part of the national calendar in the same sense as in pre–World War II Japan or pre-Communist China.

Table 15.3: Item values for `nl_langinfo()`

Item name	Category	Meaning
`ABDAY_1`, ..., `ABDAY_7`	`LC_TIME`	The abbreviated names of the days of the week. Sunday is Day 1.
`ABMON_1`, ..., `ABMON_12`	`LC_TIME`	The abbreviated names of the months.
`ALTMON_1`, ..., `ALTMON_12`	`LC_TIME`	Alternative names of the months, described shortly.
`ALT_DIGITS`	`LC_TIME`	Alternative symbols for digits, also described shortly.
`AM_STR`, `PM_STR`	`LC_TIME`	The a.m./p.m. notations for the locale.
`CODESET`	`LC_TYPE`	The name of the locale's *codeset*; that is, the character set and encoding in use.
`CRNCYSTR`	`LC_MONETARY`	The local currency symbol, described shortly.
`DAY_1`, ..., `DAY_7`	`LC_TIME`	The names of the days of the week. Sunday is Day 1.
`D_FMT`	`LC_TIME`	The date format.
`D_T_FMT`	`LC_TIME`	The date and time format.
`ERA_D_FMT`	`LC_TIME`	The era date format.
`ERA_D_T_FMT`	`LC_TIME`	The era date and time format.
`ERA_T_FMT`	`LC_TIME`	The era time format.
`ERA`	`LC_TIME`	Era description segments. This is shortly described in more detail.
`MON_1`, ..., `MON_12`	`LC_TIME`	The names of the months.
`RADIXCHAR`	`LC_NUMERIC`	The radix character. For base 10, this is the decimal point character.
`THOUSEP`	`LC_NUMERIC`	The thousands-separator character.
`T_FMT_AMPM`	`LC_TIME`	The time format with a.m./p.m. notation.
`T_FMT`	`LC_TIME`	The time format.
`YESEXPR`, `NOEXPR`	`LC_MESSAGES`	Strings representing positive and negative responses.

POSIX era specifications can describe eras before A.D. 1. In such cases, the start date has a higher absolute numeric value than the end date. For example, Alexander the Great ruled from 336 B.C. to 323 B.C.

The value returned by '`nl_langinfo(ERA)`', if not `NULL`, consists of one or more era specifications. Each specification is separated from the next by a `;` character. Components of each era specification are separated from each other by a `:` character. The components are described in Table 15.4.

The `ALT_DIGITS` value also needs some explanation. Some locales provide for "alternative digits." (Consider Arabic, which uses the decimal numbering system but different glyphs for the digits `0`–`9`. Or consider a hypothetical "Ancient Rome" locale using roman numerals.) These come up, for example, in `strftime()`'s various `%Oc` conversion specifications. The return value for '`nl_langinfo(ALT_DIGITS)`' is a semicolon-separated list of character strings for the alternative digits. The first should be used for `0`, the next for `1`, and so on. POSIX states that up to 100 alternative symbols may be provided. The point is to avoid restricting locales to the use of the ASCII digit characters when a locale has its own numbering system.

Similar logic applies to the `ALTMON_`*x* values.

Table 15.4: Era specification components

Component	Meaning
Direction	A + or '-' character. A + indicates that the era runs from a numerically lower year to a numerically higher one, and a '-' indicates the opposite.
Offset	The year closest to the start date of the of era.
Start date	The date when the era began, in the form '*yyyy*/*mm*/*dd*'. These are the year, month, and day, respectively. Years before A.D. 1 use a negative value for *yyyy*.
End date	The date when the era ended, in the same form. Two additional special forms are allowed: `-*` means the "beginning of time," and `+*` means the "end of time."
Era name	The name of the era, corresponding to `strftime()`'s `%EC` conversion specification.
Era format	The format of the year within the era, corresponding to `strftime()`'s `%EY` conversion specification.

Finally, '`nl_langinfo(CRNCYSTR)`' returns the local currency symbol. The first character of the return value, if it's a '`-`', `+`, or '`.`', indicates how the symbol should be used:

`-`	The symbol should appear before the value.
`+`	The symbol should appear after the value.
`.`	The symbol should replace the radix character (decimal point).

15.3 Dynamic Translation of Program Messages

The standard C library interfaces just covered solve the easy parts of the localization problem. Monetary, numeric, and time and date values, as well as string collation issues, all lend themselves to management through tables of locale-specific data (such as lists of month and day names).

However, most user interaction with a text-based program occurs in the form of the messages it outputs, such as prompts or error messages. The problem is to avoid having multiple versions of the same program that differ only in the contents of the message strings. The de facto solution in the GNU world is GNU `gettext`. (GUI programs face similar issues with the items in menus and menu bars; typically, each major user interface toolkit has its own way to solve that problem.)

GNU `gettext` enables translation of program messages into different languages at runtime. Within the code for a program, this translation involves several steps, each of which uses different library functions. Once the program itself has been properly prepared, several shell-level utilities facilitate the preparation of translations into different languages. Each such translation is referred to as a *message catalog*.

These functions have been available on GLIBC systems for decades. They are now standard, as they are included in the 2024 POSIX standard.

15.3.1 Setting the Text Domain: `textdomain()`

A complete application may contain multiple components: individual executables written in C or C++ or in scripting languages that can also access `gettext` facilities, such as `gawk` or the Bash shell. The components of the application all share the same *text domain*, which is a string that uniquely identifies the application. (Examples might be `"gawk"` or `"coreutils"`; the former is a single program, and the latter is a whole suite of programs.) The text domain is set with `textdomain()`:

```
#include <libintl.h>                                    GLIBC/POSIX

char *textdomain(const char *domainname);
```

Each component should call this function with a string naming the text domain as part of the initial startup activity in `main()`. The return value is the current text domain. If the `domainname` argument is `NULL`, then the current domain is returned; otherwise, it is set to the new value and that value is then returned. A return value of `NULL` indicates an error of some sort.

If the text domain is not set with `textdomain()`, the default domain is `"messages"`.

15.3.2 Translating Messages: `gettext()`

The next step after setting the text domain is to use the `gettext()` function (or a variant) for *every* string that should be translated. Several functions provide translation services:

```
#include <libintl.h>                                    GLIBC/POSIX

char *gettext(const char *msgid);
char *dgettext(const char *domainname, const char *msgid);
char *dcgettext(const char *domainname, const char *msgid, int category);
```

The arguments used in these functions are as follows:

`const char *msgid`
: The string to be translated. It acts as a key into a database of translations.

`const char *domainname`
: The text domain from which to retrieve the translation. Thus, even though `main()` has called `textdomain()` to set the application's own domain, messages can be retrieved from other text domains. (This is most applicable to messages that might be in the text domain for a third-party library, for example.)

`int category`
: One of the domain categories described earlier (`LC_TIME` etc.).

The default text domain is whatever was set with `textdomain()` (`"messages"` if `textdomain()` was never called). The default category is `LC_MESSAGES`. Assume that `main()` makes the following call:

```
textdomain("killerapp");
```

Then '`gettext("my message")`' is equivalent to '`dgettext("killerapp", "my message")`'. Both of these in turn are equivalent to '`dcgettext("killerapp", "my message", LC_MESSAGES)`'.

You will want to use `gettext()` 99.9 percent of the time. However, the other functions give you the flexibility to work with other text domains or locale categories. You are most likely to need this flexibility when doing library programming, since a stand-alone library will almost certainly be in its own text domain.

All the functions return a string. The string is either the translation of the given `msgid` or, if no translation exists, the original string. Thus, there is always some output, even if it's just the original (presumably English) message. For example:

```
/* The canonical first C program, internationalized version. */

#include <stdio.h>
#include <locale.h>
#include <libintl.h>
#include <stdlib.h>

int
main(void)
{
    setlocale(LC_ALL, "");
    printf("%s\n", gettext("hello, world"));
    return EXIT_SUCCESS;
}
```

Although the message is a simple string, we don't use it directly as the `printf()` control string, since in general, translations can contain `%` characters.

Shortly, in Section 15.3.4, "Making `gettext()` Easy to Use," page 529, we'll see how to make `gettext()` easier to use in large-scale, real-world programs.

15.3.3 Working with Plurals: `ngettext()`

Translating plurals provides special difficulties. Naive code might look like this:

```
printf("%d word%s misspelled\n", nwords, nwords > 1 ? "s" : "");
/* or */
printf("%d %s misspelled\n", nwords, nwords == 1 ? "word" : "words");
```

This is reasonable for English, but translation becomes difficult. First of all, many languages don't use as simple a plural form as English (adding an `s` suffix for most words).

Second, many languages, particularly in Eastern Europe, have multiple plural forms, each indicating how many objects the form designates. Thus, even code like this isn't enough:

```
if (nwords == 1)
    printf("one word misspelled\n");
else
    printf("%d words misspelled\n", nwords);
```

The solution is a parallel set of routines specifically for translating plural values:

```
#include <libintl.h>                                    GLIBC/POSIX

char *ngettext(const char *msgid, const char *msgid_plural,
               unsigned long int n);
char *dngettext(const char *domainname, const char *msgid,
                const char *msgid_plural, unsigned long int n);
char *dcngettext(const char *domainname, const char *msgid,
                 const char *msgid_plural, unsigned long int n, int category);
```

Besides the original `msgid`, `domainname`, and `category` arguments, these functions accept two additional arguments:

`const char *msgid_plural`
: The default string to use for plural values. Examples shortly.

`unsigned long int n`
: The number of items there are.

Each locale's message catalog specifies how to translate plurals.[8] The `ngettext()` function (and its variants) examines `n` and, based on the specification in the message catalog, returns the appropriate translation of `msgid`. If the catalog does not have a translation for `msgid`, or if the program is running in the `"C"` locale, `ngettext()` returns the original `msgid` if '`n == 1`'; otherwise, it returns the original `msgid_plural`. Thus, our misspelled words example looks like this:

```
printf(ngettext("%d word misspelled", "%d words misspelled", nwords), nwords);
```

Note that `nwords` must be passed to `ngettext()` to select a format string, and then to `printf()` for formatting. In addition, be careful not to use a macro or expression whose value changes each time, like '`n++`'! Such a thing could happen if you're doing global editing to add calls to `ngettext()` and you don't pay attention.

15.3.4 Making `gettext()` Easy to Use

The call to `gettext()` in program source code serves two purposes. First, it does the translation at runtime, which is the main point, after all. However, it also serves to *mark* the

[8] The details are given in the GNU `gettext` documentation. Here, we're focusing on the developer's needs, not the translator's.

strings that need translating. The `xgettext` utility reads program source code and extracts all the original strings that need translation. (We briefly cover the mechanics of this later in the chapter.)

Consider the case, though, of `static` strings that aren't used directly:

```
static char *copyrights[] = {
    "Copyright 2025, Jane Programmer",
    "Permission is granted ...",
    ...                                     LOTS of legalese here
    "So there.",
    NULL
};

void
copyright(void)
{
    int i;

    for (i = 0; copyrights[i] != NULL, i++)
       printf("%s\n", gettext(copyrights[i]));
}
```

Here, we'd like to be able to print the translations of the copyright strings if they're available. However, how is the `xgettext` extractor supposed to find these strings? We can't enclose them in calls to `gettext()` because that won't work at compile time:

```
/* BAD CODE: won't compile */
static char *copyrights[] = {
    gettext("Copyright 2025, Jane Programmer"),
    gettext("Permission is granted ..."),
    ...                                     LOTS of legalese here
    NULL
};
```

Read on for the answer.

15.3.4.1 Portable Programs: `"gettext.h"`

We assume here that you wish to write a program that can be used along with the GNU `gettext` library on any Unix system, not just GNU/Linux systems. The next section describes what to do for GNU/Linux-only programs.

The solution to marking strings involves two steps. The first is the use of the `gettext.h` convenience header that comes in the GNU `gettext` distribution. This file handles several portability and compilation issues, making it easier to use `gettext()` in your own programs:

```
#define ENABLE_NLS 1           ENABLE_NLS must be true for gettext() to work
#include "gettext.h"           Instead of <libintl.h>
```

If the ENABLE_NLS macro is not defined[9] or it's set to zero, then gettext.h expands calls to gettext() into the first argument. This makes it possible to port code using gettext() to systems that have neither GNU gettext installed nor their own version. Among other things, this header file defines the following macro:

```
/* A pseudo function call that serves as a marker for the automated
   extraction of messages, but does not call gettext().  The run-time
   translation is done at a different place in the code.
   The argument, String, should be a literal string.  Concatenated strings
   and other string expressions won't work.
   The macro's expansion is not parenthesized, so that it is suitable as
   initializer for static 'char[]' or 'const char[]' variables.  */
#define gettext_noop(String) String
```

The comment is self-explanatory. With this macro, we can now proceed to the second step. We rewrite the code as follows:

```
#define ENABLE_NLS 1
#include "gettext.h"

static char copyrights[] =
    gettext_noop("Copyright 2025, Jane Programmer\n"
    "Permission is granted ...\n"
    ...                                     LOTS of legalese here
    "So there.");

void
copyright(void)
{
   printf("%s\n", gettext(copyrights));
}
```

Note that we made two changes. First, copyrights is now one long string, built up by using the Standard C string constant concatenation feature. This single string is then enclosed in the call to gettext_noop(). We need a single string so that the legalese can be translated as a single entity. (Despite the statement in the comment that concatenated strings won't work, in fact they do, at least as long as you're concatenating string constants.)

The second change is to print the translation directly, as one string in copyright().

By now, you may be thinking, "Gee, having to type 'gettext(...)' each time is pretty painful." Well, you're right. Not only is it extra work to type, but it makes program source code harder to read as well. Thus, once you are using the gettext.h header file, the GNU gettext manual recommends the introduction of two more macros, named _() and N_(), as follows:

```
#define ENABLE_NLS 1
#include "gettext.h"
```

[9]This macro is usually automatically defined by the configure program, either in a special header or on the compiler command line. configure is created with Autoconf and Automake.

```
#define _(msgid)  gettext(msgid)
#define N_(msgid) msgid
```

This approach reduces the burden of using `gettext()` to just three extra characters per translatable string constant, and to only four extra characters for `static` strings:

```
#include <stdio.h>
#include <stdlib.h>
#define ENABLE_NLS 1
#include "gettext.h"
#define _(msgid)  gettext(msgid)
#define N_(msgid) msgid
...
static char copyrights[] =
    N_("Copyright 2025, Jane Programmer\n"
    "Permission is granted ...\n"
    ...                                     LOTS of legalese here
    "So there.");

void
copyright(void)
{
   printf("%s\n", _(copyrights));
}

int
main(void)
{
    setlocale(LC_ALL, "");       /* gettext.h gets <locale.h> for us too */
    printf("%s\n", _("hello, world"));
    copyright();
    exit(EXIT_SUCCESS);
}
```

These macros are unobtrusive, and in practice, all GNU programs that use GNU `gettext` use this convention. If you intend to use GNU `gettext`, you too should follow this convention.

15.3.4.2 GLIBC Only: `<libintl.h>`

For a program that will be used only on systems with GLIBC, the header file usage and macros are similar, but simpler:

```
#include <stdio.h>
#include <libintl.h>
#define _(msgid)  gettext(msgid)
#define N_(msgid) msgid
... everything else is the same ...
```

As we saw earlier, the `<libintl.h>` header file declares `gettext()` and the other functions. You still have to define `_()` and `N_()`, but you don't have to worry about `ENABLE_NLS` or about distributing `gettext.h` with your program's source code.

15.3.5 Rearranging Word Order with `printf()`

When translations are produced, sometimes the word order that is natural in English is incorrect for other languages. For instance, while in English an adjective appears before the noun it modifies, in many languages it appears *after* the noun. Thus, code like the following presents a problem:

```
char *animal_color, *animal;

if (...) {
    animal_color = _("brown");
    animal = _("cat");
} else if (...) {
    ...
} else {
    ...
}
printf(_("The %s %s looks at you enquiringly.\n"), animal_color, color);
```

Here, the format string, `animal_color`, and `animal` are all properly enclosed in calls to `gettext()`. However, the statement will still be incorrect when translated, since *the order of the arguments cannot be changed at runtime.*

To get around this, the POSIX (but *not* ISO C) version of the `printf()` family allows you to provide a *positional specifier* within a format specifier. This takes the form of a decimal number followed by a `$` character *immediately* after the initial `%` character. For example:

```
printf("%2$s, %1$s\n", "world", "hello");
```

The positional specifier indicates which argument in the argument list to use; counts begin at `1` and don't include the format string itself. This example prints the famous '`hello, world`' message in the correct order.

Any of the regular `printf()` flags, a field width, and a precision may follow the positional specifier. The rules for using positional specifiers are these:

- The positional specifier form may not be mixed with the nonpositional form. In other words, either every format specifier includes a positional specifier or none of them do. Of course, `%%` can always be used.
- If the *N*th argument is used in the format string, all the arguments up to *N* must also be used by the string. Thus, the following is invalid:

  ```
  printf("%3$s %1$s\n", "hello", "cruel", "world");
  ```

- A particular argument may be referenced with a positional specifier multiple times. Nonpositional format specifications always move through the argument list sequentially.

This facility isn't intended for direct use by application programmers, but rather by translators. For example, a French translation for the previous format string, `"The %s %s looks at you enquiringly.\n"`, might be:

```
"Le %2$s %1$s te regarde d'un aire interrogateur.\n"
```

(Even this translation isn't perfect: the article "Le" is gender specific. Preparing a program for translation is a hard job!)

15.3.6 Testing Translations in a Private Directory

The collection of messages in a program is referred to as the *message catalog*. This term also applies to each translation of the messages into a different language. When a program is installed, its translations are also installed in a standard location, where `gettext()` can find the right one at runtime.

It can be useful to place translations in a directory other than the standard one, particularly for program testing. Especially on larger systems, a regular developer probably does not have the permissions necessary to install files in system directories. The `bindtextdomain()` function gives `gettext()` an alternative place to look for translations:

```
#include <libintl.h>                                        GLIBC/POSIX

char *bindtextdomain(const char *domainname, const char *dirname);
```

Useful directories include `.` for the current directory and `/tmp`. It might also be handy to get the directory from an environment variable, like so:

```
char *td_dir;

setlocale(LC_ALL, "");
textdomain("killerapp");
if ((td_dir = getenv("KILLERAPP_TD_DIR")) != NULL)
    bindtextdomain("killerapp", td_dir);
```

`bindtextdomain()` should be called before any calls to the `gettext()` family of functions. We see an example of how to use it in Section 15.3.9, "Creating Translations," page 536.

15.3.7 Setting the Output Codeset

A *codeset* is the POSIX term for what we call a "character set"—the defined encoding of characters in a particular locale. We get into the issues of character sets and their encodings later in this chapter, in Section 15.4, "Can You Spell That for Me, Please?," page 540.

If you like, you can check and/or set the output codeset for a text domain. This means that after a translation for a string is found, it is converted to a given codeset before being returned.

You do this with the `bind_textdomain_codeset()` function:

```
#include <libintl.h>                                    GLIBC/POSIX

char *bind_textdomain_codeset(const char *domainname,
                              const char *codeset);
```

The arguments are:

`const char *domainname`
: The name of the text domain.

`const char *codeset`
: The name of the codeset to use (such as `"UTF-8"`).

An output codeset is considered to be "bound" to a text domain. To find out the current codeset in use for a domain, pass in the domain name of interest and a `NULL` pointer for `codeset`. The return value will be either the currently bound codeset or the default codeset used by the `gettext()` suite of routines.

To change the codeset, pass in the domain name of interest and a string naming the new codeset to use.

`bind_textdomain_codeset()` returns `NULL` if an error occurred, or the bound codeset. In the case of an error, `errno` indicates the error. Since that's the case, you should set `errno` to `0` before calling this function.

This function is fairly specialized. It's unlikely that you will need it for most programs, but if you do need it, it's there.

15.3.8 Preparing Internationalized Programs

So far, we've looked at all the components that go into an internationalized program. This section summarizes the process:

1. Adopt the `gettext.h` header file into your application, and add definitions for the `_()` and `N_()` macros to a header file that is included by all your C source files. Don't forget to define the `ENABLE_NLS` symbolic constant.
2. Call `setlocale()` as appropriate. It is easiest to call '`setlocale(LC_ALL, "")`', but occasionally an application may need to be more picky about which locale categories it enables.
3. Pick a text domain for the application, and set it with `textdomain()`.
4. If testing, bind the text domain to a particular directory with `bindtextdomain()`.
5. Use `strfmon()`, `strftime()`, and the `'` flag for `printf()` as appropriate. If other locale information is needed, use `nl_langinfo()`, particularly in conjunction with `strftime()`.
6. Mark all strings that should be translated with calls to `_()` or `N_()`, as appropriate.

7. We just said "mark all strings that should be translated." However, some should not be so marked. For example, if you use `getopt_long()` (see Section 2.1.2, "GNU Long Options," page 26), you probably *don't* want the long option names to be marked for translation. Also, simple format strings like `"%d %d\n"` do not need to be translated, nor do debugging messages.
8. When appropriate, use `ngettext()` (or its variants) for dealing with values that can be either one or greater than one.
9. Make life easier for your translators by using multiple strings representing complete sentences instead of doing word substitutions with `%s` and `?:`. For example:

```
if (an error occurred) {          /* RIGHT */
    /* Use multiple strings to make translation easier. */
    if (input_type == INPUT_FILE)
        fprintf(stderr, _("%s: cannot read file: %s\n"),
                        argv[0], strerror(errno));
    else
        fprintf(stderr, _("%s: cannot read pipe: %s\n"),
                        argv[0], strerror(errno));
}
```

This is better than:

```
if (an error occurred) {          /* WRONG */
    fprintf(stderr, _("%s: cannot read %s: %s\n"), argv[0],
            input_type == INPUT_FILE ? _("file") : _("pipe"),
            strerror(errno));
}
```

As just shown, it's a good idea to include a comment stating that there are multiple messages on purpose—to make it easier to translate the messages.

15.3.9 Creating Translations

Once your program has been internationalized, it's necessary to prepare translations. This is done with several shell-level tools. We start with an internationalized version of `ch-general1-echodate.c`, from Section 6.1.4, "Converting a Broken-Down Time to a `time_t`," page 164:

```
/* ch-i18n-echodate.c --- demonstrate translations */

#include <stdio.h>
#include <time.h>
#include <locale.h>
#include <stdlib.h>
#define ENABLE_NLS 1
#include "gettext.h"
#define _(msgid) gettext(msgid)
```

```
#define N_(msgid) msgid

int
main(void)
{
    struct tm tm;
    time_t then;
    int count;

    setlocale(LC_ALL, "");
    bindtextdomain("echodate", ".");
    textdomain("echodate");

    printf("%s", _("Enter a Date/time as YYYY/MM/DD HH:MM:SS : "));
    count = scanf("%d/%d/%d %d:%d:%d",
            & tm.tm_year, & tm.tm_mon, & tm.tm_mday,
            & tm.tm_hour, & tm.tm_min, & tm.tm_sec);

    /* Error checking on values omitted for brevity. */
    tm.tm_year -= 1900;
    tm.tm_mon -= 1;

    tm.tm_isdst = -1;   /* Don't know about DST */

    then = mktime(& tm);

    printf(_("Got: %s"), ctime(& then));
    exit(EXIT_SUCCESS);
}
```

We have purposely used `"gettext.h"` and not `<gettext.h>`. If our application ships with a private copy of the `gettext` library, then `"gettext.h"` will find it, avoiding the system's copy. On the other hand, if there is only a system copy, it will be found if there is no local copy. The situation is admittedly complicated by the fact that Solaris systems also have a `gettext` library that is not as featureful as the GNU version.

Moving on to creating translations, the first step is to extract the translatable strings. This is done with the `xgettext` program:

```
$ xgettext --keyword=_ --keyword=N_ \
> --default-domain=echodate ch-i18n-echodate.c
```

The `--keyword` options tell `xgettext` to look for the `_()` and `N_()` macros. It already knows to extract strings from `gettext()` and its variants, as well as from `gettext_noop()`. When processing multiple source files, `xgettext` also knows how to handle duplicates of the same string, so that each string appears only once in the output. This saves work for translators.

The output from `xgettext` is called a *portable object* file. The default file name is `messages.po`, corresponding to the default text domain of `"messages"`. The `--default-domain` option indicates the text domain, for use in naming the output file. In this case, the file is named `echodate.po`. Here are its contents:

```
# SOME DESCRIPTIVE TITLE.
# Copyright (C) YEAR THE PACKAGE'S COPYRIGHT HOLDER
# This file is distributed under the same license as the PACKAGE package.
# FIRST AUTHOR <EMAIL@ADDRESS>, YEAR.
#
#, fuzzy
msgid ""                                          Detailed information
msgstr ""                                         Each translator completes
"Project-Id-Version: PACKAGE VERSION\n"
"Report-Msgid-Bugs-To: \n"
"POT-Creation-Date: 2025-05-08 18:18+0300\n"
"PO-Revision-Date: YEAR-MO-DA HO:MI+ZONE\n"
"Last-Translator: FULL NAME <EMAIL@ADDRESS>\n"
"Language-Team: LANGUAGE <LL@li.org>\n"
"Language: \n"
"MIME-Version: 1.0\n"
"Content-Type: text/plain; charset=CHARSET\n"
"Content-Transfer-Encoding: 8bit\n"

#: ch-i18n-echodate.c:23                          Message location
msgid "Enter a Date/time as YYYY/MM/DD HH:MM:SS : "   Original message
msgstr ""                                         Translation goes here

#: ch-i18n-echodate.c:36                          Same for each message
#, c-format
msgid "Got: %s"
msgstr ""
```

This original file is reused for each translation. It is thus a *template* for translations, and by convention it should be renamed to reflect this fact, with a `.pot` (*portable object template*) suffix:

```
$ mv echodate.po echodate.pot
```

Given that we aren't fluent in many languages, we have chosen to translate the messages into pig Latin. Thus, the next step is to produce a translation. We do this by copying the template file and adding translations to the new copy:

```
$ cp echodate.pot piglat.po
$ vim piglat.po                    Add translations, use your favorite editor
```

The file name convention is *`language`*`.po`, where *language* is the two- or three-character international standard abbreviation for the language. Occasionally the form *`language_country`*`.po` is used—for example, `pt_BR.po` for Portugese in Brazil. As pig Latin isn't a real language, we've called the file `piglat.po`. Here are the contents, after the translations have been added:

```
# echodate translations into pig Latin
# Copyright (C) 2004, 2025 Arnold David Robbins
# This file is distributed under the same license as the echodate package.
# Arnold Robbins <arnold@example.com>, 2025
#
#, fuzzy
msgid ""
msgstr ""
"Project-Id-Version: 1.0\n"
"Report-Msgid-Bugs-To: arnold@example.com\n"
"POT-Creation-Date: 2025-05-08 18:18+0300\n"
"POT-Revision-Date: 2025-05-08 18:18+0300\n"
"Last-Translator: Arnold Robbins <arnold@example.com>\n"
"Language-Team: Pig Latin <piglat@li.example.org>\n"
"Language: \n"
"MIME-Version: 1.0\n"
"Content-Type: text/plain; charset=UTF-8\n"
"Content-Transfer-Encoding: 8bit\n"

#: ch-i18n-echodate.c:23
msgid "Enter a Date/time as YYYY/MM/DD HH:MM:SS : "
msgstr "Enteray A Ateday/imetay asay YYYY/MM/DD HH:MM:SS : "

#: ch-i18n-echodate.c:36
#, c-format
msgid "Got: %s"
msgstr "Otgay: %s"
```

While it would be possible to do a linear search directly in the portable object file, such a search would be slow. For example, `gawk` has approximately 780 separate messages, and the GNU Coreutils have almost 1,900. Linear searching a text file with hundreds of messages would be noticeably slow. Therefore, GNU `gettext` uses a binary format for fast message lookup. `msgfmt` does the compilation, producing a *message object* file:

```
$ msgfmt piglat.po -o piglat.mo
```

As program maintenance is done, the strings used by a program change: new strings are added, while others are deleted or changed. At the very least, a string's location in the source file may move around. Thus, translation `.po` files will likely get out of date. The `msgmerge` program merges an old translation file with a new `.pot` file. The result can then be updated. This example does a merge and then recompiles:

```
$ msgmerge piglat.po echodate.pot -o piglat.new.po     Merge files
$ mv piglat.new.po piglat.po                           Rename the result
```

```
$ vim piglat.po                                    Bring translations up to date
$ msgfmt piglat.po -o piglat.mo                    Recreate .mo file
```

Compiled `.mo` files are placed in the file *`base/locale/category/textdomain`*`.mo`. On GNU/Linux systems, *base* is `/usr/share/locale`. *locale* is the language, such as '`es`', '`fr`', and so on. *category* is a locale category; for messages, it is `LC_MESSAGES`. *`textdomain`* is the text domain of the program—in our case, `echodate`. As a real example, the Coreutils' French translation is in `/usr/share/locale/fr/LC_MESSAGES/coreutils.mo`.

The `bindtextdomain()` function changes the *base* part of the location. In `ch-i18n-echodate.c`, we change it to `.` (dot). Thus it's necessary to make the appropriate directories, and place the pig Latin translation there:

```
$ mkdir -p en/LC_MESSAGES                          Have to use a real language
$ cp piglat.mo en/LC_MESSAGES/echodate.mo          Put the file in the right place
```

A real language must be used;[10] thus we "pretend" by using `"en"`. With the translation in place, we set `LC_ALL` appropriately, cross our fingers, and run the program:

```
$ LC_ALL=en_US.utf8 ch-i18n-echodate               Run the program
Enteray A Ateday/imetay asay YYYY/MM/DD HH:MM:SS : 2025/12/15 18:19:20
Otgay: Mon Dec 15 18:19:20 2025
```

The latest version of GNU `gettext` can be found in the GNU `gettext` distribution directory.[11]

This section has necessarily only skimmed the surface of the localization process. GNU `gettext` provides many tools for working with translations, and in particular for making it easy to keep translations up to date as program source code evolves.

The manual process for updating translations is workable but tedious. This task is easily automated with `make`; in particular, GNU `gettext` integrates well with Autoconf and Automake to provide this functionality, removing considerable development burden from the programmer.

We recommend reading the GNU `gettext` documentation to learn more about both of these issues in particular and about GNU `gettext` in general. (A link to the documentation is given later in Section 15.5, "Suggested Reading," page 553.)

Of the shell-level utilities we've described, `msgfmt` is included in the 2024 POSIX standard, along with the shell-level commands `gettext` and `ngettext` for printing translated strings.

15.4 Can You Spell That for Me, Please?

In the very early days of computing, different systems assigned different correspondences between numeric values and *glyphs*—symbols such as letters, digits, and punctuation used for communication with humans. Eventually, two widely used standards emerged: the EBCDIC

[10] For the first edition of this book, we spent a frustrating 30 or 45 minutes attempting to use a `piglat/LC_MESSAGES` directory and setting '`LC_ALL=piglat`', all to no effect, until we figured this out.

[11] `https://ftp.gnu.org/gnu/gettext`

encoding used on IBM and workalike mainframes, and ASCII, used on everything else. Today, except on mainframes, ASCII is the basis for all other character sets currently in use.

The original seven-bit ASCII character set suffices for American English and most punctuation and special characters such as `$` (though there is no character for the "cent" symbol). However, there are many languages and many countries with different character set needs. ASCII doesn't handle the accented versions of the roman characters used in Europe, and some Asian languages have *thousands* of characters. New technologies have evolved to solve these deficiencies.

The i18n literature abounds with references to three fundamental terms. Once we define them and their relationship to each other, we can then present the corresponding C APIs:

Character set
: A definition of the meaning assigned to different integer values—for example, that `A` is 65. Any character set that uses more than eight bits per character is termed a *multibyte character set*.

Character set encoding
: ASCII uses a single byte to represent characters. Thus, the integer value is stored as itself, directly in disk files. More recent character sets, most notably different versions of Unicode,[12] use 16-bit or even 32-bit integer values for representing characters. For most of the defined characters, one, two, or even three of the higher bytes in the integer are zero, making direct storage of their values in disk files expensive. The encoding describes a mechanism for converting 16- or 32-bit values into (or from) one to six bytes for storage on disk, such that overall there is a significant space savings. (Initially, Unicode's UTF-8 encoding was defined to take up to six bytes; later this was changed to a maximum of four bytes.) The encoding is also relevant for characters read from the terminal, since `read()` always works on bytes.

Language
: The rules for a given language dictate character set usage. In particular, the rules affect the ordering of characters. For example, in French, `e`, `é`, and `è` should all come between `d` and `f`, no matter what numerical values are assigned to those characters. Different languages can (and do) assign different orderings to the same glyphs.

Various technologies have evolved over time for supporting multibyte character sets. Computing practice has mostly converged on Unicode and its encodings, but Standard C and POSIX support both past and present techniques. GLIBC provides support for many character encodings, not just Unicode.

15.4.1 Wide Characters

We start with the concept of a *wide character*. A wide character is an integer type that can hold any value of the particular multibyte character set being used.

[12] `https://home.unicode.org/`

Wide characters are represented in C with the type wchar_t. C99 provides a corresponding wint_t type, which can hold any value that a wchar_t can hold, and the special value WEOF, which is analogous to regular EOF from <stdio.h>. The various types are defined in the <wchar.h> header file.

Wide characters may be 16 to 32 bits in size, depending on the implementation. As mentioned, they're intended for manipulating data in memory and are not usually stored directly in files.

Some systems[13] define wchar_t to be 16 bits in size. Since Unicode requires more characters than 16 bits can hold, the C24 standard introduced an additional type, char32_t, which is explicitly 32 bits in size. (There are also related char8_t and char16_t types.) If you don't care about systems with a 16-bit wchar_t, you can continue to use wchar_t instead of char32_t.

15.4.1.1 Wide Characters in Code

Wide characters in code are represented similarly to regular characters. You write a character constant the same way but prefix it with L or l. Using L is more readable. For example:

```
wchar_t wide_A = L'A';
```

Similarly, strings of wide characters are enclosed in double quotes, prefixed with L or l:

```
wchar_t wide_saying[] = L"Here's lookin' at you, kid!\n";   // array
wchar_t *wide_saying2 = L"Don't Panic!\n";                   // pointer to string constant
```

(You should not name all your wide strings and characters with a 'wide_' prefix; we did so just for expositive purposes.)

15.4.1.2 Wide-Character Functions

For wide characters, the C standard provides a large number of functions and macros that correspond to the traditional functions that work on char data. Since we assume that you're familiar with the regular string functions, such as strlen(), strcmp(), and so on, we provide only a brief description of the corresponding wide-character functions in Table 15.5.

In addition to the functions listed in the table, the <wctype.h> header file declares functions that correspond to those in <ctype.h>:

```
#include <wctype.h>                              ISO C

int iswalnum(wint_t wc);        // Alphanumeric characters
int iswalpha(wint_t wc);        // Alphabetic characters
int iswblank(wint_t wc);        // Blanks (spaces and tabs)
int iswcntrl(wint_t wc);        // Control characters
int iswdigit(wint_t wc);        // Digits
int iswgraph(wint_t wc);        // Visible characters
int iswlower(wint_t wc);        // Lowercase characters
int iswprint(wint_t wc);        // Printable characters
```

[13] Most notably, Microsoft Windows and IBM's AIX.

```
int iswpunct(wint_t wc);        // Punctuation characters
int iswspace(wint_t wc);        // Space characters
int iswupper(wint_t wc);        // Uppercase characters
int iswxdigit(wint_t wc);       // Hexadecimal digits
```

Table 15.5: Standard wide-character functions

Wide-character function	String function	POSIX	Description
`wcscasecmp()`	`strcasecmp()`		Case-independent string comparison.
`wcscat()`	`strcat()`		String concatenation.
`wcschr()`	`strchr()`		Find character in string, first occurrence.
`wcscmp()`	`strcmp()`		String comparison.
`wcscoll()`	`strcoll()`		Compare strings according to the locale's collating sequence.
`wcscpy()`	`strcpy()`		String copy.
`wcscspn()`	`strcspn()`		Get length of prefix string from complemented characters.
`wcsdup()`	`strdup()`		String duplication.
`wcslen()`	`strlen()`		String length.
`wcsncasecmp()`	`strncasecmp()`	✓	Counted case-independent string comparison.
`wcsncat()`	`strncat()`		Counted string concatenation.
`wcsncmp()`	`strncmp()`		Counted string comparison.
`wcsncpy()`	`strncpy()`		Counted string copy.
`wcsnlen()`	`strnlen()`	✓	Counted string length.
`wcspbrk()`	`strpbrk()`		Search a string for any of a set of bytes/characters.
`wcsrchr()`	`strrchr()`		Find character in string, last occurrence.
`wcsspn()`	`strspn()`		Get length of prefix string.
`wcsstr()`	`strstr()`		Find substring in string.
`wcstoimax()`	`strtoimax()`		Convert string to `intmax_t`.
`wcstok()`	`strtok()`		Find "tokens" within a string.
`wcstoumax()`	`strtoumax()`		Convert string to `uintmax_t`.
`wcsxfrm()`	`strxfrm()`		Transform strings for use by `strcmp()`/`wcscmp()`.
`wfprintf()`	`fprintf()`		Print wide-character string to an open file.
`wmemchr()`	`memchr()`		Find a character in a string.
`wmemcmp()`	`memcmp()`		Do a binary comparison of two memory areas.
`wmemcpy()`	`memcpy()`		Copy memory.
`wmemmove()`	`memmove()`		Copy memory while handling overlapping areas.
`wmemset()`	`memset()`		Set memory to a given value.
`wprintf()`	`printf()`		Print wide-character string to `stdout`.
`wsprintf()`	`sprintf()`		Format into a wide-character string.

The previous list of functions covers the traditional set of character tests that have long been available in C. However, ISO C provides for the existence of additional, locale-specific types (or classes) of characters in character sets that extend ASCII:

```
#include <wctype.h>                                    ISO C

wctype_t wctype(const char *name);
int iswctype(wint_t wc, wctype_t desc);
```

The `wctype_t` type represents a property that a wide character may (or may not) have, such as "alphabetic" or "punctuation." It is an integer type. The functions that use it are as follows:

`wctype_t wctype(const char *name)`
: Returns the `wctype_t` value that corresponds to the property given by `name`. The standard 12 properties `"alnum"`, `"alpha"`, and so on are valid in all locales. If `name` does not represent a valid property in the current locale, `wctype()` returns zero.

`int iswctype(wint_t wc, wctype_t desc)`
: Returns nonzero (true) if `wc` has the property indicated by `desc`, or zero otherwise. `desc` must have been obtained via `wctype()`. If `wc` is `WEOF`, the return value is zero.

Finally, two more functions deal with *character widths*. Most characters take up a single column position when printed. However, there do exist a few zero-width characters in Unicode, as well as characters that take up more than one column position. This may be true of other character sets as well.

The most notable of the Unicode zero-width characters is the zero-width space character, `0x200B`, which can be used by text formatting programs to indicate where it's OK to break a word into a new line without hyphenating it. (Interestingly, such characters introduce cybersecurity concerns, but that's beyond the scope of this book. A web search will find more details.) The functions are:

```
#define _XOPEN_SOURCE          Needed on GLIBC systems
#include <wchar.h>                             POSIX

int wcwidth(wchar_t c);
int wcswidth(const wchar_t *s, size_t n);
```

`int wcwidth(wchar_t c)`
: Returns the width ("number of column positions") of `c`. If `c` is printable, the value is at least zero. For `L'\0'`, the value is zero. `-1` is returned for anything else.

`int wcswidth(const wchar_t *s, size_t n)`
: Returns the width of the wide-character string pointed to by `s`, for at most `n` wide characters. If the string contains a nonprinting character, `-1` is returned.

These two functions are the only way to determine the column width; this means you must convert a multibyte character or string to a wide character or string in order to use them.

We show an example of `wcwidth()` in use with some of the wide-character conversion functions in Section 15.4.3.4, “Example Code: GNU `ls.c`,” page 548.

15.4.2 Multibyte Character Encodings

Strings of wide characters are stored on disk by being converted to a multibyte character set encoding in memory, and the converted data is then written to a disk file. Similarly, such strings are read in from disk through low-level block I/O and converted in memory from the encoded version to the wide-character version.

Many defined encodings represent multibyte characters by using *shift states*. In other words, given an input byte stream, byte values represent themselves until a special control value is encountered. At that point, the interpretation changes according to the current shift state. Thus, the same eight-bit value can have two or more meanings: one for the normal, unshifted state, and another for a shifted state. Correctly encoded strings are supposed to start and end in the same shift state, called the *initial shift state*.

A significant advantage to Unicode is that its encodings are self-correcting; the encodings don’t use shift states, so a loss of data in the middle does not corrupt the subsequent encoded data.

The initial versions of the multibyte-to-wide-character and wide-character-to-multibyte functions maintained a private copy of the translation state (for example, the shift state, and anything else that might be necessary). This design limits the functions’ use to one kind of translation throughout the life of the program. Examples are `mblen()` (multibyte-character length), `mbtowc()` (multibyte to wide character), `wctomb()` (wide character to multibyte), `mbstowcs()` (multibyte string to wide-character string), and `wcstombs()` (wide-character string to multibyte string). We are not going to cover those functions, because you should not use them. For what you *should* do, read on.

15.4.3 Converting Bytes to Wide Characters

The newer versions of the functions that deal with multibyte encodings are termed *restartable*. This means that user-level code maintains the state of the translation in a separate object, of type `mbstate_t`. The corresponding examples are `mbrlen()`, `mbrtowc()`, `wcrtomb()`, `mbsrtowcs()`, and `wcsrtombs()`. (Note the `r`, for “restartable,” in their names.) We describe these functions shortly.

15.4.3.1 Conversion States: `mbstate_t`

The `mbstate_t` is an opaque type, similar to the `FILE` type from `<stdio.h>`. Unlike `FILE` objects, user-level code declares and initializes `mbstate_t` objects and passes pointers to them to the various functions. But user-level code never accesses or updates the contents of an `mbstate_t` object.

Initializing an `mbstate_t` object puts it into the initial shift state that we mentioned earlier. The `mbsinit()` function allows you to tell whether an `mbstate_t` is in the initial shift state:

```
#include <wchar.h>                              ISO C

int mbsinit(const mbstate_t *ps);
```

`mbsinit()` returns nonzero (true) if `*ps` is in the initial shift state, or if `ps` is `NULL`. Otherwise it returns zero.

The most portable way to initialize an `mbstate_t` object is with `memset()`:

```
mbstate_t mbs;

memset(& mbs, 0, sizeof(mbstate_t));
```

It is also possible to initialize it this way:

```
mbstate_t mbs = { 0, };
```

But that may produce compiler warnings on some systems. Initialization should be done once, before starting to process an input byte stream. Also, it's a good idea to reinitialize the `mbstate_t` object after encountering a conversion error.

15.4.3.2 Converting Bytes

Conversion from multibyte encoded characters to wide characters is done either with `mbrtowc()`, which produces a single wide character, or with `mbsrtowcs()`, which produces a wide-character string:

```
#include <wchar.h>                              ISO C

size_t mbrtowc(wchar_t *pwc, const char *s, size_t n, mbstate_t *ps);
size_t mbsrtowcs(wchar_t *dest, const char **src, size_t len, mbstate_t *ps);
```

For `mbrtowc()`, the parameters are:

`wchar_t *pwc`
: A pointer to the wide character to receive the decoded character.

`const char *s`
: A pointer to the first byte from which to start the decoding.

`size_t n`
: The maximum number of bytes left in the data pointed to by `s`.

`mbstate_t *ps`
: A pointer to an `mbstate_t` object.

Upon success, `mbrtowc()` returns the number of bytes that were read. Usually this is a positive value. It can be zero if the converted character was `L'\0'`. In that case, `*ps` is reset to the initial shift state. There are two possible error returns. If the bytes pointed to by `s` do not contain a complete multibyte character, the return value is `(size_t) -2`. If no valid multibyte character is found at all, the return value is `(size_t) -1`, and `errno` is set to `EILSEQ`.

The function is a little complicated, in that it behaves differently when `pwc` is `NULL`, `s` is `NULL`, and/or `ps` is `NULL`. For day-to-day code, none of these conditions should be true, so we won't confuse you with the details. Instead, see the *mbrtowc*(3) manpage if you're interested.

For `mbsrtowcs()`, the parameters are:

`wchar_t *dest`
: The destination wide-character string.

`const char **src`
: A pointer to a pointer to the source bytes. As wide characters are converted, `*src` is updated. The idea is that when `mbsrtowcs()` has returned, `*src` will point just past the last byte that was converted.

`size_t len`
: The maximum number of wide characters to convert.

`mbstate_t *ps`
: A pointer to an `mbstate_t` object.

The return value is the number of wide characters converted, not including the terminating `L'\0'`. As with `mbrtowc()`, if an invalid sequence was encountered, `-1` is returned and `errno` is set to `EILSEQ`.

Here, too, the function's behavior may vary if `dest` and/or `ps` are `NULL`. We refer you to the *mbsrtowcs*(3) manpage for the details.

15.4.3.3 Byte Maximums

There are two important maximum values to be aware of when converting from bytes to wide characters:

```
#include <limits.h>                          ISO C

#define MB_LEN_MAX ...
```

and:

```
#include <stdlib.h>                          ISO C

#define MB_CUR_MAX ...
```

`MB_LEN_MAX` is the maximum number of bytes that can be used for a multibyte character in *any* locale. In practice, this isn't so useful.

`MB_CUR_MAX` is the maximum number of bytes that can be used for a multibyte character in the *current* locale. In particular, when calling `mbrtowcs()` and passing in a count of how many bytes may be read, you can use `MB_CUR_MAX`, if you know that there are at least that many bytes left in the input source string.

Caveat Emptor: MB_CUR_MAX Is Not a Constant

On GLIBC systems, what looks like a constant—MB_CUR_MAX—isn't. This macro actually invokes a function to return the maximum number of bytes for the current locale.

That it does so makes sense. After all, a program can change from one locale to another simply by calling `setlocale()`, and the related value for the maximum number of bytes for a multibyte character might change.

What's the problem? If your program is never going to change its locale after starting up, and converting from bytes to wide characters is a significant part of what your program does, you will end up making possibly millions of function calls that all return the same value! This can become a major performance hit.[14]

To that end, it's good idea to have a separate global variable that you initialize in `main()` to the value of MB_CUR_MAX, as follows, and then use that in the rest of your program:

```
extern int myprog_mb_cur_max;                        In myprog.h
...
myprog_mb_cur_max = MB_CUR_MAX;                      In main()
...
n = mbrtowc(& wc, s, myprog_mb_cur_max, & mbs);      In use
```

15.4.3.4 Example Code: GNU `ls.c`

The following code fragment from GNU `ls` shows a number of the functions we discussed in action. It's from the function `quote_name_buf()`, whose purpose is to take a file name and quote it. As part of what it does, it replaces invalid multibyte characters with a single ?:

```
          /* If we have a multibyte sequence, copy it until we
             reach its end, replacing each non-printable multibyte
             character with a single question mark.  */
          {
            mbstate_t mbstate = { 0, };
            do
              {
                wchar_t wc;
                size_t bytes;
                int w;

                bytes = mbrtowc (&wc, p, plimit - p, &mbstate);

                if (bytes == (size_t) -1)
                  {
                    /* An invalid multibyte sequence was
                       encountered.  Skip one input byte, and
```

[14] As you might guess, we learned about this the hard way.

```
18                put a question mark.  */
19              p++;
20              *q++ = '?';
21              displayed_width += 1;
22              break;
23            }
24
25        if (bytes == (size_t) -2)
26          {
27            /* An incomplete multibyte character
28               at the end.  Replace it entirely with
29               a question mark.  */
30            p = plimit;
31            *q++ = '?';
32            displayed_width += 1;
33            break;
34          }
35
36        if (bytes == 0)
37          /* A null wide character was encountered.  */
38          bytes = 1;
39
40        w = wcwidth (wc);
41        if (w >= 0)
42          {
43            /* A printable multibyte character.
44               Keep it.  */
45            for (; bytes > 0; --bytes)
46              *q++ = *p++;
47            displayed_width += w;
48          }
49        else
50          {
51            /* An nonprintable multibyte character.
52               Replace it entirely with a question
53               mark.  */
54            p += bytes;
55            *q++ = '?';
56            displayed_width += 1;
57          }
58      }
59    while (! mbsinit (&mbstate));
```

(Line numbers are relative to the beginning of the fragment.) Line 5 initializes the `mbstate_t` object, named `mbstate`. The code runs a `do-while` loop, which lasts as long as `mbstate` is not in the initial state (lines 6–59). The loop test on line 59 uses `mbsinit()` to determine whether `mbstate` is in the initial shift state.

Line 12 does the conversion. Lines 14–23 handle the case of an invalid multibyte sequence, and lines 25–34 deal with an incomplete multibyte character.

Now that there is a valid wide character in hand, we have to check if it's actually printable! Line 40 calls `wcwidth()` to find that out, and then lines 41–57 handle things appropriately.

15.4.4 Converting Wide Characters to Bytes

As we've seen, wide characters are stored in files encoded as multibyte data. The multibyte encoded data is converted to wide characters in memory for processing, if necessary. You then need to be able to convert any new or processed wide-character data back to multibyte encoded data for output to a file or pipe. There are two main functions for that purpose:

```
#include <wchar.h>                          ISO C

size_t wcrtomb(char *s, wchar_t wc, mbstate_t *ps);
size_t wcsrtombs(char *dest, const wchar_t **src,
                 size_t len, mbstate_t *ps);
```

`wcrtomb()` converts the nonzero wide character `wc` into some number of bytes stored into the `char` array pointed to by `s`. It updates the shift state in `*ps`. The return value is the number of bytes written into `s`. If `wc` is `L'\0'`, the return value is zero. If `wc` cannot be converted, the return value is `(size_t) -1`, and `errno` is set to `EILSEQ`.

`wcsrtombs()` takes the wide-character string pointed to by `*src` and converts it to a multibyte encoded string, storing the bytes in the `char` array pointed to by `dest`. `len` gives the maximum number of bytes to write into `dest`, and `*ps` maintains the shift state. The return value is the number of bytes written into `dest` (not including any terminating `'\0'`), and `*src` is updated to point past the last wide character written. If an invalid character is encountered, the return value is `(size_t) -1`, and `errno` is set to `EILSEQ`.

As with `mbrtowc()` and `mbsrtowcs()`, there are additional use cases when one or the other of the pointer values is `NULL`; see the *wcrtomb*(3) and *wcsrtombs*(3) manpages for the details.

The following code, from the file `node.c` in `gawk` 5.3.0, converts a wide-character string into a multibyte string. The code does this one wide character at a time, instead of using `wcsrtombs()`, because `gawk` strings can include characters whose value is zero. (This is part of the "no arbitrary limits" GNU coding principle, discussed earlier in Section 1.4.4, "Things That Make a GNU Program Better," page 15.)

```
/* wstr2str --- convert a wide string back into multibyte one */

NODE *
wstr2str(NODE *n)
{
    size_t result;
    size_t length;
    wchar_t *wp;
```

```
958     mbstate_t mbs;
959     char *newval, *cp;
960
961     assert(n->valref == 1);
962     assert((n->flags & WSTRCUR) != 0);
963
964     /*
965      * Convert the wide chars in t1->wstptr back into m.b. chars.
966      * This is pretty grotty, but it's the most straightforward
967      * way to do things.
968      */
969     memset(& mbs, 0, sizeof(mbs));
970
971     length = n->wstlen;
972     emalloc(newval, char *, (length * gawk_mb_cur_max) + 1, "wstr2str");
973
974     wp = n->wstptr;
975     for (cp = newval; length > 0; length--) {
976         result = wcrtomb(cp, *wp, & mbs);
977         if (result == (size_t) -1)  /* what to do? break seems best */
978             break;
979         cp += result;
980         wp++;
981     }
982     *cp = '\0';
983
984     /* N.B. caller just created n with make_string, so this free is safe */
985     efree(n->stptr);
986     n->stptr = newval;
987     n->stlen = cp - newval;
988
989     return n;
990 }
```

The action starts on line 969, where `mbs` is initialized. Lines 971–972 allocate a new buffer to hold the converted bytes. It allocates the maximum possible number of bytes that might be needed. This avoids having to use `realloc()` in the middle of the conversion in case enough space wasn't allocated at first. The trade-off here is some amount of possibly wasted space versus code that is simpler to write and get correct. Note the use of `gawk_mb_cur_max` instead of `MB_CUR_MAX`, as discussed earlier.

Lines 974–982 do the conversion, one wide character at a time. Line 976 calls `wcrtomb()`. Lines 977–978 break out of the loop if there was a problem. Otherwise, line 979 moves the destination pointer along by the number of bytes written, and line 980 increments `wp` by one.

Line 982 terminates the new string with `'\0'`. Even though `gawk` handles strings with embedded zero bytes, it also stores string data with a final zero byte in case the string needs to be used with a standard C library routine.

Finally, lines 985–987 release the old string and store the new string and string length in `*n`.

15.4.5 Languages

Language issues are controlled by the locale. We've already seen `setlocale()` earlier in the chapter. POSIX provides an elaborate mechanism for defining the rules by which a locale works; see the GNU/Linux *locale*(5) manpage for some of the details and the POSIX standard itself for the full story.

The truth is, you really don't want to know the details. Nor should you, as an application developer, need to worry about them; it is up to the library implementors to make things work. Your job is to understand the concepts and make your code use the appropriate functions, such as `strcoll()` (see Section 15.2.3, "String Collation: `strcoll()` and `strxfrm()`," page 512).

GLIBC systems provide excellent locale support, including a multibyte-aware suite of regular expression matching routines. For example, the POSIX extended regular expression `[[:alpha:]][[:alnum:]]+` matches a letter followed by one or more letters or digits (an alphabetic character followed by one or more alphanumeric ones). The definition of which characters match these classes depends on the locale. For example, this regular expression would match the two characters 'eè', whereas the traditional Unix, ASCII-oriented regular expression `[a-zA-Z][a-A-Zz0-9]+` most likely would not. The POSIX character classes are listed in Table 15.6.

Table 15.6: POSIX regular expression character classes

Class name	Matches
`[:alnum:]`	Alphanumeric characters.
`[:alpha:]`	Alphabetic characters.
`[:blank:]`	Space and tab characters.
`[:cntrl:]`	Control characters.
`[:digit:]`	Numeric characters.
`[:graph:]`	Characters that are both printable and visible. (A newline is printable but not visible, whereas a `$` is both.)
`[:lower:]`	Lowercase alphabetic characters.
`[:print:]`	Printable characters (not control characters).
`[:punct:]`	Punctuation characters (not letters, digits, control characters, or space characters).
`[:space:]`	Space characters (such as space, tab, newline, and so on).
`[:upper:]`	Uppercase alphabetic characters.
`[:xdigit:]`	Characters from the set `abcdefABCDEF0123456789`.

15.4.6 Conclusion

The world has become a "global village," and software authors and vendors can't afford to be parochial. It therefore pays to be aware of internationalization issues and character set issues, and to make your code internationalized and localizable.

15.5 Suggested Reading

1. *C: A Reference Manual*, 5th ed., by Samuel P. Harbison III and Guy L. Steele, Jr. Pearson, 2002. ISBN-13: 978-0-13-089592-9.

   We have mentioned this book before. It provides a concise and comprehensible description of the evolution and use of the multibyte and wide-character facilities in the C standard library. This is particularly valuable on systems supporting C99 and newer, because the library was significantly enhanced for the 1999 C standard.

2. *GNU gettext tools*, by Ulrich Drepper, Jim Meyering, François Pinard, and Bruno Haible. This is the manual for GNU `gettext`. On a GNU/Linux system, you can see the local copy with '`info gettext`'. The manual may be found online at `https://www.gnu.org/software/gettext/manual/`. A printable PDF version is available from that site, as well.

15.6 Summary

- Program internationalization and localization fall under the general heading of *native language support*. *i18n*, *l10n*, and *NLS* are popular acronyms. The central concept is the *locale*, which customizes the character set, date, time, and monetary and numeric information for the current language and country.
- Locale awareness must be enabled with `setlocale()`. Different locale categories provide access to the different kinds of locale information. Locale-unaware programs act as if they were in the `"C"` locale, which produces results typical of Unix systems before NLS: seven-bit ASCII, English names for months and days, and so on. The `"POSIX"` locale is equivalent to the `"C"` one.
- Locale-aware string comparisons are done with `strcoll()` or with the combination of `strxfrm()` and `strcmp()`. Library facilities provide access to locale information (`localeconv()` and `nl_langinfo()`) as well as locale-specific information formatting (`strfmon()`, `strftime()`, and `printf()`).
- The flip side of retrieving locale-related information is producing messages in the local language. The System V `catgets()` design, while standardized by POSIX, is difficult

to use and not recommended.[15] Instead, GNU `gettext` implements and extends the original Solaris design, and the associated suites of routines and commands are included in POSIX.

- With `gettext()`, the original English message string acts as a key into a binary translation file from which to retrieve the string's translation. Each application specifies a unique text domain so that `gettext()` can find the correct translation file (known as a "message catalog"). The text domain is set with `textdomain()`. For testing, or as otherwise needed, the location for message catalogs can be changed with `bindtextdomain()`. The output character set for a text domain may be set with `bind_textdomain_codeset()`.
- Along with `gettext()`, variants provide access to translations in different text domains or different locale categories. Additionally, the `ngettext()` function and its variants enable correct plural translations without overburdening the developer. The positional specifier within `printf()` format specifiers enables translation of format strings where arguments need to be printed in a different order from the one in which they're provided.
- In practice, GNU programs use the `gettext.h` header file and `_()` and `N_()` macros for marking translatable strings in their source files. This practice keeps program source code readable and maintainable while still providing the benefits of i18n and l10n.
- GNU `gettext` provides numerous tools for the creation and management of translation databases (portable object files) and their binary equivalents (message object files).
- In order to handle languages with hundreds or thousands of characters, character sets that require more than one byte per character have come into use. The world has largely moved to the use of Unicode as the universal character set, but others exist and remain in use.
- Such large character sets use a multibyte encoding for storage in files, which saves space, but at the cost of processing time when reading and writing data. Unicode has the advantage of being a strict superset of ASCII. It's UTF-8 encoding is the most popular, and it has the advantage that if a few bytes in a character are lost, it's possible to find the beginning of subsequent characters. GNU/Linux stores file names in directory entries using UTF-8.
- ISO C standardizes the `wchar_t` type for holding wide characters, and the `L` and `l` prefixes for marking wide characters in source code. The "restartable" conversion routines `mbrtowc()` and `mbsrtowcs()` convert multibyte characters/strings to wide characters/strings. The routines `wcrtomb()` and `wcsrtombs()` perform the opposite conversions. All of them use an `mbstate_t` to hold the shift state of an ongoing conversion.

---

[15] GNU/Linux supports it, but only for compatibility.

Exercises

1. What is the default locale on your system?
2. Look at the *locale*(1) manpage if you have it. How many locales are there if you count them with '`locale -a | wc -l`'?
3. Experiment with `ch-i18n-compare.c`, `ch-i18n-lconv.c`, `ch-i18n-strfmon.c`, `ch-i18n-quoteflag.c`, and `ch-i18n-times.c` in different locales. What is the most "unusual" locale you can find, and why?
4. Take one of your programs. Internationalize it to use GNU `gettext`. Try to find someone who speaks another language to translate the messages for you. Compile the translation, and test it by using `bindtextdomain()`. What was your translator's reaction upon seeing the translations in use?

Chapter 16

Extended Interfaces

This chapter describes several extended APIs. The APIs here are similar in nature to those described earlier in the book or provide additional facilities. Some of them could not be discussed easily until after the prerequisite topics were covered.

The presentation order here parallels the order of the chapters in the first half of the book. The topics are not otherwise related to each other. We cover the following topics: dynamically allocating aligned memory; file locking; a number of calls that work with subsecond time values; and a more advanced suite of functions for storing and retrieving arbitrary data values. Unless stated otherwise, all the APIs in this chapter are included in the POSIX standard.

16.1 Allocating Aligned Memory: `posix_memalign()` and `memalign()`

For most tasks, the standard allocation routines—`malloc()`, `realloc()`, and so on—are fine. Occasionally, though, you may need memory that is *aligned* a certain way. In other words, the address of the first allocated byte is a multiple of some number. (For example, on some systems, memory copies are significantly faster into and out of word-aligned buffers.) Two functions offer this service:

```
#include <stdlib.h>

int posix_memalign(void **memptr, size_t alignment, size_t size);   POSIX ADV
void *memalign(size_t boundary, size_t size);                      Common
```

`posix_memalign()` is a newer function; it's part of yet another optional extension, the "Advisory Information" (ADV) extension. The function works differently from most other allocation Linux APIs. It does not return `-1` when there's a problem. Rather, the return value is `0` on success *or an* `errno` *value on failure*. The arguments are as follows:

`void **memptr`
: A pointer to a `void *` variable. The pointed-to variable will have the address of the allocated storage placed into it.

`size_t alignment`
: The required alignment. It must be a multiple of `sizeof(void *)` and a power of two.

`size_t size`
: The number of bytes to allocate.

The storage allocated by `posix_memalign()` can be modified with `realloc()` and released with `free()`.

`memalign()` is a nonstandard but widely available function that works similarly. The return value is `NULL` on failure or the requested storage on success, with `boundary` (a power of 2) indicating the alignment and `size` indicating the requested amount of memory.

Traditionally, storage allocated with `memalign()` could *not* be released with `free()`, since `memalign()` would allocate storage with `malloc()` and return a pointer to a suitably aligned byte somewhere within that storage. The GLIBC version does not have this problem. Of the two, you should use `posix_memalign()` if you have it.

16.2 Locking Files

Modern Unix systems, including GNU/Linux, allow you to lock part or all of a file for reading and writing. Like many parts of the Unix API that developed after V7, there are multiple, conflicting ways to do file locking. This section covers the possibilities.

16.2.1 File Locking Concepts

Just as the lock in your front door prevents unwanted entry into your home, a *lock* on a file prevents access to data within the file. File locking was added to Unix after the development of V7 (from which all modern Unix systems are descended), and thus for a while, multiple and conflicting file locking mechanisms were available and in use on different Unix systems. Both BSD Unix and System V had their own incompatible locking calls. Eventually, POSIX formalized the System V way of doing file locks. Fortunately, the names of the calls were different between System V and BSD, so GNU/Linux, in an effort to please everyone, supports both kinds of locks.

Table 16.1 summarizes the different kind of locks.

There are multiple aspects to locking, as follows:

Record locking
: A record lock is a lock on a portion of the file. Since Unix files are just byte streams, it would be more correct to use the term *range lock* since the lock is on a range of bytes. Nevertheless, the term *record lock* is in common use.

Whole-file locking
: A whole-file lock, as the name implies, locks the entire file, even if its size changes while the lock is held. The BSD interface provides only whole-file locking. To lock the whole

Table 16.1: File locking functions

Source	Function	Record	Whole file	R/W	Advisory	Mandatory
BSD	`flock()`		✓	✓	✓	
POSIX	`fcntl()`	✓	✓	✓	✓	No longer
POSIX	`lockf()`	✓	✓	✓	✓	No longer

file using the POSIX interface, specify a length of zero. This is treated specially to mean "the entire file."

Read locking
A read lock prevents writing on the area being read. There may be multiple read locks on a file, and even on the same region of a file, without them interfering with each other, since data is only being accessed and not changed.

Write locking
A write lock provides exclusive access to the area being written. If that area is blocked with a read lock, the attempt to acquire a write lock either blocks or fails, depending on the type of lock request. Once a write lock has been acquired, an attempt to acquire a read lock fails.

Advisory locking
An advisory lock closely matches your front door lock. It's been said that "locks keep honest people honest," meaning that if someone *really* wishes to break into your house, they will probably find a way to do so, despite the lock in your front door. So too with an advisory lock; it works only when everyone attempting to access the locked file first attempts to acquire the lock. However, it's possible for a program to completely ignore any advisory locks and do what it pleases with the file (as long as the file permissions allow it, of course).

Mandatory locking
A mandatory lock is a stronger form of lock: when a mandatory lock is in place, no other process can access the locked file. Any process that attempts to ignore the lock either blocks until the lock becomes available or will have its operation fail.

Advisory locking is adequate for cooperating programs that share a private file, when no other application is expected to use the file (for example, the shared score file for the multiuser game program, that we mentioned back in Section 11.1.2, "Setuid and Setgid Bits," page 384). Mandatory locking can be advisable for situations in which avoiding conflicting file use is critical, such as in commercial database systems.

POSIX standardizes only advisory locking. Mandatory locking is available on a number of commercial Unix systems, but the details vary. It used to be available by default on GNU/Linux, but it has since been been removed. We discuss this briefly later on in this section. The "Rationale" section of the entry for `fcntl()` in the POSIX standard provides several reasons why mandatory locking was not standardized; see there if you're interested.

16.2.2 POSIX Locking: `fcntl()` and `lockf()`

The `fcntl()` (file control) system call is used for file locking. (Other uses for `fcntl()` were described in Section 9.4.3, "Managing File Attributes: `fcntl()`," page 315.) It is declared as follows:

```
#include <unistd.h>                                    POSIX
#include <fcntl.h>
```

```
int fcntl(int fd, int cmd);                          Not relevant for file locking
int fcntl(int fd, int cmd, long arg);                Not relevant for file locking
int fcntl(int fd, int cmd, struct flock *lock);
```

The arguments are as follows:

`fd`
: The file descriptor for the open file.

`cmd`
: One of the symbolic constants defined in `<fcntl.h>`. These are described in more detail later in the chapter.

`lock`
: A pointer to a `struct flock` describing the desired lock.

16.2.2.1 Describing a Lock

Before looking at how to get a lock, let's examine how to describe a lock to the operating system. You do so with the `struct flock` structure, which describes the byte range to be locked and the kind of lock being requested. The POSIX standard states that a `struct flock` contains "at least" certain members. This allows implementations to provide additional structure members, if so desired. From the *fcntl*(3) manpage, slightly edited:

```
struct flock {
    ...
    short l_type;        Type of lock: F_RDLCK, F_WRLCK, F_UNLCK
    short l_whence;      How to interpret l_start: SEEK_SET, SEEK_CUR, SEEK_END
    off_t l_start;       Starting offset for lock
    off_t l_len;         Number of bytes to lock; 0 means from start to end-of-file
    pid_t l_pid;         PID of process blocking our lock (F_GETLK and F_OFD_GETLK)
    ...
};
```

The `l_start` field is the starting byte offset for the lock. `l_len` is the length of the byte range—that is, the total number of bytes to lock. `l_whence` specifies the point in the file that `l_start` is relative to; the values are the same as for the `whence` argument to `lseek()` (see Section 4.5, "Random Access: Moving Around within a File," page 96), hence the name for the field. The structure is thus self-contained: the `l_start` offset and `l_whence` value are *not* related to the current file offset for reading and writing. Some example code might look like this:

```
struct employee { /* whatever */ };          /* Describe an employee */
struct flock lock;                            /* Lock structure */
...
/* Lock sixth struct employee */
lock.l_whence = SEEK_SET;                     /* Absolute position */
lock.l_start = 5 * sizeof(struct employee);   /* Start of 6th structure */
lock.l_len = sizeof(struct employee);         /* Lock one record */
```

Using SEEK_CUR or SEEK_END, you can lock ranges relative to the current position in the file, or relative to the end of the file, respectively. For these two cases, l_start may be negative, as long as the absolute starting position is not less than zero. Thus, to lock the last record in a file:

```
/* Lock last struct employee */
lock.l_whence = SEEK_END;                          /* Relative to EOF */
lock.l_start = -1 * sizeof(struct employee);       /* Start of last structure */
lock.l_len = sizeof(struct employee);              /* Lock one record */
```

Setting l_len to 0 is a special case. It means lock the file from the starting position indicated by l_start and l_whence through the end of the file. This includes any positions past the end of the file, as well. (In other words, if the file grows while the lock is held, the lock is extended so that it continues to cover the entire file.) Thus, locking the entire file is a degenerate case of locking a single record:

```
lock.l_whence = SEEK_SET;                          /* Absolute position */
lock.l_start = 0;                                  /* Start of file */
lock.l_len = 0;                                    /* Through end of file */
```

The 2024 POSIX standard has this to say about l_len:

> If l_len is positive, the area affected shall start at l_start and end at l_start+l_len-1. If l_len is negative, the area affected shall start at l_start+l_len and end at l_start-1. Locks may start and extend beyond the current end of a file, but shall not extend before the beginning of the file. A lock shall be set to extend to the largest possible value of the file offset for that file by setting l_len to 0. If such a lock also has l_start set to 0 and l_whence is set to SEEK_SET, the whole file shall be locked.

Now that we know how to describe *where* in the file to lock, we can describe the *type* of the lock with l_type. The possible values are as follows:

F_RDLCK — A read lock. The file must have been opened for reading to apply a read lock.

F_WRLCK — A write lock. The file must have been opened for writing to apply a write lock.

F_UNLCK — Release a previously held lock.

Thus, the complete specification of a lock involves setting a total of four fields in the struct flock structure: three to specify the byte range and the fourth to describe the desired lock type.

The F_UNLCK value for l_type releases locks. In general, it's easiest to release exactly the same locks that you acquired earlier, but it is possible to "split" a lock by releasing a range of bytes within a larger, previously locked range. For example:

```
struct employee { /* whatever */ };                /* Describe an employee */
struct flock lock;                                 /* Lock structure */
...
```

```
/* Lock struct employees 6-8 */
lock.l_whence = SEEK_SET;                     /* Absolute position */
lock.l_start = 5 * sizeof(struct employee);   /* Start of 6th structure */
lock.l_len = sizeof(struct employee) * 3;     /* Lock three records */
... obtain lock (see next section) ...
/* Release record 7: this splits the previous lock into two: */
lock.l_whence = SEEK_SET;                     /* Absolute position */
lock.l_start = 6 * sizeof(struct employee);   /* Start of 7th structure */
lock.l_len = sizeof(struct employee) * 1;     /* Unlock one record */
... release lock (see next section) ...
```

16.2.2.2 Obtaining and Releasing Process-Based Locks

Once the `struct flock` has been filled in, the next step is to request the lock. This step is done with an appropriate value for the `cmd` argument to `fcntl()`:

`F_GETLK`	Inquire if it's possible to obtain a lock.
`F_SETLK`	Obtain or release a lock.
`F_SETLKW`	Obtain a lock, waiting until it's available.

The `F_GETLK` command is the "Mother may I?" command. It inquires whether the lock described by the `struct flock` is available. If it is, the lock is *not* placed; instead, the operating system changes the `l_type` field to `F_UNLCK`. The other fields are left unchanged.

If the lock is not available, then the operating system fills in the various fields with information describing an already held lock that blocks the requested lock from being obtained. In this case, `l_pid` contains the PID of the process holding the described lock.[1] There's not a lot to be done if the lock is being held, other than to wait awhile and try again to obtain the lock, or print an error message and give up.

The `F_SETLK` command attempts to acquire the specified lock. If `fcntl()` returns `0`, then the lock has been successfully acquired. If it returns `-1`, then another process holds a conflicting lock. In this case, `errno` is set to either `EAGAIN` (try again later) or `EACCES` (access denied). Both values are possible, to cater to historical systems.

The `F_SETLKW` command also attempts to acquire the specified lock. It differs from `F_SETLK` in that it will wait until the lock becomes available.

Once you've chosen the appropriate value for the `cmd` argument, pass it as the second argument to `fcntl()`, with a pointer to a filled-in `struct flock` as the third argument:

```
struct flock lock;
int fd;
... open file, fill in struct flock ...
if (fcntl(fd, F_SETLK, & lock) < 0) {
    /* Could not acquire lock, attempt to recover */
}
```

---

[1] The GNU/Linux *fcntl*(3) manpage points out that this may not be enough information; the process could be residing on another machine! There are other issues with locks held across a network; in general, using locks on filesystems mounted from remote computers is not a good idea.

The `lockf()` function[2] provides an alternative way to acquire a lock *at the current file position*:

```
#include <sys/file.h>                                POSIX XSI

int lockf(int fd, int cmd, off_t len);
```

The file descriptor, `fd`, must have been opened for writing. `len` specifies the number of bytes to lock: from the current position (call it `pos`) to `pos+len` bytes if `len` is positive, or from `pos-len` to `pos-1` if `len` is negative. The commands are as follows:

`F_LOCK` Sets an exclusive lock on the range. The call blocks until the lock becomes available.

`F_TLOCK` Tries the lock. This is like `F_LOCK`, but if the lock isn't available, `F_TLOCK` returns an error.

`F_ULOCK` Unlocks the indicated section. This can cause lock splitting, as described earlier.

`F_TEST` Sees if the lock is available. If it is, it returns `0` and acquires the lock. Otherwise, it returns `-1` and sets `errno` to `EACCES`.

The return value is `0` on success and `-1` on error, with `errno` set appropriately. Possible error returns include:

`EAGAIN`	The file is locked, for `F_TLOCK` or `F_TEST`.
`EDEADLK`	For `F_TLOCK`, this operation would cause a deadlock.
`ENOLCK`	The operating system is unable to allocate a lock.

The combination of `F_TLOCK` and `EDEADLK` is useful: if you know that there can never be potential for deadlock, then use `F_LOCK`. Otherwise, it pays to be safe and use `F_TLOCK`. If the lock is available, you'll get it, but if it's not, you have a chance to recover instead of blocking, possibly forever, waiting for the lock.

When you're done with a lock, you should release it. With `fcntl()`, take the original `struct lock` used to acquire the lock and change the `l_type` field to `F_UNLCK`. Then use `F_SETLK` as the `cmd` argument:

```
lock.l_whence = ... ;        /* As before */
lock.l_start = ... ;         /* As before */
lock.l_len = ... ;           /* As before */
lock.l_type = F_UNLCK;        /* Unlock */
if (fcntl(fd, F_SETLK, & lock) < 0) {
    /* handle error */
}
/* Lock has been released */
```

Code using `lockf()` is a bit simpler. For brevity, we've omitted the error checking:

```
off_t curpos, len;
```

[2]On GNU/Linux, `lockf()` is implemented as a "wrapper" around `fcntl()`.

```
curpos = lseek(fd, (off_t) 0, SEEK_CUR);       Retrieve current position
len = ... ;                                    Set correct number of bytes to lock

lockf(fd, F_LOCK, len);                        Acquire lock
... use locked area here ...
lseek(fd, curpos, SEEK_SET);                   Return to position of lock

lockf(fd, F_ULOCK, len);                       Unlock file
```

If you don't explicitly release a lock, the operating system will do it for you in two cases. The first is when the process exits (either by `main()` returning or by the `exit()` function, which was covered in Section 9.1.5.1, "Defining Process Exit Status," page 289). The other case is when you call `close()` on the file descriptor—more on this in the next section.

16.2.2.3 Observing Locking Caveats

There are several caveats to be aware of when doing file locking:

- As described previously, advisory locking is just that. An uncooperative process can do anything it wants behind the back (so to speak) of processes that are doing locking.
- These calls should *not* be used in conjunction with the `<stdio.h>` library. This library does its own buffering, and while you can retrieve the underlying file descriptor with `fileno()`, the actual position in the file may not be where you think it is. In general, the Standard I/O library doesn't understand file locks.[3]
- Bear in mind that locks are *not* inherited by child processes after a fork but that they *do* remain in place after an exec.
- A `close()` of *any* file descriptor open on the file removes *all* of the process's locks on a file, even if other file descriptors remain open on it.

That `close()` works this way is unfortunate, but because this is how `fcntl()` locking was originally implemented, POSIX standardizes it. Making this behavior the standard avoids breaking existing Unix code.

Because of the behavior of `fork()`, exec, and `close()`, these locks are referred to as *process-based*. In other words, the lock is associated with the process and not with the file descriptor.

16.2.2.4 Open File Descriptor–Based Locks

To avoid the problems with process-based locks described in the previous section, GNU/Linux introduced open file descriptor–based locks. The 2024 POSIX standard now includes them as well, so they no longer need be considered specific to GNU/Linux.

---

[3]There are several functions—`flockfile()`, `ftrylockfile()`, and `funlockfile()`—for use with `FILE *` objects. These provide locks *on the* `FILE` *objects themselves*, not on the underlying file. They are for use in threaded programs, to keep multiple threads from trying simultaneously to use the same open `FILE` pointer.

You obtain and release file descriptor–based locks with the same `struct flock` described earlier. However, the values for the `cmd` argument passed to `fcntl()` are different:

`F_OFD_GETLK`	Inquire if it's possible to obtain a lock.
`F_OFD_SETLK`	Obtain or release a lock.
`F_OFD_SETLKW`	Obtain a lock, waiting until it's available.

Open file descriptor locks are also advisory locks, but they differ from process-based locks as follows:

- You must set the `l_pid` field to zero.
- Locks are inherited across `fork()` and exec.
- Locks are propagated to new file descriptors via `dup()`.
- Locks are released only upon the *last* close of a file descriptor opened on the file.
- The Linux kernel does *not* do deadlock detection for open file descriptor locks, something it *does* do for process-based locks.

A few more points: First, locks obtained via different file descriptors, such as by calling `open()` twice on the same file, can conflict with each other. Second, these locks can also conflict with process-based locks. Third, it's a bad idea to try to lock a file descriptor inherited from a parent, especially as the Linux kernel does not do deadlock detection.

16.2.3 BSD Locking: `flock()`

4.2 BSD Unix introduced its own file locking mechanism, `flock()`.[4] It is declared as follows:

```
#include <sys/file.h>                                    Common

int flock(int fd, int operation);
```

The file descriptor `fd` represents the open file. These are the operations:

`LOCK_SH`	Create a shared lock. There can be multiple shared locks.
`LOCK_EX`	Create an exclusive lock. There can be only one such lock.
`LOCK_UN`	Remove the previous lock.
`LOCK_NB`	When bitwise-OR'd with `LOCK_SH` or `LOCK_EX`, avoid blocking if the lock isn't available.

By default, the lock requests will block (not return) if a competing lock exists. Once the competing lock is removed and the requested lock is obtained, the call returns. (This implies that, by default, there is potential for deadlock.) To attempt to obtain a lock without blocking, perform a bitwise-OR of `LOCK_NB` with one of the other values for `operation`.

[4] It is fortunate that `flock()` is a different name from `lockf()`, since the semantics are different. It is also terribly confusing. Keep your manual handy.

The salient points about `flock()` are as follows:

- `flock()` locking is also advisory locking; a program that does no locking can come in and blast, with no errors, a file locked with `flock()`.
- The whole file is locked. There is no mechanism for locking or unlocking just a part of the file.
- How the file was opened has no effect on the type of lock that may be placed. (Compare this to `fcntl()`, whereby the file must have been opened for reading for a read lock, or opened for writing for a write lock.)
- Multiple file descriptors open on the same file share the lock. Any one of them can be used to remove the lock. Unlike `fcntl()`'s process-based locks, when there is no explicit unlock, the lock is not removed until *all* open file descriptors for the file have been closed.
- Only one `flock()` lock can be held by a process on a file; calling `flock()` successively with two different lock types changes the lock to the new type.
- On GNU/Linux systems, `flock()` locks are *completely independent* of `fcntl()` locks. Many commercial Unix systems implement `flock()` as a "wrapper" on top of `fcntl()`, but the semantics are not the same.

We don't recommend using `flock()` in new programs, because the semantics are not as flexible and because the call is not standardized by POSIX. Support for it in GNU/Linux is primarily for compatibility with software written for older BSD Unix systems.

NOTE

The GNU/Linux *flock*(2) manpage explains that on NFS filesystems, `flock()` locks are emulated using `fcntl()`. As a result, a remotely mounted NFS file must be opened for writing in order to obtain a write lock with `flock()`.

16.2.4 Mandatory Locking

Most commercial Unix systems support mandatory file locking, in addition to advisory file locking. Mandatory locking works only with `fcntl()` locks. Mandatory locking for a file is controlled by the file's permission settings—in particular, by addition of the setgid bit to a file with the `chmod` command:

```
$ echo hello, world > myfile                                    Create file
$ ls -l myfile                                                  Show permissions
-rw-r--r--    1 arnold    devel          13 Apr  3 17:11 myfile
$ chmod g+s myfile                                              Add setgid bit
$ ls -l myfile                                                  Show new permissions
-rw-r-Sr--    1 arnold    devel          13 Apr  3 17:11 myfile
```

The group execute bit should be left turned off. The `S` shows that the setgid bit is turned on but that execute permission isn't; an `s` would be used if both were on.

The combination of setgid on and group execute off is generally meaningless. For this reason, it was chosen by the System V developers to mean "enforce mandatory locking." And indeed, adding this bit is enough to cause a commercial Unix system, such as Solaris, to enforce file locks.

On GNU/Linux systems, the story used to be a little different. The setgid bit had to be applied to a file for mandatory locking, but that alone was not enough. The filesystem containing the file also had to be mounted with the `mand` option to the `mount` command (see Section 8.1.3, "Mounting Filesystems: `mount`," page 225).

However, beginning with the Linux 4.5 kernel, mandatory locking must be configured into the kernel when it's built, using the `CONFIG_MANDATORY_FILE_LOCKING` configuration option. Otherwise, mounting a filesystem with the `mand` option has no effect. From version 5.15 and later of the Linux kernel, mandatory locking is no longer supported at all.

Because mandatory file locking is no longer available, we don't demonstrate it here. The program `ch-extended-mandlock.c` in the book's GitHub code repository demonstrates mandatory file locking. Look there if you're interested.

16.3 More Precise Times

The `time()` system call and `time_t` type represent times in seconds since the Epoch format. A *resolution* of one second really isn't enough; today's machines are fast, and it's often useful to distinguish subsecond time intervals. Starting with 4.2 BSD, Berkeley Unix introduced a series of system calls that make it possible to retrieve and use subsecond times. These calls are available on all modern Unix systems, including GNU/Linux.

16.3.1 Microsecond Times: `gettimeofday()`

The first task is to retrieve the time of day:

```
#include <sys/time.h>                                    Common

int gettimeofday(struct timeval *tv, void *tz);     Old POSIX definition, not GLIBC's
```

`gettimeofday()` gets the time of day.[5] The return value is `0` on success, `-1` for an error. The arguments are as follows:

`struct timeval *tv`
: This argument is a pointer to a `struct timeval`, described shortly, into which the system places the current time.

[5] The *gettimeofday*(2) manpage documents a corresponding `settimeofday()` function, for use by the superuser (`root`) to set the time of day for the whole system.

`void *tz`
: This argument is no longer used; thus, it's of type `void *` and you should always pass `NULL` for it. (The manpage describes what it used to be and then proceeds to state that it's obsolete. Read it if you're interested in the details.)

The time is represented by a `struct timeval`:

```
struct timeval {
    time_t       tv_sec;      /* seconds */
    suseconds_t tv_usec;      /* microseconds */
};
```

The `tv_sec` value represents seconds since the Epoch; `tv_usec` is the number of microseconds within the second. (Apparently an `suseconds_t` is for holding subsecond values. It's not clear where the 'b' disappeared to.)

GLIBC provides a number of macros for working with objects of type `struct timeval`:

```
#define timerisset(tvp) ((tvp)->tv_sec || (tvp)->tv_usec)

#define timercmp(tvp, uvp, cmp) \
        ((tvp)->tv_sec cmp (uvp)->tv_sec || \
        (tvp)->tv_sec == (uvp)->tv_sec && \
        (tvp)->tv_usec cmp (uvp)->tv_usec)

#define timerclear(tvp) ((tvp)->tv_sec = (tvp)->tv_usec = 0)
```

These macros work on `struct timeval *` values—that is, pointers to structures—and their use should be obvious both from their names and the code. The `timercmp()` macro is particularly interesting; the third argument is a comparison operator to indicate the kind of comparison. For example, consider the determination of whether one `struct timeval` is less than another:

```
struct timeval t1, t2;
...
if (timercmp(& t1, & t2, <))
    /* t1 is less than t2 */
```

The macro expands to:

```
((& t1)->tv_sec < (& t2)->tv_sec || \
 (& t1)->tv_sec == (& t2)->tv_sec && \
 (& t1)->tv_usec < (& t2)->tv_usec)
```

This says, "if `t1.tv_sec` is less than `t2.tv_sec`, OR if they are equal and `t1.tv_usec` is less than `t2.tv_usec`, then ..."

Two additional macros let you add and subtract `struct timeval` values:

```
#include <sys/time.h>                         GLIBC

void timeradd(struct timeval *a, struct timeval *b,      res = a + b
              struct timeval *res);
```

```
void timersub(struct timeval *a, struct timeval *b,       res = a - b
              struct timeval *res);
```

These macros arrange things such that '`0 <= res->tv_usec <= 999999`'.

See Section 5.6.4, "Changing Timestamps: `utime()` and Successors," page 148, for a discussion of the different data structures and system calls used to return time of day values, and how they have evolved.

As stated earlier, `gettimeofday()` was introduced in 4.2 BSD over 40 years ago. Although POSIX removed it from the 2024 standard, it is unlikely that it will go away anytime soon.

16.3.2 Nanosecond Times: `clock_gettime()`

The finest time resolution currently available is in nanoseconds. To get the current time, including nanoseconds within the current second, use `clock_gettime()`:

```
#include <time.h>                          POSIX

int clock_gettime(clockid_t clockid, struct timespec *tp);
```

The parameters are:

`clockid_t clockid`
: The identifier of the particular system clock to get the time from. Particularly on GNU/Linux, there are many. The only one defined by POSIX, which is the one we want, is `CLOCK_REALTIME`. (See *clock_gettime*(2) for the others.)

`struct timespec *tp`
: A pointer to a `struct timespec` that will be filled in by the system. This structure is presented later, in Section 16.3.4, "More Exact Pauses: `nanosleep()`," page 573.

As usual, the return value is `0` upon success or `-1` with `errno` indicating the error. Here is a small demonstration program:

```
/* ch-extended-nstime.c --- demonstrate nanosecond clock resolution */

#include <stdio.h>
#include <errno.h>
#include <stdlib.h>
#include <string.h>
#include <time.h>

int
main(int argc, char **argv)
{
    struct timespec now;
    struct tm *the_time;
    char buf[BUFSIZ];
```

```
    if (clock_gettime(CLOCK_REALTIME, & now) < 0) {
        fprintf(stderr, "%s: clock_gettime failed: %s\n",
                argv[0], strerror(errno));
        exit(EXIT_FAILURE);
    }

    the_time = localtime(& now.tv_sec);

    strftime(buf, sizeof buf, "%c", the_time);
    printf("It is now: %s and %ld nanoseconds\n", buf, now.tv_nsec);

    return EXIT_SUCCESS;
}
```

And a sample run:

```
$ ch-extended-nstime
It is now: Tue May 27 16:25:42 2025 and 279958485 nanoseconds
```

16.3.3 Interval Timers: `setitimer()` and `getitimer()`

The `alarm()` function (see Section 10.8.1, "Alarm Clocks: `sleep()`, `alarm()`, and `SIGALRM`," page 363) arranges to send `SIGALRM` after the given number of seconds has passed. Its smallest resolution is one second. Here, too, 4.2 BSD introduced a function and three different timers that accept subsecond times.

An *interval timer* is like a repeating alarm clock. You set the first time it should "go off," as well as how frequently after that the timer should repeat. Both of these values use `struct timeval` objects; that is, they (potentially) have microsecond resolution. The timer "goes off" by delivering a signal; thus, you have to install a signal handler for the timer, preferably before setting the timer itself.

Three different timers exist, as described in Table 16.2.

The use of the first timer, `ITIMER_REAL`, is straightforward. The timer runs down in real time, sending `SIGALRM` after the given amount of time has passed. Because `SIGALRM` is sent, you cannot mix calls to `setitimer()` with calls to `alarm()` (the latter is often implemented using the former), and mixing them with calls to `sleep()` is also dangerous; see Section 10.8.1, "Alarm Clocks: `sleep()`, `alarm()`, and `SIGALRM`," page 363.

The second timer, `ITIMER_VIRTUAL`, is also fairly straightforward. It runs down when the process is running, but only in user-level (application) code. If a process is blocked doing I/O, such as to a disk or, more importantly, to a terminal, the timer is suspended.

Table 16.2: Interval timers

Timer	Signal	Function
`ITIMER_REAL`	`SIGALRM`	Runs in real time.
`ITIMER_VIRTUAL`	`SIGVTALRM`	Runs when a process is executing in user mode.
`ITIMER_PROF`	`SIGPROF`	Runs when a process is in either user or system mode.

The third timer, `ITIMER_PROF`, is more specialized. It runs down whenever the process is running, even if the operating system is doing something on behalf of the process (such as I/O). This is useful, for example, for interpreters that wish to statistically profile the execution of an interpreted program. By setting both `ITIMER_VIRTUAL` and `ITIMER_PROF` to identical intervals and computing the difference between the times when the two timers go off, an interpreter can tell how much time it's spending in system calls on behalf of the executing interpreted program.[6] (As stated, this is quite specialized.) The two system calls are:

```
#include <sys/time.h>                                          Common

int getitimer(int which, struct itimerval *value);
int setitimer(int which, const struct itimerval *value,
                         struct itimerval *ovalue);
```

The `which` argument is one of the symbolic constants listed earlier naming a timer. `getitimer()` fills in the `struct itimerval` pointed to by `value` with the given timer's current settings. `setitimer()` sets the given timer with the value in `value`. If `ovalue` is provided, the function fills it in with the timer's current value. Use an `ovalue` of `NULL` if you don't care about the current value. Both functions return `0` on success or `-1` on error.

A `struct itimerval` consists of two `struct timeval` members:

```
struct itimerval {
   struct timeval it_interval; /* next value */
   struct timeval it_value;    /* current value */
};
```

Application programs should not expect timers to be exact to the microsecond. The *getitimer*(2) manpage provides this explanation:

> Timers will never expire before the requested time, but may expire some (short) time afterward, which depends on the system timer resolution and on the system load; see *time*(7). ... If the timer expires while the process is active (always true for `ITIMER_VIRTUAL`), the signal will be delivered immediately when generated.

Of the three timers, `ITIMER_REAL` seems most useful. The following program, `ch-extended-timers.c`, shows how to read data from a terminal, but with a *timeout* so that the program won't hang forever waiting for input:

```
/* ch-extended-timers.c ---- demonstrate interval timers */

#include <stdio.h>
#include <assert.h>
#include <signal.h>
#include <stdlib.h>
#include <unistd.h>
#include <sys/time.h>
```

[6]Doing profiling correctly is nontrivial; if you're thinking about writing an interpreter, it pays to do your research first.

```
9
10 /* handler --- handle SIGALRM */
11
12 void
13 handler(int signo)
14 {
15     static const char msg[] = "\n*** Timer expired, you lose ***\n";
16
17     assert(signo == SIGALRM);
18
19     ssize_t junk = write(2, msg, sizeof(msg) - 1);
20     exit(EXIT_FAILURE);
21 }
22
23 /* main --- set up timer, read data with timeout */
24
25 int
26 main(void)
27 {
28     struct itimerval tval;
29     char string[BUFSIZ];
30
31     timerclear(& tval.it_interval); /* zero interval means no reset of timer */
32     timerclear(& tval.it_value);
33
34     tval.it_value.tv_sec = 10;  /* 10 second timeout */
35
36     (void) signal(SIGALRM, handler);
37
38     printf("You have ten seconds to enter\n");
39     printf("your name, rank, and serial number: ");
40
41     (void) setitimer(ITIMER_REAL, & tval, NULL);
42     if (fgets(string, sizeof string, stdin) != NULL) {
43         (void) setitimer(ITIMER_REAL, NULL, NULL);  /* turn off timer */
44         /* process rest of data, diagnostic print for illustration */
45         printf("I'm glad you are being cooperative.\n");
46     } else
47         printf("\nEOF, eh?  We won't give up so easily!\n");
48
49     exit(EXIT_SUCCESS);
50 }
```

Lines 12–21 are the signal handler for `SIGALRM`; the `assert()` call makes sure that the signal handler was set up properly. The body of the handler prints a message and exits, but it could do anything appropriate for a larger-scale program. (Here too, the `junk` variable lets us avoid a compiler warning.)

In the main program, lines 31–32 clear out the two `struct timeval` members of the `struct itimerval` structure, `tval`. Then line 34 sets the timeout to 10 seconds. Having `tval.it_interval` set to `0` means there is no repeated alarm; it goes off only once. Line 36 sets the signal handler, and lines 38–39 print the prompt.

Line 41 sets the timer, and lines 42–47 print appropriate messages based on the user's action. A real program would do its work at this point. What's important to note is line 43, which cancels the timer because valid data was entered.

NOTE

There is a deliberate race condition between lines 42 and 43. The whole point is that if the user doesn't enter a line within the timer's expiration period, the signal will be delivered and the signal handler will print the "you lose" message.

Here are three successive runs of the program:

```
$ ch-extended-timers                              First run, enter nothing
You have ten seconds to enter
your name, rank, and serial number:
*** Timer expired, you lose ***

$ ch-extended-timers                              Second run, enter data
You have ten seconds to enter
your name, rank, and serial number: James Kirk, Starfleet Captain, 1234
I'm glad you are being cooperative.

$ ch-extended-timers                              Third run, enter EOF (^D)
You have ten seconds to enter
your name, rank, and serial number: ^D
EOF, eh?  We won't give up so easily!
```

It is undefined as to how the interval timers interact with the `sleep()` function, if at all. GLIBC does not use `alarm()` to implement `sleep()`, so on GNU/Linux systems, `sleep()` does not interact with the interval timer. However, for portable programs, you cannot make this assumption.

As with `gettimeofday()`, these functions have been around since 4.2 BSD, but were also removed from the 2024 POSIX standard. Nonetheless, we feel safe in describing them, as it's also unlikely that they will go away anytime soon.

16.3.4 More Exact Pauses: `nanosleep()`

The `sleep()` function (see Section 10.8.1, "Alarm Clocks: `sleep()`, `alarm()`, and `SIGALRM`," page 363) lets a program sleep for a given number of seconds. But as we saw, it only accepts an integral number of seconds, making it impossible to delay for a short period, and it also can potentially interact with `SIGALRM` handlers. The `nanosleep()` function makes up for these deficiencies:

```
#include <time.h>                                               POSIX

int nanosleep(const struct timespec *req, struct timespec *rem);
```

The two arguments are the requested sleep time and the amount of time remaining should the sleep return early (if `rem` is not `NULL`). Both of these are `struct timespec` values:

```
struct timespec {
    ...
    time_t tv_sec;          /* seconds */
    long   tv_nsec;         /* nanoseconds, may be a different type */
    ...
};
```

The `tv_nsec` value must be in the range 0–999,999,999. As with `sleep()`, the amount of time slept can be more than the requested amount of time, depending on when and how the kernel schedules processes for execution.

Unlike `sleep()`, `nanosleep()` has no interactions with any signals, making it generally safer and easier to use.

The return value is `0` if the process slept for the full time. Otherwise, it is `-1`, with `errno` indicating the error. In particular, if `errno` is `EINTR`, then `nanosleep()` was interrupted by a signal. In this case, if `rem` is not `NULL`, the `struct timespec` it points to is filled in with the remaining sleep time. This facilitates calling `nanosleep()` again to continue napping.

Although it looks a little strange, it's perfectly OK to use the same structure for both parameters:

```
struct timespec sleeptime = /* whatever */ ;
int ret;

ret = nanosleep(& sleeptime, & sleeptime);
```

The `struct timeval` and `struct timespec` are similar to each other, differing only in the units of the second component. The GLIBC `<sys/time.h>` header file defines two useful macros for converting between them:

```
#define __USE_GNU   1
#include <sys/time.h>                                           GLIBC

void TIMEVAL_TO_TIMESPEC(struct timeval *tv, struct timespec *ts);
void TIMESPEC_TO_TIMEVAL(struct timespec *ts, struct timeval *tv);
```

Here they are:

```
#ifdef __USE_GNU
/* Macros for converting between 'struct timeval' and 'struct timespec'.  */
# define TIMEVAL_TO_TIMESPEC(tv, ts) {                                  \
```

```
    (ts)->tv_sec = (tv)->tv_sec;                                  \
    (ts)->tv_nsec = (tv)->tv_usec * 1000;                         \
}
# define TIMESPEC_TO_TIMEVAL(tv, ts) {                                   \
    (tv)->tv_sec = (ts)->tv_sec;                                  \
    (tv)->tv_usec = (ts)->tv_nsec / 1000;                         \
}
#endif
```

As you can see, you must define `__USE_GNU` in order to have access to the macros. Whenever this is the case, you must define it before including *any* header files.

NOTE

It is indeed confusing that some system calls use microsecond resolution and others use nanosecond resolution. The reason is historical: the microsecond calls were developed on systems whose hardware clocks did not have any higher resolution, whereas the nanosecond calls were developed more recently, for systems with much higher resolution clocks. *C'est la vie.* About all you can do is to keep your manual handy.

For new code, we recommend using the POSIX standard `nanosleep()` function.

16.4 Advanced Searching with Binary Trees

In Section 6.2, "Sorting and Searching Functions," page 171, we presented functions for searching and sorting arrays. In this section, we cover a more advanced facility.

16.4.1 Introduction to Binary Trees

Arrays are about the simplest kind of structured data. They are easy to understand and use. They have a disadvantage, though, which is that their size is fixed at compile time. Thus, if you have more data than will fit in the array, you're out of luck. If you have considerably less data than the size of your array, you're wasting memory. (Although modern systems have large memories, consider the constraints of programmers writing software for embedded systems, such as microwave ovens or smart refrigerators. On the other end of the spectrum, consider the problems of programmers dealing with very large amounts of inputs, such as weather simulations.)

The computer science field has invented numerous *dynamic data structures*—structures that grow and shrink in size on demand and are more flexible than simple arrays, even arrays created and resized dynamically with `malloc()` and `realloc()`. Arrays also require re-sorting should new elements be added or removed.

One such structure is the *binary search tree*, which we'll just call a "binary tree" for short. A binary tree maintains items in sorted order, inserting them in the proper place in the tree

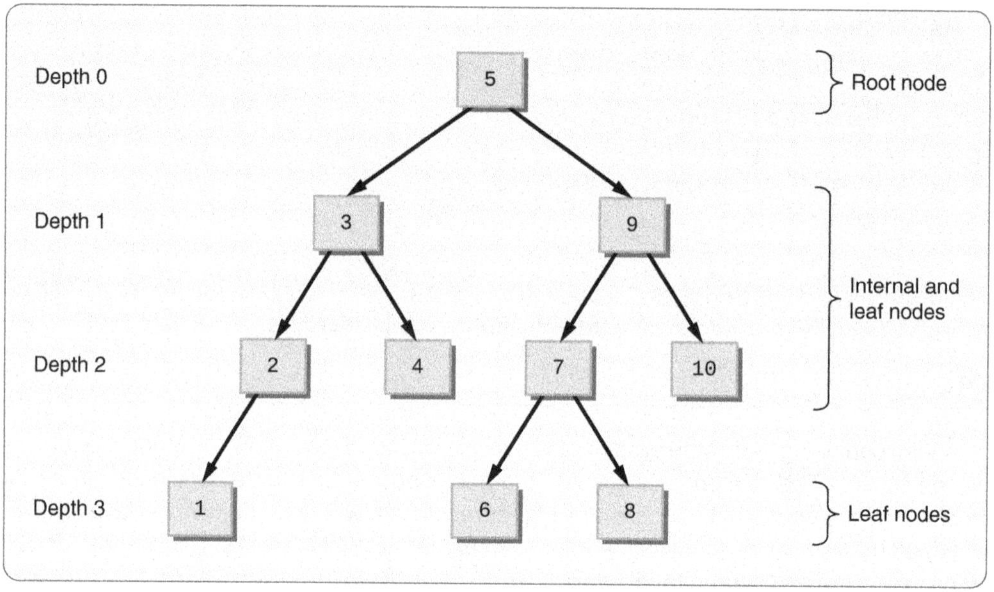

Figure 16.1: A binary tree

as they come in. Lookup in a binary tree is also fast, similar in time to binary search on an array. Unlike arrays, binary trees do not have to be re-sorted from scratch every time you add an item.

Binary trees have one disadvantage. In the case in which the input data is mostly (or already) sorted, the lookup time of binary trees reduces to that of linear searching. The technicalities of this have to do with how binary trees are managed internally, described shortly.

Some more formal data-structure terminology is now unavoidable. Figure 16.1 shows a binary tree. In computer science, trees are drawn starting at the top and growing downward. The further down the tree you go, the greater *depth* you have. Each object within the tree is termed a *node*. At the top of the tree is the *root node*, with depth `0`. At the bottom are the *leaf nodes*, with varying depth. In between the root and the leaves are zero or more *internal nodes*. Leaf nodes are distinguished by the fact that they have no *subtrees* hanging off them, whereas internal nodes have at least one subtree. Nodes with subtrees are sometimes referred to as *parent* nodes, with the subnodes being called *children*.

Plain binary trees are distinguished by the fact that nodes have no more than two children. (Trees with more than two child nodes are useful but aren't relevant here.) The children are referred to as the left and right children, respectively.

Binary search trees are further distinguished by the fact that the values stored in a left subchild are always less than the value stored in the node itself, and the values stored in the right subchild are always greater than the value in the node itself. This implies that there are no duplicate values within the tree. This fact also explains why trees don't handle presorted data well: depending on the sort order, each new data item ends up stored either to the left or to the right of the one before it, forming a simple linear list.

The operations on a binary tree are as follows:

Insertion
Adding a new item to the tree.

Lookup
Finding an item in the tree.

Removal
Removing an item from the tree.

Traversal
Doing something with every item that has been stored in the tree. (This is similar to traversing filesystem hierarchies, as we saw in Section 8.4.3.2, "Processing a File Tree Stream," page 252.) Tree traversals are also referred to as *tree walks*. There are multiple ways to "visit" the items stored in a tree. The functions discussed here only implement one such way. We will have more to say about this later.

16.4.2 Tree Management Functions

The operations just described correspond to the following functions:

```
#include <search.h>                                          POSIX XSI

void *tsearch(const void *key, void **rootp,
              int (*compare)(const void *, const void *));
void *tfind(const void *key, const void **rootp,
              int (*compare)(const void *, const void *));
void *tdelete(const void *key, void **rootp,
              int (*compare)(const void *, const void *));

typedef enum { preorder, postorder, endorder, leaf } VISIT;
void twalk(const void *root,
        void (*action)(const void *nodep, const VISIT which, const int depth));

#define _GNU_SOURCE 1
#include <search.h>

void tdestroy(void *root, void (*free_node)(void *nodep));         GLIBC
```

These functions were first defined for System V and are now formally standardized by POSIX. They follow the pattern of the others we saw in Section 6.2, "Sorting and Searching Functions," page 171: using `void *` pointers for pointing at arbitrary data types, and using user-provided comparison functions to determine ordering. As for `qsort()` and `bsearch()`, the comparison function must return a negative/zero/positive value when the `key` is compared with a value in a tree node.

The POSIX declarations are:

```
#include <search.h>

void *tdelete(const void *key,
              posix_tnode **rootp,
              int(*compar)(const void *, const void *));
posix_tnode *tfind(const void *key,
                   posix_tnode *const *rootp,
                   int(*compar)(const void *, const void *));
posix_tnode *tsearch(const void *key,
                     posix_tnode **rootp,
                     int (*compar)(const void *, const void *));
void twalk(const posix_tnode *root,
           void (*action)(const posix_tnode *, VISIT, int));
```

The POSIX standard uses a type, `posix_tnode`, for the parameters referring to the nodes. This is a simple alias for `void`, intended to make the prototypes easier to understand.

16.4.3 Tree Insertion: `tsearch()`

These routines allocate storage for the tree nodes. To use them with multiple trees, you have to give them a pointer to a `void *` variable, which they fill in with the address of the root node. When creating a new tree, initialize this pointer to `NULL`:

```
void *root = NULL;                                     Root of new tree
void *val;                                             Pointer to returned data

extern int my_compare(const void *, const void *);     Comparison function
extern char key[], key2[];                             Values to insert in tree

val = tsearch(key, & root, my_compare);                Insert first item in tree
... fill key2 with a different value. DON'T modify root ...
val = tsearch(key2, & root, my_compare);               Insert subsequent item in tree
```

As shown, the `root` variable should be set to `NULL` only the first time and then left alone after that. On each subsequent call, `tsearch()` uses it to manage the tree.

When the `key` being sought is found, both `tsearch()` and `tfind()` return pointers to the node containing it. They differ when the `key` is not found: `tfind()` returns `NULL`, and `tsearch()` inserts the new value into the tree and returns a pointer to it. The pointers returned by `tsearch()` and `tfind()` are to the internal tree nodes. They can be used as the value of `root` in subsequent calls in order to work on subtrees. As we will see shortly, the `key` value can be a pointer to an arbitrary structure; it's not restricted to a character string as the previous example might imply.

These routines store only *pointers* to the data used for keys. Thus it is up to you to manage the storage holding the data values, usually with `malloc()`.

NOTE

Since the tree functions keep pointers, be extra careful *not* to use `realloc()` for values that have been used as keys! `realloc()` could move the data around, returning a new pointer, but the tree routines would still be maintaining *dangling pointers* into the old data.

16.4.4 Tree Lookup and Use of a Returned Pointer: `tfind()` and `tsearch()`

The `tfind()` and `tsearch()` functions search a binary tree for a given key. They take the same list of arguments: a `key` to search for; a pointer to the root of the tree, `rootp`; and `compare`, a pointer to a comparison function. Both functions return a pointer to the node that matches `key`.

Just how do you use the pointer returned by `tfind()` or `tsearch()`? What exactly does it point to, anyway? The answer is that it points to a node in the tree. This is an *internal* type; you can't see how it's defined. However, POSIX guarantees that this pointer can be cast to *a pointer to a pointer* to whatever you're using for a key. Here is some fragmentary code to demonstrate, and then we show how this works:

```
struct employee {                                    From Chapter 6
        char lastname[30];
        char firstname[30];
        long emp_id;
        time_t start_date;
};

/* emp_name_id_compare --- compare by name, then by ID */

int
emp_name_id_compare(const void *e1p, const void *e2p)
{
... also from Chapter 6, reproduced in full later on ...
}

struct employee key = { ... };
void *vp = NULL, *root = NULL;
struct employee *e;
... fill tree with data ...

vp = tfind(& key, root, emp_name_id_compare);
if (vp != NULL) {  /* it's there, use it */
    e = *((struct employee **) vp);                  Retrieve stored data from tree
    /* use info in *e ... */
}
```

How can a pointer to a node double as a pointer to a pointer to the data? Well, consider how a binary tree's node would be implemented. Each node maintains at least a pointer to the user's data item and pointers to potential left and right subchildren. So it has to look approximately like this:

```
struct binary_tree {
    void *user_data;                     Pointer to user's data
    struct binary_tree *left;            Left subchild or NULL
    struct binary_tree *right;           Right subchild or NULL
    ... possibly other fields here ...
} node;
```

C and C++ guarantee that fields within a `struct` are laid out in increasing address order. Thus it's true that '`& node.left < & node.right`'. Furthermore, the address of the `struct` is *also* the address of its first field (in other words, ignoring type issues, '`& node == & node.user_data`').

Conceptually, then, here's what '`e = *((struct employee **) vp);`' means:

1. `vp` is a `void *`—that is, a generic pointer. It is the address of the internal tree node, but it's *also* the address of the part of the node (most likely another `void *`) that points to the user's data.
2. '`(struct employee **) vp`' casts the address of the internal pointer to the correct type; it remains a pointer to a pointer, but now to a `struct employee`. Remember that casts from one pointer type to another don't change any values (bit patterns); they change only how the compiler treats the values for type considerations.
3. '`*((struct employee **) vp)`' indirects through the newly minted `struct employee **`, returning a usable `struct employee *` pointer.
4. '`e = *((struct employee **) vp)`' stores this value in `e` for direct use later.

The concept is illustrated in Figure 16.2.

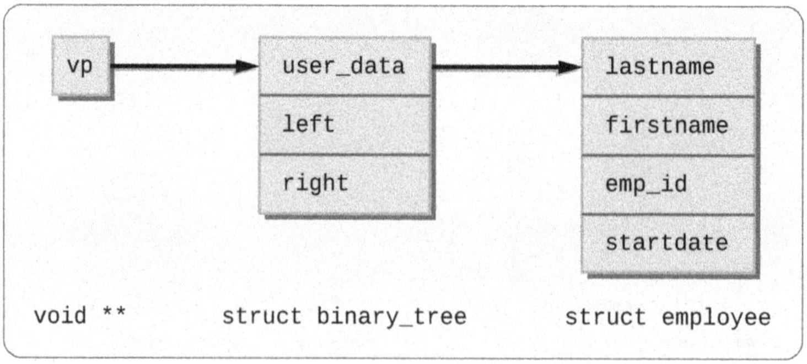

Figure 16.2: Tree nodes and their pointers

You might consider defining a macro to simplify the use of the returned pointer:[7]

```
#define tree_data(ptr, type) (*(type **) (ptr))
...
struct employee *e;
void *vp;

vp = tfind(& key, root, emp_name_id_compare);
if (vp != NULL) {  /* it's there, use it */
    e = tree_data(vp, struct employee);
    /* use info in *e ... */
}
```

16.4.5 Tree Traversal: `twalk()`

The `twalk()` function is declared as follows in `<search.h>`:

```
typedef enum { preorder, postorder, endorder, leaf } VISIT;
void twalk(const void *root,
           void (*action)(const void *nodep, const VISIT which, const int depth));
```

The first parameter is the root of the tree (*not* a pointer to the root). The second is a pointer to a callback function, which is called with three arguments: a pointer to the tree node being visited, an enumerated type indicating how the given node is being visited, and an integer indicating the depth of the current node (the root is at depth `0`, as explained earlier).

There are several ways to traverse, or "walk," a binary tree:

- Left child, node itself, right child.
- Node itself, left child, right child.
- Left child, right child, node itself.

The GLIBC `twalk()` function uses the second of these: the node first, then the left child, and finally the right child. Each time a node is encountered, the node is said to be *visited.*[8] In the course of visiting a node's child, the function must visit the node itself. Thus the values of type `VISIT` indicate at what stage this node is being encountered:

`preorder`	Before visiting any children.
`postorder`	After visiting the first child but before visiting the second child.
`endorder`	After visiting both children.
`leaf`	This node is a leaf node, without children.

[7]Thanks to Jim Meyering for this suggestion.

[8]Images come to mind of little binary data structures sitting down with each other over tea and cookies. Or at least that happens if you've been spending too much time in front of your computer.

NOTE

The terminology used here does not exactly match that used in formal texts on data structures. There, the terms used are *inorder*, *preorder*, and *postorder*, referring respectively to the three ways listed earlier for traversing a tree. Thus, `twalk()` uses a preorder traversal, but uses the `preorder` and other symbolic constants to indicate at what stage a node is being visited. This can be confusing.

In Section 8.4.3.2, "Processing a File Tree Stream," page 252, we described how the `fts()` suite of functions lets you traverse directory hierarchies. Such hierarchies can also be viewed as trees, wherein each node (directory) can have multiple children (files and/or subdirectories). In-memory binary trees are just a simplified version of this, wherein each node may have a maximum of two children.

The following program, `ch-extended-tsearch.c`, demonstrates building and traversing a tree. It reuses the `struct employee` structure and `emp_name_id_compare()` function from Section 6.2, "Sorting and Searching Functions," page 171:

```
/* ch-extended-tsearch.c --- demonstrate tree management */

#include <stdio.h>
#include <search.h>
#include <stdlib.h>
#include <string.h>
#include <time.h>

struct employee {
    char lastname[30];
    char firstname[30];
    long emp_id;
    time_t start_date;
};

/* emp_name_id_compare --- compare by name, then by ID */

int
emp_name_id_compare(const void *e1p, const void *e2p)
{
    const struct employee *e1, *e2;
    int last, first;

    e1 = (const struct employee *) e1p;
    e2 = (const struct employee *) e2p;

    if ((last = strcmp(e1->lastname, e2->lastname)) != 0)
        return last;
```

```
29
30       /* same last name, check first name */
31       if ((first = strcmp(e1->firstname, e2->firstname)) != 0)
32           return first;
33
34       /* same first name, check ID numbers */
35       if (e1->emp_id < e2->emp_id)
36           return -1;
37       else if (e1->emp_id == e2->emp_id)
38           return 0;
39       else
40           return 1;
41   }
42
43   /* print_emp --- print an employee structure during a tree walk */
44
45   void
46   print_emp(const void *nodep, const VISIT which, const int depth)
47   {
48       struct employee *e = *((struct employee **) nodep);
49
50       switch (which) {
51       case leaf:
52       case postorder:
53           printf("Depth: %d. Employee:\n", depth);
54           printf("\t%s, %s\t%ld\t%s\n", e->lastname, e->firstname,
55               e->emp_id, ctime(& e->start_date));
56           break;
57       default:
58           break;
59       }
60   }
```

Lines 9–14 define the `struct employee`, and lines 18–41 define `emp_name_id_compare()`.

Lines 45–60 define `print_emp()`, the callback function that prints a `struct employee`, along with the depth in the tree of the current node. Note the magic cast on line 48 to retrieve the pointer to the stored data.

The `main()` program reads employee data, stores it in a tree, and then prints it:

```
62   /* main --- demonstrate maintaining data in binary tree */
63
64   int
65   main(void)
66   {
67   #define NPRES 10
68       struct employee presidents[NPRES];
```

```
    int i, npres;
    char buf[BUFSIZ];
    void *root = NULL;

    /* Very simple code to read data: */
    for (npres = 0; npres < NPRES && fgets(buf, BUFSIZ, stdin) != NULL;
            npres++) {
        sscanf(buf, "%s %s %ld %ld\n",
            presidents[npres].lastname,
            presidents[npres].firstname,
            & presidents[npres].emp_id,
            & presidents[npres].start_date);
    }

    for (i = 0; i < npres; i++)
        (void) tsearch(& presidents[i], & root, emp_name_id_compare);

    twalk(root, print_emp);
    return EXIT_SUCCESS;
}
```

The goal of printing the tree is to print the contained elements in sorted order. Remember that `twalk()` visits intermediate nodes three times and that the left child is less than the node itself, while the right child is greater than the node. Thus, the `switch` statement prints the node's information only if `which` is `leaf`, for a leaf node, or `postorder`, indicating that the left child has been visited, but not yet the right child.

The data used is the list of presidents, also from Section 6.2, "Sorting and Searching Functions," page 171. To refresh your memory, the fields are last name, first name, employee number, and start time as a seconds-since-the-Epoch timestamp:

```
$ cat presdata.txt
Trump Donald 47 1737396000
Biden Joseph 46 1611165600
Trump Donald 45 1484935200
Obama Barack 44 1232474400
Bush George 43 980013600
Clinton William 42 727552800
Bush George 41 601322400
Reagan Ronald 40 348861600
Carter James 39 222631200
```

The data is sorted based on last name, then first name, and then seniority. When run, the program produces this output:[9]

[9] This output is for the U.S. Eastern time zone.

```
$ ch-extended-tsearch < presdata.txt
Depth: 2. Employee:
    Biden, Joseph   46  Wed Jan 20 13:00:00 2021

Depth: 3. Employee:
    Bush, George    41  Fri Jan 20 13:00:00 1989

Depth: 1. Employee:
    Bush, George    43  Sat Jan 20 13:00:00 2001

Depth: 3. Employee:
    Carter, James   39  Thu Jan 20 13:00:00 1977

Depth: 2. Employee:
    Clinton, William    42  Wed Jan 20 13:00:00 1993

Depth: 0. Employee:
    Obama, Barack   44  Tue Jan 20 13:00:00 2009

Depth: 2. Employee:
    Reagan, Ronald  40  Tue Jan 20 13:00:00 1981

Depth: 1. Employee:
    Trump, Donald   45  Fri Jan 20 13:00:00 2017

Depth: 2. Employee:
    Trump, Donald   47  Mon Jan 20 13:00:00 2025
```

16.4.6 Tree Node Removal and Tree Deletion: `tdelete()` and `tdestroy()`

Finally, you can remove items from a tree and, on GLIBC systems, delete the entire tree itself:

```
void *tdelete(const void *key, void **rootp,
              int (*compare)(const void *, const void *));

/* GLIBC extension, not in POSIX: */
void tdestroy(void *root, void (*free_node)(void *nodep));
```

The arguments to `tdelete()` are the same as for `tsearch()`: the key, the address of the tree's root, and the comparison function. If the given item is found in the tree, it is removed, and `tdelete()` returns a pointer to the *parent* of the given node. Otherwise, it returns `NULL`. This behavior has to be managed carefully in your code if you need the original item being deleted, for example, to free its storage:

```
struct employee *e, key;                    Variable declarations
void *vp, *root;
... fill in key for item to remove from tree ...
```

```
vp = tfind(& key, root, emp_name_id_compare);          Find item to remove
if (vp != NULL) {
    e = *((struct employee **) vp);                    Convert pointer
    free(e);                                           Free storage
}
(void) tdelete(& key, & root, emp_name_id_compare);    Now remove it from tree
```

If you delete the item stored in the root node, the returned value is "an unspecified null pointer" (POSIX). More strongly, the manpage says that "`tdelete()` returns a dangling pointer that must not be accessed."

The `tdestroy()` function is a GLIBC extension. It allows you to destroy a whole tree. The first argument is the root of the tree. The second is a pointer to a function that releases the *data* pointed to by each node in the tree. If nothing needs to be done with this data (for example, it's held in a regular array, as in our earlier example program), then this function should do nothing. Do *not* pass in a `NULL` pointer! Doing so results in a crash.

16.5 Summary

- Occasionally, it's necessary to allocate memory aligned at a certain boundary. `posix_memalign()` does this. Its return value is different from that of most of the functions covered in this book: caveat emptor. `memalign()` also allocates aligned memory, but not all systems support releasing that memory with `free()`.
- File locking with `fcntl()` provides record locks, down to the level of the ability to lock single bytes within a file. Read locks prevent writing of the locked area, and a write lock prevents other processes from reading and writing the locked area. Locking is advisory, and POSIX standardizes only advisory locking. These locks are associated with the process.
- Most modern Unix systems support mandatory locking, using the setgid permission bit on the file. GNU/Linux no longer supports mandatory locking.
- Additionally, GNU/Linux provides advisory locking associated with open file descriptors, and these are included in the 2024 POSIX standard.
- On GNU/Linux, the `lockf()` function acts as a wrapper around POSIX locking with `fcntl()`; the BSD `flock()` function's locks are (on GNU/Linux) completely independent of `fcntl()` locks. BSD `flock()` locks are whole-file locks only and do not work on remote filesystems. For these reasons, `flock()` locks are not recommended.
- `gettimeofday()` retrieves the time of day as a (seconds, microseconds) pair in a `struct timeval`. These values may be used by `utimes()` to update a file's accessed and modification times (see Section 5.6.4, "Changing Timestamps: `utime()` and Successors," page 148).
- The `getitimer()` and `setitimer()` system calls use pairs of `struct timevals` in a `struct itimerval` to create interval timers—alarm clocks that "go off" at a set time

and continue to go off at a set interval thereafter. Three different timers provide control over the states in which the timer continues to run down.

- The `nanosleep()` function uses a `struct timespec`, which specifies time in seconds and nanoseconds, to pause a process for a given amount of time. It has the happy trait of not interacting at all with the signal mechanism.
- The tree API is an additional set of data storage and search functions that maintain data in binary trees, the effect of which is to keep data sorted. The tree API is very flexible, allowing use of multiple trees and arbitrary data.

Exercises

1. Write the `lockf()` function, using `fcntl()` to do the locking.
2. If you have a non-Linux system that supports mandatory locking, try the `ch-extended-lockall` program on it.
3. Write a function named `strftimes()`, with the following API:

```
size_t strftimes(char *buf, size_t size, const char *format,
                 const struct timeval *tp);
```

   It should behave like the standard `strftime()` function, except that it allows `%q` to mean "the current number of microseconds." You can start with the version of the standard `strftime()` function that you wrote for the exercises in "Exercises for Chapter 6," page 198.
4. Using the `strftimes()` function you just wrote, write an enhanced version of `date` that accepts a format string beginning with a leading `+` and formats the current date and time. (See *date*(1).)
5. The handling of the timeout in `ch-extended-timers.c` is rather primitive. Rewrite the program to use `setjmp()` after printing the prompt and `longjmp()` from within the signal handler. Does this improve the structure or clarity of the program?
6. We noted that `ch-extended-timers.c` contains a deliberate race condition. Suppose the user enters a response within the right time period, but `ch-extended-timers` is suspended before the alarm can be canceled. What call can you make to cut down the size of the problem window?
7. Draw the tree as shown by the output of `ch-extended-tsearch` in Section 16.4.5, "Tree Traversal: `twalk()`," page 581.
8. Examine the file `/usr/share/dict/words` on a GNU/Linux system. (This is the spelling dictionary for `spell`; it might be in a different place on different systems, or it might be a symbolic link to the real dictionary file.) The words exist in the file, one per line, in sorted order. (You might need to install the `spell` program in order to get this file.)

First, use this `awk` program to create a new list, in random order:

```
$ awk '{ list[$0]++ }
> END { for (i in list) print i }' /usr/share/dict/words > /tmp/wlist
```

Next, write two programs. Each should read the new list and store each word read into a tree and an array, respectively. The second program should use `qsort()` to sort the array and `bsearch()` to search it.

Retrieve the word '`gravy`' from the tree or array. Time the two programs to see which one runs faster. You may need to put the word retrieval inside a loop that runs multiple times (say 10,000) to get running times that are long enough to show a difference.

Use the output of `ps` to see how much memory each program uses.

9. Rerun the two programs, using the original sorted dictionary file, and see how, if at all, the timing results change.

Part III

Debugging and Final Project

Chapter 17

Debugging

Some days, you just can't get rid of a bomb!
— Batman

There are many practices, starting with program logic and data design and continuing on through code breakdown and organization to implementation, that can help minimize errors and problems. We encourage you to study these; find good books on software design and software engineering, and put their advice into practice! Any program over a few hundred lines in size should be carefully thought out and designed, instead of just hacked on until it appears to work.

However, since programmers are human, programming errors are unavoidable. *Debugging* is the process of tracking down and removing errors in programs. Even well-designed, well-implemented programs occasionally don't work; when something's going wrong and you can't figure out why, it's a good idea to point a debugger at the code and watch it fail.

This chapter covers a range of topics, starting off with basic debugging advice and techniques (compiling for debugging and elementary use of GDB, the GNU debugger) before moving on to a range of techniques for use during program development and debugging that make debugging easier, and then looking at a number of tools that help the debugging process. It then closes with a brief introduction to software testing and a wonderful set of "debugging rules," extracted from a book that we highly recommend.

Most of our advice is based on our long-term experience as a volunteer for the GNU project, maintaining `gawk` (GNU `awk`). Most, if not all, of the specific examples we present come from that program.

Throughout the chapter, specific recommendations are marked **Recommendation**.

17.1 First Things First

Note that it can sometimes be maddeningly difficult to make a program fail under the debugger, and that's a separate and frustrating class of error.
— Chet Ramey

When a program misbehaves, you may be at a loss as to what to do first. Often, strange behavior is due to misusing memory—using uninitialized values, reading or writing outside the bounds of dynamic memory, and so on. Therefore, you may get faster results by trying out a memory-debugging tool *before* you crank up a debugger.

The reason is that memory tools can point you directly at the failing line of code, whereas using a debugger is more like embarking on a search-and-destroy mission, in which you first have to isolate the problem and then fix it. Once you're sure that memory problems aren't the issue, you can proceed to using a debugger.

Because the debugger is a more general tool, we cover it first. We discuss two major memory-debugging tools later in the chapter.

What about the case Chet Ramey describes, where you can't even use a debugger? In that case, some or all of the techniques described in Section 17.4.2, "Runtime Debugging Code," page 622, may be of help.

17.2 Compilation for Debugging

For a source code debugger to be used, the executable being debugged (the *target*, if you will) must be compiled with the compiler's `-g` option. This option causes the compiler to put extra *debugging symbols* into the object code—that is, extra information giving the names and types of variables, constants, functions, and so on. The debugger then uses this information to match source code locations with the code being executed and to retrieve or store variable values in the running program.

On many Unix systems, the `-g` compiler option is mutually exclusive with the `-O` option, which turns on optimizations. This is because optimizations can cause rearrangement of bits and pieces of the object code, such that there is no longer a direct relationship between what's being executed and a linear reading of the source code. By disabling optimizations, you make it much easier for the debugger to relate the object code to the source code, and in turn, single-stepping through a program's execution works in the obvious way. (Single-stepping is described shortly.)

GCC, the GNU Compiler Collection, does allow `-g` and `-O` together. However, this introduces exactly the problem we wish to avoid when debugging, which is following the execution in a debugger becomes considerably more difficult. The advantage of allowing the two together is that you can leave the debugging symbols in an optimized, for-production-use executable. They occupy only disk space, not memory. Then an installed executable can still be debugged in an emergency.

In our experience, if you need to use a debugger, it's better to recompile the application from scratch, with only the `-g` option. This makes tracing considerably easier; there's enough detail to keep track of just going through the program as it's written without also having to worry about how the compiler rearranged the code.

There is one caveat: *be sure the program still misbehaves.* Reproducibility is the key to debugging; if you can't reproduce the problem, it's *much* harder to track it down and fix it.

Rarely, compiling a program without `-O` can cause it to stop failing.[1] Usually the problem persists when compiled without `-O`, meaning there is indeed a logic bug of some kind, waiting to be discovered.

There is another possibility when your program fails if compiled with `-O` but doesn't fail when not: you've unintentionally done something that depends on *undefined behavior*, a grey area in the language that the standard specifically leaves unlighted.

A discussion of undefined behavior is well beyond the scope of this book. See the reference to `n3308.pdf` in Section 17.10, "Suggested Reading," page 655, for a little more information.

Recommendation: Don't mix `-g` with `-O`.

17.3 GDB Basics

A *debugger* is a program that allows you to control the execution of another program and examine and change the subordinate program's state (such as variable values). There are two kinds of debuggers: *machine-level debuggers*, which work on the level of machine instructions, and *source-level debuggers*, which work in terms of the program's source code. For example, in a machine-level debugger, to change a variable's value you specify its address in memory. In a source-level debugger, you just use the variable's name.

Historically, V7 Unix had `adb`, which was a machine-level debugger. System III had `sdb`, which was a source-level debugger, and BSD Unix provided `dbx`, also a source-level debugger. (Both continued to provide `adb`.) `dbx` survives on some commercial Unix systems.

GDB, the GNU Debugger, is a source-level debugger. It has many more features, is more broadly portable, and is more usable than either of `sdb` or `dbx`.[2]

Like its predecessors, GDB is a command-line debugger. It prints one line of source code at a time, prints a prompt, and reads one line of input containing a command to execute. (There are more user-friendly ways to use GDB, which we touch on later.)

GDB understands C and C++, including support for *name demangling*, which means that you can use the regular C++ source code names for class member functions and overloaded functions. In particular, GDB understands C expression syntax, which is useful when you wish to look at the value of complicated expressions, such as '`*ptr->x.a[1]->q`'. It also understands Fortran, D, Objective-C, Java, OpenCL, Pascal, Modula-2, and Ada.

If you're running GNU/Linux or a BSD system (and you installed the development tools), then you should have a recent version of GDB already installed and ready to use. If not, you can download the GDB source code from the GNU project's FTP site for GDB[3] and build it yourself.

GDB comes with its own manual, which is over 700 pages long (not including the appendices). You can generate the printable version of the manual in the GDB source code directory

---

[1] Compiler optimizations are a notorious scapegoat for logic bugs. In the distant past, pointing a finger at the compiler was more justified. In our experience, using modern systems and compilers, it is *very* unusual to find a case in which compiler optimization introduces bugs into working code.

[2] We're speaking of the original BSD `dbx`. We have used GDB exclusively for several decades.

[3] `https://ftp.gnu.org/gnu/gdb/`

and print it yourself. You can also buy printed and bound copies from the Free Software Foundation; your purchase helps the FSF and contributes directly to the production of more Free Software. (See the FSF website[4] for ordering information.) This section describes the basics of GDB; we recommend reading the manual to learn how to take full advantage of GDB's capabilities.

17.3.1 Getting a `core` File

On Unix and systems derived from it, misbehaving programs often die, leaving behind a *core dump*. Indeed, we saw in Section 10.2, "Signal Actions," page 333, that a number of signals can cause such a core dump.[5]

Originally, core dumps were created in a file named `core` in the dying process's current directory (if the process had write permission there). For some years, under GNU/Linux, such files (by default) were named `core.pid`, where *pid* was the process ID number of the running program that died. The *pid* extension meant that you could have multiple core dumps in the same directory, which is helpful, but also good for consuming disk space!

17.3.1.1 The Core File Pattern

Today, the situation is different. Most GNU/Linux systems are not used by developers, and if an application dumps core in a random directory, it's unlikely to be of much use to anyone. Instead, when an application crashes, it's useful to send a report to the application's developer, or at least to the people who create the particular GNU/Linux distribution that you are using. When this happens, at least on some systems, a pop-up window appears, similar to that shown in Figure 17.1.

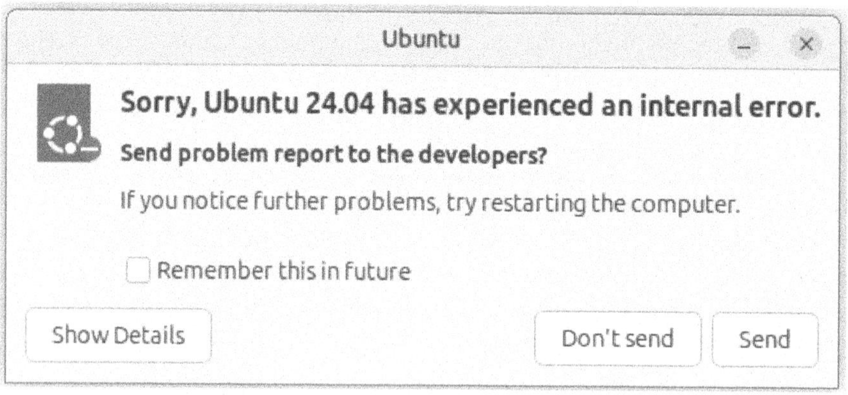

Figure 17.1: A pop-up error reporting window

[4] `http://www.gnu.org`

[5] Use of the term *core* for "memory" dates back to the early days of computers, when each bit in memory was stored in a magnetic ring, or core, with wires running through it. More information about this kind of memory can be found in the Wikipedia article on core memory (`https://en.wikipedia.org/wiki/Magnetic-core_memory`).

The mechanisms that make this possible are somewhat complicated. The full details (and there are lots of them) may be found in the *core*(5) manpage.

Basically, the file `/proc/sys/kernel/core_pattern` serves as a *template* for the name of a file to create. Within this file, certain specifiers are replaced with relevant information about the process dumping core. For example, to get the traditional `core.`*`pid`* type of core dump, you would put '`core.%p`' into `/proc/sys/kernel/core_pattern`.

If the first character in `/proc/sys/kernel/core_pattern` is a pipe character ('`|`'), then the rest of the line is a template for a user-space program to be run. The program receives the contents of the core file on standard input. The program to run must be given as an absolute pathname.

On our system, `/proc/sys/kernel/core_pattern` looks like this:

```
$ cat /proc/sys/kernel/core_pattern
|/usr/share/apport/apport -p%p -s%s -c%c -d%d -P%P -u%u -g%g -F%F -- %E
```

This runs the `apport` program, which generates the pop-up window shown in Figure 17.1 and sends an error report on to the distribution maintainers. Sadly, `apport` does not (currently) have a manpage, although an Internet search brings up useful information.

The specifiers used for the core pattern in the previous command are:

`%c` The *comm* value of the process, typically the program's name truncated to 15 characters.

`%d` The process's *dump mode*. See the `PR_GET_DUMPABLE` flag described in the *prctl*(2) manpage.

`%E` The pathname of the executable, with slash characters replaced with exclamation marks. (Why? We don't know.)

`%F` The pidfd for the crashed process. (This is an advanced feature.)

`%g` The numeric real GID of the process.

`%P` The PID of the process as seen in the initial process ID namespace.

`%p` The PID of the process as seen in the process ID namespace in which the process lives. (This is an advanced feature, used for containerized environments.)

`%s` The number of the signal causing the dump.

`%u` The numeric real UID of the process.

There are other specifiers; see the *core*(5) manpage for details.

17.3.1.2 Generating a Core Dump

Let's try to create a core dump. The following program, `ch-debugging-abort.c`, creates a few nested function calls and then purposely dies by `abort()` to create a core dump:

```
/* ch-debugging-abort.c --- produce a core dump */

#include <stdio.h>
#include <stdlib.h>

/* recurse --- build up some function calls */
```

```
void
recurse(void)
{
    static int i;

    if (++i == 3)
        abort();
    else
        recurse();
}

int
main(int argc, char **argv)
{
    recurse();
}
```

Let's compile and run it:

```
$ cc -O ch-debugging-abort.c -o ch-debugging-abort     Compile the program
$ ls                                                    Check out the directory's contents
ch-debugging-abort  ch-debugging-abort.c
$ ch-debugging-abort                                    Run the program
Aborted (core dumped)                                   It worked!
$ ls
ch-debugging-abort  ch-debugging-abort.c                Or did it? Where's the core file?
$ ulimit -c                                             Maybe we have a resource limitation?
unlimited                                               Hmm, no problem with resource limits ...
```

The problem, of course, is the core pattern file. We have to (temporarily) put a more useful (to us) pattern into the core pattern file:

```
$ cp /proc/sys/kernel/core_pattern save_core_pattern              Save the original pattern
$ sudo sh -c 'echo core.%p > /proc/sys/kernel/core_pattern'       Update the pattern, as root
[sudo] password for arnold:                                       Enter our password
$ cat /proc/sys/kernel/core_pattern                               Verify the change
core.%p
$ ch-debugging-abort a b c                                        Try again, arguments are unused
Aborted (core dumped)
$ ls                                                              Check it out, it worked!
ch-debugging-abort  ch-debugging-abort.c  core.36698  save_core_pattern
$ sudo sh -c 'cat save_core_pattern > /proc/sys/kernel/core_pattern'    Restore the original
```

Changes to the `/proc/sys/kernel/core_pattern` are ephemeral; they don't last across reboots. To make a permanent change, you will have to modify one of your system's start-up files (or create a new one) to put your desired core file pattern into place. The details will vary by GNU/Linux distribution and over time, so we won't attempt to give you specific advice.

17.3.2 Running GDB

Now that we know how to get a core file, we can look at using GDB to examine one. The basic usage is this:

gdb [*options*] [*executable* [*core-file-name*]]

Here, *executable* is the executable program to be debugged. If provided, *core-file-name* is the name of a `core` file created when a program was killed by the operating system and dumped core (see the previous section).

If you forget to name the files on the command line, you can use '`file` *`executable`*' to tell GDB the name of the executable file, and '`core-file` *`core-file-name`*' to tell GDB the name of the core file.

With a core dump, GDB indicates where the program died. First, let's recompile with debug symbols and without optimization. Then let's get a core file. We'll use `ch-debugging-abort.c`, shown previously:

```
$ rm core.36698 ch-debugging-abort                              Clean up to start over
$ cc -g ch-debugging-abort.c -o ch-debugging-abort              Recompile, no -O
$ sudo sh -c 'echo core.%p > /proc/sys/kernel/core_pattern'     Update the pattern, as root
$ ch-debugging-abort a b c                                      Get our core dump
Aborted (core dumped)
$ ls                                                            It's there
ch-debugging-abort  ch-debugging-abort.c  core.38668  save_core_pattern
```

Here's a short GDB session with this program:

```
$ gdb ch-debugging-abort core.38668                 Start GDB on the program and core
GNU gdb (Ubuntu 12.1-0ubuntu1~22.04) 12.1
Copyright (C) 2022 Free Software Foundation, Inc.
...

For help, type "help".
Type "apropos word" to search for commands related to "word"...
Reading symbols from ch-debugging-abort...
[New LWP 38668]
[Thread debugging using libthread_db enabled]
Using host libthread_db library "/lib/x86_64-linux-gnu/libthread_db.so.1".
Core was generated by 'ch-debugging-abort a b c'.   GDB prints the command line
Program terminated with signal SIGABRT, Aborted.
#0  __pthread_kill_implementation (no_tid=0, signo=6, threadid=124448894838592)
    at ./nptl/pthread_kill.c:44
44  ./nptl/pthread_kill.c: No such file or directory.
(gdb) where                                                 Print stack trace
#0  __pthread_kill_implementation (no_tid=0, signo=6, threadid=124448894838592)
    at ./nptl/pthread_kill.c:44
#1  __pthread_kill_internal (signo=6, threadid=124448894838592)
    at ./nptl/pthread_kill.c:78
```

```
#2  __GI___pthread_kill (threadid=124448894838592, signo=signo@entry=6)
    at ./nptl/pthread_kill.c:89
#3  0x0000712f84042476 in __GI_raise (sig=sig@entry=6) at ../sysdeps/posix/raise.c:26
#4  0x0000712f840287f3 in __GI_abort () at ./stdlib/abort.c:79
#5  0x000058ea51873170 in recurse () at ch-debugging-abort.c:14    <---- We need to examine here
#6  0x000058ea51873175 in recurse () at ch-debugging-abort.c:16
#7  0x000058ea51873175 in recurse () at ch-debugging-abort.c:16
#8  0x000058ea51873190 in main (argc=1, argv=0x7ffc729fb5d8) at ch-debugging-abort.c:22
```

GDB prints the command line that caused the core dump.

The `where` command prints a *stack trace*—that is, a list of all the functions called, most recent first. Note that there are three invocations of the `recurse()` function. The command `bt`, for "back trace," is an alias for `where`; it's easier to type.

Each function invocation in the stack is referred to as a *frame*. This term comes from the compiler field, in which each function's parameters, local variables, and return address, grouped on the stack, are referred to as a *stack frame*. The GDB `frame` command lets you examine a particular frame. In this case, we want frame `5`. This is the most recent invocation of `recurse()`, which called `abort()`:

```
(gdb) frame 5                                          Move to frame 5
#5  0x000058ea51873170 in recurse () at ch-debugging-abort.c:14
14          abort();                                   GDB prints source location in frame
(gdb) list                                             Show several lines of source code
9   recurse(void)
10  {
11      static int i;
12
13      if (++i == 3)
14          abort();
15      else
16          recurse();
17  }
18
(gdb)                                                  Pressing ENTER repeats the last command
19  int
20  main(int argc, char **argv)
21  {
22      recurse();
23  }
(gdb) quit                                             Leave the debugger (for now)
```

As demonstrated, pressing ENTER repeats the last command—in this case, `list`, to show source code lines. This is an easy way to step through the source code.

GDB uses the `readline` library for command-line editing, so you can use Emacs or `vi` commands (as you prefer) for recalling and editing previous lines. The Bash shell uses the same library, so if you're familiar with command-line editing at the shell prompt, GDB's works the same way. This feature saves considerable typing.

The `readline` library reads its commands from a file named `.inputrc` in your home directory. Here's ours:

```
$ cat /home/arnold/.inputrc
set editing-mode vi
set horizontal-scroll-mode On
control-h: backward-delete-char
set comment-begin #
set expand-tilde On
```

17.3.3 Setting Breakpoints, Single-Stepping, and Setting Watchpoints

Often, program failures produce a core dump. The first step is to use GDB on the `core` file to determine the routine in which the program died. If the original binary was not compiled for debugging (that is, no `-g`), GDB can tell you the function's name but no other details.

The next step is to recompile the program with debugging and without optimization and *verify that it still fails*. Assuming it does, you'll want to run the program under the control of the debugger and set a breakpoint in the failing routine.

A *breakpoint* is a point at which execution should break, or stop. You can set breakpoints by function name, source code line number, or source code file and line number together, as well as in other ways.

After setting the breakpoint, you start the program running using the `run` command, possibly followed by any command-line arguments to be passed on to the target. (GDB conveniently remembers the arguments for you; if you wish to start the program over again from the beginning, all you need do is type the `run` command by itself, and GDB starts a fresh copy with the same arguments as before. GDB uses a shell to start the program, so you may also use shell constructs, such as I/O redirection, in your `run` command.)

Running the program from within GDB can be helpful if you don't have permission to alter `/proc/sys/kernel/core_pattern` (so you can't get a core dump) but you do know the command-line arguments that caused the failure. In that case, running the program from the debugger should fail, and GDB will break in the routine that caused the problem.

Here's a short session using `gawk`:

```
$ gdb gawk                                                Start GDB on gawk
GNU gdb (Ubuntu 12.1-0ubuntu1~22.04) 12.1
...
(gdb) break do_print                                      Set breakpoint in do_print
Breakpoint 1 at 0x426471: file builtin.c, line 2321.
(gdb) run 'BEGIN { print "hello, world" }'               Start the program running
Starting program: /home/arnold/Gnu/gawk/gawk.git/gawk 'BEGIN { print "hello, world" }'
[Thread debugging using libthread_db enabled]
Using host libthread_db library "/lib/x86_64-linux-gnu/libthread_db.so.1".
```

```
Breakpoint 1, do_print (nargs=1, redirtype=0) at builtin.c:2321
2321    {                                               Execution reaches breakpoint
(gdb) list                                              Show source code
2316
2317    /* do_print --- print items, separated by OFS, terminated with ORS */
2318
2319    void
2320    do_print(int nargs, int redirtype)
2321    {
2322            struct redirect *rp = NULL;
2323            int errflg = 0;
2324            FILE *fp = NULL;
2325            int i;
```

Once the breakpoint is reached, you proceed through the program by *single-stepping* it. This means that GDB allows the program to execute one source code statement at a time. GDB prints the line it's about to execute and then prints its prompt. To run the statement, use the `next` command:

```
(gdb) next                                      Run current statement (2322, above)
2322            struct redirect *rp = NULL;     GDB prints next statement
(gdb)                                           Hit ENTER to run it and go to next
2323            int errflg = 0;
(gdb)                                           ENTER again
2324            FILE *fp = NULL;
...
2356            for (i = 1; i <= nargs; i++) {
(gdb)
2357                    tmp = args_array[i] = POP();
```

The `step` command is an alternative command for single-stepping. There is an important difference between `next` and `step`. `next` executes the next statement. If that statement contains a function call, the function is called and returns before GDB regains control of the running program.

On the other hand, when you use `step` on a statement with a function call, GDB descends into the called function, allowing you to continue single-stepping (or *tracing*) the program. If a statement doesn't contain a function call, then `step` is the same as `next`.

NOTE

It's easy to forget which command you're using and keep pressing ENTER to run each subsequent statement. If you're using `step`, you can accidentally enter a library function, such as `strlen()` or `printf()`, which you really don't want to bother with. In such a case, you can use the command `finish`, which causes the program to run until the current function returns.

You can print memory contents by using the `print` command. GDB understands C expression syntax, which makes it easy and natural to examine structures pointed to by pointers:

```
(gdb) print *tmp                              Print the structure pointed to by tmp
$1 = {sub = {nodep = {l = {lptr = 0x0, li = 0x0, ll = 0, lp = 0x0}, r = {
          rptr = 0x0, preg = {0x0, 0x0}, av = 0x0, bv = 0x0, uptr = 0x0,
          iptr = 0x0}, x = {extra = 0x0, aptr = 0x0, xl = 0, cmnt = 0x0},
      name = 0x4e <error: Cannot access memory at address 0x4e>,
      reserved = 5153936, rn = 0xc, cnt = 4294967295, reflags = 0}, val = {
      nm = {fltnum = 0, mpnum = {{_mpfr_prec = 0, _mpfr_sign = 0,
            _mpfr_exp = 0, _mpfr_d = 0x0}}, mpi = {{_mp_alloc = 0,
            _mp_size = 0, _mp_d = 0x0}}}, rndmode = 78,
        sp = 0x4ea490 "hello, world", slen = 12, idx = -1, wsp = 0x0, wslen = 0,
        typre = 0x0, comtype = 0}}, type = Node_val,
  flags = (MALLOC | STRING | STRCUR), valref = 2}
```

Note the value of `flags`. This is an `enum` field in the struct, whose values are bit fields. GDB is smart enough to understand this and print the value symbolically!

Finally, the `cont` (continue) command lets you continue the program's execution. It will run until the next breakpoint or until it exits (normally or otherwise) if it doesn't hit any breakpoints. This example picks up where the previous one left off:

```
(gdb) cont                                    Continue
Continuing.
hello, world
[Inferior 1 (process 35863) exited normally]  Informative message from GDB
(gdb) quit                                    Leave the debugger
```

A *watchpoint* is like a breakpoint, but for data instead of executable code. You set a watchpoint on a variable (or on a field in a `struct` or `union`, or on an array element), and when it changes, GDB notifies you.

GDB checks the value of the watchpoint as it single-steps the program, stopping when the value changes. For example, the `do_itrace` variable in `gawk` is true when the `--trace` option was issued. This variable is set to true by `getopt_long()`. (We covered `getopt_long()` in Section 2.1.2, "GNU Long Options," page 26.) In `gawk`'s `main.c` file:

```
bool do_itrace = false;          /* provide simple instruction trace */
...
static const struct option optab[] = {
    ...
    { "trace", no_argument, NULL, 'I' },
    ...
};
...
/* parse_args --- do the getopt_long thing */

static void
```

```
parse_args(int argc, char **argv)
{
...
        case 'I':
            do_itrace = true;
            break;
...
```

Here's a sample session, showing a watchpoint in action:

```
$ gdb gawk                                              Start GDB on gawk
GNU gdb (Ubuntu 12.1-0ubuntu1~22.04) 12.1
...
(gdb) watch do_itrace                                   Set watchpoint on variable
Hardware watchpoint 1: do_itrace
(gdb) run --trace 'BEGIN { print "hello, world" }'     Run the program
Starting program: /home/arnold/Gnu/gawk/gawk.git/gawk --trace 'BEGIN { print "hello, world" }'
[Thread debugging using libthread_db enabled]
Using host libthread_db library "/lib/x86_64-linux-gnu/libthread_db.so.1".

Hardware watchpoint 1: do_itrace

Old value = false                                       Watchpoint stops the program
New value = true
parse_args (argc=3, argv=0x7fffffffe2f8) at main.c:1681
1681                    break;
(gdb) where                                             Stack trace
#0  parse_args (argc=3, argv=0x7fffffffe2f8) at main.c:1681
#1  0x0000000000468e67 in main (argc=3, argv=0x7fffffffe2f8) at main.c:318
(gdb) quit                                              We're done for now
A debugging session is active.

    Inferior 1 [process 36043] will be killed.

Quit anyway? (y or n) y                                 Yes, really
```

If your program handles signals, it may be difficult to pass the signal through the debugger to the target. GDB is pretty good about this, though. We're told that `lldb` is not as good at it (see Section 17.3.6, "Honorable Mention: `lldb`," page 605).

GDB can do *much* more than we've shown here. The GDB manual is large, and much of its content is specialized, relating to things like remote debugging and debugging embedded systems. However, it is worthwhile to read the parts that are generally relevant so you can familiarize yourself with its commands and capabilities. After that, it's probably sufficient to look at the `NEWS` file in each new GDB distribution to see what's new or changed.

It's also worth printing the GDB reference card that comes in the file `gdb/doc/refcard.tex` within the GDB source distribution. You can create a printable PDF version of the reference card, after extracting the source, by using these commands:

`$ cd gdb-N.M`	*Change to GDB source directory*
`$ ./configure && make`	*Build everything. This takes a while*
`$ cd gdb/doc`	*Change to doc subdirectory*
`$ make refcard.pdf`	*Format the reference card*

The reference card is meant to be printed dual-sided, on 8.5 x 11-inch (letter size) paper, in landscape format. It provides a six-column summary of the most useful GDB commands. We recommend printing it and having it by your keyboard as you work with GDB. For your convenience, a copy of the reference card from GDB 16.3 (the most current as of this writing) is included in the book's GitHub repository.

Recommendation: Invest the time to learn GDB thoroughly, above and beyond what we've covered here.

17.3.4 Escaping the Line-at-a-Time Jail

Line-at-a-time debuggers are great for providing an introduction to debuggers and debugging in a book such as this one. However, even though the line-at-a-time interface is simple and easy to understand, it's not so pleasant to use, particularly when you're used to working with screenfuls of source code.

Typically, what we might call *enhanced* interfaces provide multiple windows, one of which is for entering regular GDB commands, and another of which is for showing many lines of source code. Often there is also a window for the output of the program, if any.

Here are a few options that you should explore. It's likely that at least one of them will suit you better than using vanilla GDB in a terminal window:

The built-in TUI interface
: GDB has a built-in screen-based interface called the Terminal User Interface, or TUI for short. Invoke GDB with '`gdb --tui ...`' to use it. The GDB manual has a separate chapter explaining the TUI interface.

Curses GDB (CGDB)
: The Curses GDB project[6] provides a screen-based interface to GDB, including syntax highlighting for C.

The `termdebug` package for Vim
: The Vim ("`vi` Improved") editor[7] provides a package called `termdebug`, which opens three windows: one for the GDB prompt, one for source code, and one for program output. (This is what we use.) A sample session is shown in Figure 17.2.

Emacs GDB Integration
: The GNU Emacs editor[8] also provides GDB integration.

---

[6] `https://cgdb.github.io/`
[7] `https://www.vim.org`
[8] `https://www.gnu.org/software/emacs/`

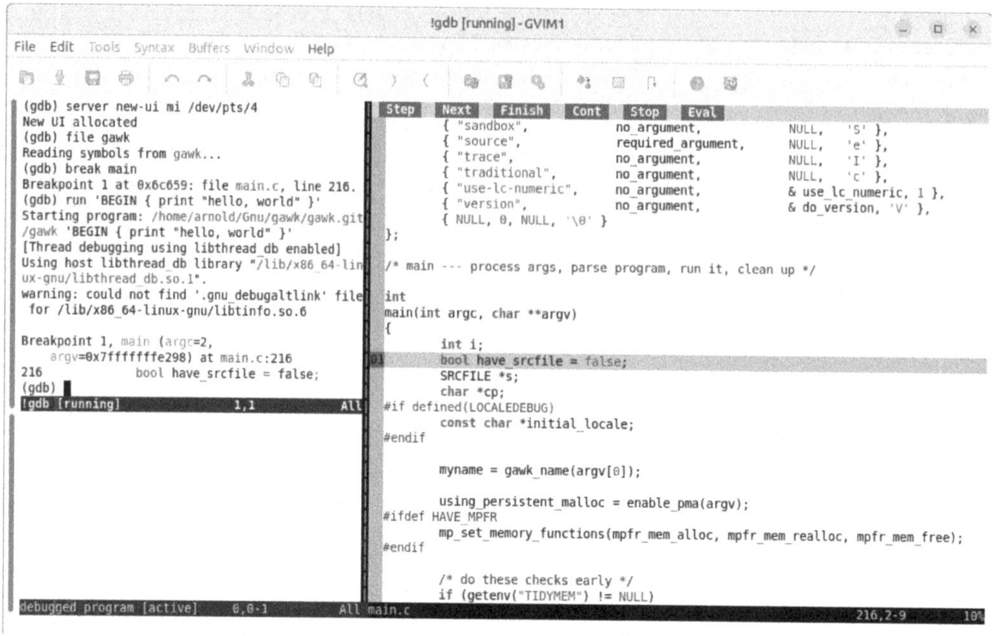

Figure 17.2: Debugging in Vim

The ddd *Debugger*

The ddd debugger[9] is a graphical debugger; it is built on top of GDB, so if you learn GDB, you can make some use of ddd right away. (ddd has its own manual, which you should read if you'll be using it heavily.)

Recommendation: Choose an enhanced interface to GDB, and use it.

17.3.5 Repeatable, Reversable Debugging with rr

As we were finishing up revising this book, we came across an interesting tool that we have yet to try out ourselves. So this section is necessarily brief, providing an introduction to rr, which we hope you will explore further.

rr provides repeatable, reversable debugging as an enhancement to facilities that already exist within GDB. The GDB manual[10] defines *reverse execution* as follows:

> When you are debugging a program, it is not unusual to realize that you have gone too far, and some event of interest has already happened. If the target environment supports it, GDB can allow you to "rewind" the program by running it backward.

[9] ddd can be installed on many GNU/Linux systems. The source code is available from the GNU Project's download site for ddd (https://ftp.gnu.org/gnu/ddd/).

[10] https://sourceware.org/gdb/current/onlinedocs/gdb.html/Reverse-Execution.html

> A target environment that supports reverse execution should be able to "undo" the changes in machine state that have taken place as the program was executing normally. Variables, registers etc. should revert to their previous values. Obviously this requires a great deal of sophistication on the part of the target environment; not all target environments can support reverse execution.
>
> When a program is executed in reverse, the instructions that have most recently been executed are "un-executed," in reverse order. The program counter runs backward, following the previous thread of execution in reverse. As each instruction is "un-executed," the values of memory and/or registers that were changed by that instruction are reverted to their previous states. After executing a piece of source code in reverse, all side effects of that code should be "undone," and all variables should be returned to their prior values.

The `rr` debugger[11] works by recording the execution of a program in a trace file, allowing you to replay the execution in a deterministic fashion, time after time. It also provides very efficient reverse execution.

A nice introduction to reverse execution and `rr` may be found at `https://stackoverflow.com/questions/1470434/how-does-reverse-debugging-work/53063242#53063242`.

The `rr` wiki[12] provides an introduction to using `rr`.

Source code may be found on GitHub.[13] We were able to install `rr` using the package tool on our system, so it's likely that you can do the same, with no need to build it from source code.

17.3.6 Honorable Mention: `lldb`

The `lldb` debugger[14] is a newer debugger that can be installed on GNU/Linux and several BSD systems. It uses infrastructure from the LLVM compiler project.[15]

As of this writing, LLDB supports fewer operating systems, languages, and machine architectures than does GDB. However, it's the native debugger on macOS, and it has a much more regular command language than GDB's. We purposely do not supply information about LLDB's operating system, language, and architecture support, as those are sure to change over time; see the website for the current status.

If LLDB is available for your system and you're just starting out learning to use a debugger, you may want to check it out.

If you're already familiar with GDB, the GDB to LLDB command map[16] may prove helpful in learning LLDB.

---

[11] `https://rr-project.org/`

[12] `https://github.com/rr-debugger/rr/wiki/Usage`

[13] `https://github.com/rr-debugger/rr`

[14] `https://lldb.llvm.org`

[15] `https://www.llvm.org`

[16] `https://lldb.llvm.org/use/map.html`

17.4 Programming for Debugging

There are many techniques for making source code easier to debug, ranging from simple to involved. We look at a number of them in this section.

17.4.1 Compile-Time Debugging Code

Several techniques relate to the source code itself.

17.4.1.1 Use Debugging Macros

Perhaps the simplest compile-time technique is the use of the preprocessor to provide conditionally compiled code. For example:

```
#ifdef DEBUG
     fprintf(stderr, "myvar = %d\n", myvar);
     fflush(stderr);
#endif /* DEBUG */
```

Adding `-DDEBUG` to the compiler command line causes the call to `fprintf()` to execute when the program runs.

Recommendation: Send debug messages to `stderr` so that they aren't lost down a pipeline and so that they can be captured with an I/O redirection. Be sure to use `fflush()` so that messages are forced to the output as soon as possible.

NOTE

The symbol `DEBUG`, while obvious, is also highly overused. It's a better idea to use a symbol specific to your program, such as `MYAPPDEBUG`. You can even use different symbols for debugging code in different parts of your program, such as file I/O, data verification, memory management, and so on.

Scattering lots of `#ifdef` statements throughout your code quickly becomes painful. And too many `#ifdef`s obscure the main program logic. There's got to be a better way, and indeed, a technique that's often been used is to conditionally define special macros for printing:

```
/* TECHNIQUE 1 --- commonly used but not recommended, see text */
/* In application header file: */
#ifdef MYAPPDEBUG
#define DPRINT0(msg)                  fprintf(stderr, msg)
#define DPRINT1(msg, v1)              fprintf(stderr, msg, v1)
#define DPRINT2(msg, v1, v2)          fprintf(stderr, msg, v1, v2)
#define DPRINT3(msg, v1, v2, v3)      fprintf(stderr, msg, v1, v2, v3)
```

```
#else /* ! MYAPPDEBUG */
#define DPRINT0(msg)
#define DPRINT1(msg, v1)
#define DPRINT2(msg, v1, v2)
#define DPRINT3(msg, v1, v2, v3)
#endif /* ! MYAPPDEBUG */

/* In application source file: */
DPRINT1("myvar = %d\n", myvar);
...
DPRINT2("v1 = %d, v2 = %f\n", v1, v2);
```

There are multiple macros, one for each different number of arguments, up to whatever limit you wish to provide. When `MYAPPDEBUG` is defined, the calls to the `DPRINTx()` macros expand into calls to `fprintf()`. When `MYAPPDEBUG` isn't defined, then those same calls expand to nothing. (This is essentially how `assert()` works; we described `assert()` in Section 13.1, "Assertion Statements: `assert()`," page 419.)

This technique works; we have used it ourselves and seen it recommended in textbooks. However, it can be refined a bit further, reducing the number of macros down to one:

```
/* TECHNIQUE 2 --- most portable to old and new compilers */
/* In application header file: */
#ifdef MYAPPDEBUG
#define DPRINT(stuff)   fprintf stuff
#else
#define DPRINT(stuff)
#endif

/* In application source file: */
DPRINT((stderr, "myvar = %d\n", myvar));        Note the double parentheses
```

Note how the macro is invoked with two sets of parentheses! By making the entire argument list for `fprintf()` into a single argument, you no longer need to have an arbitrary number of debugging macros.

Fortunately, there is an even cleaner way to do this, as long as your compiler conforms to at least the 1999 C standard:

```
/* TECHNIQUE 3 --- cleanest of all */
/* In application header file: */
#ifdef MYAPPDEBUG
#define DPRINT(mesg, ...)   fprintf(stderr, mesg, __VA_ARGS__)
#else
#define DPRINT(mesg, ...)
#endif
```

```
/* In application source file: */
DPRINT("myvar = %d\n", myvar);
...
DPRINT("v1 = %d, v2 = %f\n", v1, v2);
```

The 1999 C standard introduced *variadic macros*—that is, macros that can accept a variable number of arguments. (This is similar to variadic functions, like `printf()`.) In the macro definition, the three periods, '`...`', indicate that there will be zero or more arguments. In the macro body, the special identifier __VA_ARGS__ is replaced with the provided arguments, however many there are.

The advantage to this mechanism is that only one set of parentheses is necessary when the debugging macro is invoked, making the code read much more naturally. It also preserves the ability to have just one macro name, instead of multiple names that vary according to the number of arguments.

Recommendation: Use the C99 mechanism that relies on variadic macros. It should work with any modern C or C++ compiler.

17.4.1.2 Avoid Expression Macros If Possible

In general, C preprocessor macros are a rather sharp two-edged sword. They provide you with great power, but they also provide a great opportunity to injure yourself. That is, the preprocessor is a valuable tool, but it should be used judiciously.

For efficiency or code clarity, it's common to see macros such as this:

```
#define RS_is_null    (RS_node->var_value == Nnull_string)
...
if (RS_is_null || today == TUESDAY) ...
```

At first glance, this looks fine. The condition '`RS_is_null`' is clear and easy to understand, and it abstracts the details inherent in the test. The problem comes when you try to print the value in GDB:

```
(gdb) print RS_is_null
No symbol "RS_is_null" in current context.
```

In such a case, you have to track down the definition of the macro and print the expanded value.

Recommendation: Use variables to represent important conditions in your program, with explicit code to change the variable values when the conditions change.

Here is an abbreviated example, from `io.c` in the gawk distribution:

```
void
set_RS()
{
    ...
    RS_is_null = false;
    ...
```

```
    if (RS->stlen == 0) {
        RS_is_null = true;
        matchrec = rsnullscan;
        if (first_time || ! do_csv)
            matchrec = rsnullscan;
    }
    ...
}
```

Once `RS_is_null` is set and maintained, it can be tested by code *and* printed from within a debugger.

NOTE

With GCC, if you compile your program with the options `-gdwarf` and `-g3`, you *can* use macros from within GDB.

However, only the combination of GCC, GDB, and the special options allows you to use macros this way; if you're not using GCC, you still have the problem. We stand by our recommendation to avoid such macros if you can.

The problem with macros extends to code fragments as well. If a macro defines multiple statements, you can't set a breakpoint inside the middle of the macro. This is also true of C99 and C++ `inline` functions: if the compiler substitutes the body of an `inline` function into the generated code, it is again difficult or impossible to set a breakpoint inside it. This ties in with our advice to compile without `-O`; in this case, compilers usually don't do function inlining.

Along similar lines, it's common to have a variable that represents a particular state. It's easy, and encouraged by many C programming books, to `#define` symbolic constants for these states. For example:

```
/* The various states to be in when scanning for the end of a record. */
#define NOSTATE   1     /* scanning not started yet (all) */
#define INLEADER  2     /* skipping leading data (RS = "") */
#define INDATA    3     /* in body of record (all) */
#define INTERM    4     /* scanning terminator (RS = "", RS = regexp) */
int state;
...
state = NOSTATE;
...
state = INLEADER;
...
if (state != INTERM) ...
```

At the source code level, this looks great. But again, there is a problem when you look at the code from within GDB:

```
(gdb) print state
$1 = 2
```

Here, too, you're forced to go back and look at the header file to figure out what the 2 means. So what's the alternative?

Recommendation: Use `enum`s instead of macros to define symbolic constants. The source code usage is the same, and the debugger can print the `enum`s' values too.

An example, also from `io.c` in `gawk`:

```
typedef enum scanstate {
    NOSTATE,     /* scanning not started yet (all) */
    INLEADER,    /* skipping leading data (RS = "") */
    INDATA,      /* in body of record (all) */
    INTERM,      /* scanning terminator (RS = "", RS = regexp) */
} SCANSTATE;
SCANSTATE state;
... rest of code remains unchanged! ...
```

Now, when looking at `state` from within GDB, we see something useful:

```
(gdb) print state
$1 = NOSTATE
```

Sometimes, you may see code that looks like this:

```
typedef enum scanstate {
    NOSTATE,     /* scanning not started yet (all) */
#define NOSTATE NOSTATE
    INLEADER,    /* skipping leading data (RS = "") */
#define INLEADER INLEADER
    INDATA,      /* in body of record (all) */
#define INDATA INDATA
    INTERM,      /* scanning terminator (RS = "", RS = regexp) */
#define INTERM INTERM
} SCANSTATE;
```

What's the deal with that? Remember that in standard C, defining a macro name to itself as the value works; the macro isn't expanded recursively. This enables conditionally compiled code that will or will not be included depending on whether a value was defined, but the value will still show up correctly as an `enum` constant in the debugger, instead of as a number.

17.4.1.3 Reorder Code If Necessary

It's not uncommon to have a condition in an `if` or `while` consist of multiple component tests, separated by `&&` or `||`. If these tests are function calls (or even if they're not), it's impossible to single-step each separate part of the condition. GDB's `step` and `next` commands work on the basis of *statements*, not *expressions*. (Splitting such things across lines doesn't help either.)

Recommendation: Rewrite the original code, using explicit temporary variables that store return values or conditional results so that you can examine them in a debugger. The original code should be maintained in a comment so that you (or some later programmer) can tell what's going on.

Here's a concrete example—the function `do_input()` from the file `io.c` in version 3.1.8 of `gawk`:

```
/* do_input --- the main input processing loop */

void
do_input()
{
    IOBUF *iop;
    extern int exiting;
    int rval1, rval2, rval3;

    (void) setjmp(filebuf); /* for 'nextfile' */

    while ((iop = nextfile(FALSE)) != NULL) {
        /*
         * This was:
        if (inrec(iop) == 0)
            while (interpret(expression_value) && inrec(iop) == 0)
                continue;
         * Now expand it out for ease of debugging.
         */
        rval1 = inrec(iop);
        if (rval1 == 0) {
            for (;;) {
                rval2 = rval3 = -1; /* for debugging */
                rval2 = interpret(expression_value);
                if (rval2 != 0)
                    rval3 = inrec(iop);
                if (rval2 == 0 || rval3 != 0)
                    break;
            }
        }
        if (exiting)
            break;
    }
}
```

(The line numbers are relative to the start of the routine, not the file.) This function was the heart of gawk's main processing loop.[17] The outer loop (lines 12 and 33) steps through the command-line data files. The comment on lines 13–19 shows the original code, which reads each record from the current file and processes it.

A zero return value from `inrec()` indicates an OK status, while a nonzero return value from `interpret()` also indicates an OK status. When we tried to step through this loop, verifying the record reading process, it became necessary to perform each step individually.

Lines 20–30 are the rewritten code, which calls each function separately, storing the return values in local variables so that they can be printed from the debugger. Note how line 23 forces these variables to have known, invalid values each time around the loop: otherwise, they would retain their values from previous loop iterations. Line 27 is the exit test; because the code has changed to an infinite loop (compare line 22 to line 16), the test for breaking out of the loop is the opposite of the original test.

As an aside, we admit to having had to study the rewrite carefully when we made it, to make sure it did exactly the same as the original code; it does. It later occurred to us that perhaps this version of the loop might be closer to the original:

```
/* Possible replacement for lines 22 - 29 */
do {
    rval2 = rval3 = -1; /* for debugging */
    rval2 = interpret(expression_value);
    if (rval2 != 0)
        rval3 = inrec(iop);
} while (rval2 != 0 && rval3 == 0);
```

The truth is, both versions are harder to read than the original and thus potentially in error. However, since the code worked, we decided to leave well enough alone.

Finally, we note that not all expert programmers would agree with our advice here. When each component of a condition is a function call, you can set a breakpoint on each one, use `step` to step into each function, and then use `finish` to complete the function. GDB will tell you the function's return value, and from that point you can use `cont` or `step` to continue. We like our approach because the results are kept in variables, which can be checked (and rechecked) after the function calls, and even a few statements later.

17.4.1.4 Use Debugging Helper Functions

A common technique, applicable in many cases, is to have a set of *flag* values; when a flag is *set* (that is, true), a certain fact is true or a certain condition applies. This is commonly done with `#defined` symbolic constants and the C bitwise operators. (We discussed the use of bit flags and the bit manipulation operators in Section 8.3.1.1, "A Programming Digression: Bit Flags," page 241.)

For example, gawk's central data structure is called a `NODE`. It has a large number of fields, the last of which is a set of flag values. From the file `awk.h`:

[17] Since then, gawk's internals have been rewritten; you won't find this function in the current code base.

```
typedef struct exp_node {
    ...                                 Lots of stuff omitted
    enum flagvals {
    /* type = Node_val */
        MALLOC  = 0x0001,           /* stptr can be free'd. */
        STRING  = 0x0002,           /* assigned as string */
        STRCUR  = 0x0004,           /* string value is current */
        NUMCUR  = 0x0008,           /* numeric value is current */
        NUMBER  = 0x0010,           /* assigned as number */
        USER_INPUT = 0x0020,        /* user input: if NUMERIC then
                                     * a NUMBER */
        BOOLVAL = 0x0040,           /* this is a boolean value */
        INTLSTR = 0x0080,           /* use localized version */
        NUMINT  = 0x0100,           /* numeric value is an integer */
        INTIND  = 0x0200,           /* integral value is array index;
                                     * lazy conversion to string.
                                     */
        WSTRCUR = 0x0400,           /* wide str value is current */
        MPFN    = 0x0800,           /* arbitrary-precision floating-point number */
        MPZN    = 0x01000,          /* arbitrary-precision integer */
        NO_EXT_SET = 0x02000,       /* extension cannot set a value for this variable */
        NULL_FIELD = 0x04000,       /* this is the null field */

    /* type = Node_var_array */
        ARRAYMAXED  = 0x08000,  /* array is at max size */
        HALFHAT     = 0x010000, /* half-capacity Hashed Array Tree;
                                 * See cint_array.c */
        XARRAY      = 0x020000,
        NUMCONSTSTR = 0x040000, /* have string value for numeric constant */
        REGEX       = 0x080000, /* this is a typed regex */
    } flags;
} NODE;
```

The reason to use flag values is that they provide considerable savings in data space. If the `NODE` structure used a separate `bool` field for each flag, that would use 20 bytes instead of the four used by the `enum`. The current size of a `NODE` (on a 64-bit Intel system) is 112 bytes. Adding 16 more bytes would bump that to 128 bytes. Since `gawk` can allocate potentially hundreds of thousands (or even millions) of `NODE`s,[18] keeping the size down is important.

What's does this have to do with debugging? Although, as we showed earlier, GDB knows how to print out the OR'd combination of symbolic values, there are times when you want to do so outside the context of a debugger—for example, in a debugging log message, or on a system where you have a C compiler but no GDB.

Recommendation: Provide a function to convert flags to a string. If you have multiple independent flags, set up a general-purpose routine.

---

[18]Seriously! People often process gigabytes of data with `gawk`, storing intermediate values in memory until done. Remember, *no arbitrary limits!*

NOTE

What's unusual about these debugging functions is that *application code never calls them*. They exist *only* so that they can be called from a debugger (or from a debugging log message). Such functions should always be compiled in, without even a surrounding `#ifdef`, so that you can use them without having to take special steps. The (usually minimal) extra code size is justified by the developer's time savings.

First we'll show you how we did this initially. Here is (an abbreviated version of) `flags2str()` from a now-ancient version of `gawk` (3.0.6):

```
1  /* flags2str --- make a flags value readable */
2
3  char *
4  flags2str(flagval)
5  int flagval;
6  {
7      static char buffer[BUFSIZ];
8      char *sp;
9
10     sp = buffer;
11
12     if (flagval & MALLOC) {
13         strcpy(sp, "MALLOC");
14         sp += strlen(sp);
15     }
16     if (flagval & TEMP) {
17         if (sp != buffer)
18             *sp++ = '|';
19         strcpy(sp, "TEMP");
20         sp += strlen(sp);
21     }
22     if (flagval & PERM) {
23         if (sp != buffer)
24             *sp++ = '|';
25         strcpy(sp, "PERM");
26         sp += strlen(sp);
27     }
       ... much more of the same, omitted for brevity ...
82
83     return buffer;
84 }
```

(The line numbers are relative to the start of the function.) The result is a string, something like `"MALLOC|PERM|NUMBER"`. Each flag is tested separately, and if present, each one's action is the same: test if not at the beginning of the buffer so we can add the '|' character, copy the string into place, and update the pointer. Similar functions existed for formatting and displaying the other kinds of flags in the program.

The code is both repetitive and error prone, and for gawk 3.1 we were able to simplify and generalize it. Here's how gawk now does it. Starting with this definition in awk.h:

```
/* for debugging purposes */
struct flagtab {
    int val;                    Integer flag value
    const char *name;           String name
};
```

This structure can be used to represent any set of flags with their corresponding string values. Each different group of flags has a corresponding function that returns a printable representation of the flags that are currently set. From eval.c in gawk 5.3.0:

```
/* flags2str --- make a flags value readable */

const char *
flags2str(int flagval)
{
    static const struct flagtab values[] = {
        { MALLOC, "MALLOC" },
        { STRING, "STRING" },
        { STRCUR, "STRCUR" },
        { NUMCUR, "NUMCUR" },
        { NUMBER, "NUMBER" },
        { USER_INPUT, "USER_INPUT" },
        { BOOLVAL, "BOOL" },
        { INTLSTR, "INTLSTR" },
        { NUMINT, "NUMINT" },
        { INTIND, "INTIND" },
        { WSTRCUR, "WSTRCUR" },
        { MPFN, "MPFN" },
        { MPZN, "MPZN" },
        { NO_EXT_SET, "NO_EXT_SET" },
        { NULL_FIELD, "NULL_FIELD" },
        { ARRAYMAXED, "ARRAYMAXED" },
        { HALFHAT, "HALFHAT" },
        { XARRAY, "XARRAY" },
        { NUMCONSTSTR, "NUMCONSTSTR" },
        { REGEX, "REGEX" },
        { 0,    NULL },
    };

    return genflags2str(flagval, values);
}
```

`flags2str()` defines an array that maps flag values to strings. By convention, a `0` flag value indicates the end of the array. The code calls `genflags2str()` ("general flags to string") to do the work. `genflags2str()` is a general-purpose routine that converts a flag value into a string. It's the very next function in `eval.c`:

```
/* genflags2str --- general routine to convert a flag value to a string */

const char *
genflags2str(int flagval, const struct flagtab *tab)
{
    static char buffer[BUFSIZ];
    char *sp;
    int i, space_left, space_needed;

    sp = buffer;
    space_left = BUFSIZ;
    for (i = 0; tab[i].name != NULL; i++) {
        if ((flagval & tab[i].val) != 0) {
            /*
             * note the trick, we want 1 or 0 for whether we need
             * the '|' character.
             */
            space_needed = (strlen(tab[i].name) + (sp != buffer));
            if (space_left < space_needed)
                fatal(_("buffer overflow in genflags2str"));

            if (sp != buffer) {
                *sp++ = '|';
                space_left--;
            }
            strcpy(sp, tab[i].name);
            /* note ordering! */
            space_left -= strlen(sp);
            sp += strlen(sp);
        }
    }

    return buffer;
}
```

(Line numbers are relative to the start of the function, not the file.) As with the previous version, the idea here is to fill in a `static` buffer with a string value such as `"MALLOC|PERM|STRING|MAYBE_NUM"` and return the address of that buffer. We discuss the reasons for using a `static` buffer shortly; first let's examine the code.

The `sp` pointer tracks the position of the next empty spot in the buffer, while `space_left` tracks how much room is left; this keeps us from overflowing the buffer.

The bulk of the function is a loop (line 12) through the array of flag values. When a flag is found (line 13), the code computes how much space is needed for the string (line 18) and tests to see if that much room is left (lines 19–20).

The test '`sp != buffer`' fails on the first flag value found, returning `0`. On subsequent flags, the test has a value of `1`. This tells us if we need the '`|`' separator character between values. By adding the result (`1` or `0`) to the length of the string, we get the correct value for `space_needed`. The same test, for the same reason, is used on line 22 to control lines 23 and 24, which insert the '`|`' character.

Finally, lines 26–29 copy in the string value, adjust the amount of space left, and update the `sp` pointer. Line 33 returns the address of the buffer, which contains the printable representation of the string.

Now, what about that `static` buffer? Normally, good programming practice discourages the use of functions that return the address of `static` buffers: it's easy to have multiple calls to such a function overwrite the buffer each time, forcing the caller to copy the returned data.

Furthermore, a `static` buffer is by definition a buffer of fixed size. What happened to the GNU "no arbitrary limits" principle?

The answer to both of these questions is to remember that this is a *debugging* function. Normal code *never* calls `genflags2str()`; it's meant to be called by a human using a debugger. No caller holds a pointer to the buffer; as a developer doing debugging, we don't care that the buffer gets overwritten each time we call the function.

In practice, the fixed size isn't an issue either; we know that `BUFSIZ` is big enough to represent all the flags that we use. Nevertheless, being experienced and knowing that things can change, `genflags2str()` has code to protect itself from overrunning the buffer (the `space_left` variable and the code on lines 18–20).

As an aside, the use of `BUFSIZ` is arguable. That constant should be used exclusively for I/O buffers, but it is often used for general string buffers as well. Such code would be better off defining explicit constants, such as `FLAGVALSIZE`, and using '`sizeof(buffer)`' on line 11.

Here is an abbreviated GDB session showing `flags2str()` in use:

```
$ gdb gawk                                                    Start GDB on gawk
GNU gdb (Ubuntu 12.1-0ubuntu1~22.04) 12.1
...
Reading symbols from gawk...
(gdb) break do_print                                          Set a breakpoint
Breakpoint 1 at 0x426487: file builtin.c, line 2310.
(gdb) run 'BEGIN { print "hello, world" }'                    Start it running
Starting program: /tmp/gawk-5.3.0/gawk 'BEGIN { print "hello, world" }'
[Thread debugging using libthread_db enabled]
Using host libthread_db library "/lib/x86_64-linux-gnu/libthread_db.so.1".

Breakpoint 1, do_print (nargs=1, redirtype=0) at builtin.c:2310   Breakpoint hit
2310    {
(gdb) n                                                       Get to a NODE value
2311            struct redirect *rp = NULL;
...
```

```
2346            tmp = args_array[i] = POP();
(gdb) print *tmp                                          Print NODE
$1 = {sub = {nodep = {l = {lptr = 0x0, li = 0x0, ll = 0, lp = 0x0}, r = {
        rptr = 0x0, preg = {0x0, 0x0}, av = 0x0, bv = 0x0, uptr = 0x0,
        iptr = 0x0}, x = {extra = 0x0, aptr = 0x0, xl = 0, cmnt = 0x0},
      name = 0x4e <error: Cannot access memory at address 0x4e>,
      reserved = 5154272, rn = 0xc, cnt = 4294967295, reflags = 0}, val = {
      nm = {fltnum = 0, mpnum = {{_mpfr_prec = 0, _mpfr_sign = 0,
            _mpfr_exp = 0, _mpfr_d = 0x0}}, mpi = {{_mp_alloc = 0,
            _mp_size = 0, _mp_d = 0x0}}}, rndmode = 78,
      sp = 0x4ea5e0 "hello, world", slen = 12, idx = -1, wsp = 0x0, wslen = 0,
      typre = 0x0, comtype = 0}}, type = Node_val,
  flags = (MALLOC | STRING | STRCUR), valref = 2}
(gdb) print flags2str(tmp->flags)                         Print flag value
$2 = 0x4d3180 <buffer> "MALLOC|STRING|STRCUR"
```

Even though, for this particular case, GDB does the job for us, the technique remains valuable for cases in which flag values are stored in an `int` and not in an `enum`.

We hope you'll agree that the current general-purpose mechanism is considerably more elegant than the original one, and easier to use.

Recommendation: Careful design and use of arrays of `structs` (i.e., careful data design) can often replace or consolidate repetitive code.

17.4.1.5 Avoid Unions When Possible

There ain't no such thing as a free lunch.
— Lazarus Long

The C `union` is a relatively esoteric facility. It allows you to save memory by storing different types of items within the same physical space; how the program treats the space depends on how it's accessed:

```
/* ch-debugging-union.c --- brief demo of union usage. */

#include <stdio.h>
#include <stdlib.h>

int
main(void)
{
    union i_f {
        long i;
        double f;
    } u;

    u.f = 12.34;    /* Assign a floating-point value */
```

```
    printf("%lf also looks like %#lx\n", u.f, u.i);
    exit(EXIT_SUCCESS);
}
```

Here is what happens when the program is run on an Intel x86_64 GNU/Linux system:

```
$ ch-debugging-union
12.340000 also looks like 0x4028ae147ae147ae
```

The program prints the bit pattern that represents a floating-point number as a hexadecimal integer. The storage for the two fields occupies the same memory; the difference is in how the memory is treated: `u.f` acts like a floating-point number, whereas the same bits in `u.i` act like an integer.

Unions are particularly useful in compilers and interpreters, which often create a tree structure representing the structure of a source code file (called a *parse tree*). This models the way programming languages are formally described: `if` statements, `while` statements, assignment statements, and so on are all instances of the more generic "statement" type. Thus, a compiler might have something like this:

```
struct if_stmt { ... };                   Structure for IF statement
struct while_stmt { ... };                Structure for WHILE statement
struct for_stmt { ... };                  Structure for FOR statement
... structures for other statement types ...

typedef enum stmt_type {
    IF, WHILE, FOR, ...
} TYPE;                                   What we actually have

/* This contains the type and unions of the individual kinds of statements. */
struct statement {
    TYPE type;
    union stmt {
        struct if_stmt if_st;
        struct while_stmt while_st;
        struct for_stmt for_st;
        ...
    } u;
};
```

Along with the `union`, it is conventional to use macros to make the components of the `union` look as if they were fields in a `struct`. For example:

```
#define if_s     u.if_st                  So can use s->if_s instead of s->u.if_st
#define while_s  u.while_st               And so on ...
#define for_s    u.for_st
...
```

At the level just presented, this seems reasonable and looks manageable. The real world, however, is a more complicated place, and practical compilers and interpreters often have several levels of *nested* `struct`s and `union`s. This includes `gawk`, in which the definition of the `NODE`, its flag values, and macros for accessing `union` components takes over 130 lines![19] Here is enough of that definition to give you a feel for what's happening:

```
typedef struct exp_node {
    union {
        struct {
            union {
                struct exp_node *lptr;
                struct exp_instruction *li;
                long ll;
                const array_funcs_t *lp;
            } l;
            union {
                ...
            } r;
            union {
                ...
            } x;
            char *name;
            ...
        } nodep;

        struct {
#ifdef HAVE_MPFR
            union {
                AWKNUM fltnum;
                mpfr_t mpnum;
                mpz_t mpi;
            } nm;
            int rndmode;
#else
            AWKNUM fltnum;
#endif
            char *sp;
            size_t slen;
            int idx;
            wchar_t *wsp;
            size_t wslen;
            struct exp_node *typre;
            enum commenttype comtype;
```

[19]We inherited this design. In general it works, but it does have its problems. The point of this section is to pass on the experience we've acquired working with `union`s.

```
        } val;
    } sub;
    enum flagvals {             As shown earlier
        ...
    } flags;
    long valref;
} NODE;

#define vname sub.nodep.name

#define lnode    sub.nodep.l.lptr
#define rnode    sub.nodep.r.rptr
...
#define stptr    sub.val.sp
#define stlen    sub.val.slen
#define stfmt    sub.val.idx
#define strndmode sub.val.rndmode
#define wstptr   sub.val.wsp
#define wstlen   sub.val.wslen
...
```

The `NODE` has a `union` inside a `struct` inside a `union` inside a `struct`! (Ouch.) On top of that, multiple macro "fields" map to the same `struct`/`union` components, depending on what is actually stored in the `NODE`! (Ouch, again.)

The benefit of this complexity is that the C code is relatively clear. Something like '`NF_node->var_value->stlen`' is straightforward to read.

There is, of course, a price to pay for the flexibility that `union`s provide. When your debugger is deep down in the guts of your code, you can't use the nice macros that appear in the source. You *must* use the real expansion.[20] (And for that, you have to find the definition in the header file.)

For example, compare '`NF_node->var_value->stlen`' to what it expands to: '`NF_node->sub.nodep.l.lptr->sub.val.slen`'! You must type the latter into GDB to look at your data value. Look again at this excerpt from the earlier GDB debugging session:

```
(gdb) print *tmp                                          Print NODE
$1 = {sub = {nodep = {l = {lptr = 0x0, li = 0x0, ll = 0, lp = 0x0}, r = {
        rptr = 0x0, preg = {0x0, 0x0}, av = 0x0, bv = 0x0, uptr = 0x0,
        iptr = 0x0}, x = {extra = 0x0, aptr = 0x0, xl = 0, cmnt = 0x0},
      name = 0x4e <error: Cannot access memory at address 0x4e>,
      reserved = 5154272, rn = 0xc, cnt = 4294967295, reflags = 0}, val = {
      nm = {fltnum = 0, mpnum = {{_mpfr_prec = 0, _mpfr_sign = 0,
            _mpfr_exp = 0, _mpfr_d = 0x0}}, mpi = {{_mp_alloc = 0,
            _mp_size = 0, _mp_d = 0x0}}}, rndmode = 78,
      sp = 0x4ea5e0 "hello, world", slen = 12, idx = -1, wsp = 0x0, wslen = 0,
```

[20] Again, GCC and GDB can let you use macros directly, but only if you're using them together, with specific options. This was described earlier, in Section 17.4.1.2, "Avoid Expression Macros If Possible," page 608.

```
    typre = 0x0, comtype = 0}}, type = Node_val,
  flags = (MALLOC | STRING | STRCUR), valref = 2}
```

That's a lot of goop. However, GDB does make this a little easier to handle. You can use expressions like '`($1).sub.val.slen`' to step through the tree and list data structures.

There are other reasons to avoid `union`s. First of all, `union`s are *unchecked*. Nothing but programmer attention ensures that when you access one part of a `union`, you are accessing the same part that was last stored. We saw this in `ch-debugging-union.c`, which accessed both of the `union`'s "identities" simultaneously.

A second reason, related to the first, is to be careful of *overlays* in complicated nested `struct`/`union` combinations. For example, an earlier version of `gawk` had this code:[21]

```
/* n->lnode overlays the array size, don't unref it if array */
if (n->type != Node_var_array && n->type != Node_array_ref)
    unref(n->lnode);
```

Originally, there was no `if`, just a call to `unref()`, which frees the `NODE` pointed to by `n->lnode`. However, it was possible to crash `gawk` at this point. You can imagine how long it took, in a debugger, to track down the fact that what was being treated as a pointer was in reality an array size!

The structure of a `union` can bite you in a different way as well. When compiled for a 32-bit architecture, the members likely have different sizes and a different memory layout than when compiled for a 64-bit architecture. (There can even be differences among different architectures of the same bit size!) This can also cause problems; during the prerelease testing of `gawk` 5.3.2, a bug manifested itself only when compiled for 32 bits.

As an aside, `union`s are considerably less useful in C++. Inheritance and object-oriented features make data structure management a different ball game, one that is considerably safer.

Recommendation: Consider *very* carefully before using `union`s. Explore the design alternatives, and be sure you're justified in using them. If you are sure, then design and code them carefully!

Recommendation: Compile and test your program for different architectures and architecture sizes *before* releasing it.

17.4.2 Runtime Debugging Code

Besides things you add to your code at compile time, you can also add extra code to enable debugging features at runtime. This is particularly useful for applications that are installed in the field, where a customer's system won't have the source code installed (and maybe not even a compiler!).

This section presents some runtime debugging techniques that we have used over the years, ranging from simple to more complex. Note that our treatment is by no means exhaustive. This is an area where it pays to have some imagination and to use it!

[21] This part of the code has since been revised, and the example lines are no longer there.

17.4.2.1 Add Debugging Options and Variables

The simplest technique is to have a command-line option that enables debugging. Such an option can be conditionally compiled in when you are debugging. But it's more flexible to leave the option in the *production* version of the program. (You may or may not also wish to leave the option *undocumented* as well. This has various trade-offs: documenting it can allow your customers or clients to learn more about the internals of your system, which you may not want. On the other hand, not documenting it seems rather sneaky. If you're writing Open Source or Free Software, it's better to document the option.)

If your program is large, you may want your debugging option to take an argument indicating what subsystem should be debugged. Based on the argument, you can set different flag variables or possibly different bit flags in a single debugging variable. Here is an outline of this technique:

```
struct option options[] = {
    ...
    { "debug", required_argument, NULL, 'D' },
    ...
}

int
main(int argc, char **argv)
{
    int c;

    while ((c = getopt_long(argc, argv, "...D:")) != -1) {
        switch (c) {
        ...
        case 'D':
            parse_debug(optarg);
            break;
        ...
        }
    }
    ...
}
```

The `parse_debug()` function reads through the argument string. For example, it could be a comma- or space-separated string of subsystems, like `"file,memory,ipc"`. For each valid subsystem name, the function would set a bit in a debugging variable:

```
extern enum debug_values debugging;

void
parse_debug(const char *subsystems)
{
    char *sp;
```

```
    for (sp = subsystems; *sp != '\0';) {
        if (strncmp(sp, "file", 4) == 0) {
            debugging |= DEBUG_FILE;
            sp += 4;
        } else if (strncmp(sp, "memory", 6) == 0) {
            debugging |= DEBUG_MEM;
            sp += 6;
        } else if (strncmp(sp, "ipc", 3) == 0) {
            debugging |= DEBUG_IPC;
            sp += 3;
        ...
        }
        while (*sp == ' ' || *sp == ',')
            sp++;
    }
}
```

Finally, application code can test the flags:

```
if ((debugging & DEBUG_FILE) != 0) ...          In the I/O part of the program

if ((debugging & DEBUG_MEM) != 0) ...           In the memory manager
```

It is up to you whether to use a single variable with flag bits, separate variables, or even a `debugging` array, indexed by symbolic constants (preferably from an `enum`).

The cost of leaving the debugging code in your production executable is that the program will be larger. Depending on the placement of your debugging code, it may also be slower since the tests are always performed but are always false until debugging is turned on. And as mentioned, it may be possible for someone to figure out how your program works internally, which you may not want. Or worse, a malevolent user could enable so much debugging that the program slows to an unusable state! (This is called a *denial of service attack*.)

The benefit, which can be great, is that your already installed program can be reinvoked with debugging turned on, without requiring you to build a special version and then download it to your customer site. When the software is installed in remote places that may not have people around and *all* you can do is access the system remotely through the Internet, such a feature can be a lifesaver.

Finally, you may wish to mix and match: use conditionally compiled debugging code for fine-grained, high-detail debugging, and save the always-present code for a coarser level of output.

17.4.2.2 Use Special Environment Variables

Another useful trick is to have your application pay attention to special environment variables (documented or otherwise). This can be particularly useful for testing. We'll share another example from our experience with `gawk`, but first, some background.

gawk uses a function named `optimal_bufsize()` to obtain the optimal buffer size for I/O. For small files, the function returns the file size. Otherwise, if the filesystem defines a size to use for I/O, it returns that (the `st_blksize` member in the `struct stat`; see Section 5.4.2, "Retrieving File Information," page 131). If that member isn't available, `optimal_bufsize()` returns the `BUFSIZ` constant from `<stdio.h>`. The original function (in `posix/gawkmisc.c` from `gawk` 3.0.0) looked like this:

```
1  /* optimal_bufsize --- determine optimal buffer size */
2
3  int
4  optimal_bufsize(fd, stb)          int optimal_bufsize(int fd, struct stat *stb);
5  int fd;
6  struct stat *stb;
7  {
8      /* force all members to zero in case OS doesn't use all of them. */
9      memset(stb, '\0', sizeof(struct stat));
10
11     /*
12      * System V.n, n < 4, doesn't have the file system block size in the
13      * stat structure. So we have to make some sort of reasonable
14      * guess. We use stdio's BUFSIZ, since that is what it was
15      * meant for in the first place.
16      */
17 #ifdef HAVE_ST_BLKSIZE
18 #define DEFBLKSIZE  (stb->st_blksize ? stb->st_blksize : BUFSIZ)
19 #else
20 #define DEFBLKSIZE  BUFSIZ
21 #endif
22
23     if (isatty(fd))
24         return BUFSIZ;
25     if (fstat(fd, stb) == -1)
26         fatal("can't stat fd %d (%s)", fd, strerror(errno));
27     if (lseek(fd, (off_t)0, 0) == -1)   /* not a regular file */
28         return DEFBLKSIZE;
29     if (stb->st_size > 0 && stb->st_size < DEFBLKSIZE) /* small file */
30         return stb->st_size;
31     return DEFBLKSIZE;
32 }
```

The constant `DEFBLKSIZE` is the "default block size"—that is, the value from the `struct stat`, or `BUFSIZ`. For terminals (line 23) or for files that aren't regular files (`lseek()` fails, line 27), the return value is also `BUFSIZ`. For regular files that are small, the file size is used. In all other cases, `DEFBLKSIZE` is returned. Knowing the "optimal" buffer size is particularly useful on filesystems in which the block size is *larger* than `BUFSIZ`.

We had a problem whereby one of our test cases worked perfectly on our development GNU/Linux system and every other Unix system we had access to, but it would fail consistently on certain other systems.

For a long time, we could not get direct access to a failing system in order to run GDB. Eventually, however, we did manage to reproduce the problem; it turned out to be related to the size of the buffer `gawk` was using for reading data files: on the failing systems, the buffer size was larger than for our development system.

We wanted a way to be able to reproduce the problem on our development machine: the failing system was nine time zones away, and running GDB interactively across the Atlantic Ocean is painful. We reproduced the problem by having `optimal_bufsize()` look at a special environment variable, `AWKBUFSIZE`. When the value is `"exact"`, `optimal_bufsize()` always returns the size of the file, whatever that may be. If the value of `AWKBUFSIZE` is some integer number, the function returns that number. Otherwise, the function falls back to the previous algorithm. This allows us to run tests without having to constantly recompile `gawk`. For example,

```
$ AWKBUFSIZE=42 make check
```

runs the `gawk` test suite, using a buffer size of 42 bytes. (The test suite passes.)[22] Here is the modified version of `optimal_bufsize()` (from `gawk` 5.3.0):

```
/* optimal_bufsize --- determine optimal buffer size */

/*
 * Enhance this for debugging purposes, as follows:
 *
 * Always stat the file, stat buffer is used by higher-level code.
 *
 * if (AWKBUFSIZE == "exact")
 *  return the file size
 * else if (AWKBUFSIZE == a number)
 *  always return that number
 * else
 *  if the size is < default_blocksize
 *      return the size
 *  else
 *      return default_blocksize
 *  end if
 * endif
 *
 * Hair comes in an effort to only deal with AWKBUFSIZE
 * once, the first time this routine is called, instead of
 * every time.  Performance, dontyaknow.
 */
```

[22]While updating this section, we reran this test, just to be sure, and found a bug in a new routine. It's now fixed, and once again, the test suite passes.

```

size_t
optimal_bufsize(int fd, struct stat *stb)
{
    char *val;
    static size_t env_val = 0;
    static bool first = true;
    static bool exact = false;

    /* force all members to zero in case OS doesn't use all of them. */
    memset(stb, '\0', sizeof(struct stat));

    /* always stat, in case stb is used by higher level code. */
    if (fstat(fd, stb) == -1)
        fatal("can't stat fd %d (%s)", fd, strerror(errno));

    if (first) {
        first = false;

        if ((val = getenv("AWKBUFSIZE")) != NULL) {
            if (strcmp(val, "exact") == 0)
                exact = true;
            else if (isdigit((unsigned char) *val)) {
                for (; *val && isdigit((unsigned char) *val); val++)
                    env_val = (env_val * 10) + *val - '0';

                return env_val;
            }
        }
    } else if (! exact && env_val > 0)
        return env_val;
    /* else
        fall through */

    /*
     * System V.n, n < 4, doesn't have the file system block size in the
     * stat structure. So we have to make some sort of reasonable
     * guess. We use stdio's BUFSIZ, since that is what it was
     * meant for in the first place.
     */
#ifdef HAVE_STRUCT_STAT_ST_BLKSIZE
#define DEFBLKSIZE  (stb->st_blksize > 0 ? stb->st_blksize : BUFSIZ)
#else
#define DEFBLKSIZE  BUFSIZ
#endif
```

```
69
70     if (S_ISREG(stb->st_mode)        /* regular file */
71         && 0 < stb->st_size          /* non-zero size */
72         && (stb->st_size < DEFBLKSIZE    /* small file */
73         || exact))           /* or debugging */
74         return stb->st_size;         /* use file size */
75
76     return DEFBLKSIZE;
77 }
```

The comment on lines 3–23 explains the algorithm. Since searching the environment can be expensive and it only needs to be done once, the function uses several `static` variables to collect the appropriate information the first time.

Lines 41–52 execute the first time the function is called, and only the first time. Line 41 enforces this condition by setting `first` to false. Lines 43–52 handle the environment variable, looking for either `"exact"` or a number. In the latter case, it converts the string value to decimal, saving it in `env_val`. (We probably should have used `strtoul()` here; it didn't occur to us at the time.)

Line 53 executes every time but the first. If a numeric value was given, the condition will be true and that value is returned (line 54). Otherwise, it falls through to the rest of the function.

Lines 64–68 define `DEFBLKSIZE`; this part has not changed. Finally, lines 70–74 return the file size if appropriate. If not (line 76), `DEFBLKSIZE` is returned.

We did fix the problem,[23] but in the meantime, we left the new version of `optimal_bufsize()` in place so that we could be sure the problem hasn't reoccurred.

The marginal increase in code size and complexity is more than offset by the increased flexibility we now have for testing. Furthermore, since this is production code, it's easy to have a user in the field use this feature for testing, to determine if a similar problem has occurred. (So far, we haven't had to ask for a test, but it's nice to know that we could handle it if we had to.)

17.4.2.3 Add Logging Code

It is often the case that your application program is running on a system on which you can't use a debugger (such as at a customer site). In that case, your goal is to be able to examine the program's internal state, but from the outside. The only way to do that is to have the program itself produce this information for you.

There are multiple ways to do this:

- Always log information to a specific file. This is simplest: the program always writes logging information. You can then look at the file at your convenience.

  The disadvantage is that at some point the log file will consume all available disk space. Therefore, you should have multiple log files, with your program switching to a new one periodically.

[23] By rewriting the buffer management code!

Brian Kernighan recommends naming the log files by day of the week: `myapp.log.sun`, `myapp.log.mon`, and so on. The advantage here is that you don't have to manually move old files out of the way; you get a week's worth of log files for free. The disadvantage is that the file names don't sort numerically.

- Write to a log file only if it already exists. When your program starts up, if the log file exists, it writes information to the log. Otherwise, it doesn't. To enable logging, first create an empty log file.
- Use a fixed format for messages, one that can be easily parsed by scripting languages such as `awk`, Perl, or Python for summary and report generation.
- Alternatively, generate some form of XML, which is self-describing, and possibly convertible to other formats. (We're not big fans of XML, but you shouldn't let that stop you.) These days, JSON is a popular alternative to XML.
- Use `syslog()` to do logging; the final disposition of logging messages can be controlled by the system administrator. (`syslog()` is a fairly advanced interface; see the *syslog*(3) manpage.)

Choosing how to log information is, of course, the easy part. The hard part is choosing *what* to log. As with all parts of program development, it pays to *think before you code*. Log information about critical variables. Check their values to make sure they're in range or are otherwise what you expect. Log exceptional conditions; if something occurs that shouldn't, log it, and if possible, keep going. Also, if you have an `errno` value or equivalent piece of information, log it! In other words, log *what* went wrong, not just that "something bad happened."

The key is to log only the information you need to track down problems, no more and no less.

17.4.2.4 Runtime Debugging Files

In a previous life, we worked for a startup company with binary executables of the product installed at customer sites. It wasn't possible to attach a debugger to a running copy of the program or to run it from a debugger on the customer's system. The main component of the product was not started directly from a command line, but indirectly, through shell scripts that did considerable initial setup.

To make the program start producing logging information, we came up with the idea of special debugging files. When a file of a certain name existed in a certain directory, the program would write informational messages to a log file that we could then download and analyze. Such code looks like this:

```
struct stat sbuf;
extern bool do_logging;      /* initialized to false */

if (stat("/path/to/magic/.file", &sbuf) == 0)
    do_logging = true;
...
```

```
if (do_logging) {
    logging code here: open file, write info, close file, etc.
}
```

The call to `stat()` happened for each job the program processed. Thus we could dynamically enable and disable logging, without having to stop and restart the application!

As with debugging options and variables, there are any number of variations on this theme: different files that enable logging of information about different subsystems, debugging directives added into the debugging file itself, and so on. As with all features, you should plan a design for what you will need and then implement it cleanly, instead of hacking out some quick and dirty code at 3:00 a.m. in the morning (a not uncommon possibility in startup companies, unfortunately).

NOTE

All that glitters is not gold. Special debugging files are but one example of techniques known as *back doors*—one or more ways for developers to do undocumented things with a program, sometimes for nefarious purposes. In our instance, the back door was entirely benign. But an unscrupulous developer could just as easily arrange to generate and download a hidden copy of a customer list, personnel file, or other sensitive data. For this reason alone, you should think extra hard about whether this technique is usable in your application, or even legal in your jurisdiction!

17.4.2.5 Add Special Hooks for Breakpoints

Often, a problem may be reproducible, but only after your program has first processed many megabytes of input data. Or you may know in which function your program is failing, but the failure occurs only after the function has been called many hundreds, or even thousands of times.

This is a big problem when you're working in a debugger. If you set a breakpoint in the failing routine, you have to type the `continue` command and press ENTER hundreds or thousands of times to get your program into the state where it's about to fail. This is tedious and error prone, to say the least! It may even be so difficult to do that you'll want to give up before starting.

One solution is to add special debugging "hook" functions that your program can call when it is close to the state you're interested in.

For example, suppose that you know that the `check_salary()` function is the one that fails, but only when it's been called 1,427 times. (We kid you not; we've seen some rather strange things in our time.)

To catch `check_salary()` before it fails, create a special dummy function that does nothing but return, and then arrange for `check_salary()` to call it just before the 1,427th time that it itself is called:

```
/* debug_dummy --- debugging hook function */

void debug_dummy(void) { return; }
```

```
struct salary *check_salary(void)
{
    ... real variable declarations here ...
    static int count = 0;     /* for debugging */

    if (++count == 1426)
        debug_dummy();

    ... rest of the code here ...
}
```

Now, from within GDB, set a breakpoint in `debug_dummy()`, and then run the program normally:

```
(gdb) break debug_dummy                              Set breakpoint for dummy function
Breakpoint 1 at 0x8055885: file whizprog.c, line 3137.
(gdb) run                                            Start program running
```

Once the breakpoint for `debug_dummy()` is reached, you can set a second breakpoint for `check_salary()` and then continue execution:

```
(gdb) run                                            Start program running
Starting program: /home/arnold/whizprog

Breakpoint 1, debug_dummy () at whizprog.c, line 3137
3137  void debug_dummy(void) { return; }             Breakpoint reached
(gdb) break check_salary                             Set breakpoint for function of interest
Breakpoint 2 at 0x8057913: file whizprog.c, line 3140.
(gdb) cont
```

When the second breakpoint is reached, the program is about to fail and you can single-step through it, doing whatever is necessary to track down the problem.

Instead of using a fixed constant ('`++count == 1426`'), you may wish to have a global variable that can be set by the debugger to whatever value you need. This avoids the need to recompile the program.

For `gawk`, we have gone a step further and brought the debugging hook facility into the language, so the hook function can be called from an `awk` program. When compiled for debugging, a special do-nothing function named `stopme()` is available. This function in turn calls a C function of the same name. This allows us to put calls to `stopme()` into a failing `awk` program right before things go wrong. For example, if `gawk` is producing bad results for an `awk` program on the 1,200th input record, we can add a line like this to the `awk` program:

```
NR == 1198 { stopme() }   # Stop for debugging when Number of Records == 1198

... rest of awk program as before ...
```

Then, from within GDB, we can set a breakpoint on the C function `stopme()` and run the `awk` program. Once that breakpoint fires, we can then set breakpoints on the other parts of `gawk` wherein we suspect the real problem lies.

The hook-function technique is useful in and of itself. However, the ability to bring it to the application level multiplies its usefulness, and it has saved us untold hours of debugging time when tracking down obscure problems.

17.5 Debugging Tools I: A Modern `lint`

Besides GDB and whatever source code hooks you use for general debugging, there are several useful packages that can help find different kinds of problems. In this section we cover a static program analyzer, and in the next section we discuss memory management debugging tools.

In Original C, the compiler couldn't check whether the parameters passed in a function call matched the parameter list in the function's definition; there were no prototypes. This often led to subtle bugs, since a bad function call might produce only mildly erroneous results, which went unnoticed during testing, or might not even get called at all during testing. For example:

```
if (argc < 2)
    fprintf("usage: %s [ options ] files\n", argv[0]);        stderr is missing
```

If a program containing this fragment is never invoked with the wrong number of arguments, `fprintf()`, which is missing the initial `FILE *` argument, is never called.

The V7 `lint` program was designed to solve such problems. It made two passes over all the files in a program, first collecting information about function arguments and then comparing function calls to the gathered information. Special "`lint` library" files provided information about the standard library functions so that they could be checked as well. `lint` also checked other questionable constructs.

With prototypes in Standard C, the need for `lint` is decreased but not eliminated, since C90, C99, and C11 still allow old-style function declarations:

```
extern int some_func();            Argument list unknown
```

Additionally, many other aspects of a program can be checked *statically*—that is, by analysis of the source code text.

Secure Programming Lint[24] (`splint`) is a modern `lint` replacement. It provides too many options and facilities to list here but is worth investigating.

One thing to be aware of is that `lint`-like programs can produce a flood of warning messages. Many of the reported warnings are really harmless. In such cases, the tools allow you to provide special comments that indicate "yes, I know about this, it's not a problem." `splint` works best when you provide lots of such annotations in your code.

`splint` is a powerful but complicated tool; spending some time learning how to use it and then using it frequently will help you keep your code clean.

[24] `http://www.splint.org`

What about Compiler Warnings?

During the review process, Chet Ramey noted that GCC has many options to warn about possibly dubious constructs in the code being compiled.

OK ... So off we went to format the *gcc*(1) manpage into a PDF file to take a gander at the options. Said manpage is (currently) 399 pages long!!! The types and sheer number of warnings are amazing and, frankly, overwhelming. So the obvious question arises: which ones, in practice, should we use?

Deciding to "let someone else do the hard part," we threw the question back to Chet. Table 17.1 presents the list he supplied us with (for which we thank him).

Table 17.1: GCC options for static analysis

`-O`	`-Wmissing-declarations`
`-Wall`	`-Wmissing-prototypes`
`-Wcast-align`	`-Wno-parentheses`
`-Wcast-qual`	`-Wpointer-arith`
`-Wconversion`	`-Wredundant-decls`
`-Werror=incompatible-pointer-types`	`-Wshadow`
`-Wformat`	`-Wstrict-prototypes`
`-Wformat-security`	`-Wuninitialized`
`-Winline`	`-pedantic`
`-Wmissing-braces`	

Interestingly, `-O` is needed, since there are a number of analysis phases that GCC does only when optimizing.

Recommendation: Use compiler warnings and one or more static analysis tools to help find problems in your source code.

17.6 Debugging Tools II: Memory Allocation Debuggers

Ignoring issues such as poor program design, for any large-scale practical application, the C programmer's single biggest challenge is dynamic memory management (by `malloc()`, `realloc()`, and `free()`).

This fact is borne out by the large number of tools that have been available for debugging dynamic memory. There is a fair amount of overlap in what these tools provide. For example:

- Memory leak detection: memory that is allocated and then becomes unreachable.
- Unfreed memory detection: memory that is allocated but never freed. Never-freed memory isn't always a bug, but detecting such occurrences allows you to verify that they're indeed OK.

- Detection of bad frees: memory that is freed twice, or pointers passed to `free()` that didn't come from `malloc()`.
- Detection of use of already freed memory: freed memory that is being used through a dangling pointer.
- Memory overrun detection: accessing or storing into memory outside the bounds of what was allocated.
- Warning about the use of uninitialized memory. (Many compilers can warn about this.)
- Dynamic function tracing: when a bad memory access occurs, you get a traceback from where the memory is used to where it was allocated.

Some tools merely log these events. Others arrange for the application program to die a horrible death (through `SIGSEGV`) so that the offending code can be pinpointed from within a debugger.

While many `malloc()` debugging tools have been developed in the past and are still available, two tools that provide just about all of the features listed above have largely replaced them: Valgrind and Address Sanitizer. We cover them next.

17.6.1 Valgrind: A Versatile Tool

The GPL-licensed Valgrind program catches a large variety of problems, including those that arise from dynamic memory.

The Valgrind manual describes the program as well as or better than we can, so we'll quote from (and abbreviate) it as we go along:

> Valgrind is an instrumentation framework for building dynamic analysis tools. It comes with a set of tools each of which performs some kind of debugging, profiling, or similar task that helps you improve your programs. Valgrind's architecture is modular, so new tools can be created easily and without disturbing the existing structure.
>
> A number of useful tools are supplied as standard.
>
> 1. **Memcheck** is a memory error detector. It helps you make your programs, particularly those written in C and C++, more correct.
> 2. **Cachegrind** is a cache and branch-prediction profiler. It helps you make your programs run faster.
> 3. **Callgrind** is a call-graph generating cache profiler. It has some overlap with Cachegrind, but also gathers some information that Cachegrind does not.
> 4. **Helgrind** is a thread error detector. It helps you make your multi-threaded programs more correct.
> 5. **DRD** is also a thread error detector. It is similar to Helgrind but uses different analysis techniques and so may find different problems.
> 6. **Massif** is a heap profiler. It helps you make your programs use less memory.

7. **DHAT** is a different kind of heap profiler. It helps you understand issues of block lifetimes, block utilisation, and layout inefficiencies.
8. **BBV** is an experimental SimPoint basic block vector generator. It is useful to people doing computer architecture research and development.

In day-to-day use, the most useful tool is `memcheck`:

> Memcheck is a memory error detector. It can detect the following problems that are common in C and C++ programs.
>
> - Accessing memory you shouldn't, e.g., overrunning and underrunning heap blocks, overrunning the top of the stack, and accessing memory after it has been freed.
> - Using undefined values, i.e., values that have not been initialised, or that have been derived from other undefined values.
> - Incorrect freeing of heap memory, such as double-freeing heap blocks, or mismatched use of `malloc`/`new`/`new[]` versus `free`/`delete`/`delete[]`.
> - Mismatches will also be reported for sized and aligned allocation and deallocation functions if the deallocation value does not match the allocation value.
> - Overlapping `src` and `dst` pointers in `memcpy` and related functions.
> - Passing a fishy (presumably negative) value to the size parameter of a memory allocation function.
> - Using a size value of 0 with `realloc`.
> - Using an alignment value that is not a power of two.
> - Memory leaks.
>
> Problems like these can be difficult to find by other means, often remaining undetected for long periods, then causing occasional, difficult-to-diagnose crashes.

Finally, the manual notes:

> Valgrind is closely tied to details of the CPU and operating system, and to a lesser extent, the compiler and basic C libraries. Nonetheless, it supports a number of widely-used platforms, listed in full at `http://www.valgrind.org/`.
>
> Valgrind is built via the standard Unix `./configure`, `make`, `make install` process; full details are given in the `README` file in the distribution.

If you're on a GNU/Linux system, your package manager should be able to install Valgrind for you; you should not need to build it from source.

When we wrote the first edition of this book, Valgrind was available only for 32-bit Intel systems running GNU/Linux. In the more than 20 years since, it has been ported to a number of different CPU architectures and operating systems. As of this writing, Valgrind runs on these systems:

AMD64/Darwin	ARM64/Android	PPC32/Linux	X86/FreeBSD
AMD64/FreeBSD	ARM64/FreeBSD	PPC64/Linux	X86/Linux
AMD64/Linux	ARM64/Linux	PPC64LE/Linux	X86/Solaris
AMD64/Solaris	MIPS32/Android	S390X/Linux	
ARM/Android	MIPS32/Linux	X86/Android	
ARM/Linux	MIPS64/Linux	X86/Darwin	

Although the Valgrind manual might lead you to expect that there are separate commands named `memcheck`, `cachegrind`, and so on, this isn't the case. Instead, a driver shell program named `valgrind` runs the debugging core, with the appropriate tool as specified by the `--tool=` option. The default tool is `memcheck`; thus, running plain `valgrind` is the same as '`valgrind --tool=memcheck`'. (This provides compatibility with earlier versions of Valgrind that only did memory checking, and it also makes the most sense, since the `memcheck` tool provides the most information.)

Valgrind provides a number of options. We refer you to its documentation for the full details. The options are split into groups; of those that apply to the core (that is, work for all tools), the following are likely to be most useful:

`--help`
: List the options.

`--logfile=`*`file`*
: Log messages to *`file.pid`*. You can include special escape sequences in the file name to customize the actual file name that is used. See the *valgrind*(1) manpage.

`--num-callers=`*`number`*
: Show *num* callers in stack traces. The default is four.

`--tool=`*`tool`*
: Use the tool named *tool*. The default is `memcheck`.

`--trace-children=no|yes`
: Also run the trace on child processes. The default is `no`. There are a number of additional options related to tracing children; see the manpage for more information.

`-v`, `--verbose`
: Be more verbose. This includes listing the libraries that are loaded, as well as the counts of all the different kinds of errors.

`--vgdb=no|yes|full`
: Act like a gdbserver for values of `--vgdb=yes` or `--vgdb=full`. This lets GDB attach to the running process for interactive debugging. There are additional options for use with the gdbserver.

Of the options for the memcheck tool, the following are the ones we think are most useful:

--keep-stacktraces=alloc|free|alloc-and-free|alloc-then-free|none
: Controls which stack trace(s) to keep for dynamically allocated or freed memory blocks, as follows:

  --keep-stacktraces=alloc-then-free
  : Record one stack trace when the memory is allocated and another when it's freed; replace the first with the second. Therefore, "use after free" errors show only where the memory was freed.

  --keep-stacktraces=alloc-and-free
  : Record and keep both the allocation and the deallocation stack traces for the block. Thus a "use after free" error shows both, which may make the error easier to diagnose.

  --keep-stacktraces=alloc
  : Keep and report only the allocation stack trace.

  --keep-stacktraces=free
  : Keep and report only the deallocation stack trace.

  --keep-stacktraces=none
  : Do not record any stack trace for allocation or deallocation. This can reduce CPU and memory usage, but then you lose out on one of Valgrind's most important features.

  The default is 'alloc-and-free'.

--leak-check=no|summary|yes|full
: Find memory leaks once the program is finished. The default is 'no'.

--show-reachable=no|yes
: Show reachable blocks when the program is finished. If --show-reachable=yes is used, Valgrind looks for dynamically allocated memory that still has a pointer pointing to it. Such memory is not a memory leak, but it may be useful to know about anyway. The default is 'no'.

--track-origins=<yes|no>
: Valgrind reports the use of uninitialized memory in conditions, such as if and while. With this option, it can track where the uninitialized memory came from and report it, which can be very helpful. Note that this option can be expensive in terms of both CPU time and memory needed. The default is 'no'.

Let's take a look at Valgrind in action. We start with the program ch-debugging-badmem1.c, which abuses dynamic memory:

```
/* ch-debugging-badmem1.c --- do bad things with memory */

#include <stdio.h>
#include <stdlib.h>
```

```
#include <string.h>

int
main(int argc, char **argv)
{
    char *p;
    int i;

    p = malloc(30);

    strcpy(p, "not 30 bytes");
    printf("p = <%s>\n", p);

    if (argc == 2) {
        if (strcmp(argv[1], "-b") == 0)
            p[42] = 'a';    /* touch outside the bounds */
        else if (strcmp(argv[1], "-f") == 0) {
            free(p);    /* free memory and then use it */
            p[0] = 'b';
        }
    }

    /* free(p); */

    return EXIT_SUCCESS;
}
```

The `-b` option writes into memory that is beyond the area allocated with `malloc()`. (We see later what happens with the `-f` option.) Here's what Valgrind reports:

```
$ valgrind ch-debugging-badmem1 -b
==40682== Memcheck, a memory error detector
==40682== Copyright (C) 2002-2017, and GNU GPL'd, by Julian Seward et al.
==40682== Using Valgrind-3.18.1 and LibVEX; rerun with -h for copyright info
==40682== Command: ch-debugging-badmem1 -b
==40682==
==40682== Invalid write of size 1
==40682==    at 0x109230: main (ch-debugging-badmem1.c:20)
==40682==  Address 0x4a9d06a is 12 bytes after a block of size 30 alloc'd
==40682==    at 0x4848899: malloc (in /usr/libexec/valgrind/vgpreload_memcheck-
                                               amd64-linux.so)
==40682==    by 0x1091C5: main (ch-debugging-badmem1.c:13)
==40682==
p = <not 30 bytes>
==40682==
==40682== HEAP SUMMARY:
==40682==     in use at exit: 30 bytes in 1 blocks
==40682==   total heap usage: 2 allocs, 1 frees, 4,126 bytes allocated
```

```
17 ==40682==
18 ==40682== LEAK SUMMARY:
19 ==40682==    definitely lost: 30 bytes in 1 blocks
20 ==40682==    indirectly lost: 0 bytes in 0 blocks
21 ==40682==      possibly lost: 0 bytes in 0 blocks
22 ==40682==    still reachable: 0 bytes in 0 blocks
23 ==40682==         suppressed: 0 bytes in 0 blocks
24 ==40682== Rerun with --leak-check=full to see details of leaked memory
25 ==40682==
26 ==40682== For lists of detected and suppressed errors, rerun with: -s
27 ==40682== ERROR SUMMARY: 1 errors from 1 contexts (suppressed: 0 from 0)
```

(Line numbers in the output were added to aid in the discussion.) Line 12 is the output from the program; the others are all from Valgrind, on standard error. The error report is on lines 6–10. It indicates how many bytes were incorrectly written (line 6), where this happened (line 7), and a stack trace. Lines 8–10 describe where the memory was allocated from. Lines 14–23 provide a summary.

The `-f` option to `ch-debugging-badmem1` frees the allocated memory and then writes into it through a dangling pointer. Here is what Valgrind reports for this case:

```
$ valgrind ch-debugging-badmem1 -f
==40751== Memcheck, a memory error detector
...
==40751== Invalid write of size 1
==40751==    at 0x109266: main (ch-debugging-badmem1.c:23)
==40751==  Address 0x4a9d040 is 0 bytes inside a block of size 30 free'd
==40751==    at 0x484B27F: free (in /usr/libexec/valgrind/vgpreload_memcheck-amd64-linux.so)
==40751==    by 0x109261: main (ch-debugging-badmem1.c:22)
==40751==  Block was alloc'd at
==40751==    at 0x4848899: malloc (in /usr/libexec/valgrind/vgpreload_memcheck-amd64-linux.so)
==40751==    by 0x1091C5: main (ch-debugging-badmem1.c:13)
==40751==
p = <not 30 bytes>
...
```

This time the report indicates that the write was to freed memory and that the call to `free()` is on line 22 of `ch-debugging-badmem1.c`.

When called with no options, `ch-debugging-badmem1.c` allocates memory and uses it but does not release it. The `--leak-check=yes` option reports this case:

```
$ valgrind --leak-check=yes ch-debugging-badmem1
1 ==8720== Memcheck, a.k.a. Valgrind, a memory error detector for x86-linux.
...
8 p = <not 30 bytes>
9 ==8720==
10 ==8720== ERROR SUMMARY: 0 errors from 0 contexts (suppressed: 0 from 0)
11 ==8720== malloc/free: in use at exit: 30 bytes in 1 blocks.
```

```
12 ==8720== malloc/free: 1 allocs, 0 frees, 30 bytes allocated.
...
16 ==8720==
17 ==8720== 30 bytes in 1 blocks are definitely lost in loss record 1 of 1
18 ==8720==    at 0x40025488: malloc (vg_replace_malloc.c:153)
19 ==8720==    by 0x8048411: main (ch-debugging-badmem1.c:11)
20 ==8720==    by 0x420158D3: __libc_start_main (in /lib/i686/libc-2.2.93.so)
21 ==8720==    by 0x8048368: (within /home/arnold/progex/code/ch17/ch-debugging-badmem1)
22 ==8720==
23 ==8720== LEAK SUMMARY:
24 ==8720==    definitely lost: 30 bytes in 1 blocks.
25 ==8720==    possibly lost:   0 bytes in 0 blocks.
26 ==8720==    still reachable: 0 bytes in 0 blocks.
27 ==8720==         suppressed: 0 bytes in 0 blocks.
28 ==8720== Reachable blocks (those to which a pointer was found) are not shown.
29 ==8720== To see them, rerun with: --show-reachable=yes
```

Lines 17–29 provide the leak report; the leaked memory was allocated on line 11 of `ch-debugging-badmem1.c`.

Besides giving reports on misuses of dynamic memory, Valgrind can diagnose uses of *uninitialized* memory. Consider the following program, `ch-debugging-badmem2.c`:

```
/* ch-debugging-badmem2.c --- do bad things with nondynamic memory */

#include <stdio.h>
#include <stdlib.h>

int
main(int argc, char **argv)
{
    int a_var;  /* Both of these are uninitialized */
    int b_var;

    /* Valgrind won't flag this; see text. */
    a_var = b_var;

    /* Use uninitialized memory; this is flagged. */
    printf("a_var = %d\n", a_var);

    return EXIT_SUCCESS;
}
```

When run, Valgrind produces this (abbreviated) report:

```
$ valgrind ch-debugging-badmem2
==194322== Memcheck, a memory error detector
...
```

```
==194322== Conditional jump or move depends on uninitialised value(s)
==194322==    at 0x48E7AD6: __vfprintf_internal (vfprintf-internal.c:1516)
==194322==    by 0x48D179E: printf (printf.c:33)
==194322==    by 0x10917A: main (ch-debugging-badmem2.c:16)
==194322==
==194322== Use of uninitialised value of size 8
==194322==    at 0x48CB2EB: _itoa_word (_itoa.c:177)
==194322==    by 0x48E6ABD: __vfprintf_internal (vfprintf-internal.c:1516)
==194322==    by 0x48D179E: printf (printf.c:33)
==194322==    by 0x10917A: main (ch-debugging-badmem2.c:16)
...
a_var = 0
==194322==
==194322== HEAP SUMMARY:
==194322==     in use at exit: 0 bytes in 0 blocks
==194322==   total heap usage: 1 allocs, 1 frees, 4,096 bytes allocated
==194322==
==194322== All heap blocks were freed -- no leaks are possible
==194322==
==194322== Use --track-origins=yes to see where uninitialised values come from
==194322== For lists of detected and suppressed errors, rerun with: -s
==194322== ERROR SUMMARY: 5 errors from 5 contexts (suppressed: 0 from 0)
```

This report tells us when and where an uninitialized value was *used*. It doesn't tell us where the uninitialized value *came from*. However, Valgrind helpfully suggests that we use the `--track-origins=yes` option to find out. Let's see what happens when we try it:

```
$ valgrind --track-origins=yes ch-debugging-badmem2
==194417== Memcheck, a memory error detector
...
==194417== Conditional jump or move depends on uninitialised value(s)
==194417==    at 0x48E7AD6: __vfprintf_internal (vfprintf-internal.c:1516)
==194417==    by 0x48D179E: printf (printf.c:33)
==194417==    by 0x10917A: main (ch-debugging-badmem2.c:16)
==194417==  Uninitialised value was created by a stack allocation
==194417==    at 0x109149: main (ch-debugging-badmem2.c:8)
...
a_var = 0
==194417==
==194417== HEAP SUMMARY:
==194417==     in use at exit: 0 bytes in 0 blocks
==194417==   total heap usage: 1 allocs, 1 frees, 4,096 bytes allocated
...
```

Unfortunately, although Valgrind can report the use of uninitialized memory, all the way down to the bit level, it cannot do array bounds checking for local and global variables.

(Valgrind can do bounds checking for dynamic memory since it handles such memory itself and therefore knows the start and end of each region.)

Valgrind is a powerful memory debugging tool. It rivals several commercial offerings and has become a de facto standard tool for memory error detection. Valgrind can typically be installed using your distribution's package manager, or you can get it from its website.[25] The next section show a real example in which Valgrind was invaluable in finding a bug.

17.6.1.1 Valgrind Example: `gototab` in the One True Awk

Way back in Section 6.2.2.1, "Example: Sorting and Searching Together," page 185, we described how combining dynamic memory management with sorting and binary searching provided a large speedup in the regular expression matching functions used by the One True Awk.[26] You might want to review that section before diving into this one.

We showed how the "goto table" was set:

```
static int set_gototab(fa *f, int state, int ch, int val) /* hide gototab implementation */
{
    if (f->gototab[state].inuse == 0) {
        f->gototab[state].entries[0].ch = ch;
        f->gototab[state].entries[0].state = val;
        f->gototab[state].inuse++;
        return val;
    } else if ((unsigned)ch > f->gototab[state].entries[f->gototab[state].inuse-1].ch) {
        // not seen yet, insert and return
        gtt *tab = & f->gototab[state];
        if (tab->inuse + 1 >= tab->allocated)
            resize_gototab(f, state);
    ...
}
```

We didn't show the `resize_gototab()` function. Here it is, as originally written:

```
static void resize_gototab(fa *f, int state)
{
    size_t new_size = f->gototab[state].allocated * 2;
    gtte *p = (gtte *) realloc(f->gototab[state].entries, new_size * sizeof(gtte));
    if (p == NULL)
        overflo(__func__);
    f->gototab[state].allocated = new_size;
    f->gototab[state].entries = p;
}
```

(You can see this code by checking out commit `35d4627` in the Git repository.)

Unfortunately, there is a bug in this code. (Something is missing; think about the nature of memory allocated by `malloc()` and `realloc()`, and then take a moment before continuing

---

[25] `https://www.valgrind.org`

[26] `https://github.com/onetrueawk/awk`

to read to see if you can spot it.) The bug caused a test named `funstack` to fail, producing different output than it was supposed to.

The first thing we did was to throw Valgrind at it. Here is an abbreviated report:

```
$ valgrind --track-origins=yes ./a.out -f testdir/funstack.awk testdir/funstack.in
==217759== Memcheck, a memory error detector
==217759== Copyright (C) 2002-2017, and GNU GPL'd, by Julian Seward et al.
==217759== Using Valgrind-3.18.1 and LibVEX; rerun with -h for copyright info
==217759== Command: ./a.out -f testdir/funstack.awk testdir/funstack.in
==217759==
==217759== Conditional jump or move depends on uninitialised value(s)
==217759==    at 0x10F32A: bsearch (stdlib-bsearch.h:34)
==217759==    by 0x10F32A: get_gototab.isra.0 (b.c:616)
...
==217759==    by 0x11D750: execute (run.c:151)
==217759==    by 0x11D750: run (run.c:141)
==217759==    by 0x10CD15: main (main.c:233)
==217759==  Uninitialised value was created by a heap allocation
==217759==    at 0x484DCD3: realloc (in /usr/libexec/valgrind/vgpreload_memcheck-amd64-
                                     linux.so)
==217759==    by 0x10FB9B: resize_gototab (b.c:602)
==217759==    by 0x10FCDA: set_gototab.isra.0 (b.c:647)
==217759==    by 0x111190: cgoto (b.c:1513)
...
==217759==    by 0x118129: program (run.c:198)
...
==217759== Conditional jump or move depends on uninitialised value(s)
==217759==    at 0x499C411: msort_with_tmp.part.0 (msort.c:82)
==217759==    by 0x499C3C1: msort_with_tmp (msort.c:44)
...
==217759==    by 0x499C3C1: msort_with_tmp.part.0 (msort.c:53)
==217759==  Uninitialised value was created by a heap allocation
==217759==    at 0x484DCD3: realloc (in /usr/libexec/valgrind/vgpreload_memcheck-amd64-
                                     linux.so)
==217759==    by 0x10FB9B: resize_gototab (b.c:602)
==217759==    by 0x10FCDA: set_gototab.isra.0 (b.c:647)
...
==217759==    by 0x111190: cgoto (b.c:1513)
==217759==    by 0x118129: program (run.c:198)
==217759==
...
==217759== HEAP SUMMARY:
==217759==     in use at exit: 57,455,951 bytes in 7,048 blocks
==217759==   total heap usage: 328,826 allocs, 321,778 frees, 640,198,841 bytes allocated
==217759==
==217759== LEAK SUMMARY:
```

```
==217759==    definitely lost: 1,077 bytes in 156 blocks
==217759==    indirectly lost: 960 bytes in 30 blocks
==217759==      possibly lost: 5,600 bytes in 1 blocks
==217759==    still reachable: 57,448,314 bytes in 6,861 blocks
==217759==         suppressed: 0 bytes in 0 blocks
==217759== Rerun with --leak-check=full to see details of leaked memory
==217759==
==217759== For lists of detected and suppressed errors, rerun with: -s
==217759== ERROR SUMMARY: 4232402 errors from 62 contexts (suppressed: 0 from 0)
```

The first instance of "Conditional jump or move depends on uninitialised value(s)" occurs in `bsearch()`. The second occurs in the implementation of `qsort()`. (There were *many* instances in this report, which we've omitted for brevity.) All the instances point at `resize_gototab()` as the origin of the uninitialized memory.

Looking at the code and a little head-scratching turned the light on: after using `realloc()`, the additional memory was not initialized to anything. But the code using the memory depended on it being initialized to zero! Here is the modified routine in the current code base:[27]

```
static void resize_gototab(fa *f, int state)
{
    size_t new_size = f->gototab[state].allocated * 2;
    gtte *p = (gtte *) realloc(f->gototab[state].entries, new_size * sizeof(gtte));
    if (p == NULL)
        overflo(__func__);

    // need to initialize the new memory to zero
    size_t orig_size = f->gototab[state].allocated;  // 2nd half of new mem is this size
    memset(p + orig_size, 0, orig_size * sizeof(gtte)); // clean it out

    f->gototab[state].allocated = new_size;             // update gototab info
    f->gototab[state].entries = p;
}
```

Valgrind allowed us to pinpoint the bug quickly and easily. In short, don't leave home without it!

17.6.2 Address Sanitizer

Address Sanitizer[28] is an additional tool for finding bugs related to memory abuse. It can often catch problems that Valgrind does not. Originally a separate tool, Address Sanitizer is available as a standard part of both the GCC (`gcc`, `g++`) and LLVM (`clang`, `clang++`) compiler suites.

Valgrind does not require that you change how you build your program (other than making use of `-g` desirable to get full file line locations). Address Sanitizer takes a different approach:

---

[27] If this looks familiar, it's because we showed this version of the function back in Section 3.2.1.4, "Changing Size: `realloc()`," page 59.

[28] `https://github.com/google/sanitizers/wiki/AddressSanitizer`

you have to compile and link your program with additional compiler arguments. Because it's integrated with the compiler, it can generate additional code to perform runtime checks that aren't required by the C language.

When compiling your program, you should add at least these two options to the `gcc` or `clang` command line: `-fsanitize=address` and `-fno-omit-frame-pointer`. If you have a separate link step, supply `-fsanitize=address` there as well.

Let's see it in action. Here is a simple program that overwrites the boundaries of an array:

```
/* ch-debugging-array-bounds.c --- overstep the boundary of an array */

#include <stdio.h>
#include <stdlib.h>
#include <string.h>

int main()
{
    char buf[5];
    strcpy(buf, "hello, world");

    printf("%s\n", buf);
    exit(EXIT_SUCCESS);
}
```

```
$ gcc ch-debugging-array-bounds.c -g -o ch-debugging-array-bounds       Compile it
ch-debugging-array-bounds.c: In function 'main':
ch-debugging-array-bounds.c:10:9: warning: '__builtin_memcpy' writing 13 bytes into
a region of size 5 overflows the destination [https://gcc.gnu.org/onlinedocs/gcc/
Warning-Options.html#index-Wstringop-overflow=-Wstringop-overflow=]
   10 |         strcpy(buf, "hello, world");
      |         ^~~~~~~~~~~~~~~~~~~~~~~~~~~
ch-debugging-array-bounds.c:9:14: note: destination object 'buf' of size 5
    9 |         char buf[5];
      |              ^~~
$ ch-debugging-array-bounds                                  Run it
hello, world
```

Interestingly, GCC sees the problem at compile time. However, in a larger, more realistic program, it's unlikely that GCC would catch the problem. What happens if we run Valgrind on the program?

```
$ valgrind --leak-check=full ch-debugging-array-bounds
==35150== Memcheck, a memory error detector
==35150== Copyright (C) 2002-2017, and GNU GPL'd, by Julian Seward et al.
==35150== Using Valgrind-3.18.1 and LibVEX; rerun with -h for copyright info
==35150== Command: ./ch-debugging-array-bounds
==35150==
```

```
hello, world
==35150==
==35150== HEAP SUMMARY:
==35150==     in use at exit: 0 bytes in 0 blocks
==35150==   total heap usage: 1 allocs, 1 frees, 1,024 bytes allocated
==35150==
==35150== All heap blocks were freed -- no leaks are possible
==35150==
==35150== For lists of detected and suppressed errors, rerun with: -s
==35150== ERROR SUMMARY: 0 errors from 0 contexts (suppressed: 0 from 0)
```

Valgrind is happy. This isn't too surprising, as Valgrind focuses on problems related to dynamic memory allocation. Let's see how Address Sanitizer does:

```
$ gcc -fsanitize=address -fno-omit-frame-pointer -g ch-debugging-array-bounds.c \
>       -o ch-debugging-array-bounds
$ ch-debugging-array-bounds
=================================================================
==35175==ERROR: AddressSanitizer: stack-buffer-overflow on address 0x7fffe0be7ac5 at pc
0x7f10f6e3a2c3 bp 0x7fffe0be7a90 sp 0x7fffe0be7238
WRITE of size 13 at 0x7fffe0be7ac5 thread T0
    #0 0x7f10f6e3a2c2 in __interceptor_memcpy ../../../../src/libsanitizer/sanitizer_
       common/sanitizer_common_interceptors.inc:827
    #1 0x55e84e0032e0 in main /home/arnold/work/prenhall/progex1-2e/code/ch17/ch-debugging-
       array-bounds.c:10
    #2 0x7f10f6a29d8f in __libc_start_call_main ../sysdeps/nptl/libc_start_call_main.h:58
    #3 0x7f10f6a29e3f in __libc_start_main_impl ../csu/libc-start.c:392
    #4 0x55e84e003184 in _start (/home/arnold/work/prenhall/progex1-2e/code/ch17/
       ch-debugging-array-bounds.c:10

Address 0x7fffe0be7ac5 is located in stack of thread T0 at offset 37 in frame
    #0 0x55e84e003258 in main /home/arnold/work/prenhall/progex1-2e/code/ch17/ch-debugging-
       array-bounds.c:8

  This frame has 1 object(s):
    [32, 37) 'buf' (line 9) <== Memory access at offset 37 overflows this variable
HINT: this may be a false positive if your program uses some custom stack unwind mechanism,
      swapcontext or vfork (longjmp and C++ exceptions *are* supported)
SUMMARY: AddressSanitizer: stack-buffer-overflow ../../../../src/libsanitizer/sanitizer_
common/sanitizer_common_interceptors.inc:827 in  __interceptor_memcpy
Shadow bytes around the buggy address:
  0x10007c174f00: 00 00 00 00 00 00 00 00 00 00 00 00 00 00 00 00
  0x10007c174f10: 00 00 00 00 00 00 00 00 00 00 00 00 00 00 00 00
  0x10007c174f20: 00 00 00 00 00 00 00 00 00 00 00 00 00 00 00 00
  0x10007c174f30: 00 00 00 00 00 00 00 00 00 00 00 00 00 00 00 00
  0x10007c174f40: 00 00 00 00 00 00 00 00 00 00 00 00 00 00 00 00
```

```
=>0x10007c174f50: 00 00 00 00 f1 f1 f1 f1[05]f3 f3 f3 00 00 00 00
  0x10007c174f60: 00 00 00 00 00 00 00 00 00 00 00 00 00 00 00 00
  0x10007c174f70: 00 00 00 00 00 00 00 00 00 00 00 00 00 00 00 00
  0x10007c174f80: 00 00 00 00 00 00 00 00 00 00 00 00 00 00 00 00
  0x10007c174f90: 00 00 00 00 00 00 00 00 00 00 00 00 00 00 00 00
  0x10007c174fa0: 00 00 00 00 00 00 00 00 00 00 00 00 00 00 00 00
Shadow byte legend (one shadow byte represents 8 application bytes):
  Addressable:           00
  Partially addressable: 01 02 03 04 05 06 07
  Heap left redzone:       fa
  Freed heap region:       fd
  Stack left redzone:      f1
  Stack mid redzone:       f2
  Stack right redzone:     f3
  Stack after return:      f5
  Stack use after scope:   f8
  Global redzone:          f9
  Global init order:       f6
  Poisoned by user:        f7
  Container overflow:      fc
  Array cookie:            ac
  Intra object redzone:    bb
  ASan internal:           fe
  Left alloca redzone:     ca
  Right alloca redzone:    cb
  Shadow gap:              cc
==35175==ABORTING
```

It finds the problem, indicating the source code line, as well as giving a small memory dump.

Address Sanitizer can also find problems with dynamic memory. We show an example in the following subsection.

Programs compiled with Address Sanitizer run more slowly than regular programs do, because of the additional checking going on. You may not want to use it for the production version of your program. However, you should definitely run your test suite with it—if not all the time, then at least periodically, and especially before making a formal release.

17.6.2.1 Address Sanitizer Example: `gawk`'s `printf()` Code

After receiving a particularly disturbing bug report, for version 5.3.1 of `gawk` we decided to refactor and simplify the code that implements `printf()` and `sprintf()`. With the exception of formatting floating-point numbers, `gawk` implements these functions itself, instead of relying on the underlying C library version of `sprintf()`.

The routine in question deals with padding a value with zeros to fill out the precision part of a format specification. For an integer value, according to the *printf*(3) manpage:

> [The precision] gives the minimum number of digits to appear for `d`, `i`, `o`, `u`, `x`, and `X` conversions.

Here is the initial version of the function:

```
static char *
zero_fill_to_precision(char *number_value, struct flags *flags)
{
    char *buf1;
    char *cp, *src;
    size_t buflen;
    int prec = flags->precision;
    size_t val_len = strlen(number_value);

    buflen = flags->precision + 1;  // we know val_len < precision

    emalloc(buf1, char *, buflen, "zero_fill_to_precision");
    cp = buf1;
    src = number_value;

    if (flags->negative) {
        *cp++ = '-';
        src++;
        val_len--;
    } else if (flags->plus) {
        *cp++ = '+';
    } else if (flags->space) {
        *cp++ = ' ';
    }

    for (; prec > val_len; prec--)
        *cp++ = '0';

    strcpy(cp, src);
    free((void *) number_value);

    return buf1;
}
```

When we compiled **gawk** with Address Sanitizer and ran it through the test suite, we got this error report:

```
=================================================================
==72483==ERROR: AddressSanitizer: heap-buffer-overflow on address 0x602000007273 at pc
0x7834092544bf bp 0x7ffdea76ba60 sp 0x7ffdea76b208
WRITE of size 2 at 0x602000007273 thread T0
    #0 0x7834092544be in __interceptor_strcpy ../../../../src/libsanitizer/asan/asan_
       interceptors.cpp:440
    #1 0x50844f in zero_fill_to_precision /home/arnold/Gnu/gawk/gawk.git/printf.c:1840
    #2 0x502bd8 in format_signed_integer /home/arnold/Gnu/gawk/gawk.git/printf.c:1028
```

```
    #3 0x4ff8c3 in format_args /home/arnold/Gnu/gawk/gawk.git/printf.c:651
    #4 0x501335 in printf_common /home/arnold/Gnu/gawk/gawk.git/printf.c:792
    #5 0x501b28 in do_printf /home/arnold/Gnu/gawk/gawk.git/printf.c:868
    #6 0x49d626 in r_interpret /home/arnold/Gnu/gawk/gawk.git/interpret.h:1147
    #7 0x4e5242 in main /home/arnold/Gnu/gawk/gawk.git/main.c:543
    #8 0x783408a29d8f in __libc_start_call_main ../sysdeps/nptl/libc_start_call_main.h:58
    #9 0x783408a29e3f in __libc_start_main_impl ../csu/libc-start.c:392
    #10 0x408424 in _start (/home/arnold/Gnu/gawk/gawk.git/gawk+0x408424)

0x602000007273 is located 0 bytes to the right of 3-byte region [0x602000007270,0x602000007273)
allocated by thread T0 here:
    #0 0x7834092b4887 in __interceptor_malloc ../../../../src/libsanitizer/asan/asan_
       malloc_linux.cpp:145
    #1 0x585a43 in pma_malloc /home/arnold/Gnu/gawk/gawk.git/support/pma.c:532
    #2 0x4fc3d6 in emalloc_real /home/arnold/Gnu/gawk/gawk.git/awk.h:2080
    #3 0x508227 in zero_fill_to_precision /home/arnold/Gnu/gawk/gawk.git/printf.c:1823
    #4 0x502bd8 in format_signed_integer /home/arnold/Gnu/gawk/gawk.git/printf.c:1028
    #5 0x4ff8c3 in format_args /home/arnold/Gnu/gawk/gawk.git/printf.c:651
    #6 0x501335 in printf_common /home/arnold/Gnu/gawk/gawk.git/printf.c:792
    #7 0x501b28 in do_printf /home/arnold/Gnu/gawk/gawk.git/printf.c:868
    #8 0x49d626 in r_interpret /home/arnold/Gnu/gawk/gawk.git/interpret.h:1147
    #9 0x4e5242 in main /home/arnold/Gnu/gawk/gawk.git/main.c:543
    #10 0x783408a29d8f in __libc_start_call_main ../sysdeps/nptl/libc_start_call_main.h:58

SUMMARY: AddressSanitizer: heap-buffer-overflow ../../../../src/libsanitizer/asan/asan_
interceptors.cpp:440 in __interceptor_strcpy
Shadow bytes around the buggy address:
  0x0c047fff8df0: fa fa fd fa fa fa fd fa fa fa fd fa fa fa fd fa
  0x0c047fff8e00: fa fa fd fa fa fa fd fa fa fa fd fa fa fa fd fa
  0x0c047fff8e10: fa fa fd fa fa fa fd fa fa fa fd fa fa fa fd fa
  0x0c047fff8e20: fa fa fd fa fa fa fd fa fa fa fd fa fa fa fd fa
  0x0c047fff8e30: fa fa fd fa fa fa fd fa fa fa fd fa fa fa fd fa
=>0x0c047fff8e40: fa fa fd fa fa fa fd fa fa fa fd fd fa fa[03]fa
  0x0c047fff8e50: fa fa fa fa fa fa fa fa fa fa fa fa fa fa fa fa
  0x0c047fff8e60: fa fa fa fa fa fa fa fa fa fa fa fa fa fa fa fa
  0x0c047fff8e70: fa fa fa fa fa fa fa fa fa fa fa fa fa fa fa fa
  0x0c047fff8e80: fa fa fa fa fa fa fa fa fa fa fa fa fa fa fa fa
  0x0c047fff8e90: fa fa fa fa fa fa fa fa fa fa fa fa fa fa fa fa
Shadow byte legend (one shadow byte represents 8 application bytes):
  Addressable:           00
  Partially addressable: 01 02 03 04 05 06 07
  Heap left redzone:       fa
  Freed heap region:       fd
  Stack left redzone:      f1
  Stack mid redzone:       f2
```

```
    Stack right redzone:     f3
    Stack after return:      f5
    Stack use after scope:   f8
    Global redzone:          f9
    Global init order:       f6
    Poisoned by user:        f7
    Container overflow:      fc
    Array cookie:            ac
    Intra object redzone:    bb
    ASan internal:           fe
    Left alloca redzone:     ca
    Right alloca redzone:    cb
    Shadow gap:              cc
==72483==ABORTING
EXIT CODE: 1
```

The problem is a "heap buffer overflow." Address Sanitizer tells us both where the overflow happened and where the buffer was allocated.

Have you spotted the problem in the code yet? `buflen` allows for enough digits for the precision and the terminating NUL byte. But it does not take into account that the format specification may have included the plus or space flags, or that the number may be negative. In those cases, one additional byte is needed. Here's the corrected calculation:

```
buflen = (flags->negative || flags->plus || flags->space) +
            flags->precision + 1;    // we know val_len < precision
```

The result of the boolean test in the parentheses will be either 1 or 0, yielding the correct additional number of bytes needed.

To sum up, Address Sanitizer is a valuable weapon to have in your arsenal when you're trying to hunt down bugs!

Recommendation: Memory debugging tools are invaluable. Get in the habit of checking your programs regularly with Valgrind and/or Address Sanitizer. If possible, automate these checks with `make` or whatever other build system you use.

17.7 Asking for Help

Given enough eyeballs, all bugs are shallow.
— Linus's Law, by Eric S. Raymond

Sometimes, no matter what we do, a bug remains elusive. We become wrapped up in our code, using debuggers, different tools, `printf()` statements, and what have you, and we still can't find the bug.

When that happens, the first thing to do is to get away from your computer for a while; go for a walk, get some fresh air, enjoy a soft drink or a cup of coffee. Think about anything else *except* your program. If it's late at night, go home, relax, take a shower, and get some sleep. (Sometimes an epiphany can arrive in the middle of a shower!)

The next thing to do is to ask for help. Find a colleague and explain to them what you're trying to do, what you're seeing, and how things are supposed to work. Two different things can happen at this point.

The first is that, working together, you and your colleague find the bug.

The second is that the *very act of explaining* what you're trying to do and what is happening causes an "Aha!" moment for you, and you suddenly realize what your problem is. Your colleague can then go back to what they were doing, and you can go on to fix your bug.

It turns out that you often don't need an actual colleague. You just need to explain, *out loud*, what's going on. This fact has led to a technique known as *rubber duck debugging* (or *rubberducking*), whereby a developer keeps a favorite inanimate object (such as a rubber duck) available on their desk. When a problem comes up, they explain it to their inanimate friend and, with any luck, solve the problem and continue on.

More information about rubber duck debugging can be found at `https://rubberduckdebugging.com`. (Of course!)

Recommendation: When all else fails, ask for help, be it from a colleague, or from your favorite inanimate object.

17.8 Software Testing

Software development contains elements of both art and science; this is one aspect of what makes it such a fascinating and challenging profession. This section introduces the topic of software testing, which also involves both art and science; thus, it is somewhat more general and higher level (read: "handwavy") than the rest of this chapter.

Software testing is an integral part of the software development process. It is very unusual for a program to work 100 percent correctly the first time it compiles. The program isn't responsible for being correct; the *author* of the program is. One of the most important ways to verify that a program functions the way it's supposed to is to test it.

One way to break down the different kinds of testing is as follows:

Unit tests

These are tests you write for each separate unit or functional component of your program. As part of this effort, you may also need to write *scaffolding*—code designed to provide enough supporting framework to run the unit as a stand-alone program.

It is important to design the tests for each functional component *when you design the component*. Doing so helps you clarify the feature design; knowing how you'll test it helps you define what it should and shouldn't do in the first place.

Integration tests

These are tests you apply when all the functional components have been written, tested, and debugged individually. The idea is that everything is then hooked into place in the overall framework and the whole thing is tested to make sure that the interactions between the components are working.

Regression tests

Inevitably, you (or your users!) will discover problems. These may be real bugs, or design limitations, or failures in weird "corner cases." Once you've been able to reproduce and fix the problem, keep the original failing case as a regression test.

A regression test lets you make sure that when you make changes, you haven't reintroduced an old problem. (This can happen easily.) By running a program through its test suite after making a change, you can be (more) confident that everything is working the way it's supposed to.

Testing should be automated as much as possible. This is particularly easy to do for non-GUI programs written in the style of the Linux/Unix tools: programs that read standard input or named files and write to standard output and standard error. At the very least, testing can be done with simple shell scripts. More involved testing is usually done with a separate `test` subdirectory and the `make` program.

Software testing is a whole subfield in itself, and we don't expect to do it justice here; rather, our point is to make you aware that testing is an integral part of development and often the motivating factor for using your debugging skills! Here is a *very* brief summary list:

- Design the test along with the feature.
- Test boundary conditions: make sure the feature works both inside and at valid boundaries and that it fails correctly outside them. (For example, the `sqrt()` function has to fail when given a negative argument.)
- Use assertions in your code (see Section 13.1, "Assertion Statements: `assert()`," page 419), and run your tests with the assertions enabled.
- Create and reuse test scaffolding.
- Save failure cases for regression testing.
- Automate testing as much as possible.
- Print a count of failed tests so that success or failure, and the degree of failure, can be determined easily.
- Use code coverage tools such as `gcov` to verify that your test suite exercises all of your code.
- Test early and test often.
- Study software-testing literature to improve your ability to develop and test software.

Recommendation: Learn about software-testing best practices, and make them a standard part of how you work.

17.9 Debugging Rules

Debugging isn't a "black art." Its principles and techniques can be learned and consistently applied by anyone. To this end, we highly recommend the book *Debugging* by David J. Agans. The book has a website[29] that summarizes the rules and provides a downloadable poster for you to print and place on your office wall.

To round off our discussion, we present the following material. It was adapted by David Agans, with permission, from *Debugging*, copyright © 2002 David J. Agans, published by AMACOM,[30] a division of American Management Association. We thank him.

1. **Understand the system.** When all else fails, read the manual. You have to know what the troubled system and all of its parts are supposed to do if you want to figure out why they don't do it. So read any and all documentation you can get your hands (or browser) on.

   Knowing where functional blocks and data paths are, and how they interact, gives you a road map for failure isolation. Of course, you also have to know your domain (language, operating system, application) and your tools (compiler, source code debugger).

2. **Make it fail.** In order to see the bug, you have to be able to make the failure occur consistently. Document your procedures and start from a known state, so that you can always make it fail again. Look at the bug on the system that fails—don't try to simulate the problem on another system. Don't trust statistics on intermittent problems; they will hide the bug more than they will expose it. Rather, try to make it consistent by varying inputs, and initial conditions, and timing.

   If it's still intermittent, you have to make it look like it's not. Capture in a log every bit of information you can, during every run; then when you have some bad runs and some good runs, compare them to each other. If you've captured enough data, you'll be able to home in on the problem as if you could make it fail every time. Being able to make it fail every time also means you'll be able to tell when you've fixed it.

3. **Quit thinking and look.** There are more ways for something to fail than you can possibly imagine. So instead of imagining what could be happening, look at it—put instrumentation on the system so you can actually see the failure mechanism. Use whatever instrumentation you can—debuggers, `printf()`s, `assert()`s, logic analyzers, and even LEDs and beepers. Look at it deeply enough until the bug is obvious to the eye, not just to the brain.

   If you do guess, use the guess only to focus the search—don't try to fix it until you can see it. If you have to add instrumentation code, do it, but be sure to start with the same code base as the failing system, and make sure it still fails with your added code running. Often, adding the debugger makes it stop failing (that's why they call it a debugger).

[29] `https://www.debuggingrules.com`

[30] `http://www.amacombooks.org`

4. **Divide and conquer.** Everybody knows this one. You do a successive approximation—start at one end, jump halfway, see which way the error is from there, and jump half again in that direction. With binary search, you're there in a few jumps. The hard part is knowing whether you're past the bug or not. One helpful trick is to put known simple data into the system, so that trashed data is easier to spot. Also, start at the bad end and work back toward the good: there are too many good paths to explore if you start at the good end. Fix the bugs you know about right away, since sometimes two bugs interact (though you'd swear they can't), and successive approximation doesn't work with two target values.

5. **Change one thing at a time.** If you're trying to improve a stream-handling module and you simultaneously upgrade to the next version of the operating system, it doesn't matter whether you see improvement, degradation, or no change—you will have no idea what effect your individual changes had. The interaction of multiple changes can be unpredictable and confusing, so don't make them. Change one thing at a time, so you can bet that any difference you see as a result came from that change.

   If you make a change and it seems to have no effect, back it out immediately. It may have had some effects that you didn't see, and those may show up in combination with other changes. This goes for changes in testing as well as in coding.

6. **Keep an audit trail.** Much of the effectiveness of the preceding rules depends on keeping good records. In all aspects of testing and debugging, write down what you did, when you did it, how you did it, and what happened as a result. Do it electronically if possible, so that the record can be emailed and attached to the bug database. Many a clue is found in a pattern of events that would not be noticed if it wasn't recorded for all to see and compare. And the clue is likely to be in the details that you didn't think were important, so write it all down.

7. **Check the plug.** Everyone has a story about some problem that turned out to be "it wasn't plugged in." Sometimes it's literally unplugged, but in software, "unplugged" can mean a missing driver or an old version of code you thought you'd replaced. Or bad hardware when you swear it's a software problem. One story had the hardware and software engineers pointing fingers at each other, and it was neither: the test device they were using was not up to spec. The bottom line is that sometimes you're looking for a problem inside a system, when in fact the problem is outside the system, or underlying the system, or in the initialization of the system, or you're not looking at the right system.

   Don't necessarily trust your tools, either. The tool vendors are engineers, too; they have bugs, and you may be the one to find them.

8. **Get a fresh view.** There are three reasons to ask for help while debugging.

   The first is to get fresh insight—another person will often see something just because they aren't caught up in it like you are. The second reason is to tap expertise—they know more about the system than you do. The third reason is to get experience—they've seen this one before.

When you describe the situation to someone, report the symptoms you've seen, not your theories about why it's acting that way. You went to them because your theories aren't getting you anywhere—don't pull them down into the same rut you're stuck in.

9. **If you didn't fix it, it ain't fixed.** So you think it's fixed? Prove it. Since you were able to make it fail consistently, set up the same situation and make sure it doesn't fail. Don't assume that just because the problem was obvious, it's all fixed now. Maybe it wasn't so obvious. Maybe your fix wasn't done right. Maybe your fix isn't even in the new release! Test it! Make it not fail.

   Are you sure your code is what fixed it? Or did the test change, or did some other code get in there? Once you see that your fix works, take the fix out and make it fail again. Then put the fix back in and see that it doesn't fail. This step assures you that it was really your fix that solved the problem.

17.10 Suggested Reading

The following books are excellent, with much to say about both testing and debugging. All but the first two relate to programming in general. They're all worthwhile.

1. *GDB Pocket Reference*, by Arnold Robbins. O'Reilly, 2005. ISBN-13: 978-0-5961-0027-8.

   This is a handy quick reference guide for the GDB debugger. Note that it is *not* a tutorial.

2. *Debugging*, by David J. Agans. AMACOM, 2002. ISBN-13: 978-0-8144-3445-1.

   We highly recommend this book. Its tone is light, and amazing as it may sound, it's fun reading!

3. *Programming Pearls*, 2nd ed., by Jon Louis Bentley. Addison-Wesley, 2000. ISBN-13: 978-0-201-65788-3.

   Chapter 5 of this book gives a good discussion of unit testing and building test scaffolding.

4. *Literate Programming*, by Donald E. Knuth. Center for the Study of Language and Information, Stanford University, 1992. ISBN-13: 978-0-9370-7380-3.

   This fascinating book contains a number of articles by Donald Knuth on *literate programming*—a programming technique that he invented and used for the creation of TeX and Metafont. Of particular interest is the article entitled "The Errors of TeX," which describes how he developed and debugged TeX, including his log of all the problems found and fixed.

5. *Writing Solid Code*, 20th anniversary 2nd ed., by Steve Maguire. Greyden Press, 2013. ISBN-13: 978-1-57074-055-8.

6. *Code Complete: A Practical Handbook of Software Construction*, 2nd ed., by Steve McConnell. Microsoft Press, 2004. ISBN-13: 978-0-73561-967-8.
7. *The Practice of Programming*, by Brian W. Kernighan and Rob Pike. Addison-Wesley, 1999. ISBN-13: 978-0-201-61586-9.

   This book includes chapters on debugging and testing.
8. We've included a copy of `n3308.pdf`, *Educational Undefined Behavior Technical Report*, in the book's GitHub repository. The document states:

   > This document is an educational document that tries to explain the concept of "Undefined behavior" in the C programming language. It is the combined efforts of the ISO WG14's Undefined Behavior Study group, to clarify the term, and its implications.

   We recommend that you read it.
9. For an interesting retrospective on Valgrind, see *Twenty Years of Valgrind*[31] by Nicholas Nethercote, July 27, 2022.

17.11 Summary

- Debugging is an important part of software development. Good design and development practices should be used to minimize the introduction of bugs, but debugging will always be with us.
- Programs should be compiled without optimization and with debugging symbols included to make debugging under a debugger more straightforward. On many systems, compiling with optimization and compiling with debugging symbols are mutually exclusive. This is not true of GCC, which is why the GNU/Linux developer needs to be aware of the issue.
- The GNU debugger GDB is standard on GNU/Linux systems and can be used on just about any commercial Unix system as well. Breakpoints, watchpoints, and single-stepping with `next`, `step`, and `cont` provide basic control over a program as it's running. GDB also lets you examine data and call functions within the target.

  Graphical debuggers based on GDB are available and easily portable. Also, both Vim and Emacs (the standard text editors) have modes allowing you to run GDB from inside the editor. This makes debugging even easier.
- The `rr` debugger offers exciting possibilities for reversible, reproducible debugging.

[31] `https://nnethercote.github.io/2022/07/27/twenty-years-of-valgrind.html`

- There are many things you can do when writing your program to make life easier when you inevitably have to debug it. We covered the following topics:
  - Debugging macros for printing state.
  - Avoiding expression macros.
  - Reordering code to make single-stepping easier.
  - Writing helper functions for use from a debugger.
  - Avoiding `union`s.
  - Having runtime debugging code in the production version of a program and having different ways to enable that code's output.
  - Adding dummy functions to make breakpoints easier to set.
- A number of tools and libraries besides just general-purpose debuggers exist to help with debugging. `splint` is a modern alternative to the venerable V7 `lint` program. It is readily available on modern GNU/Linux systems and can be easily downloaded and built from source.
- Table 17.1 presents a list of GCC compiler options that are useful for static analysis of your code.
- The Valgrind program is a versatile tool for finding problems with dynamically allocated memory, as well as problems related to uninitialized memory.
- Address Sanitizer provides a complementary alternative to Valgrind, checking dynamic memory as well as local and global memory. Both programs should be used (but not together!) for finding and destroying memory-related problems.
- Having a friendly inanimate object around to explain your problems to is yet another way to find your bugs.
- Besides debugging tools, software testing is also an integral part of the software development process. It should be understood, planned for, and managed from the beginning of all software development projects, even personal ones.
- Debugging is a skill that can be learned. We recommend reading the book *Debugging* by David J. Agans and learning to apply his rules.

Exercises

1. Compile one of your programs with GCC, using both `-g` and `-O`. Run it under GDB, setting a breakpoint in `main()`. Single-step through the program, and see how closely execution relates (or doesn't relate) to the original source code. This is particularly good to do with code using a `while` or `for` loop. Examine the values of your variables as you step through the code. Some of them may have even disappeared! (GDB will tell you that the "value was optimized out.")

2. Read up on GDB's *conditional breakpoint* feature. How does that simplify dealing with problems that occur only after a certain number of operations have been done?
3. Read up on GDB's `attach` command. What possibilities does this open up for you?
4. Rewrite the `parse_debug()` function from Section 17.4.2.1, "Add Debugging Options and Variables," page 623, to use a table of debugging option strings, flag values, and string lengths.
5. (Hard.) Study the `gawk` source code—in particular, the `NODE` structure in `awk.h`. Write a debugging helper function that prints the contents of a `NODE` based on the value in the `type` field.
6. Run one of your programs that uses dynamic memory with Valgrind with leak checking enabled. Describe the problems, if any, that you found.
7. Compile the program using Address Sanitizer and run it again. Describe the problems, if any, that you found.
8. Design a set of tests for the `mv` program. (Read *mv*(1): make sure you cover all its options.)
9. Search on the Internet for software-testing resources. What interesting things did you find?

Chapter 18

A Project That Ties Everything Together

In Chapter 7, "Putting It All Together: `ls`," page 201, we rather neatly tied together everything that had been presented up to that point by looking at the V7 `ls.c`. However, as much as we would like it to be so, there is no single program small enough to include here for tying together the concepts and APIs that we presented starting with Chapter 8, "Filesystems and Directory Walks," page 221.

18.1 Project Description

In day-to-day use, the one program that does use just about everything in the book is the shell. And indeed, there are Unix programming books that write a small but working shell to illustrate the principles involved.

Real shells are large and messy creatures. They must deal with many portability issues, such as we've outlined throughout the book, and above and beyond that, they often have to work around bugs in different versions of Unix. Furthermore, to be useful, shells do many things that don't involve the system call API, such as maintaining shell variables, a history of saved commands, and so on. Providing a complete tour of a full-featured shell such as Bash, `ksh93`, or `zsh` would take a separate volume.

Instead, we suggest the following list of steps for writing your own shell, either as a (large) exercise to cement your understanding or perhaps as a cooperative project if you're in school:

1. Design your command "language" so that it will be easy to interpret with simple code. While compiler and interpreter technology is valuable when writing a production shell, it's likely to be overkill for you at this stage.

   Consider the following points:

   - Are you going to use i18n facilities?
   - What commands must be built into the shell?
   - To be useful, your shell will need a command search path mechanism, analogous to `$PATH` of the regular shell. How will you set it?
   - What I/O redirections do you wish to support? Files only? Pipes too? Do you wish to be able to redirect more than file descriptors `0`, `1`, and `2`?

- Decide how quoting will work; will you use single and double quotes, or only one kind? How do you quote a quote? How does quoting interact with I/O redirections?
- How will you handle putting commands in the background? What about waiting for a command in the background to finish?
- Decide whether you will have shell variables.
- What kind of wildcarding or other expansions will you support? How do they interact with quoting? With shell variables?
- You should plan for at least an `if` and a `while` statement. Design a syntax. We will call these *block statements*.
- Decide whether or not you wish to allow I/O redirection for a block statement. If yes, what will the syntax look like?
- Decide how, if at all, your shell language should handle signals.
- Design a testing and debugging framework *before* you start to code.

2. If you're going to use i18n facilities, do so from the outset. Retrofitting them in is painful.
3. For the real work, start simply. The initial version should read one line at a time and break it into words to use as separate arguments. Don't do any quoting, I/O redirection, or anything else. Don't even try to create a new process to run the entered program. How are you going to test what you have so far?
4. Add quoting so that individual "words" can contain whitespace. Does the quoting code implement your design?
5. Make your built-in commands work. (See Section 4.6 "Creating Files," page 101, and Section 8.4.1, "Changing Directory: `chdir()` and `fchdir()`," page 247, for at least two necessary built-in commands.) How are you going to test them?
6. Are there commands that don't have to be built into the shell that you want to have as built-ins anyway (`echo`, for example)?
7. Initially, use a fixed search path, such as `"/bin:/usr/bin:/usr/local/bin"`. Add process creation with `fork()` and execution with `exec()` (see Chapter 9, "Process Management and Pipes," page 275). Starting out, the shell should wait for each new program to finish.
8. Add backgrounding and, as a separate command, waiting for process completion (see Chapter 9, "Process Management and Pipes," page 275).
9. Add a user-settable search path (see Section 2.4, "The Environment," page 37).
10. Add I/O redirection for files (see Section 9.4, "File Descriptor Management," page 307).
11. Add shell variables. Test their interaction with quoting.
12. Add wildcard and other expansions (see Section 13.7, "Metacharacter Expansions," page 450). Test their interaction with shell variables. Test their interaction with quoting.

13. Add pipelines (see Section 9.3, "Basic Interprocess Communication: Pipes and FIFOs," page 302). At this point, real complexity starts to settle in. You may need to take a hard look at how you're managing data that represents commands to be run.

    You could stop here with a legitimate feeling of accomplishment if you get a working shell that can do everything mentioned so far.

14. If you're up for a further challenge, add `if` and/or `while` statements.
15. Add signal handling (see Chapter 10, "Signals," page 333).
16. If you'd like to use your shell for real work, explore the GNU Readline library (type '`info readline`' on a GNU/Linux system or see the source for the Bash shell). This library lets you add either Emacs-style or `vi`-style command-line editing to interactive programs. (The Readline library is distributed from `https://ftp.gnu.org/gnu/readline/`; take a look at some of the example files, such as `rl.c` and `rltest.c`.)

Keep two things constantly in mind: always be able to test what you're doing, and "no arbitrary limits!"

Once it's done, do a postmortem analysis of the project. How would you do it differently the second time?

Good luck!

18.2 Suggested Reading

1. *The UNIX Programming Environment*, by Brian W. Kernighan and Rob Pike. Pearson, 1984. ISBN-13: 978-0-13-937681-8.

   This is *the* classic book on Unix programming, describing the entire gestalt of the Unix environment, from interactive use to shell programming, programming with the <stdio.h> functions and the lower-level system calls, program development with `make`, `yacc`, and `lex`, and documentation with `nroff` and `troff`.

   Although the book shows its age, it is still eminently worth reading, and we highly recommend it.

2. *The Art of UNIX Programming*, by Eric S. Raymond. Addison-Wesley, 2004. ISBN-13: 978-0-13-142901-7.

   This is a higher-level book that focuses on the design issues in Unix programming: how Unix programs work and how to design your own programs to fit comfortably into a Linux/Unix environment.

   While we don't always agree with what the author has to say, the book does contain considerable important material and is worth reading.

Part IV

Appendices

Appendix A

Teach Yourself Programming in Ten Years

Experience, n:
Something you don't get until just after you need it.
— Olivier

This chapter is written by Peter Norvig (copyright © 2001–2014 by Peter Norvig) and is reprinted by permission. The original article, including hyperlinks, is at `https://www.norvig.com/21-days.html`. We have included it because we believe that it conveys an important message. The above quote is one of our longtime favorites, and as it applies to the point of this appendix, we've included it too.

Why is Everyone in Such a Rush?

Walk into any bookstore, and you'll see how to *Teach Yourself Java in 24 Hours* alongside endless variations offering to teach C, SQL, Ruby, Algorithms, and so on in a few days or hours. The Amazon advanced search for [title: teach, yourself, hours, since: 2000] found 512 such books. Of the top ten, nine are programming books (the other is about bookkeeping). Similar results come from replacing "teach yourself" with "learn" or "hours" with "days."

The conclusion is that either people are in a big rush to learn about programming, or that programming is somehow fabulously easier to learn than anything else. Felleisen *et al.*, give a nod to this trend in their book *How to Design Programs*, when they say "Bad programming is easy. *Idiots* can learn it in *21 days*, even if they are *dummies*." The Abstruse Goose comic also had their take.

Let's analyze what a title like *Teach Yourself C++ in 24 Hours* could mean:

- **Teach Yourself:** In 24 hours you won't have time to write several significant programs, and learn from your successes and failures with them. You won't have time to work with an experienced programmer and understand what it is like to live in a C++ environment. In short, you won't have time to learn much. So the book can only be talking about a superficial familiarity, not a deep understanding. As Alexander Pope said, a little learning is a dangerous thing.

- **C++:** In 24 hours you might be able to learn some of the syntax of C++ (if you already know another language), but you couldn't learn much about how to use the language. In short, if you were, say, a Basic programmer, you could learn to write programs in the style of Basic using C++ syntax, but you couldn't learn what C++ is actually good (and bad) for. So what's the point? Alan Perlis once said: "A language that doesn't affect the way you think about programming, is not worth knowing." One possible point is that you have to learn a tiny bit of C++ (or more likely, something like JavaScript or Processing) because you need to interface with an existing tool to accomplish a specific task. But then you're not learning how to program; you're learning to accomplish that task.
- **in 24 Hours:** Unfortunately, this is not enough, as the next section shows.

Teach Yourself Programming in Ten Years

Researchers (Bloom [1985], Bryan & Harter [1899], Hayes [1989], Simmon & Chase [1973]) have shown it takes about ten years to develop expertise in any of a wide variety of areas, including chess playing, music composition, telegraph operation, painting, piano playing, swimming, tennis, and research in neuropsychology and topology. The key is *deliberative* practice: not just doing it again and again, but challenging yourself with a task that is just beyond your current ability, trying it, analyzing your performance while and after doing it, and correcting any mistakes. Then repeat. And repeat again. There appear to be no real shortcuts: even Mozart, who was a musical prodigy at age 4, took 13 more years before he began to produce world-class music. In another genre, the Beatles seemed to burst onto the scene with a string of #1 hits and an appearance on the Ed Sullivan show in 1964. But they had been playing small clubs in Liverpool and Hamburg since 1957, and while they had mass appeal early on, their first great critical success, *Sgt. Pepper's*, was released in 1967.

Malcolm Gladwell has popularized the idea, although he concentrates on 10,000 hours, not 10 years. Henri Cartier-Bresson (1908–2004) had another metric: "Your first 10,000 photographs are your worst." (He didn't anticipate that with digital cameras, some people can reach that mark in a week.) True expertise may take a lifetime: Samuel Johnson (1709–1784) said, "Excellence in any department can be attained only by the labor of a lifetime; it is not to be purchased at a lesser price." And Chaucer (1340–1400) complained "the lyf so short, the craft so long to lerne." Hippocrates (c. 400 B.C.) is known for the excerpt "ars longa, vita brevis," which is part of the longer quotation "Ars longa, vita brevis, occasio praeceps, experimentum periculosum, iudicium difficile," which in English renders as "Life is short, [the] craft long, opportunity fleeting, experiment treacherous, judgment difficult." Of course, no single number can be the final answer: it doesn't seem reasonable to assume that all skills (e.g., programming, chess playing, checkers playing, and music playing) could all require exactly the same amount of time to master, nor that all people will take exactly the same amount of time. As Prof. K. Anders Ericsson puts it, "In most domains it's remarkable how much time even the most talented individuals need in order to reach the highest levels of performance.

The 10,000 hour number just gives you a sense that we're talking years of 10 to 20 hours a week which those who some people would argue are the most innately talented individuals still need to get to the highest level."

So You Want to Be a Programmer

Here's my recipe for programming success:

- Get **interested** in programming, and do some because it is fun. Make sure that it keeps being enough fun so that you will be willing to put in your ten years/10,000 hours.
- **Program**. The best kind of learning is learning by doing. To put it more technically, "the maximal level of performance for individuals in a given domain is not attained automatically as a function of extended experience, but the level of performance can be increased even by highly experienced individuals as a result of deliberate efforts to improve." (p. 366) and "the most effective learning requires a well-defined task with an appropriate difficulty level for the particular individual, informative feedback, and opportunities for repetition and corrections of errors" (p. 20–21). The book *Cognition in Practice: Mind, Mathematics, and Culture in Everyday Life* is an interesting reference for this viewpoint.
- **Talk with** other programmers; read other programs. This is more important than any book or training course.
- If you want, put in four years at a **college** (or more at a graduate school). This will give you access to some jobs that require credentials, and it will give you a deeper understanding of the field, but if you don't enjoy school, you can (with some dedication) get similar experience on your own or on the job. In any case, book learning alone won't be enough. "Computer science education cannot make anybody an expert programmer any more than studying brushes and pigment can make somebody an expert painter," says Eric Raymond, author of *The New Hacker's Dictionary*. One of the best programmers I ever hired had only a High School degree; he's produced a lot of great software, has his own news group, and made enough in stock options to buy his own nightclub.
- Work on **projects with** other programmers. Be the best programmer on some projects; be the worst on some others. When you're the best, you get to test your abilities to lead a project, and to inspire others with your vision. When you're the worst, you learn what the masters do, and you learn what they don't like to do (because they make you do it for them).
- Work on **projects *after*** other programmers. Understand a program written by someone else. See what it takes to understand and fix it when the original programmers are not around. Think about how to design your programs to make it easier for those who will maintain them after you.
- Learn at least a half dozen **programming languages**. Include one language that emphasizes class abstractions (like Java or C++), one that emphasizes functional abstraction (like Lisp or ML or Haskell), one that supports syntactic abstraction (like Lisp), one

that supports declarative specifications (like Prolog or C++ templates), and one that emphasizes parallelism (like Clojure or Go).

- Remember that there is a "**computer**" in "computer science." Know how long it takes your computer to execute an instruction, fetch a word from memory (with and without a cache miss), read consecutive words from disk, and seek to a new location on disk. (See "Answers," page 669.)
- Get involved in a language **standardization** effort. It could be the ANSI C++ committee, or it could be deciding if your local coding style will have 2 or 4 space indentation levels. Either way, you learn about what other people like in a language, how deeply they feel so, and perhaps even a little about why they feel so.
- Have the good sense to **get off** the language standardization effort as quickly as possible.

With all that in mind, it's questionable how far you can get just by book learning. Before my first child was born, I read all the *How To* books, and still felt like a clueless novice. 30 months later, when my second child was due, did I go back to the books for a refresher? No. Instead, I relied on my personal experience, which turned out to be far more useful and reassuring to me than the thousands of pages written by experts.

Fred Brooks, in his essay *No Silver Bullet*, identified a three-part plan for finding great software designers:

1. Systematically identify top designers as early as possible.
2. Assign a career mentor to be responsible for the development of the prospect and carefully keep a career file.
3. Provide opportunities for growing designers to interact and stimulate each other.

This assumes that some people already have the qualities necessary for being a great designer; the job is to properly coax them along. Alan Perlis put it more succinctly: "Everyone can be taught to sculpt: Michelangelo would have had to be taught how not to. So it is with the great programmers." Perlis is saying that the greats have some internal quality that transcends their training. But where does the quality come from? Is it innate? Or do they develop it through diligence? ... I think of it more as willingness to devote a large portion of one's life to deliberative practice. But maybe *fearless* is a way to summarize that. ...

So go ahead and buy that Java/Ruby/Javascript/PHP book; you'll probably get some use out of it. But you won't change your life, or your real overall expertise as a programmer in 24 hours or 21 days. How about working hard to continually improve over 24 months? Well, now you're starting to get somewhere ...

References

Bloom, Benjamin (ed.), *Developing Talent in Young People*, Ballantine, 1985.
Brooks, Fred, *No Silver Bullets*, IEEE Computer, vol. 20, no. 4, 1987, p. 10–19.

Bryan, W. L., & Harter, N., "Studies on the telegraphic language: The acquisition of a hierarchy of habits," *Psychology Review*, 1899, 8, 345–375.
Hayes, John R., *Complete Problem Solver*, Lawrence Erlbaum, 1989.
Chase, William G., & Simon, Herbert A., "Perception in Chess," *Cognitive Psychology*, 1973, 4, 55–81.
Lave, Jean, *Cognition in Practice: Mind, Mathematics, and Culture in Everyday Life*, Cambridge University Press, 1988.

Answers

Approximate timing for various operations on a typical PC:

execute typical instruction	1/1,000,000,000 sec = 1 nanosec
fetch from L1 cache memory	0.5 nanosec
branch misprediction	5 nanosec
fetch from L2 cache memory	7 nanosec
Mutex lock/unlock	25 nanosec
fetch from main memory	100 nanosec
send 2K bytes over 1Gbps network	20,000 nanosec
read 1MB sequentially from memory	250,000 nanosec
fetch from new disk location (seek)	8,000,000 nanosec
read 1MB sequentially from disk	20,000,000 nanosec
send packet US to Europe and back	150 milliseconds = 150,000,000 nanosec

Appendix: Language Choice

Several people have asked what programming language they should learn first. There is no one answer, but consider these points:

- *Use your friends.* When asked "what operating system should I use, Windows, Unix, or Mac?," my answer is usually: "use whatever your friends use." The advantage you get from learning from your friends will offset any intrinsic difference between OS, or between programming languages. Also consider your future friends: the community of programmers that you will be a part of if you continue. Does your chosen language have a large growing community or a small dying one? Are there books, web sites, and online forums to get answers from? Do you like the people in those forums?
- *Keep it simple.* Programming languages such as C++ and Java are designed for professional development by large teams of experienced programmers who are concerned about the run-time efficiency of their code. As a result, these languages have complicated parts designed for these circumstances. You're concerned with learning to program. You don't need that complication. You want a language that was designed to be easy to learn and remember by a single new programmer.

- *Play.* Which way would you rather learn to play the piano: the normal, interactive way, in which you hear each note as soon as you hit a key, or "batch" mode, in which you only hear the notes after you finish a whole song? Clearly, interactive mode makes learning easier for the piano, and also for programming. Insist on a language with an interactive mode and use it.

Given these criteria, my recommendations for a first programming language would be **Python** or **Scheme**. Another choice is Javascript, not because it is perfectly well-designed for beginners, but because there are so many online tutorials for it, such as Khan Academy's tutorial. But your circumstances may vary, and there are other good choices. If your age is a single-digit, you might prefer Alice or Squeak or Blockly (older learners might also enjoy these). The important thing is that you choose and get started.

Appendix: Books and Other Resources

Several people have asked what books and web pages they should learn from. I repeat that "book learning alone won't be enough" but I can recommend the following:

- **Scheme:** *Structure and Interpretation of Computer Programs* (Abelson & Sussman) is probably the best introduction to computer science, and it does teach programming as a way of understanding the computer science. You can see online videos of lectures on this book, as well as the complete text online. The book is challenging and will weed out some people who perhaps could be successful with another approach.
- **Scheme:** *How to Design Programs* (Felleisen *et al.*) is one of the best books on how to actually design programs in an elegant and functional way.
- **Python:** *Python Programming: An Intro to CS* (Zelle) is a good introduction using Python.
- **Python:** Several online tutorials are available at Python.org.
- **Oz:** *Concepts, Techniques, and Models of Computer Programming* (Van Roy & Haridi) is seen by some as the modern-day successor to Abelson & Sussman. It is a tour through the big ideas of programming, covering a wider range than Abelson & Sussman while being perhaps easier to read and follow. It uses a language, Oz, that is not widely known but serves as a basis for learning other languages.

Notes

T. Capey points out that the *Complete Problem Solver* page on Amazon now has the "Teach Yourself Bengali in 21 Days" and "Teach Yourself Grammar and Style" books under the "Customers who shopped for this item also shopped for these items" section. I guess that a large portion of the people who look at that book are coming from this page. Thanks to Ross Cohen for help with Hippocrates.

Appendix B
Caldera Ancient UNIX License

CALDERA
240 West Center Street
Orem, Utah 84057
801-765-4999 Fax 801-765-4481

January 23, 2002

Dear UNIX® enthusiasts,

Caldera International, Inc. hereby grants a fee free license that includes the rights use, modify and distribute this named source code, including creating derived binary products created from the source code. The source code for which Caldera International, Inc. grants rights are limited to the following UNIX Operating Systems that operate on the 16-Bit PDP-11 CPU and early versions of the 32-Bit UNIX Operating System, with specific exclusion of UNIX System III and UNIX System V and successor operating systems:

32-bit 32V UNIX
16 bit UNIX Versions 1, 2, 3, 4, 5, 6, 7

Caldera International, Inc. makes no guarantees or commitments that any source code is available from Caldera International, Inc.

The following copyright notice applies to the source code files for which this license is granted.

Copyright © Caldera International Inc. 2001–2002. All rights reserved.

Redistribution and use in source and binary forms, with or without modification, are permitted provided that the following conditions are met:

Redistributions of source code and documentation must retain the above copyright notice, this list of conditions and the following disclaimer. Redistributions in binary form must reproduce the above copyright notice, this list of conditions and the following disclaimer in the documentation and/or other materials provided with the distribution.

All advertising materials mentioning features or use of this software must display the following acknowledgement:

This product includes software developed or owned by Caldera International, Inc.

Neither the name of Caldera International, Inc. nor the names of other contributors may be used to endorse or promote products derived from this software without specific prior written permission.

USE OF THE SOFTWARE PROVIDED FOR UNDER THIS LICENSE BY CALDERA INTERNATIONAL, INC. AND CONTRIBUTORS "AS IS" AND ANY EXPRESS OR IMPLIED WARRANTIES, INCLUDING, BUT NOT LIMITED TO, THE IMPLIED WARRANTIES OF MERCHANTABILITY AND FITNESS FOR A PARTICULAR PURPOSE ARE DISCLAIMED. IN NO EVENT SHALL CALDERA INTERNATIONAL, INC. BE LIABLE FOR ANY DIRECT, INDIRECT INCIDENTAL, SPECIAL, EXEMPLARY, OR CONSEQUENTIAL DAMAGES (INCLUDING, BUT NOT LIMITED TO, PROCUREMENT OF SUBSTITUTE GOODS OR SERVICES; LOSS OF USE, DATA, OR PROFITS; OR BUSINESS INTERRUPTION) HOWEVER CAUSED AND ON ANY THEORY OF LIABILITY, WHETHER IN CONTRACT, STRICT LIABILITY, OR TORT (INCLUDING NEGLIGENCE OR OTHERWISE) ARISING IN ANY WAY OUT OF THE USE OF THIS SOFTWARE, EVEN IF ADVISED OF THE POSSIBILITY OF SUCH DAMAGE.

Very truly yours,

/signed/ Bill Broderick

Bill Broderick
Director, Licensing Services

* UNIX is a registered trademark of The Open Group in the US and other countries.

Appendix C

GNU General Public License

Version 3, 29 June 2007

Preamble

The GNU General Public License is a free, copyleft license for software and other kinds of works.

The licenses for most software and other practical works are designed to take away your freedom to share and change the works. By contrast, the GNU General Public License is intended to guarantee your freedom to share and change all versions of a program—to make sure it remains free software for all its users. We, the Free Software Foundation, use the GNU General Public License for most of our software; it applies also to any other work released this way by its authors. You can apply it to your programs, too.

When we speak of free software, we are referring to freedom, not price. Our General Public Licenses are designed to make sure that you have the freedom to distribute copies of free software (and charge for them if you wish), that you receive source code or can get it if you want it, that you can change the software or use pieces of it in new free programs, and that you know you can do these things.

To protect your rights, we need to prevent others from denying you these rights or asking you to surrender the rights. Therefore, you have certain responsibilities if you distribute copies of the software, or if you modify it: responsibilities to respect the freedom of others.

For example, if you distribute copies of such a program, whether gratis or for a fee, you must pass on to the recipients the same freedoms that you received. You must make sure that they, too, receive or can get the source code. And you must show them these terms so they know their rights.

Developers that use the GNU GPL protect your rights with two steps: (1) assert copyright on the software, and (2) offer you this License giving you legal permission to copy, distribute and/or modify it.

For the developers' and authors' protection, the GPL clearly explains that there is no warranty for this free software. For both users' and authors' sake, the GPL requires that modified versions be marked as changed, so that their problems will not be attributed erroneously to authors of previous versions.

Some devices are designed to deny users access to install or run modified versions of the software inside them, although the manufacturer can do so. This is fundamentally incompatible with the aim of protecting users' freedom to change the software. The systematic pattern of such abuse occurs in the area of products for individuals to use, which is precisely where it is most unacceptable. Therefore, we have designed this version of the GPL to prohibit the practice for those products. If such problems arise substantially in other domains, we stand ready to extend this provision to those domains in future versions of the GPL, as needed to protect the freedom of users.

Finally, every program is threatened constantly by software patents. States should not allow patents to restrict development and use of software on general-purpose computers, but in those that do, we wish to avoid the special danger that patents applied to a free program could make it effectively proprietary. To prevent this, the GPL assures that patents cannot be used to render the program non-free.

The precise terms and conditions for copying, distribution and modification follow.

TERMS AND CONDITIONS

0. Definitions.

   "This License" refers to version 3 of the GNU General Public License.

   "Copyright" also means copyright-like laws that apply to other kinds of works, such as semiconductor masks.

   "The Program" refers to any copyrightable work licensed under this License. Each licensee is addressed as "you". "Licensees" and "recipients" may be individuals or organizations.

   To "modify" a work means to copy from or adapt all or part of the work in a fashion requiring copyright permission, other than the making of an exact copy. The resulting work is called a "modified version" of the earlier work or a work "based on" the earlier work.

   A "covered work" means either the unmodified Program or a work based on the Program.

   To "propagate" a work means to do anything with it that, without permission, would make you directly or secondarily liable for infringement under applicable copyright law, except executing it on a computer or modifying a private copy. Propagation includes copying, distribution (with or without modification), making available to the public, and in some countries other activities as well.

   To "convey" a work means any kind of propagation that enables other parties to make or receive copies. Mere interaction with a user through a computer network, with no transfer of a copy, is not conveying.

An interactive user interface displays "Appropriate Legal Notices" to the extent that it includes a convenient and prominently visible feature that (1) displays an appropriate copyright notice, and (2) tells the user that there is no warranty for the work (except to the extent that warranties are provided), that licensees may convey the work under this License, and how to view a copy of this License. If the interface presents a list of user commands or options, such as a menu, a prominent item in the list meets this criterion.

1. Source Code.

   The "source code" for a work means the preferred form of the work for making modifications to it. "Object code" means any non-source form of a work.

   A "Standard Interface" means an interface that either is an official standard defined by a recognized standards body, or, in the case of interfaces specified for a particular programming language, one that is widely used among developers working in that language.

   The "System Libraries" of an executable work include anything, other than the work as a whole, that (a) is included in the normal form of packaging a Major Component, but which is not part of that Major Component, and (b) serves only to enable use of the work with that Major Component, or to implement a Standard Interface for which an implementation is available to the public in source code form. A "Major Component", in this context, means a major essential component (kernel, window system, and so on) of the specific operating system (if any) on which the executable work runs, or a compiler used to produce the work, or an object code interpreter used to run it.

   The "Corresponding Source" for a work in object code form means all the source code needed to generate, install, and (for an executable work) run the object code and to modify the work, including scripts to control those activities. However, it does not include the work's System Libraries, or general-purpose tools or generally available free programs which are used unmodified in performing those activities but which are not part of the work. For example, Corresponding Source includes interface definition files associated with source files for the work, and the source code for shared libraries and dynamically linked subprograms that the work is specifically designed to require, such as by intimate data communication or control flow between those subprograms and other parts of the work.

   The Corresponding Source need not include anything that users can regenerate automatically from other parts of the Corresponding Source.

   The Corresponding Source for a work in source code form is that same work.

2. Basic Permissions.

   All rights granted under this License are granted for the term of copyright on the Program, and are irrevocable provided the stated conditions are met. This License explicitly affirms your unlimited permission to run the unmodified Program. The output from running a covered work is covered by this License only if the output, given its content, constitutes a covered work. This License acknowledges your rights of fair use or other equivalent, as provided by copyright law.

You may make, run and propagate covered works that you do not convey, without conditions so long as your license otherwise remains in force. You may convey covered works to others for the sole purpose of having them make modifications exclusively for you, or provide you with facilities for running those works, provided that you comply with the terms of this License in conveying all material for which you do not control copyright. Those thus making or running the covered works for you must do so exclusively on your behalf, under your direction and control, on terms that prohibit them from making any copies of your copyrighted material outside their relationship with you.

Conveying under any other circumstances is permitted solely under the conditions stated below. Sublicensing is not allowed; section 10 makes it unnecessary.

3. Protecting Users' Legal Rights From Anti-Circumvention Law.

   No covered work shall be deemed part of an effective technological measure under any applicable law fulfilling obligations under article 11 of the WIPO copyright treaty adopted on 20 December 1996, or similar laws prohibiting or restricting circumvention of such measures.

   When you convey a covered work, you waive any legal power to forbid circumvention of technological measures to the extent such circumvention is effected by exercising rights under this License with respect to the covered work, and you disclaim any intention to limit operation or modification of the work as a means of enforcing, against the work's users, your or third parties' legal rights to forbid circumvention of technological measures.

4. Conveying Verbatim Copies.

   You may convey verbatim copies of the Program's source code as you receive it, in any medium, provided that you conspicuously and appropriately publish on each copy an appropriate copyright notice; keep intact all notices stating that this License and any non-permissive terms added in accord with section 7 apply to the code; keep intact all notices of the absence of any warranty; and give all recipients a copy of this License along with the Program.

   You may charge any price or no price for each copy that you convey, and you may offer support or warranty protection for a fee.

5. Conveying Modified Source Versions.

   You may convey a work based on the Program, or the modifications to produce it from the Program, in the form of source code under the terms of section 4, provided that you also meet all of these conditions:

   a. The work must carry prominent notices stating that you modified it, and giving a relevant date.
   b. The work must carry prominent notices stating that it is released under this License and any conditions added under section 7. This requirement modifies the requirement in section 4 to "keep intact all notices".

c. You must license the entire work, as a whole, under this License to anyone who comes into possession of a copy. This License will therefore apply, along with any applicable section 7 additional terms, to the whole of the work, and all its parts, regardless of how they are packaged. This License gives no permission to license the work in any other way, but it does not invalidate such permission if you have separately received it.

d. If the work has interactive user interfaces, each must display Appropriate Legal Notices; however, if the Program has interactive interfaces that do not display Appropriate Legal Notices, your work need not make them do so.

A compilation of a covered work with other separate and independent works, which are not by their nature extensions of the covered work, and which are not combined with it such as to form a larger program, in or on a volume of a storage or distribution medium, is called an "aggregate" if the compilation and its resulting copyright are not used to limit the access or legal rights of the compilation's users beyond what the individual works permit. Inclusion of a covered work in an aggregate does not cause this License to apply to the other parts of the aggregate.

6. Conveying Non-Source Forms.

You may convey a covered work in object code form under the terms of sections 4 and 5, provided that you also convey the machine-readable Corresponding Source under the terms of this License, in one of these ways:

a. Convey the object code in, or embodied in, a physical product (including a physical distribution medium), accompanied by the Corresponding Source fixed on a durable physical medium customarily used for software interchange.

b. Convey the object code in, or embodied in, a physical product (including a physical distribution medium), accompanied by a written offer, valid for at least three years and valid for as long as you offer spare parts or customer support for that product model, to give anyone who possesses the object code either (1) a copy of the Corresponding Source for all the software in the product that is covered by this License, on a durable physical medium customarily used for software interchange, for a price no more than your reasonable cost of physically performing this conveying of source, or (2) access to copy the Corresponding Source from a network server at no charge.

c. Convey individual copies of the object code with a copy of the written offer to provide the Corresponding Source. This alternative is allowed only occasionally and noncommercially, and only if you received the object code with such an offer, in accord with subsection 6b.

d. Convey the object code by offering access from a designated place (gratis or for a charge), and offer equivalent access to the Corresponding Source in the same way through the same place at no further charge. You need not require recipients to copy the Corresponding Source along with the object code. If the place to copy the object code is a network server, the Corresponding Source may be on a different server (operated by you or a third party) that supports equivalent copying facilities, provided you maintain clear directions next to the object code saying where to find the Corresponding Source. Regardless of what server hosts the Corresponding Source, you remain obligated to ensure that it is available for as long as needed to satisfy these requirements.

e. Convey the object code using peer-to-peer transmission, provided you inform other peers where the object code and Corresponding Source of the work are being offered to the general public at no charge under subsection 6d.

A separable portion of the object code, whose source code is excluded from the Corresponding Source as a System Library, need not be included in conveying the object code work.

A "User Product" is either (1) a "consumer product", which means any tangible personal property which is normally used for personal, family, or household purposes, or (2) anything designed or sold for incorporation into a dwelling. In determining whether a product is a consumer product, doubtful cases shall be resolved in favor of coverage. For a particular product received by a particular user, "normally used" refers to a typical or common use of that class of product, regardless of the status of the particular user or of the way in which the particular user actually uses, or expects or is expected to use, the product. A product is a consumer product regardless of whether the product has substantial commercial, industrial or non-consumer uses, unless such uses represent the only significant mode of use of the product.

"Installation Information" for a User Product means any methods, procedures, authorization keys, or other information required to install and execute modified versions of a covered work in that User Product from a modified version of its Corresponding Source. The information must suffice to ensure that the continued functioning of the modified object code is in no case prevented or interfered with solely because modification has been made.

If you convey an object code work under this section in, or with, or specifically for use in, a User Product, and the conveying occurs as part of a transaction in which the right of possession and use of the User Product is transferred to the recipient in perpetuity or for a fixed term (regardless of how the transaction is characterized), the Corresponding Source conveyed under this section must be accompanied by the Installation Information. But this requirement does not apply if neither you nor any third party retains the ability to install modified object code on the User Product (for example, the work has been installed in ROM).

The requirement to provide Installation Information does not include a requirement to continue to provide support service, warranty, or updates for a work that has been modified or installed by the recipient, or for the User Product in which it has been modified or installed. Access to a network may be denied when the modification itself materially and adversely affects the operation of the network or violates the rules and protocols for communication across the network.

Corresponding Source conveyed, and Installation Information provided, in accord with this section must be in a format that is publicly documented (and with an implementation available to the public in source code form), and must require no special password or key for unpacking, reading or copying.

7. Additional Terms.

   "Additional permissions" are terms that supplement the terms of this License by making exceptions from one or more of its conditions. Additional permissions that are applicable to the entire Program shall be treated as though they were included in this License, to the extent that they are valid under applicable law. If additional permissions apply only to part of the Program, that part may be used separately under those permissions, but the entire Program remains governed by this License without regard to the additional permissions.

   When you convey a copy of a covered work, you may at your option remove any additional permissions from that copy, or from any part of it. (Additional permissions may be written to require their own removal in certain cases when you modify the work.) You may place additional permissions on material, added by you to a covered work, for which you have or can give appropriate copyright permission.

   Notwithstanding any other provision of this License, for material you add to a covered work, you may (if authorized by the copyright holders of that material) supplement the terms of this License with terms:

   a. Disclaiming warranty or limiting liability differently from the terms of sections 15 and 16 of this License; or
   b. Requiring preservation of specified reasonable legal notices or author attributions in that material or in the Appropriate Legal Notices displayed by works containing it; or
   c. Prohibiting misrepresentation of the origin of that material, or requiring that modified versions of such material be marked in reasonable ways as different from the original version; or
   d. Limiting the use for publicity purposes of names of licensors or authors of the material; or
   e. Declining to grant rights under trademark law for use of some trade names, trademarks, or service marks; or
   f. Requiring indemnification of licensors and authors of that material by anyone who conveys the material (or modified versions of it) with contractual assumptions of liability to the recipient, for any liability that these contractual assumptions directly impose on those licensors and authors.

   All other non-permissive additional terms are considered "further restrictions" within the meaning of section 10. If the Program as you received it, or any part of it, contains a notice stating that it is governed by this License along with a term that is a further restriction, you may remove that term. If a license document contains a further restriction but permits relicensing or conveying under this License, you may add to a covered work material governed by the terms of that license document, provided that the further restriction does not survive such relicensing or conveying.

If you add terms to a covered work in accord with this section, you must place, in the relevant source files, a statement of the additional terms that apply to those files, or a notice indicating where to find the applicable terms.

Additional terms, permissive or non-permissive, may be stated in the form of a separately written license, or stated as exceptions; the above requirements apply either way.

8. Termination.

   You may not propagate or modify a covered work except as expressly provided under this License. Any attempt otherwise to propagate or modify it is void, and will automatically terminate your rights under this License (including any patent licenses granted under the third paragraph of section 11).

   However, if you cease all violation of this License, then your license from a particular copyright holder is reinstated (a) provisionally, unless and until the copyright holder explicitly and finally terminates your license, and (b) permanently, if the copyright holder fails to notify you of the violation by some reasonable means prior to 60 days after the cessation.

   Moreover, your license from a particular copyright holder is reinstated permanently if the copyright holder notifies you of the violation by some reasonable means, this is the first time you have received notice of violation of this License (for any work) from that copyright holder, and you cure the violation prior to 30 days after your receipt of the notice.

   Termination of your rights under this section does not terminate the licenses of parties who have received copies or rights from you under this License. If your rights have been terminated and not permanently reinstated, you do not qualify to receive new licenses for the same material under section 10.

9. Acceptance Not Required for Having Copies.

   You are not required to accept this License in order to receive or run a copy of the Program. Ancillary propagation of a covered work occurring solely as a consequence of using peer-to-peer transmission to receive a copy likewise does not require acceptance. However, nothing other than this License grants you permission to propagate or modify any covered work. These actions infringe copyright if you do not accept this License. Therefore, by modifying or propagating a covered work, you indicate your acceptance of this License to do so.

10. Automatic Licensing of Downstream Recipients.

    Each time you convey a covered work, the recipient automatically receives a license from the original licensors, to run, modify and propagate that work, subject to this License. You are not responsible for enforcing compliance by third parties with this License.

    An "entity transaction" is a transaction transferring control of an organization, or substantially all assets of one, or subdividing an organization, or merging organizations.

If propagation of a covered work results from an entity transaction, each party to that transaction who receives a copy of the work also receives whatever licenses to the work the party's predecessor in interest had or could give under the previous paragraph, plus a right to possession of the Corresponding Source of the work from the predecessor in interest, if the predecessor has it or can get it with reasonable efforts.

You may not impose any further restrictions on the exercise of the rights granted or affirmed under this License. For example, you may not impose a license fee, royalty, or other charge for exercise of rights granted under this License, and you may not initiate litigation (including a cross-claim or counterclaim in a lawsuit) alleging that any patent claim is infringed by making, using, selling, offering for sale, or importing the Program or any portion of it.

11. Patents.

A "contributor" is a copyright holder who authorizes use under this License of the Program or a work on which the Program is based. The work thus licensed is called the contributor's "contributor version".

A contributor's "essential patent claims" are all patent claims owned or controlled by the contributor, whether already acquired or hereafter acquired, that would be infringed by some manner, permitted by this License, of making, using, or selling its contributor version, but do not include claims that would be infringed only as a consequence of further modification of the contributor version. For purposes of this definition, "control" includes the right to grant patent sublicenses in a manner consistent with the requirements of this License.

Each contributor grants you a non-exclusive, worldwide, royalty-free patent license under the contributor's essential patent claims, to make, use, sell, offer for sale, import and otherwise run, modify and propagate the contents of its contributor version.

In the following three paragraphs, a "patent license" is any express agreement or commitment, however denominated, not to enforce a patent (such as an express permission to practice a patent or covenant not to sue for patent infringement). To "grant" such a patent license to a party means to make such an agreement or commitment not to enforce a patent against the party.

If you convey a covered work, knowingly relying on a patent license, and the Corresponding Source of the work is not available for anyone to copy, free of charge and under the terms of this License, through a publicly available network server or other readily accessible means, then you must either (1) cause the Corresponding Source to be so available, or (2) arrange to deprive yourself of the benefit of the patent license for this particular work, or (3) arrange, in a manner consistent with the requirements of this License, to extend the patent license to downstream recipients. "Knowingly relying" means you have actual knowledge that, but for the patent license, your conveying the covered work in a country, or your recipient's use of the covered work in a country, would infringe one or more identifiable patents in that country that you have reason to believe are valid.

If, pursuant to or in connection with a single transaction or arrangement, you convey, or propagate by procuring conveyance of, a covered work, and grant a patent license to some of the parties receiving the covered work authorizing them to use, propagate, modify or convey a specific copy of the covered work, then the patent license you grant is automatically extended to all recipients of the covered work and works based on it.

A patent license is "discriminatory" if it does not include within the scope of its coverage, prohibits the exercise of, or is conditioned on the non-exercise of one or more of the rights that are specifically granted under this License. You may not convey a covered work if you are a party to an arrangement with a third party that is in the business of distributing software, under which you make payment to the third party based on the extent of your activity of conveying the work, and under which the third party grants, to any of the parties who would receive the covered work from you, a discriminatory patent license (a) in connection with copies of the covered work conveyed by you (or copies made from those copies), or (b) primarily for and in connection with specific products or compilations that contain the covered work, unless you entered into that arrangement, or that patent license was granted, prior to 28 March 2007.

Nothing in this License shall be construed as excluding or limiting any implied license or other defenses to infringement that may otherwise be available to you under applicable patent law.

12. No Surrender of Others' Freedom.

    If conditions are imposed on you (whether by court order, agreement or otherwise) that contradict the conditions of this License, they do not excuse you from the conditions of this License. If you cannot convey a covered work so as to satisfy simultaneously your obligations under this License and any other pertinent obligations, then as a consequence you may not convey it at all. For example, if you agree to terms that obligate you to collect a royalty for further conveying from those to whom you convey the Program, the only way you could satisfy both those terms and this License would be to refrain entirely from conveying the Program.

13. Use with the GNU Affero General Public License.

    Notwithstanding any other provision of this License, you have permission to link or combine any covered work with a work licensed under version 3 of the GNU Affero General Public License into a single combined work, and to convey the resulting work. The terms of this License will continue to apply to the part which is the covered work, but the special requirements of the GNU Affero General Public License, section 13, concerning interaction through a network will apply to the combination as such.

14. Revised Versions of this License.

    The Free Software Foundation may publish revised and/or new versions of the GNU General Public License from time to time. Such new versions will be similar in spirit to the present version, but may differ in detail to address new problems or concerns.

    Each version is given a distinguishing version number. If the Program specifies that a certain numbered version of the GNU General Public License "or any later version" applies to it, you have the option of following the terms and conditions either of that numbered version or of any later version published by the Free Software Foundation. If the Program does not specify a version number of the GNU General Public License, you may choose any version ever published by the Free Software Foundation.

If the Program specifies that a proxy can decide which future versions of the GNU General Public License can be used, that proxy's public statement of acceptance of a version permanently authorizes you to choose that version for the Program.

Later license versions may give you additional or different permissions. However, no additional obligations are imposed on any author or copyright holder as a result of your choosing to follow a later version.

15. Disclaimer of Warranty.

    THERE IS NO WARRANTY FOR THE PROGRAM, TO THE EXTENT PERMITTED BY APPLICABLE LAW. EXCEPT WHEN OTHERWISE STATED IN WRITING THE COPYRIGHT HOLDERS AND/OR OTHER PARTIES PROVIDE THE PROGRAM "AS IS" WITHOUT WARRANTY OF ANY KIND, EITHER EXPRESSED OR IMPLIED, INCLUDING, BUT NOT LIMITED TO, THE IMPLIED WARRANTIES OF MERCHANTABILITY AND FITNESS FOR A PARTICULAR PURPOSE. THE ENTIRE RISK AS TO THE QUALITY AND PERFORMANCE OF THE PROGRAM IS WITH YOU. SHOULD THE PROGRAM PROVE DEFECTIVE, YOU ASSUME THE COST OF ALL NECESSARY SERVICING, REPAIR OR CORRECTION.

16. Limitation of Liability.

    IN NO EVENT UNLESS REQUIRED BY APPLICABLE LAW OR AGREED TO IN WRITING WILL ANY COPYRIGHT HOLDER, OR ANY OTHER PARTY WHO MODIFIES AND/OR CONVEYS THE PROGRAM AS PERMITTED ABOVE, BE LIABLE TO YOU FOR DAMAGES, INCLUDING ANY GENERAL, SPECIAL, INCIDENTAL OR CONSEQUENTIAL DAMAGES ARISING OUT OF THE USE OR INABILITY TO USE THE PROGRAM (INCLUDING BUT NOT LIMITED TO LOSS OF DATA OR DATA BEING RENDERED INACCURATE OR LOSSES SUSTAINED BY YOU OR THIRD PARTIES OR A FAILURE OF THE PROGRAM TO OPERATE WITH ANY OTHER PROGRAMS), EVEN IF SUCH HOLDER OR OTHER PARTY HAS BEEN ADVISED OF THE POSSIBILITY OF SUCH DAMAGES.

17. Interpretation of Sections 15 and 16.

    If the disclaimer of warranty and limitation of liability provided above cannot be given local legal effect according to their terms, reviewing courts shall apply local law that most closely approximates an absolute waiver of all civil liability in connection with the Program, unless a warranty or assumption of liability accompanies a copy of the Program in return for a fee.

END OF TERMS AND CONDITIONS

How to Apply These Terms to Your New Programs

If you develop a new program, and you want it to be of the greatest possible use to the public, the best way to achieve this is to make it free software which everyone can redistribute and change under these terms.

To do so, attach the following notices to the program. It is safest to attach them to the start of each source file to most effectively state the exclusion of warranty; and each file should have at least the "copyright" line and a pointer to where the full notice is found.

```
one line to give the program's name and a brief idea of what it does.
Copyright (C) year name of author

This program is free software: you can redistribute it and/or modify
it under the terms of the GNU General Public License as published by
the Free Software Foundation, either version 3 of the License, or (at
your option) any later version.

This program is distributed in the hope that it will be useful, but
WITHOUT ANY WARRANTY; without even the implied warranty of
MERCHANTABILITY or FITNESS FOR A PARTICULAR PURPOSE.  See the GNU
General Public License for more details.

You should have received a copy of the GNU General Public License
along with this program.  If not, see https://www.gnu.org/licenses/.
```

Also add information on how to contact you by electronic and paper mail.

If the program does terminal interaction, make it output a short notice like this when it starts in an interactive mode:

```
program Copyright (C) year name of author
This program comes with ABSOLUTELY NO WARRANTY; for details type 'show w'.
This is free software, and you are welcome to redistribute it
under certain conditions; type 'show c' for details.
```

The hypothetical commands '`show w`' and '`show c`' should show the appropriate parts of the General Public License. Of course, your program's commands might be different; for a GUI interface, you would use an "about box".

You should also get your employer (if you work as a programmer) or school, if any, to sign a "copyright disclaimer" for the program, if necessary. For more information on this, and how to apply and follow the GNU GPL, see `https://www.gnu.org/licenses/`.

The GNU General Public License does not permit incorporating your program into proprietary programs. If your program is a subroutine library, you may consider it more useful to permit linking proprietary applications with the library. If this is what you want to do, use the GNU Lesser General Public License instead of this License. But first, please read `https://www.gnu.org/philosophy/why-not-lgpl.html`.

Appendix D

License for the One True Awk

Copyright © Lucent Technologies 1997
All Rights Reserved

Permission to use, copy, modify, and distribute this software and its documentation for any purpose and without fee is hereby granted, provided that the above copyright notice appear in all copies and that both that the copyright notice and this permission notice and warranty disclaimer appear in supporting documentation, and that the name Lucent Technologies or any of its entities not be used in advertising or publicity pertaining to distribution of the software without specific, written prior permission.

LUCENT DISCLAIMS ALL WARRANTIES WITH REGARD TO THIS SOFTWARE, INCLUDING ALL IMPLIED WARRANTIES OF MERCHANTABILITY AND FITNESS. IN NO EVENT SHALL LUCENT OR ANY OF ITS ENTITIES BE LIABLE FOR ANY SPECIAL, INDIRECT OR CONSEQUENTIAL DAMAGES OR ANY DAMAGES WHATSOEVER RESULTING FROM LOSS OF USE, DATA OR PROFITS, WHETHER IN AN ACTION OF CONTRACT, NEGLIGENCE OR OTHER TORTIOUS ACTION, ARISING OUT OF OR IN CONNECTION WITH THE USE OR PERFORMANCE OF THIS SOFTWARE.

Appendix E

License for 4.4 BSD Code

Copyright © 1985, 1989, 1991, 1993
The Regents of the University of California. All rights reserved.

Redistribution and use in source and binary forms, with or without modification, are permitted provided that the following conditions are met:

1. Redistributions of source code must retain the above copyright notice, this list of conditions and the following disclaimer.
2. Redistributions in binary form must reproduce the above copyright notice, this list of conditions and the following disclaimer in the documentation and/or other materials provided with the distribution.
3. All advertising materials mentioning features or use of this software must display the following acknowledgement:

   This product includes software developed by the University of California, Berkeley and its contributors.

4. Neither the name of the University nor the names of its contributors may be used to endorse or promote products derived from this software without specific prior written permission.

THIS SOFTWARE IS PROVIDED BY THE REGENTS AND CONTRIBUTORS "AS IS" AND ANY EXPRESS OR IMPLIED WARRANTIES, INCLUDING, BUT NOT LIMITED TO, THE IMPLIED WARRANTIES OF MERCHANTABILITY AND FITNESS FOR A PARTICULAR PURPOSE ARE DISCLAIMED. IN NO EVENT SHALL THE REGENTS OR CONTRIBUTORS BE LIABLE FOR ANY DIRECT, INDIRECT, INCIDENTAL, SPECIAL, EXEMPLARY, OR CONSEQUENTIAL DAMAGES (INCLUDING, BUT NOT LIMITED TO, PROCUREMENT OF SUBSTITUTE GOODS OR SERVICES; LOSS OF USE, DATA, OR PROFITS; OR BUSINESS INTERRUPTION) HOWEVER CAUSED AND ON ANY THEORY OF LIABILITY, WHETHER IN CONTRACT, STRICT LIABILITY, OR TORT (INCLUDING NEGLIGENCE OR OTHERWISE) ARISING IN ANY WAY OUT OF THE USE OF THIS SOFTWARE, EVEN IF ADVISED OF THE POSSIBILITY OF SUCH DAMAGE.

Index

Note: Page references in **bold** *denote occurrences in programming.*

Symbols

– (dash)
  as filename, 80, 92, 463, 465
  in nl_langinfo(), 526
  in options, 23–24, 26, 32
  in permissions, 4, 130
  in regular expressions, 514
– – (dash-dash)
  in long options, 26
  as special argument, 25
_() macro, **531–532**, 535, 537, 554
, (comma)
  as decimal point, 517
  in option arguments, 26
; (semicolon)
  in getopt_long(), 35
  in nl_langinfo(), 524
: (colon)
  in getopt(), 29–31
  in nl_langinfo(), 524
  in optstring, 29
  in PATH variable, 285
  in regular expressions, 514, 552
? (question mark), in getopt(), 29–31
/ (forward slash), as root directory, 8, 151, 222–224, 269
. (dot)
  as current working directory, 8, 116, 121, 124, 127, 151, 201, 452, 515
  as decimal point, 507, 517
  in filenames, 452
  in format specifiers, 521
  in nl_langinfo(), 526
  in regular expressions, 461
.. (dot-dot), parent directory, 116, 121, 124, 127, 152, 201, 270, 452
  in the root of a mounted filesystem, 222
^ (hat), in regular expressions, 461–462
' (single quote), in format specifiers, 521–522, 535
( ) (parentheses), in regular expressions, 462–463
[] (square brackets), in regular expressions, 463, 514
{} (braces), in regular expressions, 463
$ (dollar sign)
  as currency sign, 509, 517, 520
  in format specifiers, 533–534
  as prompt, xxv
  in regular expressions, 461
\ (backslash), for continuation lines, 66, 69
(hash)
  as comment specifier, 229
  in format specifiers, 521
  as prompt, 227
#!, in scripts, 6, 284
% (per cent sign), in format specifiers, 520
+ (plus sign)
  in format specifiers, 520
  in nl_langinfo(), 526
= (equal sign), in option arguments, 26
> (greater-than)
  as operator, 104
  as prompt, xxv
>> operator, 104
| (vertical bar)
  as flag separator, 614–617
  as pipe construct, 9
|&, in gawk, 323

A

a.out (Assembler OUTput) format, 6, 84, **339**, **643**
abort(), 346, 347, 356, 420, **434**, 468, 595, **596**, **598**
accept(), 347, **483**, 486, 488, 495, 502, 504
access time, 133, 201, 237
  changing, 148–152
  formatting, 164
  retrieving, 150, 586
access(), 347, **388–390**, 402
Acorn Advanced Disc Filing System, 226
action_handler(), **354**
actions. *See* signal actions
adb debugger, 593
addmntent(), **231**, 232
address sanitizer, 644–647
address space. *See* memory
Agans, David J., xxix, 653, 655
aio_error(), 347
aio_return(), 347
aio_suspend(), 347
alarm clocks, 363–364, 570
alarm(), 281, 347, **363–364**, 378–380, 382, 470, 570, 573
alloca(), **73–76**, 77
  manpage of, 74
alphasort(), **178–180**, 197
"always check the return value" principle, 90, 342
Amiga Fast File System, 226
Andrew File System, 226
ANSI (American National Standards Institute), xxi
arbitrary-length lines, 65–70, 77
archives, 149
arg library, **29–30**, 50, 323
argc parameter, 26–32, 40, 49, 80, **205**, 206, 284, **456**, **464**, **602**
Argp library, 50
arguments, 23–32
  invalid, 83
  lists of, 83
  missing, 30–31
  optional, 25, 32
  whitespace in, 23, 25–26

Argv library, 49
argv parameter, 26–32, **37**, 39, 40, 49, 194, **205**, 206, 284–288, 328, **406**, **410**, **412**, **416**, **498**
arrays
  compared to trees, 575
  element count computation, 99
  searching, 180–185
  sorting, 171–180
artificial intelligence, 19
ASCII encoding, 541, 553
asctime(), **159–160**, 197, 209, 524
Assembler OUTput. *See* a.out
assert(), **419–423**, 434, **551**, **572**, 607, 653
assertions, 419–423, 468
AT&T, xxvi, 28, 384
atexit(), 43, **291–293**, 329, 330, 442
atoi(), **444**
atomic write, 321
Autoconf, 14, 17, 523, 540
autofs filesystem, 226
Automake, 523, 540
automounter daemon, 226
Autoopts library, 50
awk program, **6**, 15, 185, 186, 318, 323, 326, 436, 459, 460, 468, 514, **588**, 631, 632, **643**, 658, 685
  GNU version of. *See* gawk

B

b, in permissions, 7, 131
back doors, 630
Bash shell, xxv, 314, 329, 598
bc command, **100**
Beebe, Nelson H.F., xxix, 467
beepers, 653
Bell Labs, 20
Berry, Karl, xxix
bg command, 334, 365
binary data, 100
binary executables, 6, 51–52, 87, 230, 328, 392
binary trees, 575–587
  depth of, 576
  insertions in, 578–579
  lookups in, 579–581
  nodes of, 576, 585–586
  pointers in, 578–581
  removals in, 577, 585–586
  subtrees of, 576
  traversals in, 577, 581–585
bind(), 347, **481–483**, 484, **487**, **502**, 504
bindtextdomain(), 43, **534**, 535, 537, 540, 554, 555
binfmt_misc filesystem, 226, **230**
bitwise operators, 242, 612
blocks, 113, 221
  bad, 224
  boot, 235
  comparing, 425
  copying, 423–424
  fragments of, 236
  functions for, 423
  indirect, 201
  number of, 133, 201, 210, 236, 271
  size of, 133, 236
  superblock, 235
Bloom, Benjamin, 666, 668
Bourne shell, xxv, 335
break statement, 436–437
breakpoints, 599, 612, 630–632, 656
  inside macros, 609
Brennan, Michael, xxix
brk(), **72–73**, 74, 76, 77, 441
Brooks, Fred, 668
BSD Fast Filesystem, 224–225, 227
BSD Unix, 17, 108, 117, 120, 131
  core dumps in, 296
  debuggers in, 593–594
  directories in, 391
  dirfd(), 247
  file locking in, 558
  file ownership in, 146
  filesystems in, 124, 224
  4.4 BSD code, 687
  fts(), 252
  getpgrp(), 301
  group sets in, 384
  network databases in, 190
  setreuid() and setregid(), 396
  signal(), 340
  signals in, 342, 348, 350, 366, 379
  sorting functions in, 178
  st_blocks field, 211
  timezone(), 170
  wait3() and wait4(), 298, 329
bsd_signal(), **340**, **345**, 354, 379, 381
bsearch(), **180–189**, 192, 197, **643**
BSS (Block Started by Symbol), 51
BSS areas, 51, 52
BSS sections, 52–54
buffer cache, 105–106, 131
buffers
  maintaining strategy, 65–70
  overrunning, 59, 67, 617
  size of, 71, 142–144, 152, 248, 617, 625

C

c, in permissions, 7, 131
C language, xvii
  1999 Standard, xxi
  continuation lines in, 65
  NULL constant in, 56
  preprocessor in, 608
  type of character constants in, 212
  See also Original C, Standard C
C++ language
  2024 Standards, xxi
  assignment of a pointer value in, 57
  const items in, 53
  function prototypes in, 9
  GNU programs in, 17
  main(), 290
  names in, 593
  preprocessor in, 608
  sorting arrays of objects in, 177
  type of character constants in, 212
Caldera Ancient UNIX License, xx, 671–672
calloc(), **55–56**, **58–60**, **63–64**, 72, 77, 267
Capey, T., 670

carriage return character, 67
cat program, 79–80, 92–93, 95–96, 114, 119–121, 140–141, 174, 229, 234, 278, 307, 428–429, 533, 584, 595–596, 599
  GNU version of, 96
  V7 version of, 91–96, 140
catdir program, 125–127
catgets(), 508, 524, 553
cd command, 8, 146, 169, 191, 222, 228, 247–250, 314–315, 331, 391–393, 458, 603
CD-ROMs, 9, 225–227, 230–231
cfgetispeed(), 347
cfgetospeed(), 347
cfsetispeed(), 347
cfsetospeed(), 347
char type, 57, 212, 542
character sets, 508, 541, 554
characters
  classes of, 514, 552
  lowercase vs. uppercase, 509, 514, 552
  order of, 541
  wide, 541–545
chdir(), 247–248, 269, 270, 271, 347
"check every call for errors" principle, 15, 69
check_salary(), 630, 631
chgrp program, 4, 391
child(), 375, 376
client program, 477–478
  connect(), 489
  ftp, 489–492
  socket(), 489
chmod program, 4, 101, 146, 384, 385, 391, 393, 566
chmod(), 102, 146, 147, 152, 153, 347
chown program, 4, 146, 199, 250, 272
chown(), 146, 147, 152, 192, 347, 392, 396
chroot(), 221, 269–271, 276, 288, 331
  manpage of, 270
cleanup(), 341
clearenv(), 38, 39
  manpage of, 39
clock_gettime(), 115, 347, 569–570
close(), 79, 80, 89–93, 103, 108, 109, 279, 303, 305, 307, 308, 313, 325, 326, 329, 331, 347, 485, 564
closedir(), 124–126, 129, 152, 454
close-on-exec flag, 316–318, 323, 327, 329
close-on-fork flag, 316–317
Cocker, Gail, xxx
coda filesystem, 226
code formatting, 14, 647
codeset, 534–535
coding style, 18–19
COFF (Common Object File Format), 6
Coherent filesystem, 227
collating sequences, 512
Collyer, Geoff, xxix, 57, 88, 360
command line processing, 14
command substitution, 458, 469
Common filesystems on x86 hardware, 225, 270
Common Object File Format. *See* COFF
compar(), 203, 216, 217, 253
compatibility with standards, 13
compile_pattern(), 464–466
compilers, 619, 632
conditions, 610
  logging, 629
  using variables for, 608
confstr(), 411–413, 417
connect(), 347, 489, 491, 494, 502, 504
const keyword, 13, 53, 86, 244, 428
consumers, 305, 329
cont command (GDB), 601, 612, 631, 656
continuation lines, 68
continue statement, 436
Coordinated Universal Time. *See* UTC
coprocesses. *See* pipes, two-way
copyright(), 531, 532
core dumps, 54, 296, 334, 421, 434, 468, 594, 595
core file, 594–596
Cox, Russ, xxix
cp program, 208, 249, 288, 338, 339, 486, 538, 540, 551, 596, 648
cpio program, 139, 147, 149
cramfs filesystem, 226
creat(), 101, 103–104, 108, 114, 121, 136, 147, 277, 291, 305, 308, 319, 347, 391
  flags for, 319–320
critical sections, 350, 373
cryptography, 442, 447, 450
csh, manpage of, xxv, 418
ctime(), 159–160, 169, 197, 203, 209, 515, 523, 524
currency symbols, 509, 517, 520, 525–526

D

d, in permissions, 4
daemons, 271, 306
data access model, 15, 20
datagrams, 474
data sections, 51–54
data segments, 51–54
dates, 155
  current, 156
  formatting, 509, 523
daylight-saving time. *See* DST
dbx debugger, 593
dcgettext(), 528
ddd debugger, 604
deadlocks, 83, 306
debug_dummy(), 631
debuggers, 334, 421, 434, 592–593, 633–650, 653, 657
  graphical, 604, 656
  machine-level vs. source-level, 593
debugging, 591–657
  compilation for, 592–593, 599
  macros for, 606–608, 657
  memory allocation, 633–634
  rules of, 653–655, 657
  runtime, 622–632, 657
debugging files, 629–630
debugging symbols, 592, 606, 656
decimal point, 507, 517
delete operator, 55, 57, 586
DeMaille, Akim, xxix
demand paging, 392
denial of service attack, 624
determinism, 443
/dev/fd/XX files, 109, 314–315, 329, 331
/dev/random file, 447–449, 469
/dev/urandom file, 447–449, 469

device numbers, 137–138, 222
devices, 7, 20, 112, 131
  block, 7, 131, 133, 138, 152, 230
  busy, 83
  character, 7, 131, 133, 138, 152, 230
  loopback, 227, 230
  masks for, 137
  slow, 342
  types of, 137
devpts filesystem, 226, **229**, **234**
df program, 112, **235**, 236, 241, 271
dgettext(), **527**, **528**
diff program, 16, **174**, **314**, **315**, **425**, **440**
difftime(), **156**, 174, 197
DIR* objects, **124–126**, 128–129, 144, **452**, **554**
direct struct, **113**, 123–124, **213**
directories, 5, 112–115, 130, 152
  changing, 247–248
  creating, 121–123
  current position in, 129–130, 152
  current root, 8, 151, 222, 269–271, 276
  current working, 8–9, 20, 116, 228, 247, 269–271, 276
    absolute pathname to, 248
  information about, 201
  mask for, 137
  moving, 120
  parent, 116
  reading, 123–130
  removing, 118, 121
  symbolic links to, 119
  system root, 222–224, 269–270
  for temporary files, 433, 468
  walking, 250–261, 271
directory entries, 113–114, 117, 119, 124–127, 152, 201
  file types in, 129
  length of, 237
  reading, 213
  sorting, 177–180, 215
directory permissions. *See* permissions, directory
dirent struct, **124–127**, **129**, 132, 152, **178–179**, 197, **213**, **452**, 454
dirfd(), 128, 144, 247, 272
discarding data, 7
dispositions. *See* signal actions, default
do_input(), **611**
do_statfs(), 245, 246
do_statvfs(), **239**, 245
Drepper, Ulrich, xxix, 360
DST (daylight-saving time), 158, 168–170
du program, 250
  GNU version of, **261–269**, 271
dup(), **307–314**, 317, 319, 329, 347, 397, 565
dup2(), **307–314**, 317–319, 326, 329, 331, 347, 492
dup3(), **318**, 319, 329, 347
DVDs, 227, 230
dynamic data structures, 575
dynamic memory, 16, 51, 55–76
  accessing after shrinking, 60
  accessing outside the bounds, 59, 591, 634, 635
  aligned, 557–558, 586
  calculating size of, 56, 62
  changing size of, 59–61, 73
  debugging, 633–632, 657
  freed, 58, 77, 442, 634, 637
  initially allocating, 56–58, 386–387
  leaks of, 59, 61, 77, 178, 440–442, 633, 635, 639
  releasing, 58–59, 77
  tracing, 634
  unfreed, 633
  uninitialized use of, 637, 640
  zero-filling, 59, 63, 423

E

EBCDIC encoding, 540–541
echo program, 23, 27–28, 31
ed editor, 394, 435, 459, 460
ELF (Extensible Linking Format), 6, 284
Emacs editor, 14, 15, 459, 598, 661
emp_name_id_compare(), 173, **175**, **579**, 582–583
employee struct, **172–176**, 177, 181, 182, **183**, 184, **560–562**, **579**, 580, **581**, 582, **583**, **585**, **586**
ENABLE_NLS constant, **530**, 531, **532**, 533, 535, **536**
encodings, 508, 541, 554
  multibyte, 545
  self-correcting, 545
endmntent(), **232**, **234**, **239**
endpwent(), **191–192**
entropy pool, 447
env program, **40–48**
environ variable, **39–40**, **46–47**, 49, 284–286
environment variables, 8, 9, 37–39
  adding, 38, 40
  for debugging, 624–628
  with empty values, 38
  expansion of, 458, 469
  for locales, 508–510
  random order of, 40
  removing, 39, 41
environments, 9, 37–48, 276
  clearing, 39, 41
Epoch, 148, 155, 197, 567
eras, 525–526
errno variable, 56, **81–86**, 89, 91, 93, 103, 108, 115, 118, 120, 121, **123**, 125, 143, 156, **167**, 196, 247, 249, 254, 283, 284, 291, 293, 294, 321, 325, 326, 341, 344, 348, 358, 379, 394, 398, 399, 407, 449, 453, 481, 482, 485, 521, 535, 546, 547, 550, 557, 562, 563, 569, 574, 629
  examination of, 82
  manpage of, 82
  values for, 82–86
error messages, 14–16, 69, 86–87, 93, 108, 434
  diagnostic identifiers for, 86–87
  handling, 30
errors, 81
  reporting functions for, 86
Ersoy, Alper, xxix
/etc/fstab file, 228–232, 234, 270, 271
/etc/mtab file, 229–232, **233**, 234, **238**, 240, 270
/etc/vfstab file, 228
euidaccess(), **390**, 403
--exclude option, **263**, **264**, 450, 470
exec(), 47, 105, 283–289, 293, 307, 316, 327, 328, 378–379, 381, 397, 400, 454, 660
execl(), **285–286**, 326, 347
execle(), **286**, 347
execlp(), 285, 286, 297, 400
executable code, 51–54, 77

execv(), 286, 287, 347, 453, 500, 501
execve(), **284–286**, 347
  manpage of, 284
execvp(), 47, 48, 286, 312, 313, 400, 453
exit(), **87**, 291, 293, 295, 329, 434, 564
_exit(), 292, **293**, 312, 329, 347
_Exit(), 292, 293, 329, 347
EXIT_FAILURE constant, 289, 290, 328, **465**
exit status, 41, 43, 46, 48, 81, 95, 289–290, 293–300, 329, 331, 366, 375, 377, 564
EXIT_SUCCESS constant, **46**, **47**, **116**, **122**, **123**, **167**, 289, 290, 328, **465**
ext2 filesystem, 225, 226, 392
ext3 filesystem, 225, 226, **229**, 392
ext4 filesystem, 119, 133, 225, 226, 229–232, 234, **240**, **246**, 392
Extensible Linking Format. *See* ELF
Extensible Markup Language. *See* XML

F

faccessat(), 145, 347, 390, 402, 403
FAT filesystem, 225, 227, 270
fchdir(), **247–248**, 269, 271, 272, 276, 288, 347, 660
fchmod(), 102, 147, 153, 347
fchown(),145–148, 192, 347, 396
fclose(), 125, 232
fcntl(), 307, **315–323**, 329, 331, 347, **558–566**, 586, 587
  flags for, 318–320
  manpage of, 315, 320, 560, 562
fexecve(), 105, 285, 286, 347
FD_CLOEXEC flag, 317–319, 323, 479
FD_CLOFORK flag, 317–319, 323, 480, 488
fdatasync(), **107**, 108, 347
fdopen(), 327, 470
fflush(), 107, 606
fg command, 334, 365
fgets(), 67, 77, 78, 469
FIFO (first-in first-out) files, 131, 306–307, 329, 360
  creating, 306
  empty, 321
  nonblocking I/O, 320–323
  removing, 307
file descriptors, 87–96, 108, 132, 150, 196, 303
  attributes of, 315–323, 329
  bad, 83
  closing, 309, 434
  duplicating, 318–319
  functions for, 107
  leaks of, 325
  lowest acceptable value of, 318
  new, 88, 90
  obtaining, 247
  for open files, 276–279, 303, 318, 328, 432
  copying, 307–314, 326, 329
  shared, 277, 328
file modes. *See* permissions, file
file permissions. *See* permissions, file
file status flags, 319–320, 323
file table, 277
File Transfer Protocol. *See* FTP
filenames, 5
  basing program's behavior upon, 288
  changing, 117–118, 148
  functions for, 107–108
  generating, 426–430
  length of, 5, 113, 125, 254
fileno(), **90**, 95, 107, 128, 470, 564
files, 3–7, 20
  attributes of, 315–327, 329
  byte positions within, 96, 104, 563
  closing, 88–91, 279
  copying onto themselves, 95
  creating, 101–106, 108, 114–115
  existing, 83, 104
  information about. *See* metadata
  locking, 558–559, 586
  opening, 83, 88–91, 107, 108
  reading, 89, 91–94, 105–106, 108
  regular, 130, 342
    mask for, 137
  removing, 118–119
  restoring from archives, 147, 149
  shared, 90
  size of, 85, 107–108, 133, 250
  truncating, 104, 133
  types of, 129–136, 139
    macros for, 137, 138, 152
    masks for, 136–137
  writing, 89, 91–94, 104–106, 108, 133, 148
filesystems, 111–112, 124, 151, 221–228, 270
  busy status of, 228
  debugging, 201
  information about, 234
  journaling, 225, 270
  mounting, 127, 132, 221, 225, 227, 228, 271, 385, 562, 566
  read-only, 83, 226, 227, 230, 237
  unmounting, 221, 228
find program, 139, 250, 450
  manpage of, 139
finish command (GDB), 600, 612
first-in first-out. *See* FIFO files
flags, 33, 241, 345, 612
  converting to a string, 613–618
  values, 241–242
flags2str(), 614, **615**, 616, 617, **618**
flock struct, 560–562, 565
flock(), 558, 565–566, 586
  manpage of, 566
fnmatch(), 451–453, 469
folders. *See* directories
fopen(), 9, 213, 431
fork(), 275–280, **281**, 283, 284, 288, 289, **293**, 297, 298, 307, **310**, **313**, 316, 317, 325, 328, 352, 366, **370**, **372**, **376**, 378–379, 381, **397**, 400, **478**, **483**, **484**, **487**, 499, 564, 565, 660
format_num(), 367, **371**, 374
fortune program, 442
fpathconf(), 237, 249, 386, 405, 409–411, 417
fprintf(), **80**, 86, **87**, **98**, 216, **338**, 339, 543, 606, 607, 632
fpsync(), 107
Free Software Foundation. *See* FSF
free(), 55, 57–61, 64, 65, 72, 74, 77, 144, 178, 180, 218, 250, 427, 442, 558, 586, 633–634, 639
FreeBSD filesystem, 225
FSF (Free Software Foundation), xxii, xxvi, xxvii, 594
fstat(), 95, 109, **131**, 132, 136, 140, 147, 248, 272, 279, 347, 390, 486

fstatfs(), 242–246, 271
fstatvfs(), 235–243, 271
fsync(), 107, 108, 347
FTP (File Transfer Protocol), 270
ftp client code, 489–492
ftpd server code, 486–488
ftp program, xxvi, xxvii
ftruncate(), 107–109, 348
fts(), 221, 241, 252, **257**, 261, 271, 272, 582
fts_open(), 250–261
FTW struct, **251**
ftw(), 251
functions, xxi, xxv
  callback, 291, 329, 581, 583
  debugging, 614
  declarations of, 13, 27
  helper, 612–618
  low-level, 73, 77
  naming conventions for, 107–108
  recursive, 52, 62
  wrapper, 70
futimens(), 150–151, 348

G

garbage collectors, 16
gawk program, xxii, 15–16, 18, 35, 61, 65, 318, **323–327**, 387, 436, 437, 441, 527, 539, 550, **552**, 591, 599–601, **602**, 608, 610, 611, 613–615, **617**, **620**, **622**, 624–628, 631, 632, 647–650, 658
  numeric values formatting in, 521–523
  two-way pipes, 323
GCC (GNU Compiler Collection), 14, 35, **74**, **592**, 656
  macros in, 608–609, 621
GDB (GNU Debugger), 16, 593–605, 608–613, **631**, **632**, 636, 656
  distributions of, 602
  macros in, 609, 621
Gemmellaro, Anthony, xxx
Gemmellaro, Faye, xxx
General Public License. *See* GNU GPL
generality, 16
genflags2str(), 616, 617
getcwd(), 144, 248–250, **257**, 259, 271, 272
  manpage of, 250
getdelim(), 70–71, 77, 466
getdents(), **128**
  manpage of, 128
getdtablesize(), 87, 91, 108, 277, 289, **316**
getegid(), 348, **387**, 402
getenv(), 38, 49
geteuid(), 348, **386**, 402
getgid(), 348, **386**, 402
getgroups(), 348, **386–387**, 402
getitimer(), 277, 365, 570–573, 586
  manpage of, 571
getline(), **70–71**, 77, 466, 469
getmntent(), 231–234, **237**, **243**, 271
getname(), 209, 210, 218
getopt(), 25, **28–37**, 49, 205, **232**, **237**, **244**
  GNU version of, 25, 29, 31–32, 37, 49
    manpage of, 32
getopt_long(), 14, 25–26, 28–37, 41, 44, 49, 536, 601
getopt_long_only(), **32**, 49
getpeername(), 348, 486
getpgid(), 301, 329
getpgrp(), 301, 329, 348
getpid(), 277, 279–281, 328, 348, **447**, **500**
getppid(), 277, 279–281, 328, 348
getpwent(), **191**, 192, 193
getpwnam(), **191**, 192, 193
getpwuid(), **191**, 192, 193, 210
getrandom(), 449–450, 469
getrlimit(), 414–418
getresgid(), 348, **398–399**
getresuid(), 348, 398–399
getsid(), 302
getsockname(), 348, 486, 491
getsockopt(), 348
gettext program, 508, 509, 526–540, 555
gettext.h file, 67, 530–533, 535, 537, 554
gettext(), 527–535, 537, 554
gettext_noop(), 531, 537
gettimeofday(), 155, 567–569, 573, 586
  manpage of, 567
getty program, 396, 397
getuid(), 192, 348, **386**, **396**, 402
GID (group ID), 4, 20, 102, 121, 133, 147, 191, 193, 198, 383
  effective, 383–384, 386–388, 390–402
  mask for. *See* setgid bit
  real, 383–390, 393–402
  saved set, 384, 386, 397–399, 402
gid_t type, 134, 155
Glib library, 197
GLIBC (GNU C Library), 14, 18, 37, 58
  errno values, 82–86
  euidaccess(), 390
  f_flag values, 237, 241
  glob() extensions, 454–455
  libintl.h, 532–533
  rand(), 445
  superuser in, 383
  TEMP_FAILURE_RETRY(), 344
glob(), 453–458, 469
globalization, 507
globerr(), **456**, 457
globfree(), 453–458
glyphs, 540
GMT (Greenwich Mean Time), 134
gmtime(), 157–159, 197
GNOME Project, 197
GNU C Library. *See* GLIBC
GNU Coding Standards, 13–20, 26, 58, 64, 87, 288
GNU Compiler Collection. *See* GCC
GNU Coreutils, xxvi, 28, 43, 108, 115
  distribution of, 45
  du, 261–269, 271
  fts(), 261
  install, 297
  safe_read() and safe_write(), 342–344
  sort, 341
  utime(), 149
  wc, 426
  xreadlink(), 144
GNU Debugger. *See* GDB
GNU Gengetopt library, 50
GNU GPL (General Public License), xxvii, 13, 673–684
GNU Lesser General Public License, 37
GNU programs, xxi–xxii, xxvii, 13–17, 27

long options in, 26
wrapper functions in, 69
GNU Project, xxii
GNU/Linux, xvii, xviii, xix, xx, xxv, xxvi
block size in, 133
`chroot()`, 270
`clearenv()`, 39
core dumps in, 296
debuggers in, 593
`/dev/fd/XX` files in, 314–315
directories in, 391
`dirfd()`, 247
distributions of, xxvi, 226, 228, 334, 421, 508
Epoch in, 148
file formats in, 6
file types in, 136
filesystems in, 111, 124, 226–228, 270
`ftw()`, 251
inode numbers in, 224
locales in, 510
mounting in, 127, 222
numeric values formatting in, 521
preemptive multitasking in, 282
`/proc/self/cwd`, 250
`remove()`, 118, 152
renaming operation in, 118
`rsync`, xxv
`rusage struct`, 299
`signal()`, 340
signals in, 334–337, 348, 379
standard functions in, 72
`statfs()` and `fstatfs()`, 242–246
superuser in, 383
time slicing in, 429
`time_t` type, 155
time-zone information in, 169–170
`versionsort()`, 178
`wait3()` and `wait4()`, 298, 329
Gold, Yosef, xxix
`goto` statement, 435
Greenwich Mean Time. *See* GMT
`grep` program, 24, 459–463, 467, 468
`groff` program, 14
group, category of users, 4, 101–102, 383
changing, 146
databases of, 190, 193–196, 198
IDs of. *See* GID
lists of users of, 193
masks for, 136, 137
names of, 193, 198, 201, 210
passwords of, 193
`group` (`struct`), **194**, 195, 199
group sets, 193, 384, 390, 402
changing, 393–394, 402
number of groups in, 386–387, 402
retrieving, 386
`gstat()`, **203**, 206, 214–215
GTK project, 197
`gzip` program, xxvi, **xxvii**

H

`handler()`, 339, 341
handlers. *See* signal handlers
hard links, 114–117, 119–121, 152
to directories, 114, 117
to root directory, 222
hash tables, 265
`hasmntopt()`, 232
Hayes, John R., 666, 669
heap, 52–54, 441
Heisenberg, Werner, 422
heisenbugs, 422
`--help` option, 14, 26, 42, 46, 636
here documents, 119
Hesiod, 190
Hierarchical File System, 226
High Performance File System, 226
Hoare, C.A.R., xx, xxix, 171, 419, 422
Hoare's law, xx
holes, 98, 100, 133
`HOME` environment variable, 9, 38
HURD kernel, 14

I

I/O, 79, 93
asynchronous, 356
blocking, 105
nonblocking, 320–323
random access, 96, 100, 108
sequential, 96
standard functions for, 90
synchronous, 106, 108, 237
i18n. *See* internationalization
IBM, 226, 458, 541
`idtype`, **294**, 296
IEEE Standard 1003.1–2024, xxi
`#ifdef`, 18, 68, 241, 242, 288, 335, **342**, **343**, 406, **408**, 409, 508, 606, 607, 614, **620**, **625**, **627**
`ifind()`, **180**
`IFS` environment variable, 400
indentation, 256
index nodes. *See* inodes
indexing, 57, 62, 67
infinite loops, 441
`init` process, 8, 280, 293, 328, 359, 366, 396, 397
`init_groupset()`, **387**, 388
initialized data, 51
`initstate()`, **445–447**
inode change time, 133, 135, 201
changing, 148
inode numbers, 112–114, 117, 124, 132, 140, 152, 201
for root directory, 224, 270
inodes (index nodes), 5, 112–114, 152, 221
number of, 236, 271
`install` program, 297
interfaces, 17, 18
internationalized program, 535–536
International Organization for Standardization. *See* ISO
internationalization (i18n), 507, 553–554, 659
interpreters, 6, 619–620
interval timers. *See* timers
Introduction, manpage of, 28, 82, 128
invariants, 419
IPC (interprocess communication), 131, 302, 360, 473
internet building blocks, 474–475
addresses and interfaces, 476
IPv4, 475

IPC (interprocess communication) (*continued*)
IPv6, 475–476
network byte order, 476–477
networking technologies, 474
using signals for, 360, 380
isatty(), 196, 198
ISO (International Organization for Standardization), xxi
ISO 9660 CD-ROM filesystem, 225, 226, 270
ISO C. *See* Standard C
ISO/IEC International Standard 9899, xxi
ISO/IEC International Standard 14882, xxi
iswalnum(), **542**
iswlower(), **542**
itimerval struct, 571, **572**, 573, 586

J

Java language, 9
job control, 300–301, 329, 334, 365
job control shells, 300, 359, 380
Johnson, Steve, 3
Journaled File System, 226
Journaled Flash Filesystem, 226

K

K&R C. *See* Original C
K&R style of code formatting, 18
Kerberos network database, 190
Kernighan, Brian W., xvii, xxviii, 9, 18, 62, 629, 656, 661
kill program, 336, 365
kill(), 300, 326, 346, 348, 355, 358–360, 380
killpg(), 300, 326, 348, 358–360, 380
Kirsanov, Dmitry, xxx
Kirsanova, Alina, xxx
Knuth, Donald E., 197, 467, 655
ksh (Korn) shell, 323, 324, 329, 451
ksh88 shell, 314
ksh93 shell, xxv, 314, 382, 659

L

l10n. *See* localization
LANG environment variable, **509**
Lave, Jean, 669
lbuf struct, **202–203**, 206–207, **208**, **213–214**, 215, **216**, 218
invalid, 208
LC_ALL environment variable, **162–163**, 509–511, **518–519**, **521**, **524**, **540**
lchmod(), 147
lchown(), **146**, 396
lconv struct, **515–518**, 519, **521–524**
ld program, 6
LDAP (Lightweight Directory Access Protocol), 190
Lechlitner, Randy, xxix
LEDs, 653
Lehman, Manny, xxix
libintl.h file, **527–530**, **532**, 533, **534–535**
libraries, 16
general-purpose, 340
POSIX standard for, 17
shared, 54, 318
Lightweight Directory Access Protocol. *See* LDAP
limits.h file, 124, **135**, **142**, **164**, **249**, **257**, 283, 321, 330, 386, 405, **406–409**, **411**, **416**, **427**, **432**, **517**, **547**
line-at-a-time jail, 603–604
line feed character, 67
line program, 278, **597**
link count, 114, 118, 133, 152
link program, **115–116**
link(), **115–116**, 152, 347, 348
links, symbolic, 119–121, 130–132, 141–144, 151
creating, 141
to directories, 119–120, 250
levels of, 83
mask for, 137
ownership of, 146
permissions on, 147
lint program, 12, 632, 657
Linux. *See* GNU/Linux
Linux Journal, 13
list command (GDB), **598**, 599, **600**
listen(), 348, **482–483**, 488, 502, 504
lldb debugger, 605
ln program, **114–115**, **119–121**, 288
locale program, **509–513**, **521–522**
manpage of, 552
localeconv(), **515–518**, 553
locales, 507–508, 552–553
categories of, 508–510, 553
default, 508
setting, 510–511
localization (l10n), 161, 507, 553–554
localtime(), **157–158**, 159, 160, 169, 197
lockf(), 558, **559–564**, 565, 586
locks, 558–559, 586
advisory, 559, 564–565, 586
descriptor-based, 564–565
exclusive, 565
mandatory, 237, 559, 566–567, 586
obtaining, 562–564
process-based, 562–564
range, 563
read, 559, 561, 586
record, 558
releasing, 562–565
shared, 565–566
whole file, 558, 566
write, 559, 561, 586
log files, 628–630, 634, 653
logic analyzers, 653
login program, 191, **339**, 396, 397
longjmp(), 348, **436–442**, 468, 587, **646**
ls command, 4, 7, 101, 130–131, 138–139, 153, 190, 193, 196, 198, 201, 202, 217, 219, 452, 545, 548, 659
modern versions of, 201–202, 218
V7 version of, 201–218
manpage of, 201, 210
lsearch(), **419–423**
lseek(), **96–99**, 104, 108, 210, 277, 303, 347, 560, 625
whence values for, 96
lstat(), **131**, 132, 136, **141–142**, 143, 144, 152, 250, 347, **454–455**

M

MacOS X NetInfo network database, 190
magic numbers, 6, 221
converting to printable strings, 245
main program, 180, 290–291, **292**, **315**, 488, 573, 583, 606
main(), 8, 26, 29, **40**, 43, 49, **69**, 76, 79–81, 95, 125, 180, 184, 195, 203, 206, 215, 234, 239, **244**, 245, 284, **290**,

293, 295, 311, 318, 329, 339, 344, 356, 363, 369, 372, 376, 420–421, **436**, 440–441, 464, 510–511, 522, 527–528, **548**, 554, 564, 583, **645**, 657
declaring, 26
process exit status in, 80
major(), **138**, 152, 209
make program, 322, 540, 652
GNU version of, 64–70
makedev(), **138**
Makefile, 65, **66**
makename(), **203**, **212**, 213, 218
malloc() , 52, **55–58**, 59–65, 69, 70, **72**, 73, 77, 142–144, 178, **214**, 218, 249–250, 387, **412**, **423**, **434**, **440–441**, **497**, 511, 514, 558, 575, 578, 633–634, **638–640**
casting the return value, 57
manpage of, 55
MALLOC_TRACE environment variable, 634
man command, xix, xxv
manage(), **374–376**
manifest constants, 88
manpages (manual pages), xxv, 653
Marti, Don, xxix
mblen(), 545
mbrlen(), 545
mbrtowc(), 545, **546**, 547, **548**, 550, 554
mbsrtowcs(), 545, **546**, 547, 550, 554
mbstowcs(), 545
mbtowc(), 545
McGary, Greg, xxix
McIlroy, Doug, xxix
McKusick, Marshall Kirk, 328
memalign(), **557–558**, 586
memccpy(), 347, **423**, 469, 491, 543
memchr(), 347, **423**, **426**, 543
memcmp(), 347, **423**, **425**, 469
memcpy(), 347, **423–425**, 468, 491, 543
Memishian, Peter, xxix
memmove(), 18, **68**, 347, **423–425**, 468, 543
memory, 7–9, 52
address space, 51–54
dynamically allocated. *See* dynamic memory
overlapping areas of, 423
read-only, 53
setting, 423
use of, 16
memset(), 57, 63–64, 347, **423**, 543, 546
message catalogs, 526, 529, 534, 554
message object files, 539, 554
metacharacter expansions. *See* wildcard expansions
metadata, 5, 111, 118, 131–134, 151–152
modification time of. *See* inode change time
Meyering, Jim, xxix, 28, 38, 143, 251
Microsoft Windows
convention of line ending in, 67
Epoch in, 148
filesystems in, 111, 225, 227
minicomputers, 4, 7, 301
Minix filesystem, 225–227
minor(), **138–139**, 152, 209
mkdir(), **121–123**, 152, 347
manpage of, 120
mkdtemp(), 430–433, 468
mke2fs program, 111
mkfifo program, 131, 307
mkfifo(), **307**, 329, 347
manpage of, 307
mkfs program, 111
mknod program, manpage of, 138
mkostemp(), 430, 432
mkstemp(), **430–433**, 468, 470
mktemp(), **426–430**, 432, 470
mktime(), **165–167**, 169, 197
mntent struct, **231–234**, **238–239**, **244–245**
modification time, 133–135, 201
changing, 148–147, 152
formatting, 164
retrieving, 586
sorting by, 201
monetary formatting, 509, 515–520, 553
mount points, 222, 270
mount program, **119**, 222, **227–231**, **235**, **243**, **266**, 270, 385, 567
manpage of, 210, 231
mount(), 222
mounting. *See* filesystems, mounting
MS-DOS, 225
msdos filesystem, 225–227
multiuser systems, 383
mv program, 117, 288, 538–539

N

N_() macro, **531–532**, 535, 537, 554
named pipes. *See* FIFO files
nanosleep(), **573–575**, 587
native language support. *See* NLS
nblock(), **203**, **208**, **210–211**, 218
NetBSD filesystem, 225
network databases, 190
Network File System. *See* NFS
Network Information Service. *See* NIS
network technologies, 474
new operator, 55, 57, **63**, **76**, **276**, **320**, 323, 326, 328, 331, **366**, **412**, **484**, 488, **597**, **602**, **607**, **644**
newfs program, 111
next command (GDB), **600**, 656
NeXTStep system, 225
NFS (Network File System), 224, 270
nftw(), **251–264**
flags for, 251–257
manpage of, 253
private version of, 272
ngettext(), **528–529**, 536, 554
nice values, 276, 282–283, 328
nice(), **282–283**, 328
NIS (Network Information Service), 190
nl_langinfo(), **524–526**, 535, 553
NLS (native language support), 507, 553
"no arbitrary limits" principle, 15–16, 20, 51, 64–66, 613, 617, 661
nodots(), **179**, 180
nonlocal gotos, 435, 468
Norvig, Peter, xxix, 665
NTFS filesystem, 226–227
NUL character, 5, 15–16, 66, 69
NULL constant, 43, 56–64, 77, 126, 167, 184, 192, 194, 215, 232, 272, 421, 424, 453, 514, 546, 585

numbers, 33
formatting, 509, 515–524, 553
grouping digits within, 517, 520, 522–523

O

O_ACCMODE flag, 320
O_APPEND flag, **104**, 319, 320
O_ASYNC flag, 320
O_CLOEXEC flag, 105, 316
O_CLOFORK flag, 105, 317
O_CREAT flag, 99, 104, 108, 119, 319, 428
O_DIRECT flag, 320
O_DIRECTORY flag, 105
O_DSYNC flag, 105–107, 319, 320
O_EXCL flag, 104, 119, 319, 432
O_EXEC flag, 105, 285
O_NOATIME flag, 320
O_NOCTTY flag, 105, 319
O_NOFOLLOW flag, 105
O_NONBLOCK flag, 105, 319, **320–321**, 322, 330, 480
O_PATH flag, 105, 145, 285
O_RDONLY flag, 89, **92**, 104, 124, **248**, 285, 319, **320**, 321, **448**
O_RDWR flag, 89, **99**, 104, **119**, 319, **320**, **428**
O_RSYNC flag, 105, 106, 319
O_SEARCH flag, 105
O_SYNC flag, 105–107, 109, 319, 320
O_TMPFILE flag, 145
O_TRUNC flag, 99, 104, 108, 119, 319, 428
O_TTY_INIT flag, 105
O_WRONLY flag, 89, **104**, 319, **320**, 321
O_x SYNC flags, 107
object file formats, 6
obstacks, 16
off_t type, **96–98**, 107, 132, 560, **563–564**, **625**
offsets, 96, 560
Open Group, The, xxi
open(), **79–80**, **88–91**, **98–99**, 101, **104–106**, 108, 114, 121, **123**, 127, 129, 141, 247, 256, **277**, 285, 291, 308, 314, **321**, 347, 390–391, 429, 432, **470**, 565
flags for, 89, 104–106, 108, 319–321
manpage of, 106
openat(), 106, **144–145**, 150, 347, 470
OpenBSD filesystem, 225
opendir(), **124–126**, 144, 152, 252, 272, 288, 453
OpenVMS filesystem, 112
operands
order of, 25
placement of, 26
Opt library, 49
optimal_bufsize(), **625–628**
optimizations, 592, 599, 656
option struct, **32**, **34–35**, **43**, **601**, **623**
options, 14, 23
debugging, 622–624, 633
invalid, 30–31
long, 14, 26, 32–37
names of, 24, 25
placement of, 25–26
undocumented, 623
vendor-specific, 24, 35
Original C, 9–13, 20
function parameters in, 632
GNU programs in, 13
See also C language, Standard C

os_close_on_exec(), **327**
other, category of users, 4, 101–103, 383
masks for, 136–137
owner, of a file. *See* user
ownership, 4, 111
changing, 145–147, 152
masks for, 137

P

p, in permissions, 131
parameters, 26–28, 52
lists of, 632
parent process ID. *See* PPID
parse trees, 619
parse_debug(), **623**, 658
partitions, 111, 151, 270
Pascal language, 435
passwd struct, **191–193**, **497**
PATH environment variable, 9, **38–39**, **42**, 285, 286, 328, **389**, 400
pathconf(), 237, 249, 386, **409–410**, 417
pathnames, 112, 120
absolute, 248, 271
checking for validity, 390
relative, 8, 247
pause(), **339**, 347, **361–364**, 380, 382
PDP-11, 3, 113, 218, 392, 445
pentry(), **208**
Perl language, 459
permission bits, 4, 212, 218, 248
constants for, 101–102
default, 102
masks for, 136–137
permissions, 20, 111, 132, 135–141, 212
changing, 4, 102, 147–148, 152
checking, 383, 402
denied, 83
directory, 5, 118
expressed in octal, 101
file, 4, 101–103, 118
macros for, 135
perror(), **82**, 108, 109
pfatal_with_name(), 70
PGID (process group ID), 277, 294–302, 329
PID (process ID), 7–9, 276–277, 279–281, 285, 302, 328–330
parent. *See* PPID
of the process that died, 294, 297
using in seed values, 447
wrapping around, 279
pid_t type, **275–276**, **279–280**, **292**, **294**, **296**, **297–298**, **301–302**, **310**, **354**, **367**, **371**, **376**, **478**, **483–484**, **560**
Pike, Rob, 20, 656, 661
Pinard, François, xxix
pipe(), **303–305**, 309, **324**, 329, 347
PIPE_BUF constant, 321–322, **409–410**
pipes, 9, 303, 329, 361
blocking, 320
broken, 83
buffering, 305–306
creating, 303–305
empty, 321
named. *See* FIFO files
nonblocking, 320–323
nonlinear, 314, 329

  synchronization of, 306
  two-way, 323–327
Plan 9 from Bell Labs, 50, 103
`pmode()`, 212
pointers
  calculating, 55
  dangling, 58, 634
  declaring, 56
  freeing twice, 58
  generic, 55
  guaranteed valid, 69
  invalid, 56, 60–62
  passing, 58
  setting to `NULL`, 58
  sorting, 177
`poll()`, 347
Popt library, 50
portability, 14, 17–18, 21, 35, 56, 67, 74, 127, 327, 607, 659
portable object files, 538, 554
portable object templates, 538
Portable Operating System Interface. *See* POSIX standard
positional specifiers, 533–534
POSIX standard, xxi
  `bsd_signal()`, 340
  character classes in, 514, 552
  compatibility with, 13, 37
  directories in, 392
  `environ` variable, 39
  `errno` values, 82–86
  `_exit()`, 290–293
  extensions, xxi
    ADV, 557
    FSC, 107
    SIO, 107
    XSI, xxi, 72, 107, 124, 235, 295–296
  `FD_CLOEXEC` flag, 317
  file locking in, 558
  file ownership in, 4
  filesystems in, 124
  file-type and permission bitmasks in, 137
  flags for `open()`, 104–106, 319–320
  `ftw()`, 251
  `isatty()`, 196
  library and system call interfaces in, 17
  nice values in, 283
  option conventions in, 24–26, 35
  `PIPE_BUF` constant, 321–322
  `printf()`, 533–534
  process group information in, 301
  `rusage`, 299
  signals in, 341, 349, 350, 352, 357–360, 366, 379
  `st_blocks` field, 211
  superuser in, 383
  symbolic constants for permissions in, 101–102
  `time_t` type, 156
  timezones in, 168–169
  `waitpid()`, 294
`posix_memalign()`, **557–558**, 586
`posix_trace_event()`, 347
`POSIXLY_CORRECT` environment variable, 31, **263**, 411, **413**
postconditions, 419
PPID (parent process ID), 7, 277, 279–281, 328
preconditions, 419
predictable algorithms (`mktemp()`), 429
preemptive multitasking, 282
`print_emp()`, 583
`print_employee()`, **182**
`print_group()`, **195**
`print_mount()`, **234**
`printf()`, 9, 90, **122**, **125**, 160, 163–164, **178**, 207, **261**, **367**, **439**, 520–523, 528–529, 535, 553–554, 600, 653
  manpage of, 521
  POSIX version of, 533–534
priority, 282–283
private allocators, 64
privileged operations, 394
`proc` filesystem, 226, **229–231**, **234**
`/proc/mounts` file, 228–231, 234, 271
`/proc/self/cwd` file, **250**
process groups, 300–302, 329
  background, 301
  foreground, 301
  IDs of. *See* PGID
  leaders of, 300, 302, 329
  orphaned, 301
  sending signals to, 358–359
  setting, 302
process signal mask, 277, 349–353, 360, 380, 437–438, 468
  starting out, 363
process substitution, 314
`process_file()`, 267, 269
processes, 7–9, 20, 51–54
  blocking, 350, 570
  child, 8, 83, 275, 277, 279, 309–314, 324, 328
    dead, 293, 366–378
    nondeterministic order of, 312
  continuing if stopped, 334, 359, 365, 375, 377, 379
  creating, 275, 328
  executing programs in, 281, 328
  exiting, 81
  IDs of. *See* PID
  killing, 379, 422, 468
  orphan, 280
  parent, 7, 275, 277, 279, 293, 309–312, 324, 328, 366–378
  polling, 295
  reading, 305
  reaping, 293
  stopping, 294, 295, 334, 365, 379
  suspending, 361, 365
  synchronization of, 282
  terminating, 289–293, 329, 333, 341, 364, 574, 586
  writing, 305
producers, 305, 329
profiling, 571
programs
  basic structure of, 79–81
  distributions of, 37
  logging, 628–629
  messages in, 526–540, 553, 629
  names of, 24
  production versions of, 592, 623, 624
  running. *See* processes
  testing, 651–652, 657, 660
  undocumented features in, 630
prompts, xxv
prototypes, 9–12, 20, 632
`ps` program, 52, **546**, **550**
`pselect()`, 347, 501

pseudorandom numbers, 442–450, 467
pseudoterminals (pseudo-ttys), 7, 196, 226
ptrdiff_t type, 55, 74–75, 440
putenv(), 39, 49
GNU version of, 39, 49
pwd program, 117, 119–120, 153, 256, 314–315, 497, 500

Q

QNX4 filesystem, 226
qsort(), 171–181, 188, 197, 206, 216, 577, 588, 644
Quicksort algorithm, 171
quote_n(), 116

R

r, in permissions, 4
race conditions, 117, 344–346, 349, 351, 362, 373, 380, 390, 429, 467–468, 573, 636
radix point, 520, 525
Rago, Stephen, 327
raise(), 337, 341, 346–347, 355–356, 359, 365, 379
RAM disks, 226
Ramey, Chet, xxix, 38, 40, 87, 210, 249, 314, 326, 433, 591, 592, 633
ramfs filesystem, 226
rand(), 443–445, 469
compared to random(), 447
GLIBC version of, 445
manpage of, 445
random numbers, 442, 447, 467–469
random(), 445–448, 450, 469
compared to rand(), 446
manpage of, 445, 448
Raymond, Eric S., 661, 667
read build-in shell command, 65, 77, 209, 267, 278, 466, 471
read end (of pipe), 303, 305, 309
read(), 79, 80, 91–94, 105–106, 108, 127, 141, 277, 305, 321–323, 341–342, 347, 469, 473, 485, 489, 492, 541
readdir(), 124–128, 152, 207, 213–214, 452–454
GNU/Linux version of, 127
readline library, 60, 66, 598, 661
readline(), 65, 70, 77
readlink(), 141–146, 152, 250, 347
readstring(), 66
realloc(), 55, 59–64, 69, 77, 144, 249, 267, 551, 575, 579, 633
GNU version of, 64
Standard C version of, 61
recurse(), 596, 598
recv(), 347, 493–494, 504
recvfrom(), 347, 493, 504
recvmsg(), 347, 493
regcomp(), 460–463, 469
regerror(), 460, 465–466
regexec(), 460–463, 466, 469
regfree(), 460, 465
register keyword, 28, 50
registers, 52
regular expressions, 459–467, 469
basic, 460
extended, 460
ranges in, 509, 514
reiserfs filesystem, 225, 226
Remote File System. *See* RFS
remove(), 118–119, 152, 307
GNU/Linux version of, 118, 152
rename(), 117, 118, 121, 152, 347
reproducibility, 592
return values, 52–53, 289–290, 328
126 and 127 codes, 290, 293
casting, 57, 60
to void, 90
checking, 57, 60, 90, 342
negative, 290
rewinddir(), 124–125, 152
RFS (Remote File System), 224
Ritchie, Dennis M., xvii, xxix, 9, 18, 384
rm program, 5, 115, 120–121, 393, 429, 597
rmdir program, 123
rmdir(), 118, 121, 152, 347
Robbins, Miriam, xxix
Rock Ridge extensions, 226
romfs filesystem, 227–228
root (superuser), 5, 7, 36, 117, 138, 146–148, 225, 228–229, 231, 254, 269, 391–393, 359, 383–385, 388, 393–403, 567, 577–581, 584–586
rr debugger, 604–605
rsync program, xxvi
run command (GDB), 41, 286, 315, 599
runtime checks, 422, 468
rusage struct, 298–299, 329

S

S_ISXXX(), macros, 102, 135, 137, 141, 152, 153, 211
sa_flags field, 354–355, 360, 366
SA_NODEFER flag, 353–355, 360
SA_NOMASK flag, 355
SA_ONESHOT flag, 355
SA_RESETHAND flag, 355, 360
safe_read(), 342–344
safe_write(), 342–344
sbrk(), 72–74, 75, 76–77, 440, 441, 442
scandir(), 178, 179, 180, 197
scanf(), 166, 176
SCO UnixWare Boot Filesystem, 226
scripts, 6
sdb debugger, 593
searching
binary, 180–190, 197–198, 426
linear, 180, 197–198, 210, 419
in user/group databases, 192
sectors, of a disk, 236
security, 147–148, 191, 385, 399–400, 402, 422, 432, 468
sed program, 459, 460, 468
seed values, 443, 446, 469
seekdir(), 130, 152
segmentation violation, 57–58
select(), 178, 212, 347, 494–501, 504, 505
sem_post(), 347
send(), 347, 493–494, 504
sendmsg(), 348, 493
sendto(), 348, 493, 494, 504
sentinel elements, 99
server program
accept(), 483–484
bind(), 481–482
close(), 485
end of connection, 485–486

ftpd, 486–488
listen(), 482
read()/write(), 484–485
shutdown(), 485
socket(), 478–481
sessions, 300, 329, 359
IDs of, 302
leaders of, 300
setegid(), 348, **394–395**, 396, 398, 402
setenv(), **38**, 39–40, 49
seteuid(), 348, **394**, 395, 396, 398, 399, 402
setjmp(), 435–438, **439**, 440–442, 468, 587
setgid bit, 137, 237, 248, 384–385, 396–398, 402, 566–567, 586
for directories, 391–392, 402
setgid(), 348, **394–395**, 396–398, 402
setgroups(), 393–394, 397, 402
setitimer(), 277, 364–365, **570–573**, 586–587
setjmp(), 435–438, **439**, 440–442, 468, 587
setlocale(), 43, 508, **510–512**, 523, 535, 548, 552, 553
manpage of, 508
setmntent(), 231–232
setpgid(), 302, 329, 348
setpgrp(), 302, 329
setpwent(), **191–192**
setregid(), 348, **394–396**, 398, 402
setresgid(), 348, **398–399**, 402
setresuid(), 348, 398–399, 402
setreuid(), 348, **394–396**, 398, 402
setrlimit(), 414–418
setsid(), 302, 348, **500**
setsockopt(), 348
setstate(), **445–447**
settimeofday(), 567
setuid bit, 137, 237, 248, 384–385, 396–398, 402
running as root, 399, 403
setuid(), 348, **395**, 396–399, 402
Seventh Edition Research UNIX System. *See* V7 Unix
Seward, Julian, xxix
shell escapes, 394
shells, 659
separating arguments in, 23
sorting environment variables, 40
shift states, 545
shutdown(), 348, 485, 489, 504
si_code field, 354–356, 373
side effects, 423
sig_atomic_t type, 344–346, 349, 380
sigaction struct, **353**, 354, **356**, 357, **358**, **366**, **376**, 380
sigaction(), 296, 333, 340, 342, 346, 348, 350, 353–357, **358**, 360, **362–363**, 379–381, 498
manpage of, 353, 354
sigaddset(), 348, **351–352**, 360, 380, 381
sigaltstack(), 355
sigdelset(), 348, **351–352**, 360, 380, 381
sigemptyset(), 348, **351**, 352, 360, **362–363**, **369–370**, 380, 381
sigfillset(), 348, **351**, 352, 360, 380, 381
sighold(), **349**, 350, 351, 381
sigignore(), 350, 381
siginterrupt(), 357–358, 360
sigismember(), 348, **351–352**, 360, 380, 381
siglongjmp(), 348, 437–439, 442, 468
signal actions, 333, 379
default, 333–341, 350, 378–379
restoring, 335
signal handlers, 334, 337–350, 353–357, 379
functions that can be called from, 347–348
installing, 350, 364
reinstalling, 339–340, 344–345
restoring, 348
shell-level, 335
signal numbers, 295, 335
signal sets, 351–352
signal(), 334–337, 340, 346, 348–350, 354, 357, 364–365, 379–382
BSD version of, 340, 496–501
GNU/Linux version of, 340
manpage of, 334, 335
signals, 293–294, 329, 333, 346
available under GNU/Linux, 335–336
blocking, 349, 351, 353, 360, 362, 378, 380
catching, 334
death of child, 381
ignoring, 334, 335, 340–341, 357, 361, 378–379
interrupt, 7, 294, 301, 337, 348, 357–358
job control, 7, 294, 295, 301, 365–366, 380
pending, 352, 357, 366, 378, 380–381
real-time, 337
sending, 358–359, 379–380, 383
supported, list of, 336
using for IPC, 360–361, 380
sigpause(), 350, 363, 381
sigpending(), 348, **352**, 357, 360, 380
sigprocmask(), 348, 352–353, 360, 380
sigqueue(), 348, 356
sigrelse(), 350, 381
sigset(), 349–351, 354, 381
sigset_t type, 349, 351–353, 360, 380, 381
sigsetjmp(), 437–439, 468
sigsuspend(), 348, **352**, 353, 360, 363, **376**, 380–382
sigvec(), 350, 498
simplicity, 3, 7, 9, 16, 20
single-stepping, 600, 656
size program, 54, 61, 66, 76–77, 422
size_t type, 55–56, **63–70**, 71, 160, 171–172, 181, **344**, 422–425, 446, 449, 453, 460, 546–547, 557
sizeof operator, 56–58, **99**, 172, 424, **487**, **490–491**, 557, **560–562**, 617
sleep(), 281–282, 348, **363–365**, 380, 382, 470, 570, 573, 574
SMB filesystem, 227
SOCK_CLOEXEC flag, 479, 484
SOCK_CLOFORK flag, 480, 484, 488
SOCK_DGRAM flag, 479, 480, 494
SOCK_NONBLOCK flag, 480, 484
SOCK_RAW flag, 480
SOCK_RDM flag, 480
SOCK_SEQPACKET flag, 480
SOCK_STREAM flag, 479–481, 487, 489, 491, 493, 499–502
socket(), 348, 478–481, 484, **488**, 489, 491, 494, 502, 504
socketpair(), 348
sockets, 84–85, 131
mask for, 137
UPD, 494
SOCK_NONBLOCK, 480, 484

soft links. *See* symbolic links
Solaris, 271
  core dumps in, 296
  directories in, 391
  filesystem in, 225, 228
  gettext, 508
  numeric values formatting in, 521
  signals in, 338–339, 348, 379
sort program, 171, 340, 426
  manpage of, 171
sorting, 171–190, 197
  data, 185–190
  by modification time, 201
  of pointers, 177
  stable, 173–174
spaghetti code, 435
SPARC system, 225
speed, 16
Spencer, Henry, xxix, 124
splint (Secure Programming Lint) program, 632, 657
sprintf(), 160, 164, 218, 520, 521, 543, 647
srand(), 443–446, 469
srandom(), 445–447, 469
ssize_t type, 70–71, 79, 92–93, 128, 492
st_ctime field, 134, 135, 148
st_mode field, 132, 135–137, 140–141, 153
st_size field, 133, 141, 142, 144, 152, 215–216, 250, 266, 625, 628
stack, 52–54, 73
stack frames, 598
stack segments, 52–54
stack traces, 598
Stallman, Richard M., 21, 64
Standard C, 20
  1990 ISO, xxi, 9–13, 17–20
  1999 ISO, xxi, 12, 17–20
  const items in, 53
  exiting functions in, 290–293
  GNU programs in, 13
  main(), 290
  realloc(), 60
  remove(), 118
  signal functions in, 334–337
  time_t type, 155
  variadic macros in, 608
  wide characters in, 541–542
  See also C language, Standard C
standard error, xvii, 8, 20, 88, 108, 132, 196
  sending debugging messages to, 606
standard input, xvii, 8, 20, 25, 88, 93, 108, 132, 196, 303, 323, 462–463, 465
  shared by two processes, 277–278
standard output, xvii, 8, 20, 25, 88, 108, 132, 140, 196, 303, 323
  shared by two processes, 277–278
standards, xx
stat struct, 95–96, 131–132, 134–135, 146–148, 150, 152, 153, 155, 192, 203, 211, 216, 218, 222, 250, 251, 255, 261, 267, 271, 279, 455, 625, 629
stat(), 129, 131–133, 135, 136, 138, 140–141, 146, 147, 152, 153, 164, 196, 198, 205, 210, 214, 216, 250, 253, 255, 272, 348, 390, 402, 453, 455, 630
  expensiveness of, 205
  manpage of, 133
statfs struct, 243–245, 246
statfs(), 242–246, 271
static tables, 16
statvfs struct, 235, 236, 239, 241–243
statvfs(), 235–243, 246, 271
stderr variable, 7, 31, 36, 41, 69, 80, 86, 87, 90, 92–93, 95, 98, 99, 123, 126, 139, 140, 167, 179, 183, 194, 213, 214, 216, 233, 238, 239, 245, 257, 259, 280, 283, 287, 304, 325, 382, 389, 406, 410, 412, 416, 417, 444, 456, 465–467, 481, 482, 484, 486, 489–492, 494, 498–500, 536, 570, 606, 607, 632
stdin variable, 7, 71, 88, 90, 95, 175, 184, 313, 325, 464–465, 487, 513, 572, 584
stdio.h file, xvii, 68, 90, 92, 94, 107, 124–125, 128, 130, 291–292, 346, 389, 427, 430, 469, 542, 545, 564, 625, 661
stdlib.h file, 56, 430–432, 443
stdout variable, 7, 28, 43, 44, 46, 90, 92, 94–95, 116, 140, 203, 216, 313, 325, 487, 491, 513, 519, 543
step command (GDB), 600, 612, 656
Stevens, W. Richard, 327
sticky bits, 5, 248, 392
  for directories, 402
  mask for, 137
stopme(), 631–632
strcasecmp(), 515, 543
strcmp(), 123, 124, 172–173, 178, 218, 347, 425, 426, 512, 513, 514–515, 542, 543, 553, 582–583
strcoll(), 178, 512–515, 543, 552, 553
strcpy(), xxv, 347, 367–369, 374–375, 425, 543, 614, 645
strdup(), 71–72, 77, 511, 543
strerror(), 15, 86, 93, 98–99, 108, 125–126, 259–261, 304, 325, 536
strfmon(), 519–521, 535, 553
strftime(), 160–164, 166, 168–170, 197, 198, 519, 520, 523–526, 535, 553, 587
string terminator, 38, 66, 425
strings
  comparing, 509, 512–515, 553
  copying, 71
  marking for translation, 529–530
strip program, 54, 297
strip(), 297
strncmp(), 347, 515, 543, 624
strtoul(), 628
structs, in C, 601
  arrays of, 618
  nested, 620–622
  size of, 56–57
strverscmp(), 178
strxfrm(), 178, 512–515, 543, 552, 553
subshells, 278
Sun Microsystems, 190, 224, 391
superblocks, 221
superuser. *See* root
symbolic constants, 33, 88, 609, 612
  using enums for, 610
symbolic links, 119–121, 130–132, 141–144, 151
  creating, 141
  to directories, 119–120, 250
  levels of, 83
  mask for, 137
  ownership of, 146
  permissions on, 147

symbols, 54
symlink(), **120**, 141, 152, 347
  manpage of, 120
sysconf(), 386, 405–410, 417, 418
syslog(), 498, **499–501**, 629
system calls, xix, xxi, 8, 15–16, 79
  checking for errors, 93
  failing, 81, 108
  indirect, 127–128
  interrupted, 83, 341, 348
  POSIX standard for, 17
  restartable, 341–344
system console, 7
System III, 28
  debuggers in, 593
  executable files in, 288
  FIFOs in, 306
System V, 131
  directories in, 391–392
  file locking in, 558
  filesystems in, 224, 226–228
  ftw(), 251
  signals in, 338–339, 341–342, 348, 350, 360, 366, 380
  st_blocks field, 211
  UIDs in, 384
sysv filesystem, 225, 227

T

t, in permissions, 5
Taber, Louis, xxix
tar program, xxvi, xxvii, 139, 147, 149
Taub, Mark, xxix–xxx
tcdrain(), 347
tcflow(), 347
tcflush(), 347
tcgetattr(), 347
tcgetpgrp(), 347
tcsendbreak(), 347
tcsetattr(), 347
tcsetpgrp(), 347
tcsh, manpage of, xxv, 300
tdelete(), **577–578**, **585–586**
tdestroy(), **577**, **585–586**
telldir(), 130, 152
TEMP_FAILURE_RETRY() macro, **344**, 348
tempnam(), **426–427**
temporary files, 16, 340, 426–434, 468
  directories for, 119, 433
  opening, 430–433
terminals (ttys), 7, 105, 131, 140–141, 196–198, 276, 365, 396–397
  controlling, 300–301
  nonblocking, 321
  reading data from, 571
text domain, 527, 554
text sections, 51–54
text segments, 51–54, 76–77
textdomain(), 43, **44**, 527–528, 535, 554
tfind(), **577–578**, **579–581**
Thompson, Ken, 103
thousands separators, 517, 521–523, 525
thrashing, 59
threads, 54
tilde expansion, 455, 458, 469
Time Sharing Option. *See* TSO
time slicing, 282, 429
time zones, 168–170, 197
time(), 156–157, **158–161**, 164, 197, 347, 567
time_t type, 134, 148, 150, 155–157, **158–161**, 164–166, 174, 197, 536, 567
timeouts, 571
timer_getoverrun(), 347
timer_gettime(), 347
timer_settime(), 347
timerclear() macro, **568**, **572**
timercmp() macro, 568
timerisset() macro, **568**
timers, 570–573, 586–587
  expiring, 571, 573
  setting, 573
times, 155, 197
  broken-down, 157, 164, 197
  current, 156–157
  formatting, 159–164, 509, 523–524
  local, 157
  resolution of, 567–571, 575, 586
times(), 347
timespec struct, **132**, 134, **150–151**, 501, 569, **574**, 587
timestamps, 134, 148–151
timeval struct, 149, **150**, **298**, 299, 496, 501, **567–569**, 570–573, **574–575**, 586
timezone(), 170
tm struct, 157–160, **161**, **164**, **165**, 166–168, 197, 537
tm_isdst field, 158, 165
/tmp directory, 5, **117**, 119–120, **122–123**, **393**, 433, 468, 534
TMPDIR environment variable, 433–434, 468
tmpfile(), 291, **430–431**, 468, 470
tmpfs filesystem, 227, **234–235**
tmpnam(), **426–427**
tokens, 543
touch program, 164, 198
translations, 526–540, 554
  creating, 536–540
  preparing, 535–536
  testing, 534
  updating, 540
trap built-in shell command, 335
traps, 335
troff program, 14, 661
Tromey, Tom, xxix
truncate(), 107–108
tsearch(), **577**, 578–581, **584**, 585
TSO (Time Sharing Option), 3
ttys. *See* terminals
TUHS (The UNIX Heritage Society), xxv
tune2fs program, manpage of, 225, 236
Turing, Alan, 419
Turski, Wladyslaw M., xxix
twalk(), **577–578**, 581–585
two_way_open(), 324
type2str(), **244**, 245–246
TZ environment variable, 168, 170
tzset(), 168–169, 197

U

UDF filesystem, 227
UID (user ID), 4–5, 20, 102, 133, 191–193, 198, 383
  effective, 359, 383–384, 393–398

UID (user ID) (*continued*)
mask for. *See* setuid bit
real, 359, 383–384, 393–398
saved setuid, 384, 386, 394–399, 402
uid_t type, **132**, 134, 155, **191–192**, 199, 383, **385–386**, **394–396**, **398–399**
ulimit built-in shell command, 87–88, 109, 413–414, 417–418
umask built-in shell command, 101–103, 109
umask(), 102–103, 108, 109, 276, 288, 347
umasks, 102–104, 276
umount program, 222, 228, 229, 232, 270
umsdos filesystem, 225, 227
uname(), 225, 347
Uncertainty Principle, 422
Unicode character set, 508, 541
uninterruptible power supply. *See* UPS
unions, in C, 601, 618–622, 657
nested, 620–622
unistd.h file, 88, 344, 405, **406**, **408–412**
universally unique identifier (UUID), 229
Unix
archives of old versions, xxv
block size in, 133
chroot(), 270
convention of line ending in, 67
date, 161
domain sockets, 502
Epoch in, 134
file formats in, 6
file ownership in, 147
filesystems in, 111–112
ftw(), 251
inode numbers in, 224
mounting in, 127
preemptive multitasking in, 282
programs in, 16
reading directories in, 123
standard functions in, 72
time slicing in, 429
time_t type, 155
UNIX Heritage Society, The. *See* TUHS
Unix Support Group, 28–29
unlink(), 118, **119**, 152, 307, 347
unref(), 622
unsetenv(), **39**, 48, 49
UPS (uninterruptible power supply), 106
URLs
ANSI, xxi
Argp, 50
The Art of Computer Programming, 467
Autoopts, 50
Cargs, 50
ddd debugger, 604
debugging rules, 653
Free Software Foundation, 593–594
GNOME project, 197
GNU Coding Standards, 13
GNU Gengetopt, 50
GNU gettext, 540
GNU grep, 468
GNU Make, 65
GNU Project, xxii
GNU Project, The, article, 21
GTK+ project, 197
Hints On Programming Language Design, 422
ISO, xxi
Linux Journal, 13
Notes on Programming in C, 20
Open Group, The, xxi
Plan 9 From Bell Labs, 50
Protection of Data File Contents, 384
Recommended C Style and Coding Standards, 20
rsync web pages, xxv
splint program, 632
Teach Yourself Programming in Ten Years, 665
TUHS, xxv
Unicode, 541
United States Patent and Trademark Office, 384
Valgrind, 642
XFS, 227
usage(), 43, **115–116**, **464**, 466, **467**
user, category of users, 4–5, 101–103, 383
databases of, 190–193, 198
IDs of. *See* UID
masks for, 136–137
names of, 190, 198, 201, 210
passwords of, 191
See also ownership
UTC (Coordinated Universal Time), 134, 169
UTF-8 encoding, 15, 508
utimbuf struct, **148**
utime(), 148–149, 152, 156, 164, 569, 586
utimensat(), 145, 150–151, 164, 347
utimes(), 149–150, 299, 347, 496, 586

V

V6 Unix, 457–458
V7 Unix, xx, xxv, 13
cat, 94, 140
debuggers in, 593
directories in, 391
distribution of, 27
filesystem in, 224
inode numbers in, 113
ls command, 201–218
mapping names to ID numbers in, 190
rand(), 445
rmdir command, 123
signals in, 338–339, 341–342, 348, 350, 361
wait(), 294
Valgrind debugger, 634–644, 657
van der Linden, Peter, xxix
variables
for important conditions, 608
local, 52
logging, 629
temporary for debugging, 611
variadic macros, 608
VAX system, 224
--verbose option, 14, 26, 636
Veritas VxFS journaling filesystem, 227
--version option, 14, 46
versionsort(), **178**
vfat filesystem, 224, 225, 227, 271
vi editor, 459–460, 598–599, 661
vim editor, 365, 459–460, 603–604, 656

virtual circuits, 474
void * type, 55, 171–175, 181–182, 254, 355, 423–425, 449–450, 557, 568, 577–585
volatile keyword, 13, 345–346, 361, 380, 438, 439

W

w, in permissions, 4
wait(), 282, 290, 294–300, 309, 311–313, 329–331, 342, 348, 359, 366–367
wait3(), 298–300, 329
wait4(), 298–300, 329
waitid(), 282, 290, 294–298, 300, 329, 348, 359
waitpid(), 282, 290, 294–298, 300, 329, 348, 359, 369, 377
  flags for, 295
warm fuzzies, 139
watchpoints, 601–602, 656
wcrtomb(), 545, 550, 551, 554
wcsrtombs(), 545, 550, 554
wcstombs(), 545
wctomb(), 545
wget program, xxvi
wide characters
  byte maximums, 547
  converting bytes, 546–547, 550–552
  GNU, 548–550
  languages, 552
  mbstate_t, 545–546
wildcard expansions, 450–459, 469
wordexp(), 458–459, 469
wordfree(), 458–459
words
  order of, 533–534, 554
  plural forms of, 528–529, 554
wprintf(), 543
write end (of pipe), 303, 305, 309
write(), 79, 80, 91–92, 94, 105–106, 108, 127, 304, 305, 306, 320–322, 339, 341, 348, 368–369, 371, 374–375, 377, 484–485, 489, 492–494

X

x, in permissions, 5
Xenix filesystem, 225, 227
XFS filesystem, 227
xgettext program, 530, 537–538
xinetd program, manpage of, 361, 495
XML (Extensible Markup Language), 629
xreadlink(), 142, 144, 250, 389
xrealloc(), 68, 69

Z

zero-initialized data, 51–52
zombies, 293, 366

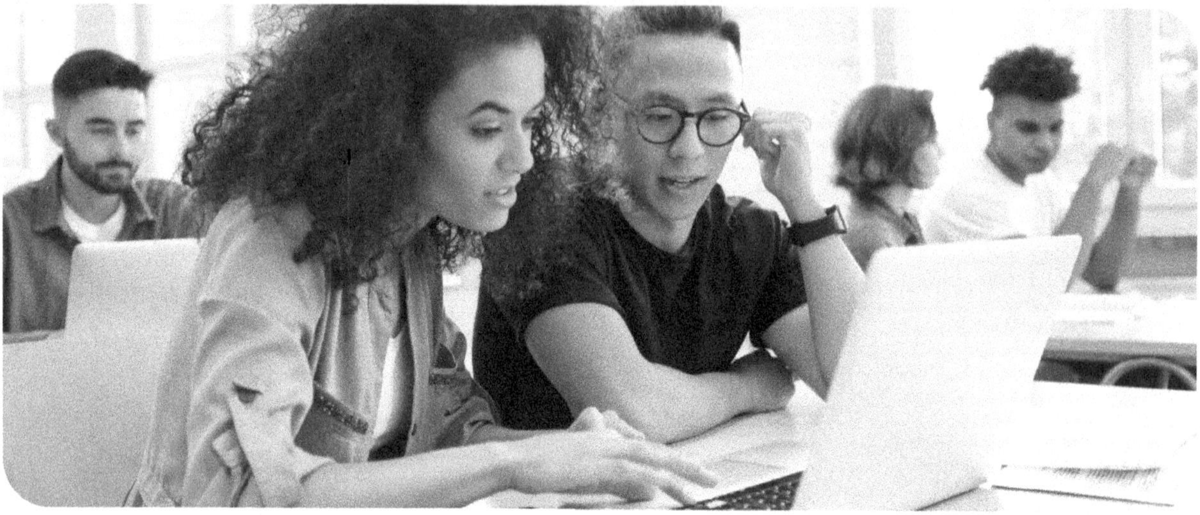